The LNICST series publishes ICST's conferences, symposia and workshops.
LNICST reports state-of-the-art results in areas related to the scope of the Institute.
The type of material published includes

- Proceedings (published in time for the respective event)
- Other edited monographs (such as project reports or invited volumes)

LNICST topics span the following areas:

- General Computer Science
- E-Economy
- E-Medicine
- Knowledge Management
- Multimedia
- Operations, Management and Policy
- Social Informatics
- Systems

Bouziane Brik · Shah Nazir
Editors

Application of Big Data, Blockchain, and Internet of Things for Education Informatization

4th EAI International Conference, BigIoT-EDU 2024
Beihai, China, August 18–20, 2024
Proceedings, Part II

 Springer

Editors
Bouziane Brik [iD]
University of Sharjah
Sharjah, United Arab Emirates

Shah Nazir [iD]
University of Swabi
Khyber Pakhtunkhwa, Pakistan

ISSN 1867-8211   ISSN 1867-822X (electronic)
Lecture Notes of the Institute for Computer Sciences, Social Informatics
and Telecommunications Engineering
ISBN 978-3-032-18630-0   ISBN 978-3-032-18631-7 (eBook)
https://doi.org/10.1007/978-3-032-18631-7

This Springer imprint is published by the registered company Springer Nature Switzerland AG
The registered company address is: Gewerbestrasse 11, 6330 Cham, Switzerland

If disposing of this product, please recycle the paper.

Preface

We are delighted to introduce the proceedings of the Fourth edition of the European Alliance for Innovation (EAI) International Conference on Application of BigData, Blockchain, and Internet of Things for Education Informatization (BigIoT-EDU 2024), held online on August 18–20, 2024. It aimed to provide an international cooperation and exchange platform for big data and information education experts, scholars and enterprise developers to share research results, discuss existing problems and challenges, and explore cutting-edge science and technology. The conference focuses on research fields such as digital education, smart classrooms, Massive Open Online Courses (MOOCs) and advanced integrated technologies for education. The use of Artificial Intelligence (AI) lies at the heart of this conference as we focused on these emerging technologies to accelerate the progress of Big Data and information education. In total, EAI BigIoT-EDU 2024 attracted 669 submissions. Upon rigorous review, only 271 papers were accepted for publication. Thus, the overall acceptance ratio of this conference is just over 40%. Each paper received a minimum of three reviews in a double-blind process.

It was a great pleasure to work with such an excellent organizing committee team for their hard work in organizing and supporting the conference. In particular, the Technical Program Committee, led by our TPC Chair, Hazrat Bilal, completed the peer-review process of technical papers and made a high-quality technical program. We are also grateful to Conference Manager Ivana Bujdakova for her constant support along with the whole of the EAI team involved during the conference. We must say that they have been wonderful and it is always a pleasant experience to work with them. Also, we would like to thank all the authors who submitted their papers to the EAI BigIoT-EDU 2024 conference.

We strongly believe that BigIoT-EDU provides a good forum for all researchers, developers and practitioners to discuss all science and technology aspects that are relevant to Big Data and Information Education. We also expect that future BigIoT-EDU conferences will be as successful and stimulating, as indicated by the contributions presented in this volume.

Bouziane Brik
Shah Nazir

Organization

Organizing Committee

General Chair

Zhang Yinjun — Guangxi Science & Technology Normal University, China

Program Chairs

Bouziane Brik — University of Sharjah, United Arab Emirates
Shah Nazir — University of Swabi, Pakistan

Technical Program Committee Co-chair

Hazrat Bilal — University of Science and Technology of China, China

Web Chairs

Islam Uddin — Abdul Wali Khan University Mardan, Pakistan
Li Anning — Guangxi Normal University of Science and Technology, China

Publicity and Social Media Chair

Mengji Chen — Hechi University, China

Workshops Chair

Rahim Khan — Abdul Wali Khan University Mardan, Pakistan

Sponsorship and Exhibits Chair

Lan Zimian — Harbin Institute of Technology, China

Publications Chair

Yar Muhammad   Beihang University, China

Panels Chair

Kong Linxiang   Hefei University of Technology, China

Tutorials Chair

Wei Rongchang   Guangxi Normal University of Science and
                               Technology, China

Demos Chair

Ryan Alturki   Umm al-Qura University, Saudi Arabia

Posters and PhD Track Chairs

Mengji Chen   Guangxi Science & Technology Normal
                               University, China
Ateeq ur Rehman   University of Haripur, Pakistan

Local Chairs

Huang Yufei   Hechi Normal University, China
Wan Haoran   Hechi Normal University, China

Technical Program Committee

Hashim Ali   Abdul Wali Khan University Mardan, Pakistan
Sohail Abbas   University of Sharjah, United Arab Emirates
Bouziane Brik   University of Sharjah, United Arab Emirates
Adil Khan Kakakhel   Abdul Wali Khan University Mardan, Pakistan
Mian Abdullah Jan   Ton Duc Thang University, Vietnam
Muhammad Bilal   Virtual University of Pakistan, Pakistan
Shaher Slehat   University of Technology Sydney, Australia
Xiangjian He   University of Technology Sydney, Australia
Farman Khan   Bacha Khan University Charsadda, Pakistan
Zia Ur Rehman   Bacha Khan University Charsadda, Pakistan

Abid Yahya	Botswana International University of Science and Technology, Botswana
Ravi Keemo	Botswana International University of Science and Technology, Botswana
Aaiza Gul	Sirindhorn International Institute of Technology, Thailand
Muhammad Sohail	Abdul Wali Khan University Mardan, Pakistan
Saad Khan	University of Peshawar, Pakistan
Bilawal Khan	COMSATS University Islamabad, Pakistan
Jamal Shah	University of Leeds, UK
Basit Kazmi	University of Peshawar, Pakistan
Jalal Turk	University of Staffordshire, UK
Umer Hussain	Indian Institute of Technology Kharagpur, India
Omer Naveed	Uppsala University, Sweden
Muhammad Ali	Uppsala University, Sweden
Hamza Khan	Hankuk University of Foreign Studies, South Korea
Tariq Khan	Abdul Wali Khan University Mardan, Pakistan
Ayaan Adeel	Abdul Wali Khan University Mardan, Pakistan
Tariq Khokar	Abdul Wali Khan University Mardan, Pakistan
Faisal Ayub Khan	Indian Institute of Technology Kharagpur, India
Faisal Khan	University of Leeds, UK
Yasir Jan	University of California Davies, USA
Ryan Alturki	Umm al-Qura University, Saudi Arabia
Walayat Hussain	University of Technology Sydney, Australia
Muhammad Usman	Federation University Australia, Australia
Naveed Khan	Abdul Wali Khan University Mardan, Pakistan
Abdul Samad	University of Nebraska Omaha, USA
Asif Khan	University of Nebraska Omaha, USA
Sohail Agha	National University of Science and Technology, Pakistan
Raza Hussain	Indian Institute of Technology Kharagpur, India
Faysal Azam	Indian Institute of Technology Kharagpur, India
Nazar Waheed	University of Technology Sydney, Australia
Mengji Chen	Hechi University, China
Yar Muhammad	Beihang University, China
Zairi Ismael Rizman	Universiti Teknologi MARA, Malaysia

Contents

The Application of Computer in Intelligence Education

Application of Model in Intelligence Education

Application of K-Means Clustering Algorithm in Intelligence Education

Construction of Intelligent Proofreading System for Chinese Writing Spelling Based on Fuzzy Clustering Algorithm

Ruiying Ma[1]([✉]) and Chunhong Wang[2]

[1] Changchun College Of Electronic Technology, Changchun 130000, Jilin, China
570108025@qq.com

[2] Shenzhen longhua vocational technical school, Shenzhen 518083, Guangdong, China

Abstract. Chinese character spelling is one of the main contents of culture, and how to effectively analyze Chinese character spelling is the main problem in Chinese calligraphy nowadays. Integrating this method with Chinese character spelling can improve the simplification rate of Chinese character spelling and promote its overall development. This article combines fuzzy analysis and cluster analysis methods to make a comprehensive judgment of Chinese character spelling, improve its decomposition effect and integrity. The results show that fuzzy analysis can promote the improvement of Chinese character spelling level and achieve the overall development of Chinese character spelling, with an improvement rate of about 10%. Therefore, mushroom analysis method can promote the overall optimization of children with anemia. Intelligent analysis methods can promote the analysis and improvement of anemia and anemia rates in children.

Keywords: fuzzy theory · fuzzy clustering algorithm · Intelligent proofreading · System Build · Chinese · Write spelling

1 Introduction

As one of the oldest characters in the world, Chinese characters carry rich cultural and historical information [1, 2]. However, with the development of society and the popularization of information technology, people are increasingly relying on electronic devices for text input and communication in daily life [3, 4]. Although the modern input method technology is quite mature, the wrong writing and spelling of Chinese characters is still a common problem [5, 6]. These problems not only affect the accuracy of information and the efficiency of communication, but can also lead to misunderstandings and the spread of errors [7, 8]. Therefore, it is of great practical significance to develop an intelligent system that can efficiently and accurately write and proofread Chinese characters. Writing and spelling errors of Chinese characters mainly come from the following aspects: first, input errors, including typing errors, stroke errors, etc.; Secondly, intellectual errors, such as typos and misuse of uncommon words; Finally, there is contextual error, that is,

B. Brik and S. Nazir (Eds.): BigIoT-EDU 2024, LNICST 659, pp. 3–13, 2026.
https://doi.org/10.1007/978-3-032-18631-7_1

inappropriate words or expressions are used in a specific context [9, 10]. The occurrence of these errors not only affects the quality of the text, but also may lead to the distortion of the information. Traditional proofreading methods mainly rely on manual work, which is not only time-consuming and labor-intensive, but also easy to omit [11, 12]. Therefore, developing an automated Chinese character writing and spelling proofreading system can significantly improve the efficiency and accuracy of text processing [13].

2 Related Concepts

2.1 The Fuzzy Clustering Algorithm Is Described Mathematically.

The Fuzzy clustering algorithm is y_i found that the unqualified value parameters in the construction of intelligent proofreading system is z_i, and the construction of intelligent proofreading system scheme is $tol(y_i \bullet t_{ij})$ integrated with the function to finally judge the feasibility of the construction of intelligent proofreading system, and the calculation is shown in Eq. (1).

$$\lim_{x \to \infty} \left(y_i \cdot t_{ij} \right) = \frac{dy}{dx} \frac{\partial^2 \Omega}{\partial u \partial v} y_{ij} \geq \max\left(t_{ij} \div 2 \right) \tag{1}$$

Equation illustrates the evaluation of outliers among them.(2).

$$\max\left(t_{ij} \right) = \partial \left(t_{ij}^2 + 2 \cdot t_{ij} \right) \succ \lim_{\delta x \to 0} \varphi \tag{2}$$

the intelligent proofreading system is t_i that the construction of intelligent proofreading system scheme is set_i, the technique for satisfying the construction of intelligent proofreading system is y_i, and the judgment function of the construction of intelligent proofreading system the scheme is $F(t_i \approx 0)$ as shown by Eq. (3).

$$F(d_i) = \prod \sum t_i \bigcap \xi \cdot \sqrt{2} \to \oint y_i \Lambda \tag{3}$$

2.2 Selection of Construction of Intelligent Proofreading System Scheme

the system function is $g(t_i)$, The weighting factor is w_i, The unqualified construction of intelligent proofreading system, as indicated in Equation, is thus required by the construction of intelligent proofreading system. (4).

$$g(t_i) = \ddot{x} \cdot z_i \prod F(d_i) \frac{dy}{dx} - w_i \Phi \Phi \tag{4}$$

The customer analysis method can analyze the comparison and if point B. can be obtained, and the results is shown in Eq. (5).

$$\lim_{x \to \infty} g(t_i) + F(d_i) \leq \cap \max\left(t_{ij} \right) \tag{5}$$

Analytical methods can optimize existing analysis content and conditions., and the results are presented in Eq. (6).

$$g(t_i) + F(d_i) \leftrightarrow \frac{\Delta y}{\Delta x} \left(\sum t_{ij} + 4 \right) \tag{6}$$

2.3   Analysis of Construction of Intelligent Proofreading System Scheme

The analysis method is used to comprehensively optimize the existing content and situation of Chinese character dictation. is $No(t_i)$ shown in Eq. (7).

$$No(t_i) = \frac{g(t_i) + F(d_i)}{mean\left(\sum t_{ij} + 4\right)} \frac{\partial^2 \Omega}{\partial v^2} y \tag{7}$$

Among them, it is $\frac{g(t_i)+F(d_i)}{mean(\sum t_{ij}+4)} \leq 1$ specified that the scheme must be $Zh(t_i)$ suggested; otherwise, the scheme integration is necessary; the outcome is illustrated in Eq. (8).

$$Zh(t_i) = \lim_{x \to \infty} \left[\sum g(t_i) + F(d_i)\right] \phi \tag{8}$$

The construction of intelligent proofreading system is $accur(t_i)$ thoroughly examined, and the threshold and index weight of the construction of intelligent proofreading system scheme are established to assure the Fuzzy clustering algorithm's correctness. The construction of intelligent proofreading system is $unno(t_i)$ a systematic test The holistic fusion of fuzzy analysis method can make overall judgments on strokes, horizontal and vertical strokes, and other contents inside. in Eq. (9).

$$accur(t_i) = \frac{\min\left[\sum g(t_i) + F(d_i)\right]}{\sum g(t_i) + F(d_i)} \frac{\partial^2 \Omega}{\partial v^2} \tag{9}$$

The Kung Fu Aircraft Forensic Medicine Team conducts a transparent judgment and research on the correlation between the content and writing style of the strokes. Is $randon(t_i)$ considered as a high analytical research. If the construction of intelligent proofreading system's stochastic function is, then the computation of Eq. (9) may be represented as eq. (10).

$$accur(t_i) = \frac{\min\left[\sum g(t_i) + F(d_i)\right]}{\frac{1}{2}\sum g(t_i) + F(d_i)} + randon(t_i) \tag{10}$$

Analysis shows that a certain analysis method can improve the strokes and overall quality of Chinese characters, promote the development of Chinese characters, and promote Chinese character culture.

3   Construction of Intelligent Proofreading System Optimization Approach

System principle fuzzy clustering algorithm is a clustering analysis method based on fuzzy set theory, which realizes soft classification of data sets through fuzzy partition of data points. In the intelligent proofreading system of Chinese character writing and spelling, fuzzy clustering algorithm can be applied to extract and classify Chinese character writing features, so as to realize intelligent recognition and proofreading of writing errors. Data preprocessing In the process of system construction, the Chinese character writing data needs to be preprocessed first. This includes the steps of collecting the written image, binarizing and denoising, so as to facilitate the subsequent feature extraction and cluster analysis. Feature extraction Feature extraction is one of the key steps to construct intelligent proofreading system. Through feature extraction of Chinese character writing images, various features reflecting writing quality can be obtained, such as stroke thickness, stroke order, writing speed and so on. These features will be used as input data of fuzzy clustering algorithm for subsequent cluster analysis. Fuzzy clustering analysis After feature extraction, the fuzzy clustering algorithm is used to cluster the writing features. Through the fuzzy partition of data points, the clustering results of different writing styles can be obtained. According to the clustering results, the system can identify writing errors or irregularities, and give corresponding proofreading suggestions. System implementation During the implementation process, a variety of technical means, such as machine learning and deep learning, can be used to improve the recognition accuracy and proofreading efficiency of the system. At the same time, the system needs to be continuously optimized and improved to adapt to different users' needs and writing habits.

4 Practical Examples of Construction of Intelligent Proofreading System

4.1 Introduction to the Construction of Intelligent Proofreading System

TFuzzy clustering algorithm is a clustering method to find fuzzy patterns and structures in data. Different from traditional hard clustering algorithms, fuzzy clustering algorithms allow data points to belong to multiple clusters, and the membership degree of each cluster is represented by a value between 0 and 1. This membership value reflects the degree to which the data points belong to a certain cluster, thus providing more flexible and accurate clustering results is shown in Table 1.

Table 1. construction of intelligent proofreading system construction of intelligent proofreading system requirements

Scope of application	Grade	Accuracy	construction of intelligent proofreading system
Education field	I	91.15	91.29
	II	89.66	85.28
Business and office	I	90.19	88.69
	II	85.68	89.80
Press and publishing	I	91.78	94.02
	II	87.91	89.96

The construction of intelligent proofreading system process in Table 1. is shown in Fig. 1.

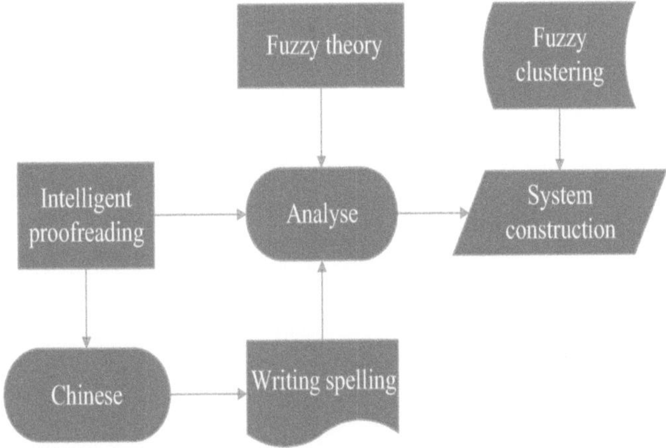

Fig. 1. Analysis process of construction of intelligent proofreading system

The basic idea of fuzzy clustering algorithm is to determine the membership matrix and clustering center of data points by optimizing an objective function. Common objective functions include those in Fuzzy C-Means FCM algorithm. This objective function aims to minimize the weighted sum of squares of distances between a data point and the cluster center to which it belongs, where the weight is some power of the membership value. The main advantages of fuzzy clustering algorithm include: 1. Flexibility: Allows data points to belong to multiple clusters, being able to handle ambiguity and uncertainty in data. 2. Robustness: It has good robustness to noise and outliers, and can effectively deal with irregular data. 3. Explanatory: Membership values provide the degree to which data points belong to different clusters, which is helpful to interpret and understand clustering results, as shown in Fig. 2.

4.2   Construction of Intelligent Proofreading System

Constructing fuzzy clustering model: Select appropriate fuzzy clustering algorithms (such as fuzzy C-means clustering) and set relevant parameters. Training model: The extracted feature data is input into the fuzzy clustering model for training to form the cluster center. Proofreading process: For the Chinese character writing samples to be proofread, their features are extracted and compared with the cluster center, and their correctness is judged according to the similarity, as shown in Table 2.

4.3   Construction of Intelligent Proofreading System and Stability

To comprehensively analyze and judge the changes in strokes and the intensity of stroke writing, and to optimize the entire structure. is shown in Fig. 2.

Figure 2 shows that the input Chinese character writing image is preprocessed, including image denoising, normalization and feature extraction. Image denoising can remove the noise in the image through median filtering, Gaussian filtering and other

Table 2. The overall situation of the construction of intelligent proofreading system scheme

Category	Random data	Reliability	Analysis rate
Education field	88.70	88.53	91.77
Business and office	90.38	88.86	88.96
Press and publishing	86.89	85.38	93.13
Mean	88.00	87.56	88.38
X6	88.41	91.68	87.16
	P = 1.249		

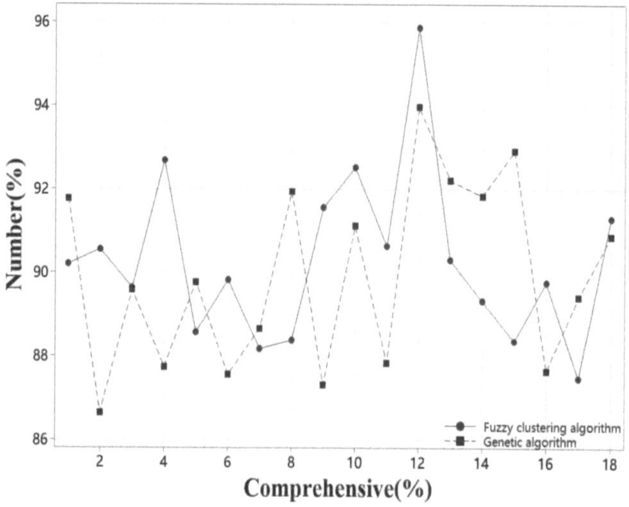

Fig. 2. Evaluation model of aging performance of different algorithms

methods; Normalization unifies Chinese character images of different sizes and directions into a standard format through scale transformation and rotation correction; Feature extraction is to extract key features from the processed image, such as stroke direction, stroke length, stroke density, etc. Initialize the cluster center: Before clustering, the cluster center needs to be initialized. The initial selection of clustering center has an important influence on the clustering results. In this study, K-means + + algorithm is used to initialize the cluster center, which avoids the randomness and instability of the initial center point selection in the traditional K-means algorithm by randomly selecting the initial center point and selecting other center points in turn according to the distance..

Table 3 shows that confusion matrix is a commonly used evaluation tool to show the classification results of a system on different categories. The rows of the confusion matrix represent the actual class, the columns represent the predicted class, and each element in the matrix represents the correspondence between the actual class and the predicted class. By analyzing the confusion matrix, we can understand the classification

Table 3 compares the accuracy of several construction of intelligent proofreading system.

Algorithm	Survey data	construction of intelligent proofreading system	Magnitude of change	Error
Fuzzy clustering algorithm	90.46	88.62	92.03	88.26
Genetic algorithm	88.77	91.26	87.98	90.98
P	89.59	93.80	89.57	87.87

effect of the system in detail, and find the advantages and disadvantages of the system. User satisfaction survey: Besides objective evaluation indicators, user satisfaction is also an important factor to measure system performance. In this study, the feedback of users' experience and satisfaction with the system was collected by questionnaire survey. The contents of the questionnaire survey include the usability, accuracy and response speed of the system. By counting the feedback results of users, the actual application effect of the system is further evaluated, as shown in Fig. 3.

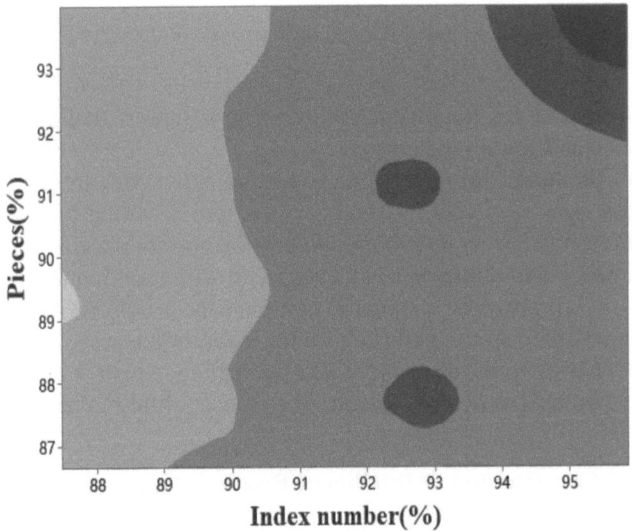

Fig. 3. construction of intelligent proofreading system of Fuzzy clustering algorithm

Figure 3 shows that Originally, it was said that the Rubik's Cube analysis method could recognize the characteristics of strokes and strokes, as well as write different styles, providing support for later stroke policies..

4.4 Rationality of Construction of Intelligent Proofreading System

The analysis and judgment of speech content require optimizing and updating the overall content based on your analysis, in order to identify key concepts. in Fig. 4.

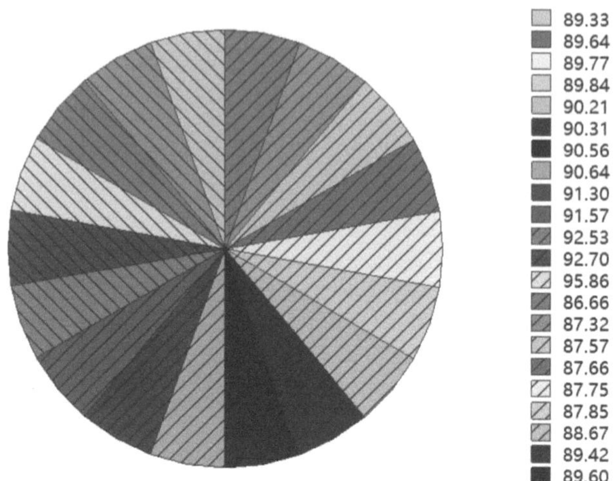

Fig. 4. Evaluation model of aging performance of different algorithms

Figure 4 shows that the intelligent proofreading system is built based on advanced technologies such as natural language processing, machine learning, and big data analysis . With the continuous progress of these technologies, the intelligent proofreading system has been able to realize fast and accurate proofreading of texts, meeting the demand for efficient and accurate proofreading in the current information explosion era. Improving efficiency and reducing costs Compared with traditional manual proofreading, the intelligent proofreading system can complete the proofreading of a large number of texts in a short time, significantly improving work efficiency . This not only saves labor costs, but also shortens the cycle of text publishing, which is of great significance to the fields of news and publication, advertising industry, film and television production.

4.5 Validity of Construction of Intelligent Proofreading System

In order to confirm the effectiveness of the Fuzzy clustering algorithm, the construction of intelligent proofreading system scheme is comprised with the Genetic algorithm, and the construction of intelligent proofreading system scheme is shown in Fig. 5 shown.

Figure 5 shows that The proofreading system can quickly complete the proofreading of a large number of texts, which greatly improves the work efficiency. Compared with traditional manual proofreading, intelligent proofreading has higher processing speed and can maintain higher accuracy to a certain extent [1]. After continuous training and optimization, the proofreading accuracy of intelligent proofreading system in some specific fields has been considerable. For common typos and grammatical errors, intelligent

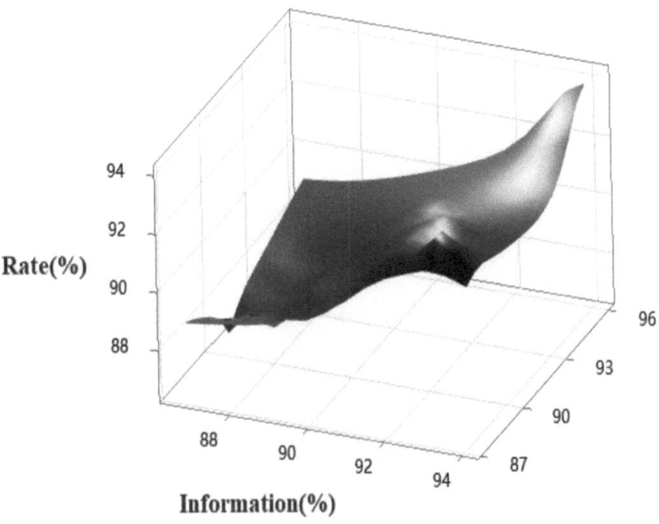

Fig. 5. construction of intelligent proofreading system of different algorithms

proofreading can often easily identify and give correct modification suggestions. Cost saving The intelligent proofreading system can greatly reduce the cost of manual proofreading and reduce the operational burden of enterprises. In scenarios that require a lot of proofreading work, intelligent proofreading is undoubtedly a more economical choice. Extensive application of intelligent proofreading tools use natural language processing and other technologies to improve writing efficiency and accuracy, and are widely used in writing platforms, academic papers, corporate copywriting, press and publication, advertising industry, film and television production, writing services, education fields, publishing industry and other fields . In these fields, intelligent proofreading system can play its efficient and accurate characteristics, helping users to improve text quality.

Table 4 compares the efficacy of several construction of intelligent proofreading system.

Algorithm	Survey data	construction of intelligent proofreading system	Magnitude of change	Error
Fuzzy clustering algorithm	89.68	86.34	85.29	89.26
Genetic algorithm	86.08	87.87	91.90	86.97
P	87.13	87.63	87.39	93.28

Table 4 shows that the Genetic algorithm has flaws in the accuracy has not altered much.The Fuzzy clustering algorithm was typically examined by numerous approaches to further validate the efficacy, as illustrated in Fig. 6.

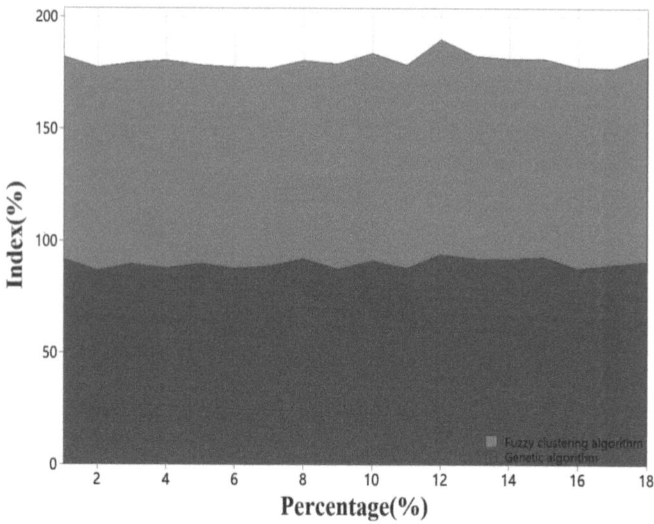

Fig. 6. Fuzzy clustering algorithm construction of intelligent proofreading system

Figure 6 shows that the construction is the Fuzzy clustering algorithm is significantly system's adjustment coefficient and sets the threshold of Internet information to eliminate the construction of intelligent proofreading system scheme that does not meet the requirements.

5   Conclusion

The application of fuzzy clustering algorithm in intelligent proofreading system of Chinese character writing and spelling has obvious advantages. Firstly, it can accurately extract and classify Chinese character writing features, thus improving the recognition accuracy of the system. Secondly, fuzzy clustering algorithm has strong adaptability and robustness, and can cope with the changes of different writing styles and writing quality. In addition, the system can also provide users with personalized proofreading suggestions to help users better standardize their writing. However, in practical applications, the system also faces some challenges. For example, for complex writing scenes and writing styles, the recognition accuracy and proofreading efficiency of the system may be affected to some extent. In addition, the implementation and optimization of the system also require a lot of time and energy. To sum up, the application of fuzzy clustering algorithm in intelligent proofreading system of Chinese character writing and spelling has broad prospects and potential. With the continuous advancement of technology and the continuous expansion of application scenarios, this system is expected to provide more comprehensive and effective support for the accuracy and standardization of Chinese character writing.

References

1. Xu Dong, Wang Lei,&Shi Shouchuang (2022) Design of an automatic information classification system for industrial intelligent application platforms based on fuzzy clustering algorithm electronic Des. Eng., 30 (14), 5
2. Gao Jie, Wei Qiang: Design and development of an intelligent lighting system based on k-means clustering algorithm Chinese Lighting Appliances (3), 8 (2022).
3. Zhou Yuan, et al.: A reactor vibration monitoring system based on LOF-FCM fuzzy clustering algorithm CN202111362866.3 (2022).
4. Bing, Y.: An Intelligent Proofreading System for English Phrase Translation Based on Deep Learning Automation and Instrumentation, vol. 008, p. 000 (2022)
5. Yao Sanjun: Method and device for extracting music melody contours based on fuzzy clustering algorithm CN115658957A (2023)
6. Yao Sanjun: Method and device for extracting music melody contours based on fuzzy clustering algorithm CN202211296379.6 (2023).
7. Haoze, W., Chenxuan, Z., Yishan, Z., Yanhua, L.: An adaptive typical day selection method based on improved fuzzy clustering algorithm Shaanxi electric. Power. **001**, 050 (2022)
8. Wang Jingang, X.U., Hang, L.I.U.H., Hanzhengnan, Y.U., Yu, L.I.U.: Construction of driving conditions for electric vehicles based on t-sne and fuzzy clustering. J. Chongqing Jiaotong Univ. (Nat. Sci Ed.). **41**(06), 126–132 (2022)
9. Shuangsheng, W., Jie, L., Zhenyu, Z.: A clustering algorithm for executed individuals based on hesitant fuzzy language decision information Operations Research and Management. **32**(3), 8 (2023)
10. Zhe, W.: Design of an intelligent inspection and analysis system for the security of charter text data based on k-means clustering algorithm Automation and Instrumentation. **003**, 000 (2022)
11. Qiuhong, Y., Li, W.: Research on System Health Status Based on Fuzzy C-means Clustering Algorithm Information and Communication Technology and Policy. **49**(4), 91–96 (2023)
12. Sisong, Z., Ming, Z.: A high-dimensional big data incremental processing method based on fuzzy clustering algorithm. J. Bengbu Univ. **002**, 011 (2022)
13. Shinan, Z., Wen, D.: A Foreign Language Database Intelligent Proofreading System Based on an Improved Phrase Translation Model Automation and Instrumentation, pp. 000–002 (2022)

Research on Classification Method of University English Teaching Resources Based on Density Clustering Algorithm

Xuke Sun[✉]

Henan Vocational College of Agriculture, Zhengzhou City, Henan province 451450, China
13526597585@163.com

Abstract. College English resources are the foundation of education and an effective means to improve the teaching effect. English resources play an important role in comprehensive classification and holistic analysis. Therefore, this paper puts forward a cluster analysis method to integrate college English education resources, promote the improvement of its reduction effect, and realize the effective utilization of resources, with the improvement degree of more than 30%. Moreover, the satisfaction and matching degree of resources and needs reach more than 80%. This shows that in the process of cluster analysis, English resources have been significantly utilized and improved.

Keywords: gradient descent theory · Density clustering algorithm;method of categorizing instructional resources plays;Stealth;Layer aging

1 Introduction

In the process of classification of college English resources, it involves the utilization of resources, the matching of customers, the narrowing of the scope of application and the integration of resources [1, 2]. Therefore, English resource matching is the foundation of college English education, resource integration and basic efficiency and effect improvement. How to effectively integrate resources and match the effect of hoist resources has become the focus of epidemic research [3, 4]. Some students believe that integrating large application resources with intelligent analysis methods and planning the authenticity of resources can improve the utilization rate of resources, and at the same time, it will deeply accompany and structure resources to realize the utilization rate of resources [5, 6]. Therefore, in the process of effectively integrating intelligent analysis methods with large medical resources, we can deepen the educational resources of college English, make logical analysis of the resources, complete the corresponding matching, and promote the role of English studies [7, 8]. Therefore, based on college English resources, this paper optimizes them with the help of intense upgrading method, and analyzes and judges them through actual cases.

© ICST Institute for Computer Sciences, Social Informatics and Telecommunications Engineering 2026
Published by Springer Nature Switzerland AG 2026. All Rights Reserved
B. Brik and S. Nazir (Eds.): BigIoT-EDU 2024, LNICST 659, pp. 14–23, 2026.
https://doi.org/10.1007/978-3-032-18631-7_2

2 Related Concepts

2.1 The Density Clustering Algorithm is Described Mathematically.

There are stages in the process of utilizing and synthesizing educational resources. So because of the clustering phase of resources is t_{ij}, and The maximum utilization of nature should be achieved [9, 10], so the maximum utilization rate of self-use is $\lim_{x \to \infty} (y_i \cdot t_{ij})$ iEnglish resources should be effectively integrated, and the comprehensiveness of English resources should be improved. As shown in Eq. (1).

$$\lim_{x \to \infty} (y_i \cdot t_{ij}) = \sqrt{b^2 - 4ac}y_{ij} \geq \max(t_{ij} \div 2) \tag{1}$$

In the process of resource integration and comprehensive analysis, it is also necessary to analyze the maximum value and average value of resources, so as to highlight the personalization of English resources. However, in the process of personalized processing of English resources, there are losses involved in Eq. (2).

$$\max(t_{ij}) = \mathbb{F}\left(t_{ij}^2 + 2 \cdot t_{ij}\right) \succ mean\left(\sum t_{ij} + 2\right)\begin{pmatrix} 1 & 0 \\ 0 & 1 \end{pmatrix} \tag{2}$$

The understanding of natural words, grammar and content requires association analysis with the help of functions is $F(d_i)$ as shown by Eq. (3).

$$F(d_i) = \frac{-b \pm \sqrt{b^2 - 4ac}}{2a} \sum \oint y_i \cdot 7 \tag{3}$$

2.2 Selection of Method of Categorizing Instructional Resources Plays Scheme

Cluster analysis is carried out on the classification of English resources, and it is classified. Partitioning process is $g(t_i)$, the division of resources and the classification of resources require weight analysis [11, 12]. The weight sequence ratio of each resource can be obtained by the formula. The specific formula is shown in Formula 4.

$$g(t_i) = \int \prod F(d_i) \frac{dy}{dx} \frac{-w_i}{k} \tag{4}$$

After the formula is obtained, the maximum value of English resources should be limited, so as to determine that the relevant research results meet the requirements. Second, the determination process is nowhere by the formula 5.

$$\lim_{x \to \infty} g(t_i) + F(d_i) \leq \bigcap kimax(t_{ij}) \tag{5}$$

The maximum value of English resource utilization, and then use the maximum value as a standard for resource matching, so as to improve the effect of the whole application utilization [13]. The specific matching process and dynamic analysis process are shown in Formula 6.

$$g(t_i) + F(d_i) \leftrightarrow \int \lim_{x \to \infty} (n) \tag{6}$$

2.3 Analysis of Method of Categorizing Instructional Resources Plays Scheme

Comprehensive analysis, the conditions of each formula in the process of English matching, English resource synthesis and overall planning. So be right. The matching process of resources is dynamically analyzed. Dynamic process is $pio(t_i)$ shown in Eq. (7).

$$pio(t_i) = \int \frac{g(t_i) + F(d_i)}{mean\left(\sum t_{ij} + 4\right)} \left\lceil \frac{n!}{r!(n-r)!} \right\rceil \tag{7}$$

Among them, The holistic division of resources is $\frac{g(t_i)+F(d_i)}{mean\left(\sum t_{ij}+4\right)} \leq 1$.Implementation effect and matching effect after resource division $h(t_i)$ suggestedIn the process of dynamic resource division, its resource matching needs to be divided into sets, and the regions of each set are divided in Eq. (8).

$$h(t_i) = \bigcap \int \mathrm{li}\left[\sum g(t_i) + F(d_i)\right] \tag{8}$$

After obtaining the corresponding resource match, to output its results, you can build a collection collection from the result output is $dataset(t_i)$. The percentage analysis of the obtained collection is carried out to verify the percentage of resource integration and resource utilization. The specific formula 9.

$$dataset(t_i) = \left(\frac{\min\left[\sum g(t_i) + F\left(d_i \pm \pi\sqrt{5}\right)\right]}{\sum g(t_i) + F(d_i)} | \mathrm{ki} \right) \tag{9}$$

After completing the overall analysis of the formula, the formula should be standardized and mapped, and input into the system matching and English learning. The database sets the corresponding result as the database result is $putdat(t_i)$ In the process of outputting the corresponding results, a virtual verification function should be set to expand the application scope of application resources. The development process is shown in the formula 10.

$$putdat(t_i) = \frac{\min\left[\sum g(t_i) + F(d_i)\right]}{\Lambda \sum g(t_i) + F(d_i)} + random(t_i) \tag{10}$$

To sum up, it is in progress. In the process of analysis, resources and needs need to be matched and dynamically developed. In the process of integration and analysis, resources should also be dynamically correlated. Achieve overall planning of resources and. Analyze and improve the utilization effect of resources.

3 Method of Categorizing Instructional Resources Plays Optimization Approach

In the process of comprehensive analysis of English teaching resources, we should also analyze the resources as a whole, so as to meet the actual needs. In the process of establishment, we should mine and match the logical relationship of English, the autonomy of words according to law and the content, so as to realize the diversification and promotion of resources. At the same time, it is necessary to output the overall planning of resources to complete the comprehensive utilization of resources. As far as life is concerned, with the help of intelligent analysis methods, resources can be effectively analyzed, the overall planning of resources can be completed, and the comprehensiveness of resources can be improved. At the same time, the diversification of resources can be judged, and the key points and contents, the overall results and structure should be explored. The matching of resources and the system should be realized, the diversification of resources should be realized, the content and planning should be realized, the diversification of resources should be realized as a whole, and the effective utilization of resources should be completed. It lays a foundation for English teaching, the application of English content and the promotion of related knowledge. Students' actual needs, classroom teaching, planning process and training analysis, through setting up certificates, can realize the matching of their own needs and complete the construction of overall resources.

4 Practical Examples of Method of Categorizing Instructional Resources Plays

4.1 Introduction to the Method of Categorizing Instructional Resources Plays

Freshman and sophomore English teaching in universities is based on the analysis and improvement of its. Analysis content, investigation process and English learning achievements, learning content and laws, correcting mistakes and third-party evaluation are the main ones. During the test, it is one to three points, and the scores are relatively few, but it has adjustment parameters and weights, which can effectively improve the scores, ensure the effectiveness of the analysis, specific score summary and data investigation as shown by the Table 1.

Table 1. Score acquisition process

Scope of application	Grade	Objective score.	Method of categorizing instructional resources plays
Listening	English content.	82.16	83.30
	External resources.	82.05	80.47
Colloquial	English content.	82.78	81.01
	External resources.	81.88	78.89
Read	English content.	82.00	81.29
	External resources.	79.43	78.56

It can be seen from the scores in Table 1 that among the obtained data, the objective score is greater than 80%, and the subjective evaluation results also meet the requirements, indicating that the obtained data is relatively complete and can be analyzed later.

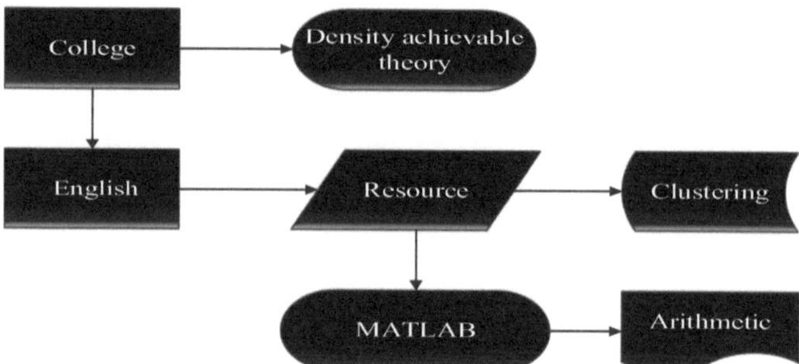

Fig. 1. Analysis process of method of categorizing instructional resources plays

Therefore, in the process of judgment, you need to describe the corresponding data values. The detailed description process is shown in Fig. 1.

According to the analysis in Fig. 1, it is necessary to change the information scores and letter contents now, and put forward the English learning scores, which should be based on objective scores, and the actual needs of students should be based on subjective scores. Through data standardization and mapping analysis, the necessary data scale is established between them, and the mapping matching is formed, and whether the resources can be utilized between them, and whether there is a significant impact on academic performance, so as to lay the foundation for the later analysis.

4.2 Method of Categorizing Instructional Resources Plays

Students' academic performance can be objectively evaluated, but students' actual needs are diversified, so it is necessary to accumulate the needs and integrate all aspects to simplify the difficulty and complexity of analysis. The specific clustering process is shown in Table 2.

Table 2. The overall situation of the method of categorizing instructional resources plays scheme

Category	Actual needs of students.	Matching of objective resources.	The actual effect of resource matching.
Listening	46.90	46.90	43.36
Colloquial	35.40	58.41	48.67
Read	57.52	36.28	40.71

4.3 Method of Categorizing Instructional Resources Plays and Stability

In the process of resource analysis and matching, the clustering results are classified and tested. Whether there is concentration of clustering results, so as to verify the effect of resource utilization. The specific test process is shown in Fig. 2

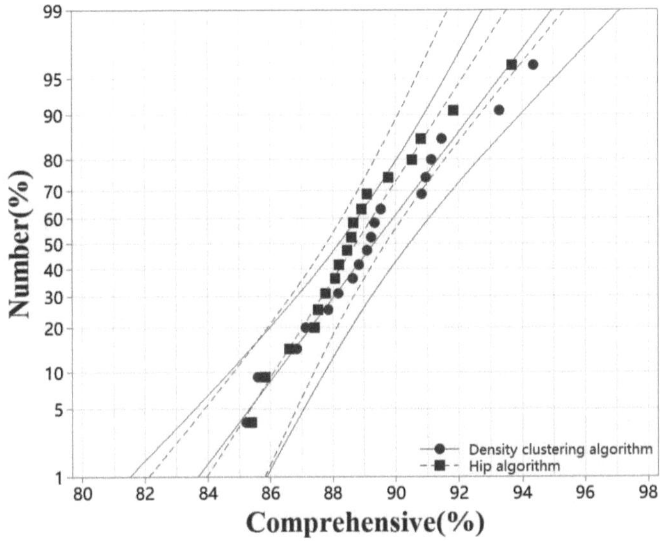

Fig. 2. Inaccurate resource classification of aging performance of different algorithms

Figure 2 shows that n the process of diversified analysis, there are big scores in students' academic performance, subjective evaluation and objective scores, and there is a big difference between them. This shows that in the process of intense analysis, the utilization rate of resources can be saved, the effectiveness of resources can be improved, the accumulation and overall analysis of resources can be completed, and the actual analysis needs can be met. The actual needs of the analysis are analyzed with the matching results, and the test results are shown in Table 3.

Table 3 Actual matching rate and comprehensiveness of overall resources.

Algorithm	Diversified analysis needs.	Student's academic performance.	Make planning.	Conversation content.
Density clustering algorithm	38.94	46.02	58.41	48.67
Bee colony algorithm	34.51	41.59	38.05	46.02
P	38.94	58.41	50.44	41.59

According to the data analysis in Table 3, in the process of overall planning and overall analysis, the specific analysis method can have a significant impact on the corresponding data, and the effect is greater than 25%. But also can promote the deepening of resources, optimize the corresponding structure, and improve the overall planning of resources. However, whether there are obvious discounts and drastic results among clusters, and whether there are similarities, is directly related to the results of resource utilization. Therefore, it is necessary to judge the clustering process, and the judgment process is as follows. As shown in Fig. 3.

Fig. 3. Method of categorizing instructional resources plays of density clustering algorithm

It can be seen from the analysis results in Fig. 3, the data is relatively reasonable, and the accumulation of grammatical content and theoretical knowledge is independent, which shows that in the process of accumulation analysis, each data value has not achieved results, and the integrity of the data also meets the requirements.

4.4 Rationality of Method of Categorizing Instructional Resources Plays

In the process of language analysis, it is necessary to verify whether there are outliers in sentences, language grammar and other analysis, so as to ensure the reasonable distribution of data and the balance of overall resource utilization. So it is necessary to perform eigenvalue analysis on it. The eigenvalue analysis process is shown in Fig. 4.

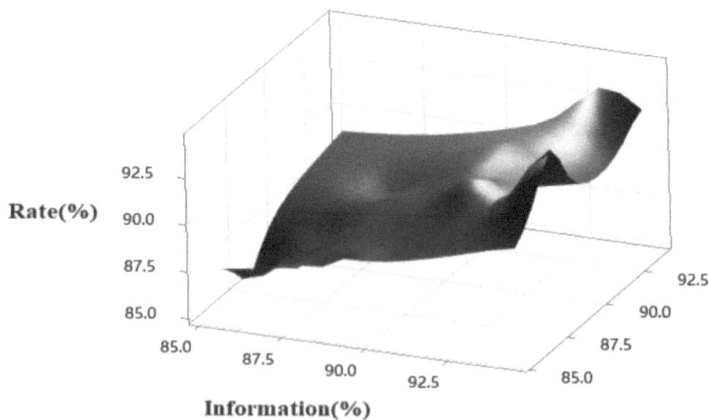

Fig. 4. Eigenvalue analysis of teaching resources.

From the decomposition in Fig. 4, it can be seen that in the overall distribution process of English, educational resources, grammar, sentences and other contents, there are direct similarities among them, and they are in balance, without significant differences, indicating that in the process of clustering, there is no significant impact on the results and English resources. In the process of analysis, English tends to be more balanced, and its contents and resources play an obvious role.

4.5   Validity of Method of Categorizing Instructional Resources Plays

In this aspect, some English contents will be virtualized and analyzed to judge whether the proportion of each indicator is the same. The specific results are shown in Fig. 5.

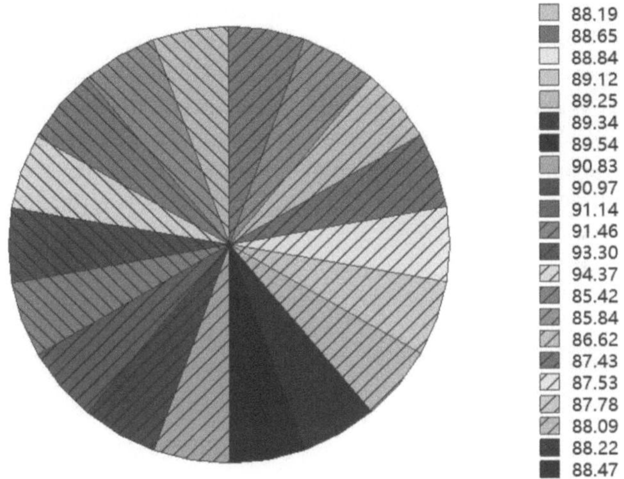

Fig. 5. The degree of balance of the contents of each index in the analysis process.

Figure 5 shows that in the analysis of English sentence content and logical relationship, the results account for the same proportion, and all of them are above 80%. It shows that in the process of technical analysis, the management and allocation of resources can be realized, so that resources can be more optimized and even, and the natural content and structure meet the requirements. In the process of holistic judgment and holistic analysis, the specific analysis results should be summarized, as shown in Fig. 4.

Table 4 Compares the efficacy of several method of categorizing instructional resources plays.

Algorithm	Holistic planning of members.	Depth of analysis.	Degree of resource utilization.	Coverage of knowledge points.
Density clustering algorithm	63.72	60.18	51.33	38.05
Bee colony algorithm	38.94	46.02	58.41	52.21

(continued)

Table 4 (*continued*)

Algorithm	Holistic planning of members.	Depth of analysis.	Degree of resource utilization.	Coverage of knowledge points.
exploitation.	34.51	41.59	38.05	38.05

Table 4 shows that the overall planning and analysis of English resources in China can realize the comprehensive judgment of resources. Moreover, through deep mining and clustering, we can realize the integration of resources, ensure the logic of resources, and provide support for corresponding scholars and university teaching. At the same time, there is a significant logical relationship between resources and many related contents such as lesson plan teaching and teaching planning, which further proves that the effectiveness of analysis results can improve and promote the comprehensiveness of resources. However, in the process of comprehensive analysis of resources, there are also three factors. Whether the three factors play a limited role and the role of interference factors require in-depth analysis. The composition process you mentioned is shown in Fig. 6.

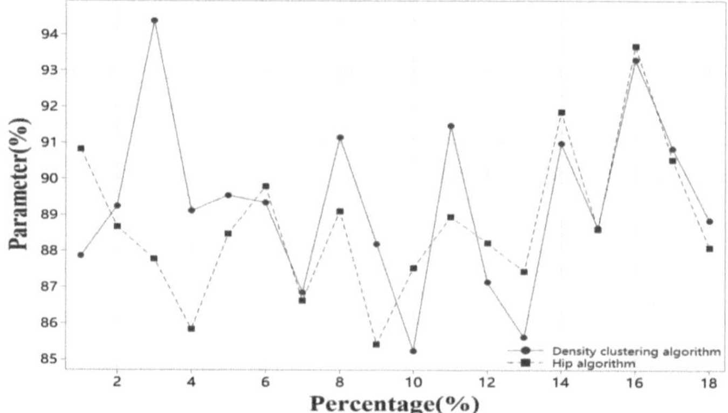

Fig. 6. Is the influence on english teaching resources.

Figure 6 shows that The integration of English and English, teaching and resource matching can improve the utilization effect of English resources, but the interference factors have not played a selective role, mainly. In the specific analysis process, the interference factors can be weakened to improve the accuracy of the analysis.

5 Conclusion

This is a complicated process of English analytical mathematics, but in the process of English teaching, whether who meets the requirements, the comprehensive utilization of resources and the matching of resources and details are the focus of research. Through the method of accumulation analysis, English resources are linked with comprehensive analysis and intense analysis, and it is found that this method can promote the promotion of English resources, with an improvement rate of more than 30%, and it can ensure that English political resources meet the requirements, and the promotion degree is greater than 80%. It shows that in the process of distance analysis and multi-faceted analysis, the needs can be met, and the logical relationship of legal content is relatively clear. Explain the indicators and contents in the process of distance, which can provide support for teaching and universities. At the same time, there exist shortcomings in my research, mainly sample data and test scope. In the future, the test scope will be expanded, and some samples will be added.

References

1. Yufei, G.: Research on classification method of college English teaching resources based on density clustering algorithm. Inf. Comput. **34**(22), 67–69 (2022)
2. Yang Zelan, Ren Yizuo, & Zhang Shaomin: Online classification method of neuronal peak potential based on density peak clustering algorithm. CN201810575804.2. (2022).
3. Guan Hongqing, Xu Liang, Wang Wei, Zhang Yuanjie, Zhang Daqian, & Yin Guangyi, et al.: Rental information retrieval method and system based on classifier and density clustering algorithm. CN202210636211.9. (2022).
4. Peng, Z., Xiaolin, L., Liyan, W.: Dynamic neighborhood density clustering algorithm based on DBSCAN. Computer Science. **50**(6A), 220400127–220400127 (2023)
5. Lü Yi, & Liu Mandan: Analysis of trajectory behavior based on improved density peak clustering algorithm. Comput. Eng. Appl.(017), 058 (2022).
6. Lin, S., Xiaoying, Q., Jiucheng, X., Zhanxi, X.: Density peak clustering algorithm based on k-nearest neighbor and optimized allocation strategy. J. Softw. (004), 033 (2022)
7. Fuqiang, L., Shihua, T., Guanghuan, H., Jinlong, M.: Point cloud extraction and monomerization of airborne lidar buildings based on spatial clustering algorithm applied by density noise. Sci. Technol. Eng. **22**(9), 7 (2022)
8. Guo Limin, & Li Dongze: A site selection method for shared bicycle stations based on density and access balance clustering. CN115879737A (2023).
9. Xinshan, Y., Xiangyin, M., Tengfei, J., Jinze, L.: Object edge detection method based on improved CANNY algorithm. Laser Optoelectron. Prog. **60**(22), 2212002 (2023)
10. Zhi, Y.: Research on visual analysis of academic data based on density clustering algorithm. Mod. Comput. Second Half Ed. (006), 028 (2022)
11. Huijuan, Q.I.: Research on hotspot mining based on improved density clustering algorithm. Manuf. Upgrade Today. (004), 000 (2022)
12. Su Guina: Research on density clustering algorithm based on standardized adaptive parameters. Electronic Technology and Wang Cheng, & Xingdong. (2022). Research on density clustering algorithm based on minimum spanning tree. Computer Technology and Development (002), 032 (2023).

Research on Dance Education Management Model Based on K-means Algorithm

Jingjing Fan[1(✉)] and Sergey Viktorovich Krivykh[2]

[1] Northeast Normal University, Changchun City, Jilin Province 130000, China
`fanjj0419@163.com`
[2] Russian State Normal University, St.Petersburg, Russian Federation 18800

Abstract. There is an issue with incorrect management positioning, despite the fact that management model research is crucial to intelligent dance education management. Intelligent dance education management presents unique challenges that conventional genetic algorithms have not been able to adequately address. Thus, this work provides an analysis of existing research on dance education management models and recommends new research based on the k-means algorithm. To begin, we use the theory of distance measurement to identify the components that will have an impact, and then we segment the indicators based on the needs of the management model research to lessen the impact of any potential interference. Next, a research plan for a k-mode algorithm management model is developed using distance measurement theory. The results show that the analysis method of educational management in the process of dance education research can improve the educational effect. Optimize the knowledge movements of dance, and the optimization rate is greater than 80%. The optimization potential and students' learning situation and content are comprehensively analyzed, and the success rate of analysis is greater than 45%.

Keywords: distance metric theory · k-means algorithm · Management model studies · Dance · Educational management

1 Introduction

An integral aspect of intelligent dance education management is management model research, which may expedite the control of management model research via accurate modeling. The management model research scheme, however, has the issue of inadequate accuracy [1, 2], which has certain negative consequences on the management model research [3] and hinders the process of management model research [4, 5]. Management model research and analysis using the k-means algorithm, according to certain academics, might produce useful results for analyzing management model research schemes [6–8]. Based on this, this work suggests a k-means method to improve the management model's research scheme and check its efficacy [9–11].

B. Brik and S. Nazir (Eds.): BigIoT-EDU 2024, LNICST 659, pp. 24–32, 2026.
https://doi.org/10.1007/978-3-032-18631-7_3

2 Related Works

2.1 K means Algorithm Mathematical Description

The k-means algorithm is y_i to use computer technology to optimize the management model research scheme, and determine the management model's unqualified value parameters based on the model's many index parameters is z_i, and integrate the management model research scheme as the function to finally judge the feasibility of the management model research, and the calculation is $tol(y_i \cdot t_{ij})$ shown in formula (1).

$$\lim_{x \to \infty} \left(y_i \cdot t_{ij} \right) = y_{ij} \div k \tag{1}$$

Among them, the judgment of outliers is shown in Eq. (2).

$$\max\left(t_{ij}\right) = \partial\left(t_{ij}^2 + io \cdot t_{ij}\right) \tag{2}$$

Management model research may be made more accurate with the use of the k-means method, which integrates the benefits of computer technology with management model research for quantification.

Teaching movements in dance is set_i, teaching skills of teachers is $F(t_i \approx 0)$ as shown in Eq. (3).

$$F\sqrt{(d_i)} = \sum t_i \oint y_i \cdot 7 \tag{3}$$

2.2 Selection of Management Model Research Protocols

Relevance of various movements in dance teaching is $g(t_i)$, difficulty in understanding the essentials of movements is w_i, comprehensive analysis of action essentials Eq. (4).

$$g(t_i) = \ddot{x} \cdot z_i \prod F(d_i)\frac{dy}{dx} - w_i \tag{4}$$

Aiming at the overall structure and logical analysis of dance teaching content. Eq. (5).

$$\lim_{x \to \infty} g(t_i) + \lim_{x \to \infty} F(d_i) \leq \bigcap imax\left(t_{ij}\right) \tag{5}$$

For the overall planning of dance teaching Eq. (6).

$$g(t_i) + F(d_i) \leftrightarrow mean\left(\sum t_{ij} + 4\right) \tag{6}$$

2.3   Analysis of Management Model Research Protocols

It is necessary to analyze the knowledge structure of learners which is $No(t_i)$. Hands-on and athletic abilities to learners are shown in Eq. (7).

$$No(t_i) = \frac{g(t_i) + F(d_i)}{mean\left(\sum t_{ij} + 4\right)} \quad \frac{-b \pm \sqrt{b^2 - 4ac}}{2a} \tag{7}$$

The individual abilities of learners are relative to the teaching conditions. Is $Zh(t_i)$ required, and the result is shown in Eq. (8).

$$Zh(t_i) = \frac{n!}{r!(n-r)!}\left[\sum g(t_i) + F(d_i)\right] \tag{8}$$

Holistic planning of learners is $unno(t_i)$. The holistic planning of dance teaching $accur(t_i)$ shown in Eq. (9).

$$Er(t_i) = \frac{\min\left[\sum g(t_i) + F(d_i)\right]}{\sum g(t_i) + F(d_i)} \tag{9}$$

During the teaching process, randomness of learning content is $randon(t_i)$. A holistic description of the requirements is formula (10).

$$FR(t_i) = \frac{\min\left[\sum g(t_i) + F(d_i)\right]}{\lim\limits_{x \to \infty} \sum g(t_i) + F(d_i)} + randon(t_i) \tag{10}$$

Therefore, the process of dance teaching is relatively complicated, and it is necessary not only to consider the learner's learning situation, personal quality and athletic ability, but also to make a collation judgment in combination with the practical teaching needs and the difficulty of dance.

3   Optimization Strategies for Managing Model Studies

By modifying the settings of the Internet information system, the k-means algorithm optimizes the management model research using a stochastic optimization method. In order to randomly choose distinct schemes, the k-means algorithm separates the management model study into multiple stages. An iterative procedure is used to optimize and assess the management model research scheme at various levels of the model. Once the optimization study is finished, we combine the management model research levels of many schemes and record the best one.

4   Results and Discussion

4.1   Introduction to Management Model Research

Art majors in universities conduct a comprehensive analysis as the research object to judge the teaching situation, teaching content and teaching form of dance. The specific data acquisition results are shown in Table 1.

Table 1. Manage model study requirements

Scope of application	grade	Athletic ability.	Understanding ability.
Dance school	I	38.05	36.28
	II	61.06	38.94
Dance Institutions	I	54.87	42.48
	II	36.28	61.06
Teacher Training	I	47.79	47.79
	II	33.63	42.48

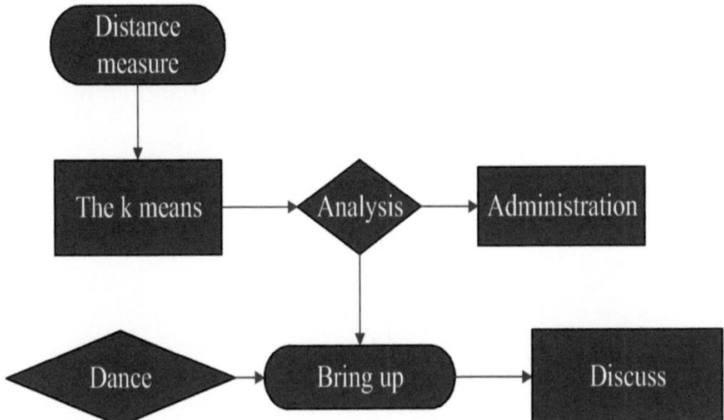

Fig. 1. Manage the analytical process of model studies

According to the analysis of No.1 Middle School, students' learning situation is relatively good in the process of judging sports ability, knowledge understanding ability and comprehensive ability, so it is necessary to analyze their judgment process and processing process. The analysis results are shown in Fig. 1.

According to the analysis of Fig. 1, in the process of learning, technical sports should be used as the technology to judge, and students' sports ability should be tested at the same time, necessary data should be obtained, data should be combined with knowledge points, and students should be taught in accordance with their aptitude, so as to realize the integration of students' learning interest, comprehensive analysis and knowledge ability.

4.2 Management Model Research

Students' knowledge should be managed as a whole, students' learning interest and content should be enhanced, and the original learning conditions should be optimized. In the analysis process of comprehensive acquisition, the learning situation and learning can be summarized, and the results can be summarized, as shown in Table 2.

Table 2. Manage the overall picture of the model study scenario

Category	Overall planning.	The perfection of the content.	The rationality of knowledge points.
Dance school	81.55	82.52	78.64
Dance institutions	82.52	77.67	82.52
Teacher training	81.55	79.61	74.76

4.3 Management Model Research and Stability

The amplitude of dance movements is displayed, and the amplitude results should be compared in the process of amplitude display. In the process of comparison, the amplitude and knowledge points should be mapped, and the content and amplitude conditions of knowledge points should be mapped.

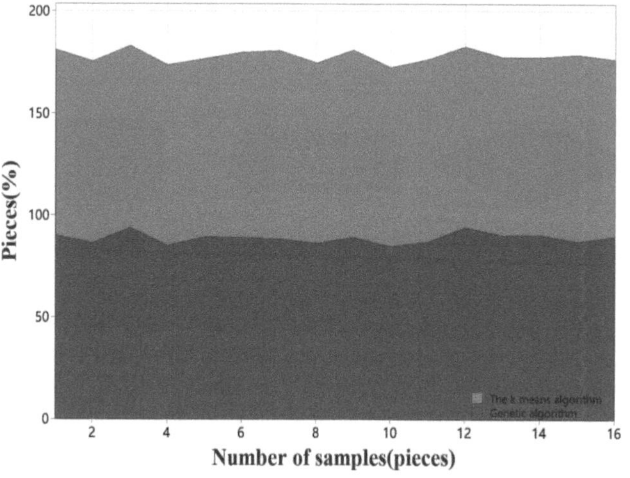

Fig. 2. Research on management models of different algorithms

Figure 2 shows that according to the actual needs of students, the exercise conditions are tested, and the exercise process is relatively reasonable. The above analysis results are compared. The analysis results are shown in Table 3.

Table 3. Comparison of the research accuracy of management models of different methods

Algorithm	Students' interest in learning is improved.	Improvement of knowledge points.	The compliance rate.	The perfection of students' dance creation.
K-means algorithm	47.79	59.29	75.73	81.55
Genetic algorithm	40.71	55.75	74.76	72.82
P	47.79	57.52	73.79	72.82

According to Table 3, compared with the movement and the overall effect, the equivalent force is greater than 80%. However, in the process of analysis, students' characteristics, personal characteristics and interests should be verified. The specific verification results are shown in Fig. 3.

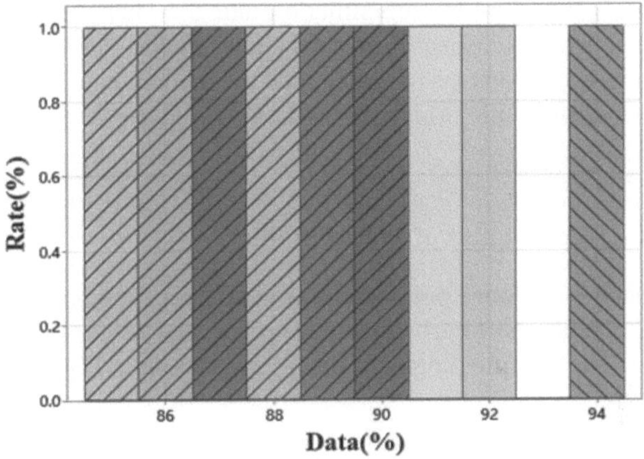

Fig. 3. Research on the management model of k-means algorithm

Figure 3 shows that the learning shape and movement process show the contrast of different colors, and between 90% and 92%, the quality of students' learning is qualitatively improved. By the way, in the process of analysis, students can better understand the knowledge points, dance, sports movements and movement essentials among students.

4.4 Rationality of Management Model Research

Each knowledge point and content are analyzed by C-chart, and the proportion and proportional relationship of each knowledge point are analyzed. The proportional relationship of each knowledge point is shown in Fig. 4.

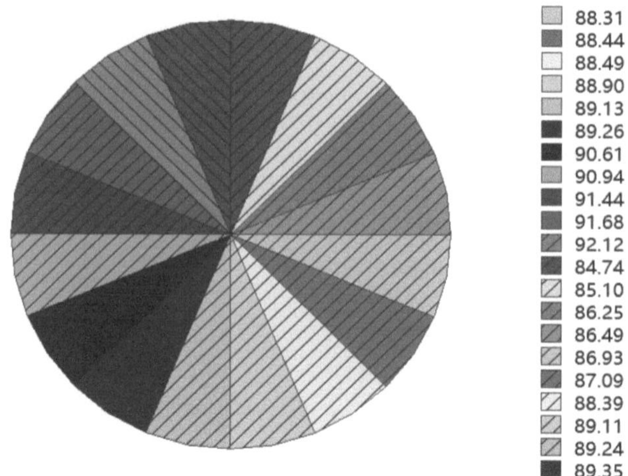

Fig. 4. Research on management models of different algorithms

Figure 4 shows that the learning situation and the changes of knowledge points are relatively reasonable. Reasonable process shows that in the process of analysis, the promotion of knowledge points is balanced, and the content and structure of knowledge points are relatively reasonable, which shows the knowledge process and analysis process can be realistic.

4.5 Manage the Effectiveness of Model Studies

The content of each knowledge point is represented by a circle graph, which represents the structure and conditions of each knowledge point, and judges the distribution of each knowledge point. The specific judgment results are shown in Fig. 5.

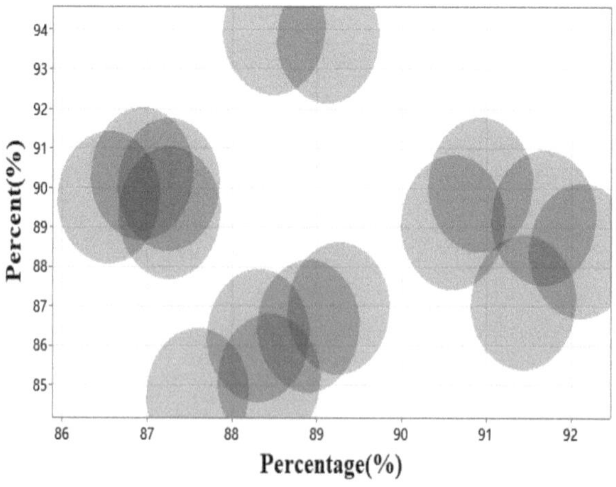

Fig. 5. Research on management models of different algorithms

Figure 5 shows that the structure and content of knowledge and the distribution of knowledge points are relatively reasonable, and the knowledge points are concentrated and different. However, whether each knowledge point is effective or not needs further excavation, and the analysis results of this paper are summarized in the form of charts. The summary results are shown in Table 4.

Table 4. Comparison of the effectiveness of management models of different methods

Algorithm	Enhancement of action expression.	Depth of understanding of knowledge points.	The connotation and relevance of knowledge.	The holistic structure of.
K-means algorithm	60.18	56.64	80.58	77.67
Genetic algorithm	46.90	40.71	72.82	77.67
P	50.44	61.06	79.61	78.64

According to Table 4, it shows that the expression of knowledge content, knowledge structure and knowledge comprehensiveness is relatively reasonable, and the real logical relationship and logical conditions also need to be judged. Through the current situation diagram to judge the changing trend of knowledge points, as illustrated in Fig. 6.

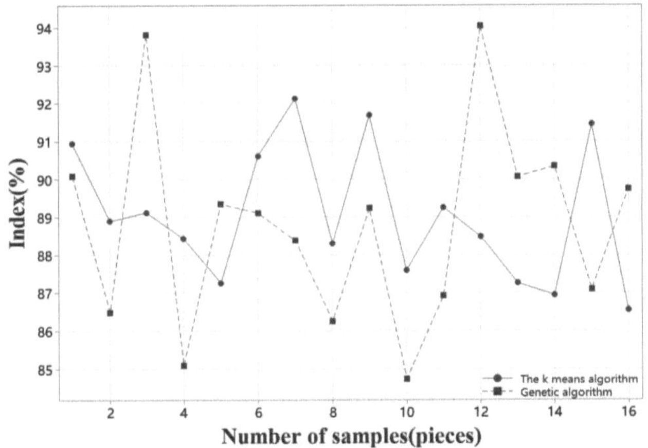

Fig. 6. Research on k-means algorithm management model

Figure 6 shows that the fluctuation of logical structure shows a uniform distribution, the contents and conditions of knowledge points, and the logical relationship of knowledge are relatively scattered, which shows that dance movements are closely related to knowledge.

5 Conclusion

Action and movement are the main contents in the existing teaching process, and they are also comprehensive judgment methods in the field of art. However, in the process of dance exercise, there are differences between its knowledge points and theories. In the process of analysis, the accuracy of dance movements has been improved, and the increase has been greater than 20%. The integration of theoretical knowledge is greater than 75%, and the exertion of individual personality is greater than 15%, which shows that the uniform analysis method can improve the analysis effect of dance education. However, we have some shortcomings, mainly due to the differences in samples and analysis time, and we will make up for the above shortcomings in the future.

References

1. Chang, F., Xu, X., Hu, Z., Zhang, Z.: Research on hierarchical teaching model based on K-means algorithm: a case study of computer network course. Comput. Knowl. Technol. Acad. Ed. **18**(26), 3 (2022)
2. Qin, X.: Research on Cloud Storage Model Based on Network Teaching Resource Consolidation. Doctoral dissertation,. Huazhong Normal University (2011)
3. Zhang, J.: Research on Privacy Protection Model and Algorithm Based on K-Anonymity. Doctoral dissertation. Tianjin University
4. Xiao, L., Zhu, X.: Research on risk prediction model of credit system based on K-means algorithm. J. Yulin Normal Univ. **5**, 6 (2018)
5. Zhao, M., Li, X., & Li, R.: Dance Generation Algorithm Based on Mixture Density Network (2019).
6. Lu, Y.: Dance Teaching Data Processing Method and System Based on Virtual Characters (2018).
7. Yu, J., Wang, Q., Chen, H.: Dance interaction system based on motion evaluation algorithm. Comput. Modernization. (6), 9 (2018)
8. Meng, X.: Dance motion interference suppression algorithm based on wearable sensors. J. Xi'an Univ Posts Telecommun. (005), 021 (2016)
9. Zhao, M.: Research on Music Choreography Algorithm Based on Mixture Density Network. Doctoral dissertation. Beijing University of Posts and Telecommunications
10. Hao, L.: Research on cloud computing-based education resource management model in universities. Electronic World. (15), 2 (2015)
11. Tian, C., Yang, W., Yang, D., Wang, Y., Sun, S.: Student behavior analysis and research based on K-means and DBSCAN clustering algorithms in the background of comprehensive university data. Heilongjiang Sci. Technol. Inf. **000**(032), 86–88 (2020)

Application of Big Data in Intelligence Education

Research on the Construction of Historical District Information Platform Based on Big Data Technology

Yuanyuan Shi[(✉)]

Changchun University of Architecture and civil engineering, Changchun 130607, Jilin, China
307007005@qq.com

Abstract. People now place a premium on cultural heritage and historical sites, and both are crucial to any nation's development. One example of this is the historic district. While exploring the historic area, one can easily sense the marks left by the past, and the knowledge provided by the blocks may help one better comprehend the district's cultural background and its origins. The challenge of understanding neighborhood information in historic neighborhoods cannot be solved using traditional approaches. Consequently, this study suggests a platform for historical district information analysis of neighborhood data that is built on big data technology. In order to minimize the block information's interference, the indicators are first segregated according to the needs of the block information, and then the historical district information platform is designed using the computer. The computer then creates the block information scheme, builds the platform for the historical district information, and produces the block information. Perform an exhaustive investigation. A MATLAB simulation demonstrates that, according to certain assessment criteria, the big data-based historical district information platform comprehends the accuracy of the neighborhood information rather well. Compared to more conventional approaches, the reliability of neighborhood data is superior.

Keywords: computer · Historic district information platform based on big data technology · Historic districts · Block information

1 Introduction

Information on individual blocks is crucial to the development of the historic district and is therefore an essential part of the district's content [1]. Nevertheless, there is an inaccuracy in comprehending the neighborhood information [4], and the neighborhood information scheme has the issue of low accuracy [3] while processing block information. There are academics who think that by analyzing historical districts using a platform built on big data technology, we may better understand the neighborhood information system and get the right kind of support for it [5]. In light of this, the article suggests a big data–powered historical district information platform to enhance the neighborhood information scheme and test the model's efficacy.

B. Brik and S. Nazir (Eds.): BigIoT-EDU 2024, LNICST 659, pp. 35–41, 2026.
https://doi.org/10.1007/978-3-032-18631-7_4

2 Related Works

A. Mathematical description of the historic district information platform based on big data technology

The historical district information platform optimizes the neighborhood information scheme by using big data technologies and identifying the unqualified values in the historic area based on n_i, and the indicators in the block information is k_i, and the block information is analyzed The scheme is $tol(n_i \cdot r_{ij})$, This historic district's feasibility was determined using the calculation shown in Eq. (1).

$$tol\left(\sum r_i \cdot n_i \cdot r_{ij}\right) = n_{ij} \geq \max(r_{ij} - 7) \div \iiint_{i=1} k_i \tag{1}$$

Eq. (2) shows the evaluation of outliers among them.

$$\max(r_{ij}) = \oiint_{JJ} n_i - \left(r_{ij}^2 + 2\right) \succ mean\left(\sum r_{ij} + 3\right) \cdot \sum_{i=1}^{n} (r_i - k_i)^2 - \hat{9} \tag{2}$$

By integrating the benefits of big data with historical districts for quantification, the historical district information platform may enhance the accuracy of neighborhood information.

Hypothesis I. The neighborhood information requirement is r_i, the neighborhood information scheme is set_i, the satisfaction of the neighborhood information scheme is n_i, and the neighborhood information scheme judgment function is $Y(r_i \approx 0)$ as shown in Eq. (3).

$$Y(x_i) = \sum r_i \bigcap \xi \cdot \oint_{i=1} x_i \iff 7 * \sqrt{6} \rightarrow \oint n_i \tag{3}$$

B. Selection of neighborhood information schemes

Hypothesis II. The historic district function is $e(r_i)$, and the weight coefficient is z_i, Finally, Eq. (4) shows the neighborhood information required for unqualified historic districts.

$$e(r_i) = \sum^{r_i} e - k_i \bullet \prod Y(x_i) + 7 \bullet \frac{\partial^2 \Omega}{\partial u^2} - z_i \bullet \frac{1}{n} \tag{4}$$

An all-inclusive function of historic district information may be derived from assumptions I and II, as seen in Eq. (5).

$$e(r_i) + Y(x_i) \leq \max\left(r_{ij}\right) \tag{5}$$

The consequences of standardizing all data may be seen in Eq. (6), which shows how to effectively increase the accuracy of neighborhood information.

$$e(r_i) + Y(x_i) \leftrightarrow mean\left(\sum r_{ij} + 3\right) \cdot \sum_{i=1}^{n} (r_i - k_i)^2 - \hat{9} \tag{6}$$

C. Analysis of the neighborhood information program

A thorough examination of the block information scheme and a mapping of the block information needs to the historical district database are prerequisites to implementing the big data technology-based historical district information platform, and eliminate the unqualified Block Information Program is $No(r_i)$, The anomaly assessment technique may be given using Eq. (6), and the outcomes can be seen in Eq. (7).

$$No(r_i) = \frac{e(r_i) + Y(x_i)}{mean\left(\sum r_{ij} + 3\right) \cdot \sum_{i=1}^{n} (r_i - k_i)^2 - \hat{9}} \tag{7}$$

Among them, $\frac{e(r_i)+Y(x_i)}{mean\left(\sum r_{ij}+3\right)\cdot\sum_{i=1}^{n}(r_i-k_i)^2-\hat{9}} \leq 1$ it is stated that the scheme needs to be proposed, otherwise the scheme integration required is $Zh(r_i)$, and the result is shown in Eq. (8).

$$Zh(r_i) = min\left[\sum e(r_i) + Y(x_i)\right] \tag{8}$$

To guarantee the accuracy of the historical district information platform based on big data technology, historic districts are thoroughly examined and the neighborhood information schemes' threshold and index weights are defined. The analysis of historic districts must be precise since they are information systems that use systematic test blocks. If a historic district is in a nonnormal distribution is $unno(r_i)$, its neighborhood information scheme is affected, reducing the accuracy of the overall neighborhood information is $accur(r_i)$, as shown in Eq. (9).

$$accur(r_i) = \frac{min\left[\sum e(r_i) + Y(x_i)\right]}{\sum e(r_i) + Y(x_i)} \times 100\% \tag{9}$$

A multidimensional distribution is presented by the neighborhood information scheme, according to the survey, which is consistent with objective facts. Because historic districts are non-directional, this research is considered to be very analytical because it shows that the neighborhood information system is quite random. If the random function of the historic district is $randon(r_i)$, then the calculation of formula (9) can be expressed as formula (10).

$$accur(r_i) = \frac{min\left[\sum e(r_i) + Y(x_i)\right]}{\sum e(r_i) + Y(x_i)} \times 100\% + randon(r_i) \tag{10}$$

Among them, the historic district satisfies typical standards; this is largely attributable to the fact that, with the help of big data technology, the district has been fine-tuned, with unnecessary and duplicate schemes removed and the default scheme supplemented to provide a robust dynamic correlation of the whole block's information scheme.

3 Optimization Strategies for Historic Districts

Utilizing big data technology, the historical district information platform implements a random optimization strategy for the district. It then tweaks the platform's settings to achieve scheme optimization for the historic district. The big data platform that tracks the historical district uses random selection to split the area into several neighborhood information tiers. Neighborhood information schemes with varying degrees of neighborhood information are optimized and evaluated iteratively. Document the best historic districts by comparing the neighborhood information levels of various scenarios when the optimization study is complete.

4 Results and Discussion

A. Neighborhood information briefing

This article utilizes the historical district as its research object, with 12 pathways and a 12-h test duration, as well as the block information of that particular historical district, in order to enable neighborhood information. Table 1 displays the scheme.

Table 1. BLOCK INFORMATION REQUIREMENTS

Scope of application	grade	accuracy	Block information
Historical city	routine	85.62	84.92
	Higher	86.97	86.83
Historical town	routine	85.96	85.50
	Higher	86.57	91.71
Historic central district	routine	88.16	85.13
	Higher	86.53	86.69

The neighborhood information process in Table 1. is shown in Fig. 1.

The neighborhood information strategy that utilizes big data technology to draw from historical district data is more in line with the real needs of the area than the conventional approach. The historical district information platform that utilizes big data technology outshines the conventional way when it comes to the veracity and logic of the data contained inside. Figure 2 shows the updated neighborhood information scheme, which demonstrates how the historical district information platform powered by big data technology is more accurate and trustworthy. Consequently, the historical district information platform that relies on big data technology offers improved neighborhood information scheme speed, accuracy, and stability of summation.

B. Historic district situation

Unstructured, semi-structural, and structural types of information are all part of a historic district's neighborhood information system. Following the pre-selection of

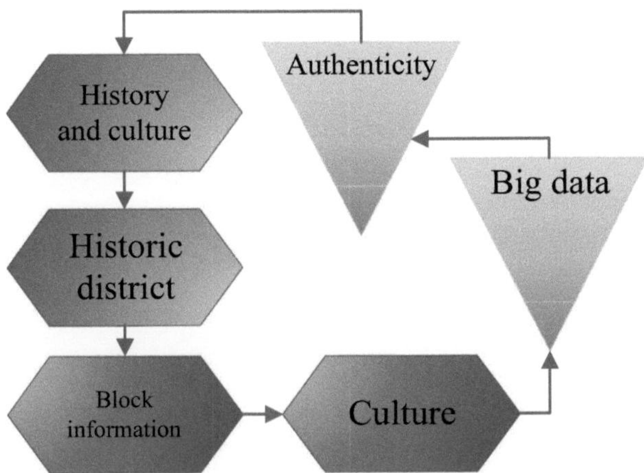

Fig. 1. The process of analysis of historic districts

the big data technology-based historical district information platform, the feasibility of the neighborhood information scheme was assessed, and the historic district's preliminary neighborhood information scheme was obtained. Referring to Table 2, you may choose from a variety of neighborhood information levels for historic districts and block information schemes to ensure that the data is correct.

Table 2. The overall situation of the neighborhood information programme

category	accuracy	Analysis rate
Historical city	83.78	88.54
Historical town	81.69	85.97
Historic central district	88.45	87.28
mean	89.03	92.06
X^6	89.30	89.92
P = 2.104		

C. Block information and stability of neighborhood information

Figure 2 shows a comparison of the neighborhood information scheme with the conventional method of comparing neighborhood information schemes in order to confirm the correctness of the historical district information platform that is based on big data technology.

From Fig. 2, we can deduce that the neighborhood information of the historical district information platform utilizing big data technology is more accurate and stable than that of the traditional method, despite having a higher neighborhood information.

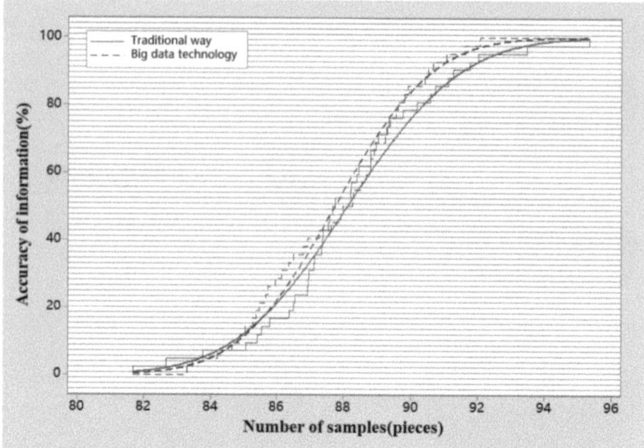

Fig. 2: Block Information for Different Algorithms

The usual method of gathering data about communities is not uniform. Table 3 displays, on average, the block information schemes of the aforementioned methods.

Table 3. Comparison of neighborhood information accuracy comparison by different methods

algorithm	Block information	Magnitude of change	error
Historical district information platform based on big data technology	94.27	93.01	96.09
The traditional way	89.80	91.21	93.07
P	88.74	90.88	90.91

Table 3 shows that there are problems with the standard method's accuracy of neighborhood information when it comes to historic districts. Additionally, the error rate is considerable, and historic districts have changed a lot. When compared to more conventional approaches, the overall outcomes of the big data-based historical district information platform are superior in terms of local data. Concurrently, the accuracy of the neighborhood data on the historical district information platform, which is based on big data technology, remains unchanged and exceeds 93%. So that the historical district's big data information platform may be further shown to be the best. The efficiency of the suggested technique is further validated by conducting a broad study of the historical district information platform based on big data technology using various methodologies, as shown in Fig. 3.

Figure 3 shows that compared to the traditional method, the neighborhood information of the historical district information platform based on big data technology is way better. This is because the platform increases the adjustment coefficient of the historic district and sets the threshold to eliminate neighborhood information schemes that don't meet the requirements.

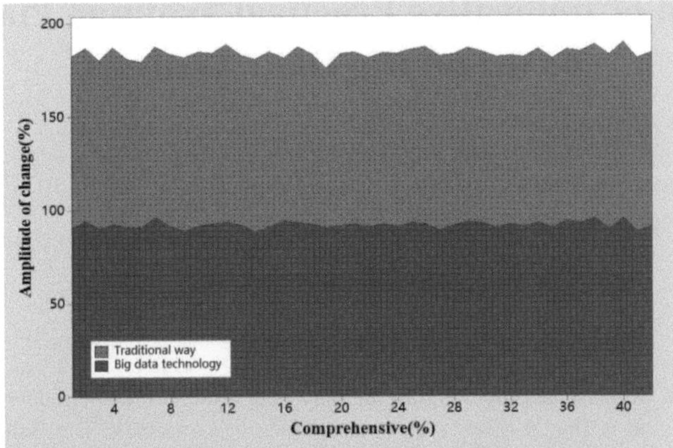

Fig. 3. Block information based on big data technology: neighborhood information based on historical district information platform

5 Conclusion

This article presents a big data technology-based historical district information platform and integrates big data technologies to optimize the historical district in an effort to address the issue of imperfect historical district information. While doing so, we compile a set of historical district information platforms and conduct an in-depth analysis of the accuracy of neighborhood information. From what we can see, a historical district information platform built on top of big data technology has the potential to enhance the district's growth and provide useful local data. But in building a big data-based historical district information platform, we focus too much on analyzing neighborhood data, which leads to an irrational choice of neighborhood data indicators.

Acknowledgements. This paper is the research result of the doctor and youth supporting project "Research of value evaluation system of commercial historical blocks in Changchun"supported by social science foundation of Jilin Province, with the project number of 2021c103.

References

1. Ying, Y., Runqiang, W.: Information graphics of public space in historic districts from the perspective of interactive determinism. J. Fine Arts. (06), 120–126 (2022)
2. Run, H.E.: Application of Digital Technology in "Restorative Construction" of Old City of Beijing. North China University of Technology (2022)
3. Ran, C.: Research on Adaptive Protection of Historic Districts Based on the Analysis of Stratification Law. Chongqing University (2020)
4. Wei, Z., Yiyu, Z.: The neighborhood culture is not only restored, but also better continued, a brief discussion on the protection of the historical and cultural district of Chaozong street in the context of the information age. Sino-Foreign Archit. (04), 16–19 (2020)
5. Qian, S.: Research on Public Participation and Platform Construction of Historic District Protection in the Era of Dataization. Huazhong University of Science and Technology (2016)

Design of Innovative Practical Training Platform Based on Big Data Analysis

Xingxing Miao$^{(\boxtimes)}$, Zhen Chen, Xiaoyu Zhang, and Guo Chen

Unit 32317, Urumqi City, Xinjiang 830000, China
119326301@qq.com

Abstract. Innovative practical training plays a crucial part in talent development, but the issue is that it often yields unsatisfactory outcomes. The issue of creative practical training in talent development remains unsolved by conventional approaches, and the outcomes are implausible. Consequently, this research suggests a novel platform for practical training analysis that is both original and practical. To begin, talent data is analyzed using big data techniques. Indicators are then classified according to the needs of creative practice training, with the goal of reducing the interference factor. The next step is for big data to examine the findings from creative practical training for talent nurturing, then create a program for innovative practical training, and finally implement the program. Perform an exhaustive investigation. According to the results of the MATLAB simulation, the unique practical training platform may be used for talent training under certain assessment conditions. Innovative practical training outperforms more conventional approaches.

Keywords: big data analysis · Innovative practical training platform · talent development

1 Introduction

There is a lot of value in talent training, and one of its key components is innovative practical training [1]. However, there is an issue with inaccurate creative practical training programs [3], which impacts talent training in some way [2], when doing innovative practical training. According to certain academics, the innovative practice training platform may be used to examine talent training in a way that is both successful and consistent with the creative practice training program [4]. Building on this foundation, this research suggests a cutting-edge platform for practice training that will optimize the training scheme and ensure the model's efficacy [5].

2 Related Works

A. Mathematical description of the innovative practical training platform

© ICST Institute for Computer Sciences, Social Informatics and Telecommunications Engineering 2026
Published by Springer Nature Switzerland AG 2026. All Rights Reserved
B. Brik and S. Nazir (Eds.): BigIoT-EDU 2024, LNICST 659, pp. 42–47, 2026.
https://doi.org/10.1007/978-3-032-18631-7_5

Using big data analysis, the innovative practice training platform optimizes the program, finds the unqualified values in talent training based on indications in innovative practice training, and trains innovation practice. Finally, the plan is put into motion, and the viability of talent development is evaluated. By integrating the benefits of big data analysis with talent training for quantification, the innovative practice training platform may enhance the outcomes of innovative practice training.

First Hypothesis: What is Necessary for Modern Practical Education is x_i, the groundbreaking hands-on education initiative is set_i, contentment with the cutting-edge hands-on training curriculum is p_i, together with the training program's novel assessment function is $H(x_i \approx 0)$, As shown in Eq. (1).

$$H(x_i p_i) = \bigcap_{i=1}^{x} x_i \int_i i + \sqrt{7} \cdot \frac{\Delta p_i}{\Delta H} \tag{1}$$

B. Selection of innovative practical training programs

We second-guess that the talent-development process is $m(x_i)$, and the weight coefficient is f_i, Consequently, as shown in Eq. (2), training for creative practice necessitates the development of untrained skills.

$$m(x_i) = \frac{1}{m} \cdot \sum_{i=1}^{x} (x_i \cdot 2 + m)^2 \overrightarrow{m} \cdot \frac{9}{7} + \int x_i \tag{2}$$

C. Analysis of innovative practical training programs

Prior to implementing the innovative practice training platform, it is essential to undertake a comprehensive evaluation of the program, determine the talent pool's capacity to meet the program's demands, and remove any programs that do not meet the program's qualifications. Initially, in order to guarantee the viability of novel practical training platforms, a thorough evaluation of talent training must be conducted, followed by the establishment of thresholds and index weights. Talent training necessitates precise analysis as it is a methodical evaluation of novel practical training methods. There will be a decrease in the overall accuracy of innovation practice training if talent training does not follow a normal distribution. Figure 1 shows the unique program selection process that should be followed to increase the quality of creative practice training and the accuracy of the innovative practice training platform.

Consistent with empirical evidence, the study of innovative practical training programs reveals that these programs have a multimodal distribution. This research is considered to be very analytical since talent training is not directed, which suggests that creative practical training methods have great unpredictability. The dynamic correlation of the whole creative practical training program is strong, and talent training fulfills the usual standards mostly because big data analysis modifies talent training, removes redundant and unnecessary schemes, and augments the default scheme.

3 Optimization Strategies for Talent Development

To optimize the talent training program, the cutting-edge practice training platform uses a random optimization technique and tweaks the parameters of the talent data set. Talent training is divided into many tiers of innovative practice training on the innovative

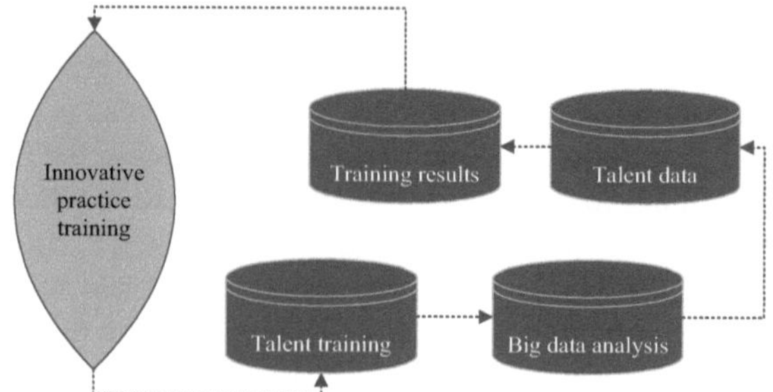

Fig. 1. Selection results of innovative practical training programs

practice training platform, and different programs are selected at random. The iterative approach involves optimizing and analyzing new practice training methods with varying degrees of instruction. Once the optimization study is finished, you may choose the best talent training by comparing the unique practical training levels of various solutions.

4   Results and Discussion

A. Introduction to innovative practical training

With 12 possible routes and a 12-h testing period, this article examines talent training in complicated contexts as its study object, with the goal of facilitating creative practical training in the area of particular talent training. Table 1 displays the scheme.

Table 1. Innovative practical training requirements

Scope of application	grade	viability	Innovative practical training
Strong skills	standard	85.04	84.95
	Higher	84.93	84.75
High quality	standard	84.44	84.90
	Higher	83.01	84.71
Wide adaptability	standard	84.52	85.26
	Higher	88.05	86.12

The innovative hands-on training process in Table 1. is shown in Fig. 2.

The innovative practical training platform's training plan is more in line with the real needs of innovative practical training than conventional techniques. The new practical training platform outperforms the old ways when comparing the logicality of talent training and training outcomes. One can see that the creative practical training platform is more stable and produces better outcomes from practical training after making the improvements shown in Fig. 2. This means that new practical training platforms have improved creative practical training program speeds, logic, and summation stability.

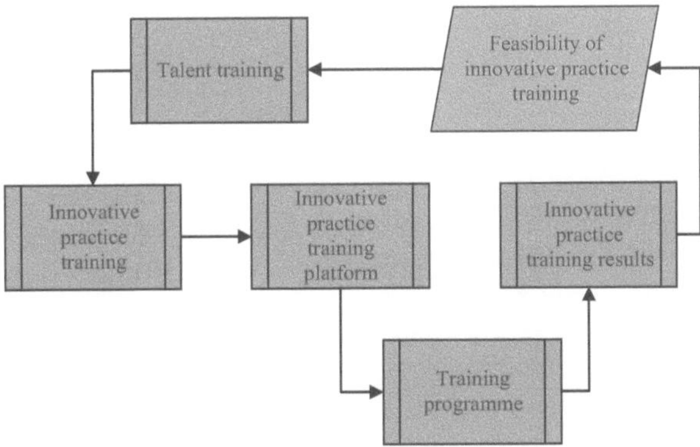

Fig. 2. The analytical process of talent development

B. Talent training

There are three types of data included in the cutting-edge practical training program for talent development: unstructured, semi-structured, and structured. The talent training process begins with the pre-selection of an innovative practical training platform and continues with the acquisition of a preliminary innovative practical training curriculum. Evaluation of potential new forms of hands-on education. Table 2 shows the novel practice training method, and selecting talent training with varying degrees of this training will allow for more precise verification of the outcomes.

Table 2. The overall situation of innovative practical training programs

category	efficiency	Analysis rate
Strong skills	88.82	88.92
High quality	88.15	85.45
Wide adaptability	85.95	85.35
mean	88.34	88.51
X^6	88.14	89.21
P = 1.66		

C. Innovative practical training and stability

The novel practice training scheme is compared with the conventional approach of the innovative practice training program in order to validate its correctness. Fig. 3 shows the innovative practice training scheme.

Figure 3 shows that the innovative practice training on the innovative practice training platform is more effective than the traditional method, with a lower error rate. This suggests that the innovative practice training on the innovative practice training platform is more stable, in contrast to the traditional method. Innovative practice training is

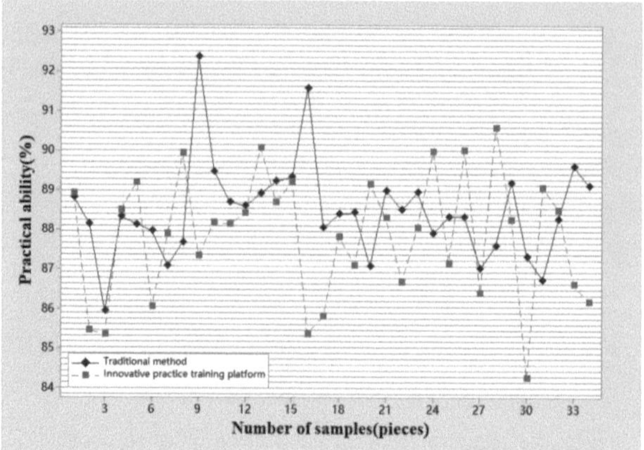

Fig. 3. INNOVATIVE Practical Training Of Different Algorithms

not uniform. The three algorithms mentioned earlier have their average novel practice training schemes shown in Table 3.

Table 3. Comparison of the accuracy of innovative practical training of different methods

algorithm	Innovative practical training	Magnitude of change	error
Innovative practical training platform	92.14	92.16	92.92
Traditional methods	91.76	90.94	90.55
P	90.59	92.23	91.96

Table 3 shows that talent training has undergone substantial changes, the mistake rate is considerable, and the old technique fails to provide outcomes that are commensurate with new practical training. In comparison to more conventional approaches, the novel practice training platform consistently produces better overall outcomes. Concurrently, the novel practice training platform has an accuracy rate of over 90% and has not seen a major shift in this area. In order to provide further evidence that the cutting-edge practical training platform is better. Figure 4 shows the results of a multi-method general study of the novel practice training platform, which is conducted to further confirm the efficacy of the suggested technique.

Figure 4 shows that compared to the conventional technique, the novel practice training platform much outperforms it. This is because the platform raises the adjustment coefficient of talent training and is Cutting out creative, hands-on training programs that fall short of expectations is the goal of talent data threshold analysis.

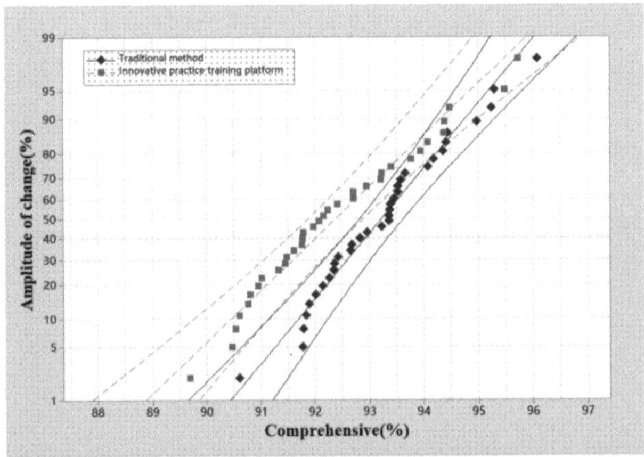

Fig. 4. Innovative practical training platforminnovative practical training of innovative practical training

5 Conclusion

This study presents a novel platform for creative practice training and integrates big data analysis to enhance talent training, in response to the issue that current innovative practice training is inadequate. Also, in order to build a talent database, extensive study of creative practice training outcomes is done. In addition to conducting general innovation practice training for talent training, research indicates that the inventive practice training platform may enhance talent training outcomes. Nevertheless, the selection of indicators for creative practice training becomes illogical due to the platform's overemphasis on innovative practice training analysis.

References

1. Rismawaty Arunglabi, A.T.I.R., Askar Taliang, M.R.: 5G Technology in Smart Healthcare and Smart City Development Integration with deep learning architectures. Int. J. Commun. Netw. Inf. Secur. (IJCNIS). **14**(3), 99–109 (2022)
2. Mubeen, S. . , Kulkarni, D. N. ., Tanpoco, M. R., Kumar, D. R., Naidu, M.L. Dhope, T. . (2022). Linguistic based emotion detection from live social media data classification using metaheuristic deep learning techniques. Int. J. Commun. Netw. Inf. Secur. (IJCNIS), 14(3), 176–186.
3. Solís, E. M. T. . , Cotrina-Aliaga, J. C. ., Calderón Samaniego, D. S. S. ., Castro-Cayllahua, F. ., Pardo Alarcon, B. N. ., & Cruz, Y. M. M. (2022). 5G with fog computing based privacy system in data analytics for healthcare system by AI techniques. Int. J. Commun. Netw. Inf. Secur. (IJCNIS), 14(3), 313–329.
4. Bhatt, R. . , Shikka, M. R., C. R. Manjunath ., Sharma, S.S.P.M. , Pandey, A. K. ., & Bala, K. . (2022). Centralized cloud service providers in improving resource allocation and data integrity by 4G IoT paradigm. Int. J. Commun. Netw. Inf. Secur. (IJCNIS), 14(3), 138–149.
5. Yadav, A. K. . , Sharma, M. B. ., Bhagat, A. K. ,Shah, D. H., Manjunath, C. R. Awasthi, A. . (2023). Edge computing in centralized data server deployment for network Qos and latency improvement for virtualization environment. Int. J. Commun. Netw. Inf. Secur. (IJCNIS), 14(3), 214–225.

Confucian Curriculum and School Cultural Management under the Background of Big Data Computing

Xiaoci Yang[1,2]([✉]) and Janaka Low Chee Kong[1,2]

[1] Malaysia University of Science and Technology, Kuala Lumpur 47810, Malaysia
yangxiaoci1978@163.com
[2] Xi'an FanYi University, Xi'an 710105, China

Abstract. The Confucian curriculum, derived from the ancient Chinese education system, and with its profound philosophical connotation and humanistic spirit, has exerted a profound influence on the education of later generations. Confucius put forward "learning while learning, not also say" emphasized the importance of continuous learning, and "those who know are not as good as the good, and those who are good are not as good as those who are happy" advocated the educational concept guided by interest. These ideas are still of great value in modern education, especially in cultivating well-rounded individuals, shaping social civic literacy and improving moral education. With the social change, modern education is facing new demands. Education in the 21st century is no longer just about the teaching of knowledge, but about the ability to cultivate the ability of innovative thinking, critical thinking and lifelong learning. The rise of big data computing has brought about revolutionary changes to educational management. By collecting and analyzing students 'learning data, educators can more accurately understand students' learning patterns, interests and challenges, thus providing personalized teaching programs. MATLAB simulation shows that under certain evaluation criteria, Confucian culture has a rational effect on school culture management and school cultural thinking All are superior to ordinary cultural ideas.

Keywords: Big Data · Confucian culture · school management · School culture

1 Introduction

Big data is also applied to the optimal allocation of educational resources. By analyzing educational data at the school, regional and national levels [1, 2], policy makers can identify patterns of educational inequalities and develop more effective policies to narrow the gap. At the same time, big data can also assist educational evaluation, evaluate the quality and effect of education in a more scientific way [3, 4], and promote the equity and quality improvement of education. In the process of integrating Confucian curriculum and modern education, big data technology can serve as a bridge to help explore the modern value of Confucianism [5, 6], combine traditional educational concepts with

B. Brik and S. Nazir (Eds.): BigIoT-EDU 2024, LNICST 659, pp. 48–56, 2026.
https://doi.org/10.1007/978-3-032-18631-7_6

scientific and technological means, and realize the personalization, intelligence and humanization of education [7, 8]. This integration can not only enrich the connotation of education, but also improve the effectiveness of education, and contribute to the cultivation of modern citizens with a global vision and traditional cultural heritage. The school culture process in Table 1. is shown in Fig. 1.

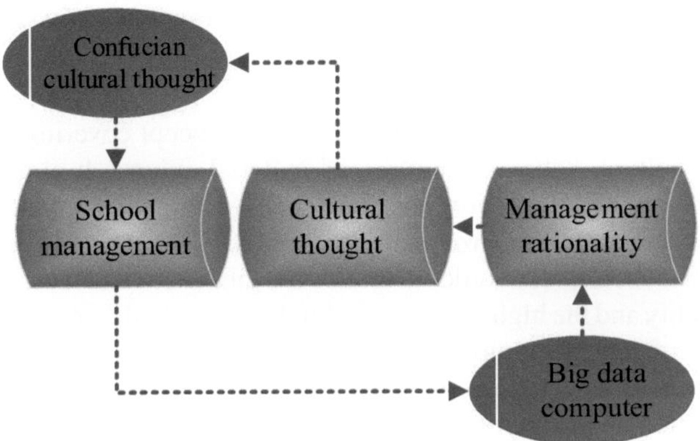

Fig. 1. The analytical process of school management

Cultural inheritance and innovation By analyzing historical data, schools can discover which cultural elements have profound effects on students and which need to be updated or innovated. This helps schools introduce new cultural elements to accommodate the changing educational environment and changing social needs while preserving tradition [9, 10].

2 Related Works

A. *The educational objectives and values of the Confucian curriculum*

1. Characteristics of Confucian culture

The Confucian curriculum, which originated from the ancient Chinese education system, takes Confucius's "benevolence, righteousness, propriety, wisdom and faith" as the core, and aims to cultivate citizens with virtue, knowledge and a sense of social responsibility. The goal of education not only focuses on the transmission of knowledge, but also pays attention to the cultivation of moral character and the perfection of personality. Confucianism emphasizes that "learning is an official" and encourages students to improve themselves through learning and then serve the society. The value of Confucian curriculum is to promote filial piety, fraternity, loyalty, trust, propriety, righteousness, integrity and shame, cultivate students' sense of social responsibility and humanistic spirit, and make them become the backbone of the society.

2. Current Situation of Confucian Cultural Management

In the modern education system, the integration of Confucian curriculum and subject education is an important way to improve the quality of education. This includes integrating the Confucian moral education concept into the teaching of various disciplines, such as exploring the influence of Confucianism on the historical course in the history class, learning the Confucian classics in the Chinese class, and emphasizing the moral norms of Confucianism in the civic education.

B. *The connotation and characteristics of school culture management*

1. The definition and importance of school culture management

School culture management is a comprehensive concept covering school spirit and culture, system culture, behavior culture and material culture. It aims to promote the growth and development of teachers and students by shaping and maintaining a positive and harmonious educational environment. It emphasizes the inheritance, innovation and integration of school culture, in order to realize the guidance of values, the improvement of education quality and the highlighting of school characteristics in educational practice. The importance of school culture management is reflected in that it plays a vital role in shaping the school atmosphere, enhancing the cohesion of education, improving the quality of education and teaching, and cultivating all-round development of talents.

2. The influence of Confucianism on school culture management

Confucianism, with "benevolence, righteousness, propriety, wisdom and faith" as the core, has deeply influenced the philosophical foundation of Chinese education. In the management of school culture, the "harmony without uniformity" advocated by Confucianism encourages the respect for individual differences and promotes the harmonious coexistence between teachers and students. The concept of "respecting teachers and valuing education" strengthens the authority of teachers and encourages students to respect and love knowledge."Learning while learning" emphasizes the importance of continuous learning and practice, which has a profound impact on forming a positive learning atmosphere and lifelong learning habits. In addition, the Confucian concept of "cultivating one's morality, regulating the family, governing the country and leveling the world" emphasizes the cultivation of individual morality, which is of guiding significance to the construction of a school culture based on moral education.

C. *The application of big data computing in School culture management*

1. Data-driven school culture management strategy

Big data computing provides a new means, through the deep mining of school historical data, we can more accurately diagnose and evaluate the status quo of school culture. This includes quantitative analysis of the school's core values, norms, behavioral norms, teaching models, and teacher-student relationship, so as to reveal its internal patterns and laws.

2. Personalized strategy formulation

Data-driven management strategies enable more targeted improvement programs based on the unique cultural characteristics of each school. Through the correlation analysis of the data from different dimensions, the school management can identify the key factors affecting the cultural development, and then design the strategies that can optimize these factors.

3. Real-time monitoring and adjustment

The real-time nature of big data enables the school management to timely understand the implementation effect of cultural management strategies, and to adjust the measures that are not adapted or not effective. Through continuous data collection and analysis, schools can form a feedback loop to ensure that cultural management strategies are always consistent with the actual situation.

Through the analysis of students 'interest, participation and other data, the school can more accurately plan campus cultural activities and improve students' enthusiasm for participation. For example, based on historical activity data, it is possible to predict which themes or forms of activity are more popular, thus optimizing activity design. Community building and interaction.

3 Optimization Strategies for School Management

The inheritance of Confucianism needs to adapt to modern educational technology while maintaining its core values. In the future, schools will not only need to use big data to improve teaching efficiency, but also need to create a school environment conducive to the all-round development of students under the guidance of Confucian culture.

A. *The association between student behavior analysis and school culture management*

Big data technology can help identify students' behavior patterns, such as study habits, participation in extracurricular activities, which are closely related to school culture. Through the analysis of these models, schools can understand the influence of culture on students' growth, and how to promote the overall development of students by adjusting the cultural environment.

$$tol\left(d_i + 5 \cdot f_{ij}\right) = d_{ij} \geq \max\left(\frac{w_i - 3}{\sigma} \cdot f_{ij}\right) \tag{1}$$

Through the predictive analysis of student behavior data, schools can detect potential problems in advance, such as learning difficulties, social difficulties, and then take interventions to prevent the problems from escalating.

$$\max(f_i) = \left(f_{ij}^2 + 2\right) \to \int E \bullet \overline{7} \succ mean\left(\frac{E!}{d_i!(E - d_i)!} \cdot \sum f_{ij} \cdot \frac{1}{4}\right) \tag{2}$$

Through the analysis of campus safety-related data, schools can more effectively prevent and respond to safety incidents. For example, by analyzing student behavior and environmental data, safety risks can be identified, and timely measures can be taken to maintain a harmonious atmosphere of the campus. To sum up, the application of big data computing in school culture management not only improves the management efficiency, but also provides scientific decision support for the healthy development of campus culture, and realizes the precise and personalized management.

$$E(t_i) = \sum f_i \cdot \sum_{i=1}^{n} (f_i - E)^2 + \bigcap \xi \rightarrow 2 \oint d_i \tag{3}$$

B. *Choice of school cultural programme*

In the era of big data, Confucian curriculum and school culture management are facing unprecedented challenges and opportunities. The challenge is mainly reflected in how to maintain the essence of Confucian curriculum in a digital environment and avoid excessive reliance on technology and ignoring humanistic care.

$$q(f_i) = \sqrt{2} + w_i \cdot \prod E(t_i) \cdot \sqrt{7} - m_i \cdot 3 \tag{4}$$

Data-driven teaching models may enable personalized education, but at the same time may weaken interpersonal interactions between teachers and students, which challenges the Confucian emphasis on mentoring and emotional communication.

$$q(f_i) + E(t_i) \leq \max(f_{ij}) \tag{5}$$

On the other hand, the opportunity is that big data can provide strong support for the dissemination of Confucian courses and personalized learning. By accurate analysis of students' learning habits and interests, Confucianism can be better integrated into teaching practice.

$$q(f_i) + E(t_i) \leftrightarrow mean\left(\frac{E!}{d_i!(E - d_i)!} \cdot \sum f_{ij} \cdot \frac{1}{4} \right) \tag{6}$$

C. *Prediction of the future trend of Confucian curriculum and school culture management*

Looking into the future, the Confucian curriculum and school culture management will show the following trends:

$$No(f_i) = \frac{q(f_i) + E(t_i)}{mean\left(\frac{E!}{d_i!(E-d_i)!} \cdot \sum f_{ij} \cdot \frac{1}{4} \right)} \tag{7}$$

Digital Confucian education: With the development of artificial intelligence and virtual reality technology, Confucian curriculum can be presented in a more vivid and interactive way, so that students can feel the depth of Confucianism in an immersive experience.

$$Zh(f_i) = \min\left[\sum q(f_i) + E(t_i) \right] \tag{8}$$

Personalization and integration: Big data will promote the deep integration of Confucian curriculum and various disciplines, and realize the personalized learning path. At the same time, the school cultural management will also focus on the cultivation of students' comprehensive quality, rather than just academic performance. Globalization perspective: In the context of globalization, the Confucian curriculum and school culture management will pay more attention to cross-cultural exchanges, and cultivate citizens with a global perspective and Confucian ethics.

$$accur(f_i) = \frac{\min\left[\sum q(f_i) + E(t_i)\right]}{\sum q(f_i) + E(t_i)} \times 100\% \tag{9}$$

To sum up, the era of big data has brought about profound changes to the Confucian curriculum and school culture management.

$$accur(f_i) = \frac{\min\left[\sum q(f_i) + E(t_i)\right]}{\sum q(f_i) + E(t_i)} \times 100\% + randon(f_i) \tag{10}$$

Among them, school management meets the normal requirements, mainly cultural ideas adjust school management, eliminate duplicate and irrelevant schemes, and supplement the default scheme, so that the dynamic correlation of the entire school cultural program is strong.

4 Results and Discussion

A. *Introduction to school culture*

Big data analysis helps to understand the social networks and interaction patterns among students, and promotes the formation of positive and healthy campus communities. By analyzing student behavior on social media, potential community leaders can be identified to support their influence and promote a positive campus culture.

Table 1. School culture requirements

Scope of application	grade	viability	School culture
administration	standard	84.35	84.53
	Higher	83.22	80.92
Faculty management	standard	84.20	83.65
	Higher	80.85	80.55
Student management	standard	77.87	80.98
	Higher	81.57	80.39

B. *School management*

Through these strategies, school cultural management can not only inherit and carry forward the fine tradition of Confucianism, but also integrate with modern educational concepts, to provide students with an educational environment that is both rich in historical deposits and has the flavor of The Times (Table 2).

Table 2. Overall situation of the school cultural programme

category	Satisfaction	Analysis rate
administration	82.06	85.55
Faculty management	84.59	86.86
Student management	87.32	87.41
mean	84.93	89.68
X^6	84.31	83.35
P = 2.111		

C. *School culture and stability*

Clear core values: Schools should establish core values based on Confucian ideas, such as respect, honesty, diligence and cooperation, to guide the behavior and decisions of all members. Create a cultural environment: through the design and layout of the campus environment, cultural activities to show the history and achievements of the school, so as to enhance the sense of identity and belonging of teachers and students to the school culture.

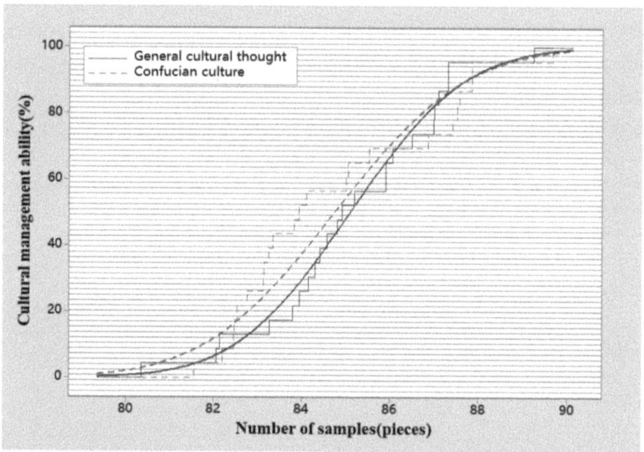

Fig. 2: School culture with different algorithms

It can be seen from Fig. 2 that the school culture of Confucian culture is higher than that of ordinary cultural thought, but the error rate is lower, indicating that the school culture of Confucian culture is relatively stable, while that of ordinary cultural thought School culture is uneven. The average school culture scheme for the above three algorithms is shown in Table 3.

Strengthen system construction: establish and improve school rules and regulations in line with Confucian ideas, such as fair evaluation system, fair reward and punishment

Table 3. Comparison of school culture accuracy of different methods

algorithm	School culture	Magnitude of change	error
Confucian culture	94.99	93.17	93.42
General cultural thought	93.75	94.07	91.90
P	92.69	92.70	91.57

system, so as to maintain school order and encourage good behavior. Teacher team construction: train and introduce teachers with Confucian spirit, and spread and practice Confucian culture through their words and deeds (Fig. 3).

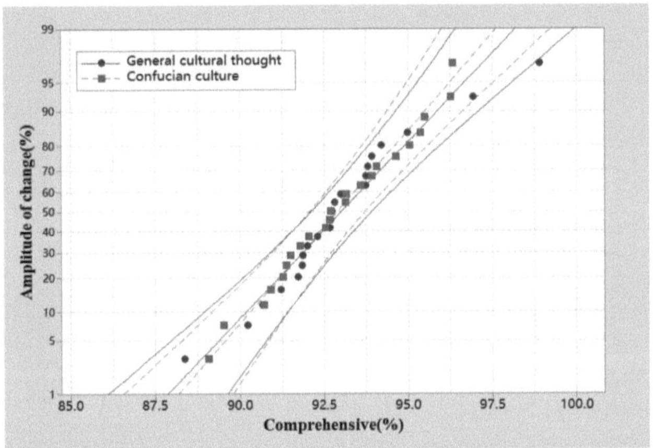

Fig. 3. Confucian cultureschool culture school culture of school culture

Curriculum integration: Integrate Confucianism, such as curriculum, morality and law curriculum and Chinese curriculum, to guide students to understand and practice Confucian values. Home-school cooperation: maintain close communication with parents, jointly cultivate students' good moral character, and form a joint force of home-school co-education.

5 Conclusion

Continuous evaluation and improvement: regularly evaluate the effect of school culture management, adjust according to feedback to ensure the continuous renewal and improvement of culture.

In the future, schools will not only need to use big data to improve teaching efficiency, but also need to create a school environment conducive to the all-round development of students under the guidance of Confucian culture. With the continuous progress of science and technology, we expect a better integration of Confucian curriculum and school cultural management to cultivate future citizens with both profound cultural heritage and modern literacy. This is both a challenge and a historic mission for educators.

Aiming at the problem that school management culture is not ideal, this paper puts forward Confucian culture and optimizes school management in combination with cultural ideas. At the same time, the school culture optimization is analyzed in depth to construct the school culture collection. Studies have shown that Confucian culture can improve the rationality of school management, and can carry out general school culture for school management。 However, in the process of Confucian culture, too much attention is paid to the analysis of school culture, resulting in irrationality in the selection of school cultural indicators.

References

1. Azaola, M.C.: Challenges of working in undervalued technical schools. A continuum between discourses of deficit and trust. Br. J. Sociol. Educ. **44**(5), 927–943 (2023)
2. Barker, R., Hartwell, G., Egan, M., Lock, K.: The importance of school culture in supporting student mental health in secondary schools. Insights from a qualitative study. Br. Educ. Res. J. **49**(3), 499–521 (2023)
3. Barnsteiner, J., Disch, J., Johnson, M., Spector, N.: Applying principles of a fair and just culture to a student scenario. J. Nurs. Educ. **62**(3), 139–145 (2023)
4. Biberman-Shalev, L., Bar-Tal, S.: The codes of school mathematics culture as mirrored in mathematics interns' reflective blogs. Asia Pac. Educ. Rev. **25**, 373 (2023)
5. Bumbungan, B., Bafadal, I., Ulfatin, N., Supriyanto, A.: School principal's Wanua Mappatuo Naewai Alena leadership: a strategy to develop school entrepreneurship. Pegem Egitim Ve Ogretim Dergisi. **13**(1), 309–318 (2023)
6. Camber Tambolas, A., Vujicic, L., Jancec, L.: Relationship between structural and social dimensions of school culture. Frontiers Educ. **7**, 1057706 (2023)
7. Castro, C.A., Castellanos, S.L.V., Souza, M.D.A.: O Lyceu Maranhense e a Construção de uma Cultura Material Escolar embasada por Discursos Modernizadores. Educação & Realidade. **48**, e118077–e118077 (2023)
8. Celik, H., Yazan, B.: Teaching culture through EFL classes in Turkey: a qualitative study of teachers' conceptualizations and pedagogical orientations. Pedagogies. (2023)
9. Celik, O.: Developing a multipronged academic integrity policy writing tool for secondary schools. Int. J. Educ. Dev. **100**, 102807 (2023)
10. Celik, O., Razi, S.: Facilitators and barriers to creating a culture of academic integrity at secondary schools: an exploratory case study. Int. J. Educ. Integr. **19**(1), 4 (2023)
11. Chalwell, K., Stanton, G.D., Grice, C.: Christian middle leadership: how the faith of middle leaders shapes and is shaped by school culture and community. Int. J. Christianity Educ. **28**, 7 (2023)
12. Coma-Rosello, T., Blasco-Serrano, A. C., Gracia, B. D., & Sierra, N. S.: Transformative schools. a path to global citizenship and agenda 2030. Contextos Educativos-Revista De Educacion (31): 27–51 (2023).
13. Farag, A.: The CRT culture war in the suburbs. Phi Delta Kappan. **104**(5), 18–23 (2023)
14. Fennie, T., Moletsane, M., Padmanabhanunni, A.: Teachers' reflections on menstrual management among urban and rural schoolgirls in South Africa. Afr. J. Reprod. Health. **27**(2), 34–44 (2023)
15. Gouedard, P., Kools, M., George, B.: The impact of schools as learning organisations on teachers' self-efficacy and job satisfaction: a cross-country analysis. Sch. Eff. Sch. Improv. **34**, 331 (2023)

Research on the Prediction of Mental Health Problems of Vocational Students Based on Big Data and Deep Learning

Qiuyue Min[✉] and Wen Liu

Weifang Engineering Vocational College, Shandong 262500, China
mqy20221122@163.com

Abstract. Directly recruited students need to adjust their psychology in the face of student pressure. Currently, for the psychological testing of students, we have proposed an intelligent method to analyze their mental health and combine big data to mine and quickly identify their psychology. The research results show that big data methods can detect students' psychological problems and improve the effectiveness of psychological recognition by more than 10%. The overall mental health of students has been greatly improved, and those who can achieve overall optimization and improvement of their mental health can do. Therefore, big data methods can predict mental health problems and improve the psychological well-being of vocational high school students.

Keywords: big data · deep learning · higher vocational students · Mental health issues

1 Introduction

As an important group of society, higher vocational students' mental health has been paid more and more attention [1, 2]. With the advent of the era of big data and the rapid development of deep learning technology, it is possible to use these technologies to predict and intervene the mental health problems of higher vocational students. This kind of research not only helps to detect potential psychological problems in advance, but also provides scientific basis for formulating effective interventions [3, 4]. Using big data and deep learning technology to study the mental health problems of higher vocational students can not only provide scientific basis for educators to formulate more effective educational strategies, but also provide more personalized mental health services for higher vocational students and promote their healthy growth is shown in Fig. 1.

This study conducted predictive analysis on the mental health issues of vocational students by integrating big data and deep learning technologies [5, 6]. The research results indicate that the widespread collection of big data and the complexity of deep learning models can significantly improve the accuracy and sensitivity of predictions. The model not only successfully captures a series of characteristics related to mental

B. Brik and S. Nazir (Eds.): BigIoT-EDU 2024, LNICST 659, pp. 57–64, 2026.
https://doi.org/10.1007/978-3-032-18631-7_7

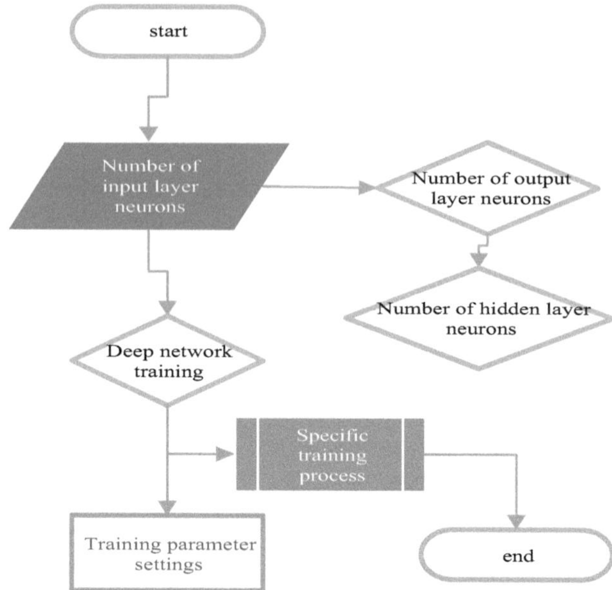

Fig. 1. The process of predicting mental health problems

health status such as learning pressure social network behavior life events etc. but also performs well in anomaly detection and early warning providing the possibility for timely intervention [6, 7]. This paper found that the mental health status of students is related to multiple factors including individual personality traits academic pressure family background social support networks and online behavior patterns. Deep learning models can learn hidden correlations from these complex data revealing patterns that traditional statistical methods find difficult to capture. In addition the study also revealed the dynamics of mental health issues indicating the importance of regular monitoring and intervention [8, 9].

2   Related Works

Improved prediction accuracy: Prediction models based on big data and deep learning can significantly improve the prediction accuracy of mental health problems of higher vocational students. Through continuous learning and optimization, the model can better identify potential risks of psychological problems and provide strong support for timely intervention [9, 10]. Individualized intervention program: According to the prediction results, individualized mental health intervention program can be provided for higher vocational students. These programs can be tailored to the student's specific circumstances to improve the pertinence and effectiveness of the intervention. This kind of personalized intervention is helpful to better meet the needs of students and promote their healthy growth [11, 12]. Auxiliary mental health education: The research results can also provide strong support for mental health education in higher vocational colleges. By understanding students' psychological condition and needs, schools can formulate more scientific and reasonable mental health education plans and curriculum arrangements, so as to improve students' psychological quality and coping ability [13, 14]. Data collection and processing: Collect data related to the mental health of higher vocational students, such as psychological assessment results, basic personal information, learning performance, social relationships, etc. Perform preprocessing operations such as cleaning, sorting, and normalizing the data to ensure the accuracy and consistency of the data. Deep learning model construction: Use deep learning algorithms, such as convolutional neural networks (CNN), recurrent neural networks (RNN), long-and short-term memory networks (LSTM), etc., to construct mental health prediction models. By training the model, it can learn the rules from massive data, and realize the intelligent identification and prediction of mental health problems of higher vocational students. Feature selection and optimization: Features related to mental health problems, such as emotional state, social ability, academic stress, etc., were extracted from raw data. Through the feature selection algorithm, the features that have great influence on the prediction results are screened out to improve the prediction performance of the model.

3 Optimization Strategy for Prediction of Mental Health Problems of Vocational Students

3.1 Mathematical Description of the Deep Learning Algorithm

The rapid development of big data and deep learning technologies has provided new possibilities for predicting and intervening in student mental health issues. This study aims to use these advanced tools to identify students who may face mental health problems in advance, to provide timely support and intervention, improve their psychological state, and promote a healthy and harmonious overall educational environment is shown in Eq. (1).

$$A_i = \frac{\sum_{i=1}^{3} a y \partial y}{\sum_{i=1}^{3} y} \tag{1}$$

3.2 Selection of Prediction Scheme for Mental Health Problems of Higher Vocational Students

Research Objectives and Scope The objective of this study is to construct a model based on big data and deep learning to predict potential mental health issues that vocational students may experience. Specifically, the research will focus on the following aspects: 1 Data collection and feature engineering: By collecting students' daily behavior data, learning data, social network data, etc., extract features that may be related to mental health issues. is shown in Eq. (2).

$$BP = \frac{(x_1, x_2, \cdots x_n)(o_1, o_2, \cdots, o_k)}{(d_1, d_2, \cdots, d_n)} \tag{2}$$

3.3 Predictive Analysis of Mental Health of Higher Vocational Students

Deep learning model construction: Using deep learning algorithms (such as convolutional neural networks, recurrent neural networks, or deep belief networks) to train prediction models to achieve accurate prediction of psychological problems as shown in Fig. 2.

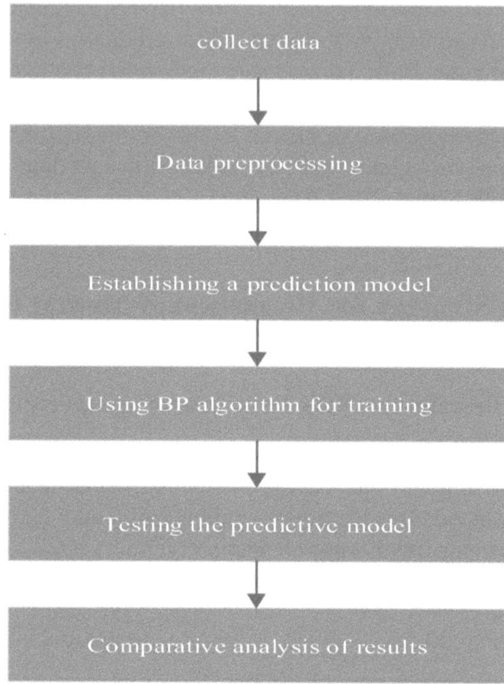

Fig. 2. Prediction scheme for mental health problems of higher vocational students

Improvement of prediction accuracy: Through the training and optimization of deep learning models, the prediction accuracy of mental health problems of higher vocational students can be significantly improved. This helps educators to find potential psychological problems in time and provide strong support for timely intervention. Ensure that students' personal information and test results are kept strictly confidential and avoid disclosure to unrelated personnel or institutions. Feedback the evaluation results to students and teachers in a timely manner, and provide them with targeted guidance and suggestions.

4 Results and Discussion

4.1 Introduction to the Prediction of Mental Health Problems of Higher Vocational Students

In the process of conducting psychological analysis and research in vocational schools, it is necessary to quantitatively analyze the researchers and make judgments on the proportion of different testers and the testing situation is shown in Table 1.

Table 1. Sample situation table

type	Constituencies	Number	Occupy proportions/%
grade	Freshman	210	75.31
	Sophomore	70	24.69
gender	man	159	61.34
	woman	104	38.66
Majors studied	Science and engineering	179	68.45
	Literature and history	44	17.30
	Art	37	14.25

4.2 Prediction of Mental Health Problems of Higher Vocational Students

The main purpose of psychological test in vocational high schools is to help students and teachers understand the information of students' psychological status, personality characteristics, hobbies, professional tendency, etc., so as to provide more personalized education and guidance for students is shown in Table 2.

Table 2. Comparison of prediction time by different methods

Different methods	Forecast time/s
Deep learning methods	18
Learn behavioral data patterns	37

4.3 The Rationality of the Prediction Scheme for Mental Health Problems of Higher Vocational Students

The main purpose of psychological test in vocational high schools is to help students and teachers understand the information of students' psychological status, personality characteristics, hobbies, professional tendency, etc., so as to provide more personalized education and guidance for students shown in Fig. 3.

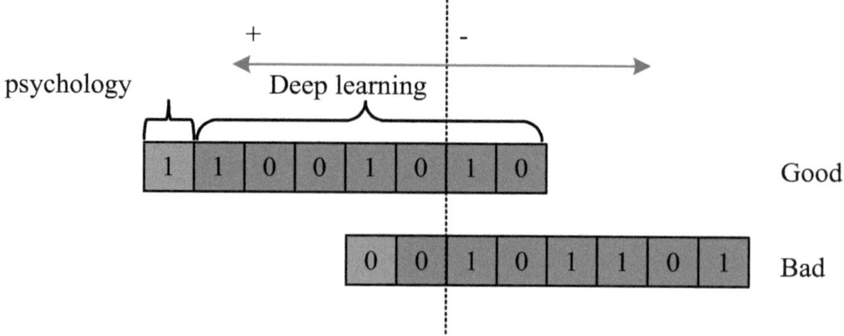

Fig. 3. Comparison of rationality of mental health problem prediction schemes of different algorithms

Learn about activities and areas that students enjoy pursuing by assessing where their interests lie. This helps students discover their own points of interest and potential career directions are shown in Table 3.

Table 3. Analysis of sample data results

serial number	Predict the output	Standard value	absolute error
1	1.79	1	−0.133
2	2.20	2	−0.097
3	1.96	1	0.076
4	1.75	1	0.122
5	2.07	2	−0.096

The application of big data in mental health research has become a new trend in modern psychology research. Big data technology can collect and integrate a large amount of unstructured data from various channels, such as social media, electronic health records, online behavioral data, etc. By analyzing these data, researchers can discover potential patterns of mental health problems and predict individual mental health risks. Language analysis on social media can reveal a user's emotional state; The data from online learning platforms can reveal the level of learning pressure and fatigue among students are shown in Fig. 4.

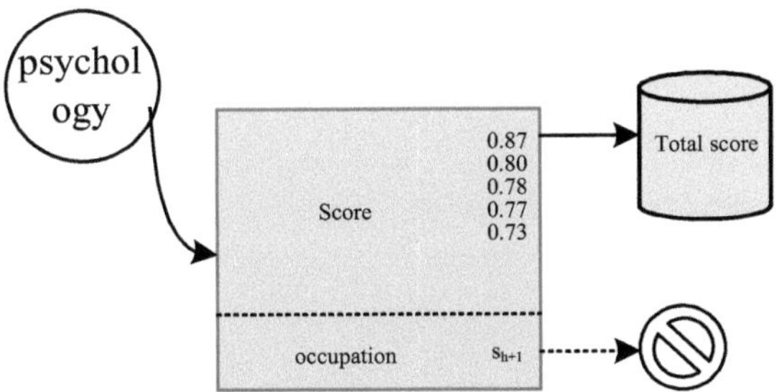

Fig. 4. Comparison of prediction performance of different methods

The application of big data not only improves the sample size and diversity of research, but also makes research more real-time and accurate. Through face-to-face communication with students, this paper can learn about their psychological situation, life experience and family background. This method can deeply understand students' inner world and provide richer and detailed information for assessment. According to students' psychological characteristics and behavioral tendencies, provide them with personalized study and life guidance. For example, for introverted students, they can be encouraged to participate in more group activities and improve their social skills; For anxious students, psychological support and counseling can be provided to help them relieve stress.

5 Conclusion

Traditional methods often rely on questionnaire survey, interview and other means, but these methods have some problems, such as strong subjectivity and low efficiency. With the rise of big data and deep learning technology, new ideas and methods are provided for the prediction of mental health problems of higher vocational students. By collecting and analyzing a large amount of data of students, we can predict their mental health more accurately and provide scientific basis for timely intervention and help. Big data and deep learning have broad application prospects and great potential in the prediction research of mental health problems of higher vocational students. In the future, with the continuous progress of technology and the in-depth development of research, it is believed that this field will achieve more fruitful results and wider applications.

References

1. Dehestani, N., Whittle, S., Vijayakumar, N., Silk, T.J.: Developmental brain changes during puberty and associations with mental health problems. Dev. Cogn. Neurosci. **60** (2023)
2. Gravrakmo, S., Henry, L., Olsen, A., Oie, M.G., Lydersen, S., Ingul, J.M.: Associations between intelligence, everyday executive functions, and symptoms of mental health problems in children and adolescents with mild intellectual disability. Int. J. Dev. Disabil. (2023)
3. Jorren, H.L., Schmidt, H., Kaman, A., Ravens-Sieberer, U., Rumpf, H.J., Pawils, S.: Children's mental health: the role of screen time, parenting behavior, and parenting stress-a secondary data analysis of KiGGS and BELLA data. Bundesgesundheitsblatt-Gesundheitsforschung-Gesundheitsschutz **66**(7), 784–793 (2023)

4. Kalaigian, A., Chaffee, B.W.: Mental health and oral health in a nationally representative cohort. J. Dent. Res. **102**(9), 1007–1014 (2023)
5. Lui, F.R.C., Finik, J., Wu, M.L., Leng, J.N.F., Gany, F.: The association of untreated mental health problems with alcohol and tobacco use among New York City taxi drivers. J. Commun. Health (2023)
6. Ma, R., Zhou, Y.Y., Xu, W.: Guardianship from being present: the moderation of mindfulness in the longitudinal relationship of loneliness to quality of life and mental health problems among the oldest old. Current Psychol. (2023)
7. Maletta, R.M., Daly, M., Goodwin, L., Noonan, R., Putra, I., Robinson, E.: Prevalence of perceived discrimination and associations with mental health inequalities in the UK during 2019–2020: a cross-sectional study. Psychiatry Res. **322** (2023)
8. McGraw, J.S., Oakey-Frost, D.N., Lefevor, G.T., Docherty, M., Tucker, R.P.: Exploring mental health and help-seeking attitudes among sexual minoritized adults in Utah. Psychol. Sex. Orientation Gender Divers. (2023)
9. Oster, C., Dawson, S., Kernot, J., Lawn, S.: Mental health outcome measures in the Australian context: what is the problem represented to be? BMC Psychiatry **23**(1) (2023)
10. Rezun, E.V., Slobodskaya, H.R., Semenova, N.B.: The structure of adolescent mental health problems: the role of effortful control and school safety. J. Adolesc. **95**(5), 947–963 (2023)
11. Saputra, F., Uthis, P., Sukratul, S.: Let's put mental health problems and related issues appropriately in social media: a voice of psychiatric nurses. Belitung Nurs. J. **9**(1), 96–99 (2023)
12. Sifat, M.S., et al.: Greater discrimination frequency and lower distress tolerance are associated with mental health problems among racially privileged and minoritized adults accessing an urban day shelter. J. Racial Ethnic Health Disparities (2023)
13. Vandamme, J., et al.: The impact of the COVID-19 pandemic on the registration and care provision of mental health problems in general practice: registry-based study. Jmir Pub. Health Surveill. **9**(1) (2023)
14. Wagner, G., et al.: Mental health and health-related quality of life in Austrian adolescents with chronic physical health conditions: results from the MHAT study. J. Clin. Med. **12**(5) (2023)

Design of College Oral English Intelligent Online Course Based on Big Data Analysis

Xiaohui Zhang[✉]

Department of Public Course Teaching, Chuzhou City Vocation College, Chuzhou 239000, China
`qianweizong188403@126.com`

Abstract. Big data features, such as a high volume of registered users, enormous amounts of actual data, and dynamic data analysis, are included in online courses that teach spoken English intelligence in higher education. From a pedagogical standpoint, the advent of big data and the advent of easily accessible information provide possibilities for educational reform, with the technical advancements made possible by big data playing a particularly pivotal role in the development of new educational models. The research and promotion value of using big data technology effectively is high because it helps to optimize the research and development mechanism of curricular resources, which in turn improves the construction quality and use efficiency of such resources. Unlike in conventional classrooms, intelligent online courses once again place an emphasis on the students as the center of attention. The online intelligent course places an emphasis on the degree to which students' oral English knowledge is transformed, necessitating oral English instruction to aid in the enhancement of students' abilities, and stresses the correspondence and collaboration between instruction and learning. This article uses big data technologies to understand how each student prefers to learn spoken English and how far along they are in their studies. This may pique their interest in the subject and lead to more personalized instruction.

Keywords: Big data analysis · Colleges and universities · Spoken English · Intelligent online courses

1 Introduction

All areas of society have been confronted with enormous potential and challenge with the advent of the big data age, which has altered people's way of life. Thanks to the widespread use of big data technologies, people's daily lives and work have been made much easier. Big data technology also has applications in education, where it may help advance digital English courses at universities. There are a lot of big data features associated with intelligent online spoken English instruction in higher education, such as a huge number of registered users, enormous amounts of actual data, and dynamic data analysis. From a pedagogical point of view, the advent of big data and the ease with which one may access its data have opened up new avenues for educational reform, with

B. Brik and S. Nazir (Eds.): BigIoT-EDU 2024, LNICST 659, pp. 65–74, 2026.
https://doi.org/10.1007/978-3-032-18631-7_8

the technical advancements made possible by this period playing a particularly pivotal role in the development of novel educational models [1]. The research and promotion value of using big data technology effectively is high because it helps to optimize the research and development mechanism of curricular resources, which in turn improves the construction quality and use efficiency of such resources. Intelligent online spoken English instruction gives educators a straightforward research tool that is easy to evaluate and has the potential to improve students' listening and speaking skills. The potential for intelligent online spoken English instruction is enormous. Online lectures, dubbing, debates, and other learning activities may be held to pique students' attention and make learning more efficient [2]. Autonomous learning manifests itself in a variety of ways, including but not limited to the following: learning content, learning progress, learning mode, and learning techniques; learning location; and learning time. The current crop of online courses, on the other hand, is based on the same model as traditional classroom instruction. If the features of learning are not taken into account, students will not be interested in taking online courses.

Intelligent instruction in spoken English at the university level has disrupted the conventional wisdom about language education. The integration of cutting-edge digital technology into the classroom has altered both the mindset of English instructors and the dynamic between them and their pupils. Online intelligent teaching of spoken English is an exciting new area of study that promises to advance online education while also shedding light on the nature of intelligent instruction. Not only will it aid online expanding students' English learning, but it will also have significant implications for intelligent spoken English instruction in higher education institutions [3]. Research on online course design of intelligent teaching of oral English based on big data analysis is still needed by scholars, especially in light of the present situation and development trend of intelligent teaching of English in college. This research would change the traditional mode of teaching oral English and is a positive exploration of innovative education and teaching methods. There is still a need for further study on how to use large data situations to support educational growth [4, 5]. Oral English instruction in higher education has begun to transcend conventional innovation practices in the age of big data, since it is the central substance of English language instruction.

2 Design of College Oral English Intelligent Online Course Based on Big Data Analysis

2.1 Proceed from the Educational Needs

The primary goal of oral English instruction is to enhance students' overall quality by enhancing their communicative competency in the language, passing on the English language and culture, and developing their practical English skills. With the new oral English teaching method, students' learning needs are better met than with traditional methods; the university classroom is no longer the front door to education; and students can make the most of their fragmented time to acquire English knowledge whenever and wherever they like [6]. Teachers and students alike have begun to acknowledge the benefits of this hybrid model of instruction. Students lack innovative consciousness, innovative thinking, and innovative ability because traditional education practices hinder the development of students' autonomous learning abilities and because students' levels are uneven, making it difficult to tailor instruction to each student's aptitude [7]. A great deal of the impact on the intelligent online course comes from the educational need, one of many reasons. Intelligent online courses must give careful thought to both the demands of students and educators when designing their curricula. Figure 1 shows the big data analysis-based approach of teaching spoken English in college.

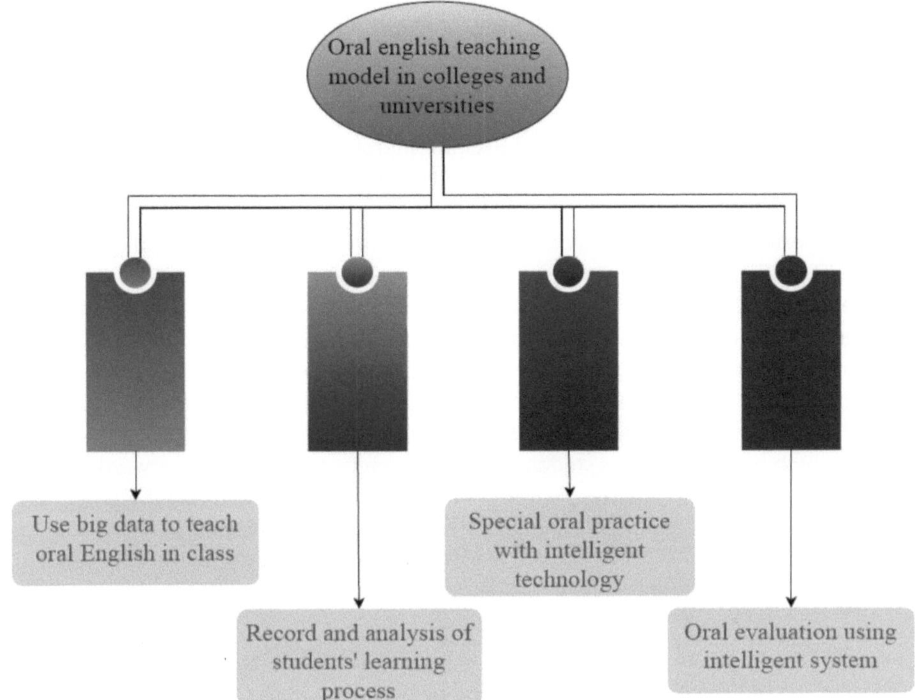

Fig. 1. College Oral English Teaching Mode in the Age of Big Data

With the help of AI, students may monitor their own learning status and identify their own knowledge gaps in real time. If IBU's own knowledge system is inadequate, then they may increase their talents in all areas via focused training. The goal of this "four step" methodology is to increase application skills and ensure that all students can speak English [8]. Concurrently, the learning platform may construct its own question bank; that is, educators can create their own oral lesson plans based on their own goals and challenges in the classroom, and students can use the materials to study, practice, and test their knowledge. Get students interested in learning spoken English by using big data to study their learning preferences, progress, etc., and then using that information to create individualized lessons.

2.2 Proceed from Learning Needs

Unlike in conventional classrooms, intelligent online courses once again place an emphasis on the students as the center of attention. The online intelligent course places an emphasis on the degree to which students' oral English knowledge is transformed, necessitating oral English instruction to aid in the enhancement of students' abilities, and stresses the correspondence and collaboration between instruction and learning. Teachers may "personalize" their teaching approaches to capture students' attention and maximize preview effectiveness by adjusting preview content and teaching progress while controlling video length. Stage in the classroom: Teachers in flipped classrooms forego the traditional method of covering foundational material in favor of responding to students' pre-class input on challenges and concerns and then testing their understanding of the material [9]. "Share, set top, edit". Teachers may construct distinct groups of pupils based on their condition and execute hierarchical instruction with the aid of class groups. Both students and instructors benefit from working in small groups for both instruction and assessment purposes.

Using performance data, educators may monitor their students' reading, engagement, and overall progress. The prepared teaching materials, instruments, and techniques should be favorable to the development and promotion of students' ability, starting with the demands of students' spoken English learning. Using performance data, educators may monitor their students' reading, engagement, and overall progress. Teachers may utilize the class group feature to assess and grade all students, in addition to daily interactive discussions and comments. It goes without saying that educators need to carry out their responsibilities and assess students' pre-class preparation, attitude toward learning, and project completion. This form of assessment in the classroom has the potential to inspire optimism among students and spark new ideas for lesson plans.

2.3 Starting from Teaching Resources

In order to help students in learning groups who are falling behind, teachers and students work together in an interactive manner. Teachers and students may bridge the gap via mutual understanding and communication, which in turn increases students' motivation to learn, creativity in thinking, and capacity to put what they know into practice. Conventional wisdom on how to teach English in higher education has become obsolete in this era of massive data sets. The usage of digital technology in the classroom is on the rise. There has been significant development in the field of digital English instruction. Adapting to and becoming experts in digital pedagogy is an inherent part of being a teacher. In intelligent online courses, teachers create short films of each lesson before class, which allows them more control over the course's goals, allows them to enhance the course material, and guarantees that students will be engaged even when the teacher isn't there [10]. Students may study at their own pace and review previously covered material by watching learning mini lesson videos many times. When it comes to intelligent oral English online course teaching in the age of big data, college English teachers can take advantage of all the resources available to them. This is particularly true when it comes to correcting students' oral pronunciation; teachers can use pre-collected cases of oral improvement, pronunciation skills, etc., to make the most of their classroom time.

Take use of smart online courses to teach English, examine data on online students' learning generally, and become an expert in students' learning traits. Simultaneously, in order to comprehend each student's learning condition, the data from their continuous learning is examined. Before class, students may use the program to practice dubbing the given video. They can also utilize the software's features, including checking phonetic symbols, following the original voice, rating the system, and interacting with netizens, to keep themselves interested in practicing. By collecting student dubbing samples, teachers may assess voice issues and provide students with individualized feedback on how to improve their voices in class.

3 Analysis and Discussion

3.1 Adhere to the "Student-Centered" Teaching Philosophy

We should follow the "student-centered" teaching idea in our online course study on college oral English intelligence based on big data analysis. These modifications to follow-up online spoken English instruction are based on findings from data analysis of students' online spoken English instruction: The first step in improving students' spoken English is to focus more on teaching them how to pronounce and intonate words correctly. This includes helping them practice vowel sounds and vivid intonation, as well as recommending films and videos that use standard pronunciation. It is "student-centered" when students learn English orally online. In order to improve their teaching methods, educators might examine and mine student data on their lessons as a whole. While students' innate intellect plays a role, ineffective teaching practices that disregard the principles of students' cognitive growth and fail to evoke their inner resonance often make it difficult for instructors to accomplish their goals.

Utilize online teaching tools to their fullest potential. For instance, you can use the oral English learning platform to upload tests and training materials for oral English, assign them to students when needed, and then use the data analysis function to keep tabs on their progress. Using visuals and conversation, instructors provide the "lead-in" connection to spoken English instruction and engage students in engaging warm-up exercises. After students have activated the appropriate vocabulary, instructors will provide oral English instruction and provide oral English assignments. In Fig. 2 we can see the strategy for delivering the oral English intelligence course online.

Students' independent oral learning may benefit from the aforementioned learning strategies. Teachers should establish class-wide artificial intelligence learning groups, standardize software selection and usage, and encourage students to utilize the program's social functions to guarantee the efficacy and quality of autonomous learning. Students should be encouraged to regularly assess their oral abilities in order to ensure that they are making full and accurate use of the learning tools and to motivate them to practice their oral skills more effectively. A high correlation value indicates that the pupils are quite similar to one another. Under the assumption that the curricular resource collection that represents student engagement and scoring is used, the similarity between student i and student j is:

$$sim(i, j) = \sqrt{\sum\nolimits_{p \in I} R_{i,p} - R_i^2} \tag{1}$$

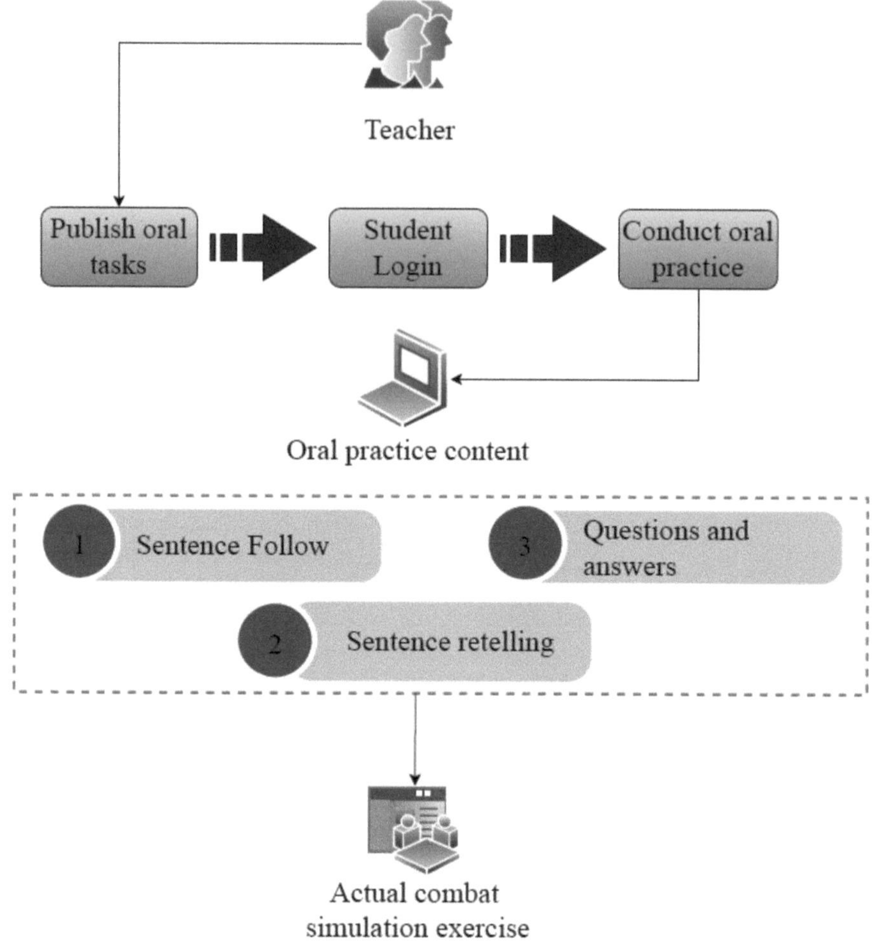

Fig. 2. Teaching Implementation Scheme in the Online Course of Oral English Intelligence

Among them, $R_{i,p}$ refers to student i score on curriculum resources p, and R_i refers to student's score on curriculum resources.

Choose the best-scoring course materials from all of them. in N and recommend them to students. It is predicted that student u will score the course resources as follows:

$$P_{u,i} = \sum_{n \in N} sim(u, n) \times R_{n,j} - R_n \tag{2}$$

Among them, $sim(u, n)$ is the similarity between student u and student n calculated previously, $R_{n,j}$ is the score of student n on course resources i, and R_n is the average score of student u on course resources.

Then use the following calculation method to find out the similarity between curriculum i resources and curriculum resources j.

$$sim(i,j) = \sqrt{\sum_{u \in U} R_{u,i} - R_u^2} \tag{3}$$

Among them, $R_{u,i}$ represents student u score on i resources of the course, and R_u represents student u average score on curriculum resources.

Students' strengths may be accentuated and their weaknesses addressed via individual instruction. The "student-centered" pedagogical approach, which ought to permeate all online course designs, is exemplified by both of them. Lastly, developing foundational skills like emphasis, rhythm, intonation, and word pronunciation provides the foundation for improving oral English fluency. You have to put in the time and effort to hone this ability. It teaches students how to employ information teaching methods like fluency in English to improve their practical application abilities and the frequency with which they use the language.

3.2 Data Analysis

As a result of his unique upbringing, each student has a unique learning style and cognitive capacity. In order to appreciate the unique qualities of each student, it is important to have a firm grasp on their unique combination of personality traits and learning styles. Only then can we tailor our recommendations and instruction to meet the needs of each individual student, allowing them to grow in self-awareness and personal development. College English instructors may better direct their students' extracurricular oral English practice with the use of big data, which also helps students practice oral English outside of the classroom. The success or failure of online courses is dependent on the level of engagement from both instructors and students. In light of this, interactive activities play a significant role in determining the efficacy of online education. Currently, all online courses have interactive learning modules that allow learners to engage in conversation and discuss what they've learned. The data analysis is objective, yet it will still ignore numerous nuanced elements. To make the most of data analysis to inform pedagogical decisions, educators should draw on their own expertise in the classroom, apply logic and reason to the results, evaluate students' spoken pronunciation based on content analysis, and assign scores. This will help students improve their pronunciation over time and provide teachers with useful feedback for evaluating their own performance. To create a more scientific approach to education, merge the findings of objective data analysis with the subjective initiative of instructors. Figure 3 displays the results of a task point exam based on the study conducted with a class of sixty students.

The students do have a basic grasp of preposition recognition, but their accuracy is lacking. The findings of the data analysis show that in the next session, we need to make sure that students learn how to use a wide variety of words, with an emphasis on adverbs and prepositions. Generally speaking, more students got the questions right than got them incorrectly, proving that clever online courses for oral English instruction are very successful.

More opportunities and a more diverse student body await educators in the years to come. The role that students play in opening up new horizons in education and shaping

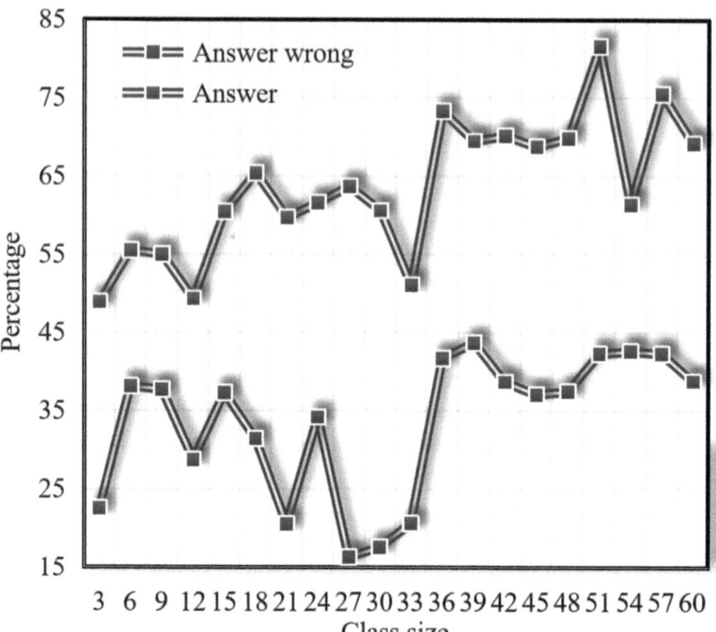

Fig. 3. Task point test diagram

the world of tomorrow is boundless. Both education and teaching are evolving from a variety of angles due to factors such as the diversification of educational practices, the deep integration of conventional pedagogical approaches, and the ongoing innovation in individualized learning. Chapter learning times for students may be used to calculate three things: the total number of students' chapter learning times (A), the number of students in their class (B), and the total number of students in the course (C). Figure 4 shows the trend chart of students' chapter learning times, which was obtained by additional experimental research based on the aforementioned three outcomes. In August 2021, the course had the most chapters taught, marking the top of the learning times trend as seen in Fig. 4, the trend chart of students' learning durations. During the other months, the quantity of chapters covered is somewhat less. Students should pay close attention to the material covered in August 2021, according to preliminary research.

Our early study suggests that intelligent online courses in college-level spoken English may benefit from big data analysis technologies. Utilizing data to inform instruction and instruction to validate data is the fundamental premise of integrating big data analysis with oral English teaching technology. In order to find the solution, a certain amount of time must be spent doing practical research on technical elements like data gathering, analysis, and characterization. Students' independent oral learning may benefit from the aforementioned learning strategies. Teachers should establish class-wide artificial intelligence learning groups, standardize software selection and usage, and encourage students to utilize the program's social functions to guarantee the efficacy and quality of autonomous learning. To ensure that students are making full use of

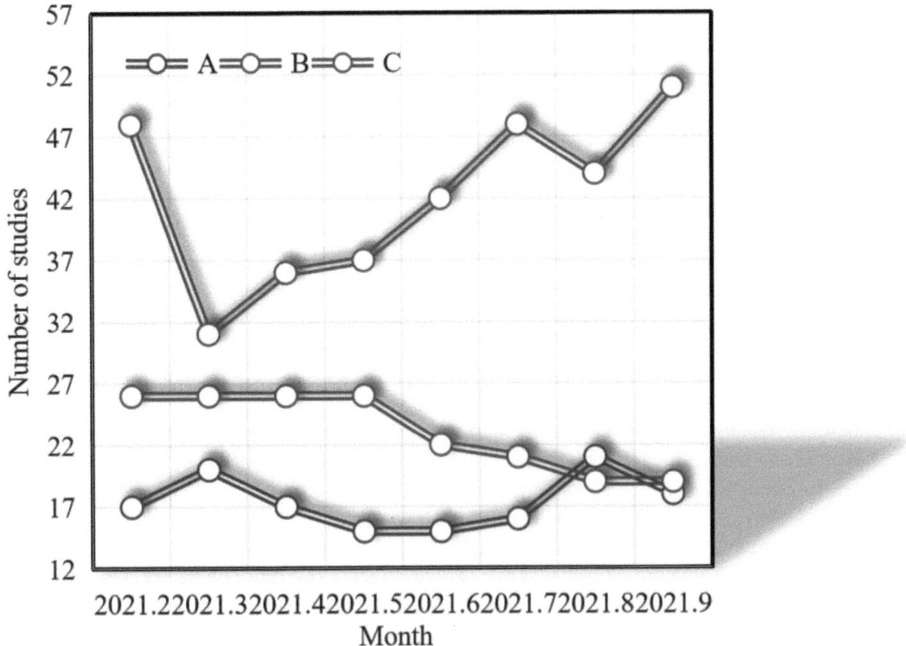

Fig. 4. The trend of students' chapter learning times

the learning software and are actively working to enhance their oral English practice abilities, it is recommended that they participate in regular oral ability testing activities.

4   Conclusions

Online spoken English intelligence courses at colleges and universities can benefit from big data analysis, which can enhance their quality and teaching efficiency. This innovation in course design can hopefully shed light on how to innovate the teaching mode of these courses. Improving the efficacy and quality of students' oral English learning may be as simple as describing its features, putting students at the center of the learning process, and making specific adjustments to the teaching tactics of higher vocational instructors. In order to meet the standards for oral English instruction in higher vocational colleges, instructors will post preview assignments and homework on the platform in advance of class, as well as a video of a micro-lesson on summarizing challenging knowledge points. Students do the preview assignments by consulting their own resources after logging onto their individual accounts and reviewing the course materials given by instructors. In addition to catering to students' broad educational requirements, it takes their unique learning styles into account, honors the objective rule that students' learning is a combination of shared and unique aspects, and uses teachers' actual classroom experiences to make targeted and dynamic adjustments to their teaching methods, allowing for a more precise evaluation of their efficacy. When it comes to actually teaching, teachers should take into account college students' professional traits and the current job market trends, come up with new ideas for the structure, content, and delivery of wisdom classes on oral English, improve the materials used to teach oral English, and encourage students to develop their oral English skills in all areas.

Acknowledgements. This work was sponsored in part by A Study on the Professional Development Path of English Teachers in Higher Vocational Colleges under the new Curriculum Standards (2021sk10).

The Integration of Excellent Chinese Traditional Culture in Higher Vocational English Teaching (Azcj2022039).

References

1. Chen, Y., Huang, M., Wang, C.: Discussion on the content system of big data courses in colleges and universities. Educ. Teach. Forum **74**(23), 67–82 (2019)
2. Yan, J., Zhou, M., Chen, Y.: Evaluation model of college English education effect based on big data analysis. J. Inf. Knowl. Manag. **21**(03), 45–68 (2022)
3. Tan, X.: Research on college English writing teaching under the background of big data: taking Leshan Normal University as an example. Theor. Pract. Lang. Stud. **9**(1), 60–82 (2019)
4. Zhang, R., Zhao, W., Wang, Y.: Big data analytics for intelligent online education. J. Intell. Fuzzy Syst. Appl. Eng. Technol. **65**(2), 40–71 (2021)
5. Chu, N., Sun, W.: The application of big data in the information of education in colleges and universities. Mod. Inf. Technol. **28**(16), 31–42 (2017)
6. Zhang, Y.: Research on college English online learning platform model based on big data technology. J. Phys. Conf. Ser. **1648**(28), 042090–042097 (2020)
7. Wang, Y.: Research on the innovation of teaching mode of the university English hierarchical listening and speaking under the "Internet+" era based on the analysis of big data. J. Phys. Conf. Ser. **1992**(2), 022125–022147 (2021)
8. Tan, Q.: Evaluation system of college English teaching based on big data. J. Phys. Conf. Ser. **1852**(2), 022014–022028 (2021)
9. Jin, L.: Application of big data technology in colleges and universities education. Wirel. Internet Technol. **38**(10), 26–54 (2017)
10. Liu, P., Chen, P., Yuan, Y., et al.: A teaching assistant system for big data analysis. J. Phys. Conf. Ser. **1678**(85), 012090–012099 (2020)

The Impact of Digital Education on Higher Education Under Big Data Algorithms and the Thinking on Coping Strategies

Yanjie Li[✉]

Shandong Institute of Commerce and Technology, Jinan 250103, Shandong, China
lyjkeke@163.com

Abstract. Digital education can stimulate the educational platform and educational process, but the corresponding factors need to be integrated in the process of digital education to find out the main influence points. This paper carries out through the digital education. Big data analysis is used to optimize the original resources and achieve effective integration of resources. The results show that big data can promote the development of digital education and integrate the relevance of education. The increase is more than 20%, and it significantly promotes the integrity of educational resources and the utilization rate of resources. The promotion rate is greater than 45%. Therefore, big data can realize the digitalization and optimization of education, the original educational effect, and the transformation of theory and practice.

Keywords: Data set theory · big data algorithms · Impact of higher education · Reflections on coping strategies · Digital · Education

1 Introduction

Digital education is the main object of educational reform and optimization [1, 2], but it needs to be digitally integrated, traditional digital integration. The establishment of big data servers can provide support for educational resources, optimize the original educational structure and model, and realize the overall structural optimization of education [3, 4]. Comprehensive, its content and results, so the linkage between socialized education and big data can be formed to promote the overall optimization of educational resources. Some people believe that the digitization of educational resources is conducive to the improvement of education level, and is also conducive to the use of resources to improve the utilization rate of educational resources [5, 6] and multi-perspective judgment of data to provide support for the synthesis of theory and practice [7, 8]. In summary, this paper integrates and analyzes big data and digital educational resources to realize the judgment of the overall structure of education and improve the actual level of education across the original results and forms [9, 10].

© ICST Institute for Computer Sciences, Social Informatics and Telecommunications Engineering 2026
Published by Springer Nature Switzerland AG 2026. All Rights Reserved
B. Brik and S. Nazir (Eds.): BigIoT-EDU 2024, LNICST 659, pp. 75–85, 2026.
https://doi.org/10.1007/978-3-032-18631-7_9

2 Related Concepts

2.1 The Big Data Algorithms is Described Mathematically

Comprehensive application of big data to system resource is y_i found. Integration of data and resources is z_i, and the overall relevance of the data is $tol(y_i \cdot t_{ij})$. Realize comprehensive judgment and analysis of data as shown in Eq. (1).

$$\lim_{x \to \infty} (y_i \cdot t_{ij}) = \sqrt{2} y_{ij} \geq max(t_{ij} \div 2) \tag{1}$$

The association of theoretical practice with practice invocation and practice operation (2).

$$max(t_{ij}) = \partial \left(t_{ij}^2 + 2 \cdot t_{ij} \right) > \sqrt{2} \left(\sum t_{ij} + 4 \right) M \tag{2}$$

Big data is used to call resources and improve classroom teaching effect is t_i, teachers' methods of teaching is set_i, teacher's instructional strategies is y_i, and student's academic performance is $F(t_i \approx 0)$ as shown by Eq. (3).

$$F(d_i) = \prod \sum t_i \cap \xi \cdot \sqrt{2} \to \oint y_i \cdot 7 \tag{3}$$

2.2 Selection of Impact of Higher Education and the Thinking of Coping Strategies Scheme

Practical teaching needs of students is $g(t_i)$, an overall development direction of teaching is w_i, comprehensive competitiveness of teaching (4).

$$g(t_i) = \ddot{x} \cdot z_i \prod F(d_i) \frac{dy}{dx} - w_i \Phi \tag{4}$$

Practical teaching needs of students are shown in Eq. (5).

$$\lim_{x \to \infty} g(t_i) + F(d_i) \leq \cap a \, max(t_{ij}) \tag{5}$$

Enhance students' overall interest in learning in Eq. (6).

$$g(t_i) + F(d_i) \leftrightarrow \Gamma \left(\sum t_{ij} + 4 \right) \tag{6}$$

2.3 Analysis of Impact of Higher Education and the Thinking of Coping Strategies Scheme

Correlation between teaching needs and theoretical practice is $No(t_i)$ shown in Eq. (7).

$$No(t_i) = \frac{g(t_i) + F(d_i)}{mean(\sum t_{ij} + 4)} \sqrt{2} \tag{7}$$

Among them, it is $\frac{g(t_i)+F(d_i)}{mean(\sum t_{ij}+4)} \leq 1$ specified that Planning of teaching $Zh(t_i)$ suggested; practical teaching steps and comprehensiveness in Eq. (8).

$$Zh(t_i) = \lim_{x \to \infty} \left[\sum g(t_i) + F(d_i) \right] \lim_{x \to \infty} \tag{8}$$

The impact of higher education and the thinking of coping strategies is $accur(t_i)$. Thoroughly built teaching information platform and database with big data is $unno(t_i)$. Carry out comprehensive information analysis and research, and output the actual test results to judge the deviation between the actual test results and the demand of teaching, as stated in Eq. (9).

$$accur(t_i) = \frac{min[\sum g(t_i) + F(d_i)]}{\sum g(t_i) + F(d_i)} \times 100\% \tag{9}$$

The auxiliary effect of big data in teachers' teaching process is $randon(t_i)$ Teachers' holistic needs and judgment process. Equation (9) may be represented as Eq. (10).

$$accur(t_i) = \frac{\sqrt{2}X}{\frac{1}{2} \sum g(t_i) + F(d_i)} + randon(t_i) \tag{10}$$

Integrate teachers' teaching process, teaching plan and students' actual needs, build a client database, and combine the databases to form a big data platform. Large-scale analysis is used to map each platform and client as a whole, form effective data analysis results, and realize data output.

3 Impact of Higher Education and the Thinking of Coping Strategies Optimization Approach

In the process of data information output and analysis, it is necessary to integrate data, establish a database and analyze it. The teaching resources of English teaching are analyzed, the comprehensive analysis of teaching strategies is realized, and the digital achievements of teaching education are evaluated by the content of achievements. Therefore, in the process of big data algorithm, it is necessary to establish a variety of databases, and review teachers' teaching plans, teaching conditions, teaching contents and resources involved in the teaching process, so as to form effective data correlation, optimize the original data content and improve the comprehensiveness and effect of the whole teaching analysis. In addition, it is necessary to analyze the multi-task points in the teaching process to form a comprehensive optimization of task points. Original analysis contents and results.

4 Practical Examples of Impact of Higher Education and the Thinking of Coping Strategies

4.1 Introduction to the Impact of Higher Education and the Thinking of Coping Strategies

Based on the teaching of college teachers, the scope involved includes main professional courses and auxiliary elective courses, among which there are twelve courses and 120 survey objects. The survey objects involve freshmen, juniors, sophomores, juniors and three majors, and the survey objects are analyzed continuously for six months. It mainly makes a comprehensive analysis of teaching resources, teaching contents, teaching effects, teaching practicality and the improvement of actual achievements, and effectively outputs the above analysis results is shown in Table 1.

Table 1. Impact of higher education and the thinking of coping strategies

Scope of application	The content of teaching	Integrity of teaching judgment	The rationality of the teaching plan
Personalized learning	Theoretical teaching	88.95	89.22
	Practical teaching	87.84	91.96
Improve learning	Theoretical teaching	89.01	91.93
	Practical teaching	85.87	87.98
Integration of educational technology	Theoretical teaching	88.83	88.26
	Practical teaching	85.93	85.83

A comprehensive analysis of teaching will reveal that the data in the teaching process are relatively complete. The proportion is relatively high, so it is necessary to judge the whole teaching content, and at the same time, it is necessary to describe the teaching analysis process and big data analysis process. Specific results are shown in Fig. 1.

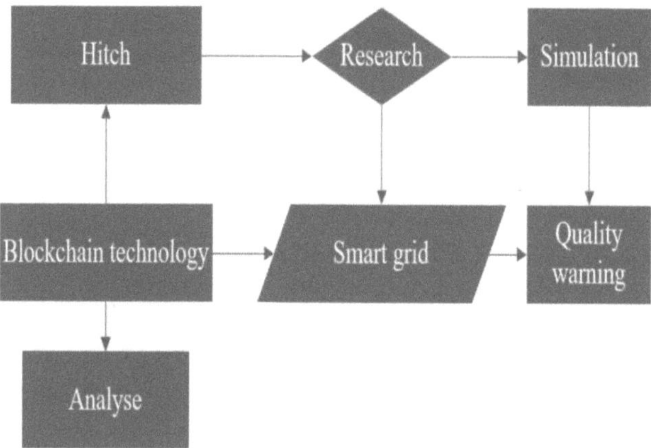

Fig. 1. Analysis process of impact of higher education and the thinking of coping strategies

From the analysis in Tongyi, it can be seen that before big data analysis, the data should be classified, and the teaching resources in the teaching process should be classified and established by establishing a classification database. Professional database, information database, practice database and achievement database, and row association of databases, establishing logical relationship tables, forming effective analysis scales, and providing support for digitalization. At the same time, it is necessary to analyze the data of each table and construct a joint analysis method.

4.2 Impact of Higher Education and the Thinking of Coping Strategies

In the process of teaching, it is also necessary to comprehensively analyze the teaching strategies, teaching forms and teaching contents, and form the final summary results. As shown in the analysis results, the valid and specific results are shown in Table 2.

Table 2. The overall situation of the impact of higher education and the thinking of coping strategies scheme

Category	Actual analysis conditions	Analyze the rationality of the results	Comprehensive content analysis
Personalized learning	88.43	85.06	87.49
Improve learning	91.52	87.41	89.09
Integration of educational technology	89.26	90.94	89.98

4.3 Impact of Higher Education and the Thinking of Coping Strategies and Stability

In the process of comprehensive analysis and data holistic description, digitalization and integration of teaching resources will also have corresponding effects. How to effectively analyze and improve the comprehensiveness in the analysis process is the focus of research, so it is necessary to analyze the big data processing process of teaching resources. The details are shown in Fig. 2.

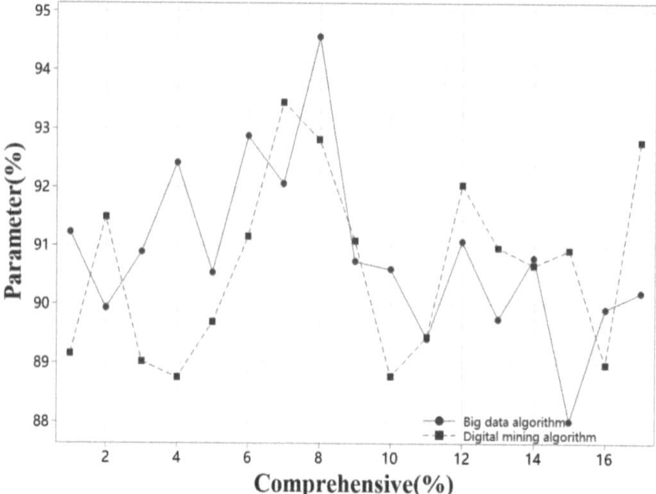

Fig. 2. Stability and volatility trend of teaching analysis performance under different algorithms

Figure 2 shows that in the process of teaching, big data analysis changes from a process with greater volatility to a process with gradual less volatility, so as to demonstrate the rationality of teaching analysis. Moreover, in the process of teaching analysis, there are correlations and similarities among data, which further proves that big data analysis can improve the effectiveness and rationality of educational analysis. On the whole, it can optimize the overall structure of education, improve the pedagogical effect, and make an overall plan for the above educational contents. The specific results are shown in the Table 3.

Table 3. Compares the accuracy of several impact of higher education and the thinking of coping strategies.

Algorithm	Comprehensive teaching planning	Dynamic analysis	Holistic analysis	Correlation analysis
Big data algorithms	88.13	89.53	88.28	88.94
Digital mining algorithms	87.49	87	89.33	91.96
P	92.03	90.9	88.43	93.46

Table 3 shows that in the process of teaching, there is inevitability between theories and practices, and whether they can be effectively integrated, and there are conditions for deep excavation of related analysis. Therefore, it is necessary to judge and verify the teaching as a whole to improve its comprehensive effect. How to analyze effectively and whether the final result meets the actual requirements is in the research process. Comprehensive content and results: Big data analysis, teaching analysis and comprehensive results are systematically displayed. Specific results, as shown in Fig. 3.

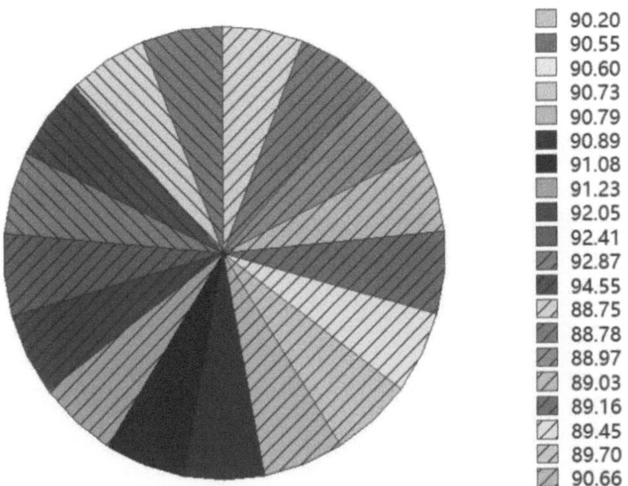

Fig. 3. Impact of higher education and the thinking of coping strategies of Big data algorithms

Figure 3 shows that the comprehensive analysis effect of big data shows that the practical and overall distribution of teaching resources is relatively reasonable, and the overall structure is relatively uniform, indicating that it is in progress. In the process of digital analysis of education in colleges and universities, big data can balance all kinds of data and improve the allocation of educational resources.

4.4 Rationality of Impact of Higher Education and the Thinking of Coping Strategies

Verify the distribution of educational resources and the utilization rate of educational resources, and judge whether they are symmetrical and the matching degree between resources and actual needs. To verify the effectiveness of this round of analysis. As well as the specific results of the role of big data in Fig. 4.

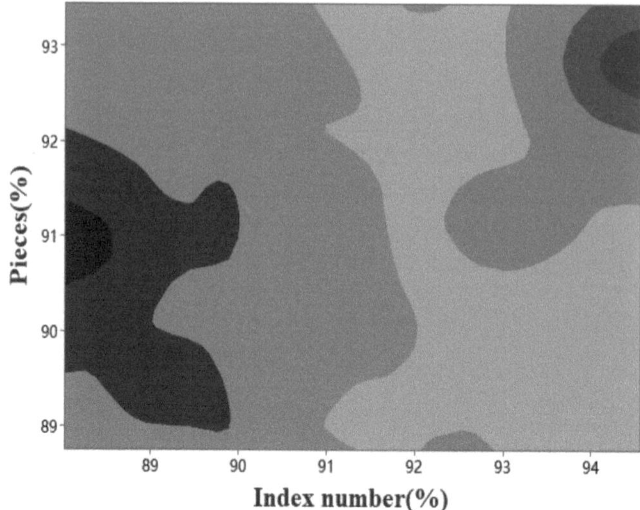

Fig. 4. Matching degree verification between educational resources and actual teaching needs based on big data analysis

Figure 4 shows that comprehensive analysis and verification of big data, and verification of relevant data and fusion. When judging, the correlation between its actual needs and practical applications verifies whether the two are reasonable. At the same time, it is necessary to verify the role, effect and scope of big data, and it will be found that the classifications are relatively balanced. The classification features are relatively obvious, indicating that in the whole. In the process of education, digitalization can improve the effectiveness of classification effect, effectively match the classification effect with actual needs and corresponding processing strategies, improve its fitting, and have a significant impact on college education.

4.5   Validity of Impact of Higher Education and the Thinking of Coping Strategies

The degree of correlation between higher education. The situation of colleges and universities, the comprehensiveness of colleges and universities is also the focus of current analysis. It is necessary to analyze the smoothness of the data, find out the main feature points, and verify its correlation degree and correlation effect. At the same time, the feature points of big data analysis should be summarized, and the specific results are shown in Fig. 5.

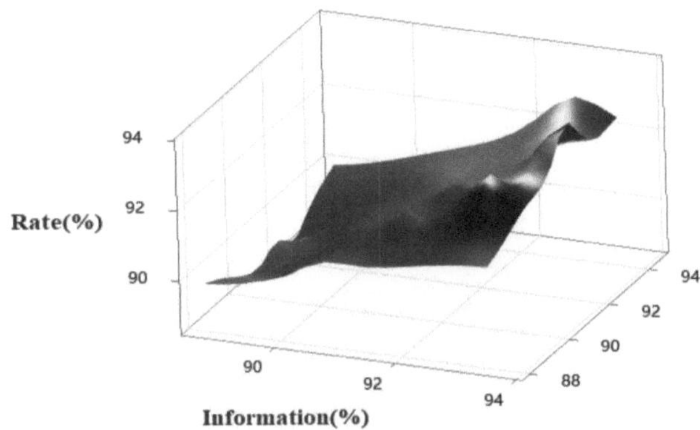

Fig. 5. Impact of higher education and the thinking of coping strategies of different algorithms

Figure 5 shows in the process of data analysis, there are volatility changes between each data and prominent points, so the volatility and surface of the data should be analyzed. At the same time, it is also necessary to determine the fusion points and outliers of big data, judge whether its feature points are actually required, and conduct an in-depth analysis of the problems to avoid redundant data and interference data, so as to prove the impact and role of big data on educational digitalization. At the same time, it is necessary to quantify the processing results and output them in the form of charts, and the specific results are summarized as shown the Table 3.

Table 4. Compares the efficacy of several impact of higher education and the thinking of coping strategies.

Algorithm	The satisfaction rate of actual needs	On the conversion rate of practice	Improve the independent innovation rate	Feel the satisfaction rate of the level
Big data algorithms	91.01	91.37	87.48	87.8
Digital mining algorithms	87.31	92.22	87.38	90.8
P	88.24	90.35	88.48	92.87

Table 4 shows that through multi-personality analysis and verification of big data, we can improve the effectiveness of analysis results and judge its analysis content. It will be found that big data can ensure that the data analysis reaches more than 90%, and has a significant impact on the comprehensive effect and characteristics of the data, indicating that big data plays a significant role in the process of classification and processing, and can reduce the interference of resources in the teaching process and reduce its complexity, Improvement of data teaching as illustrated in Fig. 6.

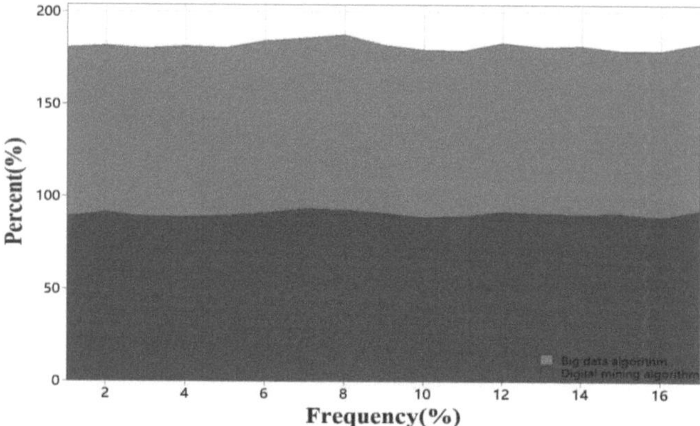

Fig. 6. Big data algorithms impact of higher education and the thinking of coping strategies

Figure 6 shows that comprehensive analysis and holistic verification of big data can improve its significant effect. Moreover, big data analysis can compare and isolate the classification effects between teaching resources and actual resource theories, forming contrast characteristics, and providing support for later in-depth analysis.

5   Conclusion

In the process of big data analysis, educational resources can be digitally analyzed, and the logical relationship between various numbers can be compared to improve their effectiveness. Through the analysis of big data, it will be shown that big data can optimize the original educational resources, with an optimization rate of more than 20%, and it will have an impact on the educational effect, with an improvement degree of more than 30%. At the same time, it can ensure that educational resources and actual needs can be effectively met, and the satisfaction rate is greater than 85%. This shows that big data can promote the comprehensive development of educational resources, and there are some shortcomings in undergraduate research, mainly due to the deviation between survey samples and survey data, which will make up for the above problems in the future.

References

1. Han, C.: Analysis on the reform strategy of hotel management and digital operations under the background of digital economy - reflections on the reform of hotel management and digital operations university. Res. Manag. (9), 48–51 (2022)
2. Wu, Y., Kan, Z., Su, C., Guo, Y., Wang, L.: Research on the construction of digital smart campus in higher vocational colleges under the background of big data. In: Taking Ordos Ecological Environment Vocational College as an Example Information Technology Education in China, no. 2, p. 4 (2023)
3. Zhang, Q., Wu, Y.: Promoting "Transformation" through evaluation: the top-level architecture and practical measures of digital transformation in OECD higher education. Higher Education Digest (10), 4 (2022)

4. Zhu, Y.: Evolutionary logic: reorganization and updating of network ideological and political carriers under intelligent algorithms. Front. Soc. Sci. **12**(5), 6 (2023)
5. Ling, F.: Opportunities, challenges, and strategies for moral education of students in the age of artificial intelligence education and equipment research **39**(5), 3–8 (2023)
6. Liang, H., Mai, Y., Jiang, Z., Xie, S.: A data sharing and exchange method and system based on big data CN116149864A (2023)
7. Yang, Y., et al.: Research progress in the application of big data and artificial intelligence technology in computer-aided drug design Drug evaluation research (2023)
8. Qian, H., Wang, M., Xiong, Q.: Research on the current situation and development of digital transformation in higher education. Big Data **9**(3), 56–70 (2023)
9. Lin, L.: Innovative strategies for digital management of archives in vocational colleges under big data Chinese Science and Technology. J. Database (Full Text Edition) Educ. Sci. (1), 33–35 (2022)
10. He, X.: Innovative thinking on teaching methods of art education in the digital era - review of "Art Education Walking with Big Data Era" Chinese University Science and Technology (10), 1 (2022)

Design of Optimization Algorithm of Information Teaching Resources Based on Big Data Analysis

Lin Cao[✉], Wenting Li, and Xiaoqian Jia

Binzhou Polytechnic, 256603 Binzhou, Shandong , China
coolcl@163.com

Abstract. The design of teaching resources optimization algorithm is critical in generator phase advance limit, however it has an issue with erroneous performance positioning. The typical Support Vector Machine SVM is unable to address the the phase limit issue in generator phase advance limit, and the result is insufficient. As a result, a Big data analysis-based optimization algorithm design of information teaching resources is provided, and the optimization algorithm design of information teaching resources is assessed. To begin, the DS theory is used to discover the influencing elements, and the indicators are split based on the design of teaching resources optimization algorithm's needs to decrease interference factors in the design of teaching resources optimization algorithm. The DS theory is then used to create a Big data analysis design of teaching resources optimization algorithm scheme, and the outcomes of the design of teaching resources optimization algorithm are thoroughly examined. The MATLAB simulation results reveal that, under particular evaluation conditions, the Big data analysis outperforms the standard Support Vector Machine SVM in terms of design of teaching resources optimization algorithm accuracy and time of influencing variables.

Keywords: DS theory · Big data analysis · Informatization;Teaching materials;Optimization

1 Introduction

Big data analysis is increasingly widely used in the field of education, behind which is the rapid development of information technology and the explosive growth of data volume [1, 2]. In the field of education, big data not only includes students' learning records, test scores, classroom interaction data, but also teachers' teaching behavior, the use of teaching resources and other information [3, 4]. The accumulation of these data provides rich resources for educational research and teaching practice [5, 6]. The application of big data technology has brought many changes to education. By analyzing students' learning behavior and achievement data, we can find the rules and problems in the learning process, thus providing support for personalized teaching. For example, by analyzing the click stream data on students' online learning platform, we can understand students'

B. Brik and S. Nazir (Eds.): BigIoT-EDU 2024, LNICST 659, pp. 86–96, 2026.
https://doi.org/10.1007/978-3-032-18631-7_10

preferences for different teaching resources, and then optimize the recommendation strategy of resources [7, 8]. Big data analytics can also help educational administrators to make decisions. For example, by analyzing students' academic performance and course selection data, curriculum settings can be optimized and teaching quality can be improved [9, 10].

2 Related Concepts

2.1 The Big Data Analysis is Described Mathematically.

Data analysis plays a vital role in the optimization of information-based teaching resources. Through big data analysis, we can more accurately understand students' learning needs, behavior patterns and teaching effects, so as to design more efficient and personalized teaching resource optimization algorithms is y_i found that the unqualified value parameters in the design of teaching resources optimization algorithm is z_i, and the design of teaching resources optimization algorithm scheme is $tol(y_i \cdot t_{ij})$, and the calculation is shown in Eq. (1).

$$\lim_{x \to \infty} \left(y_i \cdot t_{ij} \right) = \frac{n!}{r!(n-r)!} y_{ij} X \tag{1}$$

Equation illustrates the evaluation of outliers among them.(2).

$$\max\left(t_{ij}\right) = \sqrt{2}\left(\sum t_{ij} + 4\right)\mathfrak{M} \tag{2}$$

Establish a comprehensive and systematic data collection mechanism to collect students' learning process data, teachers' teaching plan and other data is t_i that the design is set_i, the technique is y_i, and the judgment function is as shown by Eq. (3).

$$F(d_i) = \mathfrak{A} \sum t_i \bigcap \xi \cdot \sqrt{2} \to \oint y_i \cdot 7 \tag{3}$$

2.2 Selection of Design of Teaching Resources Optimization Algorithm Scheme

Clean, classify and model data to ensure data accuracy and reliability is $g(t_i)$, The weighting factor is w_i, The unqualified is thus required by the design (4).

$$g(t_i) = \ddot{x} \cdot z_i \prod F(d_i) \frac{dy}{dx} - w_i \sqrt{2}\delta \tag{4}$$

the resources optimization algorithm can be obtained, and the results is shown in Eq. (5).

$$\lim_{x \to \infty} g(t_i) + F(d_i) \leq \bigcap \max\left(t_{ij}\right) \tag{5}$$

Using classification algorithms to predict students' academic performance and identify students with potential learning difficulties are presented in Eq. (6).

$$g(t_i) + F(d_i) \leftrightarrow \lim_{x \to \infty} \left(\sum t_{ij} + 4\right) \tag{6}$$

2.3 Analysis of Design of Teaching Resources Optimization Algorithm Scheme

Through clustering algorithm, students are divided into different learning groups, and customized teaching resources are provided for each group is shown in Eq. (7).

$$No(t_i) = \frac{g(t_i) + F(d_i)}{mean\left(\sum t_{ij} + 4\right)} \sqrt{b^2 - 4ac} \tag{7}$$

Among them, it is $\frac{g(t_i)+F(d_i)}{mean(\sum t_{ij}+4)} \leq 1$ specified that the scheme must be $Zh(t_i)$ suggested; Analyze the usage of school facilities and equipment, optimize procurement plan and resource allocation is illustrated in Eq. (8).

$$Zh(t_i) = \lim_{x \to \infty}\left[\sum g(t_i) + F(d_i)\right]\lim_{x \to \infty} \Theta \tag{8}$$

The design of teaching resources optimization algorithm is $accur(t_i)$ thoroughly examined, and Indicators such as teaching effect and learning resource utilization before and after algorithm optimization were compared is $unno(t_i)$, as stated in Eq. (9).

$$accur(t_i) = \frac{\min\left[\sum g(t_i) + F(d_i)\right]}{\frac{1}{2}\Lambda} \times 100\% \tag{9}$$

Big data analytics is just a tool, and it cannot be completely relied on to make decisions is $randon(t_i)$,Big data analysis has a wide application prospect in the design of information-based teaching resource optimization algorithm. Through in-depth mining and analysis of data, we can more accurately understand students' learning needs and teaching effects, so as to design a more efficient and personalized teaching resource optimization algorithm as Eq. (10).

$$accur(t_i) = \frac{\min\left[\sum g(t_i) + F(d_i)\right]}{\frac{1}{2}\sum \Gamma \overset{\sim}{\sqrt{b^2 - 4ac}}} + randon(t_i) \tag{10}$$

Big data technology can accurately understand students' learning situation and individual needs by analyzing students' learning data. By analyzing unstructured data such as students' learning behavior, achievement records, interests and hobbies, educators can tailor personalized learning programs for students.

3 Design of Teaching Resources Optimization Algorithm Optimization Approach

Data mining algorithms: such as cluster analysis, association rule mining, etc., are used to discover hidden patterns and association rules in data. These algorithms can help teachers discover students' learning characteristics and problems, so as to carry out targeted teaching optimization. Machine learning algorithms: such as decision trees, random forests, etc., are used for classification and regression analysis of students' learning data. These algorithms can provide personalized learning suggestions and resource recommendations for each student according to their learning situation and learning needs. Gradient descent algorithm: As an optimization algorithm, it is used to find the best parameters to minimize the cost function. In the field of education, the gradient descent algorithm can be used to optimize the parameters of the learning model and improve the prediction accuracy and generalization ability of the model.

4 Practical Examples of Design of Teaching Resources Optimization Algorithm

4.1 Introduction to the Design of Teaching Resources Optimization Algorithm

According to the specific teaching needs and resource optimization goals, select the appropriate optimization algorithm for design and implementation. The performance of the algorithms is evaluated and compared, and the optimal algorithm scheme is selected for application. Algorithms are continuously optimized and improved to adapt to changing teaching needs and data characteristics is shown in Table 1.

Table 1. Design of teaching resources optimization algorithm design of teaching resources optimization algorithm requirements

Scope of application	Types of resources.	Organize it.	Overall scheduling of resources.
Schooling	I	93.70	90.09
	II	91.92	90.76
Online education	I	94.68	88.73
	II	91.48	91.85
Distance learning	I	95.96	92.71
	II	91.62	91.86

The design of teaching resources optimization algorithm process in Table 1. Through algorithm optimization, we can ensure that teaching resources can be used more efficiently, reduce the waste of resources, and improve the utilization rate of resources is shown in Fig. 1.

Data-driven: The design and optimization of algorithms should be based on data. Through data analysis and mining, potential laws and patterns can be discovered to guide the optimization direction of algorithms. User-centered: Algorithms should always be user-centered, pay attention to users' needs and experiences, and ensure that recommended resources can really help users improve their learning effects. Transparency and interpretability: The decision-making process of the algorithm should be transparent and interpretable, so that users can understand the basis of recommending resources and enhance users' trust in the system. Security and privacy protection: When collecting and processing user data, we should strictly abide by relevant laws and regulations to ensure

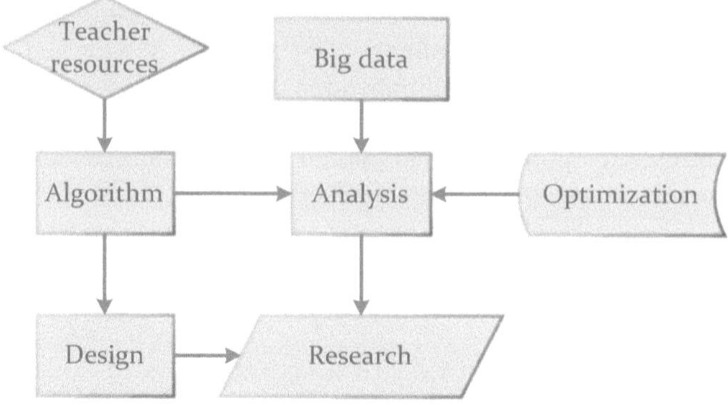

Fig. 1. Analysis process of design of teaching resources optimization algorithm

that the security and privacy of user data are not violated. Efficiency and stability: The algorithm should have efficient processing capabilities and stable performance, and be able to maintain good running status in the case of large-scale data and high concurrent access.

4.2 Design of Teaching Resources Optimization Algorithm

In the experimental design of teaching resource optimization algorithm, the selection and processing of data set is a crucial step. Two main datasets were selected for this study: one is user behavior data from an online education platform, and the other is a metadata set containing multiple types of teaching resources. The user behavior data set includes information such as user login time, browsing record, learning time, score and feedback. These data can reflect users' preferences and usage of different teaching resources. The metadata set contains multi-dimensional information such as course name, course category, course difficulty, course duration, course description, teacher information, etc. These data are helpful for the algorithm to classify and recommend teaching resources more carefully, as shown in Table 2.

Table 2. The overall situation of the design of teaching resources optimization algorithm scheme

Category	The comprehensiveness of personnel.	Overall resource optimization rate.	Middle aged balance relationship.
Schooling	92.42	92.71	91.12
Online education	90.22	88.47	92.08
Distance learning	93.50	90.82	89.01
Mean	89.27	92.98	94.90
X6	93.04	92.65	92.32
	$P = 1.249$		

4.3 Design of Teaching Resources Optimization Algorithm and Stability

Big data technology can also help educators rationally adjust the curriculum structure and optimize the allocation of teaching resources. By analyzing the teaching behavior data of teachers and students, educators can grasp the degree of correlation between each resource module, and then reasonably adjust the curriculum setting and the distribution structure of teaching resources is shown in Fig. 2.

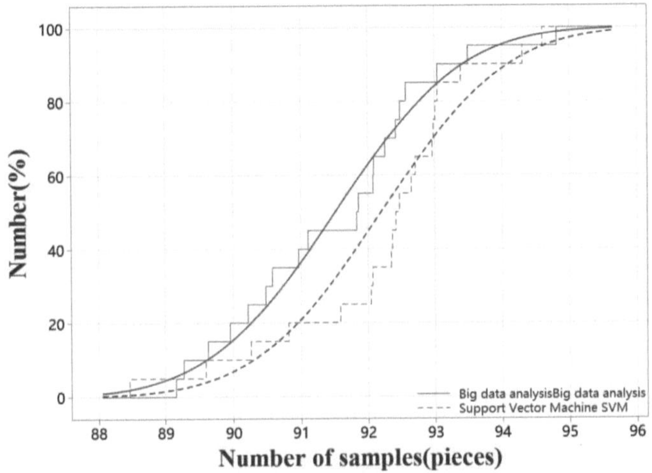

Fig. 2. Evaluation model of aging performance of different algorithms

Figure 2shows that the algorithm combines and optimizes teaching resources through genetic algorithm, so as to realize the optimal allocation of resources. Genetic algorithm continuously iteratively optimizes resource combination by simulating the process of natural selection and genetic variation. Specifically, the algorithm first generates the initial resource combination population, and then gradually evolves the optimal resource combination through selection, crossover and mutation operations. In order to ensure the diversity of optimization results, we also introduce a variety of evaluation indexes, such as resource coverage, user satisfaction, etc. Through multi-objective optimization method, we comprehensively consider these indexes, and finally get the optimal resource combination scheme,as shown in Table 3.

Table 3. Compares the accuracy of several design of teaching resources optimization algorithm.

Algorithm	Personnel data volume.	Resource comprehensiveness.	Resource adjustment rate.	Overall changes in resources.
Big data analysis	91.87	89.59	90.18	93.41
Support Vector Machine SVM	89.63	93.04	91.41	90.11

(*continued*)

Table 3. (continued)

Algorithm	Personnel data volume.	Resource comprehensiveness.	Resource adjustment rate.	Overall changes in resources.
P	90.97	92.35	90.10	91.48

Table 3 shows that the experimental results show that the proposed teaching resource optimization algorithm is excellent in many aspects. The resource recommendation algorithm based on machine learning is superior to the traditional recommendation algorithm in terms of recommendation accuracy and user satisfaction. Specifically, the algorithm's recommendation accuracy rate reached 85%, and the user satisfaction score reached 4.5 out of 5. This shows that the algorithm can effectively identify users' interests and needs and provide personalized recommendation services. Content classification and screening algorithms based on deep learning are outstanding in classification accuracy and screening efficiency. The classification accuracy of this algorithm reaches 92%, and the screening efficiency is 30% higher than that of traditional methods. This shows that the algorithm can more accurately identify the category and quality of courses, effectively screen out high-quality teaching resources, and provide users with a better learning experience, as shown in Fig. 3.

Fig. 3. Design of teaching resources optimization algorithm of Big data analysis

Figure 3 shows that The optimization of teaching resource combination based on genetic algorithm is excellent in resource coverage and user satisfaction. The resource coverage rate of this algorithm reaches 90%, and the user satisfaction score reaches 4.7. This shows that the algorithm can effectively optimize the resource combination, realize the optimal allocation of resources, and meet the diversified needs of users.

4.4   Rationality of Design of Teaching Resources Optimization Algorithm

The design of teaching resources optimization algorithm scheme is integrated with the Support Vector Machine SVM to check the correctness of the Big data analysis, and the design of teaching resources optimization algorithm scheme is depicted in Fig. 4.

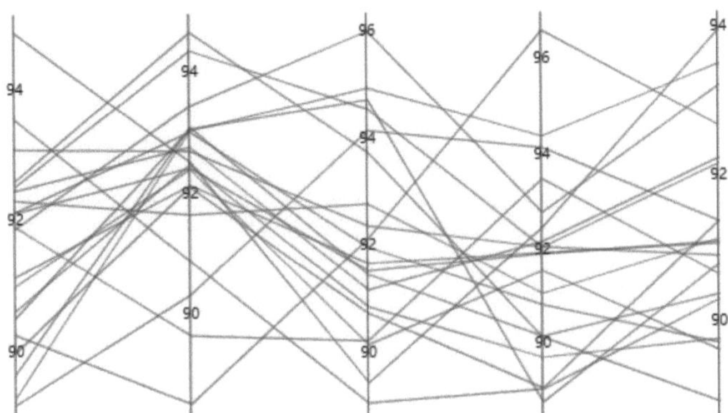

Fig. 4. Evaluation model of aging performance of different algorithms

Figure 4 shows that efficiency the efficiency of the algorithm is also an important criterion to measure its rationality. In the teaching resource optimization problem, the algorithm needs to complete a large number of calculation and analysis tasks in a limited time to provide timely resource allocation scheme. Therefore, the algorithm design should pay attention to improving computational efficiency, reducing unnecessary computational overhead, and ensuring that the algorithm can get results within a reasonable time. The optimization algorithm of teaching resources also needs to have good adaptability. With the change of teaching environment, students' needs and teaching resources, the algorithm should be able to flexibly adjust and optimize the resource allocation scheme. This requires the algorithm to have certain self-learning and self-adaptive capabilities, and be able to dynamically adjust according to real-time data and information.

4.5   Validity of Design of Teaching Resources Optimization Algorithm

In order to confirm the effectiveness of the Big data analysis, the design of teaching resources optimization algorithm scheme is comprised with the Support Vector Machine SVM, and the design of teaching resources optimization algorithm scheme is shown in Fig. 5 shown.

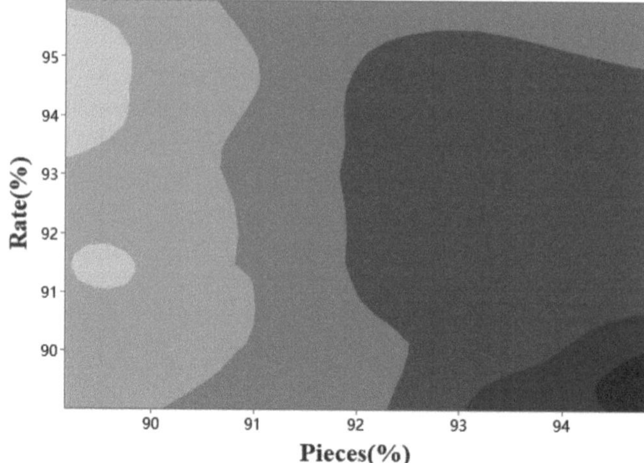

Fig. 5. Design of teaching resources optimization algorithm of different algorithms

Figure 5 shows that the primary goal of teaching resource optimization algorithm design is to ensure the effectiveness of the algorithm. This means that the algorithm should be able to accurately provide the optimal or approximately optimal resource allocation scheme for teaching activities according to various factors such as teaching needs, students' characteristics, teaching resources, etc. Effectiveness is an important index to evaluate the performance of algorithms, which is usually verified by comparative experiments, simulation tests and other methods.

Table 4. Compares the efficacy of several design of teaching resources optimization algorithm.

Algorithm	Survey data	design of teaching resources optimization algorithm	Magnitude of change	Error
Big data analysis	90.59	92.42	90.80	89.66
Support Vector Machine SVM	89.16	90.27	94.09	94.07
P	89.96	92.05	90.68	89.02

Table 4 shows that Big data technology can support the establishment and optimization of online learning platforms to provide more teaching resources and learning opportunities. Online learning platforms can use big data technology to analyze students' learning behaviors and interests and preferences, and recommend relevant learning resources and courses for them. At the same time, the platform can dynamically adjust the teaching content and difficulty according to students' learning progress and feedback to provide a more personalized learning experience., as illustrated in Fig. 6.

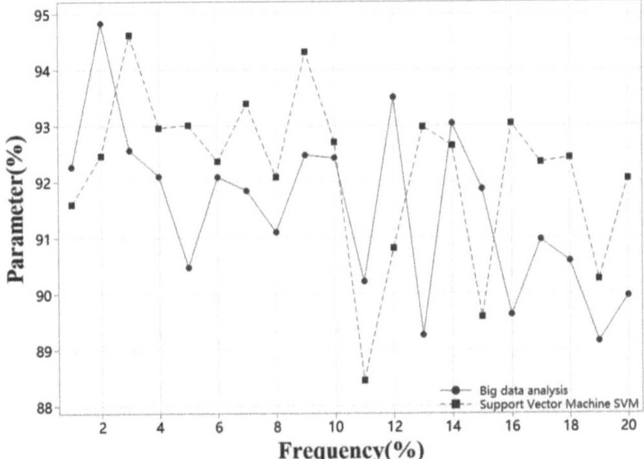

Fig. 6. Big data analysis design of teaching resources optimization algorithm

Figure 6 shows that abundance and diversity: Information teaching resources provide students with rich and diverse learning materials through the Internet and multimedia technology. Students can choose their own learning resources according to their own interests and needs, so as to improve their learning effect. Flexibility and convenience: Information teaching resources are not limited by time and space, and students can study at any time and anywhere. This flexibility allows for more autonomous and efficient learning. Interactivity and personalization: The online learning platform and multimedia courseware supported by modern information technology provide rich interactive functions, such as online discussion, instant feedback, personalized recommendation, etc. These functions help to stimulate students' interest in learning and improve their participation and enthusiasm in learning. Timeliness of updating: Information teaching resources can be updated quickly to reflect the latest development and research results of the discipline in a timely manner, so that students can get in touch with the most cutting-edge knowledge and information.

5   Conclusion

In this study, by systematically analyzing the application of big data analysis in the optimization of information teaching resources, a set of comprehensive optimization schemes based on machine learning, deep learning and genetic algorithm is proposed. Through in-depth discussion on the concept, characteristics and applicability of big data in the field of education, the importance and feasibility of big data analysis in education are clarified. This paper expounds the definition and classification of information teaching resources and their advantages and challenges in modern education in detail, which provides a theoretical basis for the subsequent algorithm design. In the aspect of algorithm design, this study proposes a resource recommendation algorithm based on machine learning, which can intelligently recommend personalized teaching resources according to students' learning behaviors and preferences, and improves the pertinence and effectiveness of learning. The content classification and screening algorithm based on deep learning can automatically identify and classify different types of educational resources, improving the efficiency and accuracy of resource management. The optimization of teaching resources combination based on genetic algorithm realizes the optimal combination of teaching resources by simulating the process of natural selection, and further improves the teaching effect.

References

1. Zang Xiaodi, Wang Zhongguan, Guo Li: A data-driven modeling based reactive power and voltage optimization control method for wind farms CN202210108334.5 (2022)
2. Bai Wenchao, Liu Yingming, Wang Xiaodong, Zhang Shuyuan: A data-driven method for identifying the optimal pitch angle of wind turbines Electric Power Science and Engineering (009), 038 (2022)
3. Lei Daozhong: Design of Speed Control System for Marine Diesel Generators Ship Science and Technology (2023)
4. Yue Wenji, Wang Hao, Wu Tianzhun, Li Jingjun: Non contact shaking pulse generator and method based on programmable nano friction power generation mechanism CN115912982A (2023)
5. Takada mason, Takazawa Plows flat: Engine driven generator CN116263141A (2023)
6. Xie Gangwen, Li Dengfeng, Liu Yuming, Xu Ruilin, Zhan Hang, Xia Hanlin, et al.: An online monitoring method and system for the margin of generator safety phase advance capability CN202010915154.9 (2022)
7. Zhang Chao, Zhang Shaofei: A method for identifying abnormal bearings at the driving end of wind turbine generators based on scada temperature data Bearing (006), 000 (2022)
8. Hongwei, W., Wenlei, S., Xiaodong, Z., Li, H.: Research on fault diagnosis method for wind turbine gearbox based on optimized VMD composite multi-scale dispersion entropy and LSTM. Journal of Solar Energy. **004**, 043 (2022)
9. Taibo, Z., Shuwei, Z., Qiming, C.: Calculation of generator loss of excitation protection setting based on admittance plane. Electr. Eng. **3**, 34–37 (2023)
10. Jiawei, Q., Deyou, Y., Guowei, C., Lixin, W., Fangwei, D.: A data-driven damping modulation strategy for AC/DC hybrid power systems. J. Power Syst. Autom. **35**(1), 59–67 (2023)

Innovative Methods of Dance Teaching in Universities under Big Data Thinking

ChuLing Wu[⊠]

Quanzhou Preschool Education College, QPEC, Zhangzhou 363000, Fujian, China
56952992@qq.com

Abstract. Dance teaching innovation is the main content of physical education in colleges and universities, and dance teaching innovation is reflected in the integration of posture, movement, and essentials. Dance content involves many aspects such as skills and skills, so it needs to be integrated with the help of big data analysis methods. This paper is based on big data thinking to make a holistic judgment. Form an effective data set, and then provide innovative guidance for dance teaching. The results showed that the average scores of students in the following areas were as follows: innovative thinking (8.5), skill level (7.5), collaboration ability (8.0), rhythm mastery (8.0), and work performance (9.0). Moreover, the average scores of students' dance skills, cooperation ability, rhythm mastery and work performance were 9.0 points, 8.0 points, 8.5 points and 9.5 points respectively, which showed a significant improvement. Therefore, big data ideas have a large application space in the process of dance teaching in colleges and universities, which can promote the development of their teaching in the direction of innovation.

Keywords: BD Thinking · Dance Teaching In Tertiary institutionsAnd Universities · Innovative · Educational Technology

1 Introduction

Due to the improvement of dance teaching content and teaching effect, dance education should develop in the direction of innovation to meet the needs. The development of dance requires innovation, but dance involves many contents, including not only students' physical strength, but also students' understanding and practical teaching environment and teaching tools [1, 2]. Therefore, in the teaching process of teachers, dance teaching innovation cannot be effectively carried out [3–5]. In addition, in the process of overall analysis of dance, dance teaching cannot achieve overall planning. In order to solve the above problems, some scholars believe that big data analysis methods should be integrated into dance teaching, and the content of dance teaching should be analyzed, including movement learning, physical fitness indicators, understanding, and the overall integration of various factors [6, 7]. Big data analysis can be used to share data with the help of cloud platforms, including dance teaching plans, teaching content, and teaching

B. Brik and S. Nazir (Eds.): BigIoT-EDU 2024, LNICST 659, pp. 97–104, 2026.
https://doi.org/10.1007/978-3-032-18631-7_11

stages, and complete comprehensive data analysis [8–10]. In the process of education, dance teaching shows significant innovation. Big data analysis and dance teaching can be integrated, including: educational content and methods, such as teaching students according to their aptitude [11–13]. Big data has theoretical feasibility in the process of dance teaching [14, 15]. Based on the above analysis conditions, this paper conducts in-depth excavation of dance teaching, learning situation, learning content, and academic performance, and integrates various indicators such as students' physical fitness, physical strength, and teaching content. In the existing dance teaching, improve the learning effect of students, promote the development of dance teaching to innovation, make up for the shortcomings in manual teaching, and expand the scope of dance teaching.

2 Related Works

2.1 Integration of Big Data and Dance Teaching

Because dance teaching involves relatively many contents, including: physical strength, physical fitness, students' understanding, teaching content and implementation conditions and other factors. Therefore, the integration of dance teaching and big data requires the establishment of cloud data, the judgment of students' learning situation, learning interests, and learning indicators, and the continuous updating of teaching indicators and content. In the teaching process, teachers make overall plans according to the teaching effect, students' physical fitness and physical properties. With the assistance of big data, record students' information, form effective feature points, and provide support for the adjustment of later teaching plans and the update of teaching content. However, the integration process of big data and dance teaching needs to be mathematically described to make it more concrete.

$$R(\beta) = \sum_{j=1}^{p} \beta_j - \frac{1}{2_k} \sum_{k=1}^{p} \beta_j \beta_k Z_k Z_j \left(y_k * y_j \right) \tag{1}$$

Where, $R(\beta)$ is the quadratic data discriminant function $y_j * y_k$ is the dot product of two vectors; Z is the classification threshold Z_j; And Z_k respectively represent the classification threshold β of β and y_j vectors as the weight vector y_j; And y_j: y_j; The weight p of the two vectors and L is the maximum vector. The ideal method for data categorization should be able to fulfill the following criteria:

$$\begin{cases} \sum_{j=1}^{p} Z_j \beta_j = 0 \\ \\ \beta_j \geq 0 j = 1, 2 \end{cases} \tag{2}$$

The auxiliary role of big data in dance teaching is mainly to continuously record students' learning situation and learning content, and supervise the overall changes of students and students' physical changes. Identify anomalous changes and support the adjustment of teaching plans.Here are some prerequisites for distributed issue solution in categorized calculation: $L(y_j, y_k)$ Replace the dot product in the optimal classification function. In order to get the transformed outcomes, the distributed solution problem has to satisfy these conditions, and the optimum data plane solution problem may do the same.

$$L(y) = \text{sgn}\left(\sum_{j=1}^{p} \beta, Z_j L(y_j * y_k) + c\right) \tag{3}$$

2.2 The Concept of BD Thinking and its Application in Education

The teaching process is a process of multi-complex data change, which includes not only physical learning content, learning interest and multi-index content, but also includes the analysis of teaching conditions in dance teaching. Therefore, big data can analyze dance teaching in stages and continuously record relevant data, including: students' learning situation, learning content and interests, as well as the understanding and transformation of dance teaching content. Therefore, in the process of big data analysis, the above process can be continuously analyzed and displayed in the form of diagrams. Figure 1 illustrates:

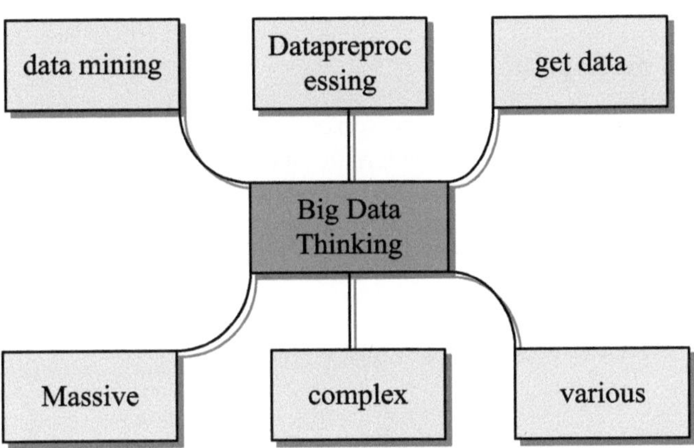

Fig. 1. Flowchart of BD Thinking

2.3 The Basis of Big Data for Dance Innovation

Dance innovation is a continuous process that includes not only the characteristics of each student, but also the needs of students' teaching. Therefore, in the process of analysis, big data can analyze the characteristics of each student in dance teaching through cloud technology, match the teaching content with students one by one, and form a teaching according to their aptitude. In addition, in the process of analysis, big data can find out the abnormalities of students, including: physical fitness changes, characteristics changes, skill changes, etc. Therefore, big data has significant significance in the dance teaching process, mainly for continuous analysis. By comparing the characteristics of the data, find out the characteristics of students to provide support for teaching. With the assistance of cloud technology, big data can record massive data, accurately identify small changes in students, make up for the shortcomings in manual analysis and manual measurement, and provide support for dance innovation and talent discovery.

The prerequisite for teaching improvement is students, and the physical factors, understanding factors, posture and body flexibility of individual students will have an impact on dance innovation. Therefore, in the process of big data analysis, the overall changes of students can be recorded and the data analysis can be compared. According to the content and form of students' data, the data is compared to form the characteristics of continuous analysis. In addition, it is necessary to integrate the characteristics of dance and student innovation to deepen students' learning interest and learning content, and provide support for the improvement of dance innovation. The application of big data can find students' good basic conditions and teach them according to their aptitude, so as to promote students' development in the direction of diversification and in-depth. Support for dance teaching and dance innovation.

3 Comparison of Dance Innovation Results in Colleges and Universities with the Assistance of Big Data

3.1 Purpose of the Experiment

With the help of massive data, the comparison of dance teaching is carried out, and the difference between students' dance characteristics and dance movements is found through the comparison of dance teaching analysis methods. Specific comparison process.

1. Expand the difference between dance teaching innovation and artificial dance innovation assisted by data.
2. Judge the innovative content of dance.
3. discover the sustainability and feasibility of dance innovation.

3.2 Analysis

Innovate comparative analysis, randomly assign students to different analysis methods and research, among which students should make judgments based on big data analysis methods and manual analysis methods. The following factors were examined to compare the two groups: 1) students' learning status, physical fitness, physical coordination, dance movement innovation level, and dance score score. 2) Guide students to conduct subjective surveys to judge their learning content and interest in learning and evaluate the rationality of education. At the same time, the application rate of theoretical content in the teaching content is compared, and the physical consumption of students is compared. 4) The effect of students' dance teaching and the rationality of the teaching plan were discovered, and whether the teaching content was optimized in a targeted manner. The specific optimization results are shown in Table 1.

Table 1 shows that in the process of comparing students' learning conditions, it will be found that the learning content and learning motivation of dance learning interest have increased significantly, and then in the process of grading dance students, it will

Table 1. Comparative experimental results of innovative methods of dance teaching in colleges and universities based on Big data thinking mode

control group	academic record	learning motivation	Utilization of teaching resources	teaching efficiency
Big data analysis methods	86.5	4.3	32	78.2
Manual analysis methods	76.8	3.8	22	65.9

be found that the analysis method of the big data group is 86.5, which is significantly greater than the original analysis method and analysis content. Therefore, the effect of dance innovation is relatively good, which can meet actual needs, and the auxiliary effect of big data will also be found in the use of learning motivation and related resources and teaching efficiency, and the effect is very obvious. The results are greater than those of manual analysis methods, which shows that under the intervention of big data, students' learning situation has been significantly improved, their learning performance has been improved, and students' learning interests and learning directions have been improved. It can also improve the overall learning effect of students, encourage students to innovate in dance, assist teachers in effective dance teaching, and save a lot of manpower and material resources.

3.3 Results

By comparing big data analysis methods and manual analysis methods, it will be found that big data can guide dance teaching innovation, and teach students according to their learning interests, learning characteristics, and physical conditions. The big data method effectively analyzes the rationality of teaching content and highlights the advantages of big data education methods. Relatively speaking, manual analysis methods mainly carry out content adjustment and empirical verification, and do not fundamentally improve students. In the process of learning, students are not satisfied with all aspects of content and teaching effect, and need to be further optimized.

4   Results and Discussion

4.1 Specific Case Description

Taking dance teaching in colleges and universities as a research case, the analysis of big data thinking and manual teaching schemes will find that big data continuously records the learning characteristics in learning, as well as the content and teaching effect of dance teaching, including students' interests, hobbies, physical fitness and other aspects. Therefore, big data analysis methods actively participate in dance teaching and guide all aspects of dance teaching, including: content, teachers, and personal interests.

4.2 Data Analysis Results

The dance situation of students is analyzed and the results of big data analysis are compared, including movement standards, students' interests, learning content, dance content, and physical fitness. Figure 2 shows specific data:

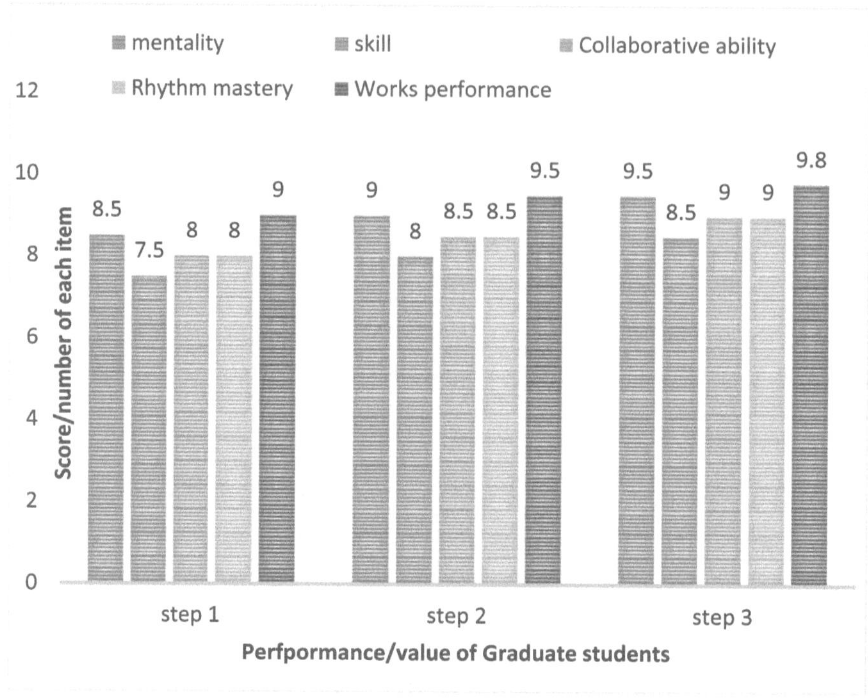

Fig. 2. The role of big data in dance teaching

Figure 2 shows that in the process of dance teaching, big data plays a significant role in improving, with the highest score of 10 points. Moreover, in terms of students' physical status, it was found that big data can improve students' physical fitness, with a physical fitness score of 8.5 points and a technical level of 7.5 points. In addition, big data analyzes students' personal physical conditions and judges their synergy, with students' learning interest being 3 points, knowledge mastery being 5 points, and dance rhythm perception and movement performance being 8 and 9 points. This shows that in the process of student analysis, big data gives full play to its continuous monitoring role. In addition, the analysis method of big data is reflected in the phase, in the first stage: students' learning interest and learning content, as well as the standard of action, have not been significantly improved. However, in the third stage, students' physical coordination and movement mastery rate are 8.5 points. This shows that in the process of in-depth analysis, students' learning interest has been significantly improved, the difficulty of learning, and practicality have been significantly improved, and big data can continuously optimize students.

4.3 Teaching Effect Evaluation

Based on the above content, it is found that the role of big data in dance teaching is mainly reflected in four aspects, namely: educational content, educational characteristics, students' physical condition, and dance movement improvement level. Among them, the educational content and educational characteristics are highlighted based on students' posture and dance understanding. After highlighting the characteristics and learning content of students, big data plays a role in continuous monitoring, finding out its focus, and teaching students according to their aptitude, so that the accuracy of their dance movement recognition is improved and students' physical fitness is significantly improved.

5 Conclusion

Dance teaching is the main content in the teaching process of colleges and universities, but dance teaching involves many factors such as physical teaching content, teaching characteristics, and talent. Therefore, it is necessary to use big data analysis methods for analysis. The results of this paper show that in the process of comparing the big data group and the manual screening group, big data can continuously analyze students' dance characteristics, discover students' learning characteristics, and teach students according to their aptitude. Big data improves dance teaching by more than 20%, and students' coordination, dance mastery, and physical fitness scores are greater than 8 points, indicating that under the guidance of big data, students can be recorded and optimized. However, there are also shortcomings in this study, mainly in terms of student analysis and related research data, and the data volume and sample size will be increased in the future to make up for the lack of research.

References

1. El Raheb, K., et al.: Towards a general framework for the annotation of dance motion sequences. Multim. Tools Appl. **82**(3), 3363–3395 (2023)
2. Abe, N.: Beyond anthropomorphising robot motion and towards robot-specific motion: consideration of the potential of artist - dancers in research on robotic motion. Artif. Life Robot. **27**(4), 777–785 (2022)
3. de Souza, F., et al.: The effects of a low volume physical training program on functional movement and strength in dancers. Int. J. Art Cult. Des. Technol. **11**(2), 1–12 (2022)
4. Fischer, C.: Analysis of current tests for assessing dance aesthetic performance: a systematic review. Int. J. Art Cult. Des. Technol. **11**(2), 1–9 (2022)
5. Ljubojevic, A., Popovic, B., Bijelic, S., et al.: Proprioceptive training in dance sport: effects of agility skills. J. Turkish J. Kinesiol. **6**(3), 109–117 (2020)
6. Hasko, J., Rivera, M.C., Erbacher, M.K., et al.: Visual analysis plus hierarchical linear model regressions: Morphosyntax intervention with deaf-and-hard-of-hearing students. J. Commun. Disord. Q. **43**(3), 195–205 (2022)
7. Matos, M.I., da Silva, E.B.: New notes on the cardiorespiratory capacity of dancers: a narrative review. Int. J. Art Cult. Des. Technol. **11**(2), 1–11 (2022)
8. Rettore, P.H.L.: The implantation of a dance workshop on the quality of life in the work environment: the Paola Rettore method. Int. J. Art Cult. Des. Technol. **11**(2), 1–9 (2022)

9. Yin, G., Wang, L.: Teaching effect analysis and behavior detection of an online dance learning platform in the context of COVID-19. Int. J. Inf. Syst. Serv. Sect. **14**(3), 1–17 (2022)
10. Hsia, L.-H., Hwang, G.-J., Lin, C.-J.: A WSQ-based flipped learning approach to improving students' dance performance through reflection and effort promotion. Interact. Learn. Environ. **30**(2), 229–244 (2022)
11. Kalita, D., Deka, D.: Ontology for preserving the knowledge base of traditional dances (OTD). Electron. Libr. **38**(4), 785–803 (2020)
12. Guo, B.: Analysis on influencing factors of dance teaching effect in tertiary institutionsBased on data analysis and decision tree model. Int. J. Emerg. Technol. Learn. **15**(9), 245–257 (2020)
13. Landry, S., Jeon, M.: Interactive sonification strategies for the motion and emotion of dance performances. J. Multimodal User Interfaces. **14**(2), 167–186 (2020)
14. Behmanesh, F., Bakouei, F., Nikpour, M., Parvaneh, M.: Comparing the effects of traditional teaching and flipped classroom on midwifery students' practical learning: the embedded mixed method. Technol. Knowl. Learn. **27**(2), 599–608 (2022)
15. Prvan, M., Ozegovic, J.: Methods in teaching computer networks: a literature review. ACM Trans. Comput. Educ. **20**(3), 1–35 (2020)

Design of Achievement Display System for Double Qualified Team Based on Network and Big Data

Xinfeng Zhou[✉]

Loudi Xiaoxiang Vocational Collage, Loudi 417000, Hunan, China
`szpthero@dingtalk.com`

Abstract. Teachers that are considered DQTs (Double Qualified Teachers) should be well-versed in both theory and practice. In addition to being an accomplished educator, he is also skilled at directing professionals in their daily work. This research delves into the features of network big data, examines the meaning of DQT, and builds a method to evaluate its performance at various points in its development. All the way through DQT's development, it assesses how well task indicators are doing their jobs. From the data, we can deduce that the theory of double ability accounts for 46% of the double certified instructors, while the theory of double professional title accounts for 26%.

Keywords: Network · Big Data · Double Qualification · Team Building

1 Introduction

In order for colleges and universities to undergo transformation and growth, it is essential to build faculty members who are both prepared academically and capable of providing social service. One important area of practical focus in the field of transformation research at regular undergraduate institutions is the development of "double qualified" teaching personnel.

The dual qualification team has been the subject of much research due to the exponential growth in computing power. Some Chinese groups, for instance, have looked at the published research on teamwork in big data project implementation and the incentive mechanism of "double qualified" instructors. Key success indicators for using big data have been developed to assist practitioners in executing their initiatives. These elements are classified in accordance with the six traits shared by mature big data companies. This paper proposes a solution to the problem of how to build DQT in our country's colleges and universities during this period of transition, drawing on empirical evidence, the successful experience of DQT in other countries, and an analysis of the current situation. The goal is to cultivate traditional teacher professionals while also meeting the demand for big data network talents. The paper bases its recommendations on a thorough examination of relevant literature. Building a system of "double qualified" teachers

B. Brik and S. Nazir (Eds.): BigIoT-EDU 2024, LNICST 659, pp. 105–112, 2026.
https://doi.org/10.1007/978-3-032-18631-7_12

necessitates recruiting new educators, as outlined in a teaching reform plan spearheaded by education management majors: revamp the training system in response to the demand for smart educators, and ramp up research and technology implementation into the DQT building process. The present state of affairs and Construction Countermeasures for "double qualified" educators have been the subject of research by some specialists. We should choose outstanding instructional leaders and fortify team construction in accordance with the recommendations of specialized construction and curriculum reform. The management strategy of teacher team building is the formation of an efficient reward mechanism and a scientific performance assessment system [2]. The construction of "double qualified" instructors has also been examined by certain specialists. This study examines the method of DQT building. Its goal, when coupled with school enterprise collaboration, is to train educators who are up to the task. This paper investigates the ways in which a "double qualified" logistics management teaching team can be formed, how to set up a developmental evaluation and guidance mechanism for DQT against the backdrop of a modern apprenticeship system, and how to increase teachers' awareness and active participation through the implementation of a "double professional title" system for "double qualified" teachers. Issues with DQT's instructional system development are examined and solutions proposed in this study. In order to understand the actual development of DQT in higher vocational colleges, this paper uses data analysis to study double qualified, randomly select samples, and conduct an interview survey. The survey focuses on the management suggestions of DQT and summarizes the number, age, existing problems, proportion of professionals with DQT degrees, and educational background of DQT in these colleges. This study examines the, and elaborates on the need of developing DQT in order to fulfill the needs of contemporary businesses for the development of highly trained individuals. Lastly, this article proposes some sound solutions for the development of professional degree graduate DQT based on an examination of particular issues and the state of our nation generally. Some gaps remain in the design and study of the network and big data based double qualified team performance display system, despite the many accomplishments in the field of double qualified team research.

This study investigates the design of a network big data double certified team performance display system based on research into both technologies. It finds that we prioritize evaluation throughout the usage process. The findings demonstrate that network big data technology promotes the development of talents with two qualifications.

2 Related Works

2.1 Network Big Data Technology

(1) Large databases

Data that is big, diversified, and processed quickly is known as big data [4]. In order to store and handle it, regular processing tools are out of the question; instead, virtualization technologies, including cloud computing, are required to transcend physical and temporal constraints [5]. While big data cannot be processed by a regular computer, it may be realized with cloud computing, which allows for a distributed architecture of data [7]. Data can only be fully used for its hidden worth via distributed deep mining, which will help individuals improve processes and make other choices more effectively [8]. The unique handling of enormous data sets is the defining characteristic of the big data age [9].

(2) Network large data information features

Features of network big data in terms of information: first, transparency [10]. After all, big data is derived from a shared and open network of information. As we go from collecting data to transforming and updating data technologies, more and more user data will be made public and utilized for several purposes. The second one is evolving. One quality of network information that evolves over time is its dynamic character. The widespread use of computers and the Internet has been the foundation for the growth of the big data age. As a result, big data is no more static information content shaped by the past or any one setting; rather, it is real-time dynamic data created on the Internet. And last, sociality. Information shared via networks has far-reaching effects, influencing not only the advancement of the hard and social sciences but also people's day-to-day lives and the way they do their jobs.

2.2 Double Qualified Team

One club that has qualified twice.

"Fusion type" is primarily responsible for promoting "double qualified" instructors, "double qualified" standards, and "double qualified" organizational framework. There is an element of both individual and collective interpretation in it. A "double qualification" instructor is both an individual and a part of a team, meeting the common requirements of both in vocational education. A DQT is built using several levels and channels. The meaning is summed up by the building of integrated instructors. Taking a broad view, this definition raises the bar for what it means to be a "double qualified" teacher. However, the notion of "knowledge, ability and quality" is difficult to define in the real operation and operating uncertainty when it comes to identifying and evaluating "double qualified" instructors.

(3) Two-pronged methods of educating

Project management style may be effectively used into "double qualification" teacher training due to its operational qualities. To promote the scientific building of the DQT training mode and to completely integrate the many resources for teacher training, it is helpful to include the concept and technique of project management into the DQT training mode. It is important to maximize the resource efficiency of DQT training by pursuing economic advantages and social effect in addition to the work efficiency of DQT training. In addition to being educators, they also operate a manufacturing. Coordination and optimization of training content, strengthening of communication and feedback before, during, and after training, and ensuring the maximum training effect are all part of the training process that aims to improve the core literacy, existing technical skills, sustainable development ability, professional standards, and job specifications of "double qualification" teachers. Schools are able to streamline their teaching and practice processes by collaborating with businesses, borrowing and sharing resources, and making use of cutting-edge experimental equipment. Concurrently, in order to prevent construction crew from becoming blind, we need to set training rules and regulations and a time restriction.

As they mature into adults, "double qualification" educators should further their education in professional ethics and ideology and politics. Following the elucidation of the scientific meaning of "double qualified" teachers, it is imperative that we evolve teacher identification criteria in accordance with the fundamental law of teacher development, enhance teacher training, and refine teacher evaluation procedures. There has to be variety in the assessment tools as well. We should institute a tutorial system and fully use the illustrious roles of renowned educators and craftspeople to help train the next generation of educators to be better in the areas of education, research, and scientific inquiry. Teacher entry into enterprises needs to be standardized, training needs to be made clear, temporary training and technical services need to be standardized as well, teachers need to be organized into batches, teachers need to be encouraged to participate in product development and technological innovation, and "double qualified" teachers need to be cultivated quickly.

2.3 Pay Attention to the Assessment During the Employment Period

After instructors finish their assignments, they fill out the quantitative assessment, which is then approved by the department. P = K1 * research and teaching workload + K2 * teaching workload + K3 * management workload is the calculation for the final score. Consider the G1 teaching workload estimate, as shown in Eq. (1).

$$G1 = S \times Z \times X \times B \times K \times A \tag{1}$$

According to Eq. (2), the matrix elements exhibit the following properties.

$$a_{ij} = {}^{1}\!/a_{ij} \tag{2}$$

The primary goal of single-level sorting is to achieve a certain standard by calculating the weight of each candidate element. As seen in Eq. (3), the first step is to determine the judgment matrix's eigenvalue.

$$AW = \lambda\, max\, W \tag{3}$$

After calculating the average random consistency index (ijr) and the consistency index (CIJ) of B-level partial factors with respect to JA single ranking, we can use these numbers in formula (4) to get the random consistency ratio for B-level total ranking:

$$CR = \frac{\sum_{j-1}^{m} a_j c_{ij}}{\sum_{j-1}^{m} a_j R_{ij}} \tag{4}$$

3 Experience

3.1 Object Extraction

A large number of educational institutions have made significant strides in their pursuit of "double qualified" faculty members. A college education, on the other hand, begins late and ends quickly. The development and establishment of DQT at academic institutions has occurred in the last few years. The study thoroughly examines the implementation of reasonable certification and the formation of the "double qualified" teacher system. It also observes, researches, and analyzes the building of the "double qualified" teaching team in the school to gather original data. Additionally, this paper provides numerous scientific and effective recommendations for managing "double qualified" professional teachers and part-time teachers, and it places particular emphasis on the importance of system construction and restraint mechanisms in building "double qualified" teacher teams and schools.

3.2 Experimental Analysis

There are a lot of moving parts in the massive "double qualification" teacher training project, which will take a long time to complete and cover a lot of ground. An extensive and thorough investigation of the meaning, scope, principles, and practices of "double qualification" teacher training is required to enhance the training impact as part of the project management implementation process. Simultaneously, based on this foundation, we should institute the idea of "double qualification" teacher training, which entails two levels: the first is the level of the instructors themselves; the second is the level of the students they teach. The first level focuses on the development of teachers' professional backbone; the second level emphasizes the development of teachers' ethics. (1) In accordance with the "Teacher Law" and other applicable laws and regulations, as well as the, progressively implement a system of DQT; this system will emphasize the features of vocational education and help bring about the uniformity of project management for double-qualified teacher training [2]. Construct a comprehensive framework for "double qualification" teacher training. We need to construct a system for training teachers who are "double qualified" with a consistent and acceptable framework, so that it can operate flawlessly and provide outstanding results. This should be the central focus of school teacher training programs.

4 Discussion

4.1 The Number of "Double Qualified" Teachers

Universities place a premium on producing "double qualified" educators, propose practical ability standards for full-time faculty, and implement policies that reflect these standards. In Table 1 we can see the overall situation of "double qualified" instructors in every field.

Based on the data shown above, it is evident that ordinary universities have 12 basic course instructors, 25 professional course instructors, and 28 practice instructors.

Table 1. Source statistics of double qualified team

Source index	Basic course teacher	Professional course teacher	critic teacher
Colleges and Universities	12	25	28
Normal University	23	36	24
Enterprise introduction	34	47	25

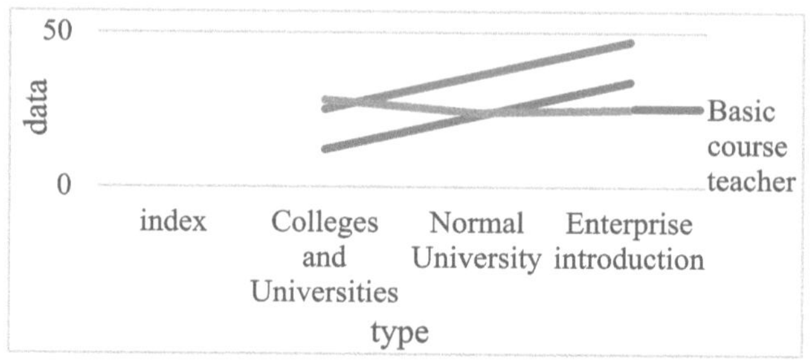

Fig. 1. Source statistics of double qualified team

On the other hand, enterprises have 34 basic course instructors, 47 professional course instructors, and 25 practice instructors. Pictured below are the outcomes (Fig. 1).

According to the data shown above, there are a maximum of 28 internship instructors at colleges and universities, 36 professional teachers at regular institutions, and 47 professional teachers at businesses.

4.2   A Survey on the Connotation Cognition of DQT

From a managerial vantage point, we have a good grasp of the policies that will help build more "double qualified" educators, as well as the strategies for attracting and retaining such educators, as well as the measures to incentivize and ensure their success. In Table 2 you can see the outcomes.

Table 2. Statistics of the connotation of "double qualified" Teachers

Understanding of connotation	Number of people	percentage
Double evidence theory	45	28%
Double title	42	26%
Dual capabilities	73	46%

The data shown above shows that 45 "DQT" (or 28% of the total) are believed to have two certifications; 42 "DQT" (or 26% of the total) are believed to hold two professional

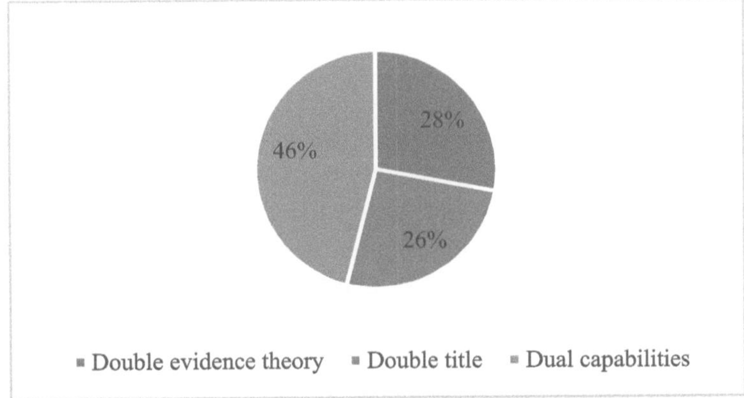

Fig. 2. Statistics on the connotation of "double qualified" Teachers

titles; and 73 "DQT" (or 46% of the total) are believed to possess two talents. Figure 2 displays the outcomes.

From the data shown above, we can deduce that 16% of people believe that "DQT" refers to the theory of dual skills, whereas 46% hold the view that it refers to the theory of dual degrees.

5   Conclusion

The number of educators is rising in tandem with the expansion of vocational education. "Double qualification" educators flourish and establish themselves as a formidable faculty. In order to improve students' abilities and the development of higher vocational colleges, this article first examines "double qualified" instructors. It then addresses the value of these teachers and proposes steps to increase the legal construction of teachers. Using the docking mechanism of business plates, strengthening the construction of teacher training bases, broadening the channels of talent training, introducing teachers, expanding the proportion of part-time teachers, making full use of relevant policies, and following policy guidance are all suggestions put forth in this paper on human resource management and teachers' professional knowledge.

References

1. An, H., Park, M.: A study on the evaluation of fashion design based on big data text analysis -focus on semantic network analysis of design elements and emotional terms. J. Korean Soc. Cloth. Text. **42**(3), 428–437 (2018)
2. Hidayat, M., Sukasno, S., Efuansyah, E.: Penerapan model student team achievement division (Stad) Pada Pembelajaran Matematika Siswa Kelas Viii Smp Negeri 2 Saling. J. Math. Sci. Educ. **3**(1), 37–44 (2020)
3. Li, J., Dong, Y., Xu, M., et al.: Genetic programming method for satellite system topology and parameter optimization. Int. J. Aerosp. Eng. **2020**(4), 1–14 (2020)

4. Cahyono, A.E.Y.: Improving achievement and attitudes towards mathematics using problem-based learning setting team accelerated instruction. J. Math. Educ. **4**(2), 52–59 (2019)
5. Astri, T.P.Y., Gunarhadi, G., Riyadi, R.: Numbered-board quiz with TGT to improve students' science achievement based on learning motivation. Int. J. Educ. Res. Rev. **3**(4), 68–76 (2018)
6. Andriani, W., Natsir, I.: Meningkatkan Hasil Belajar Matematika Siswa Melalui Model Kooperatif Tipe Student Team Achievement Division (STAD). Musamus J. Math. Educ. **2**(2), 67–73 (2020)
7. Jufri, M.: Student Team Achievement Division dalam Meningkatkan Hasil Belajar Siswa. Kuriositas Media Komunikasi Sosial dan Keagamaan **11**(2), 135–144 (2018)
8. Zhang, L., Qi, K.: The fabrication of an amperometric immunosensor based on double-layer 2D-Network (3-Mercaptopropyl) trimethoxysilane polymer and platinum-Prussian blue hybrid film. Bull. Chem. Soc. Jpn **91**(3), 368–374 (2018)
9. Kaya, M., Kawash, J., Khoury, S., et al.: Social network based big data analysis and applications. In: Extraction and Analysis of Dynamic Conversational Networks from TV Series. Lecture Notes in Social Networks, pp. 55–84 (2018). https://doi.org/10.1007/978-3-319-781 96-9. (Chapter 3)
10. Guo, C., Wang, J., Huo, Y., et al.: Sparse and dense mixed grid transit accessible network based on uneven distribution of travel demand. Discret. Dyn. Nat. Soc. **2021**(15), 1–12 (2021)

Design and Development of English Grammar Network Teaching System Based on Big Data

Yunbo Yuan[✉]

Changchun University of Chinese Medicine, Changchun, Jilin, China
evathesis@126.com

Abstract. As a result of the widespread adoption of big data technologies in the classroom, traditional pedagogical practices have seen profound shifts, and students are now able to take an active role in their own education rather than passively receiving information from their instructors. The proliferation of learning materials is another consequence of big data's meteoric rise to prominence. An online system for teaching English grammar is primarily researched and developed in this work, with a focus on big data. It begins with an examination of how big data has altered the landscape of English grammar instruction, moves on to specify the needs for online grammar instruction, develops research methodologies to meet those needs, plans the architecture and functionality of an online grammar instruction system that leverages big data, and concludes with a survey of current English teachers to gauge their level of comfort with online grammar instruction. The findings of the investigation reveal that the twenty English instructors surveyed are not very acquainted with or accepting of online grammar instruction.

Keywords: English Language Teaching,English Grammar,Network Teaching,System Design,System Development

1 Introduction

The rules of grammar are fundamental to the study of language and are present in every language. Words and phrases are connected via it. Consequently, studying English grammar is crucial, since it is a component of English instruction that is vital from the viewpoints of cognitive capacity, the nature of language itself, and the features of effective English instruction. There are a lot of issues that need fixing right now with teaching and understanding English grammar.Many researchers have looked into the topic of designing and developing big data-based English grammar network teaching systems, and they have all come up with successful solutions. Yao suggested a web-based teaching management system design approach to enhance the efficacy of English language instruction scheduling and resource sharing. It primarily consists of the following modules: MUC primary control, database, data management, human-computer interface, network management, online scheduling of English teaching materials based on C/S structure, and client-server data interchange. He utilized MBM29LV400BC Flash

B. Brik and S. Nazir (Eds.): BigIoT-EDU 2024, LNICST 659, pp. 113–119, 2026.
https://doi.org/10.1007/978-3-032-18631-7_13

memory to store the firmware for the logic decoding controller [1]. As big data continues to grow and evolve, Cai proposed for cutting-edge pedagogical concepts and practices. Using diagnostic mechanisms, computer-aided learning systems dynamically create individualized lesson plans and instructional materials, and they assess students' knowledge and progress toward learning goals, giving teachers solid data with which to fine-tune their lessons. The use of CAI has become the norm in modern English language education. Based on his research on CAI system needs, J. Wang develops a C++ and Windows-based educational system [2]. Many collegiate writing textbooks continue to promote the use of prescriptive grammar, despite many composition and rhetorical specialists urging writing instructors to abandon this practice. If you want to know how to write properly, you should look at the grammar part of Hacker's Pocket Style Manual. Even while hackers don't always want for their lectures to be considered oral, they often spend a lot of time in many courses teaching students these grammar norms. Normative grammar instruction impedes the expansion and improvement of writing instruction, according to C. Park, e. Wright, D. Beard, and R. Regal, who use the contemporary American English Corpus (COCA) to bolster the case of writers and rhetoricians [3].

The majority of a teacher's lesson plans revolve on reviewing grammar principles via various activities and other instructional strategies. Nevertheless, students sometimes find textbooks to be too academic and unapproachable. There are a lot of lesson plans but not enough classroom time, according to the way the curriculum is structured. The course method is dull, and there's a lot of pressure on grammar teachers to raise test scores in order to satisfy students' demands for higher-level English grammar tests. One of the biggest problems with both instructors' and students' ability to learn English grammar is the prevalence of inefficient techniques that use too simplistic approaches, which causes students to lose interest over time and leads to conflicting feelings [4]. This study establishes a network teaching system for English grammar with the goal of addressing the aforementioned issues, and it goes on to outline the benefits of using network technology in this context. Realizing a network-based grammar teaching mode is the fundamental premise of this project. To maximize the benefits of network multimedia instruction, classroom instruction in English grammar is supplemented with network aided learning. Using a network to enhance classroom instruction is not the same as doing away with it altogether, but it will substantially raise the bar. That is why it is highly recommended to use a network teaching system for English grammar in order to boost the quality of English grammar instruction.

2   Related Works

2.1   *The Influence of Big Data on English Network Teaching*

The significance of big data technology has been increasingly recognized by the whole industry due to the fast expansion of the internet. According to Wikipedia, "big data" refers to massive amounts of complicated data that conventional data processing techniques are ill-equipped to handle. Effective analysis of consumer consumption behavior, foundation for decision-making, and execution of focused commercial actions are all possible with big data. Improving teaching linkages and, by extension, the quality of instruction, is possible via the integration of big data with the education and training sector, which may provide teachers with a better understanding of their own knowledge, abilities, learning patterns, and other relevant information [5, 6].

2.2 *Design Requirements of English Grammar Network Teaching System*

An auxiliary English grammar teaching system built on big data may improve the English grammar classroom experience, turning what might otherwise be a tedious subject into something more engaging for students. In order to make the online English language learning system more autonomous, this article presents a network interactive environment. While developing the vocational English teaching system, users can check the content to make sure it's accurate. They can also look around the system to see if it can meet the needs of users at different levels and make the most of its features [7]. By using big data, it guarantees that all teaching materials are well-organized, makes sure that every student has access to the Internet, and makes it possible for English grammar teaching resources to be shared in the LAN. This way, it can guarantee that the intended system of instruction satisfies the demands of its users.

2.3 *Design Method of English Grammar Network Teaching System*

In academic circles, the design technique of English grammar web-based teaching systems has been extensively studied, and the fuzzy KNN algorithm has emerged as the widely acknowledged way. The following is the exact application: To begin, the training-based clustering center's distance from sample A using the standard distance measure is verified. First, choose the G-th sample that is geographically closest to the target sample; second, assign significant weight to the pattern sample's nearest neighbor; and lastly, sort the samples by their membership functions to find that they all fall into class B. According to the membership function of pattern samples to determine the type of pattern. It concludes that the pattern sample belongs to the membership function of category b, and the detailed expression is shown in expression (1).

$$W_b(G_i) = \frac{\sum_{G-1}^{G} W_b(G_i)/\|G_i - I_G\|^2}{\sum_{G-1}^{G} P/\|G_i - I_G\|^2} \tag{1}$$

In this formula, the value of membership function of cluster center is the radius of the cluster center, and the category label of cluster center is the category label b of all samples in cluster. The membership function of cluster center is shown in expression (2).

$$W_b(I_G) = \begin{cases} P_G \\ 3 \end{cases} \tag{2}$$

The fuzzy KNN method enhances the accuracy and efficiency of classification by reducing the influence of uneven sample distribution and by extracting the clustering center of training data, which in turn improves the efficiency of fuzzy KNN classification.

3 Design and Development of English Grammar Network Teaching System Based on Big Data

3.1 *System Structure Design*

The system's development mode for data analysis structures is B/S. In this mode, servers act as platform services for the cloud, and the traditional idea of the Internet has evolved from storing data to providing services. With Hadoop as the foundation of the distributed system, the file system of the distributed system is realized, allowing application programs to access data with high throughput. Databases are used to store and manage large amounts of data, which supports the system. Data is stored in a database by the server; later on, it can be used and analyzed with the help of data analysis and statistical analysis methods. The data is then processed, summarized, understood, and analyzed to get the most out of the data function [8].

3.2 *System Function Design*

Each layer's primary responsibilities are defined and needs are articulated in the system's hierarchical architecture. Assuring that the system administrator can silently handle all forms of English grammar network teaching information resources is the primary goal of designing a system for teaching the language over a network. Students may make use of the online teaching platform offered by the English grammar system, and teachers and users can also provide courses connected to the subject. The English grammar network teaching system can provide courses that are relevant to students' needs in terms of grammar [9, 10]. Thus, the system's functionality is enhanced by English grammar network teaching materials, with a focus on the needs of both students and teachers.

3.2.1 *Management Layer*

From the perspective of the system administrator, the system's primary role is to restrict access to the system's administration platform to the administrator alone, using the password associated with his account. Simultaneously, the resource-based method for managing the English grammar network teaching system allows only the administrator to post announcements.

3.2.2 *Teaching Level*

As far as the instructors are concerned, the system's purpose is to facilitate their use of the platform, which allows them to post English teaching difficulties, modify lesson plans, and accomplish their goals. The English grammar teaching system allows users and instructors to post course materials, administer quizzes, provide students with access to video resources, and interact with students via online question and answer sessions.

3.2.3 *Learning Layer*

From the student's point of view, the system's purpose is to optimize the design of the English grammar teaching system using big data as a foundation. It also makes sure that students can access the learning interface with their own login credentials, edit their personal information, and communicate with teachers through the system chat page about the important and challenging parts of learning English grammar. A better approach for teaching English grammar may be created and put into practice as a result of this [11, 12].

4 Results and Discussion

This research uses a questionnaire survey to examine the state of online grammar instruction in English against the backdrop of big data, and it draws the following conclusions.

4.1 A Survey of English Grammar Online Teaching System Between Teachers and Students

To learn more about people's emotions, views, attitudes, needs, motivations, and actions, a questionnaire is a great tool to use. The use of questionnaire surveys allows for the quick collection of substantial real-world data for the purpose of investigating the application of English teaching techniques. Questionnaires were sent to both students and teachers in order to gather data. Personal information, language usage, English teaching techniques, and English teaching status are the three aspects from which these questions are constructed, in accordance with the key features of English grammar teaching methods. Table 1 displays the obtained data.

Table 1. Structure of Questionnaires

Factors of the Investigation	Items in Teacher-questionnaire	Items in Student-questionnaire
The Status Quo of the Usage of English Teaching Methods	6	3,5,7,8,9,10
Personal Information	1,2,3,4,5	1,2
The Status Quo of English Teaching and Learning	7,8,9,10,11,12,13,14	11,12,14

Furthermore, this study's questionnaire analyzes the reliability of the questionnaire and primarily targets at the research status. What follows is a detailed breakdown of the procedure: Twenty teachers were re-surveyed 30 days after the survey ended using the same questionnaire, and 360 students were chosen from nine courses, with 40 students in each. Using SPSS 20.0, a statistical program, we summed up the two groups' scores and determined the correlation coefficient. Reliability of measurement is enhanced when the correlation coefficient approaches 1, as shown in Fig. 1:

Figure 1 shows the retest reliability correlation coefficients (r) for every item. All of the measurement items have an effective correlation higher than 0.9, and this value is statistically significant at $p < 0.02$. The findings demonstrate a strong correlation and excellent reliability of the questionnaire.

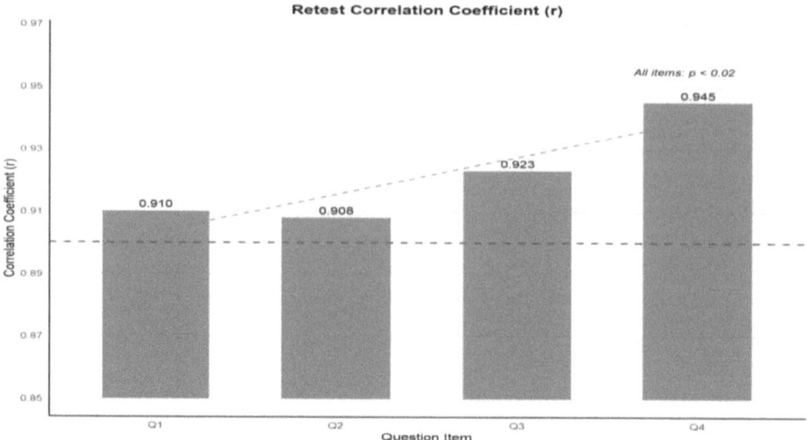

Fig. 1. Retest Correlation Efficient R

4.2 *Survey Data Analysis*

This study obtained ethical approval from relevant teachers and students, and administered questionnaires to 20 teachers and 360 students to investigate their awareness of online English grammar teaching. As shown in Fig. 2, only 10% of teachers (n=2) are familiar with the system, while 90% (n=18) are unfamiliar. Among students, 11.1% (n=40) are aware, and 88.9% (n=320) are unaware, revealing very low awareness in both groups.

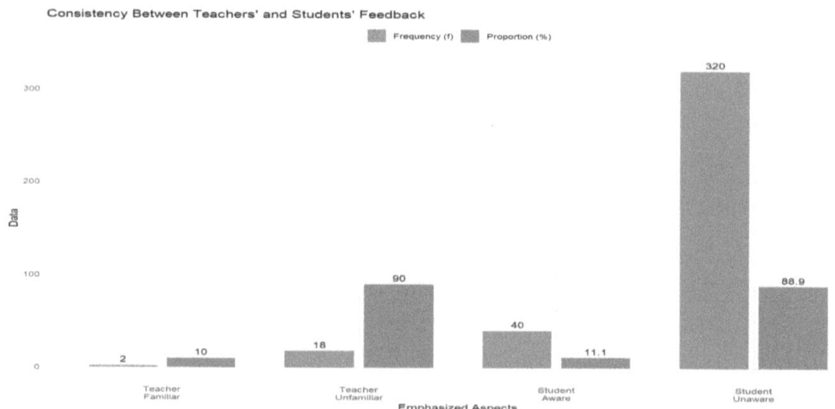

Fig. 2. Ts' and Ss' Awareness of Online English Grammar Teaching

Despite the prevalence of big data in the field of online grammar instruction, the majority of teachers still lack a solid grasp of effective online grammar teaching practices.

Few students have heard of English grammar network instruction, and even fewer teachers are familiar with the idea. The underdeveloped professional conscience of teachers is fundamentally tied to this as well.

5   Conclusions

At the moment, online English grammar instruction is not up to speed with the tactics and methods used in big data education. A method for teaching English grammar online is the primary focus of this article. This study recognizes the inconsistencies in English grammar instruction by conducting in-depth interviews with both students and instructors. It then uses this information to analyze and create the system's functional needs. The system's modules are created with their functions in mind.

References

1. Yao, N.: Design and Implementation of English Teaching Management System Based on Web. In: Proc. ICITBS 2018, pp. 58–60 (2018)
2. Wang, J.: Research on college English teaching system based on computer big data. J. Phys. Conf. Ser. **1865**(4), 042141 (2021)
3. Park, C., Wright, E., Beard, D., et al.: Rethinking the teaching of grammar from the perspective of corpus linguistics. Linguistic Res. **36**(1), 35–65 (2019)
4. Amin, M.: English language teaching methods and reforms in English curriculum in Iraq; an overview. J. Univ. Hum. Dev. **3**(3), 578–583 (2017)
5. Goh, R., Fang, Y.: Improving English language teaching through lesson study: case study of teacher learning in a Singapore primary school grade level team. Int. J. Lesson Learn. Stud. **6**(2), 135–150 (2017)
6. Polat, M.: Teachers' attitudes towards teaching English grammar: a scale development study. Int. J. Instr. **10**(4), 379–398 (2017)
7. Uskov, V.L., Howlett, R.J., Jain, L.C., et al.: Learning English grammar in the smart learning environment. In: Smart Education and e-Learning 2018. Smart Innovation, Systems and Technologies, vol. 144, pp. 142–150. Springer, Cham (2019).
8. Wang, N., Zhang, Y.: Application status and promotion strategy of integrated network teaching platform: taking northwest A&F university as an example. Agric. Res. Asia. **11**(14), 90–92 (2019)
9. Laurent, B., et al.: A prototype approach to information system design and development. Inf. Manag. **1**(1), 21–26 (1977)
10. Peterson, J.L., Bohrer, P.J., Chen, L., et al.: Application of full-system simulation in exploratory system design and development. IBM J. Res. Dev. **50**(2/3), 321–332 (2006)
11. Nyce, J.M., White III, W.G.: Normative models and situated practice in medicine: towards more adequate system design and development. Inf. Decis. Technol. **18**(2), 143–149 (1992)
12. Phuong, V.Q.: Rethinking intercultural communication competence in English language teaching: a gap between lecturers' perspectives and practices in a southeast Asian tertiary context. I-Manager's J. Engl. Lang. Teach. **7**(1), 20–22 (2017)

Construction of Physical Education Evaluation System in Colleges and Universities Under the Background of Big Data

Yi Xiao[✉]

Loudi Xiaoxiang Vocational Collage, Loudi, Hunan, China
13647385997@163.com

Abstract. Now that people's material lives have been substantially advanced thanks to the development of different high and new technologies, the government is increasingly focusing on education. Thus, all forms of assessment and the original techniques of instruction are inadequate in comparison to the present. As a result, educational institutions must adapt their policies to the features of the modern period and the many new technologies that have emerged in order to address this. Consequently, this paper's goal is to develop a model for evaluating college and university teaching using big data technologies. This paper builds a new system for evaluating the quality of physical education instruction based on big data technology and various research theories. It does this by taking into account both the theoretical and practical aspects of the field, as well as the reform measures taken by colleges and universities both domestically and abroad, and by addressing the issues plaguing our country's distinct physical education curriculum. The findings of the experiments demonstrate that theoretical and practical research may work together to improve the framework for evaluating the quality of physical education programs at higher education institutions. This will help to address and ultimately resolve some of the issues plaguing these programs.

Keywords: Big Data · Ordinary Universities Evaluation of Physical Education · Reform of Physical Education

1 Introduction

The development of modern technology and big data technology bring better counter-measures to the current college sports evaluation system [1]. But because the main object of teaching evaluation in higher education is students, and students have a strong subjective initiative, so their evaluation mainly comes from their achievements and their satisfaction with teachers and courses. But this is the previous analysis mode, so there will be a lot of uncertainty and compromise [2]. So, the evaluation system is not reasonable, so we need to find a new evaluation system to improve and solve such problems [3]. Therefore, with the development of big data, we find that we can set an algorithm function for the teaching system to count various data indicators, and apply a pair of

B. Brik and S. Nazir (Eds.): BigIoT-EDU 2024, LNICST 659, pp. 120–127, 2026.
https://doi.org/10.1007/978-3-032-18631-7_14

corresponding calculation formulas to calculate the corresponding evaluation scores [4]. Only in this way can we help students and teachers guide and complete the same course more reasonably and better. Because our ultimate goal is to help students learn [5].

2 Related Works

2.1 Construction of Physical Education Evaluation System

This study uses a status quo questionnaire survey to examine the content of college physical education evaluation based on the current state of affairs in physical education evaluation at five ordinary universities in central China. The participants included physical education instructors and students. Each school chooses ten PE instructors for a total of fifty; each school also chooses one hundred and twenty pupils, with an equal number of boys and girls for each grade (60 each) due to the absence of junior and senior classes.

2.2 Colleges and Universities Under the Background of Big Data

And in the analysis of teaching evaluation, we need to get data from two different directions of teachers and students, and get the final evaluation attitude. For teaching, we need to encourage innovation, and teachers need to have a good teaching attitude and excellent moral quality in order to have a responsible attitude towards the curriculum and students [6, 7]. Only when the teacher's attitude is positive, the students will like this course and study it wholeheartedly [8].

Physical education is a practical and applied subject, and the physical education courses provided by universities are required courses for all students [9]. The ultimate goal of physical education courses is to apply them to daily sports and exercises, but the decline in the physical health of college students has not been curbed. Abnormal work and rest eating habits, Internet addiction, and reduced exercise consumption are important reasons for the decline in physical health of college students. Most importantly, nearly half of college students did not take the initiative to participate in fitness exercises. The situational design ability of network sports courses, the innovative ability of interactive sports teaching methods, and the management ability of sports elective clubs are new challenges faced by college physical education teachers in actual teaching activities [10].

3 Experiment

3.1 Establishment of Association Rule Algorithm

Commonly, when expressing association rules, people will use the implication formula $X \Rightarrow Y$. This means that itemset X and itemset Y are really part of itemset I of transaction database D, and that X and Y do not cross. The $X \Rightarrow Y$ rule support and rule credibility are two indicators used to quantify the strength of the relationship between X and Y in the $X \Rightarrow Y$ association rules:

$$\text{Confidence}(X \Rightarrow Y) = \frac{Support(X \cup Y)}{Support} = P(Y|X) \tag{1}$$

A strong association rule is X⇒Y that meets both the Support(X⇒Y) ≥ minsup and Confidence(X⇒Y) ≥ minconf criteria, where minconf is the user-given minimal credibility barrier. If not, the association rule is weak:

$$Support(X \Rightarrow Y) = Support(X \cup Y) = 0.5$$

$$Support(X \Rightarrow Y) = \frac{Support(X \Rightarrow Y)}{Support(X)} = 1 \tag{2}$$

The connection between association and rule X⇒Y is strong because its support and credibility are currently equal to or greater than minsup and minconf.

There are a lot of different algorithms in use now for online learning that are based on big data analysis. Nevertheless, when considering the breadth of their use, perceptrons have the most wide applicability. The next step is to apply the penalty cumulatively to all misclassified samples using an algorithmic method like the one below:

$$Jp(W) = \sum_{i\epsilon r}(-W^T X_i)$$

$$W(x, i) = (1 - \alpha) + \alpha \frac{D_{si}}{LX}$$

$$r(x, j) = \sum_{i\epsilon I_x} W(j, I)xsim(i, j) \tag{3}$$

Following the above formula, the recommended value for the provided resource is as follows:

$$r(x, j) = \sum_{i\epsilon I_x} Wsim(i, j) \tag{4}$$

3.2 Construction of Optimal Model Based on Grey Relational Theory

The core tenet of gray association theory is that the similarity of objective curve shapes may be used to judge the degree of connection between sequences. The gray correlation degree is bigger for more comparable graphs and lower for less similar graphs.

3.3 Original Data Transformation

Processing the original data without quantification is important to accomplish the goal of unifying dimensions and address the issue of multiple data units for measurement. There are primarily two approaches of bringing together data dimensions:

Initial value changes:

$$X_i^{(1)}(k) = \frac{X_i^{(0)}(k)}{X_i^{(0)}(1)} \tag{5}$$

Average transformation:

$$X_i^{(1)}(k) = \frac{X_i^{(0)}(k)}{\overline{X}_i^{(0)}} \tag{6}$$

3.4 The Index System of College Physical Education Teaching Evaluation Under the Background of Big Data

Preliminary designs for an evaluation index system for PE instructors and an evaluation index system for PE students were created based on expert interview proposals, evaluation system design principles, and the features of the big data era. Level and index description. In order to determine the importance of each indicator in the assessment system, the three experts' assigned duty involves using SPSS statistical software to conduct computer-based parameter analysis.

3.5 Experimental Research Survey Objects and Research Methods

Due to the fact that first-year students in public PE did not yet grasp the specifics of the problem, only second-year students were given surveys to fill out.

3.6 Establishment of Coefficient of Variation

How well specialists work together is shown by the coefficient of variation. Coefficients of variation higher than 0.25 indicate a lack of coordination. The formula for computation is:

$$V_j = \frac{S_j}{M_j}$$

$$M_j = \frac{1}{n}\sum_{i \to 1}^{n} X$$

$$S_j = \sqrt{\frac{1}{n-1}\sum_{i=1}^{n}(X_i - M_j)^2} \tag{7}$$

V_j represents the coefficient of variation, S_j represents the standard deviation, and M_j symbolises the geometric mean. Coefficients of variance are lower.

Balanced Kendall Coefficient.

To check whether the experts' evaluations are consistent, one might use the Kendall harmony coefficient W value. In a scale from 0 to 1, a greater W value indicates more consistency. In a significance test of Kendall's harmony coefficient, the p-value is represented as follows: $P > 0.05$, which indicates that the result is not consistent; nonetheless, it is consistent. Coefficients of variance are lower.

Balanced Kendall Coefficient.

To check whether the experts' evaluations are consistent, one might use the Kendall harmony coefficient W value. A greater W number indicates more consistency; it ranges from 0 to 1. A p-value indicates that Kendall's harmony coefficient passed its significance test: There is inconsistency in the outcome; nevertheless, there is consistency in the process $(P > 0.05)$. The formula for computation is:

$$W = \frac{S}{\frac{1}{12}[K^2(N^3 - N) - K\sum_{i=1}^{K} T_i]}$$

$$S = \sum_{i=1}^{n} (R_i - \overline{R_i})^2 = \sum_{i=1}^{n} R_i^2 - \frac{1}{n}(\sum_{i=1}^{n} R_i)^2$$

$$T_i = \sum_{i=1}^{M_i} (N_{ij}^3 - N_{ij})$$

$$X^2 = K(N-1)W \tag{8}$$

In this equation, N is the number of indicators that were reviewed, K is the number of experts that were involved in the assessment, S is the sum of squared variances of all the evaluated indicators and their averages, and r is the correction coefficient.

4 Results and Discussion

4.1 Survey Results and Analysis of Teaching Evaluation Indicators for College Physical Education Teachers

Table 1 shows that all three indications are generally recognized, with an average value over 4.05 and a coefficient of variation below 0.19. The recognition is greatest for the teaching process, which also happens to have the lowest coefficient of variance and highest mean.

Table 1. Analysis table of the first-round index parameter values (N = 15)

First level indicator	Standard deviation	Average	Coefficient of Variation
Teaching process	0.87	4.05	0.22
Teaching preparation	0.93	4.1	0.25
Teaching effect	0.86	4.3	0.23

The mean for teaching preparation is the lowest, while the coefficient of variance for teaching impact is the biggest. Experts in the field have proposed: Table 2 shows that the first round's Kendall harmony coefficient was 0.07 (P > 0.05), indicating that the outcomes of the expert index assessment are inconsistent and have a poor degree of coordination.

Table 2. The first round and the consistent test statistics of the index parameter values

Rounds	Chi-square value	Kendall harmony coefficient value	Test significance value
first round	0.07	2.53	0.82 > 0.05

Figure 1 shows that the first round's five secondary indicator averages are all more than 3.7, suggesting that experts have mostly acknowledged the originally designed secondary indicators; eight items have a coefficient of variation less than 0.25, with physical fitness and physical fitness being the only two exceptions. The coefficient of variation is still more than 0.25, suggesting that these two variables need adjustment. It has been noted that the index of physical fitness incorporates physical signs; nevertheless, these two variables should not coexist. Additionally, fundamental understanding of sports theory must be taken into account.

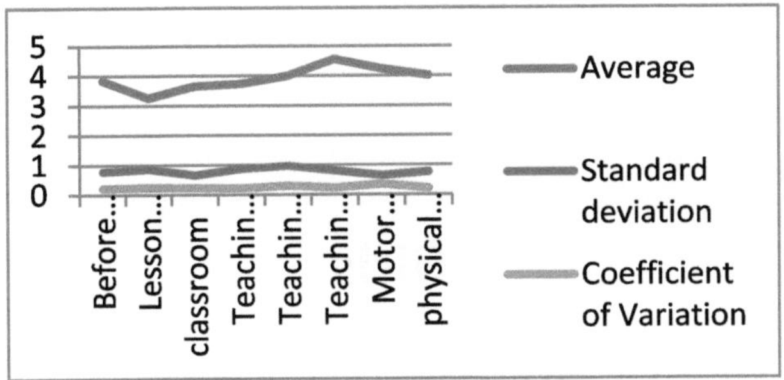

Fig. 1. The first round of secondary indicators reference map (N = 10)

The evaluation ratio of boys and girls in elective physical education
And.
Based on the data from the two polls mentioned earlier, it is clear that many college students like sports. This is further supported by a study that looked at which physical education classes were most popular. Nonetheless, as the aforementioned image makes clear, men and women choose PE courses in different ways.

4.2 Apply Big Data Technology to the Evaluation of Sports Education

Various schools and universities have various physical education needs, thus we need to establish multiple assessment standards for the same program. This is due to the fact that establishing standards for PE programs requires us to be more rational and compassionate. We should make every effort to incorporate this new technology into our teaching now that the age of big data has arrived. So, we need to step up our efforts to provide physical education courses and platforms that will assist children learn their favorite sports, as well as a variety of sports and more logical approaches to teaching them. Students will learn the most when they are enthusiastic about the material, as curiosity is the greatest teacher.

5 Conclusion

The widespread use of big data in higher education has brought about revolutionary shifts in the way sports are taught and studied. As a method of instructing pupils in the academic process at educational institutions. Combining the two approaches is not

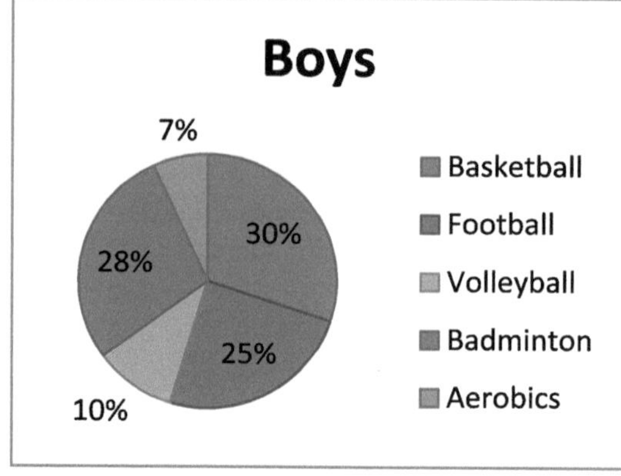

And

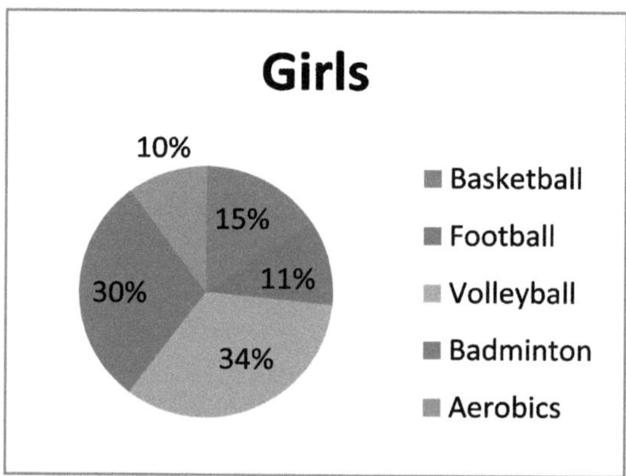

Fig. 2. Survey data show that boys and girls are evaluating the proportion of elective physical education teaching

enough; one must not mindlessly follow one. Only with complete immersion will the potential of PE be fully realized. While big data presents exciting new opportunities for PE reform, educators must not lose sight of the formidable obstacles standing in the way of its widespread adoption.

References

1. Xu, W., Zhou, H., Cheng, N., et al.: Internet of vehicles in big data era. IEEE/CAA J. Automatica Sinica **5**(1), 19–35 (2018)
2. Wang, Y., Kung, L.A., Byrd, T.A.: Big data analytics: understanding its capabilities and potential benefits for healthcare organizations. Technol. Forecast. Soc. Change **126**, 3–13 (2018)
3. Wang, X., Zhang, Y., Leung, V.C.M., et al.: D2D big data: content deliveries over wireless device-to-device sharing in large scale mobile networks. IEEE Wirel. Commun. **25**(1), 32–38 (2018)

4. Draxl, C., Scheffler, M.: NOMAD: the FAIR concept for big-data-driven materials science. MRS Bull. **43**(9), 676–682 (2018)
5. Egan, C.A., Webster, C.A., Stewart, G.L., et al.: Case study of a health optimizing physical education-based comprehensive school physical activity program. Eval. Program Plann. **72**, 106–117 (2019)
6. J, McConnell-Nzunga, P.J., et al.: Classification of obesity varies between body mass index and direct measures of body fat in boys and girls of Asian and European ancestry. Measure. Phys. Educ. Excercise Sci. Official J. Measur. Eval. Council AAPAR **22**(2), 154–166 (2018)
7. Huo, D.: Evaluation of the value of basketball players based on wireless network and improved Bayesian algorithm. EURASIP J. Wirel. Commun. Netw. **2020**(1), 1–11 (2020)
8. Ztrk, M.A., Alincak, F.: Evaluation of physical education teachers thoughts on in-service education. Online J. Recreation Sport **7**(3), 31–48 (2018)
9. Wang, Z., Lima, S., Rocha, Á.: Fuzzy comprehensive evaluation of physical education based on high dimensional data mining. J. Intell. Fuzzy Syst. **35**(3), 1–12 (2018)
10. Yusriadi, A.H., Ihsan, A.: Bureaucratic reform in public service: a case study on the one stop-integrated service. Mediterr. J. Soc. Sci. **8**(2), 253–258 (2018)

Digital Clothing Design System Style Generation Module Optimization Research

Fengyu Xue[✉]

Southwest University, College of Sericulture, Textile and Biomass Science, Chongqing 400715, China
fengyuxue@swu.edu.cn

Abstract. Since digitalization is a big deal in the world of social economics and development, it stands to reason that conventional clothing businesses' manufacturing methods would benefit greatly from applying digitalization to their design systems. In the digital production mode of clothing firms, traditional clothing design cannot address the issue of incorrect clothing design and manufacturing process, and the assessment is inappropriate. Hence, a genetic algorithm is suggested in this work as a means of analyzing digital clothing design systems in a novel and optimal way. To begin, the designer is assessed using the principles of fashion design. Then, the indicators are split according to the needs of the digital clothing design system in order to make them more concise. Challenges with digital clothing creation platforms. Afterwards, a thorough examination of the outcomes of the digital clothing design system is rectified by using the principles of fashion design theory to the digital clothing design system as it pertains to the method of production for clothing firms. The applicability of genetic algorithms to digital clothing design systems of clothing firms' production modes is superior to conventional clothing design, according to MATLAB simulations run under certain assessment criteria.

Keywords: fashion design theory · genetic algorithms · digitalization · Module

1 Introduction

Important to the growth of garment businesses, the style generating module is a foundational component of their production mode design [1]. On the other hand, the computerized clothing design system scheme has an issue with low precision, which affects the style design of garments [2]. In order to promote digital clothing design systems, several researchers have proposed using genetic algorithms to examine digital manufacturing modes of clothing businesses [3, 4]. To improve the scheme of the digital apparel design system and assess the efficacy of the model, this research presents a genetic algorithm [5].

B. Brik and S. Nazir (Eds.): BigIoT-EDU 2024, LNICST 659, pp. 128–135, 2026.
https://doi.org/10.1007/978-3-032-18631-7_15

2 Related Works

A. *Mathematical description of the genetic algorithm*

Based on the digital clothing design system's indicators, the genetic algorithm optimizes the scheme using practice test theory, and digital production mode of clothing firms' indicators point to the unqualified values is y_i, and analyzes the digital clothing design system is x_i. Finally, the plan is put into action, and the digital production mode of the garment business's viability is evaluated is $|D_i|p$, where Eq. (1) displays the result of the computation.

$$|D_i|p = \sum_{i=1}^{n} \tau F(y_i \cdot x_i) \tag{1}$$

Eq. (2) shows the evaluation of outliers among them.

$$\sum_{i=1}^{n} \tau F(y_i \cdot x_i) = \int |d + 2p|^a + pf \tag{2}$$

The genetic algorithm is able to optimize the digital clothing design system's style generation module by combining the benefits of practice test theory, using the digital production mode of clothing firms to quantify, and so on.

For the sake of argument, let's say I. the digital apparel design system's needs is a_i, the digital clothing design system scheme is z, the autonomy of the digital clothing design system scheme is p_i, the digital clothing design system is Xp_i, Here we can see the scheme judgment function in Eq. (3).

$$Xp_i = \sum_{\rightarrow}^{n} a_i \cdot (z + p_i) \tag{3}$$

B. *Selection of style generation module scheme*

Hypothesis 2: The role of digital manufacturing modes in apparel companies is d, and the weight coefficient is $D(x_i)$, the digital production method of unqualified clothing firms is required by the digital clothing design system, as illustrated in Eq. (4).

$$d + 2p = D(x_i) \cdot \prod -p_i \tag{4}$$

By using assumptions I and II, we may get the style's comprehensive function, as shown in Eq. (5).

$$Xp_i + d + 2p \leq \sum_{i=1}^{n} \tau F(y_i \cdot x_i) \tag{5}$$

Eq. (6) shows the outcome of standardizing all data, which is necessary to increase the efficacy of garment design.

$$Dp_i + \max|x_i - y_i| \leftrightarrow \sum_{i=1}^{n} \tau F(y_i \cdot x_i) \tag{6}$$

C. *Analysis of digital clothing design system scheme*

A multi-dimensional analysis of the digital clothing design system's scheme and a mapping of its requirements to the clothing enterprise's digital production mode data database are prerequisites to running the genetic algorithm and weeding out unqualified candidates. System strategy for digital garment design is FD_{ij}. Eq. (7) displays the outcomes, while Eq. (6) allows for the proposal of the anomaly assessment method.

$$FD_{ij} = \frac{Xp_i + d + 2p}{\int d\left[\left[|d + 2p|^a\right]\right] + pf}$$

(7)

Among them, it is $\frac{(Xp_i + d + 2p)}{\int d\left[\left[|d+2p|^a\right]\right]+pf} \leq 1$ stated that the scheme needs to be proposed, otherwise the scheme needs to be integrated into it is $tm(x_{ij})$, as shown by Eq. (8).

$$tm(x_{ij}) = Dp_i + \max|x_i - y_i|$$

(8)

To guarantee the genetic algorithm's correctness, we first conduct a thorough analysis of the digital production mode of clothing firms. Then, we determine the threshold and index weight of the digital clothing design system scheme. Businesses in the garment industry are shifting to digital manufacturing in order to more thoroughly evaluate the digital clothing design system solution. A clothing company's digital production method may not follow a conventional distribution is $X(p_i)$, its digital clothing design system solution will be affected, reducing the overall digital clothing design system The accuracy of the calculation is $p\tau\left(x_{ij}^n\right)$, as shown in Eq. (9).

$$p\tau\left(x_{ij}^n\right) = \frac{\min\left[\sum Xp_i + d + 2p\right]}{\sum Xp_i + d + 2p} \times 100\%$$

(9)

A multi-dimensional distribution is shown by the scheme of the style generating module in the digital clothing design system survey, which is consistent with the objective facts. Due to the high level of analysis and research involved, the digital manufacturing mode of clothing firms is considered directional, suggesting a style generating module scheme with considerable randomization. Assuming the fabric business's digital manufacturing mode is completely at random is $randon(h_i)$, then formula (10). This is the expression that represents the computation of formula (9).

$$p\tau\left(x_{ij}^n\right) = \frac{\min\left[\sum Xp_i + d + 2p\right]}{\sum Xp_i + d + 2p} \times 100\% + randon(h_i)$$

(10)

In particular, the practice test theory modifies the digital production mode of clothing enterprises, gets rid of unnecessary and duplicate schemes, and enhances the default scheme, ensuring a strong dynamic correlation throughout the digital clothing design system. This ensures that the mode of production meets the usual requirements.

3 Optimization Strategy of Digital Production Mode of Clothing Enterprises

In order to achieve the scheme optimization of the digital manufacturing mode of clothing firms, the genetic algorithm uses a random optimization strategy and modifies the designer's parameters. The genetic algorithm randomly chooses other schemes after dividing the digital production mode of clothing firms into several layers of the digital clothing design system. The iterative method included optimizing and analyzing solutions from various layers of the digital apparel design system. The optimization study is finished, and then the digital production mode of clothing firms is documented after comparing the level of digital clothing design systems of various schemes.

4 Results and Discussion

A. *Introduction to the digital clothing design system*

This article uses the digital production method of clothing firms in difficult conditions as its research target. It tests 12 pathways and takes 12 h. The goal is to make it easier to analyze digital clothing design systems. Tabulated in Table 1 is the digital garment design system's blueprint.

Table 1. Requirements for digital clothing design system for apparel enterprises

parts	grade	Innovative effect	Variant generation module
collar	Excellent product	85.17	84.87
	Good product	89.10	85.58
Coating tablets	Excellent product	81.61	84.78
	Good product	85.11	83.17
sleeve	Excellent product	86.38	86.37
	Good product	82.82	84.87

The digital clothing design system process in Table 1. is shown in Fig. 1.

The criteria of a computerized clothing design system are more closely met by a genetic algorithm scheme than by conventional methods of garment creation. When compared to conventional methods of garment design, genetic algorithms provide a more reasonable and fluctuation-free digital manufacturing mode for apparel businesses. Figure 1 shows the updated digital garment design system scheme, which demonstrates how the genetic algorithm has become more robust and innovative. Consequently, the genetic algorithm scheme for digital garment design is more practical, artistic, style-generating module-scheme, and summation-stabile than the alternatives.

B. *Digital production mode of clothing enterprises*

There is structural information, semi-structural information, and non-structural information in the digital clothing design system scheme of digital production mode of clothing firms. Once the genetic algorithm has been pre-selected, the digital production mode of clothing firms can be accessed, and afterwards, the digital clothing design system scheme may be evaluated for practicality. Choose the digital production mode of clothing enterprises with varying degrees of digital clothing design systems to more precisely

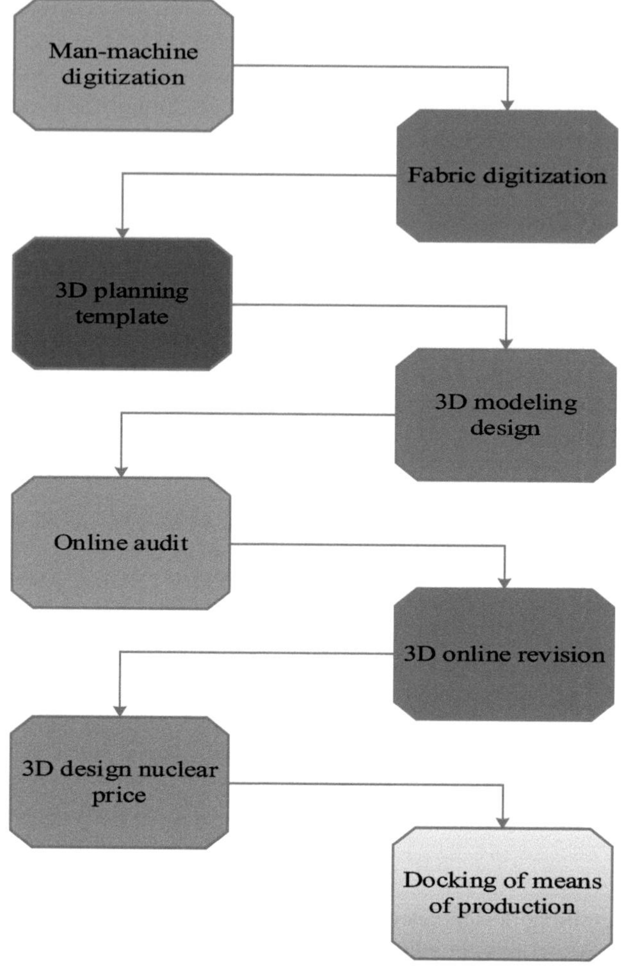

Fig. 1. Analysis process of digital production mode of garment enterprises

verify the innovative effect of digital clothing design systems; Table 2 shows the scheme of digital clothing design systems.

C. Style generation module and pioneering of digital clothing design system.

Figure 2 shows the digital clothing design system scheme, which is compared with conventional clothing design to ensure the genetic algorithm is accurate.

Figure 2 shows that conventional clothing design has a lower mistake rate and a lower style generation module compared to the evolutionary algorithm's digital clothing design system, suggesting that the latter is more stable. conventional apparel design's digital system isn't uniform. Table 3 displays the average digital garment design system layout for the two methodologies mentioned before.

Table 2. The overall picture of the variant generation module scheme

category	practicability	artistry
Design style	86.07	83.48
Fabric	85.23	85.05
Clothing color	83.77	84.74
mean	85.21	85.12
X^6	32.54	34.86
P = 3.50		

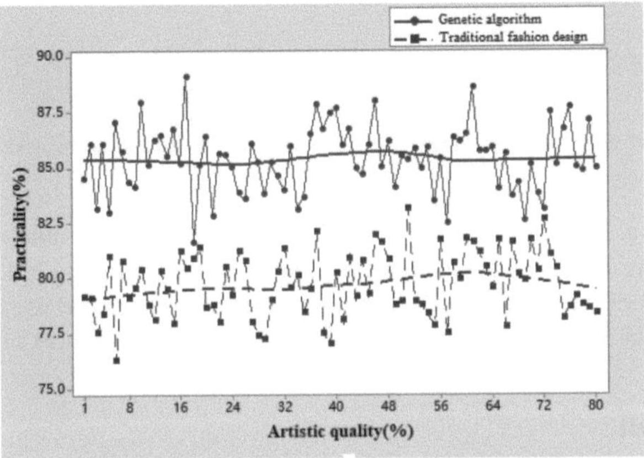

Fig. 2. Variant generation modules for different methods

Table 3. Comparison of the accuracy of digital clothing design systems with different methods

algorithm	Variant generation module	Magnitude of change	error
Genetic algorithm	83.08	83.75	0.67
Traditional clothing design	68.02	75.61	7.59
P	31.02	33.98	32.15

As seen in Table 3 Compared to the digital production mode of clothing companies, conventional clothing design suffers from style generation module flaws and unstable digital production. Additionally, the digital production mode of clothing enterprises has undergone substantial changes, leading to a high mistake rate. There is a considerable improvement over conventional garment design in the style generation module of the overall genetic algorithm output. Also, the genetic algorithm's style generation module is over 83% accurate, and it hasn't altered much over the years. Various approaches were used to assess the genetic algorithm in order to further prove its superiority and efficacy, as illustrated in Fig. 3.

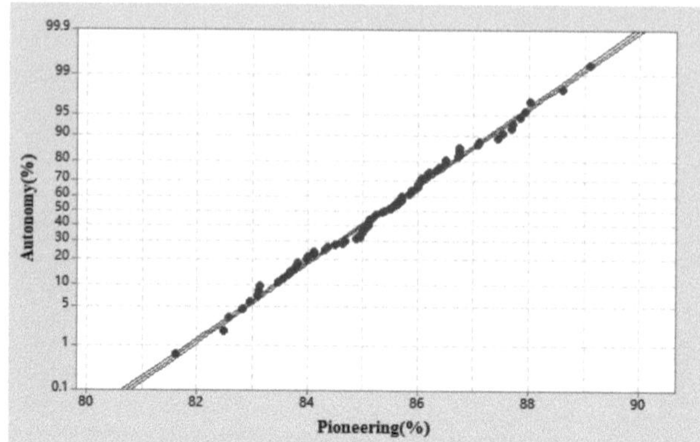

Fig. 3. Style generation module of genetic algorithm digital clothing design system

In light of Fig. 3 The genetic algorithm's style generation module outperforms conventional clothing design by a wide margin. This is because, among other things, it raises the adjustment coefficient of digital clothing production modes and uses it as a designer's threshold to weed out digital clothing design schemes that fall short of expectations.

5 Conclusion

Using the theory of practical testing as a foundation, this research suggests a genetic algorithm to improve the digital production mode of clothing firms, specifically targeting the issue of an imperfect style generating module. Simultaneously, a database of designers is established by conducting an in-depth analysis of digital garment design system innovations and threshold innovations. Scientific studies have shown that genetic algorithms may enhance the digital manufacturing method of apparel businesses' attention to detail, the overall functionality and aesthetics of garments, and bring them into harmony with the user's reasoning logic while also making them more compassionate. The system's style generating module is fine-tuned.

References

1. Harahap, S.H., Sunendar, D., Sumiyadi, & Vismaia S. Damayanti.: Requirements analysis: Drama education in high school. Educ. Adm. Theor. Pract. **28**(02), 66–73 (2022)
2. Rahmattullah, M.W., Suman, A., Witjaksono, M.: Economic learning educational practices for local values of " Baharit" culture based on the perspective of sustainable development. Educ. Adm. Theor. Pract. **27**(3), 1160–1167 (2021)
3. Sharma, A. S. ., & Hota, D. H. . (2022). ECG analysis-based cardiac disease prediction using signal feature selection with extraction based on AI techniques. Int. J. Commun. Netw. Inf. Security (IJCNIS), 14(3), 73–85.

4. Chandana, K.P., Samaniego, S.L., Chaudhary, S.S.C., Vekariya, D.M.G., Chaturvedi M. A., D.V.: Intelligent Mobile edge computing integrated with Blockchain security analysis for millimetre -wave communication. Int. J. Commun. Netw. Inf. Security (IJCNIS). **14**(3), 110–122 (2022)
5. Bernardo Tello, A. ., Xing, J. ., Lalitkumar Patil, D. A. ., Premchandra Patil, D. L. ., & Sayyad, D. S. . (2022). Blockchain Technologies in Healthcare System for real time applications using IoT and deep learning techniques. Int. J. Commun. Netw. Inf. Security (IJCNIS), 14(3), 257–268.

Research on Sculpture Art Creation Methods Combined with Digital Technology

Xue Fucheng[✉]

Shaanxi Institute of Fashion Engineering,
No. 1, Tongwen Road, Fengxi New Town, Xixian New District, Xi'an,
Shaanxi Province 712046, China
XFC1234562023@163.com

Abstract. Sculpture art creation, a form of artistic expression dating back to the dawn of human history, encompasses the process of designing, modeling, and fabricating three-dimensional forms using a wide range of materials, from stone and metal to clay and wood. It transcends functional purposes to communicate ideas, emotions, and cultural narratives. Sculptures not only serve as aesthetic objects but also function as symbols of identity, societal values, and spiritual beliefs. They enrich public spaces, museums, and private collections, inviting viewers to engage with their physical presence and interpret their meaning. MATLAB simulation shows that under the condition of certain evaluation criteria, innovative digital technology can achieve digital engraving accuracy for sculpture art creation The creation efficiency and cost are better than the traditional creation method.

Keywords: fine art engraving theory · innovative digital technologies · artistic creation · Art design

1 Introduction

Throughout history, sculpture techniques have evolved in tandem with available resources and technological advancements. From the ancient civilizations of Mesopotamia, Egypt, and Greece, where monumental works were chiseled from stone or cast in bronze, to the Renaissance period, where the likes of Michelangelo and Donatello mastered the art of marble carving, the evolution has been marked by innovation and refinement. The Baroque era introduced dynamic movement and emotional intensity, while the 20th century saw the rise of abstract and conceptual sculpture, embracing new materials like steel and concrete, as well as the use of found objects.

2 Related Works

A. *Mathematical description of innovative digital technologies*

B. Brik and S. Nazir (Eds.): BigIoT-EDU 2024, LNICST 659, pp. 136–143, 2026.
https://doi.org/10.1007/978-3-032-18631-7_16

The 21st century has witnessed a revolutionary shift in the world of sculpture, with the advent of digital technology. 3D modeling software, such as Blender, ZBrush, and Autodesk Maya, has empowered artists to create intricate forms and structures with unprecedented precision and efficiency. Rapid prototyping techniques like 3D printing have revolutionized the fabrication process, allowing artists to bring their digital designs to life in a matter of hours, bypassing traditional methods that could take weeks or even months. Additionally, virtual and augmented reality tools enable artists to visualize their works in immersive environments, fostering new possibilities for interactive and site-specific installations.

$$d\left(\vec{y} \cdot \vec{x}\right) = \sum_{i=1}^{p} \frac{(x_i - y_i)}{\sigma_i^2} \tag{1}$$

Among them, the judgment of outliers is shown in Eq. (2).

$$H(x - 1) = \sum_{x \in X} p(x, y) \log p(x_i) \tag{2}$$

Furthermore, digital technology has facilitated the documentation and preservation of sculptures. High-resolution scanning techniques allow for the creation of digital archives, ensuring that these cultural artifacts can be studied and appreciated for generations to come. The integration of digital tools has also democratized the art form, as more artists can access these resources and explore new avenues of expression.

$$\sum_{i=1}^{n} |D_i| = \sum_{i=1}^{n} \frac{|C_k|}{|D|} \log_2 \tag{3}$$

B. *Selection of work quality schemes*

This fusion of traditional craftsmanship with cutting-edge technology has opened up new dimensions in sculpture, challenging artists to explore the boundaries of form, space, and perception. The result is a dynamic, evolving landscape of contemporary sculpture that continues to redefine the very essence of this timeless art form.

$$P(|D, A|) = \frac{g(d, a)}{H(D)} \prod I + \sum_{i=1}^{n} \tag{4}$$

Digital technology has revolutionized the world of sculpture art, providing artists with a range of powerful tools and software to explore new creative possibilities. Some of the essential digital tools for sculpture include:

$$\sum_{i=1}^{n} |D_i| + P(|D, A|) \leq \sum_{i=1}^{p} \frac{(x_i - y_i)}{\sigma_i^2} \tag{5}$$

3D modeling software: Programs like Blender, ZBrush, and Maya allow artists to create intricate digital sculptures, offering features such as sculpting brushes, mesh manipulation, and advanced texturing capabilities.

$$\sum_{i=1}^{n} |D_i| + P(|D, A|) \leftrightarrow \sum_{x \in X} p(x, y) \log p(x_i) \tag{6}$$

C. *Analysis of digital engraving schemes*

CAD software: Computer-aided design (CAD) tools, like AutoCAD, are used for precise geometric modeling, often employed in conjunction with 3D printing.

Image manipulation software: Photoshop and GIMP can be used for 2D sketching, concept development, and editing of photographs or digital renderings.

$$\max_a \sum_{i=1}^{n} = \frac{\sum_{i=1}^{n} |D_i| + P(|D, A|)}{\sum_{x \in X} p(x, y) \log p(x_i)} \tag{7}$$

Digital modeling techniques in sculpture art encompass a variety of approaches, each with its unique strengths and applications:

$$\vec{w}^T \vec{x} + b = \sum_{i=1}^{n} |D_i| + P(|D, A|) \tag{8}$$

Free-form sculpting: Tools like ZBrush's DynaMesh and Sculptris' Pro Mode enable artists to shape virtual clay, adding and removing material in a manner similar to traditional sculpting.

Sculpting from reference: Using photographs or real-life objects as a basis, artists can create highly detailed digital replicas, adjusting proportions and refining details as needed.

$$p(c_i|w_i|) = \frac{\min\left[\sum \sum_{i=1}^{n} |D_i| + P(|D, A|)\right]}{\sum \sum_{i=1}^{n} |D_i| + P(|D, A|)} \times 100\% \tag{9}$$

Parametric modeling: Involves creating shapes using mathematical algorithms, allowing for precise control over forms and the ability to generate complex geometries.

Procedural modeling: This technique generates shapes automatically through a set of rules or algorithms, often useful for creating organic or abstract forms.

$$p(c_i|w_i|) = \frac{\min\left[\sum \sum_{i=1}^{n} |D_i| + P(|D, A|)\right]}{\sum \sum_{i=1}^{n} |D_i| + P(|D, A|)} \times 100\% + randon(k_i) \tag{10}$$

Among them, the sculpture art creation works meet the normal requirements, mainly because the art theory adjusts the sculpture art creation works, removes the repetitive and irrelevant schemes, and supplements the default scheme, so that the dynamic correlation of the entire digital sculpture scheme is strong.

2.1 Optimization Strategies for Sculptural Art Creation

Before a digital sculpture transitions into the physical realm, artists can simulate and test various materials and fabrication methods to ensure the desired outcome:

Material properties simulation: Software like Autodesk Maya's Arnold or Substance 3D Painter can simulate the look and feel of different materials, such as marble, bronze, or wood, allowing artists to preview the final aesthetic.

Print-ability analysis: 3D printing software like Cura and Simplify3D can analyze models for support structures, overhangs, and resolution, ensuring successful prints.

Strength and durability testing: Using finite element analysis (FEA) tools, artists can simulate the stress and strain on a sculpture under different conditions, crucial for large-scale or load-bearing works.

Color and texture mapping: Artists can apply color and texture maps to their digital models, predicting how pigments and finishes will interact with the material during casting or painting.

3 Practical Examples of Sculpture Art Creations

A. *Introduction to digital engraving*

In the digital age, sculpture artists use advanced computer-aided design (CAD) software, such as Autodesk 3ds Max, Blender, or ZBrush, for the preliminary design of the sculpture. These tools enable artists to quickly sketch, create 3D models, and even conduct dynamic simulations to explore different perspectives and light and shadow effects.

Table 1. Digital sculptural requirements for sculpture creation

Scope of application	Grade	Innovative effect	Quality of work
Material	I	92.72	95.27
	II	91.66	92.33
size	I	93.22	95.55
	II	94.64	92.54
sculpt	I	93.13	91.55
	II	94.23	93.97

The digital engraving process in Table 1. is shown in Fig. 1.

Artists can try a variety of design styles, from abstract to concrete, from surreal to futurism, not limited by traditional media. Digital design also offers endless possibilities for replication and modification, allowing the artist to iterate and optimize repeatedly throughout the creative process.

After the design phase, the artist can perform rapid typing using 3 D printing.3D printing technologies, such as Fused Deposition Modeling (FDM) or Selective Laser Sintering (SLS), can transform digital models into physical entities, providing tactile feedback to artists and further testing the feasibility of the design. By printing models of different proportions, the artist can examine the proportion and structure of the sculpture and even test its vision in different environments. In addition, the digital simulation can also be used to simulate the mechanical properties of the material, ensuring the structural stability of the sculpture.

B. *Sculpture art creation*

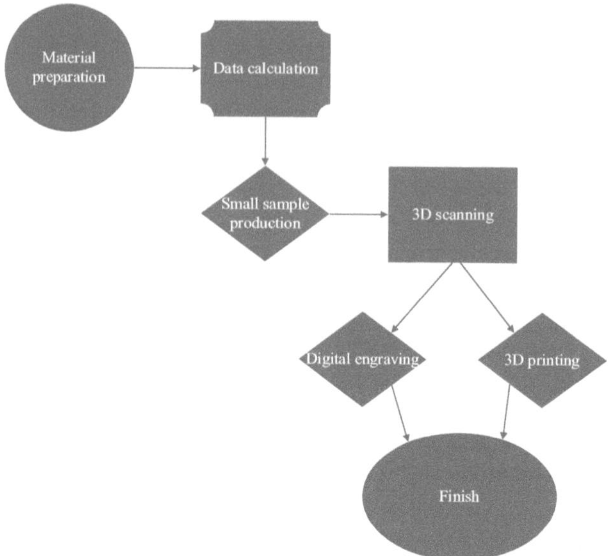

Fig. 1. The analysis process of sculpture art creation

After prototype verification, the artist enters the manufacturing and refining stage. This may include the use of CNC milling or laser cutting techniques to make sculptures on various materials such as metal, wood or stone. These techniques provide unprecedented precision, allowing complex geometries and fine details to be realized. For large sculptures, artists may use the BIM (Building Information Model) software for structural analysis and construction planning to ensure safety and efficiency. In the refining stage, artists may combine traditional handicraft techniques, such as polishing, polishing or coloring, to give digital sculpture a unique texture and personality. The combination of digital technology and traditional technology creates art works with both modern sense and humanistic temperature. At the same time, through digital recording and analysis, artists can track and copy these process steps to ensure the quality and consistency of the work (Table 2).

Table 2. The overall situation of the quality program of the work

Category	Completeness	Performance analysis
Material	96.71	96.38
size	95.93	96.11
structure	96.15	95.50
mean	96.72	95.77
X^6	44.37	45.61
P = 5.32		

C. *Quality integrity and stability of digitally engraved works*

In this process, the collaboration between artists and designers becomes crucial, and they jointly explore the intersection of digital technology and artistic creation, and constantly push the boundaries of sculpture art. Whether it is independent creation or team cooperation, the application of digital technology has greatly enriched the expression mode of sculpture art and injected new vitality into the traditional art form (Fig. 2).

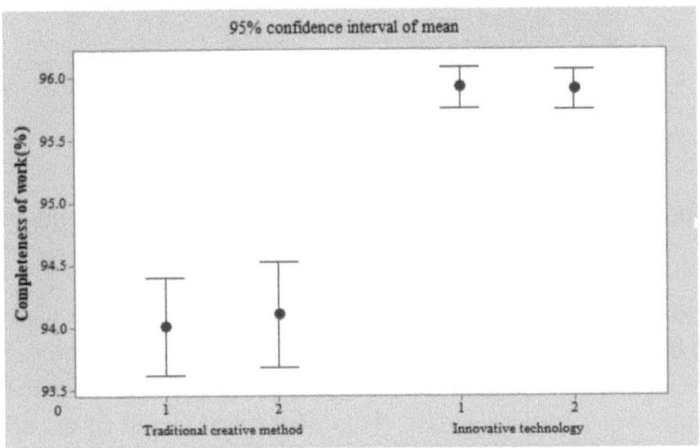

Fig. 2. Quality of works of different algorithms

Digital technology has revolutionized the way sculptors approach their craft, providing an unprecedented level of creative freedom. With 3D modeling software, artists can now explore forms and shapes that were once impossible to achieve with traditional sculpting tools. The ability to manipulate digital models in multiple dimensions allows for a level of precision and detail that surpasses the limitations of physical materials. Additionally, the ability to undo and redo actions eliminates the fear of error, fostering a more experimental and exploratory creative process (Table 3).

Table 3. Comparison of digital engraving accuracy of different methods

method	Quality of work	Magnitude of change	error
Innovative digital technologies	94.11	94.61	050
Traditional authoring methods	83.79	90.60	6.09
P	44.38	43.92	45.03

Furthermore, digital technology enables the combination of diverse materials and textures in a single work, breaking down the barriers between traditional media. Artists can virtually merge stone, metal, and organic materials, creating hybrid sculptures that challenge conventional aesthetics. This newfound freedom encourages artists to push the boundaries of their imagination and produce works that defy the conventions of the past (Fig. 3).

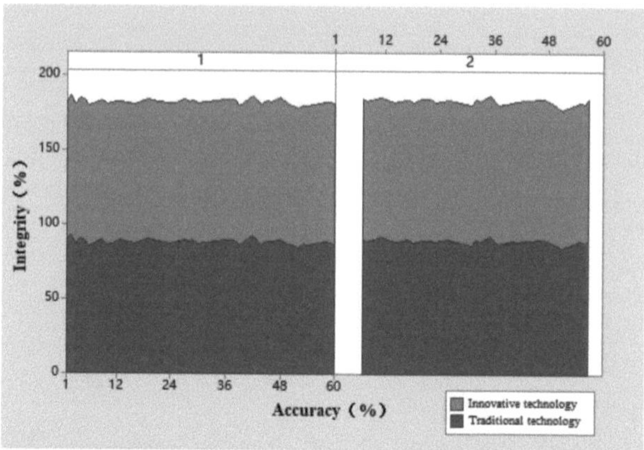

Fig. 3. Innovative digital technology digital engraving of the quality of the work

The integration of digital technology in sculpture has not only transformed the creative process but has also made art more accessible to a wider audience. Digital sculpting tools, many of which are now available for free or at affordable prices, have lowered the barriers to entry for aspiring artists. This democratization of art allows individuals with limited resources or physical disabilities to engage in sculpting, fostering a more inclusive artistic community.

Moreover, digital platforms have made it possible for artists to showcase their work to a global audience. Online galleries, social media, and digital marketplaces enable artists to share their sculptures with viewers around the world, bypassing the need for physical exhibitions. This increased visibility has led to new opportunities for collaboration, commissions, and sales, empowering artists to sustain their careers independently.

4   Conclusion

The integration of digital technology in sculpture has not only transformed the creative process but has also made art more accessible to a wider audience. Digital sculpting tools, many of which are now available for free or at affordable prices, have lowered the barriers to entry for aspiring artists. This democratization of art allows individuals with limited resources or physical disabilities to engage in sculpting, fostering a more inclusive artistic community.

Moreover, digital platforms have made it possible for artists to showcase their work to a global audience. Online galleries, social media, and digital marketplaces enable artists to share their sculptures with viewers around the world, bypassing the need for physical exhibitions. This increased visibility has led to new opportunities for collaboration, commissions, and sales, empowering artists to sustain their careers independently.

Aiming at the problem that the quality of sculpture art creation is not satisfactory, this paper proposes innovative digital technology and combines art theory to optimize sculpture art creation works. At the same time, the digital engraving innovation and threshold innovation are analyzed in depth to construct a designer collection. Research shows that innovative digital technology can improve the precision, stability and integrity of sculpture art creations, and can create works of sculpture art Do general digital engraving. However, in the process of innovative digital technology analysis, too much attention is paid to the analysis of digital engraving, resulting in unreasonable selection of digital engraving indicators.

References

1. Samala, A.D., Marta, R., Anori, S., Indarta, Y.: Online learning apps for students: opportunities and challenges. Educ. Adm. Theor. Pract. **28**(03), 1–12 (2022)
2. Al Nadi, A., M.: The effect of a critical thinking course on students at the University of Petra during the Covid-19 pandemic. Educ. Adm. Theor. Pract. **28**(03), 29–41 (2022)
3. Siregar, E.S., D, H.S.S.: Predictor of multiple intelligence in educational practice. Educ. Adm. Theor. Pract. **28**(02), 49–56 (2022)
4. Harahap, S.H., Sunendar, D., Sumiyadi, & Vismaia S. Damayanti.: Requirements analysis: Drama education in high school. Educ. Adm. Theor. Pract. **28**(02), 66–73 (2022)
5. Supraja, D.P., Salameh, A.A., V., H.R.D., Anand, D.M., Priyadi, U.: An optimal routing protocol using a multiverse optimizer algorithm for wireless mesh network. Int. J. Commun. Netw. Inf. Sec. (IJCNIS). **14**(3), 36–46 (2022)

Research on the Reform of Professional Quality Training of Accounting Professionals Under the Background of Digital Intelligence

Li Wang[✉]

Hainan Technology and Business College, Haikou 570203, China
wangjie0711@sina.com

Abstract. With the rapid development of Internet technology, the current smart city and the connection of everything have begun to take shape, and people have entered the era of digital intelligence in an all-round way. Technology has brought many changes to our way of life and work. It also affects our education system, and our education system is also being changed by technology. In this era of digital transformation, accounting professionals are also affected by it. As an important position for talent training, higher vocational colleges should be able to effectively grasp the new needs of financial and accounting talent training in the era of logarithmic intelligence. The use of digital tools and technologies in the accounting field makes it easier and more efficient for them to complete their work. This article will discuss how to use technology to improve the quality training plan of accountants to meet the needs of the changing business environment. In combination with the professional needs of higher vocational accounting and some new challenges of talent training in the era of digital intelligence, optimize the training ideas of accounting talents. We should build a modern financial and accounting talent guarantee system from multiple perspectives, such as clarifying the training direction of financial and accounting talents in higher vocational colleges, building a diversified curriculum system, and improving the construction of teaching staff, and comprehensively develop complex financial and accounting professionals in digital and intelligent higher vocational colleges.

Keywords: Digital intelligence · Accounting major · Talent training · Professional quality

1 Introduction

With the continuous development of science and technology, the society has stepped into the digital and intelligent stage, and all walks of life have been affected to a certain extent, including the accounting profession. Under the background of traditional majors, accounting mainly focuses on accounting and accounting supervision. In the era of digital intelligence, the accounting profession has entered the full-chain digital intelligence transformation stage of "online business, data operation and intelligent decision-making", and the accounting profession has also been systematized. Informatization has replaced the traditional manual bookkeeping [1].

B. Brik and S. Nazir (Eds.): BigIoT-EDU 2024, LNICST 659, pp. 144–154, 2026.
https://doi.org/10.1007/978-3-032-18631-7_17

While the accounting profession is informationalized and intelligent, it also puts forward new requirements for the knowledge reserve and skills of industry personnel. In addition to basic accounting knowledge, financial personnel also need to master certain management skills and information technology means. However, colleges and universities still continue the traditional accounting talent training mode, which exposes the disadvantages of relatively outdated curriculum content, teachers' first-line practical experience lag, lack of education and industry docking, which causes the existing accounting college graduates to deviate from the industrial demand under the background of digital intelligence, the lack of students' new business practice ability, and the disconnection between the supply side and the demand side of talent training. With the development of artificial intelligence technology, a large number of repetitive financial work will be replaced by machines, which will bring great challenges to the training of financial and accounting professionals and the employment of students in colleges and universities. The mode of talent training in colleges and universities needs to be changed urgently.

The National Medium and Long-term Education Reform and Development Plan Outline (2010–2020) issued by the State Council in 2010 clearly pointed out that we should vigorously develop vocational education, focus on improving quality, take employment as the guidance, and promote vocational education and teaching reform. The government should earnestly fulfill the responsibility of developing vocational education, improve the vocational education support system, fully mobilize the enthusiasm of industry enterprises, and promote the institutionalization of school-enterprise cooperation [2]. In 2014, the Decision on Accelerating the Development of Modern Vocational Education issued by the State Council mentioned that: promote the close connection between secondary and higher vocational education, and play the fundamental role of secondary vocational education in the development of modern vocational education. We should focus on the construction of modern vocational education system and cultivate high-quality new industrial forces; Focus on the improvement of system standards and find the breakthrough of reform; Focus on the integration of industry and education, deepen the cooperation between schools and enterprises, and form a community of shared future for schools and enterprises; To improve the quality of talent training, we should focus on the improvement of the education mechanism of combining morality and technology, and combining work and learning; We also need to focus on the next big game to enhance the synergy of the multi-party collaborative work, and issue the Vocational Education Reform Service Plan as soon as possible. Vocational education has great potential, and the basic role of higher education cannot be ignored [3].

The 2020 government work report of the State Council clearly proposes to comprehensively promote "Internet +" and create new advantages in the digital economy. The development of emerging technologies has spawned new industries and new business models, but it has also led to structural contradictions between the supply and demand sides of accounting personnel, and thus has a stronger dependence on the professional ability of accounting personnel and the application ability of digital and intelligent technology. Although the training system of accounting talents in colleges and universities has been continuously improved, there is still a gap between accounting theory education and work practice. Tang Dapeng et al. pointed out that the contradiction between the talent demand of enterprises and institutions and the current higher education supply is more prominent under the upgrading of digital and intelligent technology elements. The accounting talents trained under the current accounting college education mode are obviously insufficient in the ability to apply digital and intelligent technology. Zhu Bo and others pointed out that in the era of digital intelligence, the highest proportion of all abilities required by recruitment units nationwide for accounting college graduates is information technology ability. Jin Qinglu and others stressed that the application of digital intelligence, represented by the Internet and artificial intelligence, has led to significant changes in the accounting environment [4]. Therefore, the goal of talent training must be readjusted, especially the irreplaceable ability of accounting professionals should be highlighted. At present, accounting colleges and universities still pay insufficient attention to the training aimed at the application of digital and intelligent technology. It is difficult to match the market demand for the training of exported accounting talents, and reform is imperative.

2 Related Work

2.1 Accounting Professionals

"Talent" refers to people with outstanding talents. In Cihai, talent is defined as people with intelligence or noble character. They tend to make great contributions to the society, have good moral character, and have both moral integrity and ability. Comrade Hu Jintao once pointed out that people who are useful for social development are talents. The 2003 National Talent Work Conference proposed that talents should have three conditions: first, knowledge and ability; The second is to be able to carry out creative work; Third, make contributions to the construction of material civilization, political civilization and spiritual civilization. Most scholars believe that talents should meet the following criteria (1) Have good character; (2) Having expertise in a certain field or some fields on the basis of extensive knowledge; (3) High efficiency, methodical, insightful, hardworking, creative thinking; 4. High EQ [5].

According to the standards of talents, financial and accounting talents should meet the following standards: (1) have good character; (2) On the basis of extensive knowledge, he has expertise in the field of finance and accounting; (3) High efficiency, methodical, insightful, hardworking, creative thinking; (4) High EQ. Financial talents should have the following three requirements: first, they should have financial knowledge and skills; The second is to have the ability to creatively apply accounting knowledge and skills; Third, we should be able to transform accounting knowledge and skills into productivity.

Therefore, the author believes that financial talents refer to those who have financial knowledge and skills, can creatively apply financial knowledge and skills, transform them into productive forces, and make contributions to social progress and development. According to the level requirements, it can be divided into low-level, intermediate and high-level accounting talents. This section focuses on the concept of senior accounting talents.

There are many versions of the definition of senior financial and accounting talents. The author believes that it can be summarized into the following three views: first, the hierarchy theory. It is believed that senior financial and accounting talents are different from general financial and accounting practitioners. They are senior financial and accounting affairs and management talents in enterprises. This view starts from the level of financial and accounting talents, and proposes that the definition of senior financial and accounting talents should pay attention to the distinction between "senior" and "ordinary", and points out that senior financial and accounting talents are senior financial and accounting affairs and management talents in enterprises. Second, the theory of quality requirements holds that senior financial and accounting talents should not only master the handling of financial and accounting business, but also master modern enterprise management knowledge and have strategic development thinking and organizational management ability [6]. This view defines senior financial and accounting talents from the perspective of the ability and quality requirements that senior financial and accounting talents should have, and lists financial and accounting professional knowledge and skills, management knowledge and skills, and strategic development thinking ability as the standard to measure senior financial and accounting talents. Third, value theory. Financial personnel with an annual salary of more than 200000 are considered as senior financial personnel. This view defines senior financial and accounting talents from the perspective of human capital, and believes that it is feasible to take the annual salary as the standard to measure senior financial and accounting talents under the conditions of market economy.

Wang Jiaotong, director of the China Institute of Personnel and Talents, believes that the definition of talent depends on its talent in essence, but talent is difficult to show easily. Therefore, it is reasonable to take academic qualifications and professional titles as the criteria for evaluating talent. He believes that senior financial talents refer to high-level financial personnel with certain academic qualifications and modern financial knowledge, certain professional and technical qualifications in finance and accounting, and practical work ability.

2.2 Research Status of Professional Quality Training of Accounting Professionals

Xing Yanhui (2012, It will meet the needs of employers for high-quality skilled talents. Liu Runzhong proposed that the teaching mode of accounting courses should be studied from the aspects of school curriculum design, practical training, etc.

Luo Ling (2017) believed that due to the deep-rooted traditional teaching concept, the needs of modern and contemporary students were ignored in the practical teaching of accounting major in colleges and universities, which was mainly reflected in the mismatch between the curriculum and the practical teaching objectives of accounting major, and the lack of simulation in the practical training materials of the practical training courses, leading to the incomplete curriculum system; According to the actual situation, a series of processes of practical teaching of accounting specialty in colleges and universities should face the actual work needs of social enterprise accounting posts, so as to provide targeted training for students and ensure that students can meet the actual work requirements, which is the goal of technical training for students; In order to achieve this goal, secondary vocational schools should take the simulation module involved in learning as an important part of students' learning in the process of learning students' accounting skills, so that students can combine theory and practice in simulation [7].

In the actual simulation training, students can not only verify the knowledge they have learned, but also improve their practical ability. Schools can also find problems in the training materials through actual teaching, so as to continuously improve the training materials and ensure that the content of the teaching materials can meet the actual needs of social enterprises.

Chen Guiju (2014) believed that secondary vocational schools must reflect the characteristics of accounting specialty in the practical teaching of students, pay attention to cultivating students' professional ability, and improve students' practical ability through practical teaching, which is also a point that social enterprises attach more importance to in actual work, so school practical activities should match the actual work needs of accounting posts, Only in this way can we meet the actual work needs of enterprises. Liu Hanmei believes that in order to fully develop students' theoretical knowledge and practical ability, theoretical teaching and practical teaching should be divided into two parts. The learning of accounting theoretical knowledge and professional skills should be arranged in the teaching hours, and the training of students' various accounting skills should be arranged in the specialized courses during the practical training hours, and the professional theoretical teaching and professional practical teaching should be carried out simultaneously, so that the arrangement is more systematic. In terms of class hours, this ensures that the theoretical knowledge teaching of the school accounting course can be carried out smoothly, and can also win sufficient time for the students' professional skills training of accounting, so that the students who are proficient in various professional skills of accounting have the guarantee of course duration.

In terms of training mode, Lai Huiming (2011) believed that secondary vocational schools should take the training of students' practical ability as the main foundation, so its practical teaching reform of accounting specialty should focus on the reform of curriculum arrangement and the establishment of corresponding training bases. Two scholars, Zhu Desheng and Zhao Daoming (2013), believe that the teaching mode of secondary vocational schools in China must be reformed. Teachers in schools must carry out practical work, improve their practical level, and obtain the latest practical experience in the accounting profession. At the same time, government accounting departments and accounting practice circles should also focus on supporting accounting teachers to go out of school to carry out practical work and obtain the latest practical experience. Tang Hong believes that teachers in secondary vocational schools should improve their theoretical knowledge and practical work, and be able to combine theoretical knowledge with practical work [8]. Therefore, the practical teaching of accounting specialty must follow the principle of "step by step". When colleges and universities carry out the content arrangement of each link and each stage of practical teaching of accounting specialty, they should reasonably adopt the single-skill single-cycle teaching, To ensure that students continuously improve their practical ability in practical training, and can improve their comprehensive ability in comprehensive practice outside the school.

In addition, in the teaching of colleges and universities in China, we have gradually attached importance to the reform of practical teaching in schools. In the actual teaching, the practical teaching part is relatively large, and various practical courses are offered according to the needs of social work. The reform methods of practical teaching in colleges and universities are worthy of learning from secondary vocational schools.

From the analysis of the above contents, China's colleges and universities are constantly improving the practical teaching of accounting specialty, and the research on practical teaching is also constantly strengthening, which can effectively improve students' practical ability in practical teaching. However, there is no unified reform plan for secondary vocational schools in this regard.

3 Professional Quality Training of Accounting Professionals Under the Background of Digital Intelligence

(1) The talent training objectives are closely combined with the market demand

The training objectives of accounting talents in colleges and universities should be closely combined with the actual needs of enterprises, and the ability framework that meets the professional needs of enterprises should be formulated. The National Standard for the Quality of Professional Teaching in Colleges and Universities issued in 2018 proposed that application-oriented talents should be the basic goal of accounting talent training. On the premise of cultivating students' practical abilities such as accounting professional ability and business processing, we should also cultivate compound talents with interdisciplinary knowledge, academic research ability and practical innovation consciousness. In 2020, the Ministry of Education, the National Development and Reform Commission and the Ministry of Finance formulated the Several Opinions on the "Double First-class" Construction of Colleges and Universities to Promote the Integration of Disciplines and Accelerate the Cultivation of Postgraduates in the Field of Artificial Intelligence, encouraging colleges and universities to focus on building a training system that pays equal attention to basic theoretical talents and "AI + X" compound talents, and constantly enrich and improve the interdisciplinary core knowledge system [9].

(2) Innovate college accounting teaching mode

Innovating the teaching mode of accounting in colleges and universities should not be done behind closed doors, but should be based on the demand side of accounting education. Teachers should actively use online teaching software facilities to increase students' opportunities to actively accept knowledge. In terms of student assessment, students should be systematically assessed by combining theory with practice. For unqualified students, establish a regular return mechanism. For teacher assessment, the paper should not be the only indicator to judge teachers, but should return the focus to the classroom and set up expert and student assessment mechanism. At the same time, teachers of the same curriculum should hold regular learning sharing meetings to evaluate the curriculum model in the way of criticism and self-criticism and summarize the innovation points in teaching. Accounting teaching innovation in the era of digital intelligence is mainly reflected in the deep integration of information technology and teaching, and the diversification of teaching models. In the era of digital intelligence, college students need more opportunities for teacher-student interaction, self-display and mutual exchange, as shown in Fig. 1. Therefore, colleges and universities should actively innovate teaching models, vigorously develop online and offline hybrid classes, and make full use of new media teaching and other technologies.

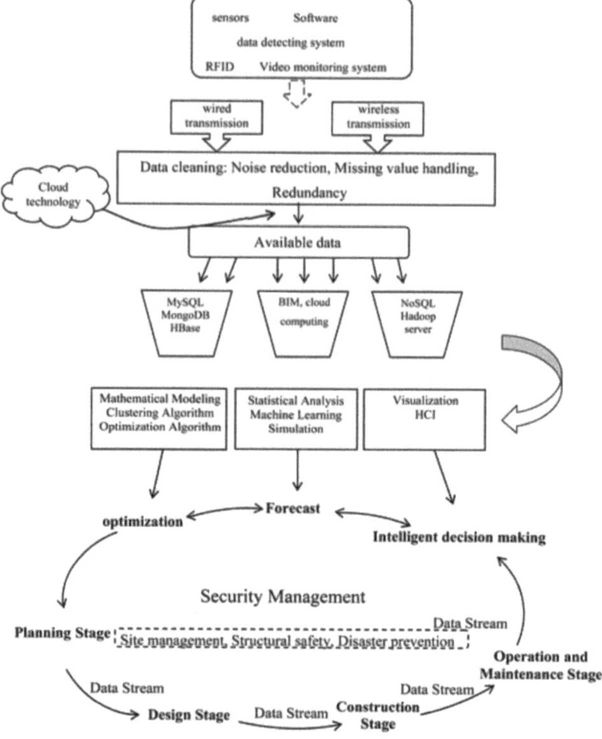

Fig. 1. College Accounting Teaching Model

(3) Optimizing the curriculum of accounting personnel training in colleges and universities

The goal of accounting education in colleges and universities in the era of digital intelligence is to cultivate comprehensive talents of "accounting + digital intelligence". At present, in addition to the general education course and the basic course of the discipline, the accounting courses set up in colleges and universities are mainly divided into two parts: professional theory course and professional practice course. On the one hand, as far as the theoretical curriculum is concerned, colleges and universities should adjust the proportion of class hours between professional compulsory courses and public compulsory courses according to their actual conditions, so as to further improve the freedom of students to choose courses. At the same time, ideological and political courses that keep pace with the times should be set up to improve students' political sensitivity [10]. On the other hand, in terms of the practice curriculum, colleges and universities should appropriately increase the proportion of practice course duration in all courses, strengthen the link between enterprise practice and college practice courses, so that accounting college talents can "recruit and use, use the best" after graduation. More importantly, colleges and universities should increase supportive courses, such as courses to cultivate students' ability of basic computer application, financial information system analysis and decision-making and comprehensive application of financial software, as shown in Fig. 2.

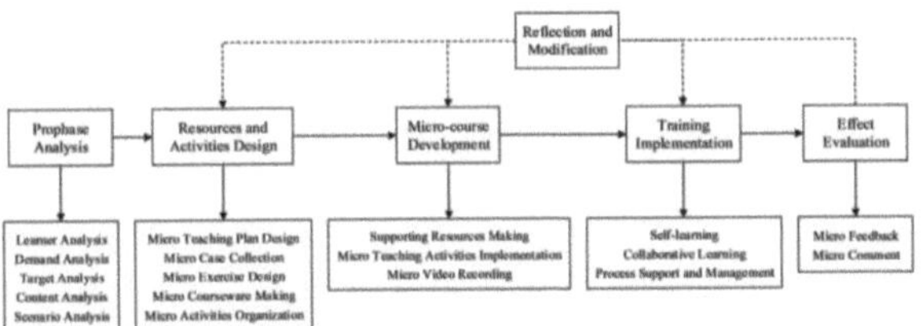

Fig. 2. Talent training mode

(4) Complement the weaknesses of accounting teachers in colleges and universities

Colleges and universities should set up a reasonable structure of teachers. For in-service teachers in colleges and universities, they should increase their opportunities for external exchange and temporary training, enrich their practical experience and enhance their ability to skillfully apply accounting software and hardware. At the same time, college teachers should be "decompressed" so that they have enough energy to devote to practical teaching. Colleges and universities should consider introducing accounting talents with multi-disciplinary backgrounds, especially engineering backgrounds, as well as talents with rich practical experience in enterprises. In addition, we should further strengthen the construction of college teachers' ethics and style of work, strictly eradicate plagiarism of papers, and oppose unhealthy lifestyles.

Although the teaching of digital and intelligent accounting specialty uses advanced digital and intelligent tools as the teaching platform, the core role of teachers is irreplaceable. In the era of digital intelligence, a number of digital intelligence teachers with a speculative thinking mode are needed.

(5) Improve teaching infrastructure

In the process of professional theory and practice teaching activities in accounting colleges and universities, the basic software and hardware facilities and the allocation of digital and intelligent accounting resources in colleges and universities have an important impact on the training quality of theoretical and practical ability of accounting talents in colleges and universities. The Outline of the Fourteenth Five-Year Plan for Accounting Reform and Development issued by the Ministry of Finance in 2021 proposed that the construction of accounting talent training base should be strengthened, and universities and enterprises should be encouraged to participate in accounting talent training. To this end, colleges and universities should enhance their support for the teaching facilities of accounting colleges and universities, update the software and hardware teaching facilities of accounting majors in time, introduce supporting resources such as the scenario-based accounting teaching platform based on virtual reality technology, and make the training of accounting talents in colleges and universities more connected with the practice of the era of digital intelligence.

Colleges and universities should improve the infrastructure conditions of colleges and universities around the goal of talent training in accounting colleges and universities. Actively reach strategic cooperation with enterprises and institutions, while creating value for enterprises, it also provides more practical opportunities for accounting college talents. In addition, colleges and universities should also build and improve the accounting education cloud platform to achieve teaching scoring and other functions. Based on the actual needs of colleges and universities, the ERP cloud accounting simulation system and other modules are introduced into it, and the accounting education cloud platform is applied to provide more reference indicators for accounting teaching, so that teachers can fully grasp the learning situation of each student, thus improving the learning efficiency and quality of students, and providing a strong guarantee for the training of accounting talents in colleges and universities.

4 Data Analysis of the Reform of Professional Quality Training for Financial and Accounting Professionals

In the context of digital intelligence, the training of financial and accounting talents in colleges and universities should not only enable students to learn and master professional knowledge, but also better broaden the training direction in combination with their future positions, so that students can grow into versatile talents, better adapt to some cross-border cooperation work, and better enable students to connect with industries in the future. In particular, some emerging positions, such as shared finance, intelligent accounting, characteristic project audit, investment analysis, tax planning, financial analysts, have put forward higher requirements for student management accounting, intelligent financial direction, big data audit ability, and strategic financial planning.

The respondents of this questionnaire are mainly secondary vocational school students. The questionnaires of students in school were distributed from December 15, 2018 to January 10, 2019. Students were studying in school. After obtaining the consent of the head teacher, the researcher himself distributed them to the respondents on the spot and asked the respondents to complete and submit them on the spot to ensure the recovery rate of the questionnaire. In combination with the class size arrangement, a total of 320 questionnaires were distributed and 296 were recovered. The questionnaire without signs of random filling and no contradictory answers was considered valid, There are 288 valid questionnaires, with the effective rate of 90%. Because grade students mainly practice in units and enterprises arranged by the school, mainly in the form of electronic questionnaires, distributed by the teachers or monitor contacted by the author, a total of 300 questionnaires were distributed, 281 of which were recovered, 258 of which were valid, with an effective rate of 86%.

According to the survey, secondary vocational students generally think that the school has more professional theory courses. According to the main teaching courses of the school accounting major and the curriculum of each grade, according to the "Teaching Standards for Accounting Major in Secondary Vocational Schools (Trial)" and "Teaching Standards for Accounting Computerization Major in Secondary Vocational Schools (Trial)" issued by the Ministry of Education in 2014, the school curriculum arrangement participating in the survey conforms to the class hour arrangement in the teaching standards. However, students are not satisfied with the length of practical courses. According to the interview with students, the main reason for the lack of time is that the content learned in the course is relatively simple and not enough to cope with the actual work. However, in terms of the length of practice, the proportion of "satisfaction" and above given by the students of the two grades is relatively consistent, as shown in Fig. 3.

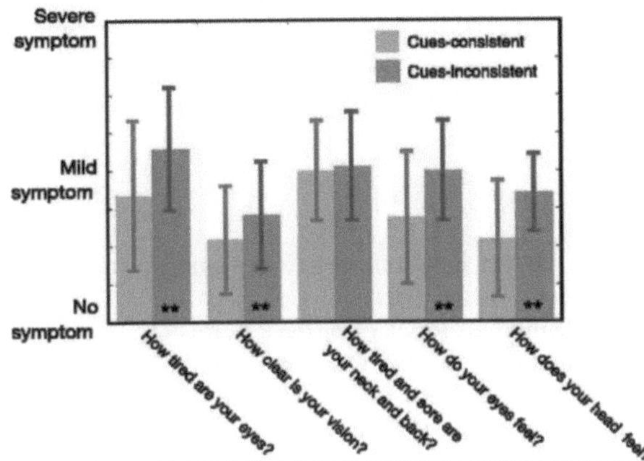

Fig. 3. Survey results

According to the survey, 62% of students said that the current teaching methods and methods of practical courses can attract their attention. The main reason is that practical courses are "more interesting" than theoretical courses. For the current secondary vocational students, there are some difficulties in understanding the theoretical courses studied in the classroom environment. Most of them are rote memorization. The students know it but do not know why. The practical course is no longer facing the textbook, but completed under the guidance of the classroom. Compared with the one-way absorption of teachers in the classroom, it is easier to arouse students' enthusiasm and initiative in learning. This reflects from another perspective that in the eyes of secondary vocational students, the theoretical teaching in the classroom is less attractive than the theoretical and practical teaching, mainly because the current classroom teaching methods are still inadequate. However, it is worth noting that the proportion of students who believe that the practical course can not arouse learning interest has also reached 37%. The main reason is that the practical teaching is a mere formality and the simulation level is not high.

5   Conclusion

The coming of the era of digital intelligence urgently needs the reform of college accounting education. Colleges and universities must actively comply with the development trend of the times, build a high-level accounting college education, form a high-level accounting talent training system, and strive to create a new situation of accounting college education. In view of the above objectives, the author puts forward corresponding countermeasures for the challenges faced by the talent training in accounting colleges and universities, hoping to play a role in the reform of talent training in accounting colleges and universities, and provide reference for the construction of high-level accounting education. At present, a large number of students' assessment methods are still based on examinations. Some information courses are still in the form of written examinations, which can not assess students' computer mastery and practical ability, and can not meet the teaching requirements. Therefore, colleges and universities need to change the way of student assessment when carrying out talent training reform, which can include computer operation, simulation practice and other methods, so that students can adapt to the requirements of the era of digital intelligence.

References

1. Wei, Q.: Research on the Teaching Reform of Accounting Course under the Background of Innovation and Entrepreneurship (2021)
2. Rui, X., Houjun, L., Jiaming, Z.: Research on the Reform of Cost-Accounting Teaching Mode under the Background of Internet-Plus. Clausius Scientific Press (2021)(4)
3. Lijunling, X.: Research on the reform of automobile testing curriculum under the background of intelligent. J. Phys.: Conf. Ser. **1939**(1), 012062 (2021)
4. Zhao, J., Ying, F.: Research on the teaching reform strategy of professional engineering survey course for architecture specialty based on the internet under the background of MOOC. J. Phys.: Conf. Ser. **1744**(3), 032114 (2021)
5. Xu, Y.: Research on the improvement of accounting work quality of new agricultural business entities under the background of big data. Acta Agric. Scandinavica Sect. B - Soil Plant Sci. **11**, 1–14 (2022)
6. Li, P.: Research on the reform of English Education based on the Internet Information Technology. J. Phys.: Conf. Ser. **1992**(2), 022097 (2021)
7. Lin, D., Xue, L.: Research on teaching reform of digital media technology under the background of new engineering course construction. In: International Conference on Web-Based Learning. Springer, Cham (2021)
8. Cheng, P., Yang, L., Niu, T., et al.: On the ideological and political education of material specialty courses under the background of the internet. J. High. Educ. Res. **3**(1), 79–82 (2022)
9. Stapleton, D., Liu, S.: Will Health Care Reform Increase the Employment of People with Disabilities?. Mathematica Policy Research, Washington, DC (2022)
10. Li, Z., Jiang, W.: Research on the teaching reform of inorganic chemistry based on SPOC and FCM during COVID-19. Sustainability **14** (2022)

Reform and Practice of Material Sorting Training Course Based on Digital Twin Technology

Zhiyuan Gao[✉] and Jiaxi Zhao

School of Intelligent Manufacturing, Guangdong Technology College, Gaoyao Campus, Zhaoqing 526100, Guangdong, China
15527315055@163.com

Abstract. Material sorting is a crucial step in the manufacturing process for businesses. There are two types of material sorting: mechanical and manual. The former involves hands-on experience, while the latter is more theoretical. Manual material sorting training has become an issue in corporate production, and standard practical training courses are unable to address it. So, to conduct a realistic examination of material sorting, this research suggests a digital twin technique. To begin, the material sorting training course is redesigned and optimized with the use of digital technology. In order to minimize interference factors, the indicators are segregated according to the needs of the training. The next step is for the digital technology to maximize the outcomes of the enterprise's material sorting training courses, create a program for material sorting training, and conduct a thorough analysis of the findings. Digital twin technology has a greater impact on the practical training of material sorting produced by enterprises and the feasibility of material sorting practical training than traditional practical training courses, according to MATLAB simulations conducted under specific evaluation criteria.

Keywords: digital technology · digital twin technology · Enterprise production · Material sorting

1 Introduction

There is a considerable deal of importance for material sorting in business production, which includes material sorting training [1]. Unfortunately, there is an issue with the material sorting training program's low feasibility [5], which impacts the material sorting training [6], while the process of material sorting training [4] is underway. According to some academics, the material sorting training program may be thoroughly examined and bolstered by using digital twin technologies into corporate production analysis [7]. Based on this, this research suggests using digital twin technology to improve the material sorting training scheme and check the model's efficacy [8].Recent years have seen the rise of digital twin technology, which bridges the gap between the digital and physical realms and offers fresh perspectives on intelligent material management and

B. Brik and S. Nazir (Eds.): BigIoT-EDU 2024, LNICST 659, pp. 155–163, 2026.
https://doi.org/10.1007/978-3-032-18631-7_18

automated sorting. There is a clear correlation between the effectiveness of logistics sorting and the timeliness and cost of logistics distribution; sorting is a key link in logistics storage. Manual sorting is the norm in traditional logistics, yet it's inefficient, wasteful of human resources, and inaccurate. With the use of digital twin technology, logistics sorting may be automated and intelligently managed, opening up new avenues for growth in the sector. This article addresses the teaching practice of material sorting practical training courses as a basis for discussing the application and reform of digital twin technology in practical training courses. The goal is to shed light on the teaching reform of logistics majors in colleges and universities in light of this trend. This paper presents a reform scheme for material sorting training courses based on digital twin technology. It applies this scheme to the teaching practice of logistics management in colleges and universities, starting from the design of practical training courses, adjusting teaching content, and optimizing practical training links. Given this background, it is critical that schools and universities update their logistics majors' curricula. Students must take a logistics management practical training course if they want to develop their practical abilities and talents. The conventional logistics sorting training course, on the other hand, relies on a single pedagogical approach and covers much too little ground to keep up with the rapidly evolving logistics sector. Thus, the purpose of this article is to investigate potential applications of digital twin technology in the material sorting training course with the goals of enhancing students' sorting skills and practical operation level, reshaping the course to align with the logistics industry's current trend of transformation and upgrading.Fig. 1 depicts the actual procedure for sorting materials as described in Table 1.

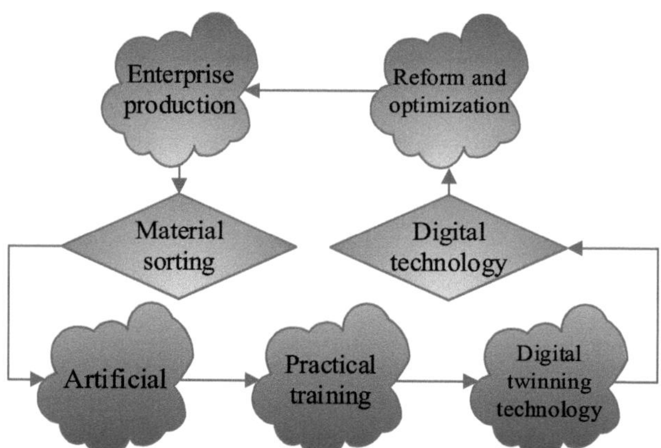

Fig. 1. Analysis process of enterprise production

2 Related Works

2.1 Digital Twin Technology

When compared to more conventional training methods, digital twin technology's material sorting training plan more closely matches the needs of the industry. A multiple dimensions distribution is shown by the material sorting training program, according to the survey, which is consistent with the objective facts. Digital twin technology outshines more conventional forms of hands-on education when comparing company production rationale and practicality. In comparison to more conventional forms of hands-on teaching, digital twin technology often yields superior material sorting instruction. This is because digital twin technology raises the enterprise's production adjustment coefficient and establishes a material sorting training course threshold that allows for the elimination of programs that fail to meet these standards.

2.2 Material Sorting Training Course Reform

In order to improve the solution for corporate production, digital twin technology uses a random optimization method and tweaks the parameters of material sorting training sessions. With the use of digital twin technology, businesses may split their production into several material processing training levels and randomly choose solutions. During the iterative process, several material sorting training levels' training schemes are optimized and evaluated. Once the optimization study is finished, you should record the best enterprise production by comparing the material sorting training levels of distinct schemes.To make material sorting training more feasible, digital twin technology combines the benefits of mirror models and quantifies via corporate production.In order to improve and assess the material sorting training program, enterprise production is going to rigorously test it. There is details about the structure, semi-structural knowledge, and non-structural information in the business's material sorting training program. Once the digital twin technology has been pre-selected, the firm may proceed to get its basic material sorting training plan and then examine its practicality.

3 Optimization Strategies for Enterprise Production

3.1 Mathematical Description of Digital Twin Technology

Utilizing the mirror model, digital twin technology optimizes the material sorting training program in accordance with the index parameters [10] is y_i, ascertain the enterprise's production's qualifying value requirements is z_i, while incorporating the material kind instruction program's capability to is, lastly, use the results from the calculation stated in formula (1) to determine the enterprise's production feasibility.

$$tol(y_i \cdot m_{ij}) = y_{ij} \geq max(m_{ij} \oplus \frac{\Delta y}{\Delta m} \cdot \frac{dy}{dm}) \tag{1}$$

Equation (2) shows the assessment of outliers among them.

$$max(m_{ij}) = (x_{ij}^2 \div 3) \succ mean(\sum m_{ij} \sum^{n}_{i=1} \sum m_i^2) \tag{2}$$

Assume I. The necessary training for material sorting is, the curriculum for training in material sorting is, said the training program for material sorting was satisfactory is, and the software's assessment feature for material sorting is, Eq. (3) demonstrates this.

$$N(p_i) = \sum m_i \cap \xi \rightarrow \left(\frac{\pi}{2} - \theta\right) \div \oint y_i \tag{3}$$

158   Z. Gao and J. Zhao

3.2 Selection of Material Sorting Training Program

The business's production function, supposing that is, and the weight coefficient is, Eq. (4) shows that in order to complete the material sorting training, unqualified firms must be produced.

$$q(m_i) = z_i \cdot \prod N(p_i) - w_i \searrow \sum \partial m \tag{4}$$

The outcome is shown in Eq. (5), which is in accordance with Hypotheses I and II, and it pertains to the complete function of material sorting training.

$$q(m_i) + N(p_i) \leq max(m_{ij}) \tag{5}$$

The outcomes of standardizing all the data are indicated in Eq. (6), which is essential for improving the efficacy of the practical training.

$$q(m_i) + N(p_i) \leftrightarrow mean(\sum m_{ij} \sum_{i=1}^{n} m_i^2) \tag{6}$$

3.3 Analysis of Material Sorting Training Program

A multi-faceted analysis of the material sorting training scheme, a mapping of the needs to the corporate production library, and the elimination of the unqualified program are all prerequisites to the use of digital twin technology is Eq. (6) allows for the proposal of the anomaly assessment system, and Eq. (7) displays the findings.

$$No(m_i) = \frac{q(m_i) + N(p_i)}{mean(\sum m_{ij} \sum_{i=1}^{n} m_i^2)} \tag{7}$$

Among them, If the scheme is not presented, then its integration will be necessary is, as shown by Eq. (8).

$$Zh(m_i) = min[\sum q(m_i) + N(p_i)] \tag{8}$$

The firm ensures the correctness of digital twin technology by conducting detailed production analyses and setting the threshold and index weight of the material sorting training program. When a non-normal distribution is seen in the enterprise's production is, This will have an impact on its material sorting training plan, which in turn will lower the overall accuracy of the training and the computation results is, shown in Eq. (9).

$$accur(m_i) = \frac{min[\sum q(m_i) + N(p_i)]}{\sum q(m_i) + N(p_i)} \times 100\% \tag{9}$$

The material sorting training program is considered to have significant levels of randomness due to the lack of directionality in business production; as a result, it undergoes extensive examination and research. In the event when the business's random function is, then Eq. (10). This allows us to state the computation of Eq. (9).

$$accur(m_i) = \frac{min[\sum q(m_i) + N(p_i)]}{\sum q(m_i) + N(p_i)} \times 100\% + randon(m_i) \tag{10}$$

Amongst them, and corporation production satisfies typical standards; the mirror model, in particular, modifies enterprise production, eliminates redundant and unnecessary schemes, and augments the default scheme, resulting in a robust dynamic correlation throughout the material sorting retraining scheme.

4   Results and Discussion

4.1   Introduction to Material Sorting Training

Companies' complicated case production is the focus of this study; the study's twelve pathways and twelve hours of testing time are detailed in Table 1, which also shows the material sorting training schemes developed by each companies.

Table 1. Requirements for Material Sorting Training in Colleges and Universities

Scope of application	grade	Reform results	Material sorting training
Enterprise One	I	84.01	83.22
	II	83.42	85.62
Enterprise two	I	83.01	83.86
	II	83.69	81.98
Enterprise three	I	85.13	85.19
	II	85.76	84.59

The improvements in the material sorting training scheme shown in Fig. 2 demonstrate that digital twin technology has a greater and more realistic level of practicality. That is why digital twin technology's material sorting training method is faster, more feasible, and more stable in terms of summation.

4.2   Production of Enterprises

Choose various degrees of material sorting training for your business's production and follow the material sorting training plan described in Table 2 to more precisely test the impact of material sorting training.

Table 2. The Overall Situation of the Material Sorting Training Program

category	Random data	Satisfaction	Analysis rate
Enterprise One	84.26	85.86	84.39
Enterprise two	86.56	84.48	89.41
Enterprise three	86.13	85.48	87.92
mean	87.35	84.02	85.55
$X6$	86.63	90.61	85.95
		$P = 1.577$	

4.3 Material Sorting Training and Stability of Material Sorting Training

Figure 2 shows the subject matter sorting training scheme, which may be used to compare the digital twin technology with the conventional training course for material sorting and ensure its correctness.

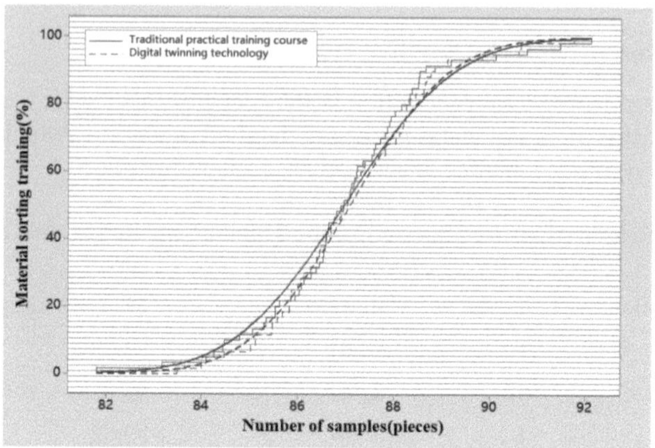

Fig. 2. Stability and Accuracy Comparison of Material Sorting Training with Different Algorithms

Figure 2 shows that compared to conventional instructional courses, digital twin technology training has a higher level of material sorting but a lower error rate, suggesting that the former is mostly stable and the latter is more prone to inconsistencies. You can see the three algorithms' average material sorting training schemes in Table 3.

Table 3. Comparison of the Accuracy of Material Sorting Training of Different Methods

algorithm	Survey data	Material sorting training	Magnitude of change	error
Digital twins	97.08	94.61	96.46	31.87
Traditional practical training courses	92.94	96.76	93.04	27.65
P	93.22	93.47	94.70	30.00

Table 3 shows that standard practical training courses fail to adequately address the impact of material sorting training on business output, which in turn leads to high mistake rates and significant changes in firm production. The precision has not altered much, and the material sorting training of digital twin technology is above 90%. In order to provide further proof that digital twin technology is better. The digital twin technology is often examined using several approaches to further confirm the efficacy of the suggested approach, as illustrated in Fig. 3.

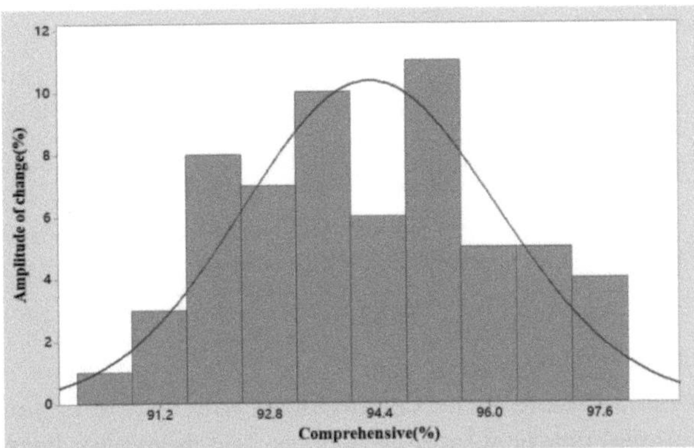

Fig. 3. Comprehensive Performance Comparison of Material Sorting Training Based on Digital Twin Technology

Figure 3 shows that digital twin technology's material sorting training is far superior to the conventional training method.

4.4 The Effectiveness of Material Sorting Training

Figure 4 shows the material sorting training scheme, which was used to evaluate the digital twin technology's efficacy with that of the standard training course.

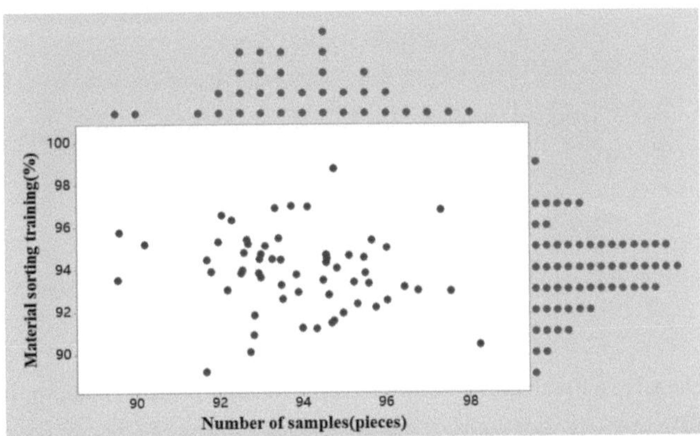

Fig. 4. Effectiveness Evaluation of Material Sorting Training with Different Algorithms

Figure 4 shows that traditional training courses have a lower error rate and lower material sorting training compared to digital twin technology, suggesting that the former is more stable. In contrast, the latter exhibits more uneven material sorting training. See Table 4 for an average of the three algorithms' resource sorting training schemes.

Table 4. Comparison of the Effectiveness of Material Sorting Training of Different Methods

algorithm	Survey data	Material sorting training	Magnitude of change	error
Digital twins	89.29	88.33	88.61	28.72
Traditional practical training courses	84.39	89.50	88.89	28.10
P	88.71	90.67	87.62	29.34

According to Table 4, there are certain problems with the stability of material sorting training in conventional practical training courses, and there have been a lot of changes in company production, leading to a high mistake rate. In comparison to more conventional forms of hands-on teaching, digital twin technology often yields superior material handling instruction. Also, there has been no discernible change in the accuracy of digital twin technology's material sorting training, which is above 92%. In order to provide further proof that digital twin technology is better. A comprehensive evaluation of digital twin technology is conducted using various ways to further confirm the efficacy of the suggested approach, as illustrated in Fig. 5.

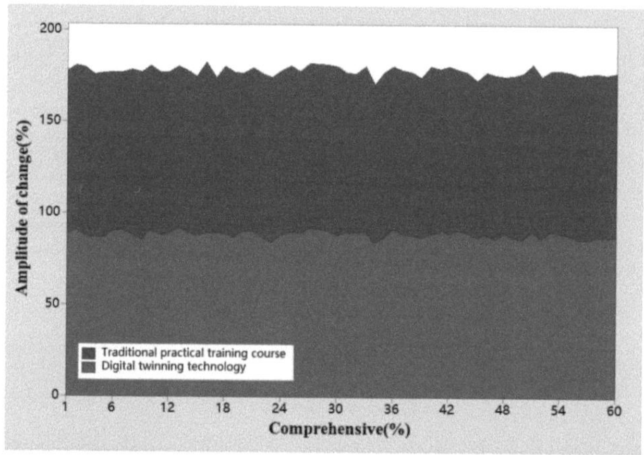

Fig. 5. Comprehensive Effectiveness Verification of Material Sorting Training Based on Digital Twin Technology

Figure 5 shows that digital twin technology's material sorting training is far superior to the conventional training method. This is because digital twin technology boosts the enterprise's production adjustment coefficient and establishes a material sorting training course threshold that allows for the elimination of programs that fail to meet these standards.

5   Conclusion

This article presents a solution to the issue of subpar material sorting training in business production via the use of the use of digital twins and a mirrored model. The goal is to optimize enterprise production. Concurrently, a set of material sorting training courses is built after an in-depth analysis of the reform of these courses. Digital twin technology may teach enterprise production staff in general material sorting and increase the stability and precision of company production, according to studies. The problem with digital twin technology is that indications for material separating training are often picked irrationally since too much emphasis is put on training assessment.

Acknowledgements. 1. The research was founded within the project No. 2022-1006 entitled Reform and Practice of Material Sorting Training Course Based on Digital Twin Technology, being a part of Higher Education Teaching Reform Project supported by Guangdong Provincial Department of Education (Guangdong, China).

2. The research was founded within the project No. S202213720011 entitled An Intelligent Control System for Active Manufacturing Workshop Manipulators Driven by Digital Twins, being a part of Innovation and Entrepreneurship Training Program for College Students supported by Guangdong Provincial Department of Education (Guangdong, China).

References

1. Cheng, Y.: Design of reconfigurable material sorting training platform. Southwest University of Science and Technology (2022)
2. Hao, M.: Application of color identification system in material sorting system. Mod. Agric. Mach. **05**, 64–65 (2021)
3. Wang, D.: Design of material sorting teaching and training platform based on industrial robot and PLC. Wirel. Internet Sci. Technol. **17**(11), 59–61 (2020)
4. Wang, L., Ge, S.: Design of control system of material sorting workbench for practical training and teaching. Precis. Manuf. Autom. **03**, 26–30 (2019)
5. Zhang, Y.: Application of annular conveyor material sorting system in express delivery industry training and teaching. Guangdong Vocat. Tech. Educ. Res. **03**, 147–151 (2019)
6. Zhong, J.: Design of material sorting teaching and training platform based on industrial robot and PLC. South China Agric. Mach. **50**(11), 171+178 (2019)
7. Zhao, X., Han, X.: Application of MPS modular production teaching and training system in practical training teaching. Equip. Maint. Technol. **02**, 54 (2019)
8. Yin, M., Xu, Y., Cui, Y., Gu, Y., Lu, H.: Design and implementation of PLC-based material sorting and conveying control system. Comput. Knowl. Technol. **15**(13), 276–277 (2019)
9. Xu, L., Liu, J.: Design of virtual simulation experimental system for material sorting. Exp. Technol. Manag. **34**(02), 105–109+115 (2017)
10. Xiong, J.: Development and research of curriculum resources of "mechanical and electrical equipment installation and adjustment technology" under the background of information teaching. New Curriculum Res. (Mid-J.) (01), 83–85 (2017)

College English Course Design and Teaching Design in a New Form of Knowledge Graph Led by Digital Technology

Cai Zheng[⊠]

Hubei Three Gorges Polytechnic, 443000 Yichang, China
13986800785@163.com

Abstract. In the new graph state, the logical relationship of English courses can be analyzed, but existing analysis methods have shortcomings. This article focuses on digital technology as the main approach to designing new export courses and studies their corresponding results. The results show that digital technology can provide the logical relationship of the new graph, playing an important role in optimizing the design of college English courses. The optimization rate is between 10% and 20%, meeting the actual graph and analysis needs of students. Therefore, digital technology can play an auxiliary role in the teaching of college English courses and promote the improvement of their teaching level.

Keywords: Big Data Theory · Digital technology · Knowledge Graph · New form · College English · Instructional Design

1 Introduction

The development of digital technology has brought unprecedented opportunities for the construction and application of knowledge graphs [1]. As a structured form of knowledge representation, knowledge graph organically organizes entities, attributes and relationships through graph structure, providing strong support for information retrieval, natural language processing, recommendation systems and other fields [2, 3]. With the continuous progress of big data, cloud computing, artificial intelligence and other technologies, the construction and application of knowledge graphs also show new characteristics and trends [4, 5]. Big data technology provides rich data sources for the construction of knowledge graphs [6, 7]. In the Internet age, various types of data are constantly generated, including multimedia data such as text, images and videos [8, 9]. These data can be effectively transformed into entities and relationships in the knowledge graph through data mining and natural language processing technology, enriching the content of the knowledge graph [10, 11]. For example, user-generated content on social media platforms, news reports on news websites, academic papers, etc. can all be used as input data for knowledge graphs to help build a more comprehensive and accurate knowledge graph [12, 13].

B. Brik and S. Nazir (Eds.): BigIoT-EDU 2024, LNICST 659, pp. 164–174, 2026.
https://doi.org/10.1007/978-3-032-18631-7_19

2 Related Concepts

2.1 The Digital Technology is Described Mathematically

Under the new form of knowledge map dominated by digital technology, the role of college English courses has been significantly expanded and improved. Knowledge graph is a graph-based data structure, which is mainly used to represent the relationships and attributes between entities. It presents a large amount of complex knowledge content in the form of logical framework is y_i found that the unqualified value parameters in the college English course design and instructional design is z_i, and the college English course design and instructional design scheme is $tol(y_i \cdot t_{ij})$ integrated with the function to finally judge the feasibility of the college English course design and instructional design, and the calculation is shown in Eq. (1).

$$\lim_{x \to \infty}\left(y_i \cdot t_{ij}\right) = \frac{n!}{r!(n-r)!}y_{ij} \geqslant \max(t_{ij} \div 2) \tag{1}$$

Equation illustrates the evaluation of outliers among them (2).

$$max(t_{ij}) = \partial(t_{ij}^2 + 2 \cdot t_{ij}) \succ \sqrt{2}(\sum t_{ij} + 4)\mathfrak{M} \tag{2}$$

Knowledge graphs can be combined with AI recommendation algorithms to provide personalized educational solutions and plan learning paths based on students' mastery of knowledge points, thereby meeting students' personalized and autonomous learning needs is t_i that the college English course design and instructional design scheme is set_i, the technique for satisfying the college English course design and instructional design is y_i, and the judgment function of the college English course design and instructional design the scheme is as shown by Eq. (3).

$$F(d_i) = \prod \sum t_i \bigcap \xi \cdot \sqrt{2} \to \oint y_i \cdot 7 \tag{3}$$

2.2 Selection of College English Course Design and Instructional Design Scheme

Teachers can use knowledge graph for instructional design, and help students form a systematic knowledge system by visually displaying the relationship between curriculum knowledge points is thus required by the college English course design and instructional design (4).

$$g(t_i) = \ddot{x} \cdot z_i \prod F(d_i)\frac{dy}{dx} - w_i\Phi \tag{4}$$

Knowledge map can also assist teachers in analyzing the learning situation and accurately grasp students' learning progress and problems, so as to provide targeted counseling is shown in Eq. (5).

$$\lim_{x \to \infty} g(t_i) + F(d_i) \leq \bigcap max(t_{ij}) \tag{5}$$

Through the knowledge map, students can interact with other students or teachers, discuss problems and share learning experiences together, and form an interactive learning atmosphere are presented in Eq. (6).

$$g(t_i) + F(d_i) \leftrightarrow \sqrt{b^2 - 4ac}\left(\sum t_{ij} + 4\right) \tag{6}$$

2.3 Analysis of College English Course Design and Instructional Design Scheme

Knowledge graph can help teachers integrate and optimize curriculum resources, associate and classify relevant knowledge points and resources, and form a structured curriculum resource library is shown in Eq. (7).

$$No(t_i) = \frac{g(t_i) + F(d_i)}{mean\left(\sum t_{ij} + 4\right)} \sqrt{b^2 - 4ac} \tag{7}$$

Among them, it is $\frac{g(t_i)+F(d_i)}{mean(\sum t_{ij}+4)} \leq 1$ specified that the scheme must be $Zh(t_i)$ suggested; Through the knowledge graph, students can self-assess their learning outcomes and receive immediate feedback and suggestions to adjust learning strategies and methods in Eq. (8).

$$Zh(t_i) = \lim_{x \to \infty} \left[\sum g(t_i) + F(d_i)\right] \lim_{x \to \infty} \tag{8}$$

Through the application of knowledge map, college English courses have realized the digitization and informatization of teaching contents, teaching methods and teaching resources, and improved the level of educational informatization. To sum up, under the new form of knowledge map dominated by digital technology $accur(t_i)$, college English courses have played an important role in teaching quality, teaching mode, resource allocation, students' autonomous learning ability and educational informatization process. These functions not only improve the teaching effect and learning experience of college English courses $unno(t_i)$, but also provide strong support for the digital transformation and innovative development of the education industry, as stated in Eq. (9).

$$accur(t_i) = \frac{min\left[\sum g(t_i) + F(d_i)\right]}{\underset{\sim}{\sum} g(t_i) + F(d_i)} \times 100\% \tag{9}$$

"Live broadcast + group task", "Live broadcast + nail group discussion", etc. These modes have changed the traditional way of teaching-oriented, completed the transformation from teaching-oriented to cooperation and discussion, and avoided the disadvantages of moving classroom teaching directly online., and hence it is $randon(t_i)$ considered as a high analytical research. If the college English course design and instructional design's stochastic function is, then the computation of Eq. (9) may be represented as Eq. (10).

$$accur(t_i) = \frac{min\left[\sum g(t_i) + F(d_i)\right]}{\frac{1}{2}\sum g(t_i) + F(d_i)} + randon(t_i) \tag{10}$$

The construction of DingTalk English communication circle broadens the scenarios for students to communicate in English, guides students to form an "online learning community", enables students to become information content providers and communicators, and improves the activity, frequency, content and depth of English communication.

3 College English Course Design and Instructional Design Optimization Approach

Innovative teaching mode: Knowledge graph can support the implementation of new teaching modes such as flipped classroom and bipartition classroom. Through the guidance of knowledge map, students can learn independently before class, and classroom time is more used for discussion and interaction, thus improving the teaching effect. Achieve accurate teaching: Teachers can understand students' mastery of knowledge points through knowledge graphs, so as to make accurate teaching design and adjustment. In view of students' weak links, teachers can design targeted exercises and explanations to help students better understand and master knowledge points. Promote teacher-student interaction: The knowledge graph can be used as an interactive platform to promote communication and interaction between teachers and students. Students can ask questions and share their learning experiences in the knowledge map, and teachers can respond and comment in a timely manner, creating a good learning atmosphere.

4 Practical Examples of College English Course Design and Instructional Design

4.1 Introduction to the College English Course Design and Instructional Design

Driven by digital technology, knowledge graphs have become an effective tool for organizing and presenting complex knowledge systems. College English curriculum design can make full use of the advantages of knowledge graph to realize the systematic and structured curriculum content is shown in Table 1.

Table 1. College English course design and instructional design college English course design and instructional design requirements

Scope of application	The level of English proficiency	The extent and effectiveness of English improvement	Your overall situation and optimization analysis content
Simulated communication	I	92.31	91.00
	II	91.37	93.98
Language skills training	I	89.71	92.41
	II	94.22	91.79
Personalized learning	I	93.27	92.28
	II	91.67	90.41

The college English course design and instructional design process in Table 1 is shown in Fig. 1.

Construct a systematic knowledge system: Using the knowledge map, we can systematically sort out the knowledge points such as words, grammar and sentence patterns

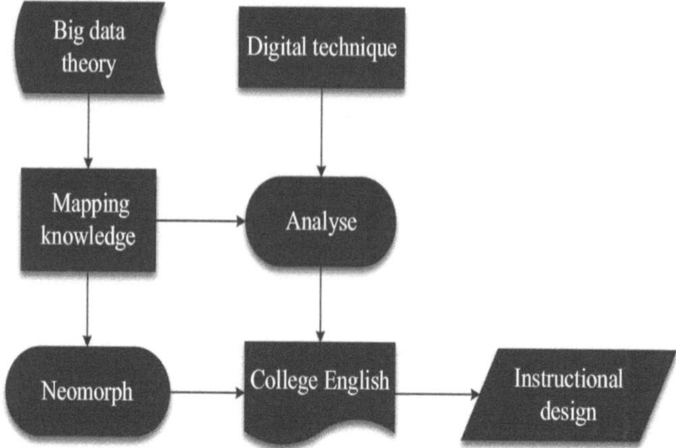

Fig. 1. Analysis process of college English course design and instructional design

in college English courses to form a clear knowledge structure. Through the presentation of knowledge map, students can intuitively see the connections and differences between knowledge points, which helps to form a complete knowledge system. Personalized learning path design: Based on the knowledge map, students' learning situation and learning needs can be analyzed to provide students with personalized learning paths. By analyzing students' learning progress and difficulties in the knowledge map, teachers can customize exclusive learning plans for each student to improve learning effects. Intelligent Recommended Learning Resources: Knowledge Graph can integrate various English learning resources, such as online courses, reading materials, listening exercises, etc. According to students' learning situation and interests, the knowledge map can intelligently recommend relevant learning resources to help students better consolidate and expand their knowledge.

4.2   College English Course Design and Instructional Design

Once applied, students can break through the limitation of time and space by scanning four-dimensional codes, and enter the simulation scenario to learn English, no longer bound by the traditional classroom time and place, as shown in Table 2.

Table 2.   The overall situation of the college English course design and instructional design scheme

Category	The logical relationship of English	The role of graph analysis in English	The contribution rate of digital technology
Simulated communication	92.19	91.16	90.34
Language skills training	97.55	91.42	87.03

(continued)

Table 2. (*continued*)

Category	The logical relationship of English	The role of graph analysis in English	The contribution rate of digital technology
Personalized learning	88.70	90.83	87.68
Mean	88.71	89.03	90.54
X6	91.66	94.41	93.33
	P =.128		

4.3   College English Course Design and Instructional Design and Stability

Digital technology supports the open sharing of educational and teaching resources. For example, high-quality English educational resources can be disseminated and taught through major short video platforms, providing new contents, models and resources, so that more college English learning resources can be widely disseminated and accessed is shown in Fig. 2.

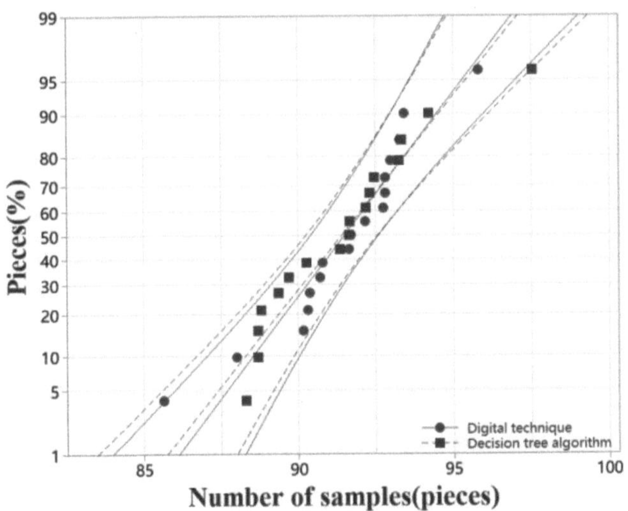

Fig. 2. Evaluation model of aging performance of different algorithms

Figure 2 shows that Digital technology supports the open sharing of educational and teaching resources. For example, high-quality English educational resources can be disseminated and taught through major short video platforms, providing new contents, models and resources, so that more college English learning resources can be widely disseminated and accessed, as shown in Table 3.

Table 3. Compares the accuracy of several college English course design and instructional design.

Algorithm	The optimization effect of course design	Course content and practical needs	Satisfaction rate	The overall improvement effect of technology
Digital technology	90.37	88.80	87.49	91.46
Decision tree algorithm	90.16	90.28	91.61	89.13
P	92.81	88.31	92.54	89.58

Table 3 shows that Advanced digital technologies such as big data can be used to screen high-quality English education resources, collect and integrate cutting-edge technologies at home and abroad, dynamic development of English knowledge and other contents, and implement optimal allocation, so as to realize higher-quality resource supply for college English courses in colleges and universities and improve the quality and pertinence of teaching resources, as shown in Fig. 3.

Fig. 3. College English course design and instructional design of Digital technology

Figure 3 shows that Advanced digital technologies such as big data can be used to screen high-quality English education resources, collect and integrate cutting-edge technologies at home and abroad, dynamic development of English knowledge and other contents, and implement optimal allocation, so as to realize higher-quality resource supply for college English courses in colleges and universities and improve the quality and pertinence of teaching resources.

4.4   Rationality of College English Course Design and Instructional Design

Under the impetus of digital technology, the professional ability training of college English is closely combined with the cultivation of digital literacy, such as building digital campus, digital library and digital resource library in Fig. 4.

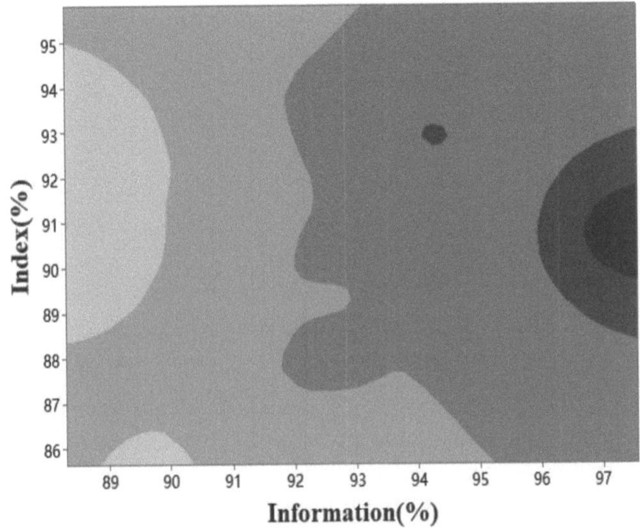

Fig. 4. Evaluation model of aging performance of different algorithms

Figure 4 shows that The achievements of digital technology can provide more information for college English teaching, help students better understand and understand the cultural customs, human history, international situation, etc., so as to broaden students' horizons, improve students' English professional ability, and better adapt to the requirements of talent cultivation in the development of digital age.

4.5   Validity of College English Course Design and Instructional Design

The traditional foreign language curriculum composition paradigm often focuses on the mode of "theory, method + textbook", that is, teaching theory and teaching method are mainly embodied in traditional paper textbooks. However, with the integration of digital technology, the paradigm of college English curriculum has gradually changed to the model of "theory, method and technology + three-dimensional teaching materials" is shown in Fig. 5 shown.

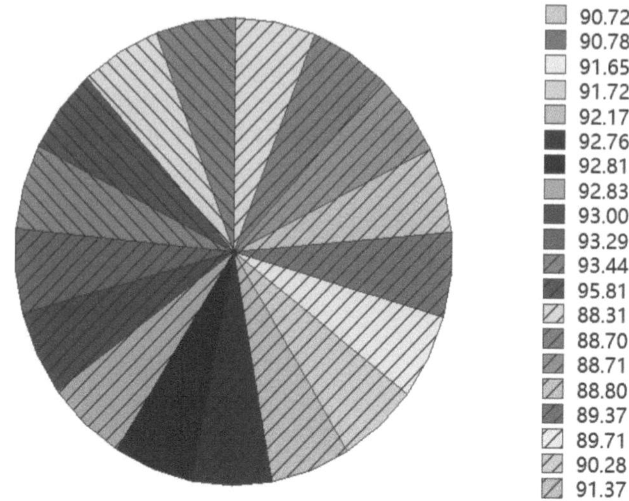

Fig. 5. College English course design and instructional design of different algorithms

Figure 5 shows that The transformation of three-dimensional teaching materials has become the foundation of ecological curriculum construction, and an important link in realizing the goal of college English curriculum. Three-dimensional textbooks not only contain the content of paper textbooks, but also integrate digital resources such as multimedia, computer network and mobile network, so as to provide students with a richer and more diverse learning experience, as shown in Table 4.

Table 4. Compares the efficacy of several college English course design and instructional design.

Algorithm	The vocabulary of English	college English course design and instructional design	Combination and phrase analysis	The conditional relationship of English
Digital technology	91.65	93.35	93.43	87.55
Decision tree algorithm	93.29	92.47	95.08	93.89
P	92.17	89.37	92.50	89.26

Table 4 shows that Three-dimensional textbooks not only contain the content of paper textbooks, but also integrate digital resources such as multimedia, computer network and mobile network, so as to provide students with a richer and more diverse learning experience, as illustrated in Fig. 6.

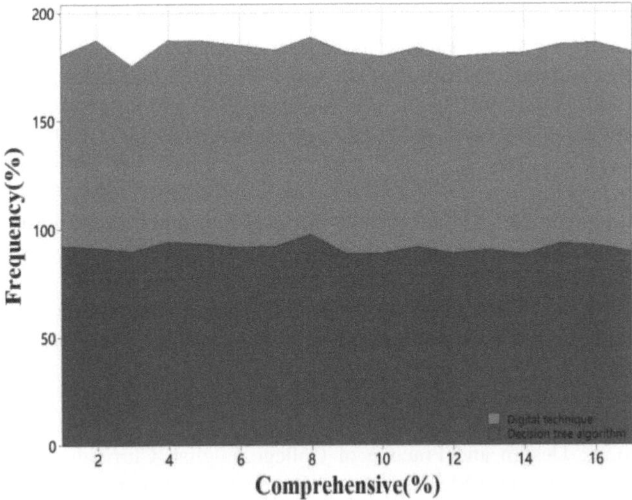

Fig. 6. Digital technology college English course design and instructional design

Figure 6 shows that the application of knowledge graph can help students grasp the internal logic of knowledge as a whole and better understand and master related knowledge. By establishing the relationship between words, word meaning and grammar, and effectively classifying vocabulary, knowledge graph can provide students with personalized learning paths.

5 Conclusion

The development of digital technology has greatly enriched the construction and application of knowledge graphs. Traditional knowledge graphs mainly rely on the knowledge and experience of experts, while digital knowledge graphs can automatically extract, organize and update knowledge through big data and artificial intelligence technology. This not only improves the accuracy and timeliness of the knowledge graph, but also provides richer resources and tools for instructional design. College English curriculum design based on knowledge graph can better meet students' learning needs. Through the knowledge map, teachers can systematically organize the course content to form a knowledge system with clear logic and distinct levels. Knowledge map can also help teachers realize the integration of interdisciplinary knowledge, broaden students' knowledge horizons, and improve their comprehensive literacy.

References

1. Lin, Q.: The Design and Practice of Ideological and Political Education in College English Curriculum under the Poa+boppps Mode - Taking Unit 3 of "New Era Mingde University English Comprehensive Course 2" as an Example Journal of Hubei Adult Education College **28**(1), 86–91 (2022)

2. Ruolan, W.: Design and exploration of ideological and political education in college english curriculum under the mixed teaching mode. J. Higher Educ. **8**(32), 177–180 (2022)
3. Qu, W.: Design and Implementation of Ideological and Political Education in College English Curriculum - Review of the "Guidelines for Ideological and Political Education in College English Curriculum" Research on Technology Management **43**(7), I0017 (2023)
4. Deng, Y., Zhang, C., Zhou, X.: A Technical Framework for Urban Form Research Supported by Historical GIS Intelligent Buildings and Urban Information (004), 000 (2022)
5. Liu, W.: Research on the Ideological and Political Design and Practice of the Course "College English Quality Expansion Course - Level 4 Intensive Training" University: Teaching and Education (5), 62–65 (2023)
6. Huang, X., Tian, X.: Research on the "Smart" Teaching Design for the Integration of Information Technology and College English Classroom University: Teaching and Education (1), 38–41 (2022)
7. Fang, J., Xu, F.: Analysis of the Visual Language Characteristics of Dynamic Posters in the Digital Media Era Design **8**(3), 6 (2023)
8. He, Y., Guo, J.: Design and Practice of College English Curriculum Teaching from the Perspective of Curriculum Ideological and Political Construction Overseas English (8), 3 (2022)
9. Jin, Y., Wang, X., Hao, Y.: Design and Practice of Ideological and Political Education in College English Curriculum Based on Output Oriented Approach China Science and Technology Economic News Database Education (8), 4 (2022)
10. Liu, Q., Zhu, X.: Design and practice of ideological and political education in college English courses based on the "output oriented approach". J. Jinzhou Med. Univ. Soc. Sci. Edition **20**(5), 104–107 (2022)
11. Li, J., Yangmei: Exploration and Practice of the Design of Ideological and Political Education in Hybrid College English Curriculum - Taking "A Love of Reading" in the New Edition of College Advanced English II as an Example Modern English (14), 4 (2022)
12. Zhu, L.: Research on the Design and Practice of Ideological and Political Education in College English Curriculum Based on Blended Teaching Language and Culture Forum (1), 237–248 (2022)
13. Fang Bao, Li Shaoli (2022) Research on the Curriculum Module Design and Teaching Model Reform of the "Five in One" College English under the Background of New Medical Science Construction Journal of Jilin Provincial Institute of Education, 38 (9), 101–108

Aesthetic Research in Digital Visual Art Design Engineering

Zhang Lan[✉]

Shanghai Institute of Visual Arts, Shanghai 201620, China
zhanglan_666@163.com

Abstract. Digital visual art design engineering relies heavily on aesthetic research, however the field sometimes makes erroneous aesthetic positioning claims. When used to the aesthetic research issues surrounding digital visual art design engineering, the conventional ant colony method yields unsatisfactory results. Refine artistic design and design connotation and content to realize intelligent analysis. Optimize the original effect. To begin, we use group behavior theory to identify potential influences; next, we categorize indicators according to aesthetic research needs in order to lessen the impact of potential interference elements. The results show that facilities engineering is able to provide. The effect of artistic design is enhanced. Art. Conditions optimize the original shape. The content of the design.

Keywords: swarm behavior theory · particle swarm algorithm · Aesthetic studies · Digital · Visual · Art design

1 Introduction

An important aspect of engineering for digital visual art is aesthetic research, which may lead to ever-increasing precision in aesthetic control [1, 2]. But there is an issue with inaccuracy in the aesthetic research scheme [3] that arises throughout the aesthetic research process [4], which has certain unintended consequences for aesthetic research. A number of academics have speculated that the particle swarm algorithm may be useful for analyzing aesthetic research schemes and providing related assistance for aesthetic research [5–7] and analysis of aesthetic research [8]. Based on this, this work suggests using a particle swarm algorithm to improve the aesthetic research method and check the model's performance [9]. The artistic design process of the body and the data collection process are shown in the Fig. 1.

B. Brik and S. Nazir (Eds.): BigIoT-EDU 2024, LNICST 659, pp. 175–184, 2026.
https://doi.org/10.1007/978-3-032-18631-7_20

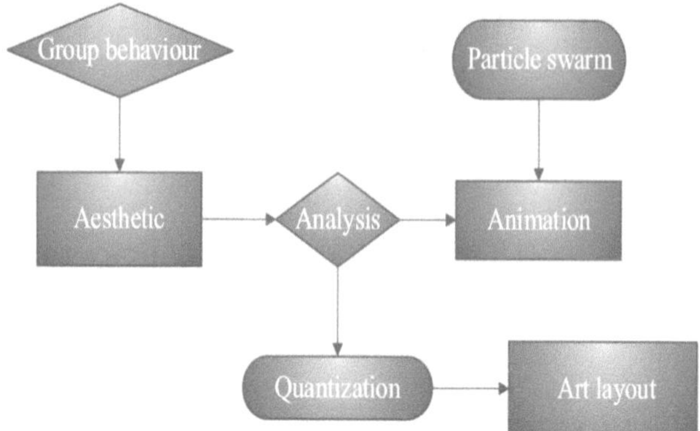

Fig. 1. The analytical process of aesthetic research

2 Related Works

2.1 Aesthetic Research

According to the results of the survey, the aesthetic study scheme complies with the objective facts as it displays a multi-dimensional distribution. Because aesthetic research is non-directional, it is considered a highly analytical study because aesthetic research methods are quite unpredictable. In the event where aesthetic research is a stochastic function is, the result of solving problem aesthetic research satisfies typical standards; primarily, computer technology modifies aesthetic research, gets rid of redundant and unneeded schemes, and augments the default scheme, resulting in a robust dynamic correlation across the whole aesthetic research scheme [10]. In order to quantify aesthetic studies more accurately, particle swarm optimization integrates the benefits of computer technology. There are three types of information included in the aesthetic research program: non-structural, semi-structural, and structural. We acquire the aesthetic research scheme of preliminary aesthetic research after the particle swarm algorithm's preference, and then we examine the viability of this scheme [11].

2.2 Digital Visual Art Design

Using computer technology, the particle swarm method optimizes the aesthetic research scheme and finds the unqualified value parameter based on the aesthetic research index parameters is include the attractiveness study plan is In order to optimize the aesthetic research scheme, the particle swarm algorithm uses a random optimization method and tweaks the settings of the Internet's information. Particle swarm method picks several schemes at random after dividing aesthetic study into various stages. The iterative approach involves optimizing and analyzing aesthetic research strategies at various stages. Following the completion of the optimization analysis, the most effective aesthetic studies are documented by combining the aesthetic research levels of several procedures.

3 Optimization Strategies for Aesthetic Research

3.1 Mathematical Description of Particle Swarm Arithmetic

The role to ultimately determine the practicability of the aesthetic study, computed is shown in Eq. (1).

$$\lim_{x \to \infty} \left(y_i \cdot t_{ij} \right) = y_{ij} \geq max(t_{ij} \div 2) \tag{1}$$

Among them, Eq. (2) displays the outlier judgment.

$$max(t_{ij}) = (t_{ij}^2 + 2 \cdot t_{ij}) \succ \left(\sum t_{ij} + 4 \right)M \tag{2}$$

Assuming I meet all of the aesthetic research criteria is, the aesthetic research plan is, having the aesthetic plan met is, The composition of art design analysis and the composition of collections. as shown in Eq. (3).

$$F(d_i) = \mathbb{R} \bigcup \sum t_i \bigcap \xi \cdot \sqrt{2} \to \oint y_i \cdot 7 \tag{3}$$

3.2 Selection of Aesthetic Research Protocols

Second Hypothesis Aesthetics in research is, the coefficient of weight is, thereafter, aesthetic study necessitates aesthetic research without any qualifications is shown in Eq. (4).

$$O(t_i) = (d_i)\frac{dy}{dx} \prod F - \int w_i \tag{4}$$

Equation (5) shows that a complete function of aesthetic research may be produced by combining Hypotheses I and II.

$$\lim_{x \to \infty} g(t_i) + F(d_i) \leq \frac{1}{2}max(t_{ij}) \tag{5}$$

Equation (6) shows the outcomes of standardizing all data, which improves the usefulness and reliability of aesthetic study..

$$g(t_i) + F(d_i) \leftrightarrow mean\left(\sum t_{ij} + 4 \right) \tag{6}$$

3.3 Analysis of Aesthetic Research Protocols

Prior to using the particle swarm technique, it is important to do a thorough analysis of the aesthetic research scheme, map the requirements to the aesthetic research library, and reject any unqualified aesthetic research schemes. The findings may be used to suggest the anomaly assessment system, (7).

$$No(t_i) = \frac{g(t_i) + F(d_i)}{mean(\sum t_{ij} + 4)} \frac{n!}{r!(n - r)!} \tag{7}$$

shown in Eq. (8).

$$Zh(t_i) = \bigcap [\sum g(t_i) + F(d_i)] \tag{8}$$

In order to guarantee that the particle swarm method is accurate, the aesthetic research scheme's threshold and index weights are defined after a thorough analysis of the aesthetic study. Aesthetic research necessitates precise analysis as it is a methodical examination of aesthetic research plans. Aesthetic research is The aesthetic research technique will be impacted by a non-normal distribution, which will reduce the overall accuracy of the study and the calculating outcome is shown in Eq. (9).

$$CU(t_i) = \sum \frac{min[\sum g(t_i) + F(d_i)]}{\lim\limits_{x \to \infty} \sum g(t_i) + F(d_i)} \tag{9}$$

4   Results and Discussion

4.1   Introduction to Aesthetic Research

Table 1 shows the aesthetic research scheme of particular aesthetic research; the research goal is aesthetic research in complicated circumstances; the test period is 12 h; and there are 12 pathways.

Table 1. Aesthetic research requirements

Scope of application	Design scope	Comprehensive element design	Combination of connotation elements
Advertising design	Master design	3.64	2.43
	Connotation enhancement	4.51	4.86
Brand design	Master design	2.99	2.81
	Connotation enhancement	4.46	4.58
Game design	Master design	79.56	81.99
	Connotation enhancement	79.10	80.11

The particle swarm algorithm's aesthetic research scheme, which is based on the ant colony algorithm, is more in line with the real needs of aesthetic research. Particle swarm optimization outperforms ant colony algorithm when it comes to the precision and logic of aesthetic study. Figure II shows the updated aesthetic research strategy that improves the particle swarm algorithm's accuracy and dependability. Consequently, particle swarm optimization has superior aesthetic research method speed, accuracy, and summation stability.

4.2 Aesthetic Research

Table 2 displays the aesthetic research methodology, which was used to more precisely confirm the aesthetic research impact. Aesthetic research with varying degrees of aesthetic research was chosen.

Table 2. The overall picture of the aesthetic research program

Category	the integral component of a design element	Comprehensive design content	Digitization of pluralistic art design
Advertising design	4	6	7
Brand design	9	9	7
Game design	4	1	4

4.3 Aesthetic Research and Stability

Figure 2 shows the aesthetic study plan that incorporates the ant colony algorithm to confirm the particle swarm technique's correctness.

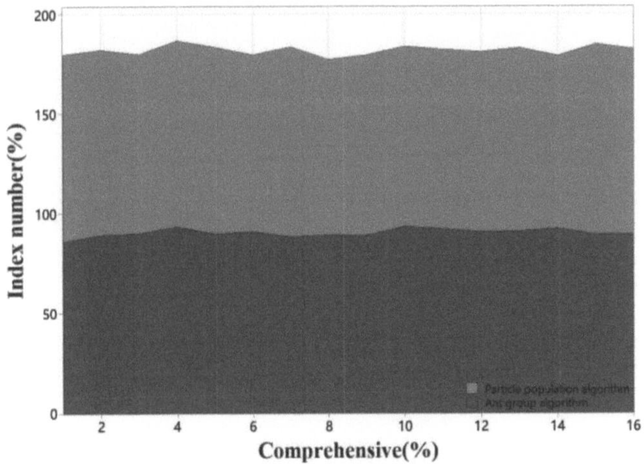

Fig. 2. Aesthetic studies of different algorithms

Figure 2 shows that compared to the ant colony algorithm, the particle swarm algorithm has more consistent aesthetic research, whereas the latter has an uneven amount of research, suggesting that the former is more stable. Table III displays the average aesthetic study plan of the three methods mentioned earlier.

Table 3. Comparison of aesthetic research accuracy of different methods

Algorithm	Design Classification	Design Composition	Core Design Analysis	Example Design Renderings
Particle swarm arithmetic	10	8	1	10
Ant colony algorithm	2	9	9	4

Table 3 clearly shows that the ant colony method isn't perfect when it comes to aesthetic research accuracy; furthermore, aesthetic research has evolved much, and the mistake rate is rather significant. Particle swarm optimization outperforms ant colony math in terms of the aesthetic evaluation of its overall outcomes. While this is going on, the accuracy has hardly budged, and the aesthetic study on particle swarm optimization is above 90%. So that the excellence of the particle swarm method may be confirmed even further. Figure 3 shows the results of several approaches used to conduct a general analysis of the particle swarm algorithm, which is done to further confirm the efficacy of the suggested method.

Fig. 3. Aesthetic research on particle swarm algorithms

Figure 3 shows that the ant colony algorithm's aesthetic research is poor compared to particle swarm optimization's. This is because optimization by particle swarm raises the adjustment coefficient of aesthetic research, establishes the threshold of Internet information, and gets rid of aesthetic research schemes that don't measure up.

4.4 Rationality of Aesthetic Research

As seen in Fig. 4, the aesthetic research scheme is constituted of the ant colony algorithm and is used to test the correctness of the particle swarm method.

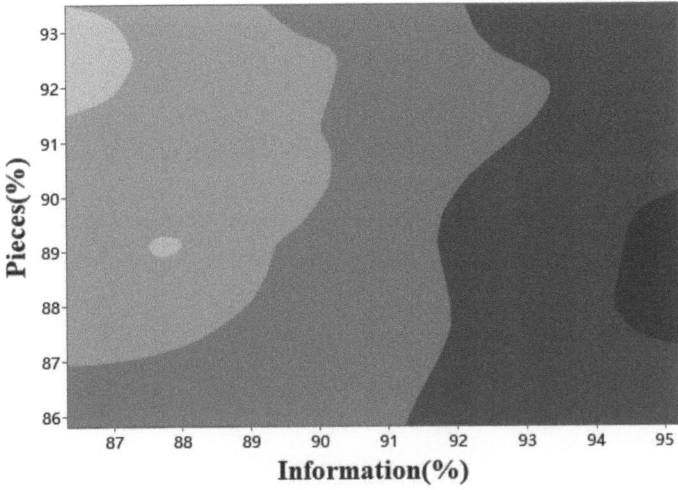

Fig. 4. Aesthetic studies of different algorithms

As shown in Fig. 4, the particle swarm algorithm outperforms the ant colony method when it comes to the rationality of aesthetic research. Furthermore, by enhancing aesthetic research using the particle swarm algorithm, the rationality of aesthetic research may be further enhanced. With the help of particle swarm algorithms, a decentralized platform for data storage and administration may be created, guaranteeing the safe recording and storage of findings. Each particle may have its own distinct identity thanks to particle swarming, which also allows for the recording of pertinent data and schemes.

4.5 Validity of Aesthetic Research

Figure 5 shows the aesthetic research plan that combines the ant colony algorithm with the particle swarm algorithm to test the method's efficacy.

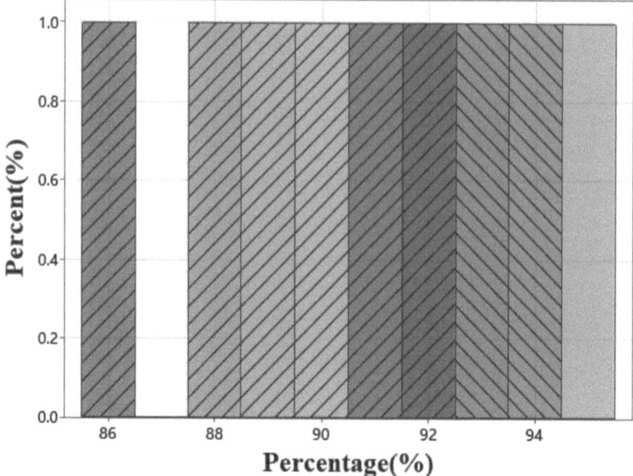

Fig. 5. Aesthetic studies of different algorithms

Figure 5 shows that compared to the ant colony algorithm, the particle swarm algorithm has more consistent aesthetic research, whereas the latter has more inconsistent results, suggesting that the former is more stable. In Table IV, you can see the typical aesthetic research plan of the three algorithms mentioned earlier.

Table 4. Comparison of the effectiveness of aesthetic studies of different methods

Algorithm	The promotion of artistic connotation	The role of digitalization	The overall structure of the building	The satisfaction rate of actual needs
Particle swarm arithmetic	4	10	7	7
Ant colony algorithm	6	2	4	2

From Table 4, we may deduce that the ant colony method isn't perfect when it comes to aesthetic research accuracy; furthermore, that aesthetic research has evolved much and has a significant mistake rate. Particle swarm optimization outperforms ant colony math in terms of the aesthetic evaluation of its overall outcomes. While this is going on, the accuracy has hardly budged, and the aesthetic study on particle swarm optimization is above 90%. So that the excellence of the particle swarm method may be confirmed even further. Figure VI shows the results of several approaches used to conduct a general analysis of the particle swarm algorithm, which is done to further confirm the efficacy of the suggested method.

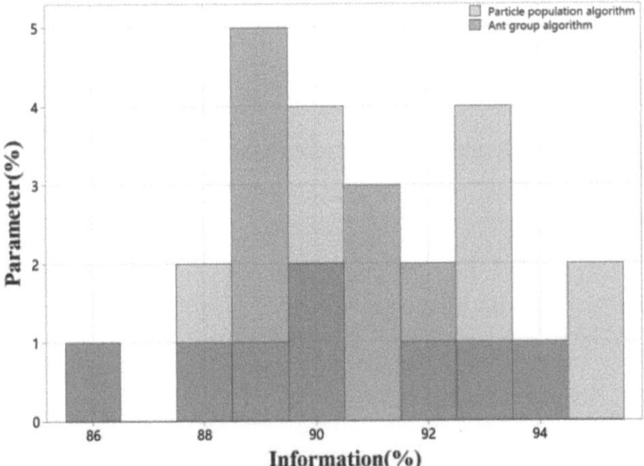

Fig. 6. Research on the aesthetics of particle swarm arithmetic

Because it raises the adjustment coefficient of aesthetic research, establishes the threshold of Internet information, and discards aesthetic research schemes that fail to fulfill the requirements, the particle swarm algorithm produces far superior results compared to the ant colony algorithm, as shown in Fig. 6.

5 Conclusion

This work sets out to solve the issue of imperfect aesthetic research by combining computer technology and proposing particle swarm optimization. While building the Internet information collection, thorough analyses of the reliability and quality of aesthetic research are conducted. Particle swarm optimization can perform general aesthetic research on aesthetic research and increase the accuracy of aesthetic research, according to studies. Unfortunately, the particle swarm algorithm pays an excessive amount of attention to aesthetic research analysis, leading to irrationality in the indicators used for aesthetic research.

References

1. He, K.: Applicaunsttion of color aesthetics of Tujia brocade from the perspective of visual art in modern bag design. Pop Color (11), 55–57 (2022)
2. Liu, L.: Research on the application of visual communication design and traditional aesthetic art elements in mobile user interface design. Shanghai Packaging (2023)
3. Li, X.: Application of modern art design in virtual implanted visual design of stage - taking the virtual implanted visual design of "Flying to the Future - Beijing 2022 Winter Paralympic Torch Relay Special Program" as an example. Film and Television Production **28**(6), 6 (2022)
4. Debo, S., Junlian, S.: Research on the application of Song Dynasty aesthetic concept "Shang Yi" in modern visual design. Art Technol. **36**(10), 181–183 (2023)
5. Tan, C.: Research on the visual art theory of Richard Wollheim. (Doctoral dissertation, Sichuan Normal University) (2022)

6. Li, M.: Innovative research on visual communication design teaching in the digital age. Educ. Res. **4**(11), 3–5 (2022)
7. Wei, L., Dasen, W., Jingbo, Y.: Digital design of architectural form based on technical aesthetics. J. Archit. Civil Eng. **004**, 039 (2022)
8. Ning, Z.: Preliminary exploration of the aesthetic form of "Zen" style in brand visual design. Footwear Craft Des. **3**(5), 55–57 (2023)
9. Lei, S.: Exploration of the application effect of digital technology in environmental art design. Environ. Eng. **001**, 040 (2022)
10. Yapei, L.: Application of intelligent digital modeling technology in the design of transformed civil structure dwellings - taking Fujian Mindong dwellings as an example. J. Jilin College Art **003**, 000 (2022)
11. Yong, T., Yuqi, Z., Xi, W.: Research on bridge aesthetics based on the perspective of design art. Beauty Era: Urban **11**, 24–26 (2022)

Data-Driven Research on Higher Education Management and Decision-Making Techniques and Their Applications

Jiajia Xu[✉]

Beijing University of Civil Engineering and Architecture Institute of Science and Technology Development, Beijing 100044, China
`xujiajia@bucea.edu.cn`

Abstract. There has been extensive usage of IT in the realm of higher education. Improving educational outcomes is a top priority for higher education administration and policymakers. When it comes to managing and making decisions in higher education, the old management approach just won't cut it. Hence, a method of data analysis for educational administration and decision-making is suggested in this work. The first step in minimizing interference factors in educational management and decision-making is to use information technology for analysis of education management. Indicators are then split according to the needs of education management and decision-making. After that, a program for educational management and decision-making is formed using the findings of IT analysis of higher education administration and decision-making, and then a thorough examination of these outcomes is carried out. Results from a MATLAB simulation demonstrate that data analysis outperforms the conventional management mode for the feasibility of education management and decision-making, and the rationality of education management and decision-making in higher education.

Keywords: information technology · Data analysis · Higher education · Educational management and decision-making

1 Introduction

Higher education places a premium on educational administration and decision-making as a core competency [1]. Nevertheless, universities face the challenge of inadequate feasibility in instructional administration and decision-making schemes[2], which impacts their image [3]. A number of academics hold the view that educational management and decision-making programs may be better studied with the use of data analysis applied to higher education[4], and that this can be backed up by the results [5]. This study optimizes school management and decision-making schemes[8], presents data analysis[7], and confirms the model's effectiveness[9] based on this premise.

B. Brik and S. Nazir (Eds.): BigIoT-EDU 2024, LNICST 659, pp. 185–193, 2026.
https://doi.org/10.1007/978-3-032-18631-7_21

2 Related Works

2.1 Mathematical Description of Data Analysis

In order to optimize education management and decision-making schemes using data analysis, one must first identify the index parameters used in these processes. Then, based on these parameters, one must determine the unqualified value parameters in higher education is z_i, and integrate the function of education management and decision-making schemes is $tol(y_i \cdot r_{ij}$, and finally judge the feasibility of higher education, calculated as shown in formula (1).

$$tol(y_i \cdot r_{ij}) = y_{ij} \geq max(r_{ij} \cdot \sum\nolimits_{i=1}^{n} r_i^2) \tag{1}$$

Equation (2) shows the evaluation of outliers among them.

$$max(r_{ij}) = \left(r_{ij}^2 \div 3 \right) \succ mean\left(\sum r_{ij} \cdot \frac{r - \mu}{\sigma} \cdot \sigma_r^2 \right) \tag{2}$$

Data analytics combines the benefits of being data-driven, quantified with higher education, and can improve the viability of education management and decision-making.

Suppose I. The requirements of educational management and decision-making is r_i, the educational management and strategy for making a choice is set_i, the satisfaction of educational management and decision-making scheme is y_i, coupled with the evaluation process of educational management and decision-making scheme is $B(r_i \approx 0)$, as shown in Eq. (3).

$$B(t_i) = \sum r_i \bigcap \xi \to \oint y_i \Rightarrow \sum\nolimits_{i=1}^{n} r_i \cdot \frac{1}{n} \tag{3}$$

2.2 Selection of Educational Management and Decision-Making Options

Assuming that the higher education function is $h(r_i)$, and the weight coefficient is w_i, then educational management and decision-making requires substandard higher education as shown in Eq. (4).

$$h(r_i) = z_i \cdot \frac{\delta y}{\delta x} \Rightarrow \frac{\partial^2 \Omega}{\partial u^2} \cdot \prod B(t_i) - w_i \tag{4}$$

An all-encompassing function of decision-making and administration in higher education may be derived from assumptions I and II, as shown in Eq. (5).

$$h(r_i) + B(t_i) \leq max(r_{ij}) \tag{5}$$

As seen in Eq. (6), standardizing all data is necessary to enhance the efficacy of decision-making and management in higher education.

$$h(r_i) + B(t_i) \leftrightarrow mean(\sum r_{ij} \cdot \frac{r - \mu}{\sigma} \cdot \sigma_r^2) \tag{6}$$

2.3 Analysis of Educational Management and Decision-Making Programs

Before data analysis, multi-dimensional analysis of educational management and decision-making schemes have to be executed, and the needs for educational administration and decision-making ought to be connected to the above education library, and unqualified educational management and decision-making schemes should be eliminated is $No(r_i)$. Equation (7) displays the outcomes, while Eq. (6) allows for the proposal of the anomaly assessment method.

$$No(r_i) = \frac{h(r_i) + B(t_i)}{mean(\sum r_{ij} \cdot \frac{r-\mu}{\sigma} \cdot \sigma_r^2)} \tag{7}$$

Among them, $\frac{h(r_i)+B(t_i)}{mean(\sum r_{ij} \cdot \frac{r-\mu}{\sigma} \cdot \sigma_r^2)} \leq 1$ It is said that in order for the strategy to be integrated, it must first be presented is $Zh(r_i)$, and the result is shown in Eq. (8).

$$Zh(r_i) = min[\sum h(r_i) + B(t_i)] \tag{8}$$

Higher education conducts comprehensive analysis, and sets decision-making and instructional management frameworks for indicator weights and thresholds to guarantee reliable data analysis. Analysis of educational management and decision-making methods is necessary in higher education since it is a systematic examination. Educational administration and decision-making in higher education will be less accurate as a whole if the data does not follow a normal distribution is $accur(r_i)$, as shown in Eq. (9).

$$accur(r_i) = \frac{min[\sum h(r_i) + B(t_i)]}{\sum h(r_i) + B(t_i)} \times 100\% \tag{9}$$

In agreement with actual realities, the examination of educational administration and decision-making schemes reveals that these systems exhibit a multi-dimensional distribution. As a highly analytical field, higher education is devoid of direction, suggesting that educational administration and decision-making systems exhibit considerable unpredictability. Assuming that the probability function for university enrollment is $randon(r_i)$, Eq. (10), which expresses the computation of Eq. (9), follows.

$$accur(r_i) = \frac{min[\sum h(r_i) + B(t_i)]}{\sum h(r_i) + B(t_i)} \times 100\% + randon(r_i) \tag{10}$$

A strong dynamic correlation between the entire education management and decision-making scheme is achieved, among other things, by ensuring that higher education meets the usual requirements, primarily through data-driven adjustment of higher education, by supplementing the default scheme, and by eliminating duplicate and irrelevant schemes.

3 Optimization Strategies for Higher Education

Data analysis optimizes higher education programs by adjusting education management parameters using a random optimization technique. Based on the data, we may randomly choose several solutions for the various tiers of administration and decision-making in higher education. Various layers of education management and decision-making processes are optimized and evaluated in the iterative process. Following the completion of the optimization study, the most effective programs are documented by comparing their educational management and decision-making levels higher education.

4 Results and Discussion

4.1 Introduction to Educational Management and Decision-Making

Table 1 shows the special educational management and decision-making scheme of higher education, and the study uses higher education in difficult instances as its research target. There are 12 pathways and a 12-h test duration.

Table 1. College Education Management and Decision-Making Requirements

Scope of application	Grade	Viability	Educational management and decision-making
One	I	81.22	81.88
	II	80.24	82.33
Two	I	81.57	81.57
	II	83.46	82.04
Three	I	83.08	84.84
	II	80.34	83.24

The educational management and decision-making process in Table 1, shown in Fig. 1.

Education management and decision-making schemes that use data analysis are more in line with the needs of real education management and decision-making than those that use conventional management modes. Data analysis is the conventional paradigm for managing academic institutions in a way that is both reasonable and practical. Figure II shows that data analysis is becoming more feasible as a result of improvements in educational management and decision-making methods. Consequently, the education management and decision-making scheme's speed, the stability of the data's summation, and both are improved.

4.2 Higher Education

Higher education's program for educational management and decision-making incorporates all three types of data: unstructured, semi-structured, and structural. We acquired the preliminary educational management and decision-making scheme of higher education after doing the pre-selection data analysis. Then, we examined its viability. Picking higher education at various tiers of educational management and decision-making allows for more precise verification of its effects, and the educational management and decision-making plan is shown in Table 2.

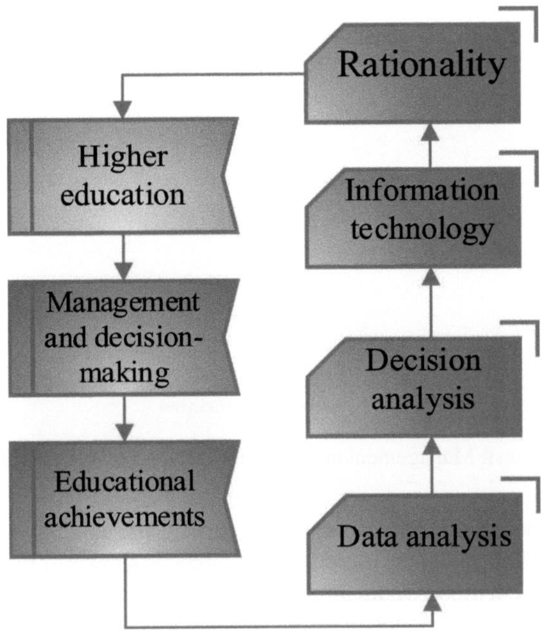

Fig. 1. Analytical Process in Higher Education

Table 2. Overall Picture of Educational Management and Decision-Making Programmes

Category	Random data	Satisfaction	Analysis rate
One	88.32	86.86	86.37
Sophomore	88.76	85.48	85.74
Junior	87.61	82.82	84.28
mean	85.60	85.77	86.71
i	84.14	89.54	87.46
	P = 2.024		

4.3   Educational Management and Decision-Making Educational Management and Decision-Making and Stability

In order to verify the accuracy of data analysis, the educational management and decision-making scheme is compared with the traditional management model, and the educational management and decision-making scheme is shown in Fig. 2.

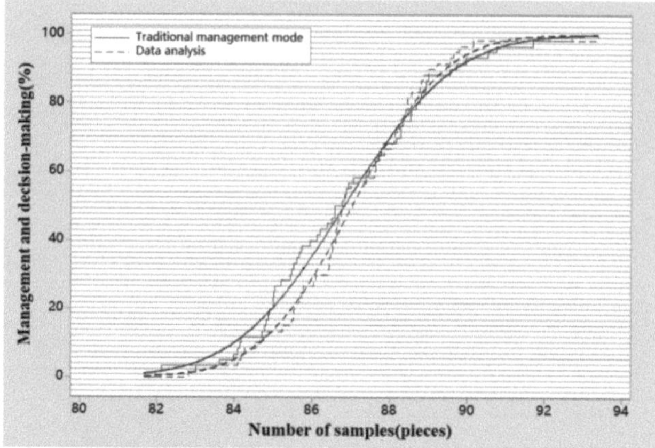

Fig. 2. Educational Management and Decision-Making with Different Algorithms

Compared to the traditional management model, the education management and decision-making of data analysis are relatively stable, as shown in Figure II, whereas the traditional management mode's education management and decision-making are uneven. This is because the error rate is lower in the former case. See Table III for an average of the three algorithms' instructional management and decision-making schemes.

Table 3. Comparison of Different Methods of Educational Management and Decision-Making Accuracy

Algorithm	Survey data	Educational management and decision-making	Magnitude of change	Error
Data analysis	92.43	93.15	95.86	92.37
Traditional management model	84.54	85.19	89.53	84.18
P	87.08	85.68	85.38	87.92

Table 4. Comparison of different methods of educational management and decision-making effectiveness

Algorithm	Survey data	Educational management and decision-making	Magnitude of change	Error
data analysis	88.03	89.13	88.87	84.14
Traditional management model	90.43	88.91	86.51	85.22
P	89.25	89.09	92.31	90.80

Table 3 shows that there are problems with the conventional management model when it comes to educational management and the feasibility of decisions in higher education. Changes in higher education have been large, and there is a high rate of errors. Compared to the conventional management paradigm, the overall outcomes of data analysis in educational administration and decision-making are superior. Also, the accuracy rate hasn't altered much, and it's above 90% for educational administration and decision-making based on data. That data analysis is better may be confirmed in additional detail. Various approaches were often used to examine the data in order to further validate the efficiency of the suggested strategy, Fig. 3 shown.

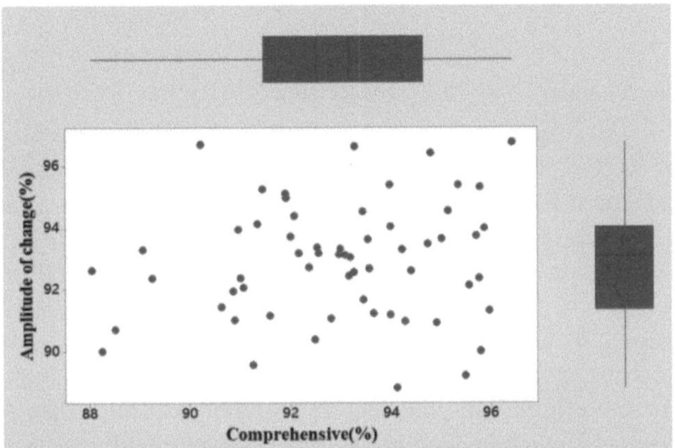

Fig. 3. Data Analysis Educational Management and Decision-Making Educational Management and Decision-Making

Figure 3 clearly shows that data-driven education management and decision-making outperforms the conventional management model. This is due to the fact that data-driven decision-making raises the higher education adjustment coefficient, establishes the education management threshold, and gets rid of unsatisfactory education management and decision-making schemes.

4.4 Effectiveness of Educational Management and Decision-Making

In order to verify the effectiveness of data analysis, the educational management and decision-making scheme is compared with the traditional management model, and the educational management and decision-making scheme is shown in Fig. 4.

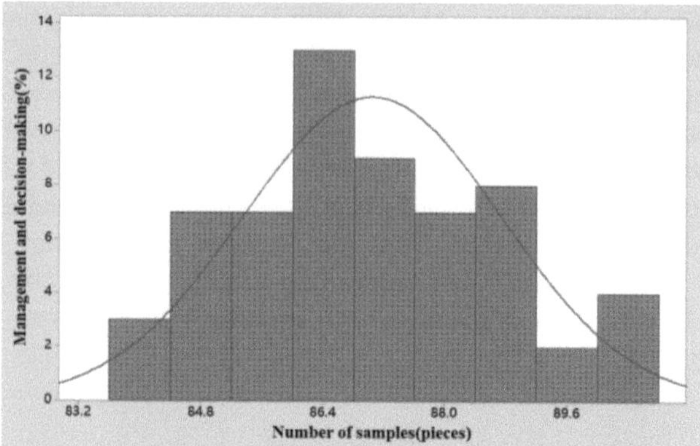

Fig. 4. Educational Management and Decision-Making with Different Algorithms

Figure 4 shows that compared to the traditional management model, data analysis education management and decision-making are higher and have a lower error rate, suggesting that they are relatively stable. In contrast, traditional management education management and decision-making are inconsistent. Table IV shows the average decision-making and education management scheme of the three algorithms mentioned earlier.

The conventional management model fails to adequately address educational management and decision-making rationality in higher education, as shown in Table IV. Additionally, the table highlights the fact that higher education has seen significant changes and a high mistake rate. Compared to the conventional management paradigm, the overall outcomes of data analysis in educational administration and decision-making are superior. Also, the accuracy rate hasn't altered much, and it's above 90% for educational administration and decision-making based on data. That data analysis is better may be confirmed in additional detail. Figure V shows the results of a general study of data analysis using various methodologies, which was conducted to further confirm the efficacy of the approach provided in this research.

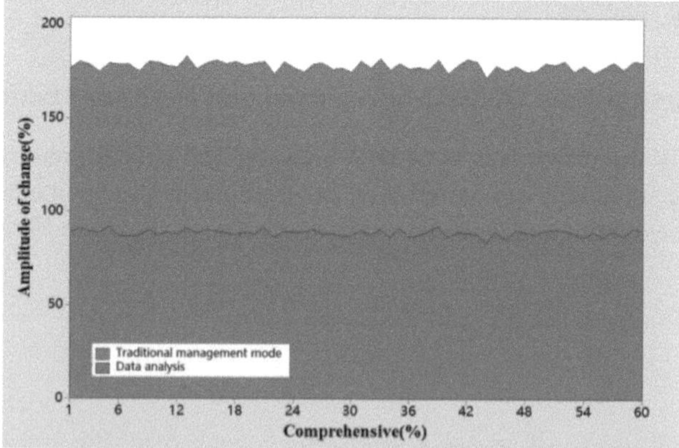

Fig. 5. Data analysis educational management and decision-making educational management and decision-making

Figure 5 clearly shows that data-driven education management and decision-making outperforms the conventional management model. This is due to the fact that data-driven education management and decision-making removes subpar schemes, raises the adjustment coefficient for higher education, and establishes the bar for effective education management.

5 Conclusion

With the goal of improving the higher education system's administration and decision-making, this study suggests using data analysis and combining data-driven optimization strategies. While doing so, we build the education management collection and conduct an in-depth analysis of the practicability of education management and decision-making. Research has shown that data analysis has the potential to enhance the precision of higher education, as well as to manage and make decisions on general education. On the other hand, educational administration and decision-making analysis get an inordinate amount of focus throughout data analysis, resulting in irrationality in the selection of educational management and decision-making indicators.

References

1. Zhang, L.: Data-driven higher education management and decision-making technology and its application. Taiyuan University of Science and Technology (2021)
2. Liu, D., Zeng, Z., Song, Y., Wang, J., Wang, S.: Reform and practice of higher education management and decision making driven by big data. Wireless Internet Technol. **16**(08), 94–95 (2019)
3. Shi, J., Wu, L.: Overview of China's higher education management decision innovation under the background of big data. Contemporary Tourism **04**, 225 (2019)
4. Chen, Y., Liu, C.: Research on the innovation of higher education management decision in China under the background of big data. J. Liaoning Inst. Educ. Administration **36**(01), 48–51 (2019)
5. Zhou, J.: Research on the rule of law in China's higher education governance. Nanchang University (2017)
6. Wang. Decision Ecology Analysis in Higher Education Management. J. Chifeng Univ. (Natural Science Edition) **28**(14), 212–213 (2012)
7. Yan, Z.: Research on macro-decision-making system and process of higher education in China. Xiamen University (2006)
8. Tang, J., Yuan, K.: Mathematical model method for higher education management decision-making——AHP method. Sci. Eng. Stud. High. Educ. **2002**(03), 21–23 (2002)
9. Hu, Y., Liao, C.: Scientific decision making in higher education management. Yunnan J. High. Educ. Res. (02), 19–21 (1999)
10. Wang, J.: Successful example of democratization and scientific democratization of higher education management and decision-making. J. Chongqing Univ. (Social Science Edition) (03), 45–47 (1996)

Research Hotspot Analysis of Nursing Simulation Teaching Based on PubMed Database

Wei Lilin[⊠], Gan Min, Zhao Qian, Li Zhuang, and Song Feng

Yunnan College of Business Management, YunNan 650000, China
43118918@qq.com

Abstract. As an innovative teaching method, nursing simulation teaching has received wide attention worldwide in recent years. With the rapid development of medical technology and the improvement of patient safety needs, nursing education is facing new challenges. Traditional clinical practice mode is often difficult to meet the teaching needs of combining theory and practice, and nursing simulation teaching, by creating a safe and controllable environment, enables students to learn and practice clinical skills under risk-free conditions, and improves the efficiency and quality of nursing education. Moreover, due to the complexity and unpredictability of the medical environment, simulation teaching provides students with training opportunities to cope with emergencies and crisis management, thereby partly reducing errors and risks in clinical practice. MATLAB simulation shows that under certain evaluation criteria, the cluster analysis algorithm has a teaching quality on the teaching strategy of nursing simulation teaching the simulation practice effect is better than the traditional nursing teaching mode.

Keywords: Thorndike theory · clustering algorithms · nursing professions · Simulation teaching

1 Introduction

This study aims to comprehensively analyze the literature on nursing simulation teaching in the PubMed database to reveal research hotspots, trends and existing problems in this field. Through in-depth study of relevant literature, we expect to understand the current practice of nursing simulation teaching, evaluate its teaching effect, explore the possibility of technological innovation and application expansion, and identify challenges in education and clinical practice. Moreover, this study attempts to provide theoretical basis and practical guidance for the future direction of nursing education and promote the continuous improvement and quality improvement of nursing education. Through this analysis, we hope to establish a comprehensive framework to guide the further development of nursing simulation teaching and provide valuable reference information for educators, policy makers and nursing students.

B. Brik and S. Nazir (Eds.): BigIoT-EDU 2024, LNICST 659, pp. 194–203, 2026.
https://doi.org/10.1007/978-3-032-18631-7_22

2 Related Works

A.Research status of nursing teaching mode

The PubMed database PubMed Is a free search engine maintained by the National Center for Biotechnology Information (NCBI) of the National Library of Medicine (NLM) and index the medical, biomedical and health sciences related literature. Since its launch in 1996, PubMed has evolved from the original Medline database to an important resource for medical researchers and professionals worldwide. As of 2024, PubMed contains over 30 million articles covering over 5,900 journals, most of which provide abstracts and in sections provide full-text links. PubMed More than 1 million new documents are added every year, ensuring that users can obtain the latest medical research results in time. PubMed During its development, new features and improvements have been introduced, such as PubMed Central (PMC) as an open access full-text repository and MeSH (Medical Subject Headings) system, a set of standardized medical subject words for users to facilitate accurate retrieval. In addition, PubMed supports retrieval of clinical trial registration information as well as provision of consumer health information through PubMed Health.

PubMed Database is widely used and far-reaching in the field of nursing, which provides massive information support for nursing education, research and practice. In nursing education, PubMed is an important tool for teachers and students to conduct literature search, curriculum design, and thesis writing. Teachers can use PubMed to find the latest nursing theory and practical research to update the teaching content; students can use PubMed to understand the latest developments in the nursing field and support their academic research and clinical practice. Decision-making In clinical care, nurses can use the PubMed to query the latest treatment options, standards of care, and disease management strategies. By searching the relevant literature, nurses were able to access evidence-supported nursing practices to improve the quality of care and patient safety.PubMed Is the main platform for nursing researchers to conduct literature reviews, design research projects, and find data sources. Researchers can look for existing research, identify research gaps, and provide a basis for new research directions. In addition, PubMed provides clinical trial registration information to help researchers track the latest clinical trials. In the area of care policy and management, the PubMed literature can help policymakers understand trends in nursing care practices worldwide, assess the effectiveness of care services, and develop or adapt care policies.

B. Improve the quality of nursing education

Part PubMed Health provides easy-to-understand health information that helps educates nurses and patients about disease prevention and self-management. In conclusion, the PubMed database plays an indispensable role in the field of nursing, providing nursing professionals with valuable resources to acquire, share and apply knowledge, and promoting the scientization and specialization of nursing practice.

Adopt diversified education methods

Nursing simulation teaching is a teaching method using simulated environments, simulated patients, and simulated clinical situations, aiming to provide a safe and controlled learning environment for nursing students and practitioners. This approach allows students to practice clinical skills, decision-making skills, and teamwork skills without harming real patients. The characteristics of nursing simulation teaching include:

Authenticity: The simulated environments and cases reproduce the real clinical situations as much as possible to improve the relevance and practicability of learning. Interactivity:

C. Innovative ways of education

Promote communication and collaboration between students through role-play and teamwork. Feedback timeliness: The immediate feedback mechanism helps students identify mistakes, adjust strategies, and improve learning efficiency. Reproducibility: Students can practice repeatedly until they master skills or concepts.

The theoretical basis of nursing simulation teaching mainly comes from some important theories in the fields of pedagogy and psychology: Learning theory: including behaviorism, cognitivism and constructivism, which emphasize the relationship between environment, experience and learning, as well as the importance of active learning and problem solving. Contextual learning theory: It emphasizes that learners build knowledge and skills through practical operation and reflection in real or simulated environments. Cognitive load theory: to guide the design of simulation teaching to reduce students' cognitive burden and improve the learning effect. Self-efficacy theory: to improve students' self-confidence through simulation training, and to enhance their sense of ability in practical clinical work.

In nursing education, simulation teaching is widely used in the following aspects: Skill training: such as cardiopulmonary resuscitation, venipuncture, catheterization and other basic nursing skills practice. Decision-making training: simulate complex cases and allow students to make clinical decisions under time pressure. Teamwork: Improve teamwork and communication skills through multi-professional team simulation exercises. Crisis management: simulate emergency, such as the patient's condition suddenly deteriorated, train students' emergency response and handling ability. Ethics and legal education: to discuss and learn about ethical and legal issues in nursing through simulated cases.

3 Optimization Strategies for Nursing Education Practices

The research methods of nursing simulation teaching are varied and cover multiple aspects of quantitative and qualitative research. Quantitative studies often employ randomized controlled trials, cohort studies, or cross-sectional surveys with quantified data to measure the impact of simulation teaching on the knowledge, skills, and attitudes of nursing students. Qualitative research included observation, interview, and focus group discussions to deeply understand the experience of simulation teaching, the students' learning process, and the impact of the teaching environment. Mixed-methods research combines both quantitative and qualitative methods to provide a more comprehensive perspective on the complexity of simulation teaching.

A. Mathematical description of the clustering algorithm

Part PubMed Health provides easy-to-understand health information that helps educates nurses and patients about disease prevention and self-management. In conclusion, the PubMed database plays an indispensable role in the field of nursing, providing nursing professionals with valuable resources to acquire, share and apply knowledge, and promoting the scientization and specialization of nursing practice.

$$D(x_i) + (d_i) = \int +(x_i, y_i) \tag{1}$$

Among them, the judgment of outliers is shown in Eq. (2).

$$\int +(x_i, y_i) = \sum\nolimits_{i=1}^{n} x(1-p) \tag{2}$$

Nursing simulation teaching is a teaching method using simulated environments, simulated patients, and simulated clinical situations, aiming to provide a safe and controlled learning environment for nursing students and practitioners. This approach allows students to practice clinical skills, decision-making skills, and teamwork skills without harming real patients. The characteristics of nursing simulation teaching include:

$$f(a_i) = \prod\nolimits_{i=1}^{n} F\gamma + p_i \tag{3}$$

B. Selection of simulation teaching programs
Authenticity: The simulated environment and cases reproduce the real clinical situations as much as possible to improve the relevance and practicability of learning. Interactivity:

$$D(x_i) = (d_i)_i \sum\nolimits_{i=1}^{n} (x_i) - u \tag{4}$$

Promote communication and collaboration between students through role-play and teamwork. Feedback timeliness:

$$f(a_i) + D(x_i) \leq \int +(x_i, y_i) \tag{5}$$

The immediate feedback mechanism helps students identify mistakes, adjust strategies, and improve learning efficiency. Reproducibility: Students can practice repeatedly until they master skills or concepts.

$$f(a_i) + D(x_i) \leftrightarrow \sum\nolimits_{i=1}^{n} x(1-p) \tag{6}$$

C. Analysis of teaching strategy schemes
The theoretical basis of nursing simulation teaching mainly comes from some important theories in the fields of pedagogy and psychology: Learning theory: including behaviorism, cognitivism and constructivism, which emphasize the relationship between environment, experience and learning, as well as the importance of active learning and problem solving. Contextual learning theory: It emphasizes that learners build knowledge and skills through practical operation and reflection in real or simulated environments.

$$z(d_i) = \frac{f(a_i) + D(x_i)}{\sum_{i=1}^{n} x(1-p)} \tag{7}$$

Cognitive load theory: to guide the design of simulation teaching to reduce students' cognitive burden and improve the learning effect. Self-efficacy theory: to improve students' self-confidence through simulation training, and to enhance their sense of ability in practical clinical work.

$$sh(p_i) = f(a_i) + D(x_i) \tag{8}$$

198   W. Lilin et al.

In nursing education, simulation teaching is widely used in the following aspects: Skill training: such as cardiopulmonary resuscitation, venipuncture, catheterization and other basic nursing skills practice. Decision-making training: simulate complex cases and allow students to make clinical decisions under time pressure. Teamwork: Improve teamwork and communication skills through multi-professional team simulation exercises.

$$d^\tau x + f = \frac{min[\sum f(a_i) + D(x_i)]}{\sum f(a_i) + D(x_i)} \times 100\% \tag{9}$$

Crisis management: simulate emergency, such as the patient's condition suddenly deteriorated, train students' emergency response and handling ability. Ethics and legal education: to discuss and learn about ethical and legal issues in nursing through simulated cases.

$$d^\tau x + f = \frac{min[\sum f(a_i) + D(x_i)]}{\sum f(a_i) + D(x_i)} \times 100\% + unno(x_i) \tag{10}$$

In practical application, nursing simulation teaching usually combines advanced mannequins (such as SimMan, SimBaby, etc.), standardized patient, situational simulation and online virtual environment. The use of these tools makes the teaching process more diversified and can meet learners at different levels and needs. In addition, through regular simulation training and evaluation, nursing simulation teaching not only improves the skill level of nursing staff, but also promotes their clinical reasoning ability and professional competence.

4 Results and Discussion

A. Introduction to teaching strategies

The key to evaluating the effectiveness of nursing simulation teaching is to determine its effectiveness in improving nursing professional skills, clinical decision-making ability, teamwork, and coping with stress. Researchers used standardized tests, skill scores, processing performance of simulated cases, student feedback questionnaire, and clinical practice performance. For example, simulation teaching was shown to significantly improve students' first aid skills, communication skills, and enhance their resilience in complex clinical situations.

The process of teaching strategies in Table 1 is shown in Fig. 1.

Compared with the traditional nursing teaching mode, the teaching strategy scheme of the cluster analysis algorithm is closer to the actual teaching strategy requirements. In terms of rationality and fluctuation range of nursing education practice, the cluster analysis algorithm is better than the traditional nursing teaching mode. It can be seen from the changes of teaching strategies in Fig. 1 that the stability of the cluster analysis algorithm is better, and the teaching quality is better. Therefore, the teaching quality, simulation teaching scheme, teaching strategy scheme and summation stability of the cluster analysis algorithm are better.

B. Nursing education practice

Table 1. Nursing Professional Teaching Strategy Requirements

Scope of application	Feedback effect	Innovative effect	Simulation teaching
Major in Nursing	84.50	83.36	86.67
Nurse Profession	86.04	83.87	85.65
Major in midwifery	83.12	85.44	85.41
Medical representative profession	86.05	83.85	85.42
Advanced Nursing Specialty	82.95	85.07	85.93
Sales reps specialize	87.08	83.53	88.72

Table 2. Simulate the overall situation of the teaching program.

Category	Simulate practical effects	Analysis rate
Major in Nursing	84.35	85.11
Nurse Profession	84.11	86.14
Major in midwifery	87.92	82.67
mean	85.10	84.22
X^6	35.62	32.61
P = 3.52		

Table 3. Comparison of the Accuracy of Teaching Strategies of Different Methods

Algorithm	Simulation teaching	Magnitude of change	Error
Clustering algorithms	84.29	85.36	1.07
Traditional nursing teaching model	74.28	79.60	5.32
P	34.91	32.84	34.77

With the progress of technology, nursing simulation teaching has also constantly introduced new technical means, such as virtual reality (VR), augmented reality (AR), mixed reality (MR) and remote simulation. These technologies provide an immersive learning experience, enabling students to practice high-risk clinical situations in a safe environment. In addition, the use of intelligent figures and advanced mannequins makes the simulation more realistic, simulating various physiological conditions and disease processes. At the same time, the application of artificial intelligence and big data also shows potential in personalized teaching, learning progress tracking and teaching feedback (Table 2).

C. Simulation teaching and stability of teaching strategies

The application of nursing simulation teaching is not limited to the educational field, but also gradually extends to on-the-job training and continuing education. In clinical

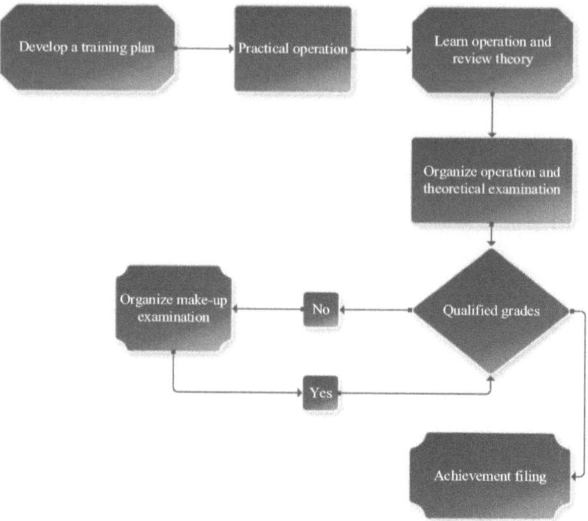

Fig. 1. Analysis Process of Nursing Education Practice

settings, simulation training helps to update caregivers' knowledge and skills, reduce medical errors, and improve patient safety (Fig. 2).

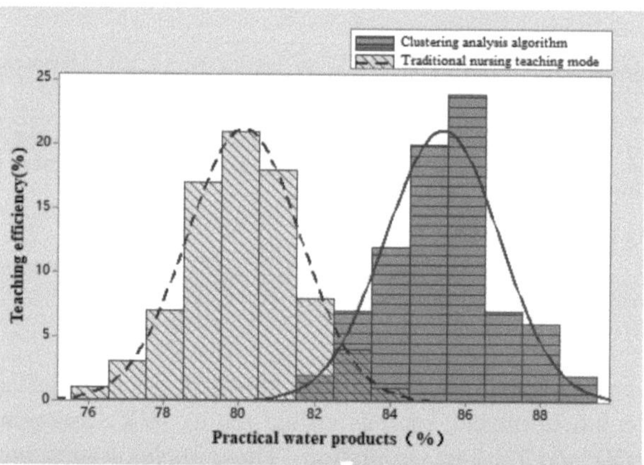

Fig. 2. Simulation Teaching With Different Methods

In addition, simulation teaching is also used in policy development and regulation training to help caregivers understand and follow new medical guidelines and standard operating procedures. Interprofessional team training is also an important application of simulation teaching, promoting collaboration and communication between different specialties (Tables 3).

Although simulation teaching shows great potential in nursing education, there are several challenges such as high equipment costs, the need for teacher training, the difficulty of simulating real clinical environments, and the standardization of assessing and validating simulation effects. In the future, researchers need to continue to explore more economical, effective, and scalable models of simulation teaching while addressing these challenges. With continued technology development, simulation teaching is expected to achieve broader and deeper integration as a core component of nursing education and clinical practice (Fig. 3).

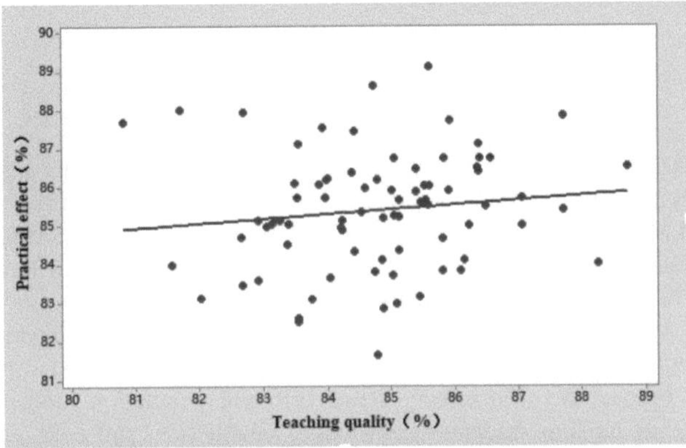

Fig. 3. Simulation Teaching of Clustering Algorithm Teaching Strategy

Nursing simulation teaching plays a crucial role in nursing education. By simulating real clinical environments, students are able to learn and practice nursing skills in a safe, controlled environment. These simulation activities include basic skills training, emergency handling, teamwork, and clinical decision-making. Using advanced mannequins (e. g., simulated patients) and virtual reality technologies, students can experience a variety of complex clinical situations, such as acute illness onset, surgical care, and intensive care. In addition, simulation teaching also promotes the development of critical thinking, allowing students both to learn to think and solve problems independently in the face of uncertainty and complexity.

5 Conclusion

In clinical nursing, simulation teaching helps to improve nurses' practical skills and ability to respond to emergencies. For example, by simulating first aid scenarios, nurses can be familiar with emergency operations such as CPR and endotracheal intubation, thus being more confident and efficient in practical work. Simulation training can also help nurses adapt to new medical technologies and equipment, such as the use of non-invasive ventilators, the management of intravenous fluids, etc. Moreover, simulation teaching helps to enhance interprofessional team collaboration, and through role-playing and team simulation, different medical professionals can learn how to work together in emergencies to improve the overall quality of care.

Aiming at the problem that nursing education practice simulation teaching is not ideal, this paper proposes a cluster analysis algorithm, combined with the search of PubMed database and Skinner's theory, to improve the practice of nursing education Optimize. At the same time, the innovation of teaching strategies and thresholds is analyzed in depth to build a collection of health professionals. The results show that the cluster analysis algorithm can improve the effect and quality of nursing education practice and can carry out general teaching strategies for nursing education practice. However, in the process of cluster analysis algorithm, too much attention is paid to the analysis of teaching strategy, resulting in irrationality in the selection of teaching strategy indicators.

References

1. Aldridge, M.D.: An at-home simulation to teach undergraduate nursing students the concept of medication adherence. Teach. Learn. Nursing **18**(3), 429–431 (2023)
2. Almotairy, M.M., Algabbashi, M., Alshutwi, S., Shibily, F., Alsharif, F., Almutairi, W., Nahari, A.: Nursing faculty perceptions of simulation culture readiness in Saudi universities: a cross-sectional study. Bmc Nursing **22**(1) (2023)
3. Altmiller, G., Wilson, C., Jimenez, F.A., Perron, T.: Impact of a virtual patient simulation on nursing students' attitudes of transgender care. Nurse Educ. **48**(3), 131–136 (2023)
4. Alwawi, A., Inkaya, B.: The effect of two different simulation modalities in palliative care teaching on nursing students' knowledge, satisfaction, self-confidence, and skills a randomized controlled trial. Cin-Comput. Inform. Nursing **41**(4), 246–257 (2023)
5. Annion, M., Ojasoo, M., Ernits, U., Puusepp, K.: Emotional coping of nursing students during mental health nursing simulation training. Proc. Est. Acad. Sci. **72**(3), 212–219 (2023)
6. Azher, S., Cervantes, A., Marchionni, C., Grewal, K., Marchand, H., Harley, J.M.: Virtual simulation in nursing education: headset virtual reality and screen-based virtual simulation offer a comparable experience. Clin. Simul. Nurs. **79**, 61–74 (2023)
7. Benko, E., Persolja, M.: Nursing students' views of the impact of geriatric role-play workshops on professional competencies: survey. Bmc Nursing **22**(1) (2023)
8. Bodempudi, S., et al.: Improving time to defibrillation following ventricular tachycardia (VTach) and Ventricular Fibrillation (VFib) cardiac arrest: a multicenter retrospective and prospective quality improvement study. Am. J. Med. Qual. **38**(2), 73–80 (2023)
9. Burrell, S.A., Ross, J.G., Keil, K.M., Heverly, M.: Pilot Testing of virtual simulation-based experiences in an oncology nursing seminar. J. Nurs. Educ. **62**(3), 167–170 (2023)
10. Calcagni, L., Lindell, D., Weaver, A., Jackson, M.: Clinical judgment development and assessment in clinical nursing education. Nurse Educ. **48**(4), 175–181 (2023)
11. Carr, K., Rhodes, K.A., Klamm, M.M., McElwain, S.: Engaging nursing students in mental health concepts through multiple teaching modalities. J. Nurs. Educ. **62**(6), 359–363 (2023)
12. Clephane, K., Heheman, C., Gardner, J., MacPherson, S., Baker, R.: Assessing a pediatric nursing simulation with an electronic health record, video-assisted debrief, and minimized group sizes. Clin. Simul. Nurs. **76**, 17–25 (2023)
13. de Campos, A.P., Polifroni, E.C.: Development of a standardized simulation advance care planning conversations for nurses. Nurs. Res. **72**(1), 74–80 (2023)
14. de Leon, C., Mano, L.Y., Fernandes, D.D., Paula, R.A.P., Brasil, G.D., Ribeiro, L.M.: Artificial intelligence in the analysis of emotions of nursing students undergoing clinical simulation. Revista Brasileira De Enfermagem, 76 (2023)

15. de Rosa, C., Frost, E., Ziegler, E., Spies, M.: Improving student perceptions of simulation effectiveness with co-facilitation from prebriefing through debriefing. Nurs. Educ. Perspect. **44**(3), 183–185 (2023)
16. Dou, C.X., Ji, Y.J., Zhou, X.Y., Wang, Y.F., Yang, Q.H.: Design and application of virtual reality simulation for rehabilitation nursing of patients with cervical spondylosis under the background of new medical science. Am. J. Health Behav. **47**(2), 297–305 (2023)
17. El-Hussein, M.T., Harvey, G.: Scaffolding safety in nursing simulation: a grounded theory. J. Prof. Nurs. **45**, 14–20 (2023)
18. Evgin, D., Sumen, A.: Effect of online case-based teaching method on professional development of nursing students. Clin. Exp. Health Sci. **13**(1), 9–17 (2023)

Research on Data Center Resource Management Technology Based on Incremental Learning

Dong Cuicui[⊠]

Nanchang Institute of Technology, Nanchang 330000, China
664810006@qq.com

Abstract. An issue with erroneous result assessment exists, despite the critical significance that resource management evaluation plays in data center resource management systems. Uneven resource consumption in the data center resource management system is an issue that traditional management strategies cannot handle, and the assessment is unreasonable. This study suggests an incremental learning algorithm to assess and analyze the most effective way to manage innovation resources. To begin, the data nodes are evaluated using the three-ring theory. The indicators are then split according to the criteria of the resource management assessment in order to eliminate interference elements. Next, a resource management assessment scheme is developed and the findings are thoroughly analyzed using the three-ring theory, which assesses the management of resources in response to the ever-changing demand for data center resources. According to MATLAB simulations, incremental learning algorithms outperform conventional management technologies in terms of resource allocation, dynamically modified evaluation accuracy, and assessment time for resource management, under certain evaluation criteria.

Keywords: three-ring theory · incremental learning algorithm · resource allocation · Data Center

1 Introduction

Using ongoing data flow input and ongoing learning and updating of previous data, the incremental learning method is a dataflow-based machine learning approach that steadily improves the model's accuracy and generalization performance. A key tenet of incremental learning is the continual incorporation of fresh data into the optimization process, with the goal of increasing the data's usage value [1].

A. Application of incremental learning method in data resource management.

1. Data cleaning

Data cleaning is a crucial component of business data management. Data cleaning efficiency and accuracy may be enhanced with the help of the incremental learning approach, which updates and improves the data cleaning model via continuous learning. In addition to enhancing data quality, this may drastically cut down on data cleaning costs [2].

B. Brik and S. Nazir (Eds.): BigIoT-EDU 2024, LNICST 659, pp. 204–212, 2026.
https://doi.org/10.1007/978-3-032-18631-7_23

2. Data analysis

The backbone of business data management is data analysis. By constantly learning and updating, incremental learning may make data analysis models more accurate and reliable. In addition to enhancing analytical efficiency and decreasing corporate running expenses, incremental learning approaches provide other benefits.

3. Data forecasting

An important aspect of managing data for a business is data forecasting. By constantly learning and updating, the incremental learning approach may improve the data prediction model's accuracy and generalization performance. Better forecasting of future trends and developments is made possible, which aids in commercial decision-making [4].

B. Optimization of data resource management by incremental learning method.

1. Improve the value of data utilization

The use value and trustworthiness of data may be enhanced by optimizing and managing data resources via incremental learning. Data models may be improved and learned continually using incremental learning approaches. This leads to more efficient and high-quality data processing, which in turn helps with business operations and decision-making [5].

2. Reduce the cost of the enterprise

Businesses may cut down on operational and managerial expenses by managing and optimizing data resources via incremental learning. By eliminating the need for costly human oversight and intervention, incremental learning may automatically train and enhance data models, leading to more precise and efficient data processing [6].

3. Improve the competitiveness of enterprises

Businesses may boost their creativity and competitiveness by managing and optimizing their data resources via incremental learning. Data models may be incrementally learned and updated in order to unearth previously unseen patterns and information, which can greatly aid in the growth and innovation of businesses [7].

Incremental learning is a novel machine learning approach that has been widely used in data resource management. Our best estimate is that as technology develops and advances, incremental learning methodologies will provide new opportunities and challenges for data resource management and commercial data applications widely would be in the future[8].

Improving the utilization rate of physical resources in data centers is of tremendous importance, and data centers must immediately address the critical issue of low resource utilization via rational resource allocation and modification [9]. However, there is an issue with the resource management assessment scheme's lack of accuracy throughout the review process, leading to data center resource waste and tenant cost hikes [10]. Data center resource management system analysis using incremental learning algorithms may successfully evaluate evaluation schemes for resource management and give commensurate assistance for assessment, according to certain researchers [11, 12]. To improve the assessment scheme for resource management and to test the model's efficacy, an incremental learning method is presented on this basis [13].

.

2 Related Works

A. Mathematical description of the incremental learning algorithm

Based on the indicators in the resource management assessment, the incremental learning algorithm optimizes the scheme for evaluating resource management using the three-ring theory. It then determines the unqualified values in the data center resource management system is a_i, integrates the resource management evaluation scheme is b_i [14], before determining if the data center's resource management system is feasible is $Z(a)$, which is calculated as shown in Eq. (1).

$$Z(a) = y(a_i - b_1) \tag{1}$$

Outlier evaluation is one of them, as indicated in Eq. (2).

$$y(a_i - b_1) = a_i \prod_{i=1}^{n} c + p_{ij} + b \tag{2}$$

The incremental learning algorithm takes use of the data center's resource management system to quantify, combining the strengths of the three-ring theory; this, in turn, may enhance the assessment of resource consumption in management.

Assume first that there are criteria for evaluating resource management is x_i, the resource management evaluation scheme is n, satisfaction with the assessment program for resource management is y_i, as well as the assessment function for programs pertaining to resource management is $A(y_i)$, as shown in Eq. (3).

$$A(y_i) = \prod_{i=1}^{n} \eta + x_i + y_i \tag{3}$$

B. Selection of resource utilization scheme

Data center administration of resources system function (Second Hypothesis) is $G_l(y)$, and the weight coefficient is d, Eq. (4) shows that a non-qualified data center resource management system is required for the resource management assessment.

$$G_l(y) = \sum_{i=1}^{n} \vartheta (d - a)\iota_{ij} + wp \tag{4}$$

An all-encompassing function of resource needs may be derived from assumptions I and II, as shown in Eq. (5).

$$A(y_i) + G_l(y) \leq y(a_i - b_1) \tag{5}$$

Equation (6) shows the outcomes of standardizing all data, which is necessary to enhance the efficacy of resource management evaluations.

$$A(y_i) + G_l(y) \leftrightarrow a_i \prod_{i=1}^{n} c + p_{ij} + b \tag{6}$$

C. Analysis of resource management evaluation programs

Prior to implementing the incremental learning algorithm, it is recommended to conduct a multi-dimensional analysis of the resource management evaluation scheme, map the requirements to the data center resource management system library, and remove any unqualified schemes is $T_{ij}(a_i)$. The findings are illustrated in Eq. (7), and the anomaly assessment method may be provided according to Eq. (6).

$$T_{ij}(a_i) = \frac{A(y_i) + G_l(y)}{a_i \prod_{i=1}^{n} c + p_{ij} + b} \tag{7}$$

Among them, it is $\frac{A(y_i)+G_l(y)}{a_i \prod_{i=1}^{n} c + p_{ij} + b} \leq 1$, informed that a proposal is required for the program, or else it will have to be included into it is $V_{ij}(m)$, and the result is shown in Eq. (8).

$$V_{ij}(m) = A(y_i) + G_l(y) \tag{8}$$

After a thorough analysis of the data center's RMS, the evaluation scheme's threshold and index weights are adjusted to guarantee that the incremental learning method is accurate. In order to evaluate the data center's resource management system, which is a test system, new and creative analysis is needed. Resource management assessment schemes may be impacted by data center resource management systems that do not follow normal distributions is $unno(h_i)$, reducing the accuracy of the overall resource management evaluation is $W_i(a_i)$, and Eq. (9) displays the outcome of the computation.

$$W_i(a_i) = \frac{min[\sum A(y_i) + G_l(y)]}{\sum A(y_i) + G_l(y)} \times 100\% \tag{9}$$

According to the survey's assessment system for resource management, the resource utilization scheme displays a multi-dimensional distribution that aligns with the objective facts. Due to the lack of direction in the data center's resource management system, which suggests a highly stochastic resource usage scheme, this research is considered to be of high analytical quality. If the data center's resource management system is a completely arbitrary operation is $arcexs(c_i)$, then the calculation of Eq. (9) can be expressed as formula (10).

$$W_i(a_i) = \frac{min[\sum A(y_i) + G_l(y)]}{\sum A(y_i) + G_l(y)} \times 100\% + arcexs(c_i) \tag{10}$$

One of them is the data center resource management system, which satisfies standard requirements. The three-ring theory, in particular, modifies this system, gets rid of unnecessary and duplicate schemes, and adds to the default scheme, resulting in a robust dynamic correlation throughout the evaluation scheme for resource management.

3 Optimization Strategy of Data Center Resource Management System

By adjusting the settings of the data nodes, the incremental learning algorithm optimizes the data center resource management system using a random optimization technique. The incremental learning algorithm randomly chooses multiple schemes after dividing the data center resource management system into several tiers of assessment for resource management. Iteratively, the system for evaluating resource management is fine-tuned and studied using varying degrees of assessment. Once the optimization study is finished, you may choose the best data center resource management system by comparing the evaluation levels of various systems.

4   Results and Discussion

A. Introduction to resource management evaluation

Table 1 shows the resource management evaluation scheme for the specific data center resource management system; this paper uses the data center resource management system in complex cases as its research object; the system is tested over 12 paths with a 12-h timeframe.

Table 1. Data center resource management evaluation requirements

Scope of application	Grade	Predict the effect	Utilization rate
CPU	I	77.36	76.32
	II	79.97	76.95
memory	I	76.62	78.64
	II	80.53	80.13
node	I	79.23	80.53
	II	78.35	77.93

Table 2. Overall picture of resource utilization scenarios

Category	Rationality	Adaptability
CPU	77.57	76.89
memory	76.75	78.52
node	77.32	78.57
mean	77.41	76.86
X^6	31.26	32.75
P = 3.42		

The resource management evaluation process in Table 1 is shown in Fig. 1.

Incremental learning algorithms' resource management evaluation schemes are more in line with the needs of real resource management evaluations than those of conventional management approaches. When compared to more conventional methods of management, incremental learning algorithms provide a data center resource management

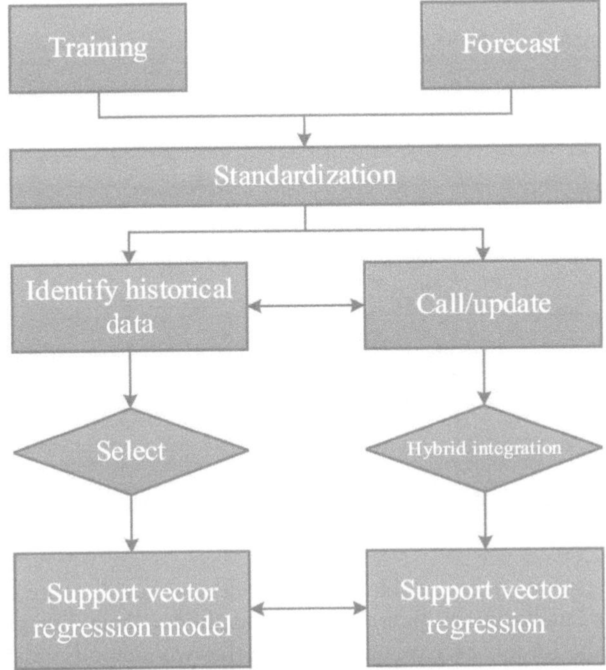

Fig. 1. Analysis process of data center resource management system

system that is more robust and resilient to fluctuations in demand. Figure I depicts a revised assessment scheme for resource management, demonstrating that the incremental learning algorithm is more stable and makes quicker judgments. Thus, the incremental learning algorithm's resource management assessment scheme is faster, more efficient, and more stable in the aggregate.

B. Data center resource management system

Information classified as either semi-structural or structural is part of the data center resource management system's assessment framework for resource management. Once an incremental learning algorithm has been pre-selected, the data center resource management system's viability may be assessed by obtaining its preliminary resource management assessment scheme. Table II shows the resource management evaluation scheme that may be used to more precisely confirm the innovative impact of a data center resource management system. To do this, choose a data center resource management system with various degrees of assessment (Table 2).

C. Resource utilization and stability of resource management evaluation

Figure 2 compares the resource management assessment scheme of conventional management technology with that of incremental learning algorithm in order to confirm the algorithm's correctness.

By comparing the two sets of data, it is clear that incremental learning algorithms outperform traditional management techniques in terms of resource utilization rate and error

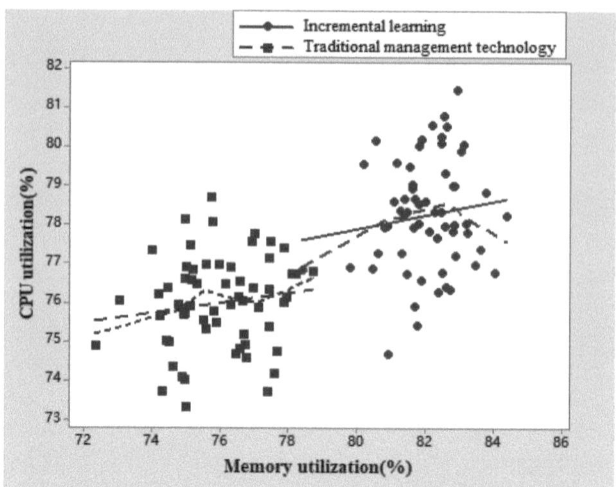

Fig. 2. Resource Utilization Of Different Algorithms

rate. This suggests that incremental learning algorithms provide more consistent evaluations of resource management than traditional methods. Table 3 displays the average assessment scheme for resource management for the two methods mentioned earlier.

Table 3. Comparison of Resource Management Evaluation Accuracy of Different Methods

Algorithm	Resource utilization	Magnitude of change	Error
Incremental learning algorithms	85.05	85.97	0.92
Traditional management techniques	76.16	79.68	3.52
P	31.61	34.29	2.72

The data center resource management system has changed a lot and has a high mistake rate, as shown in Table 3, and conventional management systems aren't very good at using resources and keeping them stable. In comparison to more conventional methods of management, incremental learning algorithms often lead to more efficient use of available resources. While maintaining essentially constant accuracy, the incremental learning algorithm uses more than 85% of available resources. As seen in Fig. 3, the incremental learning algorithm is often subjected to various analyses in order to provide more evidence of its superiority and efficacy.

Figure 3 shows that incremental learning outperforms traditional management technology in terms of resource utilization rate. This is because incremental learning raises the data center resource management system's adjustment coefficient, establishes the data node's threshold, and gets rid of evaluation schemes for resource management that don't measure up.

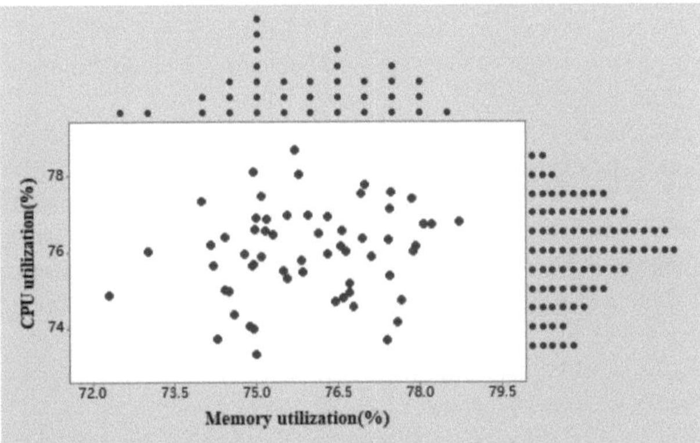

Fig. 3. Resource utilization for incremental learning algorithm resource management evaluation

5 Conclusion

This paper's goal is to improve the data center resource management system by proposing an incremental learning method and combining the three-ring theory. The resource utilization rate of the current system is not optimum. Concurrently, a data node collection is built, and there is an in-depth analysis of the threshold innovation and resource management assessment innovation. The data center resource management system can be made more accurate and stable with the help of an incremental learning algorithm, according to the research. This will allow for more precise demand-based resource allocation, more reasonable resource allocation, and more balanced utilization of all resources.

References

1. Behboudian, M., Kerachian, R., Motlaghzadeh, K., Ashrafi, S.: Application of multi-agent decision-making methods in hydrological ecosystem services management. Methodsx, 10 (2023)
2. da Silva, M.D., Gamatie, A., Sassatelli, G., Poss, M., Robert, M.: Optimization of data and energy migrations in mini data centers for carbon-neutral computing. IEEE Trans. Sustainable Comput. 8(1), 68–81 (2023)
3. Diao, H.J., Yin, L.A., Wang, L., Liang, B., Chen, Y.Y.: Sustainable multimedia service cloud platform framework based on intelligent management system. Soft Computing (2023)
4. dos Santos, P., Pinho, C.P.D., Leonte, F.I.S.: Study for the implementation of the balanced scorecard in the hospital center of west Lisbon. Revista De Gestao E Secretariado-Gesec 14(6), 9590–9614 (2023)
5. Durairaj, S., Sridhar, R.: MOM-VMP: multi-objective mayfly optimization algorithm for VM placement supported by principal component analysis (PCA) in cloud data center. Cluster Computing-the Journal of Networks Software Tools and Applications (2023)
6. Fanaei, S., Zareiyan, A., Shahraki, S., Mirzaei, A.: Determining the key performance indicators of human resource management of military hospital managers; a TOPSIS study. Bmc Primary Care 24(1) (2023)
7. Franco, L.M.Q., Lopez, R.G., Garcia, H.G., Rodriguez, J.M.D., Enguita, C.G.: Evolution and current status of the management of functional and pelvic floor pathology in the hospitals of the Community of Madrid. Actas Urol. Esp. 47(3), 187–192 (2023)

8. George, S.S., Pramila, R.S.: Fractional IWSOA-LB: fractional improved whale social optimization based VM migration strategy for load balancing in cloud computing. Int. J. Wireless Inf. Networks **30**(1), 58–74 (2023)
9. Guo, C., Zukerman, M., Wang, T.J.: Radar: reliable resource scheduling for composable/disaggregated data centers. IEEE Trans. Industr. Inf. **19**(8), 8551–8563 (2023)
10. Guo, Z. L., Li, J., Ramesh, R.: Green data analytics of supercomputing from massive sensor networks: does workload distribution matter? Inf. Syst. Res. (2023)
11. Halford, F.K., Ables, D.M.: The National Cultural Resources Information Management System (NCRIMS) New Horizons for cultural resources data management and analyses. Adv. Archaeol. Pract. **11**(1), 52–62 (2023)
12. Hamm, M.F.A., Jofri, M.H., Kadir, N.A.A., Meerengani, K.A., Sharipp, M.T.M., Suyurno, S.: Enhancing Quality of Experience (QoE) in IM-Tahfiz Framework for predictive acceptance influence of user screening test. Islamiyyat-the Int. J. Islamic Stud. **45**(1), 59–68 (2023)
13. Hogade, N., Pasricha, S.: A survey on machine learning for geo-distributed cloud data center managements. IEEE Trans. Sustainable Comput. **8**(1), 15–31 (2023)
14. Isa, F.M., Noor, S., Mohammad, N.M.N.: Critical issues of human resource management in ageing care centres: case of Malaysia. J. Health Manag. **25**(2), 382–392 (2023)

University Research Management and Decision Analysis System Based on Data Warehouse

HaoYue Gao[✉]

School of Experimental Art, Tianjin Academy of Fine Arts, Tianjin 300402, China
haoyuecamila@163.com

Abstract. Scientific research management is the main way to improve the competitiveness of universities, and data warehouse has a significant impact on the promotion and development of scientific research. However, the establishment of data storage needs to focus on two aspects, data storage technology analysis and application, so the data warehouse needs to be optimized. In order to solve this problem, this paper proposes a data warehouse analysis method and synthesizes scientific research results to realize data sharing. The experimental results show that: 1) the analysis and management of warehousing data can effectively improve the scientific research management ability of universities, with an improvement rate of more than 15%; 2) The data structure and data sharing within the data warehouse are significantly optimized; 3) Data storage analysis has a significant positive impact on scientific research, improves the competitiveness of universities, and increases the degree of influence by 20%; 4) The overall effect of data storage reaches more than 90%, indicating that the relationship between scientific research management and warehousing and application in universities is very close, which can promote the development of scientific research in universities.

Keywords: Dataset Theory · Data Warehousing · Management and Decision Analysis System · Universities · Scientific Research Management

1 Introduction

The process of scientific research and development (R&D) is essentially the improvement of teaching effectiveness, including practical innovation and practical application. However, scientific research data are fragmented and diverse, and cannot be effectively utilized, so proposing an effective method is a key focus and current research hotspot [1, 2]. At present, data collection and database construction in scientific research practice can provide support for related research [3, 4]. Some scholars believe that manual data management, LAN data management, and other traditional methods are not enough to meet the actual needs of scientific research in universities. The data storage, data sharing mechanism, data encryption, and optimization of overall scientific research data have become the focus of current research. Specifically, this study proposes to integrate databases, computing, teaching, and management technologies for comprehensive

B. Brik and S. Nazir (Eds.): BigIoT-EDU 2024, LNICST 659, pp. 213–223, 2026.
https://doi.org/10.1007/978-3-032-18631-7_24

evaluation and judgment [5, 6], and initially construct a scientific research framework scientific research data utilization. Data warehouses can generate standardized analytical content and reliable datasets to support researchers at different levels. Data warehousing can fully implement systematic data storage, management, and analysis, and establish correlation with university research achievements [7, 8]. In order to further promote warehousing construction, universities should classify scientific research data, establish standards for data structure and content system, provide guidance for researchers, institutions, and related personnel, and assist in decision-making and analysis [9, 10].

2 Related Concepts

2.1 The Data Warehouse is Described Mathematically.

The scientific research process is to carry out practical research, integrate theory and practice, and the integration conditions are strict, so a warehousing database can be established to achieve information sharing and avoid duplicate operations. It is y_i found that the unqualified value parameters is z_i, and the management is $\text{tol}(y_i \cdot t_{ij})$ integrated evaluate the comprehensiveness and integrity of scientific research activities, and the calculation is shown in Eq. (1).

$$\lim_{x \to \infty} (y_i \cdot t_{ij}) = \frac{n!}{r!(n-r)!} y_{ij} \geq \max(t_{ij}/2) \tag{1}$$

The correlation between scientific research data forms an effective fusion of data (2).

$$\max(t_{ij}) = \partial\left(t_{ij}^2 + 2 \cdot t_{ij}\right) \succ \sqrt{2}\left(\sum t_{ij} + 4\right)M \tag{2}$$

The audio, and files exist in the data warehouse, which has a complex structure and a large amount of data. Whether the content and form meet the requirements also requires in-depth judgment. Form is t_i that is set_i, the technique is y_i, and the is $F(t_i \approx 0)$ as shown by Eq. (3).

$$F(d_i) = \prod \sum t_i \bigcap \xi \cdot \sqrt{2} \to \oint y_i \cdot 7 \tag{3}$$

2.2 Selection of Management and Decision Analysis System Scheme

Specifically, it is necessary to verify whether the scientific research data analysis is methodologically reasonable and whether it meets the preset research requirements, because these two aspects are the core prerequisites for verifying the reliability of the research process. This study establishes a dataset for scientific research and analysis, denoted as $g(t_i)$. The weighting factor is w_i. Comprehensive analysis of the comprehensive formation conditions of scientific research and the rationality of the analysis need to be constrained (4).

$$g(t_i) = \ddot{x} \cdot z_i \prod F(d_i)\frac{dy}{dx} - w_i \Phi \tag{4}$$

In the process of storing science and technology warehouses, the scientific and technological content should be analyzed to judge its analysis effect, as shown in Eq. (5).

$$\lim_{x \to \infty} g(t_i) + F(d_i) \leq \bigcap \max(t_{ij}) \tag{5}$$

For the actual situation of teachers and the conditions of scientific and technological output, the corresponding level of content and experimental specifications are selected to promote the scientific and technological content to meet the corresponding requirements, and the specific evaluation results are shown in Eq. (6).

$$\overline{g(t_i) + F(d_i)} \leftrightarrow \sqrt{b^2 - 4ac}\left(\sum t_{ij} + 4\right) \tag{6}$$

2.3 Analysis of the Management and Decision-Making Analysis System Scheme

The effective implementation of comprehensive scientific and technological conditions for content technology effects, and the outcomes are shown in Eq. (7). $No(t_i)$.

$$No(t_i) = \frac{\overline{g(t_i) + F(d_i)}}{mean\left(\sum t_{ij} + 4\right)} \sqrt{b^2 - 4ac} \tag{7}$$

Among them, it is $\frac{g(t_i) + F(d_i)}{mean(\sum t_{ij} + 4)} \leq 1$ specified that the scheme must be $Zh(t_i)$ suggested; otherwise, the scheme integration is necessary; the outcome is illustrated in Eq. (8).

$$Zh(t_i) = \lim_{x \to \infty}\left[\sum \overline{g(t_i) + F(d_i)}\right] \lim_{x \to \infty} \tag{8}$$

The management and decision analysis system is $accur(t_i)$ thoroughly examined, In the actual implementation process, the results and the overall effect and content of science and technology are judged, and the effectiveness of science and technology implementation is analyzed. Teachers carry out practical scientific research and data sharing in the process of transforming scientific research results. In the process of data sharing, data matching should also be carried out according to the conditions of scientific and technological research at the scientific and technological level to form dynamic data sharing $unno(t_i)$, as specifically calculated in Eq. (9).

$$accur(t_i) = \frac{\min\left[\sum \overline{g(t_i) + F(d_i)}\right]}{\sum \overline{g(t_i) + F(d_i)}} \times 100\% \tag{9}$$

Verify the integrity of scientific and technological data and the rationality of scientific and technological data, and effectively manage data. Necessary data content Data conditions make overall judgments on data relevance, data coupling and scientific research effects, and form corresponding knowledge protection. $randon(t_i)$ The calculation process described in Eq. (9) can then be further expressed as Eq. (10).

$$accur(t_i) = \frac{\min\left[\sum \overline{g(t_i) + F(d_i)}\right]}{\frac{1}{2}\sum \overline{g(t_i) + F(d_i)}} + randon(t_i) \tag{10}$$

The implementation process of data warehouse mainly completes several aspects, data collation, data mechanism, data integrity, and data sharing. Its purpose is to use necessary data analysis for different researchers to improve the rationality of data.

3 Management and Decision Analysis System Optimization Approach

Scientific research management and comprehensive analysis of scientific research content are important links in the self-improvement of universities. The industry-university-research structure and the integration of enterprise-based research content and data can support researchers. In the initial stage of scientific research, it can provide data inspiration for researchers to write papers and research scientific research projects. In the intermediate stage, it can assist researchers to carry out standardized experiments and standardized development to ensure that scientific research projects can be applied practically. In the later stage, assist researchers to protect relevant knowledge points and scientific research content. Therefore, data warehouse management plays an important role in scientific research management, as well as in teaching and overall development processes. Its purpose is to realize data sharing and comprehensive support of data, and improve the knowledge application of scientific researchers in comprehensive analysis, as well as the overall structure and data application.

4 Practical Examples of Management and Decision Analysis System

4.1 Introduction to the Management and Decision Analysis System

Knowledge management is divided into different stages, but its main purpose is data collection, data sharing and comprehensive analysis to support scientific research results, are shown in Table 1.

Table 1. Requirements of the Management and Decision-Making Analysis System

Scope of application	Data planning	Scientific research	Sharing
Research project management	Database	89.97	88
	Scientific research decision-making	90.76	90.59
Scientific resource management	Database	91.55	88.23
	Scientific research decision-making	90.54	91.38
Research Guidelines	Database	92.4	89.85
	Scientific research decision-making	89.5	88.64

According to the data integrity and overall analysis results in Table 1, the establishment of scientific research data warehouse has a high degree of rationality, and more than 80% of the data can provide a foundation for scientific research in universities. The process of warehouse establishment, the relevant details are shown in Fig. 1.

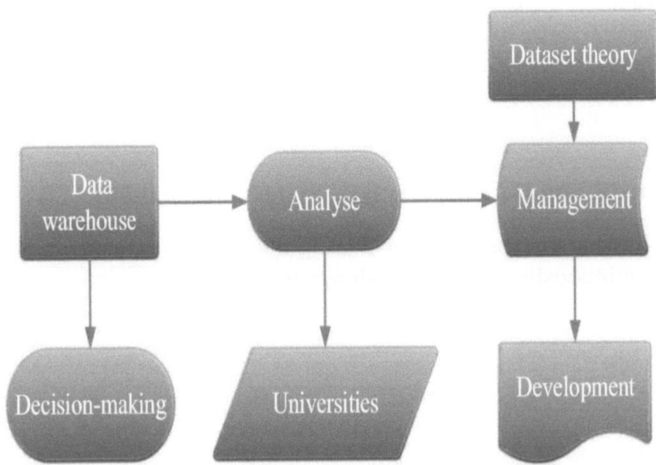

Fig. 1. The process of establishing scientific research storage data

For the dataset in Fig. 1, the research project, the content of the scientific research, and the overall nature of the scientific research can be planned, and the data should be established based on it. Video, image, text and other contents are synthesized to achieve the overall combination of scientific research, data, and warehousing, complete data sharing, and provide support for the implementation of scientific research.

4.2 Decision-Making Effect of Scientific Research Projects

The use of content, as well as the relationship between data sharing and scientific research projects, and the overall planning of scientific research practice are a development trend in the process of scientific research analysis, which plays an important supporting role in the development of competitive teaching in colleges and universities. Each indicator needs to be investigated, and the specific findings are shown in Table 2.

Table 2. The overall situation of the management and decision analysis system scheme

category	The completion rate of scientific research projects	Rationality of scientific research	Accuracy of decision-making
Research project management	88.26	88.61	89.25

(*continued*)

Table 2. (*continued*)

category	The completion rate of scientific research projects	Rationality of scientific research	Accuracy of decision-making
Scientific resource management	87.6	88.93	92.39
Research Guidelines	85.58	87.69	88.1

4.3 Management and Decision Analysis System and Stability

The changes in data storage and data sharing during the implementation of scientific research are continuously analyzed, as shown in Fig. 2.

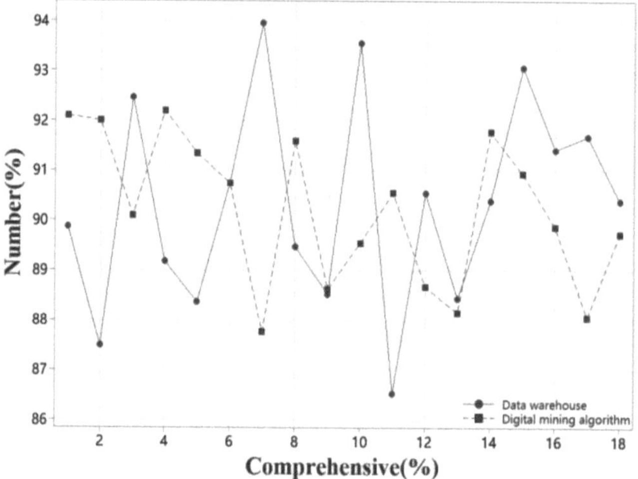

Fig. 2. Management and decision of aging performance of different algorithms

Figure 2 shows that there is a fluctuation between scientific research projects and data warehousing, and there is an effective correlation between the two, and the volatility between the completion rate of scientific research projects and the force of data warehousing is a volatility change. For the specific changes in scientific research projects, see Table 3.

Table 3. Compares the accuracy of several management and decision analysis system.

Algorithm	Journal publication	Scientific research competitiveness of universities	Scientific research projects	Project conversion rate
D	88.84	86.61	89.23	86.38
Digital mining algorithms	89.03	87.87	90.96	93.3
P	88.36	90.43	90.69	90.33

Table 3 shows that the conversion rate of scientific research projects and university competitiveness projects is greater than 80%, indicating that data storage can lay the foundation for the improvement of scientific research capabilities of universities, and realize data sharing and effective correlation of data. The relevant details are shown in Fig. 3.

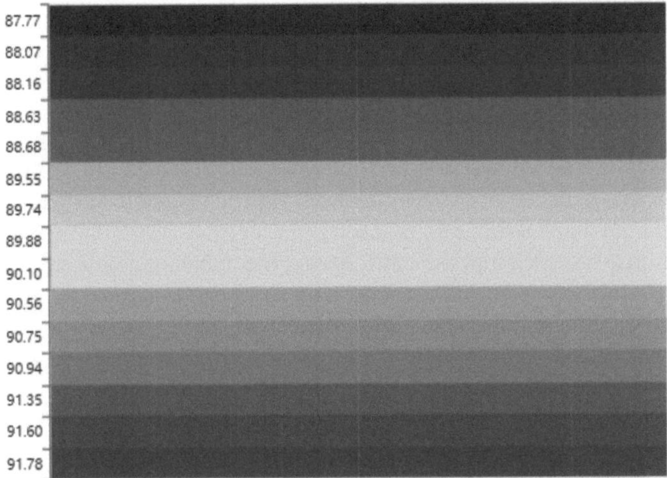

Fig. 3. The role of data warehouses on scientific research projects

Figure III shows that with the help of scientific research data, scientific research projects can be classified into levels. According to the corresponding level, video, literature, and data support is carried out to improve the relationship between teachers and scientific research projects, as well as the practical conversion rate, and complete the specific practical transformation process of scientific research projects.

4.4 Scientific Research Sharing Capabilities of Data Warehouses

The purpose of the establishment of scientific research data storage is to improve scientific research capabilities and scientific research data sharing, and reduce repetitive operations and unnecessary processing processes. The information about the sharing rate is shown in Fig. 4.

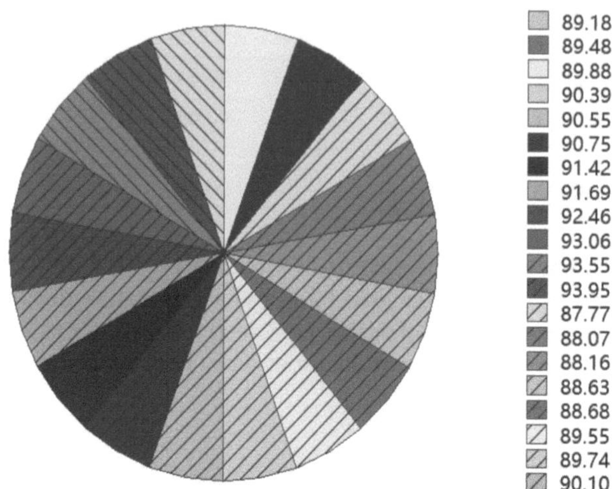

Fig. 4. The role of scientific research warehousing data on scientific research projects

Figure 4 shows that after the establishment of scientific research warehousing data, its competitiveness and completion of the entire scientific research project are completed. Its function is to equally show that the scientific research storage data has strong objectivity, and the data distribution is strictly in accordance with the governance mechanism of scientific research and the data sharing mechanism, and there is no personnel interference. Therefore, scientific research data storage can ensure the effectiveness of scientific research data and the objectivity of relevant data.

4.5   The Overall Effect of Scientific Research Project Decision-Making

The purpose of comprehensive analysis of the project is to improve the integrity of scientific research, and the development of scientific research projects and the whole can be judged by the penetration process of their infiltration forms, as shown in Fig. 5.

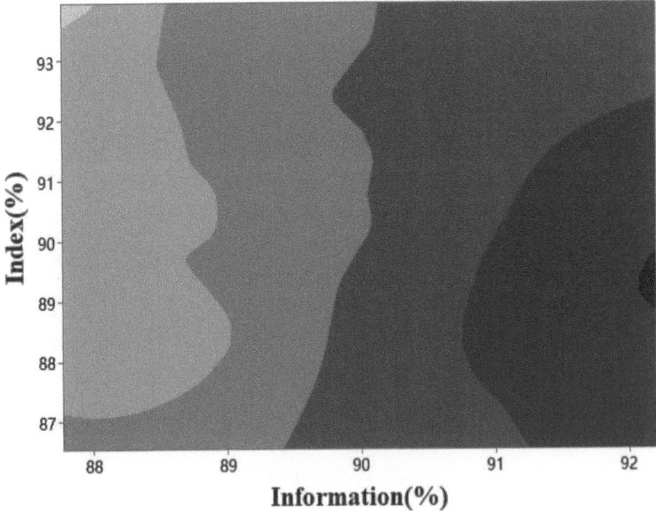

Fig. 5. Management and decision analysis system of different algorithms

Figure 5 illustrates the effective penetration between the scientific research data storage process and the competitiveness of scientific research project teachers in universities. Although it has clear boundaries, the integration effect between them is ideal. The specific summary results are shown in Table 4.

Table 4. Improvement of scientific research capacity of data storage

algorithm	Feasibility Project	Scientific research capabilities of universities	Teachers' scientific research ability	Comprehensive scientific research projects
Data warehouse	87.77	88.6	89.03	91.21
Digital mining algorithms	90.37	88.19	89.95	89.68
P	87.39	88.32	90.23	88.98

Table 4 shows that the implementation environment and implementation conditions of data and scientific research content are reasonably planned. The scientific research data warehouse can carry out effective data division and assist scientific research projects in decision-making according to the implementation of scientific research, the goal of improving competitiveness, and the participation of teachers, as shown in Fig. 6.

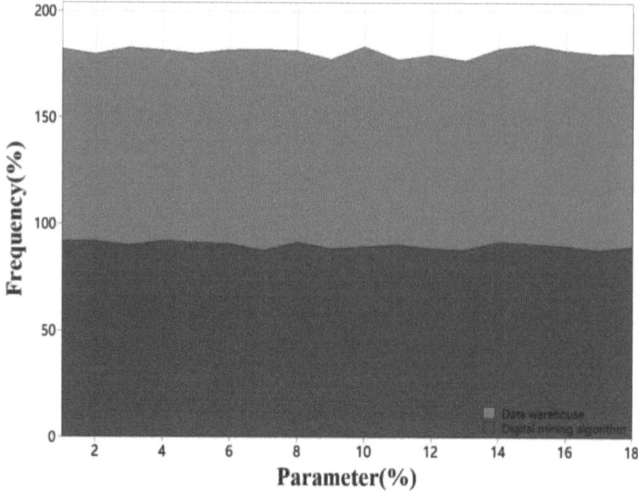

Fig. 6. The management and decision analysis system

Figure 6 shows that the fluctuations between data in the process of scientific research projects and warehousing data analysis, as well as the consistent changes in data demand and sharing, indicate that scientific research warehousing data can provide support for scientific research projects and the implementation of scientific research, and provide a guarantee for the competitiveness of universities.

5   Conclusion

The project is an important means for colleges and universities to improve their comprehensive competitiveness, and it is also the main way for college teachers to carry out self-improvement and project research. Based on scientific research data, it can promote the completion projects, realize the transformation, and bring scientific research results to society. The main purpose of data is to avoid repetitive operations and repetitive formulation of projects, although the rationality of data is closely related to the effective implementation of projects.

The data storage can promote the effective management of scientific research projects, ensure the implementation, improve the accuracy of project completion by more than 20%, and increase the bidding success rate of scientific research projects to 80%. This proves that scientific research data storage can provide support in colleges and universities and the completion of projects, and promote the integration of universities and projects. However, there are certain shortcomings in this study, mainly the establishment and authorization of data in scientific research sites, which have not been fully permitted, and the verification rate relevant data will be increased in the future.

References

1. Jin, J.: The application and research of big data correlation technology in university data warehouse information management systems Yangtze River Information and Communication (2023)
2. Wang, X.: Design of University Decision Support System Based on Data Warehouse (8) (2022)
3. Jiayi, L.: Research on the Application of Data Warehouse Technology in College Employment Decision Technology Information (014), 020 (2022)
4. Liwei, S.: Data management methods and systems based on financial cloud data warehouses and data lakes CN202111495550.1 (2022)
5. Chen, M.: Data warehouse and data mining technology for fault diagnosis of ship power systems. J. Shanghai Inst. Ship Transp. Sci. **45**(3), 8 (2022)
6. Li, H., Sun, N.: Data uniqueness identification method, device, electronic device, and storage medium CN116383196A (2023)
7. Wei, Q., Duan, G., Cai, J., Zhou, G.: The step model is implemented based on relational database mapping in a data warehouse (5) (2022)
8. Zhao, Y.: Design and Implementation of Beijing Real Estate Registration Special Data Warehouse Based on Elastic Search Beijing Surveying and Mapping (2023)
9. Li, J.: Research on big data audit methods based on data warehouse technology. Audit Abstract (5), 2 (2022)
10. Liu, X., Li, M., Xiong, C., Qin, H., Liu, X.: Research and implementation of building a high availability data warehouse based on Hadoop modern. Inf. Technol. **7**(1), 99–101 (2023)
11. Mengche: Design of public finance data analysis system based on data warehouse. Digit. Technol. Appl. **41**(3), 187–189 (2023)
12. Ye, Z.: A tobacco inventory decision support system based on data warehouse. China Inf. (7), 80–81 (2022)
13. Zhang, Y., Hu, Z.: Research on an AI based energy consumption operation management system for computer rooms. Commun. Inf. Technol. (2), 80–83 (2023)

The Design Theory of Music Education System for Higher Education Teachers Under Data Technology

Fenglei Wang[✉]

Department of Music, Xinxiang University, Xinxiang 453000, Henan, China
15617175585@163.com

Abstract. Digital technology plays an auxiliary role in music teaching, but whether it can play a role and improve the educational effect is controversial. The combination of music creation and digital logic relationship is analyzed and judged to achieve its effective optimization. Find out the fusion point, and the results show that the rationality between music creation and digital logic is relatively good, more than 75%. Moreover, the integration content and conditions are deepened, and the deepening degree is greater than 30%. Therefore, the rationality between the relationship between music creation and digital logic is relatively good, and the improvement range is large, which meets the needs of actual analysis.

Keywords: Statistical set theory · data technology; Music Education for Higher Education; System Design Theory

1 Introduction

The importance of the theoretical research on education system design in music education for higher education teachers is self-evident [1]. And the diversified analysis of digital technology to comprehensively realize the integration of music education and music teaching [2]. The traditional research scheme of education system design theory has certain deficiencies in accuracy, which limits its effect in practical application [3]. The accuracy of traditional [4] education system design theory research, researchers have introduced data technology into the research and analysis of education[5] system design theory in recent years. Data technology is a computational method based on group behavior that simulates [6] the interaction and cooperation between individuals to achieve the goal of global optimization. The algorithm has the characteristics of decentralization, immutability and smart contract [7], which can effectively solve the accuracy problems existing in traditional schemes. The optimization model [8] of education system design theory research based on data technology further improves the accuracy and reliability of simulation by optimizing the parameters [9] and algorithms in the research process of education system design theory. The model adjusts and optimizes the various [10] parameters in this process to achieve the best theoretical effect of the system design. At

B. Brik and S. Nazir (Eds.): BigIoT-EDU 2024, LNICST 659, pp. 224–230, 2026.
https://doi.org/10.1007/978-3-032-18631-7_25

the same time, the model is able to cope with complex environments [11] and interference factors, providing more realistic and reliable simulation results. Researchers use the effectiveness of the optimization model for the theoretical study of educational [12] system design based on data technology [13].

2 Theoretical Model Construction for Theoretical Research on Education System Design

Music education content is $\vec{B}$, educational outcomes is $\vec{s}$, overall changes can be referred $\left(\vec{\sigma} \cdot \vec{s}\right)\vec{s} - r^2\vec{\sigma}$ to Eqs. (1) and (2).

$$\vec{B} = -\frac{\mu_0}{4\pi}\vec{\nabla}\frac{\vec{\sigma} \cdot \vec{s}}{s^3} = \frac{\mu_0}{4\pi s^5}\left[3(\vec{\sigma} \cdot \vec{s})\vec{s} - r^2\vec{\sigma}\right] \tag{1}$$

$$\vec{s} = r\hat{e}_r + (z_{20} - u - z_1)\hat{e}_z \tag{2}$$

Data technology of education system design theory to quantify, which can improve the accuracy of education system design theory research. Planning and analyzing the conditions and holistic nature of music analysis is as follows:

$$\vec{B} = \frac{\mu_0\sigma}{4\pi}\left(\frac{3r(z_c - z)\hat{e}_r - (r^2 - 2(z_c - z)^2)\hat{e}_z}{(r^2 + (z_c - z)^2)^{5/2}}\right) \tag{3}$$

Qualifications for education is Φ_z set, and the logical relationship of creation is $z_c - z$ described as follows:

$$\Phi_z = \int_0^{2\pi}\int_0^r \vec{B}\,\hat{e}_z(rdrd\theta) = \frac{\mu_0\sigma}{2}\frac{r^2}{(r^2 + (z_c - z)^2)^{3/2}} \tag{4}$$

Music education is analyzed with actual needs and comprehensive content, and the results is shown in Eq. (5).

$$\theta_e = -N_c\xi\frac{d\Phi_a}{du} = N_c\xi\frac{d\Phi_a}{d(z_c - z)} \tag{5}$$

The overall structure of musical digital creation, it is necessary to standardize all data, and the results is shown in Eq. (6).

$$\theta_e = \frac{N_c\xi\mu_0\sigma}{2A_c}\sum_{i,j=1}^2 (-1)^{i+j} \tag{6}$$

Considering the changes of music, the integrity of music is $No(t_i mii$ shown in Eq. (7).

$$No(t_i m\ddot{u} = F_z - c\dot{u} - ku \tag{7}$$

The grade of education is $\overline{k}_e^2$, the comprehensiveness of education is $u(t)$ shown in Eq. (8).

$$\overline{k}_e^2 = \frac{\omega_r}{2\pi} \int_{t_0}^{t_0+(2\pi/\omega_r)} k_e^2(u(t))dt \tag{8}$$

According to the above research on the theory of education system design, the continuous operator of the theoretical study of education system design is ζ obtained, and the calculation results is F_z shown in Eq. (9).

$$2\omega_n(\zeta + \zeta_p + \zeta_e)\dot{u} + \omega_{nr}^2 u = \frac{F_z}{m} \tag{9}$$

Among them, the performance coefficient of the theoretical study of the education system is designed, as shown in Eq. (10).

$$B = \frac{1}{n_1 n_2} \sum_{i=1}^{n_1} \sum_{j=1}^{n_2} \frac{1}{\pi r_i^2} \Phi_z(r_i, z_j) \tag{10}$$

The above-mentioned contents and forms of music education plan and analyze the structure and content of music education as a whole, and improve the overall efficiency of English education.

3 Practical Examples of Theoretical Studies of Education System Design

3.1 Theories of Education System Design, Research and Model Construction

Simulate the theoretical research process of education system design, as shown in Fig. 1.

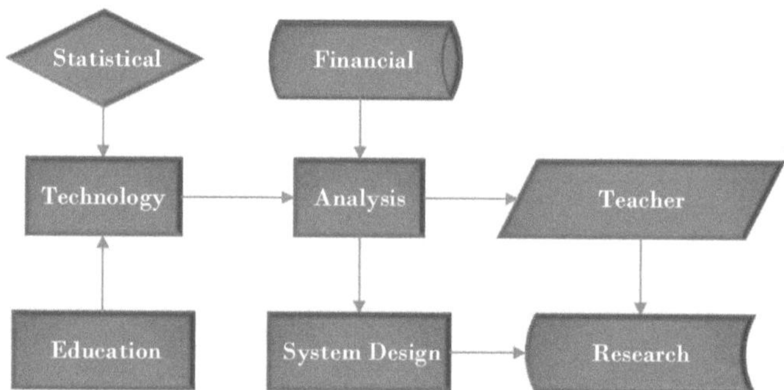

Fig. 1. The analytical process of theoretical research on the design of educational systems

Education is a continuous analysis process, but in the process of music education, it is also necessary to collect corresponding data to meet the actual needs and enhance the interest in learning. The learning content is comprehensive and legal, the overall structure of music education is learned, and then the diversified analysis of music education is realized.

3.2   Research on the Theory of Education System Design

Music education is based on the profession, and questionnaires and interviews are conducted for economic judgment and analysis to improve the integrity of music education, as shown in the table below (Table 1.).

Table 1. Performance of various data on education.

Category	Content	Structure of attention	The style of music	The overall form of music
Researcher	90.41	91.26	94.74	91.38
Management and referrals	94.54	92.73	92.38	88.99
Data Collection	90.89	92.87	89.93	91.09
Processing and analysis	88.25	95.54	93.89	90.27

3.3   Theoretical Research and Stability of Education System Design

To achieve the stability of the system design theory system, the following strategies are usually required: Education system design theory research continuous performance monitoring: real-time monitoring of system performance and user behavior in order to detect potential problems in time and make adjustments. The theory of education system design studies load balancing: the reasonable allocation of system resources and search load can improve the pressure resistance and stability of the system. Regular maintenance and update of education system design theory: Regularly maintain and update the system, fix known problems, and enhance system stability, design is shown in Fig. 2.

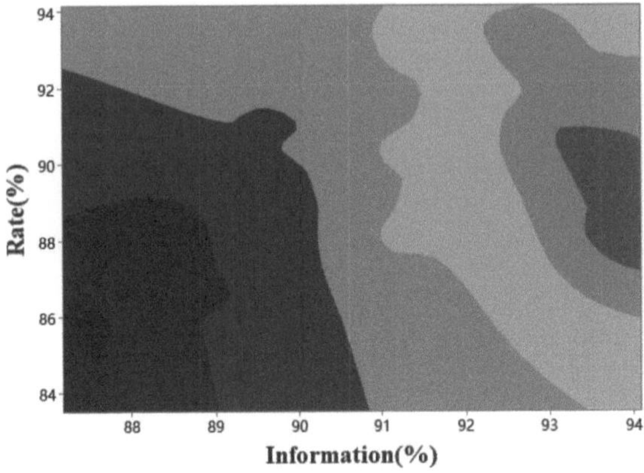

Fig. 2. Theoretical research on the design of educational systems with different algorithms

As can be seen from the analysis in Fig. 2, music education is integrated with digital education and digital technology. The core point of English education and the core point of digital education present a cross-integration mode, which shows that technology plays a role in the process of music education, and can enhance the overall form of music education, optimize the content of music education, judge each point in music education, form a multi-surface form and analysis of music education, and complete the diversification of music education. The specific analysis process is shown in Fig. 3.

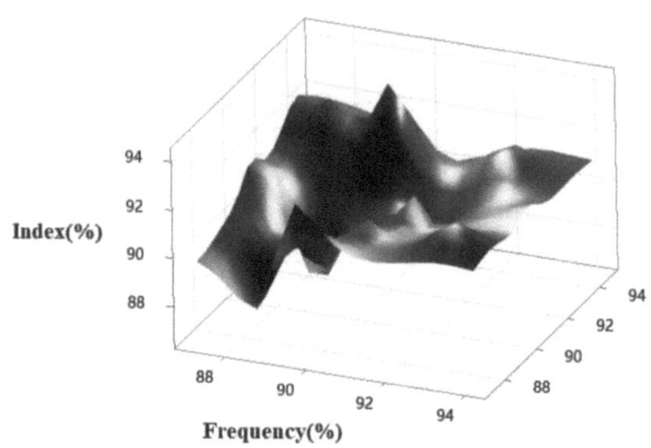

Fig. 3. Research on the theory of education system design based on data technology

Figure 3 shows the experimental results of using data technology to obtain better performance than the improved k-means algorithm in the theoretical study of education system design. There may be several key factors that make data technology outstanding: Introduction of adjustment coefficients: In system design theory process simulations, data technology may introduce adjustment coefficients to fine-tune the parameters in the simulation process. In the process of diversified analysis of music education, its educational content and results also need a continuous comprehensive process. As shown in Table 2.

Table 2. Rationalization and comparison of different approaches to education system design theory

Algorithm	Music Education Data Acquisition Point	The dispersion of the results	Justification of educational outcomes	The improvement of education	The emphasis of educational content	Actual fullness of education
Data technology	642	0.5008	0.6350	0.5722 ~ 0.6294	0.6362	1.3513
Improved k-means algorithm	631	0.6985	3.6818	0.5700 ~ 0.7270	0.2542	4.2704

From the analysis in Table 2, it can be seen that in the process of music education, comprehensive education and multi-content analysis of multiple indicators, their coincidence values are relatively good, and there is no significant difference between them, indicating that digital technology has been very deepened in the form and content of music education. Moreover, digital education also plays a subtle role in the process analysis, improving the form and content of education. However, in the process of analysis, it is also necessary to continuously track the overall change trend of music education and judge the ratio of digital technology and music education, the change process is shown in Fig. 4.

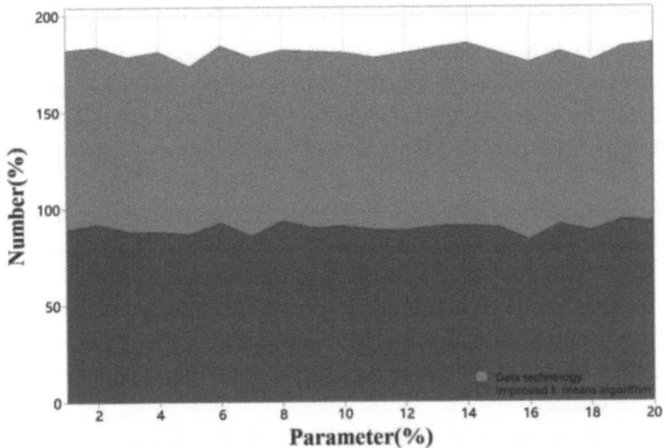

Fig. 4. Digital convergence of music creation

It is evident from Fig. 4 that the theoretical study of the design of educational systems using data technology far outperforms the design using the improved k-means algorithm in terms of performance. This significant gap is mainly due to the fact that data technology introduces a special moderation coefficient in the theoretical research process of education system design. The introduction of this coefficient enhances the flexibility and adaptability of the algorithm, allowing it to better adjust the strategy according to different situations. In addition, data technology sets a specific threshold for the processing of information on the Internet. Through this threshold setting, the algorithm can effectively identify and exclude those educational system design theory research schemes that do not meet the predetermined standards. This intelligent screening mechanism makes the data technology more efficient when processing a large number of candidates, ensuring that only the best meets the requirements is selected to continue to participate in the further design and evaluation phases.

4   Conclusion

There is a correlation between applied education and digital education, but whether digital education has a sustainable effect on applied education requires further judgment and analysis. The results show that English education and mathematics education form an effective integration because of the concentration of education. The technological improvement of architectural digital education, the influence of its content differentiation period style, makes it more in line with the requirements with its creative form. More than 80%, which shows that under the action of mathematics education, applied education has changed significantly. However, there may be some shortcomings in the research, mainly in the samples and styles of music education industry chain, which will make up for the above shortcomings in the future.

References

1. Jiang, L. Exploring the Integration Path of Music Theory Curriculum in Normal Universities from the Perspective of New Liberal Arts: Taking the Course of Western Music History and Masterpiece Appreciation as an Example Chinese Music Education, vol. (6), p. 7 (2022)
2. Liu, J., Wang, X.: Research on the reform of music theory curriculum in normal universities from the perspective of "Chinese Music School" Art Research: J. Art at Harbin Normal Univ.. (3), 4–6 (2023)
3. Kuang, Y., Li, Y.: Research on response strategies for music education in normal universities under the influence of the "Double Reduction". Policy Chin. Univ. Teach. (11), 48–52 (2022)
4. Zhang, X.: Research on the Curriculum Design and Teaching of Music Education in Normal Universities from the Perspective of Employment Music Education and Creation (4), 4 (2022)
5. Wei, W.: Research on music education and teaching in higher normal universities based on core competencies in the music discipline. J. Nanning Normal University: Philos. Soc. Sci. Edition **43**(3), 13 (2022)
6. Zhang, P., Lv, L.: Research on the Application of Siphon Rainwater Drainage System Technology and Building Water Supply and Drainage Design China Science and Technology Journal Database Industry A (011), 000 (2023)
7. Liu, F., Han, Y.: Research on Key Technologies for Network Security of Railway Design Enterprise Management Information System Railway Computer Applications **32** (11), 68–72 (2023)
8. Gao, H., Yang, J., Zhang, K., Li, H.: Design and experimental research of 921a steel crack detection system based on ACFM Manufacturing Technology and Machine Tools (12), 150–157 (2023)
9. Huang, D., Huang, W., Hu, X., Liu, L.: Social Work Intervention in College Ideological and Political Education from the Perspective of Ecosystem Theory: A Practical Exploration Based on Community Building Frontiers in Educational Research 3(1) (2023)
10. Wang Yihong's foliage A correlation study on the improvement of practical skills in music education majors in normal universities under the new curriculum reform - taking piano lessons as an example The House of Drama (29), 173–175 (2022)
11. Zhou, Y., Cao, J.: Research on the O2O model of music education in normal universities under the Track framework People's Music (2), 4 (2022)
12. Wang, Z., Wang, Y.: Research on the Construction of a Case Library for the "Ideological and Political - Aesthetic Education" Course in Music Majors of Higher Normal Schools in Ethnic Minority Areas Chinese Science and Technology Journal Database Research (8), 3 (2022)
13. Han, M., Huang, H.: Exploration of Teaching Graduation Thesis (Design) in Normal University Music Education Meimei (10), 0163–0165 (2022)

The English Teaching Mode of Colleges and Universities Has Been Improved Under the Background of Information Technology

Hui Li[✉]

Ordos Institute of Technology, Ordos City 017000, Inner Mongolia Autonomous Region, China
eyydzblihui@oit.edu.cn

Abstract. While the mode of instruction plays a crucial role in university English classes, the results of these classes are often disappointing. Teaching English as a foreign language in a university setting using the conventional wisdom is both ineffective and illogical. As a result, the research suggests using IT to assess the method of instruction. The first step in reducing the teaching mode as an intervening factor is to use the teaching results as an evaluation of the teaching mode. The indicators are then divided according to the needs of the teaching mode. Afterwards, the model's outcomes inform the model's planning, which in turn evaluates the English teaching method at higher education institutions. Perform an exhaustive investigation. The impact of IT on college English classroom practices may be shown by MATLAB simulations, provided that certain assessment criteria are met. This method of instruction is more practical than the conventional one.

Keywords: teaching outcomes · information technology · English teaching in colleges and universities · Teaching mode

1 Introduction

There have been a lot of new opportunities and challenges that have been brought to English teaching as a result of the development of information technology [1]. It is possible to say that information technology has become an important driver for the development of English teaching, which has promoted the modernization and internationalization of English teaching [2]. One of the topics that will be covered in this article is the enhancement of information technology in English language instruction.

A. Improvements in English language teaching by information technology.

1. Utilization of multimedia pedagogical tools

Multimedia tools, including audio recordings, videos, PowerPoint presentations [3], images, etc., have become more popular in English language classrooms as the use of computers and the Internet has grown. Students' listening, speaking, reading, and writing skills, as well as their interest in and ability to learn English, can all benefit from multimedia instruction, which can also optimize the English teaching process and bring about classroom diversity and innovation [4].

B. Brik and S. Nazir (Eds.): BigIoT-EDU 2024, LNICST 659, pp. 231–239, 2026.
https://doi.org/10.1007/978-3-032-18631-7_26

2. How voice recognition and NLP technologies are being used

Natural language processing and speech recognition are two of the most talked-about IT technologies right now [5]. These tools have the potential to revolutionize the way we teach English by allowing for the automated detection and assessment of both spoken and written English. By using voice recognition and natural language processing technologies, students may have their grammar and pronunciation mistakes quickly corrected [6], allowing them to acquire the ability to speak and write English more quickly [7].

3. Using VR software

Virtual reality technology remains one of the most promising technologies in computing, which can realize the simulation and reproduction of the actual setting, providing a more intuitive and vivid teaching method for English teaching [8]. Through use from virtual reality equipment, students can have a more intuitive understanding of the past, present, and everyday living habits of the English-speaking locations [9], so that the pupils can have a deeper understanding of the societal and cultural context of countries that speak English, so as to enhance their English communication ability and cultural literacy.

4. Using a platform for online courses

The online course platform is a web-based learning environment that facilitates the launch of online courses and gives students a space to work on their skills and network with one another [10]. Students are able to study English whenever and wherever they like by utilizing the online course platform, which allows them to make the most of their limited free time.

5. Mobile learning applications

Mobile learning is a new style of learning that can be learned anytime, anywhere, and incorporates the use of resources such as mobile devices and smartphones[11]. Through the app of mobile education, learners no longer need to go to the education for classroom instruction, and can learn language anytime, anywhere through mobile devices, providing them with a more simple and free means to learn [12].

B. The impact of information technology on English language teaching.
Here are just a few ways in which IT has changed the face of ESL classrooms:

1. Optimized teaching methods

Through the use of multimedia, speech recognition, virtual reality, and other technologies, students can gain a deeper understanding of the English language and culture. Moreover, by tailoring English teaching programs to each student's unique needs and differences, we can enhance the effectiveness of our lessons and move beyond the traditional teacher-centered, practice-based approach to teaching English [13].

2. Enhanced efficiency in learning

Online and mobile learning allow students to make the most of their limited study time, which in turn improves the quality and efficiency of their English language education. Simultaneously, using voice recognition and natural language processing technology [15] has greatly enhanced students' ability to speak and write English, as well as their learning outcomes.

3. Students' enthusiasm for learning has grown

The use of information technology has made English language instruction more intuitive, vivid, and engaging than the traditional model, which relies on instructors speaking and students listening and has a singular impact on learning. Multimedia, VR, and other technological advancements allow students to have a more profound familiarity with the English language and culture. Simultaneously, students may enhance their motivation and passion for learning by studying autonomously using resources like online course platforms and mobile learning.

4. What lies ahead

Despite the undeniable breadth and depth of IT's influence on ESL classrooms, the medium will inevitably encounter new obstacles down the road, such as maintaining a healthy IT-security balance, as it pushes forward with its plans to modernize and internationalize ESL curricula. Therefore, further study and investigation are required in the future to develop a more comprehensive education system and security system integrating information technology and English education, so as to optimize the use of information technology in English teaching.

The application of information technology in English teaching has become an important direction of educational reform, which optimizes the way of English teaching and improves students' learning efficiency and interest, but also faces various challenges. Teachers and students alike will need to evolve with the times in order to keep up with the rapid pace of technological change and make the most of the opportunities presented by it in order to foster an environment conducive to the continued growth and improvement of English language instruction.

The teaching method is one of the key topics of English teaching in colleges and universities, which is of considerable relevance to English teaching. But there's an issue with the teaching method scheme's lack of reason, which causes some problems for college students. Some researchers argue that the use of information technology to the study of English teaching in colleges and universities may effectively assess the teaching mode scheme and give suitable support for the teaching mode. In light of this, the research suggests using IT to strengthen the model's efficacy and enhance the teaching mode scheme..

2 Related Works

A. Mathematical description of information technology
Information technology involves utilizing computers to optimize teaching methods, identifying unqualified values in college English teaching based on teaching mode

indicators, integrating these methods, and ultimately judging the feasibility of teaching English in colleges and universities. By combining the advantages of computers with quantitative methods used in college English teaching, information technology can improve the feasibility of teaching models.

Hypothesis 1: The needs of the educational approach is v_i, the teaching mode scheme is set_i, the contentment with the instructional approach is h, and the instructional manner strategy judging function is $D(v_i \approx 0)$, As shown in Eq. (1).

$$D(v_i h) = D_1, \ldots, D_n \rightarrow \frac{3}{h} \div \sum_{i=1}^{h} v_i h \tag{1}$$

B. Choice of teaching mode scheme

My Second Hypothesis Concerning the Role of College English Instructors is $q(v_i)$, and the weight coefficient is a_i, then the teaching style demands unqualified college English instruction as illustrated in Eq. (2).

$$q(v_i) = \sqrt{3v^2 + a_i{}^2} + \oint_{v_i} q \cdot \sqrt[i]{v_i} \tag{2}$$

C. Analysis of teaching model schemes

A multi-dimensional study of the current teaching mode scheme, a mapping of the current teaching mode requirements to the English teaching libraries of colleges and universities, and the elimination of the current unqualified teaching mode scheme must precede the use of information technology. First, the English teaching in colleges and universities is completely examined, and the threshold and index weight of the teaching mode scheme are defined to assure the correctness of information technology. Examining the methods used to teach English in higher education is essential, since it is structured like an exam. The general correctness of college and university English instruction will suffer if its distribution is non-normal. This is because the teaching mode scheme is impacted. Choosing the right teaching mode scheme is essential for enhancing the precision of IT and the quality of instruction; Fig. 1 shows the details of one such program.

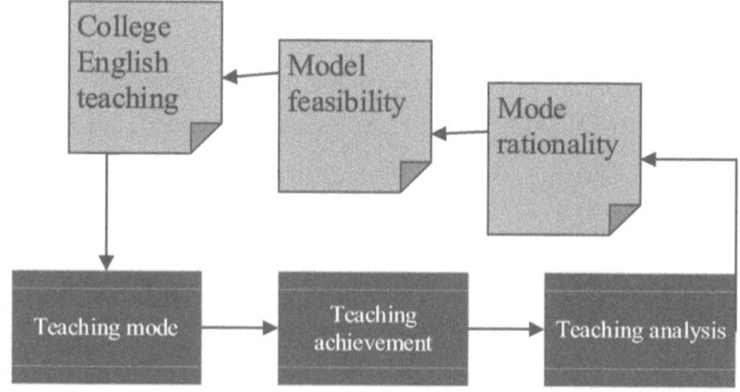

Fig. 1. The results of the selection of the teaching model scheme

Consistent with the objective facts, the teaching mode scheme survey reveals that it exhibits a multi-dimensional distribution. College and university English instruction is highly analytical since it is not directed, suggesting a highly randomised teaching mode system. College English instruction is up to par, mostly because computers tweak the instruction, filter out unnecessary and redundant plans, and augment the default plan, resulting in a robust dynamic correlation of the whole teaching mode scheme.

3   Optimization Strategies for English Teaching in Colleges and Universities

In order to optimize the scheme for teaching English in college, IT uses a random optimization technique and tweaks the parameters of the teaching mode. The use of IT in higher education has led to the randomization of pedagogical approaches and the division of English classes into many levels. The iterative process involves optimizing and analyzing the teaching mode schemes of various levels of teaching mode. After the optimize analysis is completed, the instructional approach level for different programs is evaluated in order to determine the best college English instruction.

4   Results and Discussion

A. Introduction to the teaching mode

Table 1 shows the specific scheme that this paper uses to facilitate the teaching mode of college English teachers in complex situations. The research object has 12 paths and a test time of 12 h.

Table 1. University Teaching Mode Requirements

Scope of application	grade	viability	Teaching mode
Freshman	routine	78.64	85.39
	Higher	86.13	88.15
Sophomore	routine	85.01	83.50
	Higher	86.28	86.76
Junior	routine	86.08	90.63
	Higher	85.33	84.83

The teaching mode process in Table 1 is shown in Fig. 2.

The information communication methods of instruction scheme is more in line with the needs of the real teaching mode than the conventional method. In terms of the logic and teaching successes of English educators in colleges and universities, information technology is superior than conventional teaching mode. Through the adjustments in the teaching mode plan in Fig. 2, it can be observed that the practicality of information

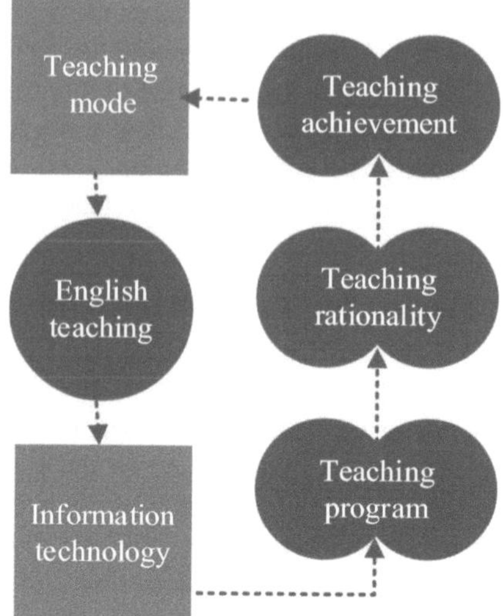

Fig. 2. The analytical process of English teaching in colleges and universities

technology is greater. This leads to improved information technology teaching mode speed, teaching mode feasibility, and summation stability.

B. English teaching in colleges and universities

Unstructured, semi-structured, then structure-based data are the three pillars of the college English teaching method system. Following the IT pre-selection, one might acquire the college English teaching mode plan and proceed with the actual teaching of the subject. Evaluate the practicability of the instructional approach. Table 2 displays the teaching mode scheme that may be used to more precisely confirm the innovative impact of English instruction at the college level.

Table 2. The overall picture of the teaching model program

category	Satisfaction	Analysis rate
Freshman	86.97	87.15
Sophomore	85.69	84.86
Junior	86.73	87.17
mean	88.82	87.09
X^6	83.55	88.50
$P = 2.06$		

C. Teaching mode and stability of teaching mode

In order to test the correctness of computer technology, the teaching mode system is checked against with the traditional methods of instruction mode, and the teaching mode scheme is displayed in Fig. 3.

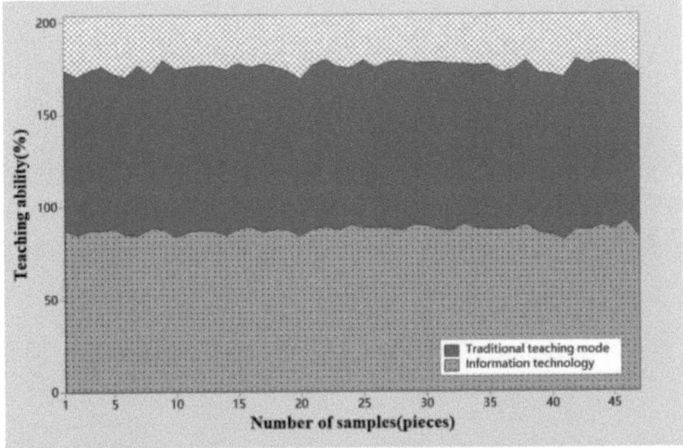

Fig. 3. Teaching modes of different algorithms

Compared to the traditional teaching mode, the data produced by the technology teaching mode has a greater likelihood of errors (Fig. 3), suggesting that it is relatively stable, in contrast to the traditional teaching mode. Models of instruction vary. Tabulated in Table 3 is the mean instructional mode scheme of the aforementioned three algorithms.

Table 3. Comparison of the accuracy of teaching modes of different methods

algorithm	Teaching mode	Magnitude of change	error
Information technology	93.75	92.14	92.30
Traditional teaching mode	91.28	89.72	90.94
P	89.17	89.49	88.36

It can be shown from Table 3 the fact the traditional teaching technique has problems in the rationality of the instruction mode in terms of the language educating in colleges and college campuses, and the language instruction in colleges or universities has undergone significant changes, and the error rate is relatively high. The overall outcomes of IT education are superior than those of more conventional curricula. Simultaneously, the accuracy rate has not altered much and the IT teaching method is above 92%. In order to further prove the supremacy of information technology. As seen in Fig. 4, several methodologies are used to conduct a comprehensive study of information technology in order to further confirm the efficacy of the suggested strategy.

Figure 4 clearly shows that IT-based instruction is vastly superior to more conventional methods. This is due to the fact that IT-based instruction raises the adjustment coefficient for English language classes at universities and colleges and establishes mode thresholds to weed out non-compliant model schemes.

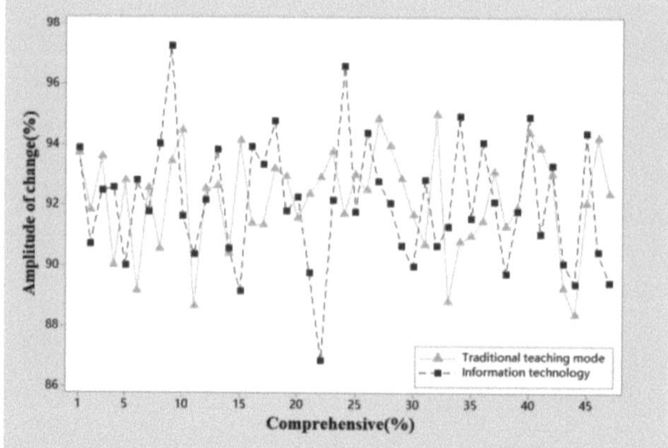

Fig. 4. The teaching mode of the information technology teaching model

5   Conclusion

The purpose of this article is to provide solutions based on information technology and computer integration in order to improve the current state of English instruction in higher education institutions. Also, in order to compile a set of teaching modes, we conduct in-depth analyses of each new method of innovation. Based on the findings, IT can implement the standard method of teaching English in higher education while also increasing its accuracy and stability. But in IT, we focus on analyzing the method of instruction too much, which leads to illogical indications of that style of instruction being chosen.

References

1. Angioni, S., Lincoln-DeCusatis, N., Ibba, A., Reforgiato Recupero, D.: A transformers-based approach for fine and coarse-grained classification and generation of MIDI songs and soundtracks. PeerJ. Comput. Sci. **9**, e1410–e1410 (2023)
2. Ashraf, M., et al.: A hybrid CNN and RNN variant model for music classification. Appl. Sci.-Basel **13**(3) (2023)
3. Bhattacharjee, M., Prasanna, S.R.M., Guha, P.: Clean vs. overlapped speech-music detection using harmonic-percussive features and multi-task learning. IEEE-ACM Trans. Audio Speech Lang. Process. **31**, 1–10 (2023)
4. Han, X., Chen, F., Ban, J.: Music emotion recognition based on a neural network with an inception-GRU residual structure. Electronics **12**(4) (2023)
5. Hecker, L., van Elst, L.T., Kornmeier, J.: Source localization using recursively applied and projected MUSIC with flexible extent estimation. Front. Neurosci. **17** (2023)
6. Ho, H.Y., Loo, F.Y.: A theoretical paradigm proposal of music arousal and emotional valence interrelations with tempo, preference, familiarity, and presence of lyrics. New Ideas Psychol. **71** (2023)
7. Hossain, S.A., Rahman, M.A., Chakrabarty, A., Rashid, M.A., Kuwana, A., Kobayashi, H.: Emotional state classification from MUSIC-based features of multichannel EEG signals. Bioeng.-Basel **10**(1)

8. Istvanek, M., Miklanek, S., Spurny, L.: Classification of interpretation differences in string quartets based on the origin of performers. Appl. Sci.-Basel **13**(6) (2023)
9. Jaishankar, B., Anitha, R., Shadrach, F.D., Sivarathinabala, M., Balamurugan, V.: Music genre classification using African buffalo optimization. Comput. Syst. Sci. Eng. **44**(2), 1823–1836 (2023)
10. Jena, K.K., Bhoi, S.K., Mohapatra, S., Bakshi, S.: A hybrid deep learning approach for classification of music genres using wavelet and spectrogram analysis. Neural Comput. Appl. (2023)
11. Lang, Y., Yang, Z., Kong, D., Zhang, W., Chen, X.: Forward-propagation-free focusing MUSIC algorithm for Lamb waves. Structural Health Monit. Int. J. (2023)
12. Lee, D.: Organising music's structures: the classification of musical forms in Western art music. J. Inf. Sci. (2023)
13. Liu, J.: An automatic classification method for multiple music genres by integrating emotions and intelligent algorithms. Appl. Artif. Intell. **37**(1) (2023)
14. Liu, Z., Bian, T., Yang, M.: Locally activated gated neural network for automatic music genre classification. Appl. Sci.-Basel **13**(8) (2023)
15. Ma, T., Xiao, Y., Lei, X.: Channel reconstruction-aided MUSIC algorithms for joint AoA&AoD estimation in MIMO systems. IEEE Wirel. Commun. Lett. **12**(2), 322–326 (2023)

Research on the Application of Information Security Technology in the Construction of Smart Education Platform

Yingying Yue[(✉)]

Lanzhou Vocational and Technical University of Resources and Environment,
Lanzhou City 730021, Gansu Province, China
`yueingying@lzre.edu.cn`

Abstract. Smart education is based on the Internet of Things and cloud data, cloud computing, artificial intelligence and other intelligent technologies, and its characteristics include strong perception, intelligence, materialization, etc., and the new teaching mode and education form of the education and teaching ecosystem combined with intelligent technology are vividly embodied. Traditional teaching facilities are difficult to adapt to the current requirements of intelligent teaching, especially in recent years, the application scenarios of education and teaching have been greatly expanded, and people's requirements for the network have become more and more engaged, such as operation and maintenance management, multi-network integration, network speed and broadband Internet of Things, etc., at this time, people urgently need a strong security, and have a fast operation speed of the intelligent education platform. Based on this, this paper will build an intelligent education platform based on the support of information security technology, so as to better promote the further development of intelligent education and enable it to achieve better digital and intelligent advantages.

Keywords: smart education · information security technology · platform construction · Education

1 Introduction

With the rapid development of digital technology, smart education platforms have become an indispensable part of the education industry [1, 2]. These platforms integrate multiple technologies such as artificial intelligence, big data analysis, and cloud computing to provide students and teachers with personalized learning, distance education, resource sharing, and other services. For example, through AI algorithms, the smart education platform can recommend course content suitable for students' ability levels, while teachers can use big data analysis to track students' learning progress for targeted teaching [3, 4].

The evaluation process of smart classroom teaching effect in Table 1 is shown in Fig. 1.

B. Brik and S. Nazir (Eds.): BigIoT-EDU 2024, LNICST 659, pp. 240–248, 2026.
https://doi.org/10.1007/978-3-032-18631-7_27

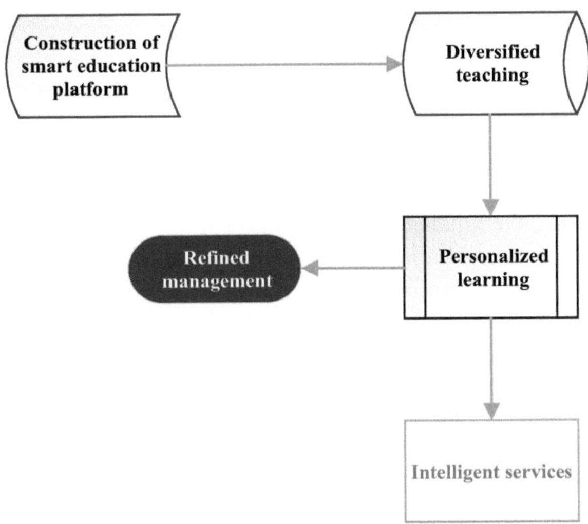

Fig. 1. The construction process of the smart education platform

Implement a multi-factor authentication mechanism, combined with passwords, biometrics and other means, to restrict access to educational resources and student information to prevent unauthorized access and data leakage [5, 6].

Configure firewalls and intrusion detection systems to monitor network traffic and prevent malicious attacks and virus intrusions. Regularly update and patch system vulnerabilities to keep your network security protection up to date.

Conduct security reviews and regular updates for all applications on the education platform to ensure the security and compliance of the application code and avoid security issues caused by software vulnerabilities [7, 8].

2 Related Works

A. Information Security Technology

However, with the popularity of the platform, a series of problems have become increasingly prominent. First of all, the smart education platform has a huge user base and involves a large amount of personal privacy data, such as student information, grades, learning behaviors, etc., which makes the platform a potential target for hacker attacks. Second, the digitization of educational resources complicates copyright protection, and illegal distribution and misappropriation of content occur from time to time. In addition, technical failures and system failures can also lead to disruptions to teaching and learning activities, affecting the quality and efficiency of education [9, 10].

In the face of the current situation of smart education platform, the application of information security technology is very important. Ensuring data security not only protects users' privacy and maintains educational fairness, but also enhances the credibility of the platform and attracts more users. For example, by implementing a strict identity authentication mechanism, illegal users can be prevented from accessing sensitive information. The use of encryption technology can protect the security of data during transmission and prevent it from being stolen or tampered with. At the same time, the urgency of information security technology stems from the growing threat of cybersecurity. Cybercriminals may exploit the platform's vulnerabilities for data theft or even extortion attacks on the platform. In addition, with the implementation of regulations such as GDPR (European Union General Data Protection Regulation), educational institutions must adhere to strict data protection standards or face serious legal consequences. Therefore, the smart education platform must take information security as its core competitiveness, and build a comprehensive security protection system through the introduction of advanced information security technology to protect the rights and interests of users and maintain the stability and sustainable development of education services.

B. Construction of smart education platform

Information security, or InfoSec for short, refers to a set of measures to protect information resources from unauthorized access, use, disclosure, interruption, modification, or destruction. This concept encompasses the confidentiality, integrity, and availability of data, ensuring that information is delivered to the right people at the right time and in the right form:

The basic principles of information security include: (1) Confidentiality. Ensure that information can only be accessed by authorized individuals or systems. This is usually achieved through encryption and access control mechanisms. (2) Integrity. Protect information from modification or destruction and ensure its accuracy. This requires data validation and validation mechanisms. (3) Availability. Ensure authorized users have timely, reliable access to information when they need it and prevent denial-of-service attacks. (4) Authentication. Determine the resources and operational permissions that users can access. (5) Non-repudiation. Ensuring that the sender of the message cannot deny the message they sent, usually through a digital signature.

3 Construction of Safety Management System

First, the structure of the security organization. Establish a dedicated security organization, including a security management team, a technical team, and a business team, to ensure that security responsibilities are clear and a mechanism for working together to effectively respond to various security challenges. Second, safety training and awareness-raising. Regularly conduct information security training for the platform's faculty and staff to enhance their awareness of cybersecurity threats, raise awareness of prevention, and ensure that everyone can follow security norms in their daily work. Third, risk assessment and management. Conduct regular risk assessments to identify potential security threats, prioritize through risk analysis, and develop appropriate risk mitigation strategies.

A. Mathematical description of information security technology

In the daily operation of the smart education platform, information security threats cannot be ignored. These threats not only affect the stable operation of the platform, but also can cause serious damage to the user's privacy and educational resources. Here are some of the major information security threats:

First, data breaches. Due to the large amount of student personal information, learning records, and educational resources contained in the platform, hackers may try to illegally obtain this sensitive information. Second, malware attacks. This includes viruses, worms, and Trojans, which can disrupt the normal functioning of the platform, resulting in data loss or system disability. Third, phishing. By disguising itself as a legitimate education platform interface, it tricks users into entering accounts and passwords, thereby stealing user information. Fourth, distributed denial-of-service (DDoS) attacks. The large amount of malicious traffic causes the platform server to be overloaded, making it inaccessible to normal users. Fifth, internal threats. Employee negligence, misoperation, or malicious behavior by insiders may also pose a threat to the security of the platform. Sixth, privacy violations. Illegally obtaining and misusing students' personal information, including location information, academic performance, etc., may infringe on students' privacy.

$$R = E\left\{xx^H\right\} = R_c + R_j + R_n \tag{1}$$

In view of the above threats, the information security requirements of the smart education platform mainly include the following aspects:

First, data protection. It is necessary to ensure the integrity, confidentiality and availability of user data, and to protect data from illegal access and tampering through encryption technology. Second, access control. Implement strict permission management to ensure that only authorized users have access to specific information and functions and prevent unauthorized intrusion. Third, cybersecurity. Build firewalls and intrusion detection systems to prevent malware and DDoS attacks, while monitoring and blocking anomalous network behavior. Fourth, privacy compliance. Comply with relevant laws and regulations, such as GDPR, etc., to ensure the legality of the collection, storage and use of personal information.

$$\widehat{R}_{SCM} = \frac{1}{T}\sum_{l=1}^{L}x_l x^H{}_l \tag{2}$$

These information security requirements are the foundation for the continuous and secure operation of the smart education platform, and an important guarantee to protect the rights and interests of users and the fairness of education. Only by comprehensively considering and effectively implementing these needs can the smart education platform provide users with safe and reliable education services in the digital era.

$$R_c = A\sum A^H \Theta\left(\Xi\,\Xi^H\right) \tag{3}$$

B. Data encryption and transmission security

Identity authentication is the first line of defense to ensure information security in the smart education platform. Ensure that only authorized users can access educational resources through multi-factor authentication (MFA) mechanisms such as usernames and passwords, biometrics, hardware tokens, and more. For example, students and teachers can use fingerprint or facial recognition to log in, along with randomly generated verification codes for added security. Access control policies, such as the principle of least privilege, ensure that users only have access to data and functions that are relevant to their responsibilities, preventing malicious or unintentional misuse.

$$T(k, n) = a_d(f_{dk}) \otimes a_s(f_{sn}) \tag{4}$$

In the smart education platform, sensitive information such as students' personal information, grades, and teaching materials need to be stored and transmitted encrypted.

$$R_c + T(k, n) = T^H{}_D x \tag{5}$$

Encryption algorithms such as AES (Advanced Encryption Standard) and RSA are widely used to encrypt data, ensuring that even if the data is stolen, it cannot be read.

$$R_T = T^H{}_D R T_D \tag{6}$$

At the same time, the HTTPS protocol is used to protect the security of data during transmission and prevent man-in-the-middle attacks. The platform should also employ SSL/TLS certificates to ensure that communication with the server is secure.

C. Firewalls and intrusion detection systems

The firewall acts as the perimeter protection of the smart education platform to prevent unauthorized network access. It filters incoming and outgoing network traffic based on predefined rules such as IP addresses, ports, and protocols. An intrusion detection system (IDS) monitors network activity in real time, identifies anomalous behaviors, such as scanning, brute force attacks, etc., and immediately alerts and takes preventive measures if a potential attack is detected.

$$w_T = \mu_T R^{-1}{}_T S_T \tag{7}$$

Security audits are a critical part of assessing the security of a platform. By recording and analyzing events such as system operations, login attempts, and resource access, potential security vulnerabilities and attack patterns can be discovered. Log management ensures that these records are properly preserved and analyzed for traceability in the event of a security incident. At the same time, regular security audits can verify the effectiveness of security policies and make necessary improvements based on the audit results.

$$T_{3DT} = \left[a_d(f_{di-1}), a_d(f_{di}), a_d(f_{di+1}) \right] \otimes I_N \tag{8}$$

The security strategy of smart education platforms needs to be continuously iterated and updated to deal with increasingly sophisticated cyber threats. Through the comprehensive application of these information security technologies, the data security of the platform can be effectively protected, the privacy of students and teachers can be guaranteed, and the integrity of educational resources can be guaranteed, so as to create a safe and reliable online learning environment.

$$T_{JDL3\times3} = \left[a_d(f_{di-1}), a_d(fd_i), a_d(f d_{i+1}) \right] \otimes \left[a_s(f_{si-1}), a_s(f_{si}), a_s(f_{si+1}), \right] \tag{9}$$

The security management system of the smart education platform first needs to establish a clear information security policy, which includes regulations on data protection, user privacy, access control, network security, etc., to ensure that all operations follow the established guidelines.

$$T_{STMB} = \left[a_d(f_{ai-2}), a_d(f_{ai-1}), a_d(f_{ai+1}), a_d(f_{ai+2}) \right] \otimes a_s(f_{si}) \tag{10}$$

4   Results and Discussion

A. Data protection strategy

Encryption technology is used to protect sensitive data, and a data classification and marking system is formulated to ensure the security of data during storage and transmission.

Table 1. Evaluation of the effectiveness of smart classroom teaching

Evaluation of the effectiveness of smart classroom teaching	Evaluation of the effectiveness of smart classroom teaching	Evaluation of the effectiveness of smart classroom teaching	Evaluation of the effectiveness of smart classroom teaching
Diversified teaching	66.1503	71.3070	70.6288
Personalized learning	69.8213	70.8782	71.4273
Intelligent service	67.1041	70.1246	72.3641
Refined management	66.7616	70.5576	67.0684

B. Emergency response and handling of security incidents

First, develop a detailed emergency response plan for security incidents, including steps for incident identification, isolation, investigation, recovery, and subsequent improvement, to ensure that you can respond quickly and effectively when a security incident occurs. Secondly, establish a 24/7 monitoring mechanism to monitor abnormal behavior of the system in real time, and once a security incident is found, the response mechanism will be activated immediately, and it will be reported to superiors and relevant departments in accordance with the prescribed process. Then, conduct post-mortem analysis and improvement. Conduct in-depth analysis of security incidents, find out the root cause of problems, fix vulnerabilities in a timely manner, improve security policies, and prevent similar incidents from happening again. At the same time, the incident handling experience is incorporated into the security training and education content to improve the overall security protection capability. Finally, cooperation and exchanges. Maintain communication with relevant industry organizations and security agencies, share threat intelligence, and keep abreast of the latest security threats for better prevention and response (Table 2).

It can be seen that information security technology plays a key role in the construction of smart education platform, and the discussion of this can provide theoretical support and practical guidance for ensuring the security, stability and sustainable development of education informatization (Fig. 2).

Through the analysis of the security threats of the existing smart education platform, we find that information security technologies such as identity authentication, data encryption, access control, and security audit are the cornerstones of platform security. The average smart classroom teaching effect evaluation scheme of the above algorithm is shown in Table 3.

We emphasize the importance of identity authentication and use multi-factor authentication and biometrics to prevent unauthorized users from accessing educational

Table 2. The overall picture of the blended learning program

Teaching content	Initiative	personalize
Learning resources	82.5498	77.7880
Learning tasks	83.1398	79.8971
Curriculum resources	81.0585	79.3184
Blended teaching	84.4752	80.9656
Remote class tours	86.2074	78.9966
Intelligent management	84.3756	80.4137
Teaching live	82.5498	80.2899

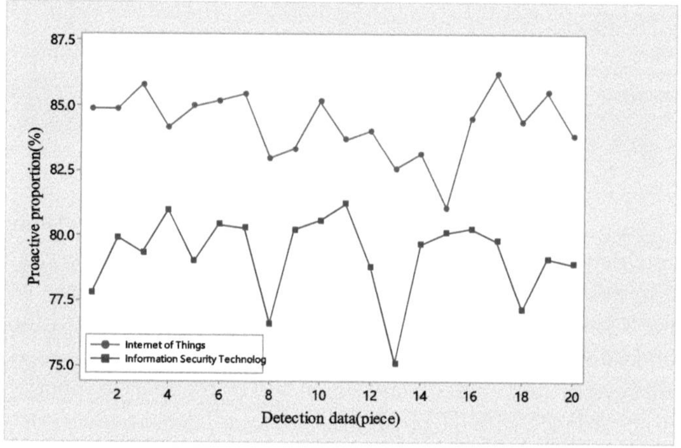

Fig. 2. Blended teaching of different algorithms

Table 3. Comparison of the evaluation accuracy of smart classroom teaching effect of different methods

algorithm	Blended teaching efficiency	Magnitude of change	error
Information security technology	80.7557	81.8599	83.2716
Internet of Things	78.7719	81.2157	76.5955

resources. Data encryption and secure transmission technology ensure the security of students' and teachers' personal information and teaching content during transmission, preventing data theft or tampering. At the same time, firewalls and intrusion detection systems build the first line of defense against malicious attacks and virus intrusions. Security audit and log management provide a monitoring and traceability mechanism for the platform, which helps to detect and deal with security issues in a timely manne. In order to further verify the effectiveness of the proposed method, the general analysis of information security technology is carried out by different methods, Fig. 3 shown.

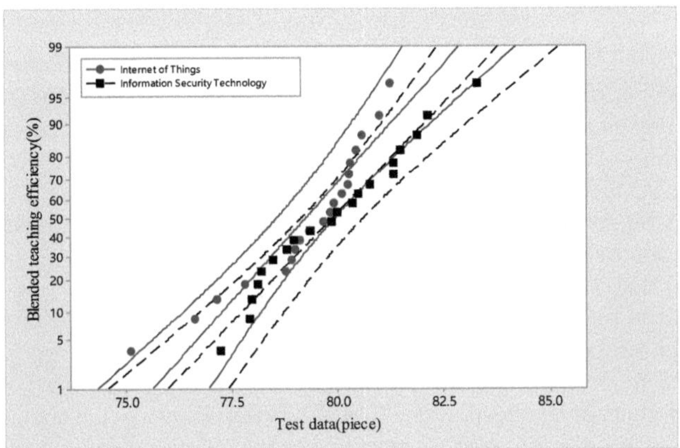

Fig. 3. Hybrid teaching for the evaluation of the teaching effect of information security technology smart classroom

5   Conclusion

We propose the construction of a security management system for the smart education platform, including the formulation of a clear security strategy, the implementation of regular safety training and drills, and the establishment of an emergency response mechanism. The implementation of these measures has improved the overall security level of the platform, providing a safer and more reliable online learning environment for educators and students. Finally, the security of education platforms not only depends on technology, but also needs to improve users' security awareness. Therefore, future research should focus more on educating users on how to use the platform correctly, understand and follow security norms, and form good cyber literacy. At the same time, at the policy level, it is also necessary to formulate more complete data protection regulations to provide legal guarantee for the healthy development of smart education.

Acknowledgements. Department of Education of Gansu Province: College Teachers Innovation Fund Project 2023B-303.

References

1. Alfoudari, A.M., Durugbo, C.M., Aldhmour, F.M.: Exploring quality attributes of smart classrooms from the perspectives of academics. Educ. Inf. Technol. (2023)
2. Alshammari, A., Alanazi, M.F.: Use of technology in enhancing learning among nurses in Saudi Arabia; a systematic review. J. Multidiscip. Healthc. **16**, 1587–1599 (2023)
3. Asamoah, K.O., et al.: A blockchain-based crowdsourcing loan platform for funding higher education in developing countries. IEEE Access **11**, 24162–24174 (2023)

4. Bai, L., et al.: A smart metasurface for electromagnetic manipulation based on speech recognition. Engineering **22**, 185–190 (2023)
5. Beck, N.M., Murray, P., Quintanilla, B.: Reimagining critical care education during COVID-19 with high-level technology. J. Nurses Prof. Dev. **39**(2), 92–96 (2023)
6. Chen, R., Wu, X., & Liu, X.: RSETP: a reliable security education and training platform based on the alliance blockchain. Electronics **12**(6) (2023)
7. Diaconita, V., Belciu, A., Stoica, M.G.: Trustful blockchain-based framework for privacy enabling voting in a university. J. Theor. Appl. Electron. Commer. Res. **18**(1), 150–169 (2023)
8. Esfandiari, E., Miller, W.C., King, S.: Usability of self-management for amputee rehabilitation using technology (SMART): an online self-management program for users with lower limb loss. Prosthet. Orthot. Int. **47**(2), 172–180 (2023)
9. Essa, M.E.-S.M., et al.: Reliable integration of neural network and internet of things for forecasting, controlling, and monitoring of experimental building management system. Sustainability **15**(3) (2023)
10. Geuer, L., Lauer, F., Kuhn, J., Wehn, N., Ulber, R.: SmaEPho-smart photometry in education 4.0. Educ. Sci. **13**(2) (2023)
11. Gharaibeh, M.K.: Measuring student satisfaction of Microsoft teams as an online learning platform in Jordan: an application of UTAUT2 model. Hum. Syst. Manag. **42**(2), 121–130 (2023)

Design and Implementation of Corpus Management System for English Teaching Based on C/S Environment

Weiwei Mao(✉)

Shandong Institute of Commerce and Technology, No. 4516, Lvyou Road, Jinan, Shandong 250103, China
cathy1521@163.com

Abstract. An issue with incorrect system placement exists, notwithstanding the importance of corpus management system design and execution in English language instruction. The English teaching corpus has design issues that traditional manual administration cannot fix, and the results are unsatisfactory. As a result, this study analyses the corpus management system and suggests its design and implementation based on a C/S environment. Then, based on the theory of computer network architecture, a plan is developed for the design and execution of an environmental corpus management system (C/S), and the outcomes of this plan are thoroughly evaluated. According to the MATLAB simulation results, when compared to traditional manual management, the C/S environment the accuracy and timeliness of corpus management system design, according to certain evaluation criteria.

Keywords: computer network architecture theory · C/S environment · Corpus management system design and implementation · English · Teaching · Corpus

1 Introduction

A crucial component of any English language learning dataset is the creation and deployment of an effective corpus management system [1–3], which, if executed properly, enables quicker, more precise, and better-regulated access to the data [4, 5]. Regrettably, there are issues with accuracy in the development and deployment of this system, negatively impacting both its design and implementation throughout the entire process of its creation and operation. Some experts believe that integrating a client/server (C/S) framework into the evaluation of the system's development can provide deeper insights into its structure and functioning, offering useful support in these areas. Using this approach, this study proposes adopting a C/S model to refine the system's design and execution strategy, and also tests the proposed model's effectiveness [6–8] is illustrated in Fig. 1.

B. Brik and S. Nazir (Eds.): BigIoT-EDU 2024, LNICST 659, pp. 249–259, 2026.
https://doi.org/10.1007/978-3-032-18631-7_28

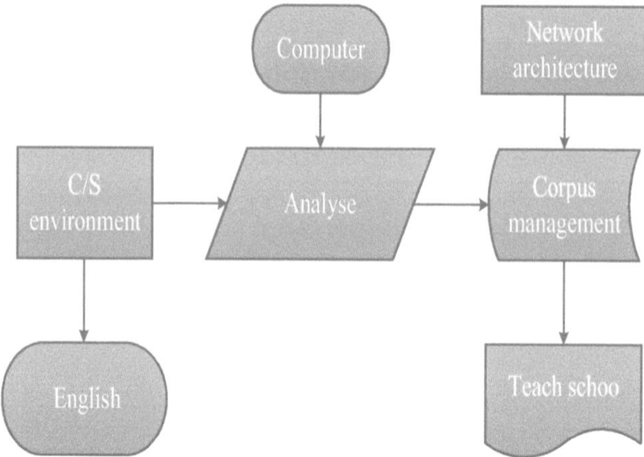

Fig. 1. The analytical process of corpus management system design and implementation

2 Related Works

2.1 Corpus Management System

Manual management brings the corpus management system's design and execution plan in a C/S environment one step closer to what's really needed. When compared to manual management, C/S environments provide more logical and accurate corpus management system design and execution.With the help of manual management, the corpus management system was designed and implemented to ensure the C/S environment is accurate. Planning and Execution of a Corpus Management System There are three types of data included in the plan for the corpus management system: non-structural, semi-structured, and structural. Following the pee-selection of the C/S environment, the corpus management system derives a preliminary design and implementation plan, and then analyzes the plan's feasibility.

2.2 C/S Environment

The C/S environment uses a random optimization method and tweaks the Internet information settings. Multiple tiers of corpus management system design and implementation are used in a C/S environment, with various schemes being chosen at random. An iterative method is used to optimize and examine the design and execution of corpus management system at various stages. Following the completion of the optimization study, several schemes are compared in terms of their corpus management system design and implementation level. The optimal system is then documented.

3 Optimization Strategy for Corpus Management System Design and Implementation

3.1 Mathematical Description of the A.C/S Environment

In a C/S environment, computer technology is used to optimize the corpus management system's design and implementation. From there, the system's unqualified value parameters are found the design and implementation. The corpus management system, calculated is a formula (1) shown.

$$\lim_{x \to \infty} \left(y_i \cdot t_{ij} \right) = y_{ij} \geq max(t_{ij} \div 2) \tag{1}$$

The processing of corpus requires data comparison and analysis of basic data of corpus is shown in Eq. (2).

$$max(t_{ij}) = \partial(t_{ij}^2 + 2 \cdot t_{ij}) \succ mean\left(\sum t_{ij} + 4\right)\mathfrak{M} \tag{2}$$

Improving the correctness of the corpus management system's design and execution is possible in the C/S environment because it combines the criteria for developing and launching the corpus management platform is, creating and launching the system for managing corpora is, content with the corpus management system's design and execution is, and the plan for designing and implementing the corpus management system's judgment function is as shown in Eq. (3).

$$F(d_i) = \int \sum t_i \bigcap \xi \cdot \Delta\sqrt{kp} \cdot \oint y_i \tag{3}$$

3.2 Selection of Corpus Management System Design and Implementation Scheme

The corpus management design and implementation are characterized by a certain weight coefficient [9, 10]. Following this, Eq. (4) details the specifications necessary for designing and executing a substandard corpus management system.

$$g(t_i) = \sqrt{\ddot{x} \cdot z_i} \prod F(d_i)\frac{dy}{dx}\frac{ki}{n}w_i \tag{4}$$

An all-encompassing function of the corpus management system's design and execution may be derived from assumptions I and II, and the outcome is shown in Eq. (5).

$$\lim_{x \to \infty} g(t_i) = F(d_i)max(t_{ij}) \tag{5}$$

Equation (6) shows the outcomes of standardizing all data, which is necessary to enhance the efficacy of corpus management system design and execution.

$$g(t_i) + F(d_i) \leftrightarrow mean\left(\sum t_{ij} + 4\right) \tag{6}$$

3.3 Comprehensive Analysis of Material Warehouse.

Prior to the client-server context, all components of the data management system's creation and execution need scrutiny. Following this, the specifications for the creation and execution should be mirrored in their actualization. Ultimately, any substandard design and execution strategies must be eliminated. Equation (6) suggests an irregularity assessment approach, with outcomes detailed in Eq. (7).

$$No(t_i) = \frac{g(t_i) + F(d_i)}{mean(\sum t_{ij} + 4)} \sqrt{b^2 - 4ac} \tag{7}$$

The comprehensive management of the material warehouse and the overall judgment of the corpus require in-depth mining and actual measurement. However, in the overall judgment process of corpus, data integration is needed, and the specific results are shown in Formula 8.

$$IOI(t_i) = \bigcap Qi[\sum g(t_i) + F(d_i)] \tag{8}$$

Upon a detailed examination of the corpus management system's design and operation, the validity of the C/S environment is assured by adjusting the scheme's threshold and index weights. Such an in-depth analysis of the corpus management system's development process acts as a critical system evaluation. If the design and implementation deviate from a normal distribution, it will adversely affect the overall precision of the corpus management system and impact its design and execution, as depicted by Eq. (9).

$$accur(t_i) = \frac{min[\sum g(t_i) + F(d_i)]}{\sum g(t_i) + F(d_i)} \times 100\% \tag{9}$$

The study on the design and implementation plan of the corpus management system reveals a distribution that is multifaceted and aligns with reality. The research is deemed of high analytical value because there's no specific direction in its design and implementation; indicating that the scheme for designing and executing the corpus management system is quite arbitrary. $Aca(t_i)$ is given that the corpus management system has a random generation feature, can be represented as per Eq. (10).

$$Aca(t_i) = \int Zi + randon(t_i) \tag{10}$$

Among these, the corpus management system's design and implementation are up to standard. This is largely due to the fact that, with the help of computer technology, the system's design and implementation are fine-tuned, any unnecessary or duplicate schemes are removed, and the default scheme is supplemented.

4 Results and Discussion

4.1 Holistic Planning and Analysis of Corpus System

Based on college students' English teaching, this paper makes a comprehensive analysis of the corpus, and judges the contents and survey data of the corpus. The analysis process is improved through data, sampling and holistic analysis. The survey results are in the form of questionnaires, and diversified judgments are made on each indicator and content to form an overall planning content. The specific results are shown in Table 1.

Table 1. Corpus management system design and implementation requirements

Scope of application	The content hierarchy of the corpus	Data of the remaining materials	Synthesis of corpus materials
Teacher	I	41.59	58.41
	II	51.33	40.71
Student	I	62.83	61.95
	II	42.48	50.44
Academic administrators	I	38.94	51.33
	II	60.18	58.41

Figure 2 shows the upgraded C/S environment's correctness and dependability as a result of the corpus management system's revised design and execution plan. As a result, the C/S environment is ideal for designing and implementing corpus management systems because of the speed, precision, and overall stability of these systems.

4.2 Corpus Management System Design and Implementation

In the process of comprehensive judgment and overall planning of corpus, it is necessary to realize the overall analysis and integration of remaining materials. The specific results are shown in Table 2.

Table 2. The overall situation of the design and implementation of the corpus management system

Category	Implementation conditions of warehouse transfer	The calling situation of data	Integrative analysis of data
Teacher	41.59	37.17	61.95
Student	38.05	40.71	58.41
Academic administrators	42.48	43.36	59.29

4.3 Diversification Analysis of Corpus to Overall Planning

Change and planning and integration of corpus. As in. As shown in Fig. 2.

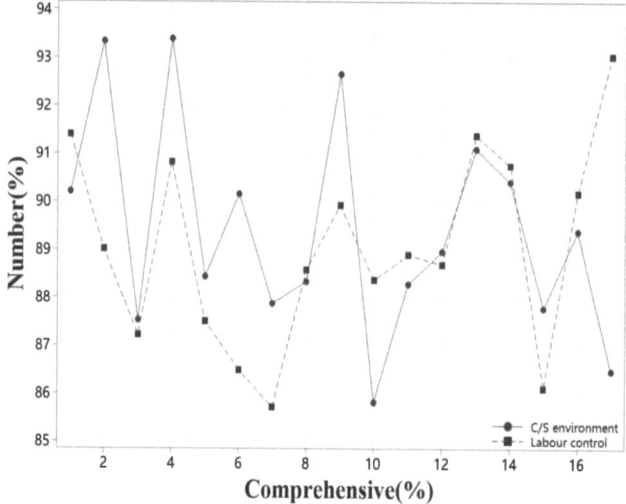

Fig. 2. Fluctuations in recreation library data calls

Figure 2 shows that compared to manual management, the C/S environment has higher standards for corpus management system design and implementation, but a lower error rate. This suggests that the C/S environment's standards are more consistently met, in contrast to the manual management environment's inconsistent standards. By comparing the actual data of the corpus, the data is summarized, and the summary results are shown in Table 3.

Table 3. Integration and comprehensive analysis of the results

Algorithm	Corpus evaluation	Multivariate planning of corpus resources	The integration judgment of data	Corpus integration comparison
C/S environment	44.25	49.56	55.75	54.87
Artificial management	52.21	47.79	38.05	35.40
Comprehensive integration of resources	47.79	53.10	56.64	54.87

Table 3 shows that there are problems with manual management when it comes to the correctness of corpus management system design and execution, as well as a high mistake rate and significant changes in both areas. When compared to manual management, the corpus management system's design and execution provide better overall outcomes in a C/S context. Meanwhile, the C/S environment's corpus management system is over 90% complete, and there has been no discernible drop in accuracy. For the purpose of providing more evidence that the C/S environment is better, various methodologies were used to conduct a broad study of the C/S environment, as shown in Fig. 3, in order to further validate the usefulness of the strategy provided in this article.

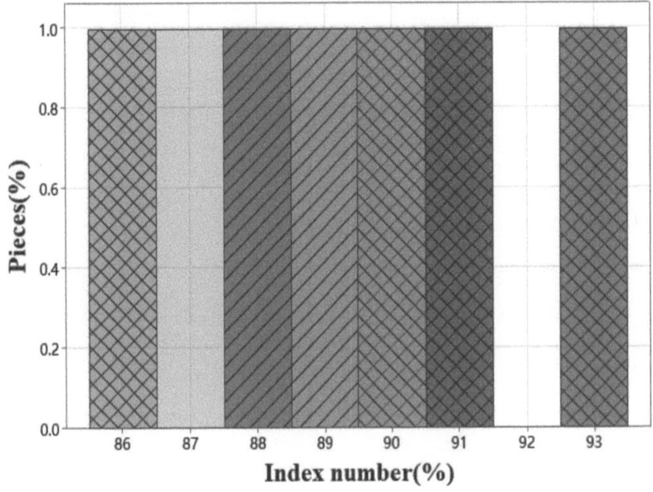

Fig. 3. Multiple data integration of language databases.

Figure 3 clearly shows that the C/S environment provides far superior corpus management system design and implementation compared to manual management. Through the right. Integrated analysis and comprehensive judgment of language databases to improve the utilization effect of data resources.

4.4 Rationality of the Design and Implementation of Corpus Management System

The data calling situation and data distribution of language database are judged and analyzed by graphical form. The specific results are shown in Fig. 4.

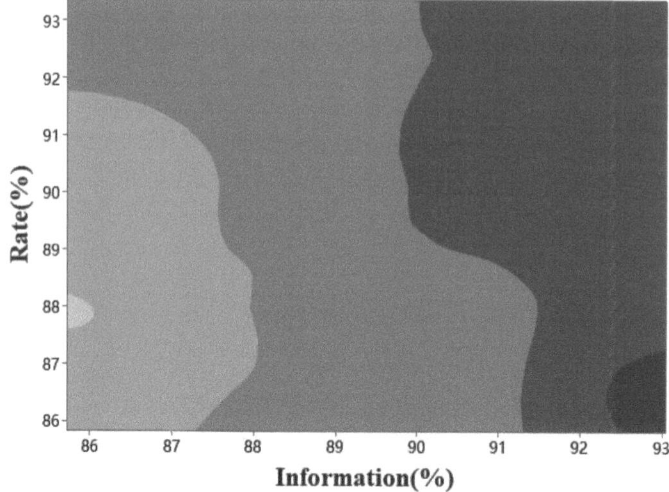

Fig. 4. Design and implementation of corpus management system with different algorithms

Figure 4 shows that Integration analysis and comprehensive judgment of linguistic data database. To guarantee the safe recording and storage of findings, a decentralized data storage and management platform may be provided by implementing a C/S environment. The C/S environment allows for the creation of unique identifiers for each and the recording of necessary data and schemes.

4.5   Effectiveness of Corpus Management System Design and Implementation

The efficacy of the C/S environment may be tested by comparing the corpus management system's design and execution with manual management. Figure 5 shows the schematic of this system.

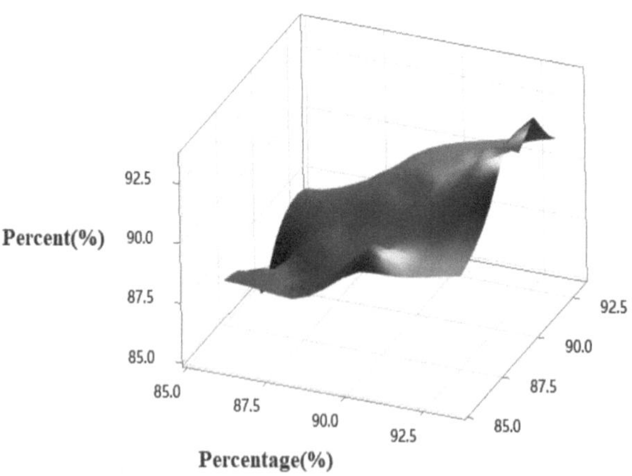

Fig. 5. Fluctuations in the database of linguistic materials

Figure 5 shows that compared to manual management, the C/S environment's corpus management system has higher design and implementation standards but lower error rates. This suggests that the C/S environment's system is relatively stable in terms of design and implementation, in contrast to the manual management system, which is uneven in this regard. After the above analysis, it can be found that in the process of integrating the language data database, the data distribution is relatively uniform, but the specific results of the distribution are not shown. Therefore, the distribution result is judged, and shown in Table 4.

Table 4. Comprehensive analysis of linguistic data database and summary of results

Algorithm	Utilization of language data databases	Integration of data databases	The degree of utilization of database information	Comparison of data and demand
C/S environment	57.52	42.48	56.64	36.28
Artificial management	38.94	41.59	51.33	58.41
The overall utilization effect of resources	53.98	48.67	53.10	49.56

Based on the data in Table 4, it is clear that manual management is not ideal when it comes to the accuracy of corpus management system design and implementation. Not only that, there have been considerable changes in both areas, and the error rate is rather high. When compared to manual management, the corpus management system's design and execution provide better overall outcomes in a C/S context. Meanwhile, the C/S environment's corpus management system is over 90% complete, and there has been no discernible drop in accuracy. For the purpose of providing more evidence that the C/S environment is better. The C/S environment is carried out using various approaches to further confirm the efficacy of the suggested approach, as seen in Fig. 6.

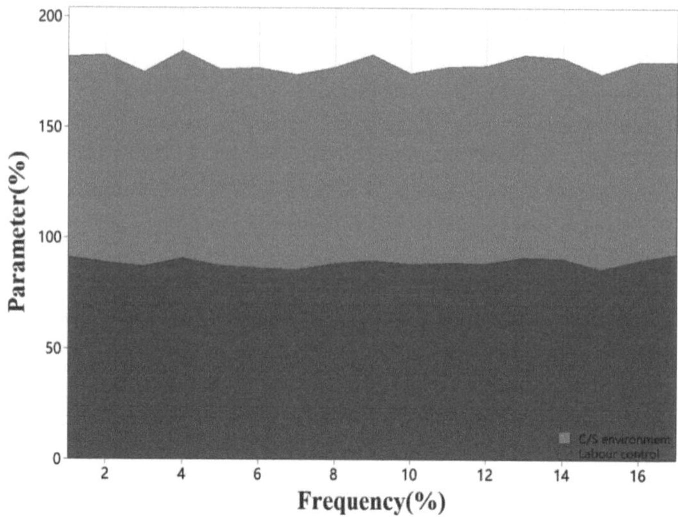

Fig. 6. Design and implementation of C/S environmental corpus management system

As can be seen from Fig. 6, in the process of data database comparison, the data call matches the actual demand, each accounting for half. Therefore, the analysis method proposed in this paper can promote the utilization of linguistic data database. At the same time, it can also integrate the resources of the data database and promote their rational distribution.

5 Conclusion

In response to the fact that current corpus management system design and implementation practices are far from optimal, this article suggests a C/S environment that would improve these processes via the use of computers. The Internet data collecting is built while the correctness and dependability of the corpus management system's design and execution are examined thoroughly. The results show that the analysis method in this paper can promote the utilization of language database, make it more reasonable, and the improvement degree is greater than 20% to 30%. Moreover, in the process of result distribution, its processing effect also meets the requirements, so that it can meet 70% of the requirements. Therefore, the method proposed in this paper can promote the utilization of language data, but the analysis in this paper also has some shortcomings, which will make up for the above analysis in the future.

Acknowledgment. A Study on Integration of Virtue Education into English Writing Teaching, Project number: 23A3018.

References

1. Rao, X.: Design and implementation of an English language and literature teaching management system (3), 5 (2022)

2. Li, B., Qian, Z., Zhang, L.: Design and implementation of a clinical medical teaching management system based on browser and server architecture. Chin. Med. Equip. **19**(1), 5 (2022)

3. Tian, Y., Song, Q., Bao, S.: Design and Implementation of a "River Chief System" River Management System Based on GIS - Taking Liyang City, Jiangsu Province as an Example (Doctoral dispersion) (2022)

4. Wu, E., et al.: Design and implementation of a workflow based geological exploration project management system. Resource Environ. Eng. **37**(3), 350–356 (2023)

5. Duan, L., et al.: A virtual reality based simulation teaching system for automotive mold design and manufacturing CN202210156430.7 (2022)

6. Meng, R., Du, S.: Design and implementation of a university student file management system based on alliance blockchain. Gansu Sci. Technol. **39**(2), 24–27 (2023)

7. Peng, T.: Design and implementation of a customer relationship management system based on SSM. Framework Information and Computers (034–008) (2022)

8. Gao X., Wang, H.: Design and implementation of an animal borne disease monitoring and management system based on Webgis. Heilongjiang Animal Husbandry and Veterinary Medicine (10), 6 (2022)

9. Liao, J., Wang, D., Lin, H.: Design and implementation of a student affairs management system based on PHP (9) (2022)

10. Kong, X., Xu, C., Wang, S., Ding, L.: Design and Implementation of a Smart Management System for River Discharge Outlets Based on Sky Map - Taking Lanling County, Shandong Province as an Example Leather Making and Environmental Protection Technology, **4**(3), 157–159 (2023)

11. Li, Y.: Design and implementation of a question bank management system based on the MVC framework. Modern Educ. Equip. China (19), 16–18 (2022)

12. Xiang, P.: Design and implementation of an intelligent greenhouse environmental monitoring and management system based on STM32. Internet Things Technol. (006), 012 (2022)

13. Wei M.: Design and implementation of a question bank management system based on Java EE architecture. Comput. Program. Skills and Maint. (10), 11–12 (2022)

Design and Implementation of Recommendation System on Education Management

Liang Zhiqiang[✉]

Shenyang University of Technology, Liaoyang, Liao Ning 111003, Liao Yang, China
yaopf-ly@petrochina.com.cn

Abstract. Educational management system is the main content of physical education and comprehensive education analysis. Analyzing how to integrate the management level of the system and optimize the original content has become the focus of current research. Therefore, in the process of recommendation, systematic management and comprehensive management can be carried out to optimize, and the overall optimization rate can be optimized by more than 75%, and comprehensive comparison and comprehensive analysis can be realized. Therefore, the overall educational analysis and the effective integration of educational management and educational system promote the improvement of teaching level.

Keywords: Pearson theory · Collaborative Filtering Algorithm · Educational Management · Recommend system · Implementation

1 Introduction

Promoting system management and educational management is the focus of current research, but there are some problems whether recommendation system and educational management can be effectively integrated, as well as the comprehensiveness, level and degree of integration [1, 2]. Some scholars believe that integrating the education system with the recommendation system, improving and optimizing the educational content, realizing multi-index analysis and multi-index optimization to improve and optimize the integrity of the system can also realize the comprehensive management of the system [3, 4]. At the same time, it is necessary to analyze the overall structure of educational management and recommended content, realize comprehensive management and optimization, and enhance the correlation between education, practice and students [5, 6]. In the process of recommendation system, recommendations should be made according to students' interests and hobbies and students' actual needs. The recommendation process can adopt practical recommendation, comprehensive recommendation and diversified recommendation. Multi-content steps are used to improve, and there are also significant problems and advantages in the recommended holistic access [7, 8]. On this basis, this paper optimizes the recommendation system, and the scope of optimization includes content, methods and results [9, 10].

B. Brik and S. Nazir (Eds.): BigIoT-EDU 2024, LNICST 659, pp. 260–266, 2026.
https://doi.org/10.1007/978-3-032-18631-7_29

2 Theoretical Model Construction for the Design and Implementation of Recommend Systems

Recommended Method is W_i, The recommended process is E_i Recommended holistic structure is $\hat{e}_i = E_i/|E_i|$, $\hat{h}_i = H_i/|H_i|$. Make comprehensive judgment and analysis on the recommended content. The result is shown in Eq. 1.

$$W_i = \frac{1}{k}E_i \times H_i^* |W_i| = \frac{|E_i|^2}{2\eta_o}\frac{\partial^2 \Omega}{\partial u \partial v} \tag{1}$$

Correlate the relationship between the data in the advancement process. The correlation process is shown in Eq. 2.

$$P = \sigma |W_i| = \frac{\Delta y}{\Delta x}\frac{dy}{dx}|E_i|^2 \sum\nolimits_{i=1}^{n} X_i \tag{2}$$

The process of meta-analysis is W_s, the recommended content is integrated with diversified analysis, and the specific process is shown in Formula 3.

$$|W_s| = k \sum\nolimits_{i=1}^{n} (X_i - \overline{X})^2 \tag{3}$$

Optimize comprehensive analysis and diversified system to provide knowledge for multiple recommendations and matching results [11–13]. Results is E_s set, and the matching process is η_o, The matching results and the process are fused. The fusion formula is as in the formula 4.

$$|W_s| = \frac{x}{k\eta_o}|E_s|^n \tag{4}$$

Integrate multiple contents and multiple indicators, and judge the actual situation of each recommendation effect. The judgment of the actual situation in the formula 5.

$$\sigma = 4\pi R^2 \frac{|E_s|^2}{|E_i|^2}\sqrt{a^2 + b^2} \tag{5}$$

It is recommended as a continuous recommendation, so it is necessary to make a continuous judgment and analysis. The continuity of the recommendation is shown in the formula 6.

$$\iint \sigma = \lim_{R \to \infty} \pi R \int \frac{E_s \times E_s^*}{E_i \times E_i^*} \sum\nolimits_{i=1}^{n} \prod X_i Y_i \tag{6}$$

In the process of recommendation, it is also necessary to realize the integration of multiple indicators to meet the actual recommendation needs. The fusion process is $Ao(t_i)$ shown in Eq. (7).

$$Ao = \frac{g(t_i) + F(d_i)}{mean(\sum v_{ij} + n)}\sqrt{\lim_{\delta x \to 0} X_1, \ldots, X_n} \tag{7}$$

3 Practical Examples of the Design and Implementation of Recommend Systems

3.1 Design and Implementation of Recommend System and Related Concepts of Model Construction

Recommendation is a systematic process, which is mainly divided into two aspects: quantifying the data of teaching content, teaching, curriculum and educational management, and comprehensively analyzing the management indicators and structures to form an effective comparison situation and output the comparison results. The comparison results should also be optimized as a whole in the analysis situation and process. Therefore, it belongs to the quantitative analysis process of data, as shown in Fig. 1.

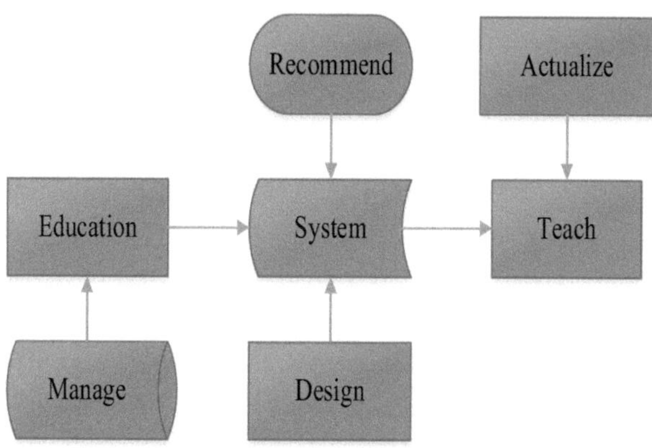

Fig. 1. The analysis process of the design and implementation of the recommend system

It can be seen from the results of Figure. Quantitative analysis, quantitative content, multi-index judgment and multi-index results need to be optimized as a whole. The overall optimization and comprehensive judgment and judgment content also need to be continuously optimized. Therefore, in the process of management analysis, teaching and comprehensive judgment, logic should be formed. The logical relationship shows that the data is analyzed first, and then the necessary system is constructed to carry out teaching and the actual content of teaching, and the actual content and teaching are integrated to realize the theory and. The integration and complementarity of practices, and ultimately, Form a recommendation system and recommendation scheme.

3.2 Design and Implementation of the Recommend System

The actual teaching analysis is based on the judgment, and the relationship between freshmen, sophomores, juniors and seniors, and the actual needs of students are investigated and analyzed. The survey contents include learning situation, hobbies and academic achievements, etc., and the corresponding database and data scale are established. The specific data collection is shown in Table 1.

Table 1. Subject-related parameters of the study

Category	Data survey and analysis	Comprehensive analysis	Diversification analysis	Overall analysis results
Resource recommendations	38.05	77.67	80.58	81.55
Teachers teach	55.75	75.73	76.70	77.67
Teachers teach	56.64	78.64	81.55	73.79
Student navigation	38.05	72.82	75.73	73.79

3.3 Design, Implementation and Stability of the Recommend System

Students' learning situation and advancement degree are progressively analyzed to judge the progressive effect, and the specific results are analyzed by images is shown in Fig. 2.

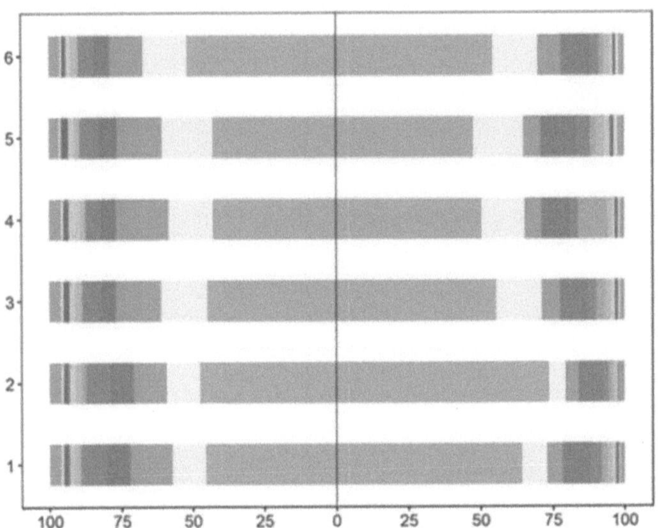

Fig. 2. Design and implementation of recommendation system with different algorithms

Through image analysis and comprehensive result judgment, the overall planning is realized. The planning content and planning effect are also diversified. Effective recommendation analysis and recommendation range measurement can realize the overall optimization and the formation of diversified indicators. Therefore, it is necessary to carry out educational analysis, management analysis and recommendation analysis, and at the same time, it is necessary to judge the effect and distribution of each recommendation. The specific results are shown in Fig. 3.

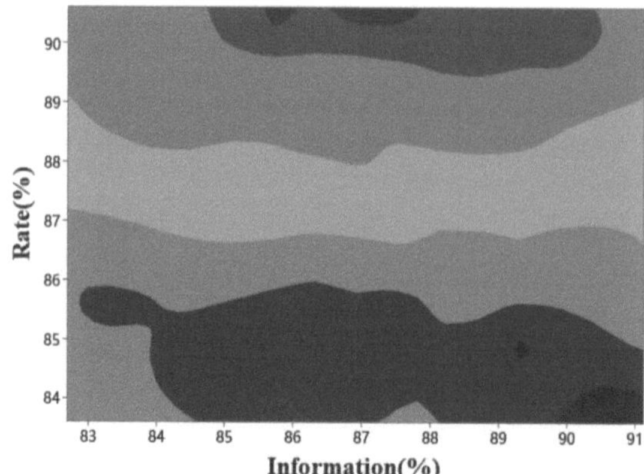

Fig. 3. Design and Implementation of Recommendation System Based on Collaborative Filtering Algorithm

Figure 3 shows that the analysis in the third book will find that there are gradual changes in the recommendation process. In the gradual change, the boundaries between the indicators are clear, and the boundary conditions and boundary results are relatively clear and effective. Correlation analysis and reference analysis are carried out to realize data fusion, comprehensive fusion and analysis fusion, so as to form the optimization of education management and education level. How to effectively determine and analyze the recommended direction and object, and the specific results are summarized as shown in Table 2.

Table 2. Rationalization and comparison of the design and implementation of recommendation systems with different methods

Algorithm	Internal recommendations	On practical recommendation, build	Comprehensive recommendation	Recommended in the original words
Collaborative filtering algorithms	49.56	46.90	76.70	80.58
Hybrid recommendation algorithms	54.87	49.56	80.58	74.76

It can be seen from Table 2, through diversified recommendations and holistic judgments, data integration, data integration and fusion are realized, presenting multi-indicators and multi-directionality. Therefore, it is necessary to optimize the recommendation system, and the optimization of the recommendation system can also be displayed through bars, so as to compare whether the recommended content is effectively matched with the actual needs. The specific results are shown in Fig. 4.

Fig. 4. Comparative study of the research scheme of the algorithm

As can be clearly seen from Fig. 4, it can be found that there is a communicative change between recommendation and actual demand, which shows that in the process of education, management and education system, recommendation and actual demand show a trend of satisfaction. Moreover, the overall change is 82.69% to 85.97%, indicating that there is an effective integration between demand and recommendation, and the consumption of the integration effect between them is greater than 80%. It also further proves the rationality of the propulsion system.

4 Conclusion

Teaching recommendation, content recommendation and teaching system planning are all conditions for effective analysis and comprehensive analysis. If the fusion and promotion of the two are effectively carried out, the optimization of the effect and content of fusion analysis is the main research direction at present. Instinctively use the recommendation system to carry out relevant optimization to realize the corresponding content and actual needs, meet students' teaching and knowledge needs, and realize its comprehensive management and optimization management. The specific optimization degree is greater than 80%. Therefore, both design analysis and recommendation analysis meet the actual requirements and can provide support for practical teaching. The main deficiency is that there are differences in the analysis of data and samples.

References

1. Cheng, H., Fu, G., Jia, J., Liu, Y.: Design of intelligent management system for digital technology museum modern electronic technology **46**(22), 165–169 (2023)
2. Wang, T., Zhang, L., Zhu, L., Yang, Y., Wang, X.: Design and implementation of a personalized agricultural product recommendation system based on collaborative filtering. Wirel. Internet Technol. **20**(14), 87–90 (2023)
3. Liu, M., Jiang, W.: Design of educational resource recommendation system based on knowledge graph Electronic Technology (Shanghai) (2023)

4. Editorial department (2023) Analyze the industry recommended standards for home theater audio system design by the Cedia Custom Electronic Design and Installation Association in the United States Home theater technology
5. Lu, R., Zhu, Y., Liang, X., Duan, H., Liu, P.: A multi behavior recommendation method and system based on multi graph semantic fusion CN202211198942.6 (2023)
6. Long, C.: Research on the realistic relief and optimization path of innovation and entrepreneurship education management system in vocational colleges educational progress **13**(12), 5 (2023)
7. Jiang, X., Zhang, Y.: Design and Implementation of Electronic Approval Management System for Customs Government Procurement Manufacturing automation, 45 (12), 9-13 (2023)
8. Yang, L.: Research and application of automation system technology for small and medium-sized reservoir management. Hydropower Water Conser. **7**(2), 101–103 (2023)
9. Zhang, Y., Zheng, J., Liu, L.: Design and implementation of a job recommendation system based on collaborative filtering algorithm. Modern Comput. **29**(13), 109–112 (2023)
10. Wang, Z., Chen, L., Deng, X.: Design of a college student employment recommendation system based on blockchain and user tags. Inf. Comput. **35**(11), 140–142 (2023)
11. Yu, Y., Cao, Z.: Design and implementation of student information management system under the informatization of education management electronic. Compon. Inf. Technol. (2023)
12. Yang, M.: Design of an enterprise level intelligent knowledge search and recommendation system solution. Inf. Comput. **35**(4), 136–139 (2023)
13. Gao, H.: Analysis and Design of the Management System for Ideological and Political Education of College Students Electronic Technology and Software Engineering (4), 211–214 (2023)

The Application of Computer in Intelligence Education

The Design of Computer Aided Wisdom Classroom Teaching System for College English

Jia Lu[✉]

Wuhan University of Engineering Science, Wuhan 430060, China
LuJia@wues.edu.com

Abstract. With the development of modern society, English is an international communication language, and many colleges and universities have gradually begun to pay attention to the reform and innovation of English teaching. With the continuous emergence of emerging technologies, the reform direction of college English teaching has turned to the construction of informatization and intelligence. This article mainly analyzes the meaning of smart classroom, and the application practice of smart classroom in college English teaching, and it also studies the design of multimedia teaching system in college English smart classroom.

Keywords: International communication language · English teaching · Smart classroom

1 Introduction

With the release of new curriculum reforms in colleges and universities, traditional teaching models can no longer meet the needs of talent training. In order to effectively improve the quality of talent training in universities, they should retain the relatively good parts of the traditional education model, and combine modern technology to make college English teaching classrooms more intelligent and informatized. This article mainly describes the application of smart classroom to English teaching and how to effectively improve the effect of English teaching [1].

2 The Overview of the Smart Classroom

With the reform of college education, smart classrooms have played a huge role in the reform of college education. The meaning of smart classroom has the following two aspects:

A. *Make the teaching classroom more intelligent.*

With the introduction of multimedia technology, teachers in college classrooms generally use multimedia equipment to display teaching content in the form of PPT courseware, and teachers can also query the video, audio, etc. of relevant teaching content

B. Brik and S. Nazir (Eds.): BigIoT-EDU 2024, LNICST 659, pp. 269–274, 2026.
https://doi.org/10.1007/978-3-032-18631-7_30

through the Internet. This not only effectively enriches students' learning resources, but also greatly expands students' learning horizons. Of course, the application of multimedia equipment effectively concentrates the students' attention in the classroom, and strengthens the students' learning enthusiasm and initiative [2]. However, college teachers still have some problems when using multimedia for classroom teaching. For example, teachers rely too much on multimedia equipment, thus neglecting the interaction with students. When teachers use multimedia courseware, they just switch courseware blindly, which makes students feel tired easily, thereby reducing their interest in learning the content of the classroom. The use of smart classroom teaching system enables students and teachers to interact with each other across time, region and space. Not only that, the smart classroom teaching system can show the students' learning conditions based on the learning records of classmates and students. And students can adjust their teaching content and methods in a timely manner according to the relevant display results, which can enhance the student's learning effect [3].

B. *Make the teaching mode more intelligent.*

The teaching stage of English theoretical knowledge is the education of junior high school and high school, so the teaching mode in the English teaching classroom of junior high school and high school is "speak + listen". This teaching mode is mainly for teachers to explain theoretical knowledge to students and students to understand the content explained by teachers. However, if college English classroom teachers still use the traditional teaching model, then students' thinking about learning will not change, and it will be difficult to get rid of the current teaching dilemma. The purpose of intelligent classroom teaching is to strengthen students' intellectual development, improve students' creative thinking and problem-solving abilities, and cultivate the necessary skills for English learning. The Smart Classroom combines information technology with modern learning environment. It combines multiple teaching methods and deep thinking for teaching[4].

III. *The construction and implementation of smart classrooms.*

The construction and implementation process of the smart classroom covers three stages of teaching links before class, during class, and after class.

- Pre-class academic analysis. Under the traditional teaching model, the teacher's pre-class preparation content is mainly to understand the core content, secondary content and extra-curricular content that needs to be taught in this section of the course, and the teacher must make corresponding teaching plans. The pre-class preparation content of students is mainly a preview of the course content of this section. Under the traditional teaching mode, teachers cannot understand the students' preview situation, and thus cannot determine the progress of classroom teaching. In a smart classroom, teachers can send relevant content and videos of this section to the smart classroom teaching system before class. Students can preview according to these contents and record their notes. In this way, the teacher can learn about the students' preview situation through the students' preview notes, and then start the design of classroom teaching. In addition, students can write out what they don't understand or send them to the teacher when recording the preview notes[5]. The teacher can directly explain to the students after receiving the message, or solve these problems for the students in the classroom.

- Instructional design in class. Under the traditional teaching model, both the teacher's explanation content and the classroom teaching atmosphere are very serious and rigid, which makes it impossible for students to learn and practice classroom content more flexibly. The teaching mode in smart classroom teaching is "offline classroom education + online platform education". Among them, offline classroom teaching still uses traditional teaching methods. Of course, teachers need to add various teaching situations in the classroom. This kind of contextualized teaching method can effectively enhance students' interest in learning, but the disadvantage of offline education is that the teaching time is fixed. Online teaching is mainly carried out through the online teaching system[6].This teaching mode can effectively overcome the constraints of time, place and space, which allows students to communicate with teachers more frequently, thereby enhancing students' learning effects.

- Personalization and intelligent tracking of after-school tutoring. The work after class in the Smart Classroom is mainly assessment. The teacher publishes the after-school exercises and assessment content of this lesson in the teaching system, so that students must complete the daily word recitation and punch in to show the task is completed, and the students must complete the exercises of this lesson and submit them to the teacher. The teacher understands the student's learning and recitation based on the content submitted by the student.

3 The Practice of Smart Classroom in English Teaching

A. *Increase video teaching content.*

In college English teaching, the smart classroom learning model can display the content of teaching materials in the form of multimedia courseware, and this can display the teaching content to students more intuitively through video, audio, pictures, animation and other methods. This method effectively strengthens students' understanding of teaching content. When making instructional videos, teachers should give detailed explanations around key content, so as to alleviate the difficulties faced by students during their studies [7].

B. *Enhance communication between students and teachers.*

The communication between students and teachers in the smart classroom includes online communication and offline communication. Online communication means that students and teachers communicate through an online teaching system. Students can send the knowledge content they don't understand to the teacher, and the teacher can explain it in detail to the students after receiving it. Offline communication means that students should be good at asking questions in the classroom teaching process, and take the initiative to tell what they don't understand, so that teachers can solve students' problems in a timely manner and avoid the phenomenon of continuing problems. Whether it is online communication or offline communication, both can enhance students' communication skills, promote emotions between students, and allow students to deepen their influence on knowledge points. At the same time, it can also improve the quality of

English teaching [8]. After the classroom teaching is over, teachers and students make a timely summary after class so that the smart classroom can be used in college English teaching.

III. *Effectively strengthen after-school exercises.*

The smart classroom teaching method effectively strengthens the students' after-school exercises. That is to say, in a teaching system where teachers can publish the teaching PPT, audio, video, etc. used in the course after class, students can conduct detailed reviews. In addition, teachers can publish after-school exercises and related tasks through the teaching system. Students must complete the content of after-school exercises and related tasks in a timely manner, and submit the completion status to the teacher, so that the teacher can also understand the student's learning through the completion of the student condition [9].

4   Design of Smart Classroom Teaching System

A. *Architecture of the teaching system.*

This system adopts a three-tier system structure of B/S structure (see Fig. 1). The three-tier model mainly includes an interaction layer, an intermediate layer and a data layer.

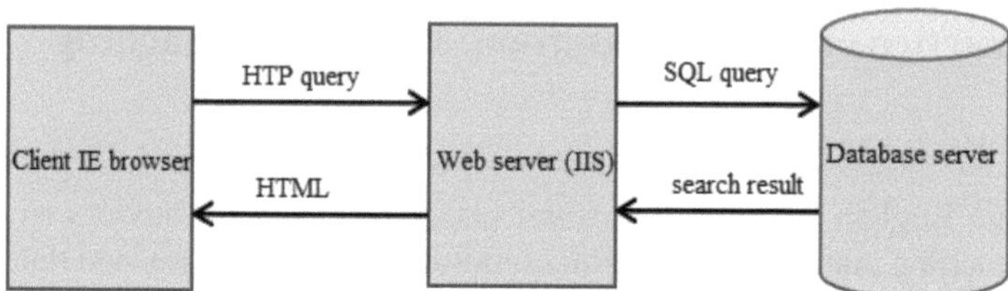

Fig. 1. Three-tier architecture

B. *System function design.*

This system includes three kinds of users: students, teachers and administrators, so the system function design for these three kinds of users is shown in Fig. 2.

III. *The main implementation mode of the system.*

The system mainly implements 4 modes (see Fig. 3). The data standardization algorithm formula in the data analysis algorithm is shown in formula (1), and the data normalization formula is shown in formula (2).

$$S = (X - \text{Mean})/(\text{standard deviation}) \tag{1}$$

$$S = \sqrt{\frac{\sum_{i=1}^{n}(s_i - \bar{s})^2}{n}} \tag{2}$$

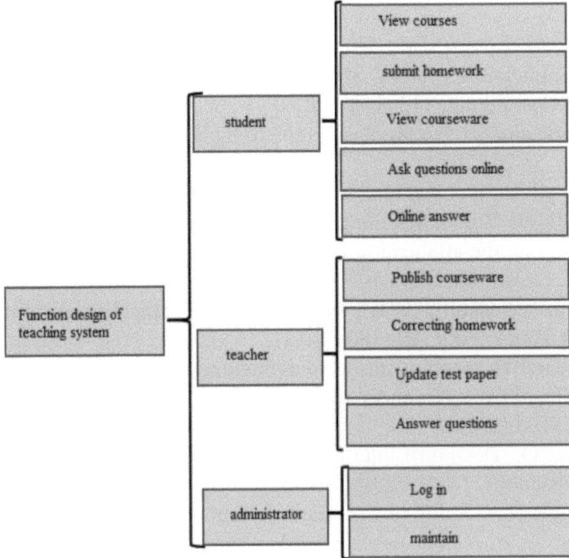

Fig. 2. System function design

5 Conclusion

With the application of smart classrooms, the teaching quality has been significantly improved. Of course, smart classrooms bring greater breakthroughs and opportunities to college education, but also bring more problems and challenges to college classroom education. Therefore, college teaching staff should continue to strengthen the application of smart classrooms, so as to further enhance the reform process of college education. Of course, with the emergence and application of various emerging technologies, these problems will also be solved [10].

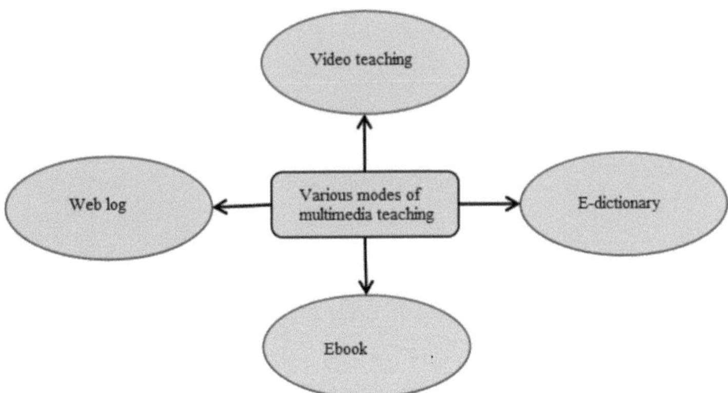

Fig. 3. The main implementation patterns of the system

References

1. Wei, L.: The application strategy of wisdom classroom. High School English Writing Teaching. New Curriculum, 115–115 (2019)
2. Li, S.: The application of "smart classroom" in high school english reading teaching. New Educ. (Hainan), 20–21 (2019)
3. Liao, S.: The application of teaching wisdom in the internet + high school english classroom environment. Middle School Teaching Reference, 29–30 (2019)
4. Yan, T.: Research on the application of information elements in the construction of college english wisdom classroom. Campus English (2017)
5. Jiang, J.: Optimizing teaching design with wisdom and achieving efficient english classroom. Primary School Times: Educ. Res. 80 (2014)
6. A review of research on teaching design and implementation of Intelligent English classroom in higher vocational Colleges under the Background of Internet +. Science & Technology Vision, pp. 102–103 (2018)
7. Zhao, H.: Zeng, Q.: Design of intelligent classroom teaching and learning system. Softw. Guide (Educ. Technol.), 14–16 (2013)
8. Guo, L.: A Comparative Study of Cultural Innovation, 102+201 (2018)
9. Liu, L.: An analysis of college english wisdom classroom teaching from the perspective of second language acquisition. English on Campus, 9–10 (2019)
10. Lian, D.: An empirical study on english wisdom classroom teaching in higher vocational colleges. China Educ. Inform. 73–75 (2017)

The Application of Computer Simulation Technology in College Physical Education Teaching

Shao Yi[✉] and Zhang Xue Feng

Shanghai Customs University, Shanghai 201204, People's Republic of China
shaoyi@shcc.edu.cn

Abstract. Using computer simulation technology to simulate the real situation of the teaching method, not only make students into the virtual scene, but also can improve the interest in learning and sports ability, which is a brand-new teaching method. Computer simulation technology can simulate the activity function of teachers and students themselves and bring physical education teaching and students into the virtual space, providing new experience for physical education teaching in colleges and universities.

Keywords: computer · simulation technology · university physical education teaching · application

1 Introduction

With the rapid development of modern science and technology, many universities, cultural courses and professional courses have set up computer simulation courses, and many courses adopt interactive multimedia teaching system [1]. Traditional education methods and today's college students' strong thirst for new knowledge do not adapt, make them think that physical education is a burden, and physical education teachers think they are not enough attention to physical education, intense exercise and college students' physical lack of science, lack of more reasonable, more novel teaching methods [2]. With the rapid development of the times and the rapid development of science and technology, the educational concept of the university is also undergoing great changes, and the physical education teaching is being comprehensively reformed [3]. Therefore, it is necessary to reform the traditional physical education teaching methods, establish more scientific, reasonable and innovative teaching methods, and strengthen the students' physical fitness and interest in physical education [4, 5].

2 Related Works

A. *Feasibility of computer simulation technology in colleges and universities.*

B. Brik and S. Nazir (Eds.): BigIoT-EDU 2024, LNICST 659, pp. 275–284, 2026.
https://doi.org/10.1007/978-3-032-18631-7_31

Because of the rapid development of artificial intelligence, virtual reality, and big data analysis technology, computer simulation technology has a good enough application foundation in college physical education and has both technical capabilities and realistic conditions [6]. Computer simulation technology can establish a high-fidelity simulation environment, and then achieve the functions of action reproduction, scene simulation, and detailed simulation analysis in physical training, which greatly enriches the teaching methods [7]. From the point of view of software and hardware, it also has the basic conditions. Among them, in terms of hardware, motion capture capabilities and sensors can make it compatible and have the advantage of cost control [8]. In terms of software, various teaching assistance platforms and motion simulation models have become more and more mature, so they can meet the requirements of personalized teaching and intelligent evaluation. From the perspective of education management, the state actively promotes the construction of smart education, so that colleges and universities can better carry out information-based teaching and allows the further application of simulation technology to get the soil [9]. Computer simulation technology has been able to obtain comprehensive conditions to be put into college physical education teaching and then play an important role in it [10].

B. *Key points of using computer simulation technology to improve the quality.*

In college physical education teaching, it is necessary to make reasonable use of relevant technologies for teaching design, and computer simulation technology can do this, which is conducive to the needs of technology integration and teaching evaluation. Teachers need to integrate the application of simulation technology into their teaching plans based on teaching objectives, such as using virtual reality to carry out tactical drills, and using action analysis to optimize training paths, to strengthen the pertinence and effectiveness of teaching. A simulation platform with strong interaction and timely feedback should be established, so that students can actively participate in the simulation environment and obtain timely error correction, so as to improve learning efficiency. At the same time, a data-based teaching evaluation mechanism can be established, and the dynamic adjustment of the teaching plan can be carried out by collecting and analyzing relevant data, so as to optimize teaching.

3 Computer Simulation Technology the Importance of Physical Education Teaching

A. *Simulation modeling and virtual scene setting of teaching objectives.*

In this regard, it is necessary to set a clear teaching goal based on the content of the course and the characteristics of the students. The goal needs to include skill mastery and include physical development, tactical understanding, and cooperation skills. To use computer simulation technology to establish a multi-dimensional target model, the system will transform the abstract target into parameters that can be measured and monitored, so as to facilitate the subsequent evaluation and adjustment of the teaching effect, as shown in Eq. (1).

$$T_g = \alpha S_k + \beta P_f + \gamma T_c + \delta C_o \tag{1}$$

In Eq. (1), T_g represents the degree of achievement of the total goal of teaching (between 0 and 1), S_k represents the skill mastery index, P_f represents the physical fitness index, T_c represents the tactical cognitive level, C_o represents the collaborative participation, α, β, γ, δ represents the importance of each one, and the sum is 1, which can be set based on the nature of the course. Through simulation modeling, the teaching objectives are concretized. Teachers can accurately control the focus and progress of all aspects of training.

Based on the computer simulation platform, the virtual sports scenes of various sports that meet the teaching needs are established. The above environment can simulate different weather, terrain and equipment conditions, which can allow students to train in a variety of situations and improve their ability to adapt and adapt, and the parameters of scene setting can adjust the difficulty, so as to provide more reliable technical support for hierarchical teaching, as shown in Eq. (2).

$$E_s = M\sqrt{f(W_c, F_d, O_t, I_r)} \tag{2}$$

In Eq. (2), M represents the model. E_s represents the value of the virtual environment simulation effect, W_c represents the complexity of weather conditions, and F_d represents the difficulty level of the venue, O_t represents the type and accuracy of the equipment, and I_r represents the interactive realism index, so that the changing environment can cope with the training, and at the same time, the simulation setting can better improve the flexibility and challenge of teaching.

B. *Motor skills motion capture and analysis.*

With the help of sensors and simulation systems, the data generated by students in training, including movement trajectory, angle and speed, can be captured and analyzed in real time. By automatically identifying incorrect movements and providing correction suggestions, students can optimize their movement skills and improve learning efficiency in the process of feedback, as shown in Eq. (3).

$$M_q = \frac{1}{n}\sum_{i=1}^{n} m_i \tag{3}$$

In Eq. (3), M_q represents the action quality index and n represents the number of action elements. $\epsilon\in_i$ represents the error rate of the i-th action element. This step can help with precise capture and improve movement standardization. The data feedback step can also better drive further skill refinement.

The system will automatically generate a personalized teaching path based on each student's performance data, mainly including training content, frequency, and difficulty. This allows teachers to optimize their teaching strategies and differentiate their instruction. This process will take into account students' interests and abilities, and enhance their motivation to learn and achieve their goals, as shown in Eq. (4).

$$P_i = A_s \cdot \left(1 + \frac{I_f}{L_d + 1}\right) \tag{4}$$

In Eq. (4), P_i represents the individualized path intensity index, and A_s represents the student's current athletic skill level, I_f represents the interest matching factor, L_d

stands for learning disability coefficient. Pathways can be customized to help students learn according to their aptitude, while at the same time, combining interests to increase efficiency.

III. *Real-time interaction and feedback mechanism construction, teaching evaluation and continuous optimization.*

In the process of simulated teaching, the system can provide real-time feedback on students' performance, and provide interactive guidance based on multimodal methods such as voice, image, and prompt light. Teachers will also be able to intervene remotely and complete synchronous evaluations. This kind of interactive feedback will make the physical education teaching in colleges and universities have a higher degree of immediacy in the classroom, and at the same time, enhance the linkage between teachers and students and the sense of student participation, as shown in Eq. (5).

$$F_r = R_t + V_m + T_s \tag{5}$$

In Eq. (5), F_r represents the degree of feedback response, R_t represents the delay of real-time data update, and V_m represents the multimodal interaction score, which mainly includes images and sounds. T_s represents the synchronicity score for teacher involvement. Interactive feedback allows the system to better help users build an immersive experience that stimulates active learning among students.

At the end of the teaching, the system will also carry out a comprehensive analysis of the teaching process and student performance, and at the same time, further generate an evaluation report. Teachers need to diagnose teaching bottlenecks based on data content, and use the simulation system to adjust teaching content, strategies, and goals, so as to form a closed-loop system of continuous optimization, as shown in Eq. (6).

$$E_t = \frac{O_g - I_g}{T_c} \tag{6}$$

In Eq. (6), E_t represents the efficiency of teaching, O_g represents the degree of goal achievement after teaching, I_g represents the starting level before teaching, and T_c represents the length of the teaching cycle. Assessment reports can help to better achieve precise improvements, thereby closing the loop and driving continuous improvement in teaching quality.

4   Results and Discussion

A. *The case study of computer simulation technology in college physical education teaching.*

For a long time, a university has adopted the traditional physical education teaching model, focusing on unified courses, fixed venues, and standardized movement training, so its teaching methods are relatively simple, and the participation of students is not high. In this case, some students are resistant due to lack of interest and physical differences, and the school's teaching evaluation also relies more on the subjective judgment of teachers, without data support. Because colleges and universities have relatively high requirements for the comprehensive quality of students' sports, the original teaching methods of the school can no longer meet the goals of personalized development and high-quality education. Based on this, the school decided to introduce a method of computer simulation technology application to use virtual training scenes, motion capture analysis, and intelligent feedback systems to achieve accurate teaching and real-time evaluation and then improve the overall quality of physical education. The architecture diagram of the simulation teaching system is shown in Fig. 1.

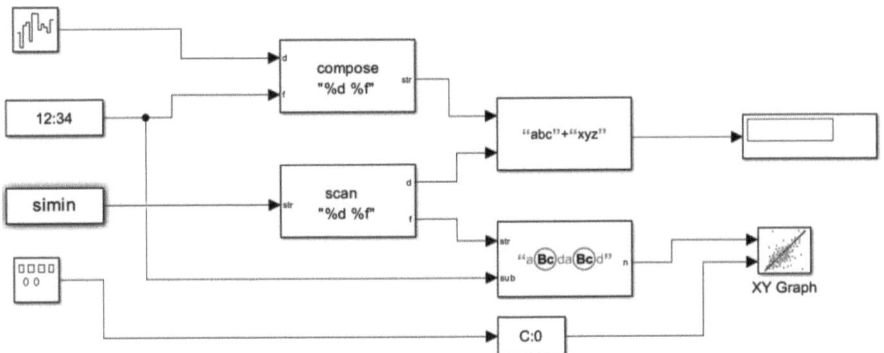

Fig. 1. Architecture diagram of the simulation teaching system

As can be seen from Fig. 1, the components of the system mainly include teaching modeling, virtual scene generation, motion capture analysis, personality path recommendation, feedback interaction module and evaluation optimization. This shows that the system is complete and has covered the whole process of physical education teaching in colleges and universities.

In physical education teaching, teachers 'teaching skills, students' learning enthusiasm, learning effect, teaching venues, teaching equipment and other factors all occupy a large proportion. Therefore, how to correctly understand the students' learning characteristics, the strength of physical quality and adaptability is the key to physical education teaching. College students are the main body of college physical education teaching, how to systematically understand and train it, to its scientific understanding and training, it is particularly important. Traditional physical education classes (as shown in Table 1) take PE teachers as the main body, and students are passive. Teachers often use the "indoctrination style" way to complete their homework. After a PE class, if the students only feel physical and mental destruction, no practical harvest, then, the quality of the classroom is difficult to reflect. As a result, many teachers will focus on the interpretation of movement skills and knowledge understanding. In such an overall environment, we must constantly improve this teaching method, and seek new ways to improve its teaching quality, as shown in Table 1.

As can be seen from Table 1, the "football manager", "like" live football "," like "FIVA", "like" NBA " -like competitive games are all a simulation of football games and training, allowing participants to experience their fighting skills and will to fight. Can cheer for the audience in the simulation, blood boiling, immersive. For those who

Table 1. Comparison between traditional PE teaching and simulation technology

	Emulation technique	Traditional classroom
Way	Teach	Teaching and learning
Point of penetration	How to teach?	How to teach and learn?
Degree of difficulty	Centre	Big
Time	Short	Long
Content	Few	More
Teaching object	Participants and virtual students	Student

like sports and sports games, although they are not qualified to participate in real sports competitions, they can also operate virtual players and conduct virtual competitions in the competitions to personally experience the fun of sports and experience the real scene of sports. Moreover, due to the high viewing value of competitive games, many people will choose sports games to meet their leisure and physical needs.

B. *Students' motion capture analysis and further teaching application.*

The real-time analysis interface for student motion capture is a key part of the system. In this way, the learning situation of students in teaching can be better reflected, which is conducive to the subsequent analysis of the system, and is conducive to the analysis and optimization of teaching quality, as shown in Fig. 2.

As can be seen in Fig. 2, the system can accurately present a variety of data, including movement trajectory, joint angle, velocity, etc. This shows that the technology has achieved highly detailed teaching intervention and action correction.

After the students learn the physical education courses, the teachers can introduce the students into the actual training, and use the computer simulation system to simulate some scenarios. Test students, such as badminton, table tennis, rugby, basketball, volleyball, tennis and other sports, they can establish a virtual arena through the computer simulation system to feel the field atmosphere in daily teaching and training, which can promote students' interest in learning, experience the exciting arena, and conduct daily simulation practice. Through the computer simulation, the students can have a better understanding of the formation mechanism of the movement process and skills. The simulation system can also provide accurate feedback for the students' physical fitness. If a student is injured in the physical education class and needs to know the information of the injured part, the computer simulation system can also simulate the injured part according to the simulation signal of the system; let the student and the teacher know whether the specific injury can continue the race, as shown in Table2.

As can be seen from Table 2, it analyzes the specific application of computer simulation in teaching activities, and expounds its characteristics and functions. Secondly, combined with the purpose, requirements and practical needs of teaching and research, the research and determination of the scale characteristics and restriction conditions of computer simulation technology are comprehensively studied.

III. *The virtual teaching scene.*

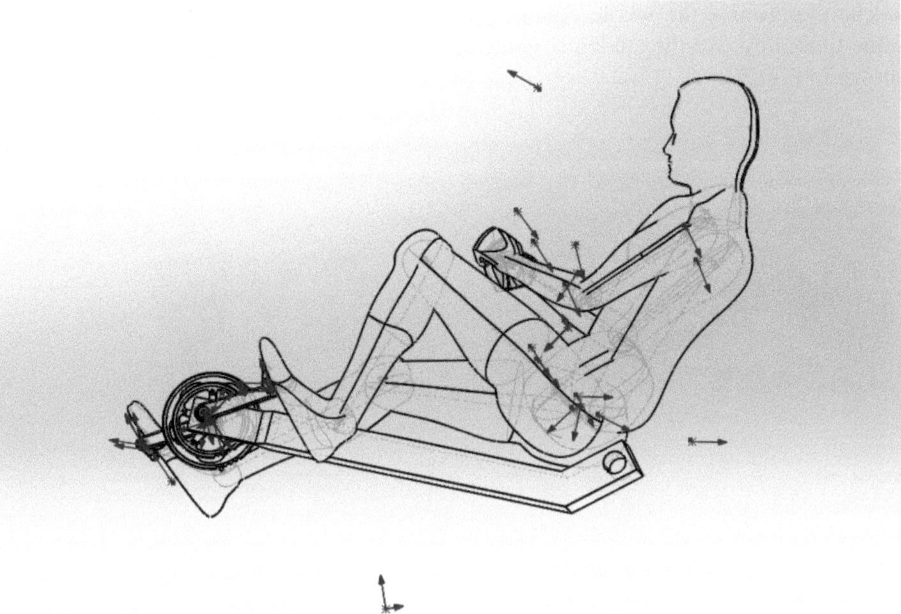

Fig. 2. Schematic diagram of the real-time analysis interface for student motion capture

Table 2. Main Application Process of Computer Simulation Technology

Implementation on the problem	Analyze the specific application, elaborate the characteristics and functions, combined with the purpose, requirements and practical needs of teaching and research
Actively construct primitive mathematical models	Active construction of the original mathematical model to ensure the quality of the model
Mathematical model of the practical construction of the simulation system	Based on the original mathematical model, the deficiencies found are corrected
Enter the programming and debugging stage	According to the established mathematical model, the shortcomings found in each link
Implement the concrete practice to the simulation experiment	The simulation experiments were performed by computer simulation techniques and the results will be recorded accurately
Careful verification of the experimental results	Meet the intended construction purpose according to the test results obtained

Through further application, the virtual teaching scene can be obtained, whereby, people can better see the whole simulation process of the system simulation scene, and realize the analysis of multi-person confrontation and tactical drills, and further help teachers, optimize the whole college physical education teaching process, and at the same time, improve the students' enthusiasm and performance in practical training, as shown in Fig. 3.

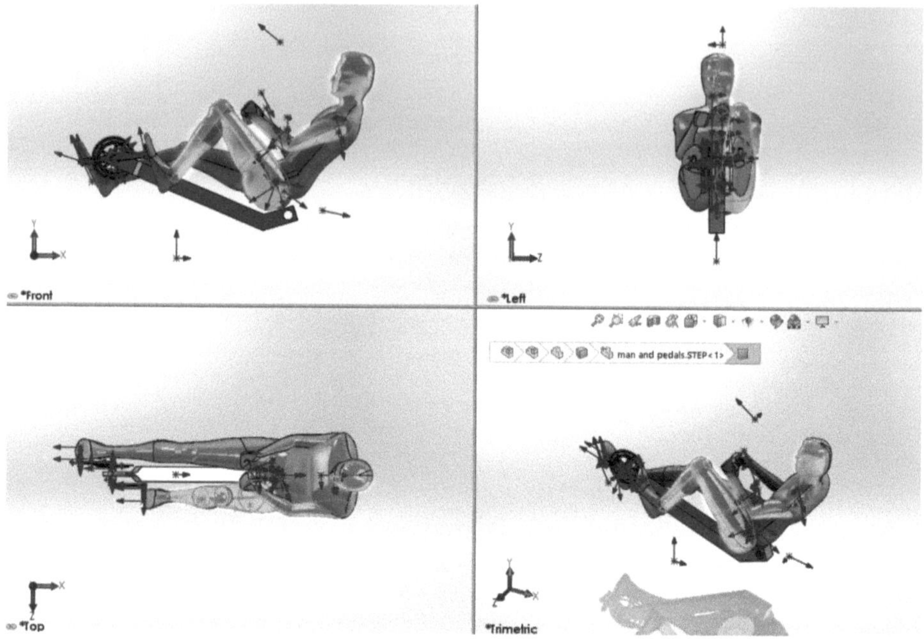

Fig. 3. Schematic diagram of the virtual teaching scene

As can be seen from Fig. 3, the system simulation scene is highly realistic, and multi-person confrontation and tactical drills can be simulated. This shows that the system has high interactivity and authenticity, which improves the immersion and efficiency of teaching.

To better analyze the practical application of computer simulation technology in physical education teaching in colleges and universities, it is necessary to evaluate its teaching effect, which is also the focus of this paper. The indicators that need to be considered mainly include skill mastery rate, physical fitness improvement value, learning interest index, collaboration ability score, and tactical comprehension score, and the specific situation of the above indicators will determine the results of this study, as shown in Table 3.

As can be seen from Table 3, The performance of the simulation system in all aspects is excellent, especially in the "skill mastery rate" and "learning interest index", and the students' physical training performance is quite outstanding. This results show that simulation teaching can greatly improve the quality of physical education teaching in colleges and universities, especially to significantly improve students' sports performance and improve their learning initiative. At the same time, it also shows that computer simulation technology can be well applied in physical education teaching in colleges and universities, and has excellent application value.

Table 3. The final evaluation of the teaching effect

Project \ Metrics	Skill Mastery Rate (%)	Physical fitness boost value	Learning Interest Index	Collaboration ability scores	Tactical understanding scores
Achievement of teaching goals	89.32	76.58	84.91	70.13	81.47
Adaptability to the environment	75.62	68.29	83.21	65.94	72.85
Accuracy of movements	93.17	80.46	79.54	74.82	77.39
Interaction response efficiency	78.64	72.13	88.40	73.20	80.51
Teaching feedback satisfaction	86.49	74.05	91.33	76.96	83.68

5 Conclusion

In short, although simulation and simulation technology is a new science and technology, and it is still in the early stage, it can more fully realize multiple forms of education, more in line with human multi-channel learning mechanism; it can greatly improve its learning effect. Therefore, the application of simulation technology to modern physical education teaching and training will have a great space for development and great value.

Acknowledgements. 2020 Shanghai Education Science Research General Project "Research on the Association Mechanism of Physical Education and Innovation and Entrepreneurship Education" Project No.: C2–2020042.

References

1. Alghadeer, M., Aldawsari, E., Selvarajan, R., Alutaibi, K., Kais, S., Alharbi, F.H.: Psitrum: an open source simulator for universal quantum computers. Iet Quantum Commun. **5**(4), 586–600 (2024)
2. Cui, J., Du, Z., Liu, K., Cao, J.: The simulation design of smart home system based on Internet of Things. J. Comput. Methods Sci. Eng. **23**(6), 2937–2947 (2023)
3. Guo, Z., Yuan, Z., Yang, Y., Jin, Y., Zhao, J., Li, T.: Co-simulation of self-propelled artillery based on virtual prototype technology. J. Mech. Sci. Technol. **37**(12), 6617–6627 (2023)
4. Hjellvik, S., Mallam, S., Giskeodegard, M.F., Nazir, S.: Review on competency assessment instrumentation in computer-based simulation. Technol. Knowl. Learn. **29**(4), 2171–2200 (2024)

5. Lin, B., Tan, Z., Mo, Y., Yang, X., Liu, Y., Xu, B.: Intelligent oncology: the convergence of artificial intelligence and oncology. J. National Cancer Center **3**(1), 83–91 (2023)
6. Mandal, N.K., Azad, A.K., Rasul, M.G.: On students learning experience of fluid power engineering - Impact of simulation software. Int. J. Mech. Eng. Educ. **52**(2), 143–156 (2024)
7. Masly, D.: Application of advanced computational building performance analysis tools in the architectural design of net-zero energy buildings - case study. Architecture Civil Eng. Environ. **18**(1), 49–62 (2025)
8. Nikitchenko, S.L., Lyashchenko, Z.V., Ignat'eva, O.V., Lyashchenko, A.M., Glazunov, D.V., Zhuravlev, D.S.: Development of a virtual simulator for studying the technology of turning on the ST16K20 machine. J. Mach. Manuf. Reliab. **53**(8), 958–963 (2024)
9. Song, C., Yao, L., Chen, H., Liu, L.: Analysis of hot spots and frontiers of nursing scenario simulation teaching research at home and abroad. Educ. Inf. Technol. **28**(9), 11951–11961 (2023)
10. Wang, X., Liang, H.: Application of physical modeling and virtual simulation technology in measuring the performance of subway train tracking and operation. Scalable Comput.-Pract. Exper. **25**(5), 4274–4282 (2024)

Research on the Construction and Language Evaluation of Computer-Based Business French Corpus

Zexiong Xiao[✉]

Department of French, College of Foreign Languages and Literature, Wuhan Donghu University,
Wuhan 430212, Hubei, China
494317918@qq.com

Abstract. In order to enhance the integrity of corpus, and optimize and analyze its data, it can enhance its integrity effect. Therefore, smart approaches are incorporated. The purpose of this study is to explore the construction and language evaluation of a computer-based business French corpus. The corpus consists of a group of texts for business courses, such as job advertisements, letters, etc. The corpus is constructed by qualitative analysis of texts from different sources (recruitment advertisements, letters, etc.). The data was collected through an interview with a native speaker who has been teaching French in college for many years. In addition to this interview, we also tested the participants' knowledge. With the help of computer, the integrity level of corpus can be improved, the results and contents of corpus can be optimized and judged, and a reasonable logical structure can be formed. Make it clearer and match the actual calling requirements. Among them, the response time has been greatly reduced, from the original two minutes to 30 s, and the result has also been improved to 80% in the way of corpus rationality. Computer technology can provide support for corpus analysis and promotion and optimize the original analysis effect.

Keywords: Data analysis · Data extraction · Corpus construction · Language assessment

1 Introduction

The relationship between language and thought has long been a controversial topic. Does language affect thinking, or does thinking affect language? Different people have different opinions on this issue. The theory of linguistic relativity holds that language can affect the habitual way of thinking and worldview of people who use the language for a long time. In other words, the theory does not focus on the ancient and interesting question of whether there is language first or thinking first, that is, "chicken" or "egg", at the stage of the original origin of the language, but on people who use the language for a long time after the invention or formation of the language, whether its habitual thinking mode and conceptual categorization mode will be affected by the language, and this theory only emphasizes the influence of language, not the decisive role [1].

B. Brik and S. Nazir (Eds.): BigIoT-EDU 2024, LNICST 659, pp. 285–295, 2026.
https://doi.org/10.1007/978-3-032-18631-7_32

So, will language affect thinking? The answer to this question has been proved to be yes by many language relativists. At the same time, the hypothesis of language relativity holds that only after acquiring another language, the original way of thinking and the way of conceptual categorization can be adjusted or changed. This view has also been confirmed by many experimental studies. However, after the theory was put forward, many scholars misunderstood the theory, so that the theory remained silent for many years in the academic background of the prevalence of universalism. Only after the rise of new cognitivism did people re-examine the theory, and proved the rationality of the theory through various experiments. The theory was revived, and was supported by a group of new Wolfs. However, in spite of this, there are still many scholars who have not grasped the true meaning of the theory [2]. Especially in China, the understanding of the theory is mostly limited to the interpretation of a few words. Therefore, it is necessary to systematically interpret and clarify the theory.

Since language will affect the habitual way of thinking and worldview of people who use the language for a long time, will the habitual way of thinking or conceptual categorization system formed under the influence of their mother tongue affect the French expression of Chinese learners who use Chinese as their mother tongue for a long time while learning another language (such as French)? In other words, will the conceptual category system of their mother tongue transfer in French learning? The issue of the conceptual category system transfer of their mother tongue has been studied by foreign scholars, but in China, the previous studies of mother tongue transfer mostly stay on the surface of the form and meaning of transfer, without involving its cognitive roots, and no one has studied the conceptual transfer of their mother tongue when learning French by Chinese learners with Chinese background [3].

Under the current research background, this study, guided by the basic philosophy of linguistic relativity and neo-cognitive linguistics, adopts the perspective of second language concept transfer theory, proposes the "theoretical framework of French learning concept transfer in Chinese context", and based on this theoretical framework, from the two language performance levels of Chinese French learners in French output. This paper discusses the systematic transfer of three conceptual categories in his French learning.

Under the influence of the linguistic relativistic hypothesis, the second language concept transfer theory has gradually formed. Although the issue of mother tongue transfer is an ancient research issue, many scholars have studied this language phenomenon, previous studies have often only focused on exploring the transfer of mother tongue form and meaning from various angles, and few have studied and analyzed the cognitive mechanism behind the transfer of form and meaning, that is, the nature of mother tongue transfer. After the formation of the second language concept transfer theory, some scholars began to re-examine the issue of mother tongue transfer from the perspective of conceptual category system transfer (see Chapter 3 for details). Based on the in-depth discussion of "history, culture, language, cognitive/thinking mode, concept category" and their relationship in the theory of linguistic relativity and new cognitive linguistics, this study further demonstrates the importance of the theory of second language concept transfer, and combines the learning characteristics of French learners in the context of Chinese language, and puts forward a theoretical framework for the study of second language concept transfer - "French learning concept transfer framework in Chinese context"; This theoretical framework not only lays a theoretical foundation for the empirical study of this study, but also provides a new way to further understand the basic issues of linguistics "history and culture, language, cognitive/thinking mode, conceptual category" and their relations [4]. At the same time, since the theoretical framework is mainly aimed at French learners in China's special linguistic and cultural environment, it can also contribute to the development of theoretical and empirical research on second language concept transfer in China.

Based on the "conceptual transfer framework of French learning in Chinese context", this study adopts a corpus-based research method to systematically analyze the systematic and differential characteristics of French vocabulary, syntax and grammatical metaphor used by Chinese French learners, and explore the cognitive root of its occurrence. On the one hand, the analysis results prove that the systematic and differential characteristics of Chinese French learners' use of French are largely affected by the transfer of mother tongue concepts (such as lexical concepts, grammatical concepts, grammatical metaphorical concepts), on the other hand, it also supports the basic views of linguistic relativism and new cognitivism to a certain extent. At the same time, It also proves the feasibility of the second language concept transfer research under the guidance of the basic viewpoints of linguistic relativity and neo-cognitive linguistics, and in turn verifies the scientific rationality of the "French learning concept transfer framework in Chinese context" proposed in this study [5].

2 Related Work

A. *Research status of French corpus construction.*

The case analysis of He Xianbin has confirmed to some extent that the phenomenon of salience does exist in the Franco-Chinese translation, but Ke Fei (2005) believes that the length of the text that He Xianbin examined is small, and the translator and other factors are not considered, and the argument is not sufficient. Therefore, he analyzed a large number of examples of Franco-Chinese translation by using the corresponding corpus of Chinese and French commonly used in Beiwai, and found that the occurrence of explicit and implicit translation was caused by many factors, such as language, text, translator and social culture. He proposed that explicit (implicit) includes not only the formal manifestation of language cohesion, but also the manifestation of meaning. He also believes that explicit and implicit translation is related to the direction of translation, and puts forward the hypothesis of the relationship between the degree of language formalization and explicit [6].

Wang Lirong (2006) 2 explained from the perspective of cognitive linguistics that the explicit and implicit phenomenon in translation is directly related to the cognitive differences of different language and culture recipients about the same thing. He also pointed out that both implicit and explicit translation should take meaning as a reference, which provided a theoretical basis for the meaning explicitation proposed by Ke Fei.

Wang Jianguo (2008) 3 believes that Wang Lirong emphasizes the explicit and implicit meaning of concepts. Based on the perspective of relevance theory, Wang Lirong believes that the explicit and implicit meaning in translation is not only reflected in the form of conceptual meaning, such as nouns, synonyms that extend the conceptual meaning of nouns, but also in the form of procedural meaning, such as topic markers, modal particles, conjunctions, word order, punctuation, etc. In addition, he also pointed out that speech forms such as modal particles, conjunctions, topic markers and carrying some cultural information may be more prone to explicit and implicit.

Huang Guowen and Yu Juan (2015), based on the theoretical perspective of systemic functional linguistics, designed the explicit analysis framework of the functional discourse analysis model, and took the empirical function as an example to analyze the process, participants and environmental elements in the French version of the Analects of Confucius, and pointed out that the explicit means include addition, explanation and reconstruction.

Huang Libo (2008), according to the object of comparison, classifies manifestation into interlingual manifestation and intralingual analogical manifestation. He also pointed out that both of them are the contents discussed in the manifestation of one of the "translation commonalities". He used the Franco-Chinese parallel corpus and the original Chinese reference corpus to investigate the number, frequency and conversion types of personal pronoun subjects in the two literary and non-literary styles in Franco-Chinese translation, and found that the inter-lingual explicit and implicit are not obvious in Franco-Chinese translation, whether literary or non-literary, but the intralingual explicit of the translated Chinese text is prominent[7]. At the same time, he also further improved and explained the hypothesis of the relationship between the degree of language formalization and the manifestation put forward by Ke Fei by combining the inter-lingual and intra-lingual manifestation, That is, "from language translation with low formalization to language with high formalization (such as Chinese translation, Finnish translation, Russian translation, etc.), the trend of interlingual manifestation is relatively prominent; from language translation with high formalization to language with low formalization, the characteristics of intralingual manifestation of translated text are relatively obvious."

Zhang Dandan and Liu Zequan (2016) investigated the interpersonal meaning representation of the reporting verbs in Wang Xifeng's discourse in the four French versions of A Dream of Red Mansions, and found that the translation of the reporting verbs in the four versions showed different degrees of salience. Their research supports Wang Jianguo's proposition that "speech forms that carry specific cultural information tend to be implicit and explicit". The latter also points out that although the number and types of reporting verbs in some translated versions are rich and varied, they do not fully consider the communicative objects and discourse content of the characters in the source language context, and fail to well reproduce the interpersonal meaning of reporting verbs and highlight the character image of Wang Xifeng; There are also translations that are influenced by the source language, and the imitation of the original text leads to a higher degree of salience of the translation. The research of Zhang Dandan and Liu Zequan put forward the thinking of the context and the applicability of the manifesting strategy, let people understand the shortcomings of the manifesting strategy, and also provide a reference for the study of the gains and losses of the manifesting strategy.

B. *Significance of educational practice.*

Traditional language teaching and learning tend to focus on the form and meaning of language (including the form and meaning of vocabulary, grammar/syntax, and grammatical metaphor). When realizing the positive or negative effects of mother tongue in second language learning, they often only observe the superficial effect/influence of mother tongue form and meaning. Therefore, whether teachers teach or students learn, they often only compare the similarities and differences between the form and meaning of the mother tongue and the second language, deliberately teach or memorize some similarities and differences, to take advantage of these similarities to promote the second language learning, while avoiding the negative impact of those differences on the second language learning. This traditional method of teaching and learning often only aggravates the memory burden of learners, because this simple method of memorizing the similarities and differences between French and Chinese language representations cannot fundamentally play the role of promoting mother tongue, nor fundamentally get rid of the negative impact of mother tongue, and learners need to memorize these representations repeatedly, which is also easy to make them afraid of the complicated vocabulary and grammatical rules of French, As a result, there is a vicious circle between French teaching and learning [8]. The fundamental way to change the current situation of teaching and learning is to find a way out from the cognitive root of language phenomena.

The representation of the transfer of form and meaning of mother tongue often has its cognitive motivation. From the perspective of categorization, due to different language types, there are some differences between French and Chinese in terms of lexicon, grammar, grammatical metaphor categorization, and some categorization methods are also quite different. Under the long-term influence of their respective languages, the French and Chinese people have formed their own unique ways of thinking and the perspective of observing world phenomena (including language phenomena). There are some differences in the way of conceptual categorization (including lexical categorization, grammatical categorization and grammatical metaphor categorization). For example, due to the influence of the language characteristics of "hypotaxis", the French and American people have formed a habitual way of thinking and a perspective of observing the world, such as paying attention to the individual, rational, logical, abstract and so on. In the category of lexical concepts, they pay attention to the logicality and structure of world phenomena, and in the category of grammatical concepts, they pay attention to grammatical forms. As a result of the long-term use of the "paratactic" language of Chinese, the Chinese nation has gradually formed a habitual way of thinking focusing on the whole, understanding, intuition, concrete and other aspects, as well as a perspective of observing world phenomena. In the category of lexical concepts, more attention is paid to the integrity and intentionality of world phenomena, while in the category of grammatical concepts, more attention is paid to the integrity and smoothness of the overall semantic expression, and less attention is paid to grammatical forms. According to the second language concept transfer theory, people's habitual thinking mode will be affected in the process of acquiring a certain language, which will affect their conceptual categorization mode, and then affect the structural forms used by other languages. As for Chinese learners, in the process of acquiring Chinese (mother tongue), their habitual mode of thinking will gradually form under the influence of Chinese, and gradually form their unique conceptual categorization mode [9]. In the process of French learning, the language category system or conceptual category system of their mother tongue may be activated, resulting in the phenomenon of transfer. The transfer may only occur at the level of language form, that is, the formal transfer of the original language category system, for example, Speech transfer and spelling transfer are called "language transfer"; The transfer may also involve the meaning level of language, that is, the meaning transfer of the original language category system, which is called "meaning transfer"; if the transfer also involves the misappropriation, adjustment or re-establishment of the original conceptual category system of Chinese, this transfer will reach the cognitive concept level, which is called "concept transfer". In other words, the essence of some forms and meanings of mother tongue transfer lies in the transfer of mother tongue conceptual category system, including lexical conceptual category system transfer, grammatical conceptual category system transfer, grammatical metaphor conceptual category system transfer, etc.

Therefore, in the process of French teaching and learning, we should explore more the cognitive roots of the transfer of form and meaning of the mother tongue, and carefully analyze the transfer of various conceptual category systems at the bottom of cognition reflected by different types of transfer of form and meaning by comparing the differences of conceptual category systems between French and Chinese. At the same time, efforts should be made to adjust or reconstruct the conceptual category system through various ways, so as to fundamentally promote the role of mother tongue in second language learning and fundamentally avoid the negative impact of mother tongue on second language learning [10].

Guided by the basic viewpoints of linguistic relativity and neo-cognitive linguistics, this study, based on the theoretical framework of second language concept transfer - "French learning concept transfer framework in Chinese context", analyzes the systematic and differential characteristics of second language acquisition, and finds the reasons (mother tongue concept transfer) from the cognitive root of interlanguage acquisition/bias, so as to make more effective use of concept transfer, And to fundamentally reduce the occurrence of errors.

3   Computer-Based Construction of Business

A. *Construction principles and key technologies of French corpus.*

Computer technology constructs classification corpus, and judges and analyzes the remaining results to form it. Logical relationship, so as to meet the actual calling requirements, and make in-depth judgment on the content and corpus conditions between each corpus, so as to form an effective beverage mapping effect. After using the software to count the small French corpus, and summarize the common words and specific habits in the news, a new vocabulary is formed, and four categories of vocabulary grades with different degrees of difficulty are divided, as shown in Fig. 1.

(2) Key technologies.

The analysis of remaining materials also needs to reduce the content of computer analysis through mapping, so as to improve the calling efficiency of remaining materials. Therefore, it is necessary to map and match the content of the corpus with the actual

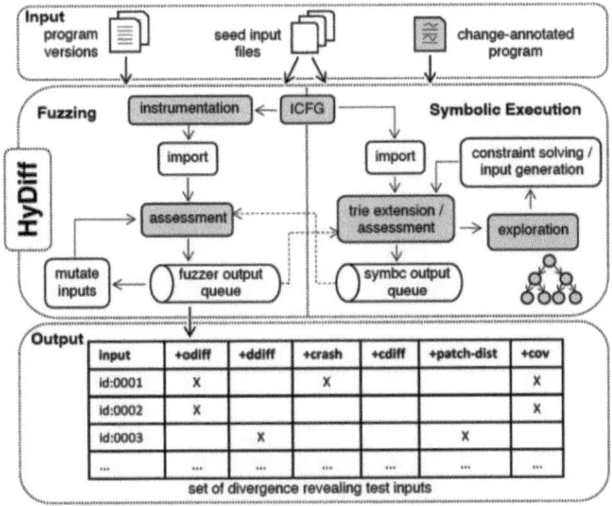

Fig. 1. Corpus analysis software

demand, compare and analyze it, and form a corresponding mapping. The XML markup set can be divided into chapters, paragraphs, sentences and words, as shown in Fig. 2.

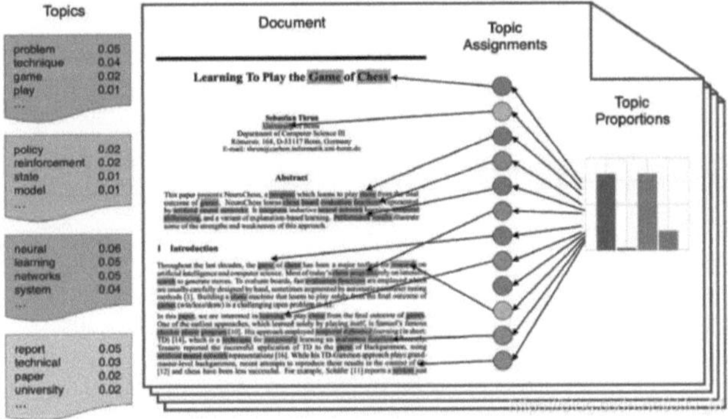

Fig. 2. Corpus storage and annotation function

Mapping analysis was performed to identify relationships between data. Through the logical dialogue and logical comparison of the identification data, the corresponding corpus resources of silver are called to form an effective corpus data table, and the remaining feed data table is summarized to assist the corresponding work. At the same time, it is also necessary to integrate and analyze the entertainment data as a whole to verify the actual call effect of the remaining materials.

B. *Construction and implementation of French corpus.*

In the process of comprehensive data analysis, the data resource database should be mapped and called through their respective logical tables. Realize the active distribution and proportion of corpus, and effectively verify and read corpus. At the same time, it is necessary to integrate the data contents in the scale, effectively make comprehensive judgment and analysis, classify the necessary margins, map them to the necessary mapping relationships, and optimize the original contents and conditions. Word segmentation, statistics of word frequency information and compilation of dictionaries, alignment of segmentation, and timely filtering of stop words, as shown in Fig. 3.

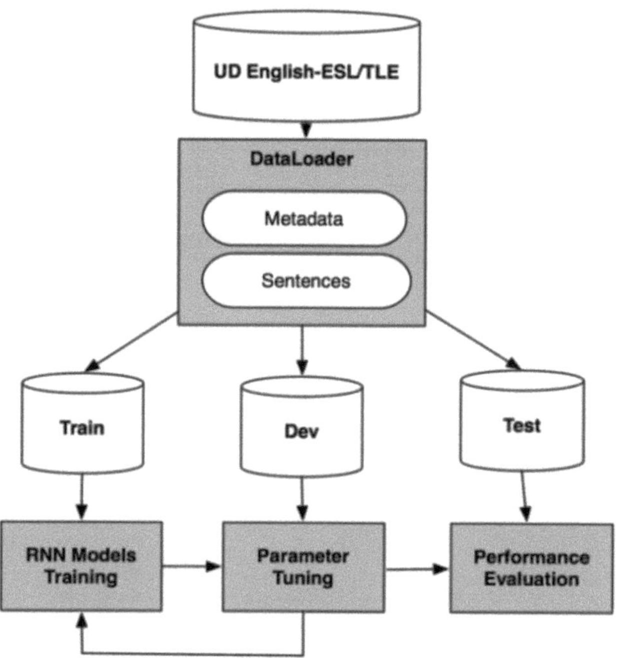

Fig. 3. French corpus platform construction scheme

In the process of remaining material mapping, it can be divided into three directions, including standard language training, mapping, logical classification of data and data correlation, and the data is transmitted according to needs to improve the matching degree of data. At the same time, it is necessary to map the matching data and grammatical content, test the logic and logical relationship between each corpus, and effectively improve the integrity of corpus analysis. At the same time, we should also pay attention to each corpus. The verification and logic mapping between associations can improve the comprehensive analysis effect of corpus. Compare and analyze the data with the actual situation, and finally output the corresponding results and contents to improve the integrity of corpus analysis., and make corresponding marks in time to ensure that the two marked documents of French and Chinese can successfully identify the specific location of the corresponding domain words, and timely complete the statistics of the main word frequency in the field based on the corresponding information.

4 Computer-Based Business French Corpus Language Evaluation

For some language learners, it is necessary to make a personalized analysis. According to language learners' learning knowledge, knowledge characteristics and future learning direction, corpus matching and data transmission are carried out to improve the comprehensiveness of the remaining materials. At the same time, it is also necessary to go to all the contents of the corpus. Matching to avoid repetitive analysis, repetitive data calling and other aspects. French learners in the learning process, as shown in Fig. 4.

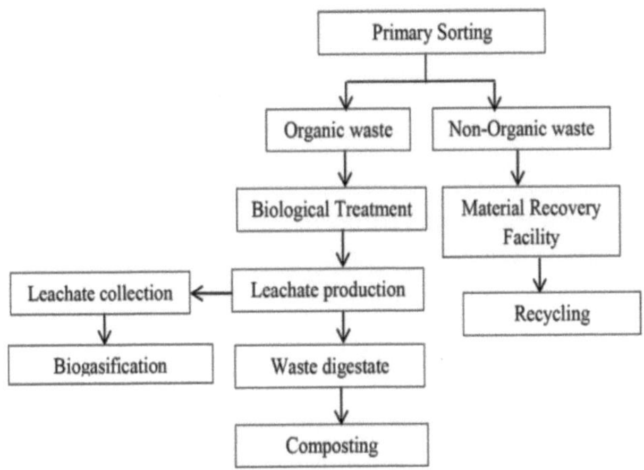

Fig. 4. Corpus language evaluation framework

This article uses WordSmith 4.0 and CUC_ The search function of Paraconc is to search L'etranger, Guo translation, Liu translation, Zheng translation of The Outsider, and the original Chinese "Chess King · Tree King" with explicit logical connectors in Chinese and French as the search items, and to count the number and frequency of their occurrence in different texts.

However, because of the wide grammatical meaning of some conjunctions, they have both logical and illogical meanings, such as putting si at the beginning of a sentence to express suggestions, wishes or regrets; Si + adj/adv means "so"; In demander si, si means "yes" and so on. These usages have no logical meaning, so it is necessary to exclude the non-logical meaning usages of connectives in combination with context. In addition, connecting adverbs such as "jiu", "du", "cai", "hui", "bian", and "ye" are often used together with related conjunctions. Therefore, this section will make statistics as a whole. The final statistical results are shown in Fig. 5.

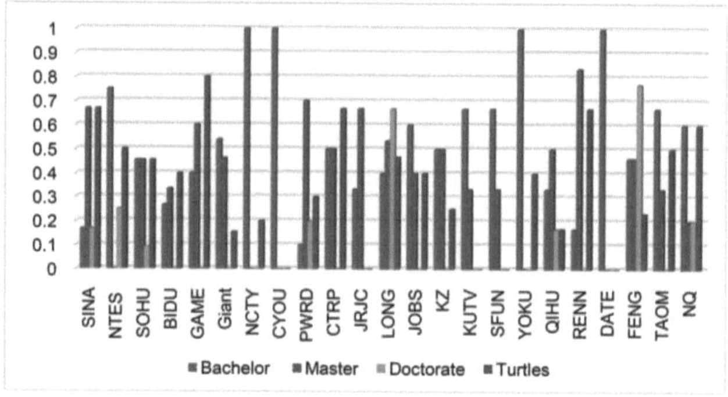

Fig. 5. Statistical results

5 Conclusion

Analysis is an important part in the process of language learning, but how to effectively improve its effect and optimize the original resources is the focus of current research. Originally, the related entertainment content was analyzed by computer technology, so as to improve its distribution effectiveness and the accuracy of corpus learning. The results show that computer technology can optimize the original residual materials, methods and methods, so that its improvement degree is greater than 10% and 20%. At the same time, it is necessary to correlate the contents in the corpus, optimize the original logic, and make it better meet the actual needs. The optimization rate is greater than 75%. Therefore, computer technology can meet the requirements of corpus learning to rationalize the allocation of corpus resources and improve the accuracy of its analysis.

References

1. Zhang, X.: Research on the construction of subject group English corpus based on computer network informatization. J. Phys. Conf. Ser. **1915**(2), 022033 (5pp) (2021)
2. Yan, C.: Research on the Construction of English Translation Corpus Based on Network Electronic Technology (2021)
3. Klimova, B.: Are there any cognitive benefits of computer-based foreign language training for healthy elderly people? – a mini-review. Front. Psychol. **11**, 573287 (2021)
4. Khairuddin, Z., Supie, H, Zahari, N S., et al.: Students' perceptions on the implementation and challenges of computer-based language test for diploma course assessment. Inter. J. Asian Social Sci. **12** (2022)
5. Zhang, C.: Research on the construction of chinese argument corpus. Open J. Mod. Linguist. (2022)
6. Wang, S., Ding, N., Lin, N., et al. Language Cognition and Language Computation -- Human and Machine Language Understanding (2023)
7. Business, J.O.: One truth and one standard for its telling: Reporting on and about scientific business research (2023)
8. Zhang, X.: Research on the language characteristics of agricultural english and its translation strategies. J. Higher Educ. Res. **3**(1), 5–8 (2022)

9. Li, R., Gou, X : Research on multi-modal corpus construction technology in ELAN-Based communicative competence cultivation. In: International Conference on Innovative Computing. Springer, Singapore (2022)
10. Granger, S.: The computer learner corpus: A versatile new source of data for SLA research (2022)

Research on Teaching Reform and Innovation of Computer-Aided Design Courses Majoring in Environmental Design

Guorui Li[(✉)]

Shaanxi Fashion Engineering University, Shaanxi 712046, China
`lgr0928@163.com`

Abstract. Curriculum teaching reform relies heavily on computer-aided design, however this tool isn't always producing the desired results. Conventional approaches to education are less creative and fail to address the issue of education reform. Thus, in order to build a model of educational innovation and change, this article suggests using a computer-aided design approach. Initially, the plant reform scheme is categorized using the auxiliary design knowledge. Then, the reform plan is split according to the teaching standards in order to achieve the quantitative processing of program teaching reform. The supplementary design knowledge then sorts the course's lesson plans, compiles a set of recommendations for improving instruction, and repeats the process until it finds the best solution. Computer-aided design (CAD) is more accurate and innovative than conventional teaching strategies under typical educational situations, according to MATLAB simulations.

Keywords: auxiliary design · designing courses · teaching content · Environmental design

1 Introduction

Key to the educational reform movement is the course material, which serves as a key assessment tool for environmental design majors [1]. But there is an issue with poor outcomes in the real process of teaching reform, and this has an effect on the curriculum. A number of academics have proposed using AI algorithms in the field of design to evaluate the reform plan and provide related pedagogical assistance [2]. In light of this, the research suggests using a computer-aided design technique to improve the course material and test the model's efficacy.

2 Related Works

A. Mathematical Description of Computer-Aided Design

B. Brik and S. Nazir (Eds.): BigIoT-EDU 2024, LNICST 659, pp. 296–301, 2026.
https://doi.org/10.1007/978-3-032-18631-7_33

Computer-aided design is the use of computer technology to optimize the reform plan, and according to the indicators in the design profession, find outliers in teaching reform [3]. At the same time, the reform plan is integrated to finally judge the feasibility of the teaching reform results. Computer-aided design combines environmental design knowledge [4], uses course teaching content mining, intelligent algorithms, optimizes course teaching content, and can improve course teaching Reform effect.

Hypothesis 1: The teaching content is x_i, the scheme set is $set \sum x_i$, the teaching standard is $f(x_i)$, and the judgment function of teaching y_i reform is shown in Eq. (1).

$$f(x_i) = \sum x_i \left| \prod y_i \right. \langle \xi \tag{1}$$

B. Choice of Reform Plan

Hypothesis 2: The reform option selection function is $F(x_i)$ and the innovation coefficient is q_i, then the reform [5] option selection is shown in Eq. (2).

$$F(x_i) = \sqrt{z_i \cdot \sqrt{f(x_i|y_i)} \cdot q_i \cdot \xi} \tag{2}$$

C. Processing of Professional Data

In order to assess the reform plan's reasonableness, it is necessary to study the teaching reform indicators and record the appropriate information in the teaching reform table before doing computer-aided design analysis [6]. The correctness of computer-aided design is guaranteed by first conducting a thorough analysis of the reform plan and then setting the reform plan's threshold and weight. If the reform plan follows a normal distribution, the outcomes of the education reform will be impacted [7], and quantitative assessment of the curriculum material is necessary. Lessen the precision of educational changes. Choose the curriculum teaching reform plan to increase the degree of reform and the accuracy of computer-aided design; Fig. 1 shows the particular program option.

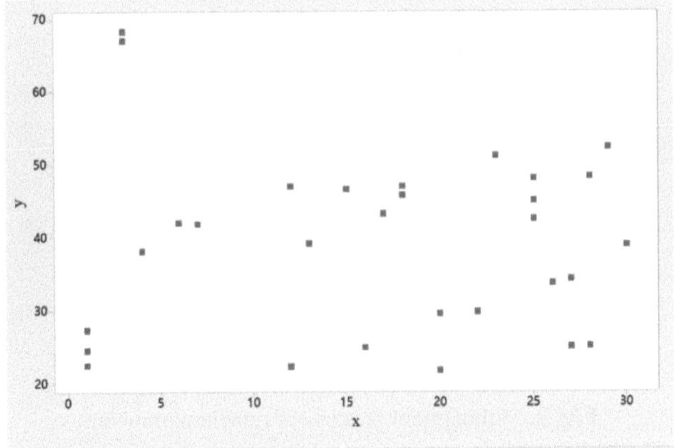

Fig. 1. Scheme selection for computer-aided design

The reform plan demonstrates a diverse distribution and satisfies the instructional criteria, as shown in Fig. 1. By modifying the reform strategy, doing away with the duplication scheme, and fixing the reform strategy, the computer-aided design technique satisfies the needs of curriculum teaching reform and has high relevance. To make the whole reform proposal more realistic, the parameters have been adjusted.

3   Results and Discussion

A. Course Teaching Content

This paper's study object is the program data, and Table 1 shows the particular course teaching material, in order to ease the examination of the reform plan.

Table 1. Characteristics of professional data

Reform programmed	Innovative	Number of scenarios	rationality	threshold
2D design	1/4	5.26	12.63	5.79
	1/2	7.37	17.89	9.47
3D design	1/4	21.05	15.79	2.63
	1/2	18.95	8.42	5.26
Comprehensive design	1/4	20.00	5.26	8.95
	1/2	12.63	20.00	3.68

The process of processing the reform parameters of the course teaching content in Table 1 is shown in Fig. 2.

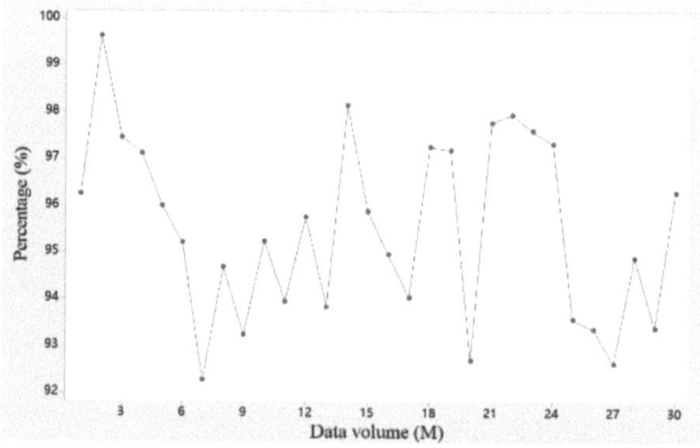

Fig. 2. Adjustment process of reform parameters

According to Table 1, the outcomes of using computer-aided design for curricular teaching material are more in line with real needs as compared to conventional teaching methodologies. When compared to more conventional methods of instruction, computer-aided design yields much higher rates of correctness and compliance. It is clear that the computer-aided design technique offers quicker reform schemes and greater accuracy from the modifications in the reform parameters shown in Fig. 4. Thus, when considering both course material and innovation, computer-aided design is superior.

B. Outlier Recognition Rate of Course Teaching

The course teaching material was examined after the screening of computer-aided design threshold standards [21]. Then, the first findings of curriculum teaching reform were achieved. Table 2 shows the findings of the investigation that was conducted using several approaches to more precisely verify the impact.

Table 2. Overall status of the parameters of the reform programmed

parameter	Reform rate	Innovation rate
two-dimensional	5.26	13.68
three-dimensional	8.42	20.00
Comprehensive design	6.32	9.47
mean	12.63	13.68
X^2	17.89	13.68
P = 0.036		

3.1 Stability and Accuracy of Curriculum Teaching Reform

Figure 3 shows the results of comparing computer-aided design with conventional teaching methodologies, which may be used to test the correctness of the former.

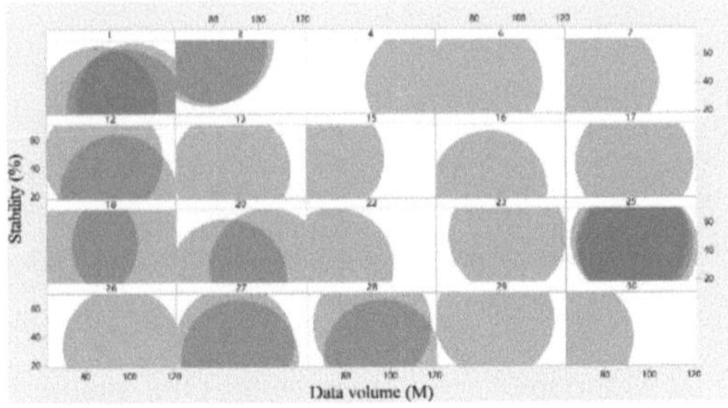

Fig. 3. Stability of computer-aided design

Figure 3 shows that compared to conventional teaching strategies, computer-aided design methods have a greater rate of innovation and a lower rate of mistake, suggesting that computer-aided design methods include the curriculum teaching reform. It makes more sense, in contrast to the less creative reform approach that relies on conventional methods of instruction. In Table 3, we can see how well the algorithm in question performed.

Table 3. Comparison of the accuracy of reforms of different methods

algorithm	Time for reform	Reformed precision	error
Computer-aided design methodology	93.93	98.93	7.86
Traditional teaching strategies	88.93	88.57	8.71
P	0. 064	0. 014	0. 029

Table 3 demonstrates that although the conventional approach to education is novel, it has certain drawbacks, such as a long reform period and a high mistake rate when it comes to implementing new curricula. Compared to more conventional approaches to education, the time required to implement changes brought about by computer-aided design is much shorter. Simultaneously, with no significant modification, the computer-aided design process reform now has an accuracy of above 90%. Just to be sure that computer-aided design is the best option. A thorough evaluation of the vegetation reform plan was conducted using several approaches to confirm the method's efficacy; the results are shown in Outcome 4.

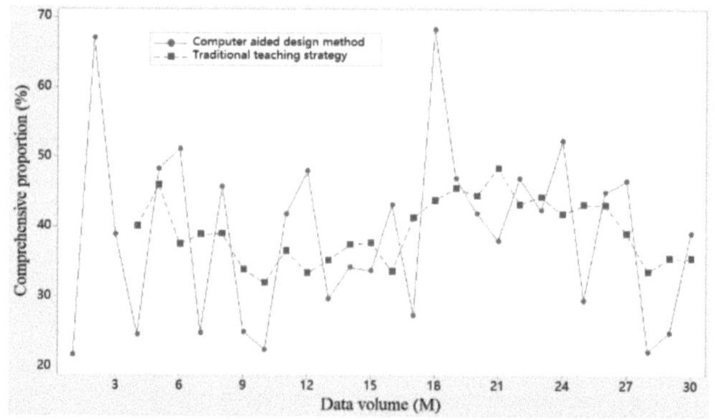

Fig. 4. Comprehensive evaluation results of computer-aided design

Figure 4 shows that compared to more conventional methods of instruction, the comprehensive outcomes of using CAD methods are more superior. This is because CAD methods have led to more curricular change in the classroom. Change the parameters of the reform plan, tweak the coefficient, and establish the threshold.

4 Conclusion

With the goal of enhancing the course material via the application of environmental design expertise, this article suggests a computer-aided design approach to environmental design development in light of the reform of curriculum teaching. Concurrently, a set of reform criteria for curriculum instruction is constructed after an exhaustive analysis of the current set. Research has shown that CAD software may optimize the delivery of courses and enhance the precision of curricular reform efforts. But computer-aided design pays much too much attention to analyzing lesson plans and not enough to allocating various indicators.

References

1. Liu, L., Zhang, C.F., Wu, T.: Application of computer simulation in innovation and entrepreneurship teaching reform of economics and management specialty. Sci. Program. **2022** (2022a)
2. Liu, Z., et al.: Teaching reform to the biology major during the COVID-19 pandemic: a study of the method of teaching industrial innovation and entrepreneurial talents. Front. Psychol. **13** (2022b)
3. Ma, Y.H.: Research on the reform and innovation of higher education teaching mode and management method from the perspective of college students' mental health. Psychiatr. Danub. **34**, S745–S746 (2022)
4. Tian, C., Zhou, Q., Yang, B.: Reform and intelligent innovation path of college football teaching and training based on mixed teaching mode. Mobile Inf. Syst. **2022** (2022)
5. Xie, Z., He, X.H.: Application of 5G network technology in basketball teaching innovation and reform. Mobile Inf. Syst. **2022** (2022)
6. Yu, H.X.: Research on multimedia teaching and teaching reform innovation of accounting major in higher vocational colleges under the background of big data and internet of things. Wirel. Commun. Mobile Comput. **2022** (2022)
7. Zhang, W.: Improved RRT-based moving path planning algorithm for teaching reform and innovation in western orchestral ensemble classes in colleges and universities. Comput. Intell. Neurosci. **2022** (2022)

Design and Implementation of Visualization Teaching System of Computer Image Science Algorithm

Qingqiong Zhu[✉]

Yunnan Technology and Business University, Kunming, Yunnan, China
zhuxq_2005@163.com

Abstract. In order to improve the teaching effect of computer image and learning introduction analysis, I propose an intelligent analysis method and analyze and display it. Computer images and teaching effects, realize comprehensive analysis in the process of teaching computer imaging science. Visualization technology and visualization system have been significantly improved, and the efficiency has been improved by more than 20%. The teaching content can be matched with the teaching image image, and the matching degree is greater than 45%. Therefore, it is explained that this can be realized in the process of comprehensive analysis. And the overall planning improvement rate of resources and teaching content is greater than 45%. Therefore, the private machine image teaching method is combined with image analysis and strength analysis, which can effectively improve its teaching content.

Keywords: Signal processing theory · Computer iconography algorithm · visualization teaching · Resource Query · Systems research

1 Introduction

In the actual teaching process, images can improve visualization, optimize teaching content and effect, and improve the overall teaching planning and level [1–3]. Therefore, a comprehensive comparison can meet the actual requirements. In order to solve the accuracy problem of traditional security and system design [4, 5] research, researchers have introduced Computer iconography algorithm into the research and analysis of planning and execution of the educational curriculum in recent [6] years. Computer iconography algorithm is a calculation method based on group behavior, which simulates the interaction and cooperation between individuals [7] to achieve the goal of global optimization. The algorithm has the characteristics of decentralization, immutability and smart contract [8], which can effectively solve the accuracy problems existing in traditional schemes. The research optimization [9] model of planning and execution of the educational curriculum based on Computer iconography algorithm further improves the accuracy and reliability of simulation by optimizing the parameters and algorithms in the research process of security and system design [10] research. The model adjusts

B. Brik and S. Nazir (Eds.): BigIoT-EDU 2024, LNICST 659, pp. 302–311, 2026.
https://doi.org/10.1007/978-3-032-18631-7_34

and optimizes various parameters in this process to achieve the best system design effect. At the same time, the model is able to cope with complex environments and interference [11] factors, providing more realistic and reliable simulation [12, 13] results. The model can provide more accurate research results of the planning and execution of the educational curriculum and describe the changes and trends in the system design process in a more detailed manner. The research and optimization model of planning and execution of the educational curriculum based on Computer iconography algorithm has great potential to improve the accuracy and quality of practical application. In the future, we can further explore and optimize the model, and use the advantages of Computer iconography algorithm in the research of planning and execution of the educational curriculum to promote the innovation and development of technology.

2   The Concept of Planning and Execution of the Educational Curriculum Research Model Construction

In the process of science teaching and image-based teaching, it is necessary to display pictures, texts and pronunciation. Among them, images can effectively improve the teaching effect and teaching conditions, and realize comprehensive judgment and analysis. Some scholars also believe that the integration of comprehensive analysis and formatted analysis can deepen students' understanding of knowledge, optimize the original resources and improve the education system. Through the comparison and analysis of images, graphics and knowledge points it can help students to establish logical relationships and help them to study and analyze in depth. Therefore, in the process of holistic judgment and animal analysis, computer graphics technology and image display technology can improve the life system of teaching, making teaching consistent with actual analysis and comprehensive needs. At the same time, it can also analyze the integrity and process of education, find out the difficulties and problems left over, and effectively conduct overall dialogue and analysis. Therefore, the computer data and comprehensive analysis are used to judge, complete the corresponding data and contents, and make a comprehensive comparison. Through comprehensive comparison and comprehensive analysis, the learning content, learning conditions, images and key points in images can be judged, and the overall display of images can be completed.

3   Optimization Strategies for Planning and Execution of the Educational Curriculum Research

Computer iconography algorithm is a computational algorithm designed to imitate the collaborative behavior of biological groups such as ant colonies, bird colonies and fish colonies. The phenomenon of collective intelligence exhibited by them in solving specific problems has great potential for the optimization of complex problems. In the field of bioengineering and chemical engineering, such algorithms are used to simulate and optimize off-test tube processes, such as system design processes. During optimization, the planning and execution of the educational curriculum study may be divided into different levels to represent different qualities or precis ions. Ultimately, by comparing the simulation performance of each solution, the best option is selected, and the laboratory's system design process may be adjusted based on the results, thereby improving the yield and quality of the product. The use of such optimization strategies can greatly improve the accuracy and efficiency of the simulation of the system design process, especially when dealing with complex and nonlinear biological processes. At the same time, due to its highly parallel and distributed characteristics, the Computer iconography algorithm shows better performance in finding the global optimal solution in the large-scale parameter space, which reduces the risk of falling into the local optimal solution in the traditional optimization method.

4 A Practical Case Study of a Planning and Execution of the Educational Curriculum

4.1 Introduction to the Research of Planning and Execution of the Educational Curriculum

Simulate the research process of the planning and execution of the educational curriculum, as shown in Fig. 1.

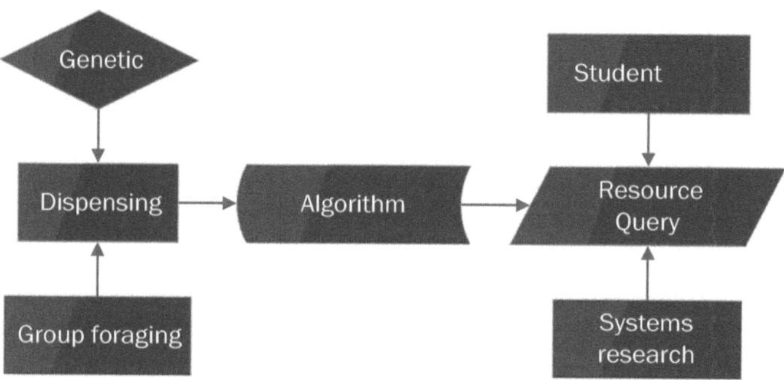

Fig. 1. The analytical process of a planning and execution of the educational curriculum study

From the data analysis in Fig. 1, it can be seen that in the process of integrity judgment and image integration of image analysis, it is necessary to combine the logical relationship of knowledge points and logical points to make judgment, fuse and compare the corresponding knowledge points and contents with images, and list the corresponding knowledge points. At the same time, a logical knowledge mapping database is established, and the mapping data of mapping music angle mapping conditions are displayed, and finally the system is output and studied.

4.2 Research on Planning and Execution of the Educational Curriculum

Based on the content of actual teaching, this paper makes a judgment. The test conditions are mainly the achievements, teaching conditions, teaching environment and teaching comprehensiveness. Complete the comprehensive comparison of teaching and improve students' academic performance. The test results are shown in Table 1.

Table 1. The overall situation of the planning and execution of the educational curriculum research program

Category	Classroom teaching content	Transformation of practice	Actual investigation	Comprehensive survey
Preschool education	88.59	85.08	87.17	85.95
Basic education	90.83	89.79	87.65	88.42
Occupational education	84.78	85.52	88.77	91.02
Distance learning	87.92	87.93	88.63	87.82
The combination of text and text	83.78	87.10	87.43	84.50

4.3 Research and Stability of Planning and Execution of the Educational Curriculum

The information of the graph is displayed through the hospitalization diagram, and the relationship between the information is verified, and the overall identification and mapping of the data are completed by color identification. The specific results are shown in Fig. 2.

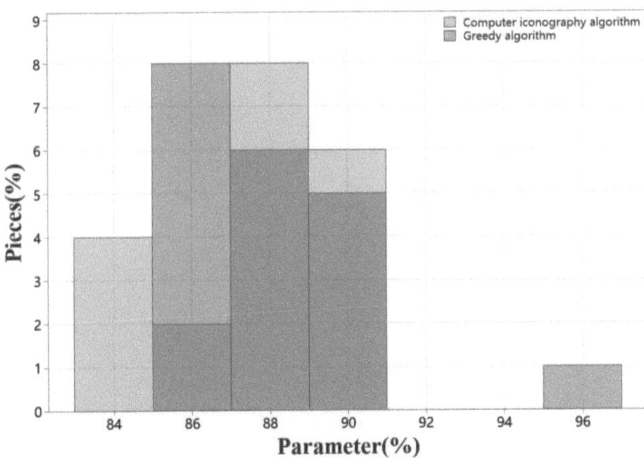

Fig. 2. Research on planning and execution of the educational curriculum with different algorithms

From the analysis in Fig. 2, it can be seen that in the process of computer scene simulation, students' academic performance is red and orange, indicating that the academic performance meets the actual requirements. However, the original analysis method has some shortcomings, and the blue color shows that the graphic display can better meet the actual requirements. For in-depth illustration and explicit presentation, the results of the analysis are summarized. The summary results are shown in Table 2.

Table 2. Comparison of research accuracy of planning and execution of the educational curriculum with different methods

Algorithm	Students' learning situation	Learning interest	Depth of understanding of knowledge points	Actual unerstanding of the effect
Computer iconography algorithm	88.05	87.41	84.39	90.20
Greedy algorithm	89.12	89.60	87.79	86.15
P	88.63	90.59	86.14	90.62

From the analysis in Table 2, it can be seen that in the process of analyzing students' learning situation and interest in learning, they all meet the requirements by more than 80%. Explain that during the comprehensive analysis. Computer scene simulation can realize the overall planning and optimize the original content. However, its distribution and the distribution of students' achievements need to be deeply analyzed. The specific results are shown in Fig. 3.

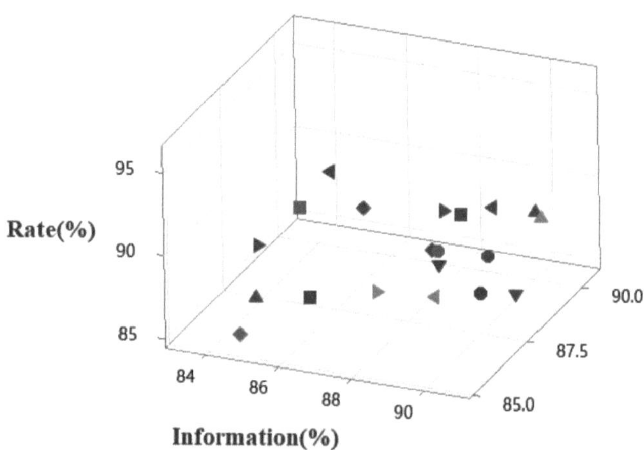

Fig. 3. Research on planning and execution of the educational curriculum of Computer iconography algorithm

From the analysis in Fig. 3, it can be seen that the color and data gathering points between scene analysis and data and logic are different, which shows that in the process of comprehensive analysis, scene simulation can enhance students' interest in learning, and effectively label each knowledge point to facilitate students' comprehensive learning.

Improve the content and effect of learning. Synthesize the original learning knowledge points to realize the effective distribution of resources. In order to make further in-depth judgment, it is also necessary to judge each point of learning and the content of each point. The specific results are shown in the Table 3.

Table 3. Rationalization and comparison of planning and execution of the educational curriculum research with different methods

Algorithm	Integrity of the comprehensive data	Demonstration of difficult knowledge	Depth of understanding of graphics	Comparison of combined teaching effects	Planning of overall analysis
Computer iconography algorithm	87.25	95.99	85.41	87.95	87.25
Greedy algorithm	88.95	88.60	89.69	89.92	88.95

4.4 Comparison of the Effectiveness of the Research on Planning and Execution of the Educational Curriculum

Analysis of computer courses and teaching contents. Is zk found that the unqualified value parameters of the planning and execution of the educational curriculum research is as, and the integration function of the planning and execution of the educational curriculum research scheme is z_i to finally judge the feasibility of the planning and execution of the educational curriculum research, and the calculation is $tol(z_i \cdot v_{ij})$ shown in Eq. (1).

$$\frac{n!}{r!(n-r)!}(z_i \cdot v_{ij}) \geq max\,(v_{ij} \div 2) \tag{1}$$

Comprehensive information comparison, complete graphic display, feature point analysis and overall planning. The specific results are shown in Eq. 2.

$$max(v_{ij}) = \partial(v_{ij}^2 \cdot v_{ij}) \succ \frac{x-\mu}{\sigma}\left(\sum v_{ij}\right) \tag{2}$$

A comprehensive analysis of the content is t_i as follows, the research scheme of the planning and execution of the educational curriculum is set_i and execution of the educational curriculum is y_i as follows, and the judgment function of the research scheme of the planning and execution of the educational curriculum is $F(t_i \approx 0)$ as shown in Eq. (3).

$$F(d_i) = \sum_{i=1}^{n} X_i Y_i \sum t_i \bigcap \xi \cdot \sqrt{2} \rightarrow \oint z_i \cdot 7 \tag{3}$$

Hypothesis II The planning and execution of the educational curriculum research function is $g(t_i)$, and the weight coefficient is w_i, then, the planning and execution of the educational curriculum research requires the unqualified planning and execution of the educational curriculum study as shown in Eq. (4).

$$g(t_i) = \ddot{x} \cdot z_i \prod F(d_i) \frac{dy}{dx} - w_i \frac{\partial^2 \Omega}{\partial u \partial v} \frac{x - \mu}{\sigma} \tag{4}$$

Based on assumptions I and II, we can obtain the synthesis function of the planning and execution of the educational curriculum study, and the results is shown in Eq. (5).

$$\lim_{x \to \infty} g(f_i) + F(x_i) \leq \frac{x - \mu}{\sigma} max(v_{ij}) \tag{5}$$

To comprehensively advance retrograde judgment, it is necessary to establish a connection between the graph and the known points of the image, and the establishment process is shown in Formula 6.

$$g(t_i) + F(d_i) \leftrightarrow mean(\sum t_{ij} + 4) \frac{\Delta y}{\Delta x} \tag{6}$$

In the process of logical analysis, knowledge point judgment and comprehensive result judgment, it is also necessary to distinguish knowledge points, knowledge contents and key contents, and complete the feature extraction of knowledge points and the effective simulation of teaching and scenes, and the outcome is $No(t_i)$ given in Eq. (7).

$$No(t_i) = \frac{g(t_i) + F(d_i)}{mean(\sum v_{ij} + 4)} \frac{n!}{r!(n - r)!} \tag{7}$$

To make sure the word segmentation method for Chinese is accurate, the planning and execution of the educational curriculum research does a thorough examination and determines the scheme's threshold and index weight. An appropriate analysis is $unno\sqrt{2}(t_i)$ required of the study on the planning and execution of the educational curriculum as it is $accur\mathfrak{A}(t_i)$ a systematic evaluation of the planning and execution of the educational curriculum research plan. Equation (8) shows that the RAISF study scheme will be impacted if the RASS dataset is not in a normal distribution, which will reduce the overall accuracy of the RAISF study.

$$accur(t_i) = \frac{min[\sum g(t_i) + F(d_i)]}{\sqrt{2} \sum g(t_i) + F(d_i)} \sqrt{b^2 - 4ac} \tag{8}$$

The research scheme of the planning and execution of the educational curriculum shows that the research scheme of the planning and execution of the educational curriculum depicts a multidimensional distribution that corresponds to objective facts. The research on planning and execution of the educational curriculum has no direction, This shows that the research scheme of the planning and execution of the educational curriculum has a high level of unpredictability, indicating that it is $randon(t_i)$ a high analytical study. If the random function analyzed by the resource inquiry system is, then Eq. (8) may be represented as Eq. (9).

$$accur(t_i) = \frac{min[\sum g(t_i) + F(d_i)]}{\sqrt{a^2 + b^2}} \tag{9}$$

So that we can confirm the effectiveness of the Computer iconography algorithm, the research scheme of the planning and execution of the educational curriculum is compared with the Greedy algorithm, and the research scheme of the system design Fig. 4 shows the system.

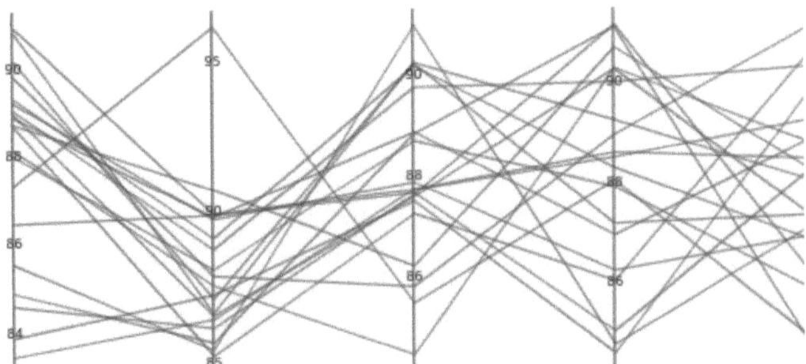

Fig. 4. Research on planning and execution of the educational curriculum with different algorithms

Figure 4 shows that research on the planning and execution of the educational curriculum of the Computer iconography algorithm is more extensive than research on the Greedy algorithm. Establishing connections between knowledge points and knowledge associations fully meets the corresponding needs. However, whether the results meet the requirements or not also requires in-depth judgment. The depth judgment process is shown in the Table 4.

Table 4. Display of comprehensive knowledge points and comparison of contents of comprehensive knowledge points

Algorithm	Scene restoration	Environmental display	Comparison of feature points	Feature point fusion
Computer iconography algorithm	89.71	87.73	85.74	88.87
Greedy algorithm	83.34	86.29	87.66	88.52

According to the data in Table 4, The extraction of feature points, features, contents, etc. is greater than 80%, and the feature problems and feature comprehensiveness are also greater than 80%. It shows that in the process of scene restoration, knowledge points and contents can be effectively identified, and effective links and logical relationships can be established. The index comparisons, and possible experimental verification may be involved. It may also include testing the suitability and robustness of the algorithm during different simulation settings or different types of resource queries to ensure that the algorithm maintains its high performance in a variety of situations. Through such comprehensive comparison and analysis, it is not only possible to clarify the performance of different algorithms in specific fields, but also to further promote the development of optimization algorithms, providing more accurate simulation and prediction tools for laboratory and industrial-scale biological processes. Continuous analysis, analysis process and continuous judgment of computer graphics display. The judgment process is shown in Fig. 5.

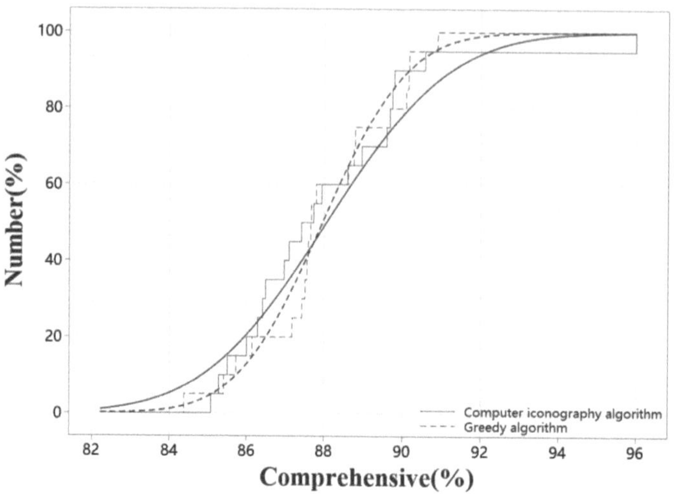

Fig. 5. Research on planning and execution of the educational curriculum of Computer iconography algorithm

As can be seen from Fig. 5, The extraction of feature points shows a parabolic trend, and the feature points also show a logical relationship in the process of correlation, and a logical curve is established in the middle. Cross-analysis between feature points and continuous quantitative explanation. In the process of analysis, the corresponding analysis can be realized, the analysis effect can be improved, and the logical relationship and comprehensive judgment can be completed.

5   Conclusion

In the actual teaching process, scene simulation, computer knowledge analysis and knowledge judgment process all meet the requirements, and can promote the improvement of its fishing effect. However, in the process of analysis, whether the scene can be effectively displayed requires in-depth judgment. Based on this judgment, this paper will find that computer scene simulation can improve the content of students' knowledge points, with an improvement rate of more than 60%, and effectively identify the key points. The recognition rate is greater than 90%, reducing the data error. Data association and data deviation reduction is greater than 10%. It shows that in the analysis process, computer scene analysis can improve the teaching effect and complete the comprehensive evaluation of teaching. There are also shortcomings in the research process. The main shortcomings are that the sample size is too small and the continuous monitoring time is short. In the future, more sample sizes will be added to make up for the research deficiency.

References

1. Shi, R.: Design and implementation analysis of visualization teaching system of computer image science algorithm. Manage. Inf. China **21**(16), 2 (2018)
2. Li, H.: Design and implementation of visualization teaching system of computer image science algorithm. Comput. Knowl. Technol. Acad. Edn. (12), 3 (2013)
3. Li, H.: Design and implementation of visualization teaching system of computer image science algorithm. Comput. Knowl. Technol. Acad. Exchange (2013)
4. Zhang, Z.: Design and implementation of the digital image processing demonstration system. (Doctoral dissertation, Jilin University) (2012)
5. Cao, H.: Research and design of virtual laboratory. (Doctoral dissertation, Shandong University of Technology)
6. Yuan, G.: Design and implementation of schistosomiasis egg image recognition algorithm. (Doctoral dissertation, Nanjing University of Aeronautics and Astronautics)
7. Zheng, R.: Design and implementation of the 3 D reconstruction system for medical images. (Doctoral dissertation, University of Xidian University)
8. Huo, Y., Tongwendi, Li, X., Wu, Y., Yao, Y.: Design and implementation of the standard section navigation visualization system for transesophageal echocardiography. Comput. Appl. **000**(0z2), 212–215, 241 (2015)
9. Zhuo, T.: Design and implementation of the laboratory teaching auxiliary system based on Android. (Doctoral dissertation, Central China Normal University) (2016)
10. Min, X.: Research on key techniques for surgical planning and simulation system of NPC brachytherapy. (Doctoral dissertation, Xiamen University) (2009)
11. Ye, L., Li, F.: Design and implementation of laboratory multimedia teaching auxiliary system. Comput. Netw. (2015)
12. Jin, H.C.: Research on the 3 D visualization and reconstruction algorithm of medical images based on GPU. (Doctoral dissertation, Guilin University of Electronic Science and Technology) (2007)
13. Jian, Z.: Research on the image monitoring system based on the improved orb algorithm. Comput. Sci. Appl. **13**(12), 7 (2023)

Higher Education Evaluation System Based on Computer Networks

Hongmei Zhang[✉]

Yunnan Technology and Business University, Kunming 651701, Yunnan, China
hongmeiz562@gmail.com

Abstract. The role of education quality evaluation in higher education of various institutions is very important, but there is a problem of inaccurate outcome evaluation. In the globalized educational environment, higher education evaluation systems play a crucial role, not only affecting the quality of teaching, but also having a profound impact on students' academic development and career prospects. Traditional evaluation methods usually rely on the subjective judgment of teachers, focusing on final exam results, while ignoring process evaluation and diversified evaluation. This approach may lead to one-sided evaluation results that do not fully reflect students' learning abilities and potential. MATLAB simulation shows that under certain evaluation criteria, the fuzzy algorithm evaluates the accuracy and rationality of the educational quality of college students' innovation All are superior to the traditional education model.

Keywords: computer network · fuzzy algorithm · innovation in education · Theory

1 Introduction

With the continuous development and wide application of computer technology, the role of computers in college education has received more and more attention [1]. Computer technology can be used to evaluate higher education, due to the limitation of geography and resources, the data collection and analysis efficiency of the traditional evaluation system is low, and the information feedback cycle is long, which is not conducive to timely teaching improvement [2]. This paper will discuss the evaluation role of computers in college education and its impact on college education.

1.1 The Evaluation Role of Computers in College Education

1. Assess learning outcomes

The rapid development of computer networks has brought about a revolutionary change in the evaluation system of higher education. Through the online platform, educational evaluation can realize real-time data collection and analysis, such as online quizzes, discussion forum interaction, project collaboration, etc., which can

© ICST Institute for Computer Sciences, Social Informatics and Telecommunications Engineering 2026
Published by Springer Nature Switzerland AG 2026. All Rights Reserved
B. Brik and S. Nazir (Eds.): BigIoT-EDU 2024, LNICST 659, pp. 312–321, 2026.
https://doi.org/10.1007/978-3-032-18631-7_35

be used as an important basis for evaluating students' learning process and ability. Cloud computing technology makes it possible to store and process large-scale data, and big data analysis can reveal in-depth information about students' learning patterns and teachers' teaching effectiveness, so as to provide more accurate evaluation results [4].

2. Assess the quality of teaching

At the same time, the online evaluation system can break the geographical restrictions and promote international academic exchanges and the unification of evaluation standards. For example, through the online course platform, students around the world can share high-quality educational resources, and the evaluation criteria can be based on international consensus, improving the fairness and transparency of education. In addition, the application of artificial intelligence (AI) technology, such as natural language processing and machine learning, can assist teachers in automating homework correction and feedback, reducing the burden on teachers and improving the efficiency of evaluation [6].

3. Assess student learning behavior

Computer technology can be used to assess the learning behavior of college students [7]. How to use network technology to optimize the evaluation system while ensuring data security and user privacy, and how to balance the relationship between technology and the essence of education are the problems that need to be solved urgently in the future development of higher education evaluation system [8].

1.2 The Impact of Computers on College Education

1. Improve teaching and learning

Computer technology can help teachers teach better. The system should be able to collect, process, and feedback evaluation data in real time to support immediate adjustment of educational decision-making [9]. The system should be seamlessly connected with the existing education information platform and support multi-device access [10].

2. Promote pedagogical innovation

The microservice architecture is adopted, and each service is deployed independently to improve the flexibility and maintainability of the system [12]. At the same time, Design architectures that support horizontal scaling to handle high concurrent access [13].

3. Enrich the student learning experience

Computer technology can provide students with a richer learning experience [14]. Responsible for user registration, login, permission management, as well as the storage and update of user information., and then stimulating students' learning potential [15].

4. Promote self-directed learning

Computer technology can facilitate students' self-directed learning. Through online courses, online handouts and learning management systems, computers can make it easier for students to access learning resources [16], and at the same time, they can also allow students to learn anytime, anywhere, thereby stimulating students' independent learning ability and learning motivation [17].

5. Reduce the cost of education

Database design should follow the principle of normalization to reduce data redundancy and improve data consistency. At the same time, use indexes to optimize query performance to ensure that the system can still run efficiently when processing large amounts of data. In addition, database backup and recovery strategies are adopted to ensure data security [18].

In conclusion, leveraging computer technology within university education not only aids in assessing educational quality but also positively influences it. This technology enhances teaching outcomes, fosters pedagogical innovation, diversifies students' learning experiences, encourages their autonomous study, and cuts educational expenses, all contributing significantly to the ongoing progression of higher education. As a crucial component of China's educational sector, tertiary education holds immense value for student development. Nonetheless, evaluations of educational quality often suffer from imprecision, tarnishing the reputation of top-tier university graduates. Some experts advocate that employing fuzzy logic algorithms to examine higher education can precisely analyze these evaluation systems, offering essential backing. Consequently, this study introduces a fuzzy algorithm aimed at refining educational quality assessment methods and affirms its model's efficacy.

2   Related Works

2.1   Mathematical Description of the Fuzzy Algorithm

Data collection is a core part of higher education evaluation systems, and it involves obtaining a wealth of information from a variety of sources, including student achievement, engagement, teacher evaluation, program completion, and more. Using modern technologies such as automated data scraping tools and API interfaces, data can be fetched from campus management systems, online learning platforms, forums, etc., in real-time or on a regular basis. Data pre-processing is essential, including cleansing, deduplication, formatting, to ensure data quality and consistency. In addition, using big data analytics tools such as Hadoop and Spark, massive amounts of data can be processed for real-time or batch analysis to reveal learning patterns and assessment trends.

Suppose I. Cloud computing provides elasticity and scalability for higher education evaluation systems is $C.I$, For example, with storage and compute services provided by Amazon Web Services (AWS) or Google Cloud Platform (GCP) is n, the education quality evaluation program is max, such as Google Cloud AI Platform and AWS Sage-Maker, enable rapid building and deployment of predictive models that can be used to predict student performance or optimize evaluation algorithms is $A(n_i \approx 0)$, As shown in Eq. (1).

$$C.I = \frac{\lambda\sqrt{a^2 + b^2}^{max}}{n - 1\frac{n}{r(n-r)}} \tag{1}$$

2.2 Choice of Higher Education Programmes

Hypothesis II Analyze a student's essay, discussion post, or assignment to understand its content and quality, and provide an objective textual assessment is $ci(x_i)$, and the weight coefficient is w_i, then, Train models to predict student learning outcomes, such as pass rates or GPAs, identify potential academic risks, and intervene in advance as shown in Eq. (2).

$$CI(x_i) = z_i \cdot \sum_{i=1}^{m} ki/m \tag{2}$$

2.3 Analysis of Educational Quality Evaluation Programmers

In handling vast amounts of sensitive educational information, prioritizing system security and user privacy is crucial. Compliance with stringent data safeguarding norms like GDPR is essential, employing encryption methods to secure the data during both transfer and storage phases. Further, implementing strict access restrictions and authentication procedures helps in preventing unauthorized access to the information. The use of differential privacy allows for data evaluation without disclosing personal details. Regular security assessments and vulnerability checks are vital to maintain a secure environment. Educational organizations must establish clear guidelines on data usage and sharing, ensuring students' privacy rights are respected and upheld, as depicted in Fig. 1.

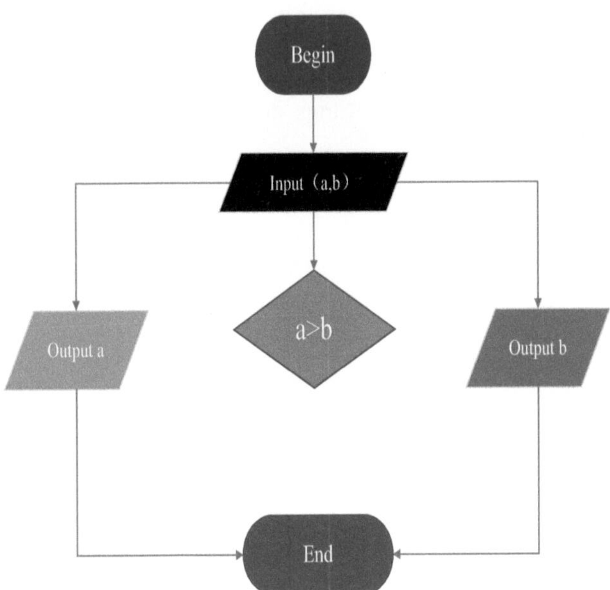

Fig. 1. Results of the Selection of Higher Education Programmes

The evaluation of the education quality scheme reveals a multi-dimensional distribution in higher education, consistent with objective reality. This suggests that students' higher education is not targeted, highlighting the program's inherent unpredictability, thereby deeming it a profound analytical endeavor. Students' higher education fulfills standard criteria, where primarily computer network principles refine their educational experience by removing redundant and irrelevant elements and enhancing default strategies, ensuring a robust dynamic interaction among scenarios within the entirety of the education quality assessment.

3   Optimization Strategies for Student Higher Education

The fuzzy algorithm utilizes a random optimization strategy for students' higher education and adjusts the talent parameters to realize the optimization of students' higher education. It categorizes students' higher education into various education quality evaluation levels and randomly selects different plans. During iteration, the education plans with diverse education quality evaluation levels undergo analysis and enhancement. Post-optimization, the educational quality evaluation level of different programs is compared, and the optimal higher education plan is noted.

4   Results and Discussion

4.1   Introduction to the Evaluation of Education Quality

In the traditional higher education evaluation system, the evaluation process often relies on traditional methods such as paper-and-pencil tests, subjective evaluations by teachers, and final assessments. Although these methods reflect students' learning outcomes to a certain extent, they have many shortcomings shown in Table 1.

Table 1. Requirements for the Evaluation of the Quality of Higher Education

Scope of application	grade	Boost performance	Faculty
Freshman	I	90.23	90.31
	II	93.50	91.20
Sophomore	I	91.41	90.06
	II	91.16	89.95
Junior	I	90.48	92.62
	II	90.80	90.76

The process of evaluating the quality of education in Table 1 is shown in Fig. 2.

In contrast to conventional educational paradigms, the fuIn contrast to conventional educational paradigms, the full quality appraisal methodology the fuzzy algorithm's education quality appraisal methodology aligns more closely with authentic evaluation

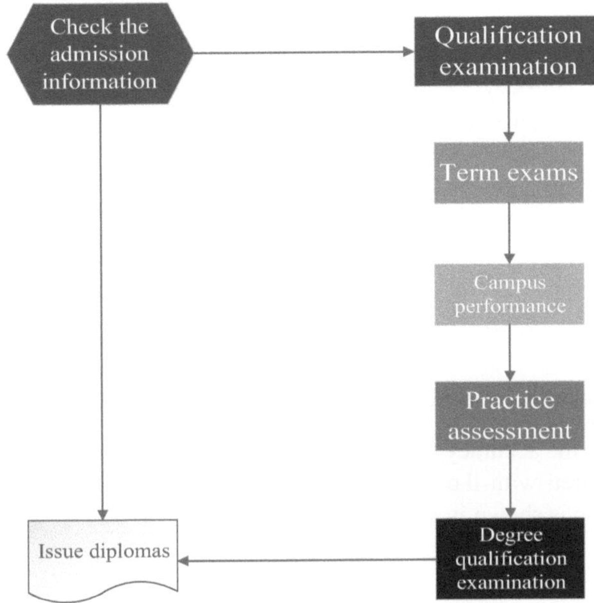

Fig. 2. The Analytical Process of Higher Education for Students

standards. Firstly, the assessment duration is extensive and outcome feedback is sluggish, preventing timely detection of learning challenges. Additionally, assessment inconsistencies may arise from personal teacher biases. Lastly, a singular appraisal technique might not fully gauge multifaceted student traits like collaborative skills or inventive reasoning.

4.2 Higher Education of Students

The student higher education quality assessment scheme incorporates unstructured and semi-structured data. With computer network technology, the evaluation process becomes digital and immediate. An online system gathers learning metrics like quiz results, forum engagement, and collaborative project logs. These metrics contribute to a holistic assessment framework. Automated analysis enables instructors to monitor student progress instantly, while the platform offers individualized feedback for strategic learning adjustments. Integrating peer and self-assessments into the digital review enhances its range and objectivity as detailed in Table 2.

Table 2. The Overall Situation of the Higher Education Programme

category	Quality of teaching	Innovative effect
Freshman	90.20	65.87

(continued)

Table 2. (*continued*)

category	Quality of teaching	Innovative effect
Sophomore	91.08	68.37
Junior	92.05	66.38
mean	92.78	67.02
X^6	45.29	43.27
P = 5.061		

4.3   Higher Education and Stability in the Evaluation of Educational Quality

In order to verify the accuracy of the fuzzy algorithm, the education quality evaluation scheme is compared with the traditional education model, and the education quality evaluation scheme is shown in Fig. 3.

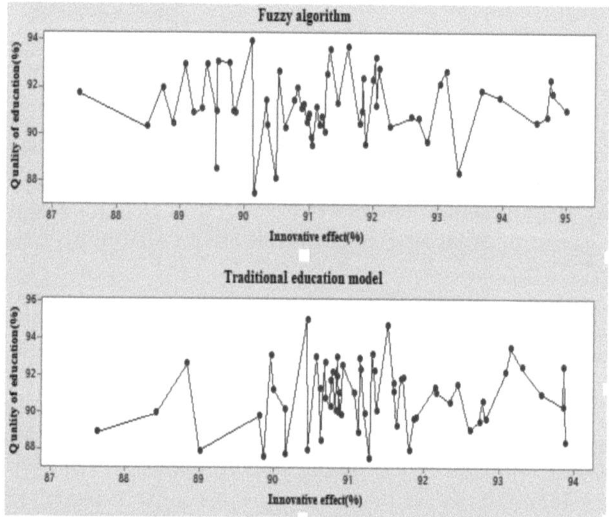

Fig. 3. Higher Education with Different Algorithms

Figure 3 reveals that the fuzzy algorithm's advanced teaching surpasses conventional models, merging diverse online platform data into one assessment system to ensure smooth data integration and analysis. The average quality of education for these methods is detailed in Table 3.

Table 3. Comparison of the Accuracy of Education Quality Evaluation by Different Methods

algorithm	higher education	Magnitude of change	error
Fuzzy algorithm	95.22	94.67	0.65
Traditional education model	82.79	75.26	7.53
P	36.216	34.537	36.412

By Table 3 It can be seen that the traditional education model has deficiencies in educational methods and stability in terms of students' higher education, and the level of education has changed significantly. High error rate. In higher education evaluation systems, user experience is one of the key factors that determine the success of the system. The user base mainly includes students, teachers, administrators, and management. Students expect the system to be simple and easy to use, and to be able to obtain evaluation results quickly. Teachers expect the system to provide fair and transparent evaluation criteria while simplifying the evaluation process. Administrators pay attention to the management convenience and data statistics function of the system; Management is concerned about the overall performance of the system and whether it can provide decision support. Therefore, the system design must fully consider these diverse requirements to ensure that each role can be used efficiently, as shown in Fig. 4.

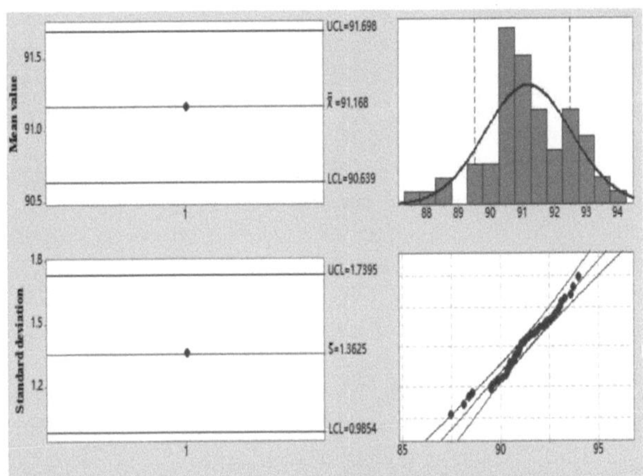

Fig. 4. Fuzzy Algorithm for Higher Education Quality Evaluation of Education

By Fig. 4 It can be seen that the higher education of the fuzzy algorithm is significantly better than the traditional education model, Simple form design supports multiple authentication methods, such as username/password, email verification, social media account login, etc. Provides clear evaluation indicators and scoring criteria, previews evaluation results, and supports the saving and submission of evaluations. Teachers can view and manage their own evaluation data, including viewing student evaluations, submitting self-evaluations, etc. Data statistics interface: Administrators can view various statistical charts, such as evaluation distribution, trend analysis, etc., and support the export of data reports.

5 Conclusion

In today's era, characterized by the swift progression of computer networking technologies, an evaluation system that leverages these networks holds profound implications for assessing higher educational outcomes. Primarily, it enables real-time evaluation, enabling educators to monitor student progress closely and modify their instructional methods accordingly. Moreover, this system introduces a broad spectrum of evaluation criteria, encompassing not just academic proficiency but also crucial soft skills such as creativity, collaborative abilities, and analytical reasoning. Furthermore, this digital assessment tool can amass extensive datasets, offering invaluable insights for educational endeavors and furthering both teaching and scholarly advancements. Ultimately, employing such an evaluation approach fosters the transcendence of physical barriers, advocates for the open exchange of top-tier educational content, and champions educational inclusivity.

References

1. Samala, A.D., Marta, R., Anori, S., Indarta, Y.: Online learning apps for students: opportunities and challenges. Educ. Adm. Theory Pract. **28**(03), 1–12 (2022)
2. Al Masud, A., Hossain, M.A., Biswas, S., Ruma, A.P., Rahman, K.S., Tagore, S.: The emergence of digital learning in higher education: a lesson from the COVID-19 pandemic. Int. J. Inf. Learn. Technol. **40**(3), 202–224 (2023)
3. Almufarreh, A., Noaman, K.M., Saeed, M.N.: Academic teaching quality framework and performance evaluation using machine learning. Appl. Sci. - Basel **13**(5) (2023)
4. Bai, L., Yang, B., Yuan, S.: Evaluating of education effects of online learning for local university students in China: a case study. Sustainability **15**(13) (2023)
5. Chen, C., Zhe, C., Zheng, Y., Xiong, X., Xiao, T., Lu, X.: Evaluation of scientific research in universities based on the theories for sustainable competitive advantage. Sage Open **13**(2) (2023)
6. del Gobbo, E., Guarino, A., Cafarelli, B., Grilli, L., Limone, P.: Automatic evaluation of open-ended questions for online learning. A systematic mapping. Stud. Educ. Eval. **77** (2023)
7. Di, H., Zhang, H., Li, P.: Teaching quality of ideological and political education in colleges based on deep learning. Int. J. E-Collab. **19**(4), 18 (2023)
8. Ding, Y., Hao, J.: Research on recommendation model of college English MOOC based on hybrid recommendation algorithm. Int. J. Adv. Comput. Sci. Appl. **14**(4), 584–593 (2023)
9. Gonzalez-Rabanal, M.C., Blanco, A.J.A.: An experience of service-learning at UNED and its evaluation with a mixed method. Prisma Soc. (41), 66–94 (2023)
10. Hahn, J., et al.: An innovative academic/practice partnership to support nursing workforce needs and student clinical education. J. Nurs. Adm. **53**(2), 88–95 (2023)
11. Hambrick, E.P., et al.: Disseminating early interventions for disaster mental health response using the ECHO model. J. Community Psychol. **51**(5), 2213–2228 (2023)
12. Han, Y., Ni, R., Gao, J.: Regional inequality of higher education development in China: comprehensive evaluation and geographical representation. Sustainability **15**(3) (2023)

13. Han, Y., Yan, R., Gou, C.: An integrated multiple attribute decision making methodology for quality evaluation of innovation and entrepreneurship education with interval-valued intuitionistic fuzzy information. J. Intell. Fuzzy Syst. **44**(2), 2231–2249 (2023)

14. Hu, W., Shao, Y., Liu, Y.: A novel MADM-based efficient methodology with 2-tuple linguistic neutrosophic numbers and applications to physical education teaching quality evaluation. J. Intell. Fuzzy Syst. **44**(5), 7351–7365 (2023)

15. Hutchinson, M., Coutts, R., Massey, D., Nasrawi, D., Fielden, J., Lee, M., Lakeman, R.: Student evaluation of teaching: reactions of Australian academics to anonymous non-constructive student commentary. Assess. Eval. High. Educ. (2023)

16. Jang, H.W., Park, J.: Evaluation of medical school faculty members' educational performance in Korea in 2022 through analysis of the promotion regulations: a mixed methods study. J. Educ. Eval. Health Prof. **20** (2023)

17. Karrenbauer, C., Brauner, T., Koenig, C.M.M., Breitner, M.H.H.: Design, development, and evaluation of an individual digital study assistant for higher education students. Etr&D-Educ. Technol. Res. Dev. (2023)

18. Kharkivska, A., Khmil, N., Dmytrenko, K., Kapustina, O., Dziuba, O.: Methodological principles of pedagogical education in the context of finding and substantiating directions for quality renewal of content and process. Synesis **15**(3), 218–232 (2023)

19. Kistaubayev, Y., Mutanov, G., Mansurova, M., Saxenbayeva, Z., Shakan, Y.: Ethereum-based information system for digital higher education registry and verification of student achievement documents. Future Internet **15**(1) (2023)

20. Li, F., Zhang, X.: Artificial intelligence facial recognition and voice anomaly detection in the application of English MOOC teaching system. Soft. Comput. **27**(10), 6855–6867 (2023)

21. Licen, S., Cassar, M., Filomeno, L., Yeratziotis, A., Prosen, M.: Development and validation of an evaluation toolkit to appraise eLearning courses in higher education: a pilot study. Sustainability **15**(8) (2023)

22. Liu, C.: GRA method for probabilistic simplified neutrosophic MADM and application to talent training quality evaluation of segmented education. J. Intell. Fuzzy Syst. **44**(5), 8637–8647 (2023)

23. Liu, X., et al.: Medical education systems in China: development, status, and evaluation. Acad. Med. **98**(1), 43–49 (2023)

Exploration and Research on Teaching CAD Method Based on Artificial Intelligence Supporting Mechanical Innovation Design

Xiaoxia Chen[✉], Chaofan Zhao, and Xuefu Li

Zhengzhou University of Aeronautics, Zhengzhou 450000, Henan, China
xxchen2002@163.com

Abstract. The role of innovative design in mechanical design is very important, but there are problems that innovative design cannot be realized. Ordinary methods cannot solve the problem of innovative design in mechanical design, and the design is not reasonable. Therefore, this paper proposes a CAD method for innovative design analysis. First, artificial intelligence is used to analyze the design scheme, and the indicators are divided according to the requirements of innovative design to reduce innovative design in the interfering factor. Then, artificial intelligence identifies the innovative design of the machine, forms an innovative design scheme, and conducts the innovative design results Comprehensive analysis. MATLAB simulation shows that under certain evaluation criteria, the feasibility of CAD methods for innovative mechanical design, The rationality of innovative designs is superior to ordinary methods.

Keywords: artificial intelligence · CAD methods · mechanical design · Innovative design

1 Introduction

1.1 Importance of Teaching Methods in CAD

Computer-aided design (CAD) is an indispensable tool in modern engineering design, which greatly improves the design efficiency and accuracy. CAD teaching not only teaches students how to use the software, but also develops their spatial imagination ability, innovative design thinking and engineering practice ability. In the era of rapidly developing technology, CAD skills become essential skills for engineers and designers, providing them with powerful tools to solve complex design problems. Through CAD teaching, students are able to understand the iteration, optimization and simulation in the design process to better adapt to the industry needs.

B. Brik and S. Nazir (Eds.): BigIoT-EDU 2024, LNICST 659, pp. 322–332, 2026.
https://doi.org/10.1007/978-3-032-18631-7_36

1.2 Overview of the Application of Artificial Intelligence in Mechanical Innovation Design

With the rapid development of artificial intelligence (AI) technology, its application in the field of CAD is gradually changing the traditional design mode. Through machine learning and deep learning algorithms, AI can learn rules from large amounts of design data, and automatically complete preliminary design, parameter optimization and even innovative design. In mechanical innovative design, AI can assist designers to quickly generate multiple design schemes, make performance predictions, reduce design cycles, while improving design quality and efficiency. For example, AI can perform structural analysis, automatically adjust design parameters to meet performance metrics, or optimize topology under satisfying constraints to generate lighter, more intense structures. In addition, AI can combine big data analysis to draw inspiration from historical design cases and assist designers in conceptual innovation. This intelligent design method is expected to lead the mechanical design into a brand-new intelligent era.

1.3 Foundation of the Integration of Artificial Intelligence and CAD Teaching

1) Core principles of artificial intelligence technology

Artificial intelligence (Artificial Intelligence) is a science and technology that simulates human intelligence or cognitive abilities such as learning, reasoning, perception and understanding. In CAD teaching, AI is mainly reflected in the following core principles:

Machine learning (Machine Learning): Data-driven computer systems to learn from experience and improve their prediction and decision-making capabilities. In CAD, it can be used to optimize the design parameters to automatically generate complex shapes.

Deep learning (Deep Learning): A machine learning method based on multi-layer neural networks that can process large amounts of data and extract high-level features. In CAD, it can be used for image recognition to assist in the automatic identification and construction of design elements.

Natural Language processing (Natural Language Processing, NLP): enables computers to understand, interpret, and generate human language. In teaching, NLP can be used for intelligent q & A and interactive learning.

2) Development status of CAD design software

Computer-aided design (Computer-Aided Design, CAD) software has become the cornerstone of modern engineering design. The current trends include:

3 D modeling (3D Modeling): Evolved from 2 D sketches to 3 D solid modeling, which provides a more intuitive design environment and supports the construction of complex geometries.

Parametric design (Parametric Design): The change of design parameters can automatically update the model to improve the flexibility and adjustment of the design.

Collaborative design (Collaborative Design): Through cloud technology, team members can share and edit designs in real time to improve design efficiency.

Integrated Simulation (Integrated Simulation): CAD software integrates with engineering analysis tools to allow designers to evaluate performance at the design stage.

3) Technical basis and prospects of the integration of the two

The integration of AI and CAD is based on data, algorithms, and computing power:

Big Data (Big Data): A large number of design cases and user behavior data provide rich resources for AI learning, and enable AI to understand and imitate excellent design.

Advanced algorithm (Advanced Algorithms): such as genetic algorithm, particle swarm optimization, etc., can solve complex optimization problems and realize intelligent design.

High performance computing (High-Performance Computing): Strong computing power enables AI to handle a large number of computing tasks in a short period of time and accelerate the design process.

1.4 Convergence Prospects

Personalized design: AI can generate customized design solutions according to users' needs and preferences.

Adaptive design: The AI can automatically adjust the design parameters according to the environmental changes or the performance requirements.

Predictive maintenance: By analyzing the design data, the AI can predict the equipment failure and maintenance requirements.

Education and training: AI-assisted teaching can provide real-time feedback, enhance the learning experience, and improve the learning results.

In the future, the deep integration of AI and CAD will further promote design innovation, improve design efficiency, reduce design costs, and potentially lead to new design methods and industry standards.

2   Related Concepts

2.1   Innovation of Teaching Mode

With the rapid development of artificial intelligence (AI) technology, the CAD (computer-aided design) teaching model is also undergoing unprecedented changes. Traditional CAD teaching often focuses on the teaching of software operation skills, while the new teaching mode pays more attention to stimulating students' innovative thinking and problem-solving ability. Through the introduction of AI, teachers can use the intelligent auxiliary design system to provide personalized learning paths and feedback according to students' learning progress and understanding degree, so as to make the learning process more targeted and efficient. At the same time, the integration of virtual reality (VR) and augmented reality (AR) technology provides students with immersive design experience, and combines abstract theoretical knowledge with intuitive visual simulation to further improve the learning effect.

$$T(b_i y_i) = \begin{pmatrix} 1 & 0 \\ 0 & 1 \end{pmatrix} \iff \frac{T}{y_i} \cdot \sum_{i=1}^{y} b_i^2 \tag{1}$$

2.2 Strengthening of Practical Teaching

In the new CAD teaching mode, the importance of practice is increasingly prominent. By simulating real design projects, students can repeatedly experiment in a virtual environment to learn how to use CAD software to solve practical problems. The AI-driven automatic optimization function can help students to quickly explore multiple design solutions, reduce the error cost, and improve the design efficiency. In addition, through the online collaboration platform, students can work remotely with their partners to complete the design tasks together, and develop teamwork skills and project management skills. Such practical teaching not only exercises students' hands-on ability, but also lays a solid foundation for their future career.

$$v(b_i) = \iiint_{b_i} 2 + \sqrt{b_i^2 - s_i \cdot 3vb_i} \cdot \coprod v \tag{2}$$

2.3 Teaching Model of Interdisciplinary Integration

In today's engineering field, a single-subject knowledge is often inadequate to address complex design challenges. Therefore, CAD teaching should encourage interdisciplinary integration to integrate the knowledge of multiple disciplines, including machinery, electronics, materials, and biology, into the design process. For example, with AI algorithms, students can learn how to apply biomechanical principles of biomechanics to medical device design or how to optimize structural strength using material science knowledge. At the same time, the introduction of data science and machine learning enables students to use big data analysis to optimize design parameters and realize intelligent decision-making. This interdisciplinary teaching model not only broadens students' knowledge horizon, but also improves their ability to solve comprehensive problems.

In short, the innovation and reform of CAD teaching aims to adapt to the pace of the development of science and technology, and to cultivate future designers with innovative spirit and practical operation ability through AI technology, strengthening practice and interdisciplinary integration (Fig. 1).

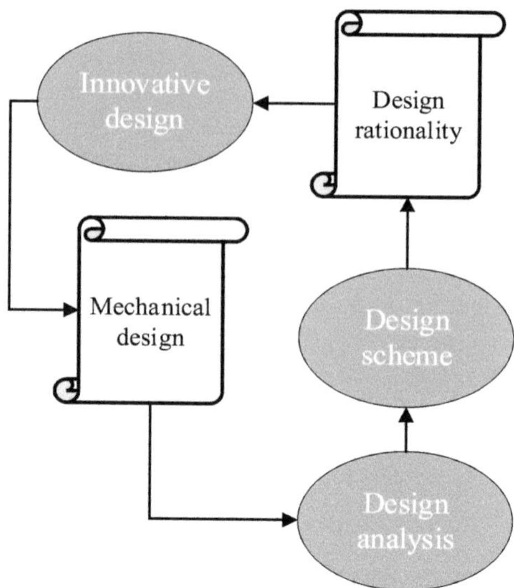

Fig. 1. The Result of the Selection of Innovative Ideas and Solutions

2.4 Challenges and Countermeasures of the Integration of Artificial Intelligence and CAD Teaching

In the process of integrating artificial intelligence (AI) and computer-aided design (CAD) teaching, the following technical challenges are mainly faced:

1. Data quality and quantity: Training of AI models requires large amounts of high-quality CAD design data, but the acquisition and annotation of these data can be time-consuming and costly.
2. Real-time and interactivity: The application of AI in CAD requires real-time feedback and interaction, which puts high requirements for computing resources and algorithm performance.
3. Model complexity and interpretability: Complex AI models may be difficult to understand and interpret, causing difficulties in teaching and student understanding.

3 Practical Examples of Mechanical Design

3.1 To Overcome These Challenges, the Following Strategies:

1. Construction and sharing of data sets: establish public CAD design data sets to enrich and annotate data through open source and cooperation.
2. Lightweight AI algorithm: develop an AI algorithm suitable for real-time interaction, optimize the computational efficiency, and improve the user experience.
3. Visualization and interpretability: Design an intuitive visual interface to make the AI decision-making process transparent and enhance its interpretability.

Table 1. Innovative Design Requirements

Scope of application	grade	Innovative effect	Innovative ideas
New design	standard	85.63	84.58
	Higher	85.65	85.27
Inherit the design	standard	87.72	86.43
	Higher	84.38	87.10
Variant design	standard	85.92	84.86
	Higher	86.60	87.07

The innovative design process in Table 1. is shown in Fig. 2.

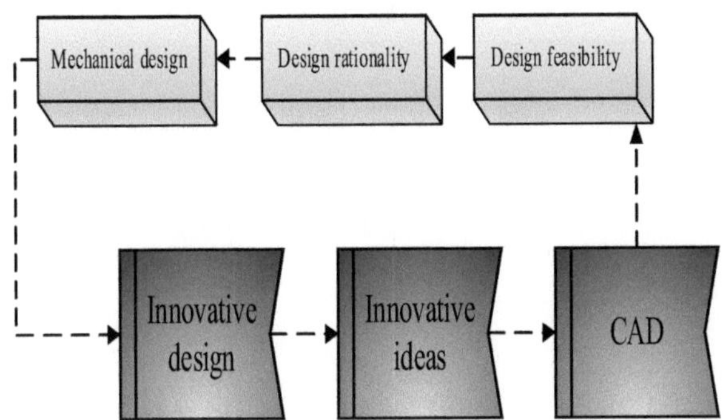

Fig. 2. The Analysis Process of Mechanical Design

Optimization of educational resources and learning environment resources integration

1. Hybrid learning materials: Combining online courses, video tutorials, interactive exercises, providing a variety of learning resources.
2. Virtual laboratory: establish virtual CAD design environment, let students practice in simulated reality.

Environmental innovation

1. Cloud computing and collaboration platform: Use cloud services to provide high-performance computing resources, and support remote collaboration and real-time communication.
2. Feedback and evaluation system: Build an AI-driven automatic feedback and evaluation system to evaluate students' designs in real time and provide suggestions for improvement.

3.2 Mechanical Design

Teacher training and ability improvement
    Skills update

1. Teacher AI training: Regular teacher training courses combining AI and CAD to ensure that teachers master the latest technology.
2. Teacher-student cooperation: Encourage teachers and students to study together, apply AI to teaching practice, and improve teachers' understanding of new technologies.

Reform of teaching methods

1. Project-oriented teaching: Through practical projects, students can learn and apply AI-CAD technology in solving real problems.
2. Continuous evaluation and feedback: Establish a continuous teaching feedback mechanism and adjust teaching strategies according to students' performance (Table 2).

Table 2. The Overall Picture of the Innovative Thinking Program

category	Satisfaction	Analysis rate
New design	89.31	89.45
Inherit the design	89.64	90.80
Variant design	89.00	89.23
mean	90.30	89.27
X^6	87.85	89.44
$P = 1.03$		

3.3 Innovative Ideas and Stability of Innovative Design

In order to verify the accuracy of the CAD method, the innovative design scheme is compared with the ordinary method, and the innovative design scheme is shown in Fig. 3.

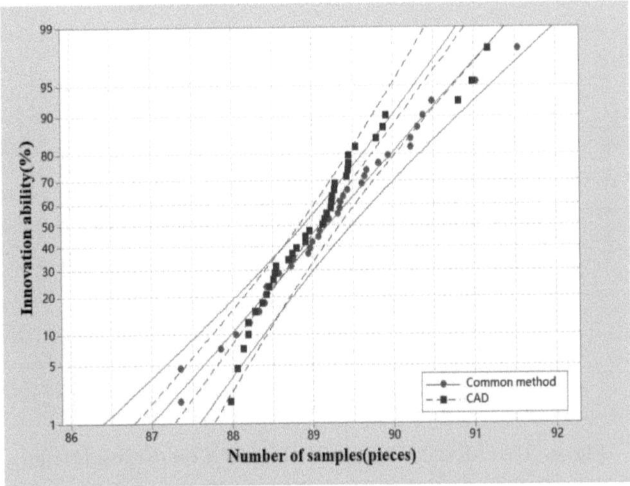

Fig. 3. Innovative Ideas of Different Algorithms

Through the response of the above challenges, the optimization of educational resources, as well as the training of teachers, the integration of AI and CAD teaching is expected to be deeper and more advanced and effective, laying a solid foundation for the training of future innovative designers.

Table 3. Comparison of Innovative Design Accuracy of Different Methods

algorithm	Innovative ideas	Magnitude of change	error
CAD method	93.83	93.47	93.75
Normal method	92.79	92.82	92.80
P	89.44	91.79	91.06

It can be seen from Table 3 that ordinary methods have deficiencies in innovation in mechanical design, mechanical design has changed significantly, and the error rate is high. The general results of CAD methods are more innovative ideas than ordinary methods. At the same time, the innovative ideas of CAD methods are greater than 93%, and the accuracy has not changed significantly. To further verify the superiority of the CAD method. In order to further verify the effectiveness of the proposed method in this paper, the CAD method is generally analyzed by different methods, as shown in Fig. 4.

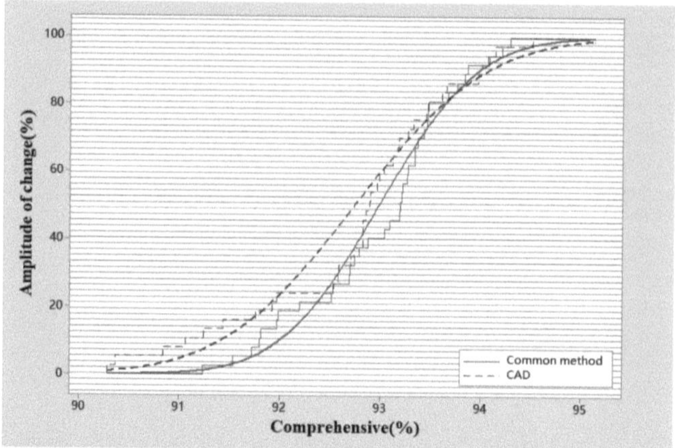

Fig. 4. Cad Method, Innovative Ideas for Innovative Design

Looking ahead, we see the following key trends:

Deep integration of deep learning and CAD: With the continuous development of deep learning technology, the future CAD systems will be able to learn and adapt by themselves, and further improve the design efficiency and accuracy. AI models will be able to extract patterns from a large number of design cases to provide intelligent suggestions for innovative designs.

Educational application of augmented reality and virtual reality: AR and VR technology will make CAD teaching more immersive, enabling students to intuitively understand the design principles in three-dimensional space, and improve the ability of design perception.

Personalized and adaptive teaching: AI will have a deeper understanding of students' learning behaviors and abilities, provide more accurate and personalized teaching programs, and realize "teaching students in accordance with their aptitude".

4 Conclusion

This study discusses the innovation of CAD teaching method in mechanical innovation design based on artificial intelligence support, aiming to improve students' innovative design ability and practical skills. By combining artificial intelligence technology, we observe that CAD teaching has changed from the traditional theoretical explanation and mechanical operation to a new teaching mode dominated by intelligent assisted design, automatic optimization and simulation verification. This shift not only enhances students' understanding of complex design problems, but also cultivates their ability to solve practical engineering problems.

Aiming at the problem that the innovative ideas of mechanical design are not ideal, this paper proposes a CAD method and combines artificial intelligence to optimize mechanical design. At the same time, the innovative ideas of mechanical design are analyzed in depth to construct a collection of design schemes. Studies have shown that CAD methods can improve the accuracy of mechanical design and can generally carry out mechanical design Innovative design. However, in the process of CAD method, too much attention is paid to the analysis of innovative design, resulting in irrationality in the selection of innovative design indicators.

References

1. Afshariantorghabeh, S., Pesonen, A., Karki, T., Leminen, V.: Effects of thermoforming operation and tooling on the thermoformability of plastic-coated fibre-based materials. Packag. Technol. Sci. (2023)
2. Bai, L., Wang, W., Xu, W., Cheng, S., Yu, X.: Dual-constituent anti-tetra-chiral lattice metamaterial with tailorable coefficient of thermal expansion and excellent bandgap. Mater. Today Commun. **34** (2023)
3. Bao, R., Duan, F., Fu, X., Yu, Z., Liu, W., Guo, G.: Frequency-scanning interferometry for axial clearance of rotating machinery based on speed synchronization and extended Kalman filter. Opt. Lasers Eng. **164** (2023)
4. Brandao, D.A.d.L., et al.: Hybridization of a backhoe loader: electric drive system design. Machines **11**(4) (2023)
5. Brkic, V.S., Misita, M., Perisic, M., Brkic, A., Veljkovic, Z.: Validating measurement structure of checklist for evaluating ergonomics risks in heavy mobile machinery cabs. Mathematics **11**(1) (2023)
6. Cheng, Z., Lu, Z.: Research on HMCVT parameter design optimization based on the service characteristics of agricultural machinery in the whole life cycle. Machines **11**(6) (2023)
7. Dai, M., et al.: Research on holographic visualization verification platform for construction machinery based on mixed reality technology. Appl. Sci.-Basel **13**(6) (2023)
8. Fang, G., Yang, R., Shen, H., Wang, H., Han, Z., Li, G.: Investigation of the aerodynamic optimization design of fluid machinery based on machine learning. Neural Comput. Appl. (2023)
9. Fieguth, D.M., Anglin, J.R.: Open system control of dynamical transitions under the generalized Kruskal-Neishtadt-Henrard theorem. Phys. Rev. E **107** (2023) (3)
10. Fraccaroli, E., Vinco, S.: Modeling cyber-physical production systems with system C-AMS. IEEE Trans. Comput. **72**(7), 2039–2051 (2023)
11. Gardner, L.: From underwear to outerwear: the influence of machinery on creativity and garment styling in the Scottish Knitwear Industry, 1920s-1970s. Textile-Cloth Cult. (2023)
12. Ge, N., Li, R., Gao, L., Wang, L., Ouyang, B.: An accumulated imaging method with phase-locking for rotor pressure-sensitive paint measurements. Exp. Fluids **64**(6) (2023)
13. Goeddecke, J., Goehrs, T., Meschut, G., Gehling, M.G.: Design method for bonding ultra-high-strength steel materials in agricultural machinery construction. Stahlbau (2023)
14. He, T., et al.: Design and experiment of a multiple vegetable block seedling transplanter for large ridge double row planting. Agric. Res. Arid Areas **41**(2), 282–290, 300 (2023)
15. Jiang, W., Chen, W., Song, C., Yan, Y., Zhang, Y., Wang, S.: Obstacle detection and tracking for intelligent agricultural machinery. Comput. Electr. Eng. **108** (2023)
16. Jing, W., Wang, P., Zhang, N.: Study on damage fatigue test method of metal materials for rotating machinery. Int. J. Mater. Prod. Technol. **66**(1), 17–30 (2023)
17. Lee, K., Willi, J.A., Cho, N., Kim, I., Jewett, M.C., Lee, J.: Cell-free biosynthesis of peptidomimetics. Biotechnol. Bioprocess Eng. (2023)
18. Li, H., Gao, F.: Improvement design of separation and conveying machinery and equipment of potato excavator in heavy soil. Phys. Chem. Earth **130** (2023)
19. Lin, J., Chen, X.: Application of digital design technology in the design of intelligent agricultural machinery and equipment. Appl. Math. Nonlinear Sci. (2023)

20. Lin, J., Zhu, Y.: Research on the identification of common faults of agricultural machinery based on vibration characteristics. Appl. Math. Nonlinear Sci. (2023)
21. Liu, X., Li, X.: The influence of agricultural production mechanization on grain production capacity and efficiency. Processes **11**(2) (2023)
22. Liu, Y., Jin, Y., Cui, G., Shen, G.: Study and application on the early damage signal characteristics of ultra-low-speed and heavy-load rolling bearings of large amusement machinery. Insight **65**(5), 270–277 (2023)
23. Loercher, M., et al.: Vorstellung eines Leitfadens zum Evaluieren der hygienegerechten konstruktiven Ausfuhrung von Susswarenmaschinen (Guidelines for evaluating the hygienic design of confectionery machines). Chemie Ingenieur Technik (2023)
24. Ma, Y., Wang, Q., Ye, M., Lian, G.: Robust control for the hybrid energy system of an electric loader. Machines **11**(4) (2023)
25. Miao, Y., Zhang, B., Li, C., Lin, J., Zhang, D.: Feature mode decomposition: new decomposition theory for rotating machinery fault diagnosis. IEEE Trans. Industr. Electron. **70**(2), 1949–1960 (2023)
26. Periyasamy, M., Quartapella, C.J., Piacente, N.P., Reichl, G., Lynn, B.: Smart quantum tunneling composite sensors to monitor FKM and FFKM seals. Sensors **23**(3) (2023)
27. Ruiperez-Valiente, J.A., Kim, Y.J., Baker, R.S., Martinez, P.A., Lin, G.C.: The affordances of multivariate Elo-based learner modeling in game-based assessment. IEEE Trans. Learn. Technol. **16**(2), 152–165 (2023)
28. Shang, Y., et al.: Design and test of obstacle detection and harvester pre-collision system based on 2D Lidar. Agronomy-Basel **13**(2) (2023)
29. Shi, Q., Zhao, X., Zhang, H., Si, B., Song, Z., Zhang, Y.: Analysis of nonlinear dynamics characteristics of a kind of hinged connection structures. Arch. Appl. Mech. **93**(4), 1725–1746 (2023)
30. Stefanov, T., Varbanova, S., Stefanova, M., Ivanov, I.: CRM system as a necessary tool for managing commercial and production processes. Tem J.-Technol. Educ. Manag. Inform. **12**(2), 785–797 (2023)

Application of Computer-Based "Task-Based" Teaching Mode in University English Teaching

Caiyuan Sun[✉]

School of Humanities, Shandong Agriculture and Engineering, Jinan 250000, Shandong, China
sunamber1978@163.com

Abstract. With the rapid development of network technology, English teaching has also been reformed, and the teaching mode has also undergone corresponding changes and improvements. The combination of computer and teaching mode has led to the emergence of a new teaching model to change the limitations of teaching mode. Therefore, this paper proposes a task-based teaching mode and analyzes the innovative teaching mode. Firstly, computer technology is used to analyze the teaching mode, and the indicators are divided according to the requirements of the teaching mode to reduce the interference factors in the teaching mode. Then, the computer technology analyzes the results of the university English teaching mode, forms the teaching model plan, and conducts the results of the teaching mode Comprehensive analysis. MATLAB simulation shows that under the condition of certain evaluation standards, the task-based teaching mode is effective in improving the comprehensive English ability of college students. The teaching efficiency is better than the traditional teaching mode.

Keywords: computer technology · task-based teaching mode · University English Teaching

1 Introduction

As the educational landscape and technological advancements continue to evolve, the realm of college-level English instruction encounters a myriad of challenges coupled with promising opportunities [1]. The pressing issue within English pedagogy now is to efficiently facilitate student engagement, collaboration, and constructive feedback [2]. The project-based learning approach, recognized for its dynamic classroom environment and its role in fostering self-directed learning among students, has gained popularity across various academic disciplines [3]. This paper will delve into the intricacies of integrating the project-based learning approach into college English curriculum, examining its practical merits and limitations is visually represented in Fig. 1.

B. Brik and S. Nazir (Eds.): BigIoT-EDU 2024, LNICST 659, pp. 333–342, 2026.
https://doi.org/10.1007/978-3-032-18631-7_37

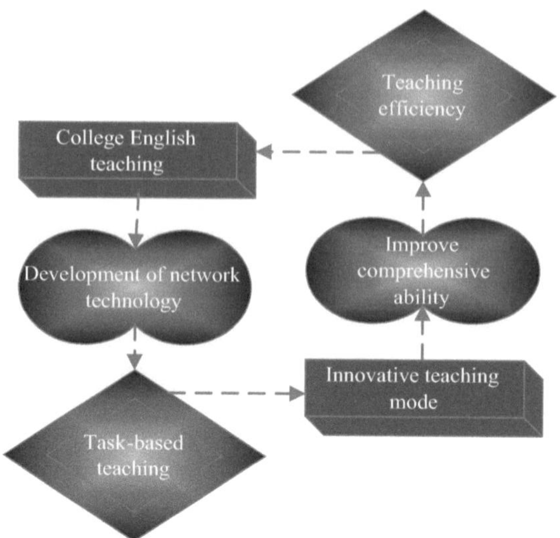

Fig. 1. The analytical process of university English teaching

2   Related Works

The "activity-centered" educational model employs a stochastic enhancement strategy for the instruction of university English, tweaking the parameters of the teaching framework to achieve its optimization. This model categorizes university English instruction into various levels of teaching frameworks and randomly selects diverse programs for implementation. Throughout the iterative process, the schemes of these frameworks at different levels are refined and scrutinized. Upon completion of the optimization and analysis, a comparison is made across the levels of different programs to document the most effective university English teaching practices.

A. Task teaching mode

The project-based learning strategy is an activity-focused educational approach, distinguished by these fundamental traits: grounding instruction in real-world scenarios, centering on educational projects as the nucleus [4], spurring students' self-driven and collaborative study, and enhancing their abilities in dialogue and tackling issues [5]. Typically, the project-based learning strategy is marked by the following attributes:

1. Task-driven

In the context of the project-driven instruction model, the essence of education is anchored in projects, which serve as the focal point of the learning process. Students are motivated to engage proactively in educational endeavors by the introduction of projects that mirror real-life situations [6], thereby fulfilling the objective of fostering autonomous learning among students.

2. Self-directed learning

The project-based learning approach fosters autonomy in student learning, where learners acquire knowledge [7], hone skills, and develop analytical methods through their own initiative. This process nurtures a sense of intrinsic motivation and capability for learning, ultimately enhancing the outcomes of their educational journey [8].

3. Cooperative learning

The task-based educational model highlights the importance of collaborative learning, where students undertake and accomplish tasks collectively through interactive dialogue [9], collaborative division of tasks, and mutual assistance. This approach is designed to enhance students' abilities in communication and problem-solving.

B. The application of task teaching mode in university English teaching

1. Task design

In the domain of collegiate English instruction, educators have the opportunity to devise linguistic exercises that are intricately tied to practical life experiences, tailored to the specific educational aspirations and requirements of their students. For instance, instructors might craft an assignment involving a persuasive essay on a topical societal matter, prompting learners to gather data through research [10], field investigations, and other similar activities. Subsequently, students are tasked with crafting a comprehensive essay that reflects their individual insights and viewpoints. Such an assignment not only serves to bolster the students' proficiency in English composition but also equips them with the tools to comprehend and address issues within the social fabric [11].

2. Student involvement

Within the framework of the task-oriented teaching approach, learners occupy the central role in the educational process, gaining knowledge and skills through the completion of tasks [12]. Consequently, it is imperative for educators to facilitate an active engagement of students in classroom activities and to foster an environment where students are encouraged to articulate their perspectives and thought processes. In the context of English language teaching, instructors can stimulate interaction and collaboration among students by employing group assignments, discussions, and presentation [13].

3. Teacher coaching

In the task-based educational paradigm, the educator's role transcends that of a mere disseminator of knowledge, evolving into a mentor and facilitator for the students. It is essential for teachers to provide timely guidance and support, assisting students in overcoming challenges and honing their competencies [14]. In the sphere of English language instruction, educators can enhance students' proficiency by offering valuable learning materials and imparting essential skills like reading, writing, and listening comprehension.

C. Pros and cons analysis

The task-based instructional framework offers both considerable strengths and potential drawbacks within the context of university English education:

1. Pros

The task-oriented educational strategy has the potential to ignite students' curiosity and passion for learning, nurturing their capacities for self-directed and collaborative study, and significantly enhancing their linguistic expression and interactive competencies [15]. Moreover, this model also offers students educational materials and practical experiences that are more closely aligned with real-life scenarios, facilitating a smoother transition into societal and everyday life contexts.

2. Deficiencies

Deploying the task-based teaching approach necessitates that educators possess advanced pedagogical skills and substantial experience, along with the capability to design tasks effectively and provide students with constructive guidance; otherwise, there is a risk of causing confusion and a sense of being lost among students [16]. Furthermore, this method demands a considerable investment of time and effort for both preparation and execution, which may not be ideal for scenarios with limited teaching material and a compressed timetable.

As information technology advances and becomes more integrated into educational practices, the task-based teaching model is poised to gain even broader application in English instruction. The prospective trajectory of its evolution includes:

(1) The incorporation of artificial intelligence to augment the efficiency and efficacy of the teaching process.
(2) The creation of novel task formats designed to pique students' interest and cater to their individual learning preferences [17].
(3) The establishment of a framework for tasks that foster cross-cultural communication, aiming to enhance students' intercultural dialogue and comprehension.

With these developmental thrusts, the task-based teaching model is set to emerge as a pivotal instrument and methodology in university English education, offering substantial backing for the development of individuals with a global perspective and well-rounded attributes.

In the educational landscape, the evolution of instructional paradigms has simplified the English learning journey for tertiary students, aligning more closely with contemporary academic standards. Yet, within the framework of crafting instructional models, there exists a challenge pertaining to the suboptimal coherence of the teaching strategies, which in turn, impacts the English proficiency of university learners. Certain academicians posit that the integration of a task-based educational model into the scrutiny of university English instruction could significantly refine the instructional blueprint and furnish pertinent reinforcement for the pedagogical approach. Building upon this premise, the present discourse introduces a task-based instructional paradigm, refines the teaching blueprint, and substantiates the efficacy of this model.

3 Optimization Strategies for University English Teaching

A. Mathematical description of the task-based teaching model

The "activity-oriented" educational approach leverages digital technologies to enhance the instructional framework, set. It scrutinizes the metrics within the teaching framework to identify deficiencies in university English instruction, set, and assimilates these findings into the teaching scheme, and set. Ultimately, the viability of the university English teaching is appraised, as delineated in the formulaic representation Eq. (1).

$$tol\left(y_i \cdot p_{ij} \cdot \frac{1}{5}\right) = y_{ij} \geq \max\left(p_{ij} \div \sqrt{7}\right) \tag{1}$$

Within this context, the identification of outliers is articulated through Eq. (2).

$$\max(p_{ij}) = \left(p_{ij}^2 \cdot 2 + \frac{1}{o_i}\right) \succ mean\left(\sum p_{ij} \div \sum_{i=1}^{o}\left(y_i - 4 + \frac{1}{3}^2\right) \cdot \int p_{ij}\right) \qquad (2)$$

The "activity-centric" educational framework amalgamates the strengths of online technologies, set, employing university English instruction to quantify and refine the pedagogical approach.

Hypothesis I posits that the criteria for the teaching approach are established, the blueprint of the teaching strategy is formulated, the fulfillment of the teaching strategy's blueprint is assessed, and the evaluative function for the teaching strategy is delineated, set $J(p_i \approx 0)$, as depicted in Eq. (3).

$$J(k_i) = \sum + \frac{7}{4} \cdot \iint_i k \cdot p_i \bigcap \xi \cdot e^{i\theta} \to \sqrt{3} \cdot \oint y_i \qquad (3)$$

B. Choice of teaching mode scheme

Hypothesis II delineates that the function of university English instruction is characterized by specific parameters, with the weight coefficients being integral to the assessment. Subsequently, it posits that the teaching model necessitates a reevaluation of substandard university English teaching, as outlined in Eq. (4).

$$q(p_i) = \sqrt{q^2 + 4b_i k_i} \cdot o_i \cdot \prod J(k_i) + \sqrt{3} - b_i \qquad (4)$$

Drawing from the premises of Hypotheses I and II, an encompassing function for university English instruction can be formulated, with the outcome presented in Eq. (5).

$$q(p_i) + J(k_i) \leq max(p_{ij}) \qquad (5)$$

To enhance the efficacy of the educational framework, it is imperative to normalize the entire dataset, with the outcomes articulated in Eq. (6).

$$\widetilde{q(p_i)} + J(k_i) \leftrightarrow mean\left(\sum p_{ij} \div \sum_{i=1}^{o}\left(y_i - 4 + \frac{1}{3}^2\right) \cdot \int p_{ij}\right) \qquad (6)$$

C. Analysis of teaching model schemes

Prior to the implementation of the task-based teaching approach, a multidimensional analysis of the instructional framework is essential. It involves aligning the teaching model criteria with the university English teaching repository to discard any substandard educational schemes. The teaching model scheme is identified as such. In accordance with Eq. (6), an anomaly assessment plan can be conceptualized, with the findings presented in Eq. (7).

$$No(p_i) = \frac{\widetilde{q(p_i)} + J(k_i)}{mean\left(\sum p_{ij} \div \sum_{i=1}^{o}\left(y_i - 4 + \frac{1}{3}^2\right) \cdot \int p_{ij}\right)} \qquad (7)$$

Within this context, it is posited that a plan must be formulated; otherwise, the amalgamation of schemes necessitated is absent, with the outcome delineated in Eq. (8).

$$Zh(p_i) = min[\sum q(p_i) \overset{\sim}{+} J(k_i)] \tag{8}$$

In a comprehensive examination of university English instruction, the thresholds and index weights of the teaching framework are calibrated to affirm the viability of the task-based teaching approach. University English teaching constitutes a holistic experimental educational model that necessitates innovative analysis. Should university English teaching follow a non-normal distribution, denoted as instructional framework may be compromised, diminishing the precision of the overall teaching strategy. The analysis of the instructional framework reveals a multifaceted distribution pattern, aligning with empirical realities. University English instruction exhibits a non-directional nature, signifying that the instructional model possesses considerable unpredictability, thus classifying it as a complex analytical subject. Should the probabilistic function for university English teaching be denoted by, then the computation detailed in Eq. (9) can be reformulated as expression (9).

$$accur(p_i) = \frac{min[\sum q(p_i) \overset{\sim}{+} J(k_i)]}{\sum q(p_i) \overset{\sim}{+} J(k_i)} \times 100\% + randon(p_i) \tag{9}$$

Within this context, university English instruction adheres to standard criteria, primarily due to the influence of web-based technology that modulates university English teaching. It filters out redundant and extraneous schemes and augments the default framework, thereby enhancing the dynamic interconnectivity of the overall instructional blueprint.

4 Results and Discussion

A. Introduction to the teaching mode

To streamline the teaching framework, this study focuses on university English instruction within intricate scenarios, featuring 12 distinct pathways and a duration of 12 h for testing. The specifics of the university English teaching framework are detailed in Table 1.

Table 1. University teaching mode requirements

Scope of application	grade	viability	Teaching mode
Freshman	standard	83.94	83.43
	Higher	82.05	84.99
Sophomore	standard	84.62	84.86
	Higher	84.93	85.60
Junior	standard	84.83	85.53
	Higher	83.87	85.83

Contrasting the conventional instructional approach, the framework of the task-based teaching model aligns more closely with the practical demands of the teaching process. Regarding the coherence and practicality of university English instruction, the task-based model outperforms the traditional one. By examining the shifts in the instructional framework depicted in Fig. 2, it is evident that the task-based teaching model boasts high learning efficiency and enhanced academic proficiency. Consequently, the swiftness of the instructional framework, its feasibility, and the overall stability of the task-based teaching model are superior.

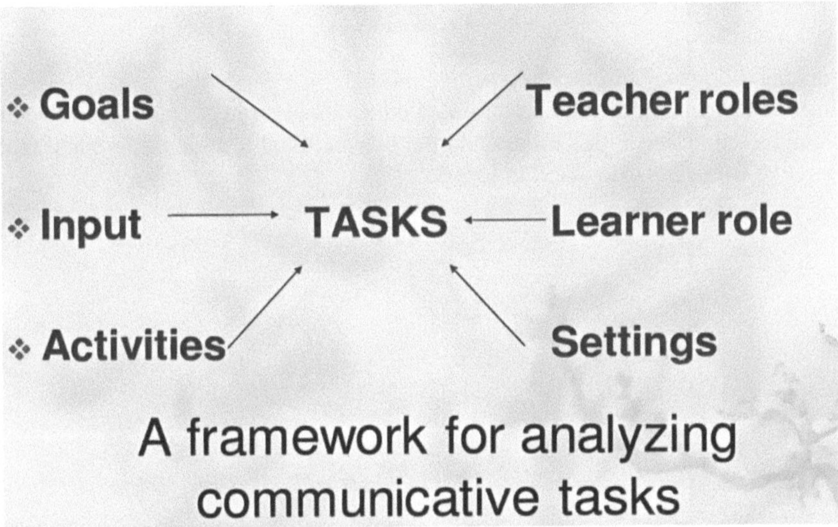

Fig. 2. Teaching modes of different content

B. University English teaching

The instructional framework for university English encompasses a spectrum of information types, ranging from unstructured to semi-structured and structured data. Following an initial filtering process through the task-based teaching approach, a preliminary scheme for university English instruction is formulated. This is then subjected to an analysis to assess the viability of the educational model's plan. To further refine the verification of the innovative impact within university English teaching, a selection of university English courses with varying levels of instructional frameworks is made, with the comparative instructional schemes detailed in Table 2.

Table 2. The overall picture of the teaching model program

category	rationality	Analysis rate
Freshman	89.02	88.97
Sophomore	88.88	87.33
Junior	89.74	88.25
mean	89.40	89.85
X^6	87.17	88.07
P = 1.204		

C. Teaching mode and stability of teaching mode

To affirm the precision of the task-oriented educational strategy, a comparative analysis is conducted between this model and the conventional teaching approach, with the comparative framework depicted in Fig. 3.

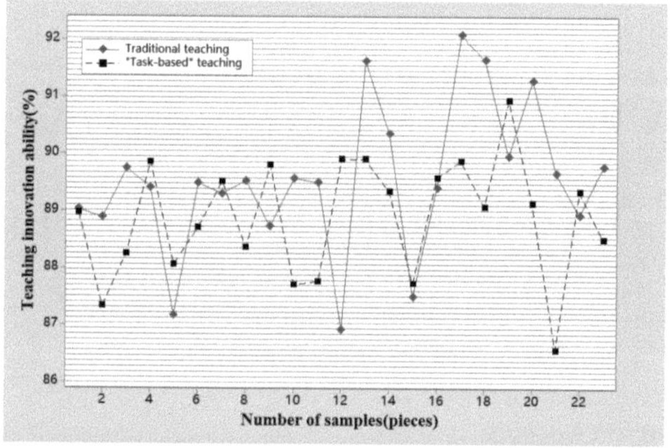

Fig. 3. Teaching modes of different algorithms

Upon reviewing Fig. 2, it is apparent that the task-based teaching approach surpasses the traditional method in terms of effectiveness, yet it exhibits a lower error rate, which suggests a more consistent performance. In contrast, the traditional teaching model demonstrates variability in its execution. Table 3 presents a comparative overview of the average instructional schemes across the aforementioned trio of methodologies.

Table 3. Comparison of the accuracy of teaching modes of different methods

algorithm	Teaching mode	Magnitude of change
"Task-based" teaching mode	94.52	92.05

(continued)

Table 3. (*continued*)

algorithm	Teaching mode	Magnitude of change
Traditional teaching mode	92.43	91.74
P	92.52	92.16

Upon examining Table 3, it is evident that the conventional teaching approach exhibits deficiencies in the rationality of its framework for university English instruction. There have been notable shifts in the way university English is taught, accompanied by a relatively elevated rate of errors. Comparatively, the overall outcome of the task-based teaching model is superior, with a higher performance than that of the traditional method. Additionally, the effectiveness of the task-based teaching model consistently exceeds 92%, with the precision remaining relatively stable. To further substantiate the advantages of the task-based teaching model, the paper conducts a comprehensive analysis of the model using various methods, as illustrated in Fig. 4, to validate the efficacy of the proposed approach.

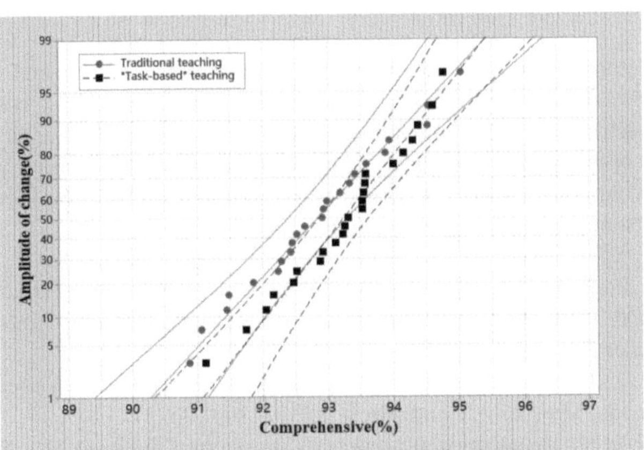

Fig. 4. "Task-Based" teaching mode the teaching mode of the teaching mode

From Fig. 4, it is discernible that the task-oriented educational strategy markedly outperforms the conventional teaching approach. This superiority stems from the task-oriented model's heightened modulation of the university English instruction parameters, the establishment of a threshold for the teaching framework, and the exclusion of teaching schemes that fail to meet the stipulated criteria.

5   Conclusion

Addressing the suboptimal state of university English instructional methods, this discourse introduces an activity-driven teaching approach and enhances the teaching of university English through the integration of web-based technologies. Concurrently, it delves into the innovation of instructional paradigms to construct a diverse array of teaching frameworks. Studies indicate that the activity-driven teaching model has the potential to elevate the academic caliber and the pace of learning within university English education. Nevertheless, the implementation of the activity-driven teaching model may overly emphasize the dissection of the instructional framework, leading to an imbalance in the selection of instructional metrics.

References

1. Almulla, M.A., Al-Rahmi, W.M.: Integrated social cognitive theory with learning input factors: the effects of problem-solving skills and critical thinking skills on learning performance sustainability. Sustainability **15**(5) (2023)
2. Aubrey, S., Philpott, A.: Second language task engagement in face-to-face and synchronous video-based computer-mediated communication modes: performances and perceptions. System **115** (2023)
3. Avsec, S.: Design thinking to envision more sustainable technology-enhanced teaching for effective knowledge transfer. Sustainability **15**(2) (2023)
4. Carswell, D., Conway, P.F.: An ethico-political analysis of a national teacher competence framework: Unravelling a 'preferred' teacher identity. British Educational Research Journal (2023)
5. Fang, Z.: Reforming spatial thinking knowledge system setting under the continuous cultivation of bachelor, master and doctor degrees. J. Geomatics **48**(1), 164–166 (2023)
6. Ge, Y.: Research on innovative cultivation mode of English and American literature translation talents based on internet environment. Applied Mathematics and Nonlinear Sciences (2023)
7. Goh, H.H., Wong, H.M., Kwek, D.: Home-based learning during school closure in Singapore: perceptions from the language classrooms. Educational Research for Policy and Practice (2023)
8. Hallstrom, J., Frejd, J.: University Teachers' Experiences of Teaching Hands-On Components in Science and Technology in Primary Teacher Education during COVID-19. Journal of Science Teacher Education (2023)
9. He, X., Zuo, Q., Chen, W.: Practice of improving the teaching ability of young teachers by team chain mode. Microbiol. China **50**(3), 1337–1344 (2023)
10. Huang, P.-H., et al.: What impacts students? Satisfaction the most from Medicine Student Experience Questionnaire in Australia: a validity study. J. Educ. Eval. Health Prof. **20** (2023)
11. Kwong, C.-Y. C., Churchill, D.: Applying the activity theory framework to analyse the use of Eportfolios in an international baccalaureate middle years programme sciences classroom: a longitudinal multiple-case study. Comput. Educ. **200** (2023)
12. Lai, Y.-L.: A fast task planning system for 6R articulated robots based on inverse kinematics. Int. J. Adv. Manufact. Technol. (2023)
13. Li, C., Peng, P., Cao, L.: Robust SSRL analysis framework for intervention strategy construction in CSCL environment. Heliyon **9**(3) (2023)
14. Li, W., Li, M., Li, F., Xue, S.: Application of MiniQuest teaching mode in virtual simulation experiment of undergraduate midwifery. Chinese J. Nurs. Educ. **20**(2), 140–145 (2023)
15. Li, Z., Liontas, J.I.: English VP idiom learning and Wechat: developing idiomatic competence among Chinese EFL learners. Iranian J. Lang. Teach. Res. **11**(2), 95–117 (2023)
16. Liu, Y.: Design and practice of physical chemistry experiment based on outcome-based education: taking the preparation of mixed-CeNiOxand characterization as an example. J. Fudan Univ. Nat. Sci. **62**(1), 31–36 (2023)

Analysis and Application of Computer 3D Software Technology in Environmental Art Courses

Ling Chen[(✉)]

School of Environmental Design, Wuhan Institute of Design and Sciences, Hubei 430000, China
Chenling0070@126.com

Abstract. As an important part of art and design education, environmental art curriculum usually includes many fields such as interior design, landscape design and public art. The current teaching mode is mainly the combination of theoretical teaching and practical operation. The class explanation covers basic knowledge such as art history, design theory and spatial planning, supplemented by case analysis to guide students to understand design principles. In practice, students exercise their design thinking and expression ability through hand-drawn sketches and model making. In addition, some of the courses also take the form of group cooperation to develop teamwork and project management skills. MATLAB simulation shows that under the condition of certain evaluation criteria, computer three-dimensional software technology has a rational effect on environmental art design The feasibility of artistic design is better than traditional design methods.

Keywords: computer · Computer three-dimensional software technology · environmental design · Environmental art design

1 Introduction

Although the traditional teaching model ensures the transmission of knowledge to some extent, environmental art courses face multiple challenges in the current rapidly developing digital age. First of all, traditional teaching methods may not be able to fully stimulate students 'awareness of innovation, and rely too much on teachers' demonstration and guidance, resulting in students' weak ability in independent thinking and problem solving. Secondly, the design tools update rapidly, such as computer-aided design (CAD), 3 D modeling software, etc., while the course content update speed is relatively slow, which may lead to the dilemma of backward skills after graduation.

2 Related Works

A. *Application of 3D modeling in environmental design.*

B. Brik and S. Nazir (Eds.): BigIoT-EDU 2024, LNICST 659, pp. 343–352, 2026.
https://doi.org/10.1007/978-3-032-18631-7_38

Twith the sustainable development and the popularization of green design concept, the curriculum needs to integrate more environmental protection and ecological awareness into the teaching, but it is often difficult to go deeper due to the limitation of the curriculum capacity. Finally, in the face of the global design vision, how to cultivate students' cross-cultural understanding and international competitiveness is also a big challenge.

As an important part of art and design education, environmental art curriculum usually includes many fields such as interior design, landscape design and public art. The current teaching mode is mainly the combination of theoretical teaching and practical operation. The class explanation covers basic knowledge such as art history, design theory and spatial planning, supplemented by case analysis to guide students to understand design principles. In practice, students exercise their design thinking and expression ability through hand-drawn sketches and model making. In addition, some of the courses also take the form of group cooperation to develop teamwork and project management skills.

B. *Application of virtual reality in environmental design*

Although the traditional teaching model ensures the transmission of knowledge to some extent, environmental art courses face multiple challenges in the current rapidly developing digital age. First of all, traditional teaching methods may not be able to fully stimulate students 'awareness of innovation, and rely too much on teachers' demonstration and guidance, resulting in students' weak ability in independent thinking and solving problems. Secondly, the design tools are updated quickly, such as computer-aided design (CAD), 3 D modeling software, etc., while the course content update speed is relatively slow, which may lead to the dilemma of backward skills after graduation. Moreover, with the sustainable development and the popularization of green design concept, the curriculum needs to integrate more environmental protection and ecological awareness into the teaching, but it is often difficult to go deeper due to the limitation of the curriculum capacity. Finally, in the face of the global design vision, how to cultivate students' cross-cultural understanding and international competitiveness is also a big challenge.

Computer 3D software technology is based on the principle of digital modeling and rendering, through computer generation of depth and space. This process usually consists of three main stages: modeling, texture mapping, and rendering. Modeling is the basis of creating 3 D objects, including the combination of points, lines, and planes to form geometry; texture maps give these geometry surface color, material, and details to make the model more realistic; rendering is the process of finally transforming the model into an image, involving the calculation of illumination, shadow, and reflection. The core of 3 D software technology lies in its algorithms, such as linear algebra, geometric transformation, illumination model, etc. These mathematical principles and algorithms are the basis of building a realistic 3 D environment. At the same time, software interaction and user interface design are also key to provide an efficient and intuitive workflow.

III. *Mainstream 3D software introduction*

3D software Autodesk 3ds Max: Widely used in the film, television and game industries, 3ds Max provides powerful modeling, animation and rendering tools, especially in the field of architectural visualization and visual effects. Autodesk Maya: Maya is another all-around 3D software, known for its advanced animation and visual effects features, often used in film and TV special effects, game development and advertising design. Blender: As open source 3D software, Blender not only provides comprehensive modeling, rendering and animation capabilities, but also has a built-in video editor and game engine, the choice for many independent artists and small studios. SketchUp: It is welcomed by architects and interior designers for its intuitive interface and fast modeling tools, which is suitable for beginners and professionals. Cinema 4D: Very popular in the field of broadcast design and visual effects, known for its stability and ease of use, especially in the dynamic graphics and short film production is widely used. Softimage (Now stopped): Once the first choice for large film and television production, known for its powerful character animation tools and hydrodynamic simulation. Houdini: Developed by Side Effects Software, known for its nodal workflow and powerful special effects functions, it is often used in advanced production of film special effects. Each of these software features, and which choice usually depends on the specific application requirements, user skill level and budget. With the continuous progress of technology, 3D software is also continuing to evolve, providing users with more innovation and possibilities.

3 Optimization Strategies for Environment Design

Hybrid learning models will become more popular, combining online and offline teaching to allow students to find a balance between theoretical learning and practical operation. For example, the theoretical explanation and discussion can be conducted in class, while the actual model production and scene construction can be carried out through 3 D software. This can not only ensure the teaching of theoretical knowledge, but also ensure that students have enough time for practical operation and improve their skills.

A. *Improve the design efficiency and accuracy*

Computer 3 D software technologies, such as Autodesk 3ds Max, SketchUp, Revit, provide powerful tools for environmental art design and greatly improve design efficiency. With these software, designers can quickly create three-dimensional models that visually show the spatial layout, material texture, and light and shadow effects.

$$tol(y_i \cdot g_{ij}) = y_{ij} \geq max(g_{ij} \frac{g - \mu}{\sigma} \int \frac{1}{n} \lim_{g \to \infty} \frac{1}{2}) \tag{1}$$

In environmental arts courses, the use of computer 3D software enables students to move from theoretical knowledge to practical operation.

$$max(g_{ij}) = (g_{ij}^2 \times 3) \succ mean(\sum g_{ij} \times \sum_{i=1}^{n} g_i^2 \frac{\Delta y}{\Delta g} \frac{dy}{dg}) \tag{2}$$

Computer 3D software technology combines the advantages of computer simulation and uses environmental design to quantify, which can improve the rationality of art design.

Students can repeatedly try and modify design schemes while in a virtual environment, which not only exercises their hands-on skills, but also improves their understanding of spatial perception and design principles. In addition, the real-time preview function provided by the software enables students to quickly see the design effect, so as to make timely feedback and adjustment. This immediate feedback mechanism is incomparable to traditional teaching methods.

$$R(l_i) = \sum g_i \bigcap \xi \to \oint y_i \leftrightarrow \sum\nolimits_{i=1}^{n} g_i^2 \frac{g - \mu}{\sigma} \tag{3}$$

B. *Selection of art design schemes*

The flexibility and scalability of 3D software bring infinite possibilities for environmental art design. Designers can import a variety of materials, such as texture, mapping, lighting, etc., to simulate the real environment, to create a rich variety of visual effects. Through VR (virtual reality) and AR (augmented reality) technology, the design works can become more three-dimensional and interactive, providing an immersive experience for the audience. In addition, the software-supported animation and rendering functions allow designers to dynamically display the design scheme, present the design intention more comprehensively, and stimulate innovative thinking.

$$s(g_i) = z_i \cdot \prod R(l_i) - w_i \notin \int \lim_{g \to \infty} \frac{1}{2} \cdot \left(\frac{\pi}{2} - \theta\right)\frac{1}{n} \tag{4}$$

In environmental art courses, the optimization of teaching content is crucial. Combined with the 3D software technology, the course design should highlight the practicality and innovation.

$$s(g_i) + R(l_i) \leq max(g_{ij}) \tag{5}$$

First of all, the course should cover the basic 3d modeling, material and texture, light rendering, spatial layout and other core modules, so that students can master the basic operation of the software. Secondly, practical project cases are introduced to let students learn in the simulated real work scenarios, such as designing interior space, public environment or landscape planning. At the same time, combining the design theory and history, let the students understand the integration of technology and art, improve the aesthetic and design thinking.

$$\overbrace{s(g_i) + R(l_i)} \leftrightarrow mean(\sum g_{ij} \times \sum\nolimits_{i=1}^{n} g_i^2 \frac{\Delta y}{\Delta g} \frac{dy}{dg}) \tag{6}$$

III. *Analysis of art design schemes*

Practice is the best way to test a theory. In the environmental art course, rich practical links should be set up, so that students can apply what they have learned in practice. For example, organize students to participate in beautification projects on campus or community, or work together to design a virtual exhibition space. Through these practical programs, students can exercise teamwork, project management, and time planning. At the same time, regular software operation training and design challenges are set to let students consolidate their skills in practice. In addition, the simulation studio environment is set up, so that students can experience the design process in a full range of aspects in the simulation workflow, from conceptual design to model making, and then to the later rendering.

$$No(g_i) = \frac{s(\widetilde{g_i}) + R(l_i)}{mean(\sum g_{ij} \times \sum_{i=1}^{n} g_i^2 \frac{\Delta y}{\Delta g} \frac{dy}{dg})} \tag{7}$$

Through the optimization of teaching content, the innovation of teaching methods and the strengthening of practical teaching links, environmental art courses can make better use of 3 D software technology, cultivate students' innovative thinking, technology application ability and practical operation skills, and lay a solid foundation for their future career.

$$Zh(g_i) = min[\sum s(\widetilde{g_i}) + R(l_i)] \tag{8}$$

With the continuous progress of computer 3D software technology, its application in environmental art curriculum has changed from auxiliary design tools to an important driving force for promoting the innovation of educational mode. The development of virtual reality (VR) and augmented reality (AR) technologies enables students to directly interact and design them in a three-dimensional space, providing an immersive learning experience. For example, through VR technology, students can simulate real scenes in the virtual environment and make real-time design modification and observation, which not only enhances the interest of learning, but also improves the learning effect.

$$accur(g_i) = \frac{min[s(\widetilde{g_i}) + R(l_i)]}{\sum s(\widetilde{g_i}) + R(l_i)} \times 100\% \tag{9}$$

In addition, the application of cloud computing and big data makes it possible to share educational resources and make personalized learning possible. Teachers can provide customized learning materials and exercises according to students' learning progress and needs, so as to realize individualized teaching. At the same time, the rise of distance education platforms has broken the geographical restrictions and enabled the integration of global educational resources, and students can have access to more diversified design concepts and practical cases.

$$accur(g_i) = \frac{min[\sum s(\widetilde{g_i}) + R(l_i)]}{\sum s(\widetilde{g_i}) + R(l_i)} \times 100\% + randon(g_i) \tag{10}$$

In the future, the teaching environment of environmental art courses will be more intelligent and dynamic. The intelligent teaching system can automatically analyze students 'learning behavior, provide accurate feedback and suggestions, and help teachers to more effectively evaluate students' learning progress and understanding degree. At the same time, these systems can also recommend appropriate learning resources according to students' learning style and interests, to realize personalized learning.

4   Results and Discussion

A. *Introduction to art and design.*

In addition, collaborative design will be an important part of the future environmental arts curriculum. Through an online collaboration platform, students can complete projects with partners around the world to develop teamwork and cross-cultural communication skills. This cross-regional and cross-disciplinary cooperation mode will greatly broaden students' horizons and promote the formation of innovative thinking (Tables 2 and 3).

Table 1. Art Design Requirements

Scope of application	grade	rationality	Art design
Indoor environment	standard	83.73	86.83
	Higher	89.56	79.81
Outdoor environment	standard	84.01	83.82
	Higher	82.28	83.97
Working environment	standard	83.37	83.01
	Higher	83.73	84.47

Table 2. The Overall Picture of the art Design Program

category	viability	Analysis rate
Indoor environment	91.76	85.20
Outdoor environment	86.43	87.02
Working environment	87.09	83.72
mean	84.41	88.25
X^6	83.50	86.50
P = 2.464		

The art design process in Table 1. is shown in Fig. 1.

it can be seen that the rationality of computer three-dimensional software technology is higher. Therefore, the speed of art design scheme, feasibility and summation stability of art design scheme of computer three-dimensional software technology are better.

B. *Environmental design*

Table 3. Comparison of Artistic Design Accuracy of Different Methods

algorithm	Art design	Magnitude of change	error
Computer three-dimensional software technology	94.20	95.81	95.44
Traditional design methods	93.64	92.17	93.43
P	90.47	92.47	91.53

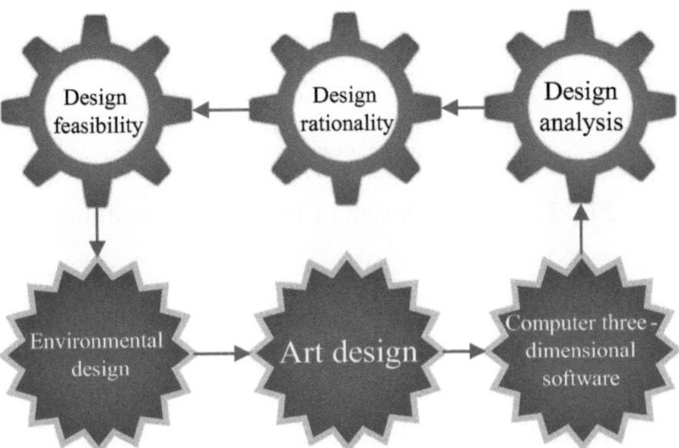

Fig. 1. The analysis process of environmental design.

To sum up, the development of computer 3D software technology not only provides a more powerful design tool at the technical level, but also brings about profound changes in the educational model. With the continuous progress of technology, the teaching of environmental art courses will pay more attention to practice, interaction and individuation, and cultivate more designers with innovative spirit and practical ability.

III. *Artistic design and stability of art design.*

With the further application of computer 3D software technology in environmental art education, the role of educators has gradually changed from the traditional knowledge imitator to the guide and facilitator. In the teaching of 3D design, teachers no longer just explain the design theory, but need to be familiar with and master the software operation, and guide students on how to combine artistic ideas with technical means. They need to stimulate students' innovative thinking, guide them to explore different design solutions, and also help students solve the technical problems they encounter in practice. In addition, educators need to follow industry trends and constantly update their teaching content to ensure that students can master the latest design tools and technologies (Fig. 2).

With the help of computer 3D software technology, students' learning experience and ability improvement have also changed significantly. They are no longer limited to 2D drawings, but can intuitively understand and display design concepts through 3D models. This change not only exercises the students' spatial perception ability, but also improves

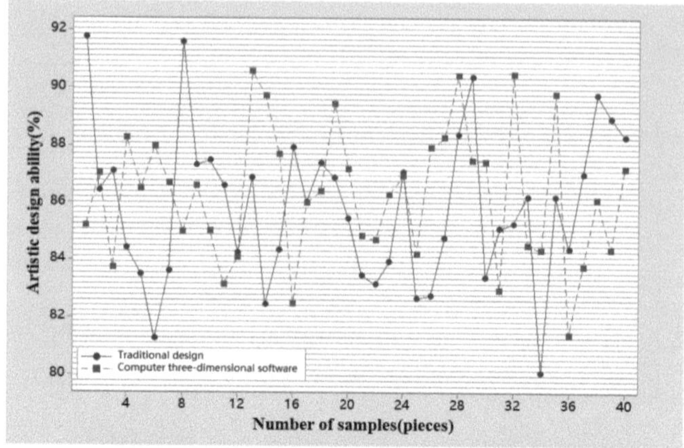

Fig. 2. Artistic Design of Different Algorithms

their practical ability and problem-solving ability. At the same time, through project-based learning, students can experience the complete design process from concept to realization, and cultivate comprehensive qualities such as teamwork, time management and communication. In addition, mastering 3D software skills also provides students with broader employment prospects, who can adapt to the changing market demands in their future careers.

With the development of technology, the resources of environmental art education have become more rich and diverse. Online tutorials, virtual reality simulation, open source software and so on all provide new possibilities for teaching. Educators can use these resources to enrich the curriculum content so that students can self-learn and practice outside the classroom. At the same time, the integration of educational resources also makes cross-regional and cross-school cooperation possible. Through the network platform, students can communicate with peers around the world, share design ideas and cases, and broaden their horizons (Fig. 3).

In addition, with cloud computing and big data technology, educators can more accurately assess students' learning progress, provide personalized learning paths and feedback, and further optimize the teaching results.

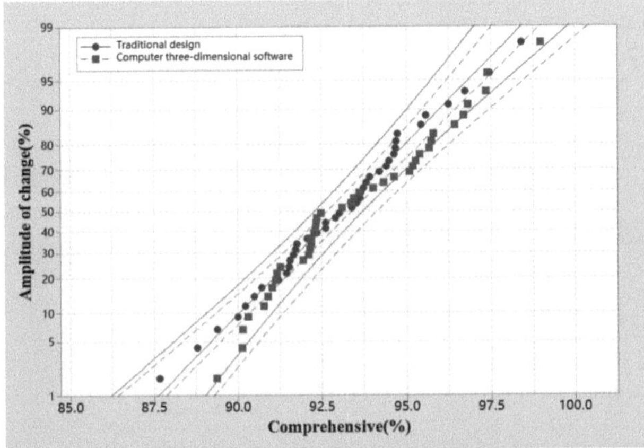

Fig. 3. Computer 3D software technology art design art design.

5 Conclusion

The introduction of computer 3D software technology has not only changed the way of environmental art education, but also brought a profound impact on educators, students and educational resources. As technology continues, we look forward to seeing more innovative teaching models and more efficient learning experiences realized in future education. Aiming at the problem of unsatisfactory environmental art design, this paper proposes computer three-dimensional software technology, combined with computer simulation, to optimize environmental design. At the same time, the feasibility of art design is analyzed in depth, and an environmental art design collection is constructed. Research shows that computer three-dimensional software technology can improve the rationality of environmental design, and can carry out general art design for environmental design. However, in the process of computer three-dimensional software technology, too much attention is paid to the analysis of art design, resulting in irrationality in the selection of art design indicators.

References

1. Agliardi, E., Alexopoulos, T., Karvelas, K.: The environmental pillar of ESG and financial performance: A portfolio analysis. Energy Econ. **120** (2023)
2. Ahmed, H.T., Aly, A.M..: Recycled waste materials in landscape design for sustainable development (Al-Ahsa as a Model). Sustainability **15**(15) (2023)
3. Ambrogio, S.: Fengshui: a moral technique-art (jiyi(sic)) for contemporary environmental awareness. Asian Studies-Azijske Studije **11**(2), 149–174 (2023)
4. Burkart, P., Vamos, I.: Getting to yes: an interview with Igor Vamos. Int. J. Cult. Stud. **26**(4), 481–494 (2023)
5. El Baz, J., Cherrafi, A., Benabdellah, A.C., Zekhnini, K., Nguema, J., Derrouiche, R.: Environmental supply chain risk management for industry 4.0: a data mining framework and research agenda. Systems **11**(1) (2023)

6. Hogan, M.: Environmental media" in the cloud: the making of critical data center art. New Media Soc. **25**(2), 384–404 (2023)

7. Ison, M., Bramwell-Lalor, S.: The arts in environmental education: connecting learners with their talents and nature. Environ. Educ. Res. **29**(7), 964–979 (2023)

8. Kuruppuarachchi, J., Hemadila, P., Madurapperuma, B.: Comparison of the literacy level on major environmental issues of the GCE (A/L) students of different disciplines in Kandy District, Sri Lanka. Sustainability **15**(5) (2023)

9. Riart, O.P., Sanz, M.A.: Artists in the mines, quarries and saltworks. Land art or earthworks and ecological art. Boletin Geologico Y Minero **134**(1), 147–164 (2023)

10. Smilan, C.: Visualizing climate change: Here we come to save the day! Inter. J. Educ. through Art **19**(1), 93–111 (2023)

11. Strehovec, J.: The upcycling and reappropriation - on art-specific circular economy in the age of climate change. Cultura-Inter. J. Philos. Culture Axiol. **20**(1), 27–41 (2023)

12. Thompson, B., Jurgens, A.S., Bohie, Lamberts, R.: Street art as a vehicle for environmental science communication. Jcom-J. Sci. Commun. **22**(4) (2023)

13. Ward, D.: The art of environmental personhood and the possibility of environmental statehood. Artnodes (32), 1–11 (2023)

Practical Discussion of Computer Multimedia Technology in Teaching

Liyuan Fu[✉] and Yuxin Fang

Shandong Communication and Media College, Jinan 250200, Shandong Province, China
`97102@163.com`

Abstract. Within the framework of the exponential growth of computer networks, educational institutions have fully embraced the use of information technology in the classroom. Improving the quality of instruction is one of the primary goals of effective pedagogy. But we can't put off reforming and innovating our teaching techniques any longer; the standard manner of instruction isn't up to the task. As a result, the article suggests using computer multimedia technology to assess various instructional techniques. To start, the use of computer technology enhances the mode of instruction, and to decrease interference factors, the indicators are split according to the needs of the method of instruction. Next, computer technology builds teaching methods schemes, enhances teaching method outcomes, and analyzes teaching method results thoroughly. When compared to more conventional forms of instruction, MATLAB simulations reveal that computer multimedia technology for teaching techniques is more practical and reliable, subject to certain evaluation criteria.

Keywords: computer technology · computer multimedia technology · Teaching · Teaching methods

1 Introduction

The cornerstone of effective teaching and a major factor in student achievement is the chosen style of instruction [1]. Problems with education and teaching arise, however, from the process of developing techniques of instruction [2] and the lack of practicality of such approaches [3]. The use of computer multimedia technology in the examination of teaching techniques is seen by some researchers to be a powerful tool for both analyzing and supporting these approaches [5]. In light of this, the authors of this work suggest using computer multimedia technology to enhance the instructional scheme and validate the model's efficacy [6]. The teaching method process in Table 1 is shown in Fig. 1.

B. Brik and S. Nazir (Eds.): BigIoT-EDU 2024, LNICST 659, pp. 353–361, 2026.
https://doi.org/10.1007/978-3-032-18631-7_39

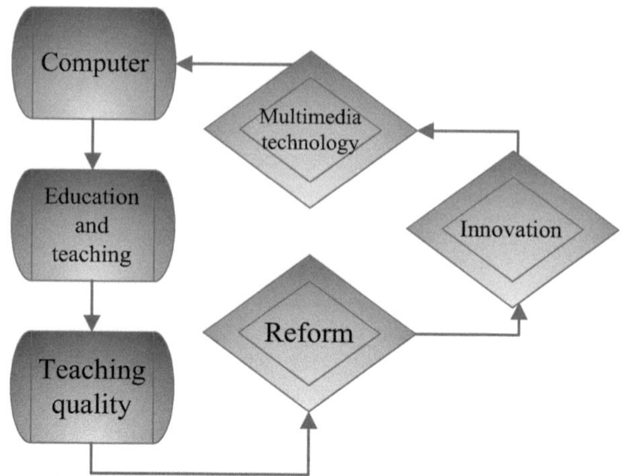

Fig. 1. Teaching the analytical process

2 Related Works

There has been extensive use of the practical discussion of computer multimedia technology in the classroom. By enhancing the use of multimedia in the classroom, teachers may make lessons more engaging for students and boost their retention of material. A discussion of the practical applications of computer multimedia technology in the classroom follows: Video resources for educators: Students' ability to observe and comprehend course material might be enhanced with the use of instructional films. Text, interactive graphics, music, and other multimedia may enhance the presentation of key points in teaching films.

(1) Engaging students: Students' engagement and learning outcomes may be significantly enhanced via the use of interactive multimedia instruction. In order to get a more thorough grasp of the material, students may engage in interactive learning, exercises, assessments, and other activities made possible by multimedia technology.
(2) Virtual experiment: Students may use computer multimedia technology to create virtual labs where they can perform experiments. This eliminates the need for physical locations and time constraints, while also reducing the expense and potential dangers of the experiments.
(3) Thirdly, gamified learning makes learning more engaging and encourages student participation by using computer multimedia technologies into games. Learning results and student engagement may be significantly enhanced via the use of gamified learning.
(4) Online interaction: In order to better answer students' questions and enhance the quality of instruction, instructors and students may engage in real-time question and answer sessions, discussions, and other activities using multimedia technology.

3 Strategies for Teaching Optimization

Using a stochastic optimization method, computer multimedia technology optimizes the teaching scheme by adjusting the characteristics of the mode of instruction. With the use of computer multimedia technology, lessons can be organized into several levels of instruction and programs may be chosen at random. Various degrees of teaching styles are optimized and assessed in the iterative process. Once you've finished the optimization analysis, it's time to evaluate and record the best teaching approaches across various programs.

A. Mathematical description of computer multimedia technology

Optimization of the teaching method scheme according to the numerous index parameters in the technique may be achieved via the use of computer multimedia technology is [7], discover the instructional approach's unqualified value parameter is [8], with the purpose of incorporating the instructional strategy to is [9], lastly, use the results from formula (1) to determine the practicability of teaching [10].

$$tol(y_i \cdot r_{ij}) = y_{ij} \geq max(r_{ij} \cdot \sum_{i=1}^{n} r_i) \tag{1}$$

Equation (2) shows the evaluation of outliers among them.

$$max(r_{ij}) = (r_{ij}^2 + 2) \succ mean(\sum \frac{1}{n} \oplus \frac{r - \mu}{\sigma} \frac{1}{2} r_{ij}) \tag{2}$$

The use of quantitative techniques in education may enhance the practicality of teaching approaches, and computer multimedia technology integrates the benefits of multimedia technology.

So what if I What is needed for the form of instruction is, the teaching method scheme is, thow happy he is with the instructional plan is, together with the evaluation function for instructional schemes is, as shown in Eq. (3).

$$P(u_i) = \sum r_i \bigcap \xi \rightarrow \oint y_i \rightarrow \frac{\delta y}{\delta r} \otimes \frac{dy}{dr} \tag{3}$$

B. Choice of teaching mode scheme

Second Hypothesis: The Role of the Instructor is, the weight coefficient is, Consequently, as shown in Eq. (4), the approach of instruction necessitates unqualified instruction.

$$s(r_i) = z_i \cdot \prod P(u_i) - w_i \cup \frac{\Delta y}{\Delta r} \partial r \tag{4}$$

Equation (5) shows the outcome of obtaining a full function of the teaching style, in accordance with assumptions I and II.

$$s(r_i) + P(u_i) \leq max(r_{ij}) \tag{5}$$

The standardization of all data is necessary to enhance the efficacy of the instructional approach, and Eq. (6) shows the outcome.

$$s(r_i) + P(u_i) \leftrightarrow mean(\sum \frac{1}{n} \oplus \frac{r - \mu}{\sigma} \frac{1}{2} r_{ij}) \tag{6}$$

C. Analysis of teaching style schemes

Computer multimedia technology cannot be implemented without first doing a multi-dimensional analysis of the teaching method scheme, mapping the needs of the method to the teaching library, and then eliminating any unqualified methods is. The findings are illustrated in Eq. (7), and the anomaly assessment method may be provided according to Eq. (6).

$$No(r_i) = \frac{s(r_i) + P(u_i)}{mean(\sum \frac{1}{n} \oplus \frac{r-\mu}{\sigma} \frac{1}{2} r_{ij})} \tag{7}$$

Among them, If the scheme is not presented, then its integration will be necessary is, and the outcome is shown in Eq. (8).

$$Zh(r_i) = min[\sum s(r_i) + P(u_i)] \tag{8}$$

In order to guarantee the precision of computer multimedia technology, teaching is thoroughly examined, and the threshold and index weights of instructional techniques and schemes are established. Innovation in analysis is necessary since teaching involves a systematic evaluation of pedagogical approaches. If the distribution of the instruction is not typical is, As a consequence, the general correctness of the teaching style and the calculation result will be diminished, and the teaching style scheme will be impacted is, shown in Eq. (9).

$$accur(r_i) = \frac{min[\sum s(r_i) + P(u_i)]}{\sum s(r_i) + P(u_i)} \times 100\% \tag{9}$$

Consistent with empirical evidence, the teaching mode scheme has a multi-dimensional distribution, according to the study of instructional strategies. It is considered a very analytical research since the instruction is not directed, which suggests that the teaching mode scheme has considerable unpredictability. If the haphazard process of education is, then Eq. (9). This allows us to state the computation of Eq. (10).

$$accur(r_i) = \frac{min[\sum s(r_i) + P(u_i)]}{\sum s(r_i) + P(u_i)} \times 100\% + randon(r_i) \tag{10}$$

Of these, the instruction satisfies typical standards; more specifically, multimedia technology modifies the instruction, eliminates redundant and unneeded schemes, and augments the default scheme, resulting in a robust dynamic correlation across the whole teaching method scheme.

4 Results and Discussion

A. Introduction to teaching methods

Table 1 shows the unique teaching technique scheme, and the research aim is the instruction in difficult circumstances. There are 12 pathways, and the test period is 12 h.

Table 1. Requirements for teaching methods in colleges and universities

Scope of application	grade	viability	Teaching mode
Teaching objectives	I	87.37	81.59
	II	84.61	84.07
Curriculum	I	88.69	82.61
	II	82.53	86.29
Teaching session	I	87.32	84.81
	II	82.85	83.48

The computer multimedia technology teaching method scheme is more in line with the real needs of the method of instruction than the conventional mode of instruction. Compared to more conventional methods of instruction, computer multimedia technology is more logical and produces higher-quality results in the classroom. Figure 2 shows the pedagogical shifts that have taken place, making the use of computer multimedia technology more practical and yielding better learning outcomes. Consequently, computer multimedia technology instruction is more efficient, has a more well-designed scheme for teaching modes, and produces more stable summations.

B. Teaching situation

Information that is not structured, information that is somewhat organized, and information that is structured are all components of the teaching technique scheme. Following the first computer multimedia technology pre-selection, a tentative teaching technique plan is produced and its practicability is assessed. As demonstrated in Table 2, several degrees of teaching styles and method schemes are chosen to more precisely validate the outcomes of teaching style innovation.

Table 2. The overall picture of the teaching model program

category	Random data	Satisfaction	Analysis rate
Teaching objectives	89.54	87.36	90.53
Curriculum	91.04	89.36	88.78
Teaching session	85.59	88.45	87.72
mean	88.65	87.02	87.86
$X6$	89.52	86.69	88.87
$P = .053$			

C. Teaching mode and stability of teaching methods

As illustrated in Fig. 2, the teaching method scheme is compared with the conventional mode of instruction in order to confirm the correctness of computer multimedia technology.

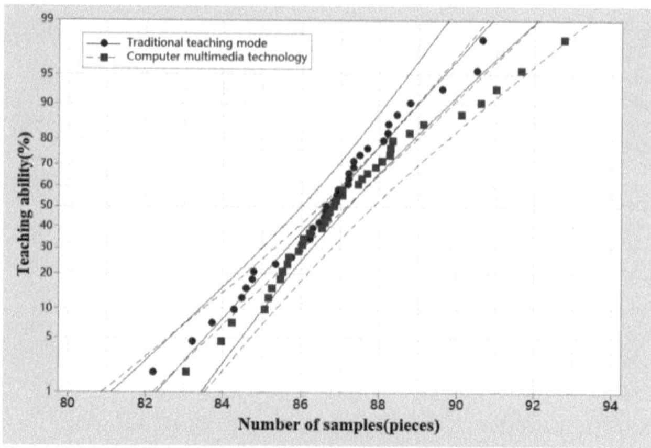

Fig. 2. Teaching modes of different algorithms

Figure 2 shows that compared to the traditional teaching mode, the computer multimedia technology teaching mode is higher, but has a lower error rate. This suggests that the computer multimedia technology teaching mode is consistent, whereas the traditional teaching mode is not. In Table 3, we can see the typical instructional plan for the three algorithms mentioned before.

Table 3. Comparison of the accuracy of teaching methods of different methods

algorithm	Survey data	Teaching mode	Magnitude of change	error
Computer multimedia technology	93.78	95.86	93.24	93.93
Traditional teaching mode	87.13	86.38	86.68	88.16
P	85.76	87.95	86.64	87.25

Table 3 shows that there are problems with the conventional method of instruction, such as a high mistake rate, a lack of adaptability to new circumstances, and a lack of practicality in the classroom. In comparison to more conventional methods of instruction, computer multimedia technology often produces superior learning outcomes. Simultaneously, the accuracy rate has not altered much, and the computer multimedia technology teaching method is above 90%. Just to make sure that computer multimedia technology is still the best. Various methodologies are used to conduct a comprehensive examination of computer multimedia technology, as illustrated in Fig. 3, in order to further confirm the efficacy of the suggested method.

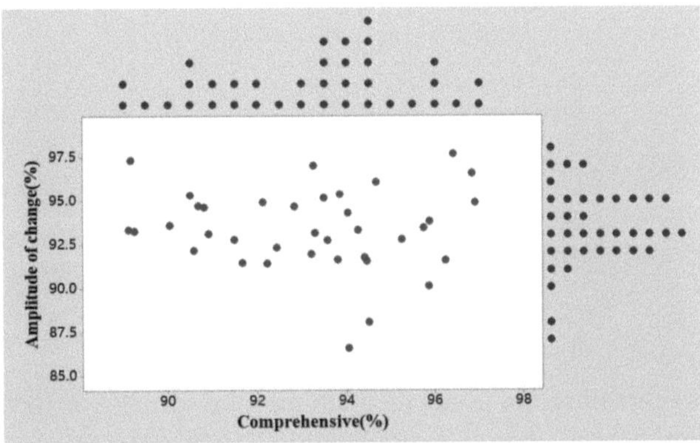

Fig. 3. The teaching mode of computer multimedia technology teaching method

By increasing the teaching adjustment coefficient and setting the threshold of the mode to eliminate the teaching method scheme that does not meet the requirements, computer multimedia technology significantly improves the teaching mode compared to the traditional teaching mode (Fig. 3).

D. Effectiveness of teaching methods

Figure 4 shows the teaching technique scheme that was used to compare computer multimedia technology with conventional teaching methods in order to validate the efficacy of the former.

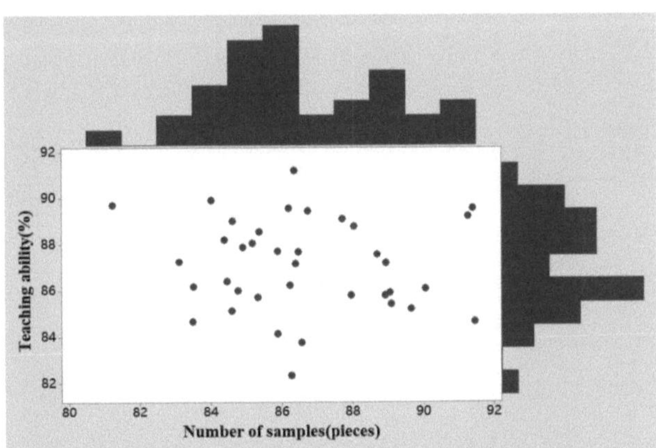

Fig. 4. Teaching modes of different algorithms

The figure shows that the error rate is lower in the computer multimedia technology teaching mode, which suggests that it is relatively stable, compared to the traditional teaching mode, which is uneven. This suggests that the computer multimedia technology teaching mode is higher in quality. Table 4 displays the average teaching strategy of the three methods mentioned before.

Table 4. Comparison of the effectiveness of teaching methods of different methods

algorithm	Survey data	Teaching mode	Magnitude of change	error
Computer multimedia technology	89.65	87.77	93.70	84.95
Traditional teaching mode	92.41	90.50	91.63	92.36
P	85.98	90.91	89.35	88.59

Table 4 shows that there are problems with the conventional method of instruction, such as a high mistake rate, a lack of adaptability to new circumstances, and a lack of practicality in the classroom. In comparison to more conventional methods of instruction, computer multimedia technology often produces superior learning outcomes. Also, there has been no discernible change in the accuracy of computer multimedia technology as a teaching modality, which is above 91%. Just to make sure that computer multimedia technology is still the best. Various methodologies are used to conduct a broad study of computer multimedia technology, as illustrated in Fig. 5, in order to further validate the usefulness of the method described in this work.

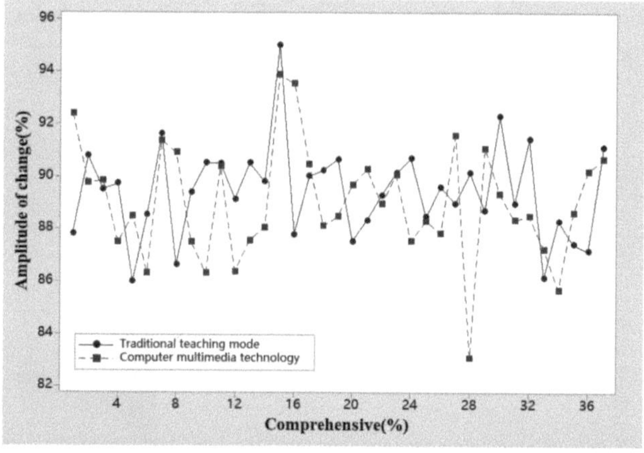

Fig. 5. The teaching mode of computer multimedia technology teaching method

Figure 5 shows that computer multimedia technology's teaching mode is far superior to the traditional one. This is because, among other things, it raises the teaching adjustment coefficient, establishes the mode's threshold, and gets rid of any teaching method schemes that don't measure up.

5 Conclusion

In response to the fact that current methods of instruction are far from optimal, this study suggests using computer multimedia technology in conjunction with other forms of multimedia technology in the classroom. Simultaneously, a comprehensive analysis is conducted on the reform and invention of teaching techniques, and a compilation of teaching modes is put together. Computer multimedia technology has the potential to carry out common teaching techniques with more precision and quality, according to studies. The problem with computer multimedia technology is that it focuses too much on analyzing teaching techniques, which leads to illogical indications of teaching modes being chosen.

References

1. Ayatiguli. Application of computer multimedia technology in teaching. Inform. Recording Mater. **20**(01), 125–126 (2019)
2. Su, L.: Advantages and current situation of computer multimedia technology in teaching. E-education Primary Secondary Sch. (Second Half of Month) (05), 4 (2018)
3. Zheng, T.: Research on the application of computer multimedia technology in teaching. Electron. World (06), 45 (2017)
4. Zhong, C.: Application of computer multimedia technology in teaching. Electron. Technol. Softw. Eng. (15), 102 (2014)
5. Yang, X.: On the role and value of computer multimedia technology in teaching. Wireless Internet Technol. (09), 168 (2012)
6. Liu, S.: Application of computer multimedia technology in teaching. Modern Marketing (Xueyuan Edition) (03), 274 (2012)
7. Guo, C., Li, J.: Application of multimedia computer technology in teaching. Wireless Internet Technol. (10), 63–64 (2011)
8. Zhang, P.: Application of computer multimedia technology in teaching. Sci. Technol. Inform. (27), 239 (2011)
9. Hou, F.: Application of computer multimedia technology in teaching. Road Success (18), 14 (2011)
10. Zhuang, X.: Application of computer multimedia technology in teaching in information age. Wireless Internet Technol. (05), 61+66 (2011)

Research on Computer Network Security Management and Related Technologies

Jilin Li[✉] and Man Wang

Shandong Institute of Commerce and Technology, Jinan, Sandong, China
`lijl0213@163.com`

Abstract. Computer network security is a key field to ensure the security of information in the process of transmission, storage and processing, prevent data from being illegally accessed, tampered with or destroyed, and protect users' privacy from infringement. With the development of the digital society, computer networks have penetrated into every aspect of our lives, from financial transactions, medical records to government services, all of which rely on the Internet. Therefore, the importance of network security is self-evident. Network system paralysis or data leakage may not only lead to economic losses, but also may cause social chaos, and even affect national security. For example, cyber attacks on critical infrastructure can have serious impacts on power supply, transportation systems, and public services. Therefore, strengthening the computer network security management and improving the defense ability is an indispensable link to ensure social stability and economic development. The feasibility analysis of network security shows that the database transparent encryption algorithm is better than the common information encryption technology in terms of the accuracy and detection time of firewall technology for computer network security under the condition of certain security system evaluation standards.

Keywords: firewall technology · Transparent encryption algorithm for database · Computer network security management · Security system assessment

1 Introduction

At present, the global network security situation is grim, and the network attacks are frequent and the means are increasingly complex. New threats such as ransomware, distributed denial of service (DDoS) attacks, zero-day attacks, and social media phishing are emerging. The global economic damage due to cybercrime is worth billions of dollars each year, and that number continues to grow. With the popularity of Internet of Things (IoT) devices, the attack surface is expanding, making the traditional security protection means face challenges. For example, smart home devices may become a springboard for malicious attackers to enter the internal network, while network security issues in industrial control systems (ICS) may directly affect the country's infrastructure security. In addition, with the development of big data and cloud computing technologies, the centralized storage and processing of data bring new security risks. The technical process of firewall in Table 1 is shown in Fig. 1.

B. Brik and S. Nazir (Eds.): BigIoT-EDU 2024, LNICST 659, pp. 362–370, 2026.
https://doi.org/10.1007/978-3-032-18631-7_40

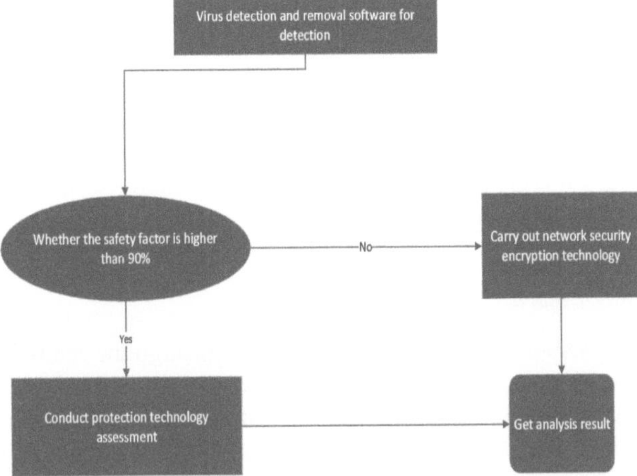

Fig. 1. Analysis Process of Computer Network Security Management and Related Technology Exploration

Data breach protection technology is designed to prevent data from being illegally acquired during transmission or storage. These technologies include firewalls, intrusion detection system (IDS), intrusion defense system (IPS), data leakage prevention (DLP) software, etc. Firewalls block unauthorized network traffic, while IDS and IPS monitor network activity to detect and block potential attacks in a timely manner. The DLP system prevents sensitive data information through email, file sharing or USB devices. In addition, access control strategies, such as the minimum authority principle and multi-factor authentication, can also effectively prevent internal unintentional or malicious data leakage.

2   Related Works

A. *Computer network security management.*

Data leakage, account hijacking, and service disruptions in the cloud environment are becoming increasingly prominent. At the same time, cyber warfare and cyber espionage among countries have intensified, and cyber security has become a new battlefield of international political game. In the face of this situation, governments and enterprises are strengthening the formulation and implementation of network security regulations, investing in the research and development of advanced security technology, enhance the public awareness of network security, in order to build an effective protective barrier in the complex and changeable network environment. However, cyber security is a never-ending offensive and defensive battle, which requires continuous innovation, collaboration and adaptation to cope with evolving threats. The Secure Sockets Layer (SSL) and Transport Layer Security (TLS) protocols are widely used secure communication protocols on the Internet, which provide end-to-end encryption to ensure that data is not stolen during transmission. HTTPS is a combination of HTTP and TLS, ensuring the security of web browsing. Security Protocol provides secure communication for IP networks, including data encryption, authentication, and tamper prevention. It is often used in virtual private networks (VPN) for remote secure access. The Secure Shell protocol is used for remote login and file transfer, which uses encryption technology to ensure privacy for command-line interaction and data transfer. Pretty Good Privacy (PGP) and GNU Privacy Guard (GPG) are open source tools for e-mail and file encryption, which use asymmetric encryption and digital signatures to provide end-to-end communication security.

B. *Related technical research.*

Network security should be based on prevention, through the establishment of multi-level protection mechanisms, such as firewall, intrusion detection system and security strategies, to prevent malicious attacks and illegal access. Cybersecurity management emphasizes dynamic adaptation, as threats and attacks constantly change. Therefore, it is necessary to update security policies regularly, monitor network behavior, and timely detect and respond to new threats. Ensure that each user and system process only has the minimum permission required to complete their tasks to limit the extent of potential damage. In the system design and development stage, security should be considered, and security is part of the system architecture. Improving users' safety awareness, letting them understand the potential risks and observing safety regulations is an important means to prevent internal threats.

3 Optimization Strategy of Computer Network Security Management and Related Technology Exploration

These encryption technologies and secure communication protocols play a key role in many fields, including email, online transactions, file sharing, and web browsing, ensuring the privacy and security of information. With the development of technology, encryption technologies are constantly evolving to address the increasingly complex cybersecurity challenges.

A. *Mathematical description of database transparent encryption algorithm.*

Effective network security management usually involves a multi-level, cross-departmental organizational structure.

$$\bigcup_{i=1}^{n} X_i(y_i \cdot x_{ij}) = y_{ij} \geq max(x_{ij}) \tag{1}$$

Including senior management, responsible for developing and approving cybersecurity policies that ensure compliance with regulatory requirements and business objectives.

$$max(x_{ij}) = (x_{ij}^2 + 2) \succ mean(\sum x_{ij}) \tag{2}$$

Responsible for executing and maintaining security policies, monitoring network activities, handling security incidents, and conducting regular security assessments.

Responsible for auditing network activities, ensuring compliance with security policies, and providing audit reports.

$$F(d_i) = \sum x_i \uplus \oint y_i \qquad (3)$$

B. *Selection of information encryption technology scheme.*

Provide technical support, including installation, configuration, and maintenance of security equipment and software, as well as security updates and patch management. Department Design and implement the staff safety training plan to improve the safety awareness and skills of all staff. Work with other departments and external agencies, such as coordinating with legal issues and working with suppliers to obtain the latest security solutions. To sum up, network security management is a multi-level and multi-angle work, which requires the participation of all members of the organization to form a comprehensive and coordinated defense system to cope with the increasingly complex network security challenges.

$$g(x_i) = z_i \cdot \prod F(d_i) \pm w_i \qquad (4)$$

Phishing attacks are a social engineering tool that often trick users into leaking sensitive information such as usernames, passwords, and credit card numbers by masquerading as trusted entities such as banks or social media platforms. A DoS attack is by sending a large number of invalid requests to the target system to service normal users. Distributed denial-of-service (DDoS) attacks are more powerful with multiple devices.

$$g(x_i) + F(d_i) \oplus max(x_{ij}) \qquad (5)$$

Malware includes viruses, worms, trojans, etc., which can replicate themselves, destroy systems, or steal data. Modern malware, such as ransomware, encrypts user data and demands a ransom to decrypt it. An attacker attempts to obtain an unauthorized data access or control system by inserting a malicious SQL code in the input field. Zero-day attacks are attacks against software vulnerabilities that were exploited before the software vendor issued the patch.

$$g(x_i) + F(d_i) \leftrightarrow min\left(\sum x_{ij}\right) \qquad (6)$$

III. *Analysis of firewall technical scheme.*

Firewall as the first line of defense of network security, by defining rules to prevent unauthorized network traffic. Intrusion Defense System (IPS) The IDS monitors network traffic and identifies suspicious behavior, while the IPS proactively blocks potential attacks. Regular updates to software and operating systems to promptly apply security patches to fix newly discovered vulnerabilities. Use encryption technology to secure data transfers, while verifying that only authorized users have access to the system. Improve the overall cyber security awareness of the organization by educating employees to identify and avoid cyber threats.

$$No(x_i) = \frac{g(x_i) + F(d_i)}{min\left(\sum x_{ij}\right)} \qquad (7)$$

Secret technology is an important means to protect information security. By transforming plaintext information into ciphertext, unauthorized users cannot understand the meaning of information.

$$Z(x_i) = min[\sum g(x_i) + F(d_i)] \qquad (8)$$

The basic principle includes two main processes: encryption and decryption. Encryption is to convert the plaintext with the key to form the ciphertext that cannot be read directly; Decryption is the reverse process of encryption and can restore the ciphertext to the original text using the same key. Encryption algorithms are usually divided into symmetric encryption and asymmetric encryption. Symmetric encryption uses the same key for encryption and decryption, while asymmetric encryption uses a pair of keys, one for encryption and the other for decryption.

$$accur(x_i) = \frac{min[\sum g(x_i) + F(d_i)]}{\sum g(x_i) + F(d_i)} \times 100\% \qquad (9)$$

RSA (Rivest-Shamir-Adleman) is the earliest asymmetric encryption algorithm, based on the difficulty of large number factorization. It generates a pair of public keys and private keys, which are used for encryption and the private key is used for decryption, ensuring that the information can be transmitted safely even if the public key is disclosed.

$$accur(x_i) = \frac{min[\sum g(x_i) + F(d_i)]}{\sum g(x_i) + F(d_i)} \times 100\% + randon(x_i) \qquad (10)$$

MD5 and SHA-1 were early hash functions, but with the discovery of collision attacks, the safer SHA-256 or SHA-3 series are now used. The hash function transforms the information of any length into a fixed length summary, which is often used for password storage and data integrity check. Asymmetric encryption algorithms such as RSA and elliptic curve encryption (ECC) are often used in digital signatures. They combine hash functions and asymmetric encryption to verify the integrity of the data and the identity of the sender.

4   Results and Discussion

A. *Introduction of firewall technology.*

Data encryption is one of the core technologies to protect information security. It converts plain-text information into incomprehensible ciphertext through specific algorithms, thus preventing unauthorized access and use. Common encryption algorithms include symmetric encryption (such as AES) and asymmetric encryption (such as RSA), the former is more efficient in large data encryption, while the latter is more advantageous in security and authentication. Desensitization is another way to protect data privacy and reducing the risk of data leakage by replacing, deleting, or blurring sensitive information, such as personal identification information (PII). For example, processing sensitive fields with a hash function maintains data availability while preventing direct leakage of raw data (Table 2 and 3).

Table 1. Technical Requirements for Network Security Firewall

Area of application	Grade	Safety effect	Privacy effect
Enterprise software	I	33.65	33.07
	II	34.28	34.65
System container	I	33.23	34.40
	II	33.77	35.10
Personal computer	I	35.60	33.67
	II	33.82	32.79

Table 2. Overall situation of network security management scheme

category	degree of satisfaction	Confidentiality rate
decision-making level	84.36	73.04
Treatment layer	83.01	73.54
Executive layer	83.52	75.27
average/mean value	82.63	73.34
X6	34.25	33.34
P = 3.074		

Table 3. Comparison of Technical Accuracy of Firewall With Different Methods

algorithm	degree of safety	amplitude of variation	error
Transparent encryption algorithm for database	93.67	93.41	95.61
General information encryption technology	82.79	83.08	84.32
P	35.012	33.827	35.810

B. *Computer network security management and related technologies.*

There are laws and regulations on data privacy worldwide. For example, Europe's General Data Protection Regulation (GDPR) sets out strict standards for personal data processing, requiring companies to obtain explicit consent from users, provide data access and deletion rights, and promptly notify them in case of data leakage. The California Consumer Privacy Act (CCPA) also gives California residents control over their personal information. In addition, there are the Health Insurance Portability and Accountability Act (HIPAA) and other regulations specifically for medical data. Following these regulations, businesses need to establish data protection systems, including data mini-mization, data lifecycle management, security audit, and compliance training, to ensure that user data is processed legally and transparently.

III. *Security management and stability of firewall technology.*

In order to verify the accuracy of database transparent encryption algorithm, the firewall technical scheme is compared with ordinary information encryption technology, and the firewall technical scheme is shown in the figuration shown (Fig. 2).

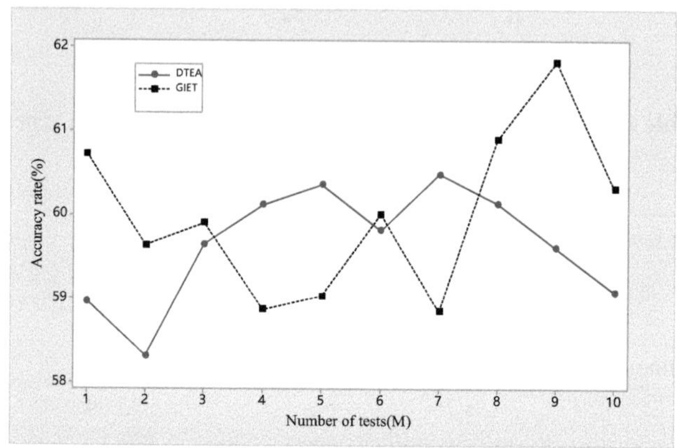

Fig. 2. Accuracy of Different Algorithms

In the era of cloud computing and big data, the challenges of data security and privacy protection are increasingly intensified. Companies not only need to continuously update their security strategies, adopt advanced encryption and protection technologies, but also constantly adapt to changing laws and regulations to protect the privacy of users' data and maintain the trust relationship between enterprises and users.

Artificial intelligence (AI) is increasingly widely used in network security, especially in automatic threat detection. Through machine learning algorithms, AI can identify and learn abnormal behavior patterns and detect potential network attacks in time. For exam-ple, deep learning models can analyze large amounts of network traffic data, identify patterns that deviate from normal behavior, thus warning and preventing malicious activ-ity.AI technology makes firewalls and intrusion defense systems more intelligent, and they can learn from themselves and adapt to changing attack strategies. The intelligent system can analyze the flow mode, dynamically adjust the protection strategy, improve the defense efficiency, and reduce false reports and missing reports (Fig. 3).

AI can also be used for adaptive security response, automatically adjusting defense strategies according to the nature and severity of the attack. When attacks are detected, the AI system responds quickly, isolates the infected system, limits the range of damage, and provides repair advice.

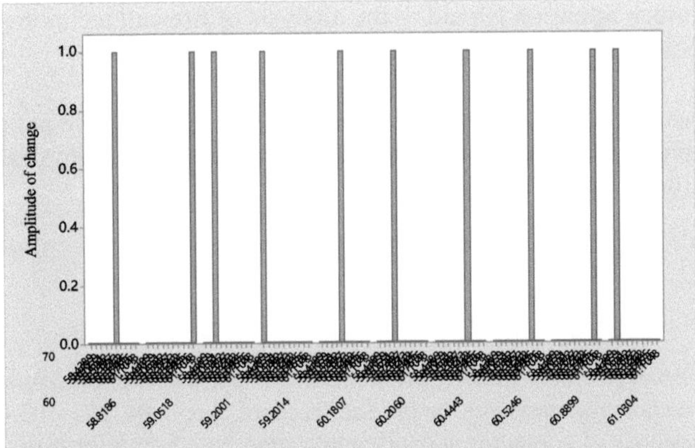

Fig. 3. Security Management of Firewall Technology of Database Transparent Encryption Algorithm

5 Conclusion

Research and practice in the field of computer network security have made remarkable progress in the past few decades. At the basic theory level, we have gained a deep understanding of network security management, including its basic concepts, principles and organizational structure. Encryption technologies, such as symmetric encryption, asymmetric encryption, and hash functions, have become the key tools for data protection, providing a basic guarantee for the confidentiality and integrity of information. In the defense of network attack, firewall, intrusion detection system, security strategy formulation and implementation and other technologies have been widely used in all kinds of network environments, effectively improving the anti-attack ability of the network. In the field of data security and privacy protection, we have witnessed the continuous development of data encryption and privacy protection laws and regulations, such as GDPR in the European Union and CCPA in California, these regulations not only enhance the public awareness of data security, but also promote enterprises to strengthen data management. Furthermore, secure communication protocols, such as TLS and IPSec, provide a standard framework for secure communication on the Internet, ensuring the security of information during transmission.

Aiming at the problem that the quality of computer network security management and its related technical exploration is not ideal, this paper puts forward a transparent encryption algorithm for database and optimizes computer network security management and its related technical exploration in combination with the running environment. At the same time, the firewall technology optimization and threshold innovation are deeply analyzed to build a network security collection. The research shows that the database transparent encryption algorithm can improve the accuracy and stability of computer network security management and related technology exploration and can carry out general firewall technology for computer network security management and related technology exploration. However, in the process of database transparent encryption algorithm, too much attention is paid to the analysis of firewall technology, which leads to the unreasonable selection of firewall technical indicators.

Acknowledgements. Shandong university humanities and social science project: Research on the theory and practice of higher vocational education on students' physical education core accomplishment(Item number 23C2007)

References

1. Feng, C.J.: Analysis of the security problems in computer network teaching in colleges and universities and countermeasures. Netw. Sec. Technol. Appli. **06**, 102–103 (2023)
2. Feng, A.: Analysis of computer network application based on information security. Netw. Sec. Technol. Appli. **06**, 170–171 (2023)
3. Liu, J., Yang, L., , Wang, H., et al.: Research and exploration of computer network virtual simulation experiment system. Comput. Knowl. Technol. **19**(15), 72–74 (2023)
4. Cao, C., Qin, D.: Analysis of security problems in computer network engineering and its countermeasures. Comput. Knowl. Technol. **19**(15), 77–79 (2023)
5. Yu Xia, Z.: Analysis on the application of artificial intelligence technology in the development of computer network. Comput. Knowl. Technol. **19**(14), 90–92 (2023)
6. Peng, P.: Analysis of computer network security issues and prevention technologies from the perspective of Informaionization. Wireless Internet Technol. **20**(08), 138–140 (2023)
7. Jiao, M., Liu, Y.G., Zhou, X., et al.: Computer network principal demonstration and virtual simulation teaching training platform under the background of new engineering. China Mod. Educ. Equipm. (07), 5–8 (2023)
8. Xu., J.: Analysis of technical integration of computer network and artificial intelligence. Electron. Technol. **52**(04), 94–95 (2023)
9. Yang, F.T.: Research on countermeasures of computer network engineering construction under the background of information technology development. Inform. Syst. Eng. **04**, 113–115 (2023)
10. Xu, Y.: The application of artificial intelligence in computer network technology in the era of big data. Television Technol. **47**(04), 142–144 (2023)

Research and Application of Blender Based 3D Design Curriculum

Guoji Liu[(✉)]

Software Engineering Institute of Guangzhou, Guangzhou 510990, Guangdong, China
lgj0328@tom.com

Abstract. With the widespread application of 3D technology, Blender based 3D design courses have become a topic of concern and importance for more and more educational institutions. However, there is currently a lack of systematic research and exploration on this course in China. This article aims to delve into the implementation of Blender based 3D design courses, study its advantages and limitations, and explore how to better apply it to the field of education. Firstly, this article summarizes and sorts out the implementation content of Blender based 3D design courses, including basic object modeling, material mapping, animation production, etc. Then, this article analyzes the application advantages of the course, including advanced technology, easy to learn, intuitive and vivid, and elaborates on the limitations of the course, such as high software configuration requirements and high technical barriers. Most importantly, this article also proposes relevant strategies and suggestions for teaching implementation, including prioritizing the selection of appropriate teaching resources, flexible teaching of technical methods, and emphasizing students' practical operations. Practice has shown that the teaching implementation of Blender based 3D design courses depends on the teacher's level and instructional design, so it is necessary to tailor it to students' learning willingness and learning situation. Therefore, the successful implementation of this course not only depends on teaching resources and equipment, but also requires a high-level teaching team and continuous innovation in teaching models. In the future, we need to further deepen our research on Blender based 3D design courses, expand their educational application fields, improve educational quality, and promote the modernization of education construction.

Keyword: Blender · 3D Design Course

1 Introduction

With the widespread application of 3D technology, the educational demand for 3D design technology is growing day by day. However, there are still some problems in the education of 3D design courses in China, such as uneven course difficulty, relatively single teaching content, and so on. Therefore, there is an urgent need for a new curriculum system to meet market demand [1]. With the continuous maturity and development of Blender 3D software, 3D design courses based on Blender have gradually become a

B. Brik and S. Nazir (Eds.): BigIoT-EDU 2024, LNICST 659, pp. 371–382, 2026.
https://doi.org/10.1007/978-3-032-18631-7_41

course module that people pay attention to and value. Due to its free, open source, and powerful features, it has attracted the favor of many novice and professional designers. The wide range of applications, user-friendly design, and easy to learn characteristics of this course module have also attracted the attention of many practitioners in the 3D field. However, so far, there is a lack of systematic research and analysis on this module [2]. Therefore, it is necessary to conduct in-depth exploration from both theoretical and practical perspectives to achieve the goal of applying Blender based on 3D design technology in the field of education.

At present, there have been many studies on Blender based 3D design courses both domestically and internationally. Most research focuses on the following aspects:

(1) The research practice of explaining Blender 3D software is mainly to explain various features and development techniques of Blender to students in a simple and easy to understand way, and improve students' practical operation skills through practical explanation.
(2) The research on Blender's teaching strategies and their impact on student performance mainly focuses on the evaluation of Blender's curriculum teaching strategies and the analysis and research of their impact on student performance, with a focus on exploring teachers' teaching.

This article aims to explore the practical application of Blender based 3D design courses in the field of education, study the teaching mode, implementation methods, teaching strategies, and their impact on students' learning outcomes of Blender based 3D design courses, and propose corresponding teaching plans and suggestions [3]. The specific research significance is as follows:

(1) We provide guidance for various design educators and students on teaching practice based on Blender 3D software, exploring as many examples as possible to better apply them to practical design.
(2) This provides a reference basis for educational institutions to formulate development and teaching plans, in order to improve the quality and efficiency of system design and curriculum implementation.
(3) By analyzing teaching models and strategies, we can explore how to better cultivate students' skills and abilities, and promote their comprehensive development.
(4) Expand the application scope of Blender based 3D design courses to become an important component of a wider range of 3D design fields, and enhance people's flexibility in using this application program in future technological applications.
(5) By comparing and analyzing multiple existing 3D design courses, we can better meet market demand and develop more flexible, comprehensive, and scientific teaching plans for 3D design courses [4].

The development of 3D graphics engines in China is relatively backward and lacks its own brand engine. Therefore, studying the key technologies in 3D graphics engines is a meaningful attempt. Scene rendering is one of the most important sub modules in a 3D engine, responsible for rendering basic primitives, ray processing, texture processing, etc. It is actually the process of reproducing 3D realistic graphics. In many application fields, there is a high demand for real-time scene performance[5]. If a certain display rate is not achieved, the value of practical applications will be lost. Therefore, how to control scene complexity and accelerate graphics rendering speed in 3D graphics engines has become a focus of current research. It can be said that the efficiency and practicality of a 3D engine largely depend on the graphics rendering speed [6].

2 Related Work

A. *Blender rendering engine.*

Blender comes with two rendering engines, both developed based on OpenGL. One is the built-in rendering engine that Blender has long had, which is very powerful (although slightly outdated). It uses multiple technical means to create the final rendered image, exchanging speed and flexibility by avoiding absolute physical accuracy. However, poor physical accuracy does not mean that Blender's built-in rendering engine cannot render sufficiently realistic images [7]. It can quickly render scenes using various complex materials, achieving a final balance between highly realistic aesthetics and a lack of photo realistic and stylized effects.

Cycles is a newly added rendering engine for Blender and is still in the active development stage. Unlike the built-in rendering engine, it focuses on simulating lighting effects more realistically, including effects that are difficult to achieve using the Blender built-in renderer, such as complex light refraction in transparent objects such as glass, multiple reflections of bounced light in the scene, and self illumination of objects with physical accuracy [8]. The characteristic that comes with the Cycles rendering engine is that even with a simple lighting scheme, its rendering speed is slower than the Blender built-in rendering engine. Meanwhile, as Cycles is still in the active development stage, it lacks some important features, such as subsurface scattering and fur rendering properties.

These two rendering engines each have their own advantages and disadvantages. Blender has a built-in rendering engine that takes a long time to develop. Developers have enough time to provide it with various efficient rendering algorithms to improve rendering speed and quality, and to add rich special effects to meet user needs [9]; Although Cycles is relatively young, lacks complete functionality, and lacks high performance, it supports GPU multithreaded rendering based on OpenCL, which is 3–4 times faster than CPU rendering in the same era. Now, it has received strong support from the development team and will definitely become Blender's main rendering engine in the future [10].

Data structure is the way computers store and organize data. A data structure is a collection of data elements that have one or more specific relationships with each other. Usually, carefully selected data structures can lead to higher operational or storage efficiency. 3D image processing generally has the following standards for data structure:

(1) Allow multiple people to work together.
(2) Build complex animation projects on top of one project (or file).
(3) Allow efficient reuse of data.
(4) Allow templates (or backgrounds). Blender has designed a 3D data world that is different from traditional scene maps, allowing for the creation of all necessary scene maps (displays, images, animations, etc.), and based on this, designs a non-standard database.

Although the optimization directions of these two rendering engines are different - the built-in rendering engine focuses on material simulation, while Cycles focuses on light simulation, these differences are more reflected in the calculation methods during data processing, and the rendering processes of both are actually similar [11]. As shown in Fig. 1.

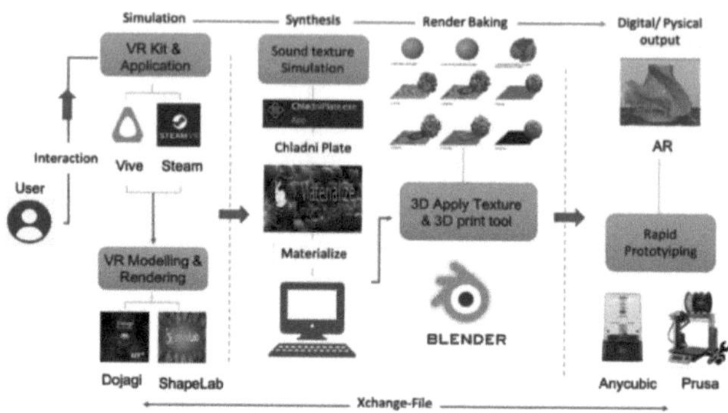

Fig. 1. Blender rendering process

Blender's rendering engine is essentially a re encapsulation of OpenGL (in fact, Blender's UI interface rendering also uses OpenGL). Compared to OpenGL storing data in the form of a display list, in Blender, rendering data is stored in the form of blocks (structure type RenderResult) and layers (structure type RenderLayer)[12]. When rendering files, data is extracted in blocks and layers, Then, the extracted data is combined with elements and rasterized, and finally the view is cropped to output the rendered image.

B. *3D data representation*

After obtaining 3D data, it is necessary to choose a form to represent it, which will serve as input data and affect the subsequent data processing method. Therefore, before specifically introducing the two 3D neural networks used in this article, the four commonly used representations of 3D data are first introduced.

Multi view representations are a collection of 2D images projected from a rendered polygonal mesh under different simulated perspectives. It is necessary to establish a complete 3D model and render the model from multiple viewpoints to fully demonstrate the underlying geometric structure and achieve the goal of reconstructing 3D objects from 2D images [13]. It should be noted that multi view images are mostly used to convert 3D data into formats that are easy to process or visualize, without retaining the data in 3D form.

Qi et al. conceived and tested three different ideas, including pre ordering, recurrent neural network and symmetric function, to solve the ranking invariance of point cloud data [14]. The pre sorting approach is very simple, as long as a stable sorting rule is determined to define the point cloud sorting standard and applied to all point clouds. However, in practical operations, this approach is almost impossible to achieve due to the difficulty of finding rules with sufficient universality. Recursive neural network traversing N! After sorting (N is the number of points), it can process continuously expanding input data and complete the training of recurrent neural networks, which is quite cumbersome. The symmetric function strategy uses a symmetric function with ranking invariance to approximate the feature learning function on the point set, namely:

$$f(x_1, \cdots, x_n) \approx g(h(x_1), \cdots, h(x_n)) \tag{1}$$

where function g ($\cdot$) is a symmetric function whose output result does not change with the recombination of the input order of the input variable.

To better understand pooling layers, give a specific example. Split a 4-order square matrix into 4 regions and mark them with different colors for differentiation, as shown in Fig. 2.

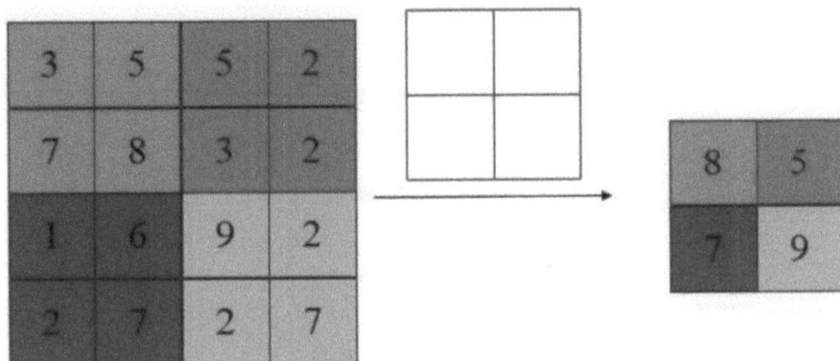

Fig. 2. Schematic diagram of maximum pooling

Regarding the specific division method of the area, the size of the filter needs to be determined first. In the above example, each divided region is a second-order square matrix, which means the filter is a second-order square matrix (f = 2). The difference in position between the first digit of a row or column between the four regions divided is 2, which means the step size is 2 (s = 2). These are the parameters for maximum pooling. In the partitioned second-order matrix, the element to be output for maximum pooling is the greatest element value in the partitioned region. In the upper left area, there are four values: 3, 5, 7, and 8, with the maximum value being 8. By performing the same operation, it is not difficult to draw a conclusion: the upper right region is 5, the lower left region is 7, and the lower right region is 9 [15].

The following describes some commonly used activation function in neural networks:

(1) ReLU function

The ReLU function is defined as the maximum value of an input element and 0, providing a very simple nonlinear transformation:

$$\text{Re}LU(x) = \max(x, 0) \tag{2}$$

(2) Sigmoid function

For an input with a defined domain in R, the sigmoid function transforms the input into the output on the interval (0,1), i.e.:

$$\sigma(x) = \frac{1}{1 + \exp(-x)} \tag{3}$$

The sigmoid function, also known as the logistic function, has a value interval of (0,1). By mapping a real number to the interval of (0,1) for binary classification, the sigmoid function can perform well in situations where the feature differences are complex or not particularly large.

The Sigmoid function is still widely used as the activation function on the output unit (see it as a special case of the Softmax function). However, it should be noted that the use of the Sigmoid function is already less common in hidden layers, and in most cases, the ReLU function can be used instead of the Sigmoid function. The derivative of the sigmoids function is:

$$\sigma'(x) = \sigma(x)(1 - \sigma(x)) \tag{4}$$

(3) Tanh function.

The function of Tanh (hyperbolic tangent) activation function is similar to that of Sigmoid function, which can compress its input to the interval (- 1, 1). Its formula is as follows:

$$Tanh(x)a = \frac{Sinhx}{Coshx} = \frac{e^x - e^{-x}}{e^x + e^{-x}} \tag{5}$$

The main difference between the Tanh function and the Sigmoid function is that the mean of the Tanh function is 0, and the Sigmoid function is only sensitive to changes in input values when the input is between [-1,1]. If it approaches or exceeds this range, it loses sensitivity. Therefore, in practical applications, the Tanh function has always been more advantageous and has better results. The derivative of the Tanh function is:

$$Tanh'(x) = 1 - Tanh^2(x) \tag{6}$$

The core of PointNet network consists of two parts: MLP and maximum pooling layer. Firstly, MLP trains a corresponding MLP to extract the features of each point in the point cloud, and then "projects" each point into a 1024 dimensional space. Next, under the action of the maximum pooling function, the characteristic that the point cloud is independent of the arrangement order of points is solved, and a 1 is provided × 1024, these feature points are sent to the nonlinear classifier. Finally, the rotation problem was solved using T-net, a "mini network".

3   Research on Blender Based 3D Design Curriculum

A. *Blender's rendering pipeline.*

There are two renderers in Blender: Blender render and Cycles render. Blender render is a traditional renderer that mainly uses CPU for image rendering, while Cycles render is a newly developed renderer in recent years that can use GPU for rendering. The design goal of Blender Render is to quickly render, but this means that users must spend a lot of time setting up numerous complex parameters (including material and rendering parameters) in advance. The design of the Cycles rendering engine, on the other hand, tends to allow you to easily and quickly set material and rendering parameters, but the cost is that Cycles needs to spend more time calculating rendering, To accelerate rendering speed, Cycles can call GPU to assist in calculations.

Blender encapsulates the data required for rendering functions in the form of structures, and designs a total of three structures: Scene, RenderResult, and RenderLayer.

The scene data of Blender is saved in the Scene. A Blender file can contain multiple Scenes, and the rendering parameters of each Scene are independent of each other. However, the rendered object may be shared by multiple Scenes or only owned by one Scene. Blender only processes one scene separately at a time, without involving other scenes, to ensure thread safety in the rendering process under multi-threading. After the Blender reads the data in the Scene, it stores them in the RenderLayer. That is to say, once the geometry or raster is created and initialized, the Blender rendering pipeline will put the data in the Scene into the RenderLayer as rendering parameters. The RenderLayer can store various parameters, such as color values, normal vector values, and vertex coordinate values. As long as there is no memory limit, theoretically a rendering thread can read countless RenderLayers.

The first step of Blender rendering a scene is to create a RenderResult, which stores all the RenderLayers required for rendering, as well as the synthesis method of these RenderLayers. A scene can have one or more RenderResults, but a RenderResult can only correspond to one scene.

Blender's rendering pipeline is actually roughly the same as OpenGL, as shown in Fig. 3.

The use of these rendering modes is determined by the user, providing them with a variety of choices. Solid rendering is actually a backside removal function, which, like Zbuffer rendering, determines whether an object's backside is occluded by reading its Zbuffer (depth). If it is occluded, it discards the rasterization of the corresponding vertex data; Light rendering simulates the physical characteristics of real-world light, such as reflection and refraction; Halo rendering appears to be similar to ray rendering, but in reality, the rendering method is completely different. Its implementation method is to filter brighter pixels, blur them, and then overlay them on the original pixel positions; Wireframe rendering removes the face attributes (materials, textures, etc.) of polygons and only renders their wireframes.

B. *3D Mathematical Computing Library.*

This article uses the Cartesian coordinate system (i.e. XYZ coordinate system) to represent points and vectors. In the Cartesian coordinate system, a set of XYZ (2D is XY) values can represent not only the position of a point, but also the direction and length of a vector. This program uses Vector and Vector3 to abstractly represent vectors and points, where Vector represents points and vectors in the 2D plane and Vector3 represents points

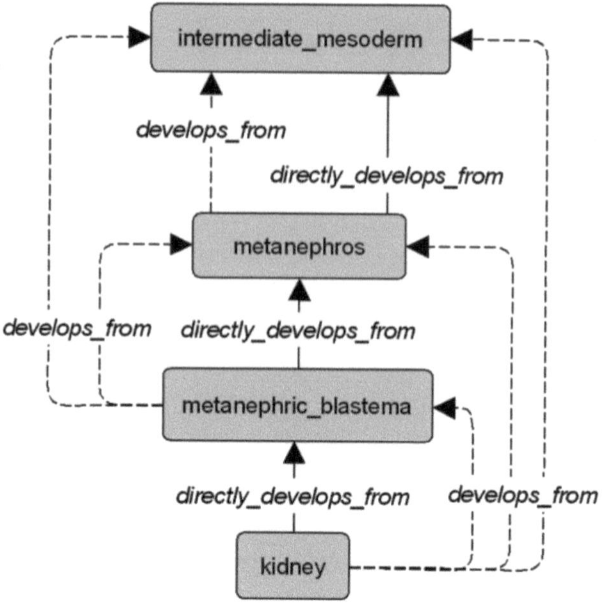

Fig. 3. Blender rendering pipeline

and vectors in the 3D space. Due to the simple calculation method between points, only subtraction is used. The main introduction is the calculation formula between vectors.

(1) Length and Normalization.

The length of a vector is called a norm, and $| u |$ represents the length of vector u. The formula for calculating $| u |$ is as follows:

$$| u | = sqrt(u_x^2 + u_y^2 + u_z^2) \tag{7}$$

After knowing the length of a vector, it can be normalized by scaling it to a length of 1 while maintaining the same direction.

(2) Addition and subtraction.

To add multiple vectors, simply add each component separately. And the subtraction of vectors is actually adding a vector in the opposite direction. The formula is as follows:

$$\text{u+v} = \langle u_x, u_y, u_z \rangle + \langle v_x, v_y, v_z \rangle = \langle u_x + v_x, u_y + v_y, u_z + v_z \rangle \tag{8}$$

$$\text{u} - \text{v} = \langle u_x, u_y, u_z \rangle - \langle v_x, v_y, v_z \rangle = \langle u_x - v_x, u_y - v_y, u_z - v_z \rangle \tag{9}$$

(3) Dot product.

The dot product of a vector multiplies each component and adds them to obtain a scalar, as follows:

$$\text{u} \cdot \text{v} = u_x * v_x + u_y * v_y + u_z * v_z \tag{10}$$

(4) Cross product.

Cross product is only meaningful when a vector contains three or more components. Cross product can determine the angle between vectors u and v, as well as the normal vectors of u and v. A third order determinant can be used:

$$u \times v = (u_y v_z - u_z v_y)i + (u_z v_x - u_x v_z)j + (u_x v_y - u_y v_x)k \tag{11}$$

From a geometric perspective, the left multiplication transformation matrix can achieve position transformation (including translation, rotation, and scaling) of one or more three-dimensional vectors (or coordinates). When calculating, first change the vector (or coordinate) to column vector, and add one dimension to ensure correct calculation. For example, Formula (12), this dimension is called the w axis, with the value of w set to 0 in the vector and 1 in the coordinate:

$$u \cdot M = \langle u_x, u_y, u_z, w \rangle \cdot M \tag{12}$$

The reason for using column vector to multiply transformation matrix by left is to learn the rules of 3D calculation in OpenGL. In fact, in Direct3D, the transformation matrix is multiplied by row vector by left, and the transformation matrix is the transposition of the above matrix.

4 Experimental Simulation Analysis

After the program is completed, various tests need to be conducted to verify whether it meets my requirements. During the testing process, the program code also needs to be continuously adjusted and optimized to meet various testing requirements.

Cross platform testing using sys_ When using version to represent different platforms, the same method can also be used when testing different versions of Blend-file. In the previous introduction to the file structure of Blend-file, it was mentioned that the identifier and version number of the Blend-file are stored in the Blend-file head. For example, the first seven bytes of Blend-file created by Blender 2.71 should be converted into ASCII code equal to BLENDER-v271, and this program will use ble_ The version variable represents this information and will be displayed in the bottom right corner of the graph.

In Fig. 4, the relationship between bending modulus and flight density is plotted. For all geometric shapes, it was observed that the strength of the specimen increased with increasing flight density. The same behavior can be observed for bending stress. As shown in Fig. 5, it can be observed that the mechanical properties of the sample at 90° (HOR 90°) are slightly higher than those of samples with other geometric shapes. Based on these results, a 90° horizontal position was selected to test different materials.

In the experimental context, we have shown the properties of the 11 materials analyzed in Table 1.

The completion of the model in this program has achieved the expected goal, but the effect of light simulation is significantly different from that of Blender rendering. The main reason is that the program aims to fully display the 3D model in Blender, and the highly simulated light simulation is not included in it. Therefore, during the program design, there was no plan to read all the light source data in the scene, Instead, customize all the data required for ray simulation.

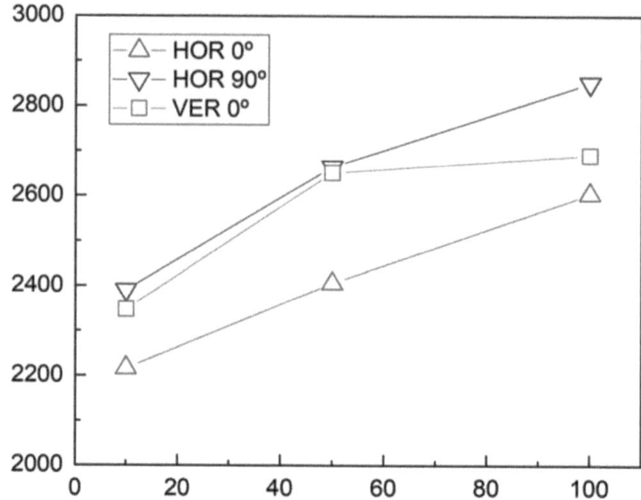

Fig. 4. The Relationship between the Bending Modulus and Inflow Density of Samples at Different Positions

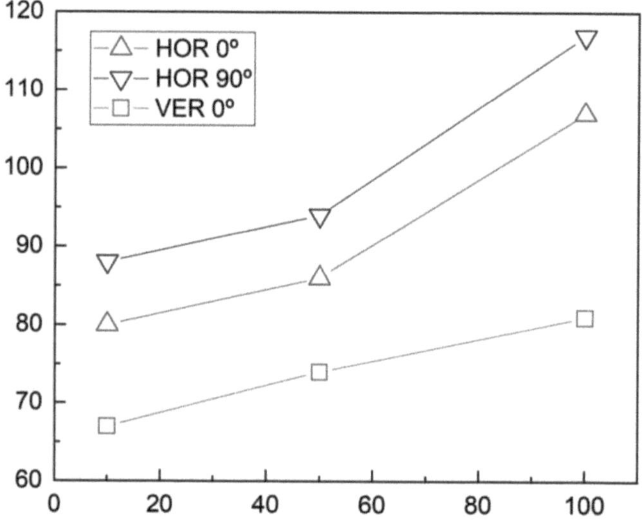

Fig. 5. The Relationship between Bending Stress and Inflow Density of Samples at Different Positions

Table 1. Test Result

Specimens	Printing material	Orientation	Filling density (%)	Printing time per specimen
ABS	ABS Acrylonitrile Butadiene Styrene	Horizontal 90°	100	91 min
PL3	PLA 3D870 Polylactic acid	Horizontal 90°	100	79 min
PET	PETG Polyethylene Terephthalate	Horizontal 90°	100	79 min
ASA	ASA Acrylonitrile Styrene Acrylate	Horizontal 90°	100	63 min

5 Conclusion

Through research on Blender based 3D design courses, we can see that this course has broad advantages in its application in education. Firstly, Blender based 3D design course is an open source, free, powerful, and user-friendly course that provides an intuitive interface and comprehensive toolset, making it easy for students to master and suitable for students of different ages and educational levels. Secondly, Blender based 3D design courses can not only improve students' 3D design skills, but also enhance their imagination and creativity, and cultivate their comprehensive qualities. Finally, Blender based 3D design courses can be widely applied in different fields, such as games, architecture, industrial products, etc., bringing more opportunities and choices for students' growth. However, there are also some problems and challenges in Blender based 3D design courses. Firstly, using Blender requires a certain amount of learning time and skills. Secondly, Blender based 3D design courses have high software configuration requirements, resulting in higher classroom environment requirements. In addition, Blender based 3D design courses need to establish a suitable teaching system and provide corresponding textbooks and tools.

References

1. Zhang, L., Shen, J., Zhu, B.: A review of the research and application of deep learning-based computer vision in structural damage detection. Earthq. Eng. Eng. Vib. **21**(1), 1–21 (2022)
2. Zca, B., Rui, M.B., Yda, B., et al.: State-of-the-art review on research and application of original bamboo-based composite components in structural engineering (2022)
3. Liu, Q., He, L., Jiang, Z.: Research and application of wavelet transform-based two-dimensional pinning potential stochastic resonant system. Fluctuation Noise Lett. **22**(02) (2023)
4. Chen, Y., Xie, W., Yu, X., et al.: Research and application of power engineering science and technology project management based on all life-cycle. EDP Sciences (2021)
5. Feng, Z., Wu, J., Ni, T.: Research and application of multifeature gesture recognition in human-computer interaction based on virtual reality technology. Hindawi Limited (2021)

6. Ruan, L.F., Wang, J.W., Ying, S.M.: Research progress and application of modified silicon-based anode materials for lithium-ion batteries. Mater. Sci. Forum **1036**, 35–44 (2021)
7. Gao, D., Xie, J., Huang, S., et al.: Research and application of evaluation methods for functional characteristics of oil-based drilling fluid in shale gas wells. Geofluids **2021**(3), 1–9 (2021)
8. Hao, C., Zheng, M.: Research and application of display system of component-based virtual instrument for land and air platforms. J. Phys. Conf. Ser. **2218**(1), 012083 (2022)
9. Zhang, C., Luo, C., Ye, L., et al.: Research and application of anti-collapse lubricant compound polyalcohol for water-based drilling fluid . Open J. Yangtze Oil and Gas (2022)
10. Fan, X., Guo, Y., Zhao, Q., et al.: Structural optimization and application research of alkali-activated slag ceramsite compound insulation block based on finite element method. Mathematics 9 (2021)
11. Zhou, Y.: The application of curriculum ideology and politics in the training of judicial vocational education talents. J. Higher Educ. Res. **3**(2), 155–159 (2022)
12. Jia, L., Kumar, B.S., Parthasarathy, R.: Research and application of artificial intelligence based integrated teaching-learning modular approach in colleges and universities. J. Interconnection Netw. **22**(Supp02) (2022)
13. Du, W.Y., Zhang, L., Sun, L.T., et al.: Research and application of semantic understanding based on Attention-RNN. Proc. Comput. Sci. **183**(8), 337–340 (2021)
14. Yang, J., Liu, K., Zhang, M., et al.: Research and application of business ability evaluation based On DBSCAN algorithm and entropy method. J. Phys. Conf. Ser. **1881**(3), 032064 (2021)
15. Zheng, Y.: Research and application of LDA model in movies images based on the visual effects of computer images. J. Phys. Conf. Ser. **1952**(2), 022060 (7pp) (2021)

Design and Implementation of Music Education Teaching Management System in Colleges and Universities

Jia Liu[✉]

Yunnan College of Business Management, Kunming 650000, China
liujia2022202212@163.com

Abstract. There is an issue with the management outcomes being unsatisfactory, despite the critical function of teaching management in college music education. Teaching management in college music education is a challenge that the conventional management model fails to address and provide the desired outcomes. In light of this need, the authors of this work suggest a framework for managing classroom instruction. The first step is to examine the TM system using the J2EE architecture, and then to implement indicators in accordance with the TM needs. Separate and minimize disruptions in classroom management instruction. The next steps include developing a program for managing music education in higher education, designing the J2EE architecture for use in that program, and finally, conducting a thorough evaluation of the program's efficacy. The MATLAB simulation demonstrates that the college music education teaching management system is quick and efficient under certain assessment conditions. Compared to the standard management style, the amount of time spent educating and supervising is superior.

Keywords: J2EE architecture · Teaching management system · College Music Education · Instructional management

1 Introduction

3D design and related technologies are gaining more and more attention as computer technology continues to evolve and become more widely used [1]. Blender is gaining popularity as a strong 3D design tool that is free, open-source, and compatible with several platforms. In order to better guide educational teaching practice, this study will examine the benefits and drawbacks of Blender, as well as its implementation and optimization in 3D design courses [2].

1.1 Application of Blender in 3D Design Course

Many 3D design classes make use of Blender, a robust piece of software for creating 3D models and animations [3]. What follows is a comprehensive introduction to Using Blender in 3D design courses:

B. Brik and S. Nazir (Eds.): BigIoT-EDU 2024, LNICST 659, pp. 383–391, 2026.
https://doi.org/10.1007/978-3-032-18631-7_42

1. Drawing in Three Dimensions

Blender is capable of supporting several modeling formats, such as NURBS and polygon modeling, among others. Students may enhance their modeling abilities, study the fundamentals of 3D modeling, and become proficient with Blender's modeling function [4].

2. Animated

In addition to creating static 3D models, Blender also allows users to create animated 3D scenes. By studying the fundamentals of 3D animation and becoming proficient with Blender's animation production features, students may swiftly create high-quality 3D animations [5].

3. creating visuals and SFX

Cycles and Eevee are only two of the many rendering engines that Blender is compatible with [6]. Students may master rendering technology and special effects production abilities by mastering Blender's rendering and effects production functions [7]. This will allow them to create works of higher quality and impact.

4. Augmented and virtual reality

Virtual and augmented reality may be easily created using Blender, and students can acquire the necessary skills to create top-notch VR and AR apps [8].

1.2 Blender's Optimization in 3D Design Courses

Although there are many positive outcomes that may result from using Blender in 3D design classes, there are also some places where it might be improved [9]. In the section that follows, we will talk about how to improve Blender in 3D design classes:

1. There is a severe learning curve

It takes some time and effort for novices to understand Blender's operation and functionality, since it is a sophisticated 3D design program with a steep learning curve. To address this issue, there are several strategies that may be used to assist students in getting started and improving their learning efficiency. These approaches include instructional films, classroom demonstrations, practical operations, and more.

2. The user interface might need some improvement

Beginners may find Blender's UI to be less than user-friendly. To get around this, you may either switch to a more user-friendly program like SketchUp or rework Blender's UI to make it more intuitive and easy to use.

Blender is very useful in 3D design classes since it is free, open-source, cross-platform, and powerful. Nevertheless, there are a few ways Blender may be improved for the 3D design course. For example, the learning curve is high, the interface is less user-friendly [12], and there isn't a Chinese version. Taking these issues into consideration, we can create instructional videos, in-class demonstrations, practical operations, etc., to aid students in getting up and running with Blender; enhance its usability and friendliness by optimizing its interface and functional design; and create and use software based on Blender in China to increase its popularity and usefulness in 3D design courses. Better applications and promotion of Blender, as well as the development and implementation of 3D design, may be achieved by ongoing investigation and practice [13].

College music programs place a premium on teaching management as a core component of their curricula. On the other hand, college and university music education is affected by the issue of poor rationality in the teaching management plan [14] that arises throughout the process of teaching management. College and university music education administration has been the subject of some academics' claims that a TMS implementation may provide useful insights into the scheme's inner workings and complementary pedagogical reinforcement. In light of this, the article presents a teaching management system, refines the teaching management plan, and confirms the model's efficacy.

2   Related Works

2.1   Mathematical Description of the Teaching Management System

Finding the unqualified values in college music education, optimizing the teaching management program based on the teaching management indicators, integrating the teaching management plan, and lastly judging are all tasks performed by the teaching management system. Whether or whether music programs in higher education are feasible. By integrating AI's benefits with quantitative insights gained from college music education, the teaching management system aims to raise the bar for effective classroom instruction.

One hypothesis is that there is a need for instructional management is w_i, an approach of managing instruction is set_i, the program's teaching management graduates is u, and the teaching management program judgment function is $K(w_i \approx 0)$, As shown in Eq. (1).

$$K(w_i u) = \frac{w_i - u^2}{2K} + K_1, \ldots, K_i \cdot \sum_{i=1}^{a} a_i \tag{1}$$

2.2   Choice of Teaching Management Program

Theory No. 2: The Role of Music Education in Higher Education is $x(w_i)$, together with the weighted average is a_i, Eq. (2) shows that unqualified college music education is required for teaching management.

$$x(w_i) = \frac{2x!}{u!(a_i - w_i)!} \to \bigcap_{i=1}^{w} x_i \cdot \frac{1}{x} \tag{2}$$

2.3   Analysis of Teaching Management Programs

It is important to remove the unqualified teaching management scheme before implementing the teaching management system, map the requirements of the system to the music education libraries of colleges and universities, and perform a multi-dimensional analysis of the scheme. To start, in order to make sure the teaching management system is feasible, college music education does a thorough study and determines the plan's threshold and index weight. It is necessary to standardize college music education in order to conduct systematic tests of teaching management methods. Overall teaching management accuracy could be compromised if college and university music education follows a non-normal distribution. Picking the right teaching management software may raise both the system's accuracy and its degree of management; Fig. 1 shows the details of one such program.

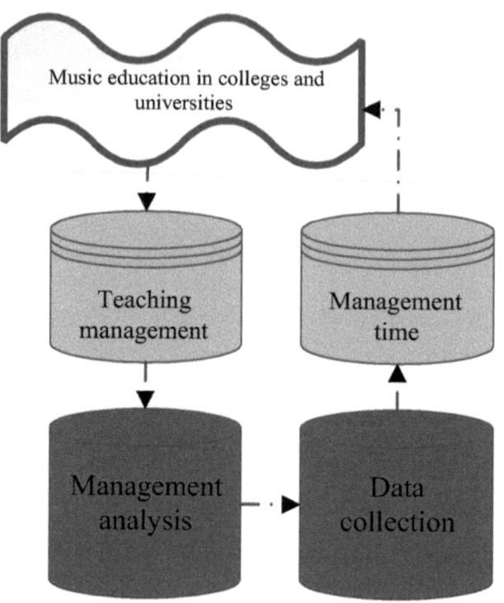

Fig. 1. The results of the selection of instructional management programs

In agreement with actual realities, the study of instructional management systems reveals that these schemes exhibit multi-dimensional distribution. The lack of direction in college and university music education suggests a very random teaching management system; as a result, this research is considered to be highly analytical. In order to ensure that the whole teaching management scheme has strong dynamic correlation, artificial intelligence primarily modifies college music education, removes redundant and unnecessary schemes, and augments the default scheme. This ensures that college music education satisfies the usual standards.

3   Optimization Strategies for College Music Education

In order to optimize college music education, the teaching management system uses a random optimization technique and tweaks the system's settings. The mechanism for managing education in higher education randomly assigns students to various music degree programs across many tiers of management. The iterative approach optimizes and analyzes various instructional management strategies at different levels. Following the completion of the optimization study, the finest college music education is documented by comparing the teaching management levels of various programs.

4   Results and Discussion

4.1   Introduction to Teaching Management

This study uses college music education as its research object, examining it via 12 pathways and a 12-h test period; moreover, it delves into the specifics of college music education teaching management in an effort to ease teaching management. Table 1 displays the scheme.

Table 1. College music teaching management requirements

Scope of application	grade	Teaching level	Instructional management
Music theory	standard	86.37	86.37
	Higher	84.73	87.66
vocality	standard	83.72	86.40
	Higher	86.05	87.52
instrumental music	standard	87.72	83.53
	Higher	85.85	86.17

The instructional management process in Table 1 is shown in Fig. 2.

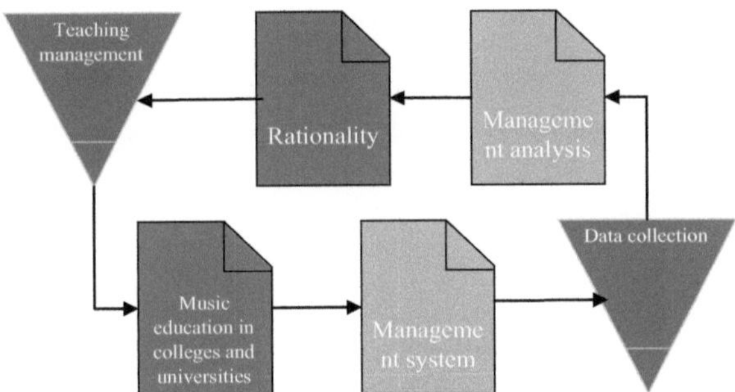

Fig. 2. The analytical process of music education in colleges and universities

The teaching management system's teaching management scheme is more in line with the real teaching management needs than the general management mode. The teaching management system outperforms the conventional management mode when it comes to the practicality and efficacy of music instruction in higher education. Figure 2 shows the revised instructional management scheme, which has improved both the system's accuracy and the management speed. Consequently, the learning management system's summation stability, program level, and program speed are all improved.

4.2   Music Education in Colleges and Universities

Unstructured, semi-structured, and structured data are all part of music education college and university teaching management programs. Following the pre-selection of the pedagogical management system, the college music education preliminary pedagogical management plan and the college music education itself are acquired. Determine if management degree programs are feasible to teach. Choose college music education and teaching management systems with varying degrees of management, as shown in Table 2, to more precisely validate the teaching outcomes of college music education.

Table 2. The overall picture of the teaching management program

category	Satisfaction	Analysis rate
Music theory	85.72	84.62
vocality	86.55	84.42
instrumental music	89.64	90.77
mean	83.43	86.04
X^6	88.70	90.10
P = 2.39		

4.3   Teaching Management and Stability of Teaching Management

Figure 3 shows the teaching management scheme, which is evaluated with the general management model to ensure the teaching management system is accurate.

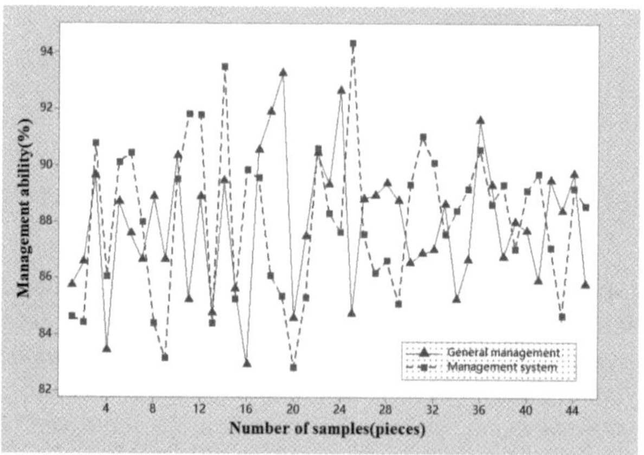

Fig. 3. Teaching management of different algorithms

Figure 3 shows that unlike the ordinary management mode, the teaching management of the teaching management system is relatively stable, with a higher teaching management but a lower error rate. This suggests that both modes of management are stable. Teaching is not uniformly managed. Table 3 displays the mean instructional management plan for the aforementioned three methods.

Table 3. Comparison of the accuracy of teaching management of different methods

algorithm	Instructional management	Magnitude of change	error
Teaching management system	92.21	92.96	93.07
Normal management mode	88.76	90.41	90.35
P	88.39	84.66	90.39

Table 3 shows that there are problems with the general management model's standardization of college music education's teaching management, that there have been significant changes to college music education, and that the error rate is rather high. Overall, the teaching management system outperforms the standard management model and produces superior outcomes. Additionally, there has been no discernible change in the accuracy of the teaching management system, which has a teaching management of more than 92%. In order to provide further proof why the TMS is the best option. Various methodologies are used to conduct a general analysis of the teaching management system, as illustrated in Fig. 4, in order to further validate the efficiency of the suggested method.

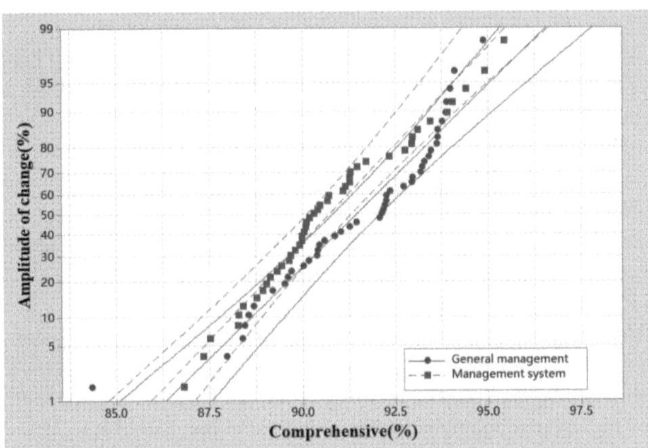

Fig. 4. Teaching management system teaching management of teaching management

Figure 4 shows that the TMS's teaching management is much superior to the traditional management mode. This is because TMS raises and sets the adjustment coefficient for college music education, which is a key component of effective teaching management. The cutoff point at which a certain instructional management plan is considered to have failed to fulfill the system's standards.

5   Conclusion

In order to improve college and university music education, this article presents a teaching management system that incorporates artificial intelligence in an effort to address the issue of inadequate music education teaching management. Meanwhile, a plethora of teaching management systems are being built and scientific and standardized approaches to teaching management are being thoroughly examined. According to studies, university music programs may benefit from using a teaching management system. The field of music education oversees the administration of general education. Irrationality in the selection of teaching management indicators occurs when the process of developing a teaching management system focuses too much on study of teaching management.

References

1. Afesi-Dei, C., Appiah-Brempong, M., Awuah, E.: Health-care waste management practices: the case of Ho Teaching Hospital in Ghana. Heliyon **9**(4) (2023)
2. Bush, H., Phaup, E., Brogan, K., Edgemon, A.K., Richling, S., Rapp, J.T.: An interdisciplinary approach to treating severe behavior in a juvenile justice facility: teaching behavioral self-management via telehealth. Behav. Soc. Issues **32**(1), 23–50 (2023)
3. Calero, L.M.P., Basantes-Arias, E.A., Verdezoto, M.A.: Proposals to develop knowledge management in the teaching-learning of English. Bibliotecas-Anales De Investigacion **19**(1), 1–10 (2023)
4. Chen, K.W., Wang, Z.Y.: Online flipped learning methods for teaching hospitality skills and management practices in an epidemic situation: a study on learning attitude and effectiveness. Front. Psychol. **13** (2023)
5. D'Anjour, M.F., Medeiros, B.C., de Lima, M.P.: Proposal for a teaching methodology for strategic management: building a non-linear view through the prism of complexity. Revista De Gestao E Secretariado-Gesec **14**(2), 1389–1412 (2023)
6. Davey, B., Lindsay, D., Cousins, J., Glass, B.: "Why didn't they teach us this?" A qualitative investigation of pharmacist stakeholder perspectives of business management for community pharmacists. Pharmacy **11**(3) (2023)
7. de Morais, P.M., et al.: Laboratory of practices in teaching management: perceptions in a public university. Revista De Gestao E Secretariado-Gesec **14**(3), 4220–4234 (2023)
8. De, P., Bakhshi, M.: An experiential learning approach for teaching appropriate assertiveness: an example of Indian management students. J. Teach. Int. Bus. **34**(1–2), 7–32 (2023)
9. Fierke, K.K., Lepp, G.A., Jones, K.M.: Teaching conflict management: an approach to increasing students' value, confidence, and ability. Curr. Pharm. Teach. Learn. **15**(3), 252–257 (2023)
10. Flatland, B., et al.: Guidelines for resident training in veterinary clinical pathology. IV: Laboratory quality management-Teaching domains, competencies, and suggested learning outcomes. Vet. Clini. Pathol. (2023)
11. Gupta, O.J., Yadav, S.: Determinants in advancement of teaching and learning in higher education: in special reference to management education. Int. J. Manag. Educ. **21**(2) (2023)

12. Hall-Mills, S.S., Marante, L.M.: Teaching expository text management and proficiency skills for comprehension for students with language/learning disabilities. Learn. Disabil. Q. (2023)
13. Junger, A.P., de Oliveira, V.I., Yamaguchi, C.K., de Oliveira, M., de Aguiar, H.M., de Lima, B.L.S.: The role of school management in technological practices as a tool for futuristic teaching. Revista De Gestao E Secretariado-Gesec **14**(7), 10749–10765 (2023)
14. Karakose, T., et al.: Assessment of the relationships between prospective mathematics teachers' classroom management anxiety, academic self-efficacy beliefs, academic a motivation and attitudes toward the teaching profession using structural equation modelling. Mathematics **11**(2) (2023)

Research on the Teaching Model of Medicinal Chemistry Based on ChemOffice

Yane Kong and Yan Liu[(✉)]

Qujing Medical College, Qujing 655000, Yunnan, China
1962789048@qq.com

Abstract. Pharmacology requires medicinal chemistry, which employs scientific approaches to examine drug structure, preparation, and properties. Typically, teaching relies on lecture-style delivery by educators, with minimal classroom engagement, and lacks immediate feedback on instructional effectiveness. This outdated and uniform method fails to meet contemporary educational requirements. Nowadays, information technology teaching has become prevalent, updating conventional methods with technological innovations. Consequently, this study introduces a ChemOffice-based instructional model for analysis. Initially, information systems optimize the teaching process, categorizing metrics according to educational needs and minimizing disruptions. Subsequently, the enhancements from applying IT to medicinal chemistry education are consolidated into a model, followed by a thorough evaluation. MATLAB simulations confirm that, under specific criteria, the ChemOffice-centric approach surpasses traditional methods in terms of practicality and dependability for medicinal chemistry's teaching strategies.

Keywords: information technology · ChemOffice-based teaching model · medicinal chemistry

1 Introduction

ChemOffice is a widely used chemical software suite that can be used to process chemical data and documents and supports a wide range of chemical file formats. In the teaching of medicinal chemistry [1], ChemOffice has important application value. This article will explore the impact of ChemOffice on the teaching mode of medicinal chemistry from the following aspects.

2 Related Concepts

2.1 Improve the Teaching Efficiency of Medicinal Chemistry Courses

Using ChemOffice for medicinal chemistry course teaching can improve the teaching efficiency of the course. ChemOffice provides a variety of chemical tools and functions, including molecular modeling, reaction simulation, thermodynamic calculations, etc. [2], which can help teachers more visually display chemical phenomena and theories, making it easier for students to understand and remember what they have learned, thereby improving teaching efficiency [3].

B. Brik and S. Nazir (Eds.): BigIoT-EDU 2024, LNICST 659, pp. 392–401, 2026.
https://doi.org/10.1007/978-3-032-18631-7_43

2.2 Promote Students' Understanding and Practical Ability in Medicinal Chemistry

By using ChemOffice software for teaching, students can enhance their understanding and practical ability in medicinal chemistry [4]. In the learning process, students can use ChemOffice software to carry out molecular modeling, reaction simulation and other experimental designs, and deepen their understanding and memory of chemical knowledge through practical operation [5]. At the same time, students can also use ChemOffice software to analyze and compare the properties and characteristics of different compounds, so as to cultivate their practical application ability to medicinal chemistry [6].

2.3 Enrich Medicinal Chemistry Teaching Resources

Using ChemOffice software for medicinal chemistry courses can also enrich teaching resources. ChemOffice software provides a variety of chemical data and document formats [7], including structural formulas, energy maps, reaction flow diagrams, etc., which can be used as teaching resources to help teachers better demonstrate what they have learned. At the same time, teachers can also create their own teaching resources, such as presentations, courseware, etc., through ChemOffice software to provide students with a better teaching experience [8].

2.4 Promote the Digital Transformation of Medicinal Chemistry Education

Using ChemOffice software for medicinal chemistry course teaching can drive the digital transformation of medicinal chemistry education. In the context of the digital era, digital transformation has become a trend in all walks of life [9], and the use of ChemOffice software can provide digital support and technical foundation for medicinal chemistry education, and promote the development of education in the direction of digitalization [10].

Overall, the impact of ChemOffice on the model of teaching medicinal chemistry has been positive. It can improve the teaching efficiency of medicinal chemistry courses, promote students' understanding and practical ability of medicinal chemistry, enrich teaching resources, and promote the digital transformation of medicinal chemistry education [11]. In the future, with the continuous development and advancement of technology, we believe that ChemOffice will play a greater role in the field of medicinal chemistry teaching, and provide more efficient and high-quality technical support and theoretical guidance for medicinal chemistry education [12].

In the field of medicinal chemistry education, the enhancement, refinement, and novel introductions in teaching methods are crucial, offering significant value to the discipline. Nevertheless, during the implementation of these educational approaches, challenges arise due to the limited practicality of certain teaching strategies, thereby affecting the instructional outcomes in medicinal chemistry. According to a number of academics, employing an educational framework that leverages ChemOffice can adeptly evaluate teaching strategies and offer pertinent support for them. Building on this perspective, this study presents a ChemOffice-centric educational model, refines the approach's design, and ascertains the model's efficacy. Pharmaceutical chemistry is an interdisciplinary subject involving chemistry, biochemistry, pharmacology and molecular biology, aiming at designing and synthesizing new drugs. In recent years, ChemOffice, a computer-aided molecular design tool, has attracted more and more attention in pharmaceutical chemistry education, because it is helpful to promote drug design and analysis. The Medicinal Chemistry Teaching Model is an educational method designed to enable students to understand important concepts such as drug molecular structure, drug synthesis, drug metabolism, and drug action. The traditional teaching model of medicinal chemistry usually adopts classroom lectures and book reading, which has some shortcomings, such as monotony, difficulty in understanding and memorizing by students.The ChemOffice-based medicinal chemistry teaching model provides a more interactive and engaging learning experience. ChemOffice is a computer-aided molecular design tool that helps students better understand the molecular structure and chemistry of drugs. At the same time, ChemOffice can perform operations such as molecular simulation and drug design, which helps improve students' practical skills. Therefore, the ChemOffice-based medicinal chemistry teaching model has the following advantages:

1. Increase students' interest in learning. The teaching mode based on ChemOffice can stimulate students' interest through visual molecular structure diagrams, 3D images and molecular simulations, so that students can be more active in learning.
2. Enhance students' comprehension and memory. Through hands-on operations such as molecular structure, simulation and design, students can better understand the molecular structure and chemical properties of drugs, making learning more in-depth and targeted, and also easier to remember.
3. Improve students' practical operation ability. The teaching mode based on ChemOffice can help students carry out practical operations such as molecular simulation and drug design, and improve students' practical operation ability and problem-solving ability.
4. Improve teaching effectiveness and student satisfaction. Through the ChemOffice-based teaching model, students can have a deeper understanding of medicinal chemistry, improve learning outcomes and teaching effects, and also improve student satisfaction. At present, the research shows that the teaching mode of pharmaceutical chemistry based on ChemOffice has proved its effectiveness in promoting students' learning achievements and satisfaction. The results show that using ChemOffice can enhance students' understanding of pharmaceutical chemistry and promote drug design and analysis. Therefore, ChemOffice-based teaching model can be regarded as a promising method in pharmaceutical chemistry education.

2.5   Mathematical Description of the Teaching Model Based on ChemOffice

ChemOffice-based teaching model employs computer technology to refine the instructional scheme. By evaluating the index parameters within this model, it identifies and adjusts substandard value parameters in medicinal chemistry, integrating these adjustments into the functional teaching scheme. This process ultimately assesses the viability of the medicinal chemistry approach, as illustrated by Eq. (1).

$$tol\left(y_i \cdot 2 - e_{ij}\right) = y_{ij} \geq max(e_{ij} \cdot \sqrt{5}) \tag{1}$$

Among them, the judgment of outliers is shown in Eq. (2).

$$\max(e_{ij}) = \left(e_{ij}^2 - 7\right) \succ \text{mean}\left(\sum e_{ij} * \frac{1}{n}\right) - \sum 5 \cdot \bigsqcup z_i \qquad (2)$$

The educational model that leverages ChemOffice synergizes computer benefits and employs medicinal chemistry for quantification, enhancing the practicality of the teaching approach.

Assuming I. the educational model's prerequisites are, its plan is, the contentment derived from the educational plan is, and the educational plan's judgment function stands as, as illustrated in Eq. (3).

$$T(d_i) = \frac{x - \mu}{\sigma} - \sum e_i \cdot \int d_i + \bigcap \xi \to \sqrt{9} - \oint y_i \qquad (3)$$

2.6 Choice of Teaching Mode Scheme

Let's assume II. The role of medicinal chemistry is denoted by and carries a weight factor of. Accordingly, the instructional framework mandates that subpar medicinal chemistry be depicted in Eq. (4).

$$g(e_i) = z_i \cdot \overline{X} + \sqrt{4} - \prod T(d_i) + \oiint z_i \cdot w_i \qquad (4)$$

According to hypothesis I and II, a comprehensive function of the teaching model of medicinal chemistry can be obtained, and the result is shown in Eq. (5).

$$g(e_i) + T(d_i) \leq \max(e_{ij}) \qquad (5)$$

In order to improve the effectiveness of the pedagogical model, all data needs to be standardized and the results are shown in Eq. (6).

$$\overline{g(e_i) + T(d_i)} \leftrightarrow \text{mean}\left(\sum e_{ij} * \frac{1}{n}\right) - \overline{)5} \cdot \bigsqcup z_i \qquad (6)$$

2.7 Analysis of Teaching Model Schemes

Before the implementation of the ChemOffice-based teaching model, it is necessary to analyze the teaching scheme in multiple dimensions, and map the teaching mode requirements to the medicinal chemistry library, so as to eliminate the teaching mode scheme that does not meet the conditions. According to Eq. (6), an anomaly assessment scheme can be proposed, and the results are presented in Eq. (7).

$$No(e_i) = \frac{\overline{g(e_i) + T(d_i)}}{\text{mean}(\sum e_{ij} * \frac{1}{n}) - \overline{)5} \cdot \bigsqcup z_i} \qquad (7)$$

It states that a scheme must be proposed, otherwise the scheme that needs to be integrated is the result as shown in Eq. (8).

$$Zh(e_i) = \min[\sum g(\widetilde{e_i)} + T(d_i)] \tag{8}$$

Medicinal chemistry conducts a comprehensive analysis, and sets the thresholds and index weights of the teaching mode scheme to ensure the accuracy of the teaching mode based on ChemOffice. Medicinal chemistry is a systematic testing teaching mode scheme, which needs to be analyzed innovatively. If the medicinal chemistry is in a non-normal distribution, the teaching mode scheme will be affected, and the accuracy of the overall teaching mode will be reduced, and the calculation results are shown in Eq. (9).

$$accur(e_i) = \frac{min[\sum g(\widetilde{e_i)} + T(d_i)]}{\sum g(\widetilde{e_i)} + T(d_i)} \times 100\% \tag{9}$$

The survey of the teaching mode scheme shows that the teaching mode scheme presents a multi-dimensional distribution, which is in line with the objective facts. Medicinal chemistry is not directional, indicating that the teaching model scheme has strong randomness, so it is regarded as a high analytical study. If the random function of medicinal chemistry is $randon(e_i)$, then the calculation of Eq. (9) can be expressed as Eq. (10).

$$accur(e_i) = \frac{min[\sum g(\widetilde{e_i)} + T(d_i)]}{\sum g(\widetilde{e_i)} + T(d_i)} \times 100\% + randon(e_i) \tag{10}$$

Among these, medicinal chemistry satisfies the usual standards, primarily computer technology modifies it, removes redundant and irrelevant strategies, and adds the default plan, ensuring a robust dynamic connection in the overall teaching model layout.

3 Optimization Strategies for Medicinal Chemistry

Using the ChemOffice teaching model, a random optimization approach is employed for medicinal chemistry. This involves adjusting the teaching model parameters to achieve an optimized medicinal chemistry process. Within this framework, medicinal chemistry is categorized into various teaching model levels. Different strategies are then randomly chosen during an iterative process. As this process unfolds, teaching model strategies across different levels are refined and evaluated. Once this evaluation is finalized, a comparison between the performance levels of distinct protocols allows for the identification and documentation of the most effective medicinal chemistry methods.

4 Practical Examples of Medicinal Chemistry

4.1 Introduction to the Teaching Mode

To enhance the teaching method, the subject of study. To enhance the teaching method, the subject of study chemistry for intricate scenarios is the subject of study in medicinal chemistry for intricate scenarios is testing duration. The detailed instructional approach for medicinal chemistry is presented in Table 1.

Table 1. Teaching model requirements

Scope of application	grade	viability	Teaching mode
organic chemistry	I	81.81	84.49
	II	81.41	81.21
physiology	I	81.99	81.79
	II	77.49	78.64
pharmacology	I	80.27	78.84
	II	82.05	79.23

The teaching mode process in Table 1 is shown in Fig. 1.

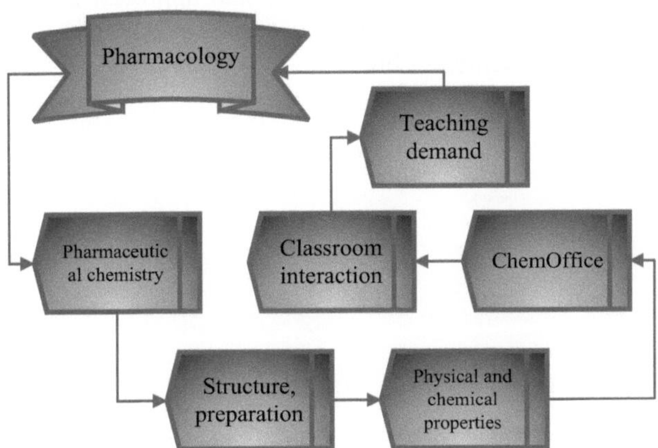

Fig. 1. Analytical process of medicinal chemistry

The teaching scheme that employs ChemOffice as its base offers advantages over conventional pedagogical methods. This is evident when considering the suitability and practicality for teaching medicinal chemistry. The stability and feasibility of this new approach are superior, as illustrated by the shifts in the instructional strategy outlined in Fig. 2. Thus, in terms of instructional speed, reliability, and overall robustness, the ChemOffice-based educational model proves to be more effective.

4.2 Medicinal Chemistry

The instructional model plan for medicinal chemistry encompasses non-structural, semi-structural, and structural data. Following the preliminary screening of the teaching approach using ChemOffice, we derived an initial educational model blueprint for medicinal chemistry, subsequently assessing the viability of this educational strategy. To more precisely evaluate the improvements in the medicinal chemistry teaching method, we chose a variety of instructional model levels as depicted in Table 2.

Table 2. The overall picture of the teaching model program

category	Random data	Satisfaction	Analysis rate
organic chemistry	81.99	85.90	83.85
physiology	84.42	88.59	82.98
pharmacology	82.99	85.13	87.77
mean	80.46	86.54	86.69
$X6$	84.60	85.73	82.98
	P = 2.095		

4.3   Teaching Mode and Stability of Teaching Mode

In order to confirm the precision of the educational approach utilizing ChemOffice, this teaching method is contrasted with conventional pedagogies. The details of the educational strategy are presented in Fig. 2.

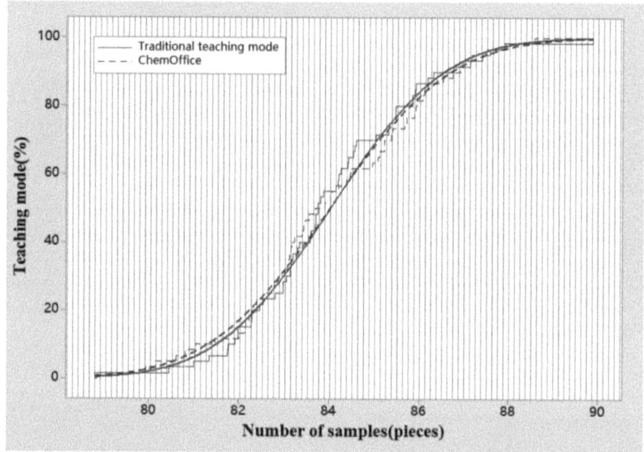

Fig. 2. Teaching modes of different algorithms

In Fig. 2, the ChemOffice-based instructional approach surpasses traditional modalities in effectiveness yet boasts a reduced error rate. This suggests the ChemOffice method's robustness compared to the fluctuations seen in conventional techniques. A summary of the average outcomes for these three strategies is detailed in Table 3.

From Table 3, it is clear that traditional instruction in medicinal chemistry faces challenges in terms of its feasibility and high error rates. In contrast, the ChemOffice-based approach shows improved results and lower error rates. Additionally, the accuracy remains consistently high, above 90%, indicating stability. To further validate the efficacy of the ChemOffice method, various analytical techniques were employed as shown in Fig. 3.

Table 3. Comparison of the accuracy of teaching modes of different methods

algorithm	Survey data	Teaching mode	Magnitude of change	error
Teaching model based on ChemOffice	93.56	87.86	89.81	30.32
Traditional teaching mode	87.98	93.43	92.26	29.41
P	93.54	90.27	91.27	32.63

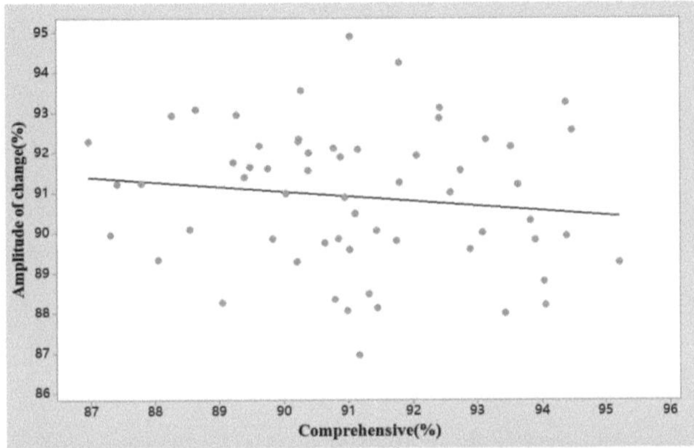

Fig. 3. The teaching mode based on the teaching mode of ChemOffice

Figure 3 reveals the superiority of the ChemOffice-based teaching method over traditional techniques. This advantage stems from an enhanced pharmacochemical adjustment factor in the ChemOffice approach, coupled with a set threshold that excludes subpar teaching strategies.

4.4   The Effectiveness of the Teaching Model

To assess the efficacy of ChemOffice-based instruction, this teaching approach is juxtaposed with conventional pedagogical methods, as depicted in Fig. 4.

Figure 4 reveals that the ChemOffice-based instructional method outperforms the traditional approach and has a reduced error rate, suggesting its superior reliability. Conversely, the traditional method's teaching outcomes are inconsistent. Table 4 summarizes the average teaching strategy for these three methods.

Table 4 reveals that traditional teaching methods in medicinal chemistry lack reliability and have undergone significant changes, resulting in a high error rate. In contrast, the teaching model based on ChemOffice's general outcomes surpasses traditional models in both height and quality. Additionally, the ChemOffice-based model maintains accuracy over 90%, with little fluctuation. To further validate the efficacy of the proposed approach, a comprehensive analysis of the ChemOffice-based teaching method is conducted using various techniques, as illustrated in Fig. 5.

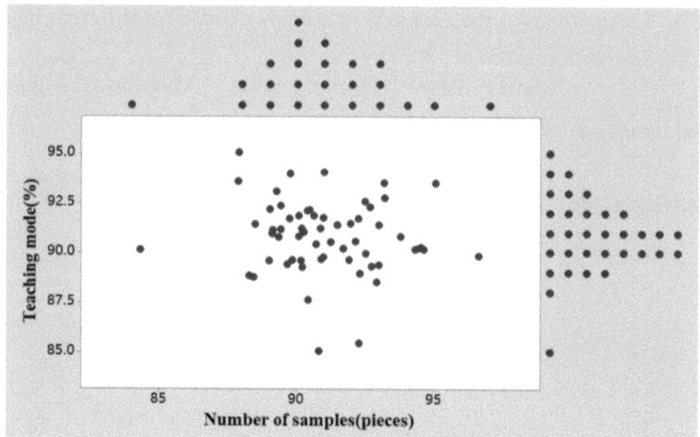

Fig. 4. Teaching modes of different algorithms

Table 4. Comparison of the effectiveness of teaching models of different methods

algorithm	Survey data	Teaching mode	Magnitude of change	error
Teaching model based on ChemOffice	86.84	85.85	84.35	31.23
Traditional teaching mode	87.21	83.41	86.96	30.28
P	86.86	84.20	83.72	27.28

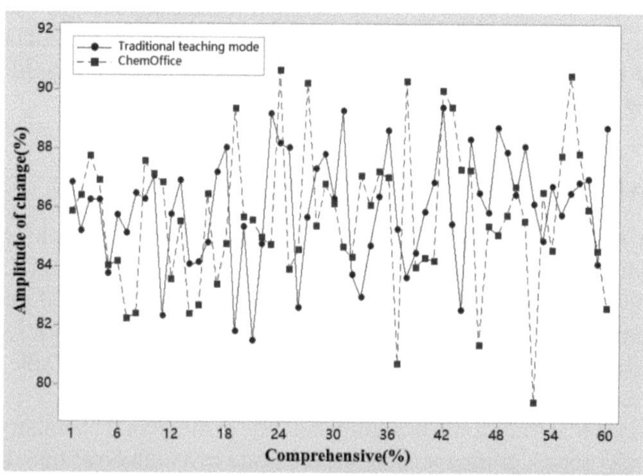

Fig. 5. The teaching mode based on the teaching mode of chemoffice

Figure 5 illustrates that the ChemOffice-based teaching approach significantly outperforms the conventional method. This superiority stems from an enhanced pharmacochemical adjustment coefficient and a set threshold for the instructional model, which eliminates inadequate schemes.

5 Conclusion

In response to suboptimal teaching methods in medicinal chemistry, this study introduces a ChemOffice-centric approach integrated with computer technology to refine the discipline. Concurrently, an in-depth analysis of instructional innovation is undertaken to establish a comprehensive set of teaching models. Research indicates that adopting the ChemOffice-based model can enhance accuracy in medicinal chemistry, and its efficacy can be generalized across standard teaching paradigms. Nonetheless, during the implementation of this ChemOffice-focused strategy, an excessive focus on analyzing pedagogical patterns has led to impractical choices in selecting instructional metrics.

References

1. Zhou, Q.: Exploration and practice of ideological and political teaching mode in medicinal chemistry course—special topic on penicillin antibiotics. Chem. Educ. (Chin. English) **43**(20), 92–97 (2022)
2. Wu, D., Zheng, X., Zheng, S., Tang, Q., Wei, T., Gao, Y.: Exploration on teaching mode of medicinal chemistry course under the background of "Internet+". Sci. Technol. Vis. (29), 136–138 (2022)
3. MA, M., Li, R., Wang, M.: Teaching reform practice of natural medicinal chemistry laboratory courses, application of MOOC+SPOCs online and offline hybrid teaching model. Straits Pharm. **34**(07), 74–77 (2022)
4. Wen, S., Rui, H., Wang, Y., Mou, Y.: A preliminary study on hybrid teaching mode of medicinal chemistry. Pharm. Educ. **38**(03), 67–70 (2022)
5. Yang, H., Tan, X., Zhang, L., Liu, S.: Practice of blended teaching mode in medicinal chemistry teaching. J. Hebei North Univ. (Nat. Sci. Edn.) **38**(04), 50–53 (2022)
6. Batista, J.M., Nicu, V.P.: Simplified and enhanced VCD analysis of cyclic peptides guided by artificial intelligence. Phys. Chem. Chem. Phys. **25**(33), 22111–22116 (2023)
7. Feng, Y., et al.: Phenotypic hit discovery oriented workshop for undergraduates: integrating cutting-edge knowledge and discovery-based laboratory experiences. J. Chem. Educ. (2023)
8. Schiesser, S., et al.: A mild synthesis of aryl triflates enabling the late-stage modification of drug analogs and complex peptides. Chem.- Eur. J. (2023)
9. Xu, X., Gao, D.D., Wang, J.H., Tang, X.Y., Wang, L.: The B(C6F5)(3)center dot H2O promoted synthesis of fluoroalkylated 3, 3′, 3″-trisindolylmethanes from fluorocarboxylic acids and indoles. Org. Biomol. Chem. **21**(7), 1478–1486 (2023)
10. Yanagihara, M., et al.: Synthesis and biological evaluation of simplified ansellone analogues with lipophilic side chains as HIV latency-reversing agents. Chem. Eur. J. (2023)
11. Yazdani, K., et al.: Machine learning informs RNA-binding chemical space. Angew. Chemie-Int. Edn. **62**(11) (2023)
12. Zhao, H.T., Branalt, J., Perry, M., Tyrchan, C.: The role of allylic strain for conformational control in medicinal chemistry. J. Med. Chem. (2023)

Design and Application of Distributed University Library and Archive Management Information System Based on Hadoop

Cui Hong[(✉)] and Wang Jing

Shangdong Institute Commerce and Technology, Jinan 250103, Shangdong, China
15605318986@163.com

Abstract. University libraries and archives have been slowly transitioning from paper-based to digital-based management strategies, thanks to the ever-increasing capabilities of information technology. The administration of libraries and archives may be substantially enhanced via the use of digital management systems. Unfortunately, conventional, standalone storage and processing systems are struggling to keep up with the ever-increasing data volumes handled by university library archives. Consequently, this article suggests using Hadoop as a tool for analyzing and evaluating creative design techniques. To minimize interference elements in design strategy assessment, we first apply data analysis theory to the data information and then split the indicators according to the needs of the evaluation. The next step is to use data analysis theory to assess the university library and archive management information system's design strategy. After that, they'll create an assessment scheme for the design strategy and thoroughly examine the outcomes. Hadoop technology outperforms conventional management approaches in terms of assessment accuracy and efficiency when it comes to the design strategy of university library and archive management information systems, according to MATLAB simulations conducted under certain evaluation criteria.

Keywords: data analysis theory · Hadoop technology · innovation and entrepreneurship of college students · Education

1 Introduction

When it comes to managing university libraries and archives, a management information system is a crucial tool that cannot be overlooked [1]. But there's an issue with the design strategy assessment system – it's not accurate enough to suit the demands of university library and archive management anymore [2]. A number of academics have proposed using Hadoop for academic library and archive administration and analysis in the hopes of better understanding and supporting design strategy evaluations [3]. Accordingly, this research suggests using Hadoop technology to fine-tune the assessment scheme for design strategies and confirm the model's efficacy [4]. The design strategy evaluation process in Table 1 is shown in Fig. 1.

B. Brik and S. Nazir (Eds.): BigIoT-EDU 2024, LNICST 659, pp. 402–413, 2026.
https://doi.org/10.1007/978-3-032-18631-7_44

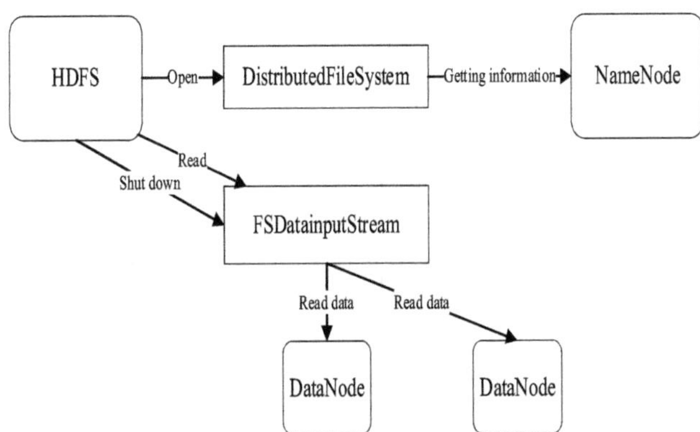

Fig. 1. The analysis process of university library and archive management.

2 Related Works

2.1 Hadoop

Hadoop technology's design strategy assessment scheme is more in line with the real needs of design strategy evaluation when compared to conventional management approaches. Hadoop technology outperforms more conventional approaches to managing university libraries and archives in terms of both rationality and fluctuation range. University library and archive management design plan assessment schemes include structural, semi-structural, and non-structural information. The process begins with the collection and cleaning of library and archive data using Hadoop technology. However, the error rate is lower, suggesting that Hadoop technology's design strategy evaluation is relatively stable, in contrast to traditional management methods' uneven design strategy evaluation.

2.2 Distributed University Library and Archive Management Information System

With Hadoop, university library and archive administration may be optimized by adjusting data information parameters using a random optimization technique [5]. Using Hadoop, university library archives are managed using several layers of design strategy review, with alternative schemes being randomly selected [6]. An iterative method is used to optimize and assess the design strategy evaluation scheme with multiple degrees of design strategy evaluation [7]. The best university library and archive administration is documented when the optimization study is finished, and various schemes are contrasted based on the design strategy assessment level. In the end, a management information system that is highly efficient, scalable, and capable of handling increasing data quantities is what you get when you use Hadoop technology.

3 Optimization Strategy of University Library and Archive Management

3.1 Mathematical Description of Hadoop Technology

Hadoop, an open-source platform for distributed computation and storage, is primarily comprised of the MapReduce and HDFS modules [8]. Data access services with high throughput and great fault tolerance are provided by HDFS, a Hadoop distributed file system [9]. One Hadoop distributed computing architecture, MapReduce, may improve data processing performance by dividing large-scale data into several tiny pieces for parallel processing [10]. The first step is to optimize the design strategy evaluation method using data mining theory is, and thereafter in accordance with the assessment criteria for the design strategy's index parameters is, University library and archive management's unqualified value parameters are determined, and the scheme for evaluating design strategies is merged with the function to determine the viability of these systems is, which is calculated as shown in Eq. (1).

$$Sp(x_{ij}) = \sum_{i=1}^{n} \eta - f_i \tag{1}$$

Equation (2) shows the evaluation of outliers among them.

$$\sum_{i=1}^{n} \eta - f_i = \int s \rightarrow \sum (x_{ij}, p_{ij}) \tag{2}$$

The design strategy assessment management information system may be enhanced using Hadoop technology, which integrates the benefits of data mining theory with the quantitative capabilities of university library and archive administration.

Assume that I. The criteria for evaluating the design approach is, the distributed file system is, the satisfaction of the processing results is a_i, and the design strategy evaluation scheme judgment function is, as shown in Eq. (3).

$$D(p_i) = \prod_{i=1}^{n} h\xi + a_i \tag{3}$$

3.2 Selection of MIS Programs

The role of university archives and libraries, supposing that II. is, and the weight coefficient is, Eq. (4) shows that in order to evaluate the design approach, competent university library and archive administration is required.

$$N(x_i) = \prod a(f) - y_i \tag{4}$$

Equation (5) displays the outcome of obtaining a full function of management information based on hypothesis I and II.

$$D(p_i) + N(x_i) \leq \sum_{i=1}^{n} \eta - f_i \tag{5}$$

Equation (6) shows the outcome of processing all data in parallel, which improves the efficacy of the design strategy assessment.

$$D(p_i) + N(x_i) \leftrightarrow \int s \rightarrow \sum (x_{ij}, p_{ij}) \tag{6}$$

3.3 Analysis of Design Strategy Evaluation Scheme

High scalability and dependability are two of Hadoop's advantages. Hadoop is capable of quickly scaling up due to the fact that it distributes data storage and computation over several nodes. Hadoop also uses data replication as a technique to get rid of assessment systems for design strategies that aren't up to scratch. is. Equation (6) allows for the proposal of the anomaly assessment system, and Eq. (7) displays the findings.

$$A(y_i) = \frac{D(p_i) + N(x_i)}{\sum (x_{ij}, p_{ij})} \tag{7}$$

Among them, it is, said that the plan must be put forward before the plan may be integrated is, and Eq. (8) displays the outcome.

$$A(d_i \cdot y_i) = min[\sum D(p_i) + N(x_i)] \tag{8}$$

In order to guarantee the data's dependability and fault tolerance, the administration of university libraries and archives does thorough analyses and determines the design strategy assessment scheme's threshold and index weight. Innovative analysis is required of university library and archive management systems since they are developed for systematic testing and strategic assessment schemes. If university library and archive administration follows an irregular distribution is, The total accuracy of its design strategy assessment will be reduced as a result of this impact on its evaluation methodology is, and Eq. (9) displays the outcome of the computation.

$$p(x_i \cdot z) = \frac{min[\sum D(p_i) + N(x_i)]}{\sum D(p_i) + N(x_i)} \times 100\% \tag{9}$$

In accordance with the objective facts, the survey design strategy assessment scheme reveals that the management information system scheme displays a multi-dimensional distribution. This study is considered to be of a high analytical quality since the university library and archive management is non-directional, suggesting that the management information system scheme is very random. When it comes to managing university libraries and archives, if is, then the calculation of Eq. (9) can be expressed as Eq. (10).

$$p(x_i \cdot z) = \frac{min[\sum D(p_i) + N(x_i)]}{\sum D(p_i) + N(x_i)} \times 100\% + don(b_i) \tag{10}$$

The data mining theory enhances the default scheme, eliminates duplicate and irrelevant data, and adjusts the management of university library archives to meet normal requirements. This results in a strong dynamic correlation of the entire design strategy evaluation scheme.

4 Results and Discussion

4.1 Introduction to the Evaluation of Design Strategies

Table 1 shows the design strategy evaluation scheme for university library and archive management; the paper uses university library and archive management in complex cases as its research object; the study has 12 paths; and the testing period is 12 h.

Table 1. Management system design strategy evaluation requirements

Scope of application	use	System performance	Optimize performance
HDFS	Store data	69.99	71.22
MapReduce	Process data	72.14	72.50
	Analyze data	75.25	74.10
HBase	Query the data	70.99	74.99
	Modify the data	74.47	73.41
Zookeeper	Node communication	72.47	71.25
	Task scheduling	73.55	73.98
Web Server	UI	73.99	73.68
	interface	71.60	74.70

It is clear that Hadoop technology offers quicker management efficiency and improved stability from the change in the design strategy assessment scheme shown in Fig. 2. As a result, Hadoop's design strategy evaluation scheme, the summation stability, and the administration information system solution design strategy evaluation scheme are all improved.

4.2   Management of Books and Archives in Colleges and Universities

The cleaned data is then stored in HDFS. The data is processed and analyzed using MapReduce. The results are stored in HBase. Lastly, a web server is created and put into operation, offering an interface and user interface. The last step is to test the system and evaluate its performance. Table 2 shows the assessment levels and schemes for university library and archive management's design strategies, which may help in more precisely confirming the innovative impact of these strategies.

Table 2. Overall status of the mi system programmer

Information category	Specific data	facticity	Analysis rate
Book information	Book name	80.83	74.57
	author	80.84	73.34
	publishing house	79.73	71.61
	Date of publication	81.32	70.61
	Inventory levels	80.99	75.90
User Information	Username	82.00	72.80
	Library card number	82.49	72.77
	Contact	79.94	72.37
	Borrowing records	82.61	72.79

(*continued*)

Table 2. (continued)

Information category	Specific data	facticity	Analysis rate
	Historical behavior	82.84	70.84
Borrow information	Borrowing time	84.64	72.39
	Return time	83.99	75.11
	Borrowing status	80.37	75.12
	Lease expiration date	81.70	73.14
Profile information	Student Profile	83.29	75.59
	Teacher Profile	83.45	74.25
	Library archives	82.05	76.70
Statistics	Number of borrowings	80.23	73.05
	Borrowing rate	80.09	74.11
	Book circulation rate	82.72	75.90
	Seat utilization	85.97	67.78

4.3 System Performance Evaluation and Stability of Design Strategy Evaluation

Figure 2 shows the results of the functional tests and performance evaluations conducted on the university's library and archive management information system, which were used to confirm the correctness of Hadoop technology.

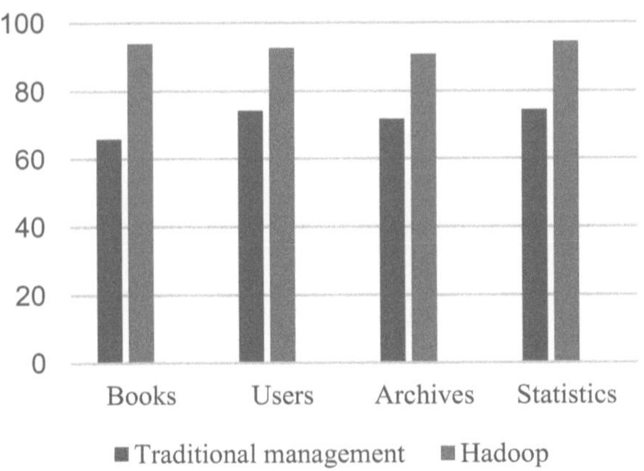

Fig. 2. System performance evaluation of different algorithms

Figure 2 shows that Hadoop technology's management information system is better than traditional management methods, but with a lower error rate. This suggests that Hadoop technology's system performance evaluation is stable and effective for managing university libraries and archives. Table 3 displays the average design strategy assessment scheme for the various algorithms mentioned before.

Table 3. Comparison of design strategy evaluation accuracy of different methods

Algorithm	Survey data	Efficiency	Extensibility	error
Hadoop technology	Book name	92.78	93.19	0.46
	Book inventory	92.38	92.25	0.49
	Username	91.50	93.24	0.56
	Library card number	91.87	94.36	0.46
	Contact	93.33	93.39	0.90
	Borrowing records	92.55	91.82	0.80
	Historical behavior	92.22	92.27	0.58
	Borrowing time	92.01	92.46	0.66
	Return time	91.82	94.16	0.78
	Borrowing status	93.09	93.86	0.66
	Lease expiration date	93.58	90.94	0.88
	Student Profile	91.79	91.91	0.44
	Teacher Profile	93.16	93.54	0.92
	Library archives	92.81	92.76	0.61
	Number of borrowings	93.32	93.26	0.85
	Borrowing rate	92.93	94.28	0.89
	Book circulation rate	93.81	92.50	0.40
	Seat utilization	91.87	92.25	0.41
Traditional management	Book name	87.88	82.59	5.72
	Book inventory	82.53	85.42	4.66
	Username	82.40	84.39	3.22
	Library card number	86.09	85.45	5.68
	Contact	81.82	86.94	3.93
	Borrowing records	85.85	84.91	4.29
	Historical behavior	86.33	83.53	5.72
	Borrowing time	91.44	88.53	3.74
	Return time	85.54	85.35	4.08
	Borrowing status	83.58	86.23	4.06
	Lease expiration date	87.48	87.07	3.27
	Student Profile	83.91	83.05	5.60
	Teacher Profile	82.87	85.41	6.24

(continued)

Table 3. (*continued*)

Algorithm	Survey data	Efficiency	Extensibility	error
	Library archives	84.01	79.03	4.65
	Number of borrowings	81.31	87.44	4.67
	Borrowing rate	85.83	80.59	5.67
	Book circulation rate	86.08	86.64	5.23
	Seat utilization	87.61	82.52	5.71

Based on the results shown in Table 3, it is clear that the conventional approach to managing university libraries and archives suffers from poor management information system performance and a high rate of calculation errors. Hadoop technology is examined using several approaches to further confirm its superiority, as illustrated in Fig. 3.

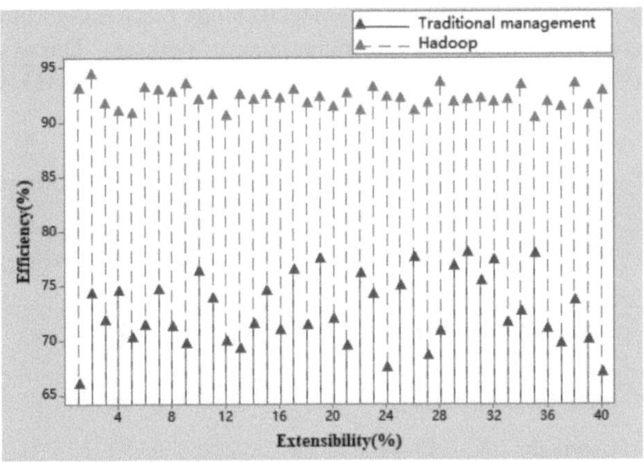

Fig. 3. The effect of hadoop technology system function testing

Figure 3 shows that compared to the old management approach, the Hadoop technology's management information system is much superior. This system can handle the data processing and storage demands of university libraries and archives.

4.4 Design Strategies to Evaluate the Effectiveness of Information Management

Figure 4 shows the design strategy assessment scheme, which is contrasted with the old management approach to validate the efficacy of Hadoop technology.

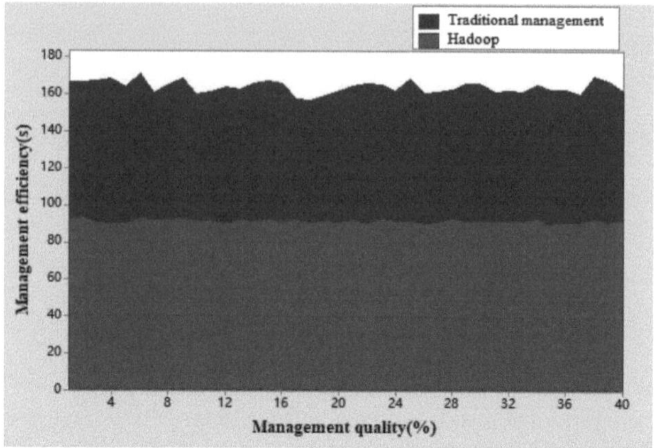

Fig. 4. Management information systems with different algorithms

Based on Fig. 4, it is evident that Hadoop technology has a higher management information system compared to traditional management methods. The assessment system for the average design strategy of the various algorithms mentioned before is shown in Table 4.

Table 4. Comparison of the effectiveness of design strategies of different methods

algorithm	Test data	Management information systems	effectiveness	Error rate
Hadoop technology	Book name	91.66	93.09	0.69
	Book inventory	93.06	93.46	0.88
	Username	93.44	93.32	0.81
	Library card number	93.44	92.43	0.62
	Contact	94.36	93.41	0.83
	Borrowing records	93.79	93.35	0.54
	Historical behavior	92.77	91.85	0.82
	Borrowing time	93.95	92.62	0.62
	Return time	92.16	91.67	0.68
	Borrowing status	93.50	93.47	0.78
	Lease expiration date	92.86	93.64	0.67

(continued)

Table 4. (*continued*)

algorithm	Test data	Management information systems	effectiveness	Error rate
	Student Profile	92.32	92.30	0.65
	Teacher Profile	93.02	92.30	0.56
	Library archives	92.85	93.74	0.96
	Number of borrowings	92.89	92.74	0.99
	Borrowing rate	93.17	92.51	0.61
	Book circulation rate	93.51	93.94	0.65
	Seat utilization	92.84	93.65	0.49
Traditional management	Book name	84.12	88.18	4.52
	Book inventory	82.82	87.40	4.82
	Username	85.39	82.02	5.39
	Library card number	88.24	87.60	4.47
	Contact	80.69	87.84	4.99
	Borrowing records	82.53	87.59	5.33
	Historical behavior	90.31	84.02	5.91
	Borrowing time	84.59	82.20	4.37
	Return time	81.42	82.62	5.06
	Borrowing status	84.91	79.66	4.85
	Lease expiration date	83.43	82.34	4.70
	Student Profile	85.23	84.81	6.29
	Teacher Profile	87.45	84.61	5.73
	Library archives	84.42	83.50	4.92
	Number of borrowings	81.37	82.43	3.77
	Borrowing rate	86.47	89.22	4.22

(*continued*)

Table 4. (continued)

algorithm	Test data	Management information systems	effectiveness	Error rate
	Book circulation rate	84.49	83.03	4.53
	Seat utilization	83.57	89.07	5.37

Table 4 shows that traditional methods of management aren't very good at managing management information systems or university libraries and archives, and that there have been a lot of changes in these areas recently, with a relatively high error rate. Hadoop technology, in general, produces a better management information system than more conventional approaches to management. Also, there has been no discernible impact in the accuracy of Hadoop's management information system, which is above 90%. Figure 5 shows the results of a comprehensive examination of Hadoop technology using various approaches, which is conducted to further confirm the efficacy of the strategy described in this research.

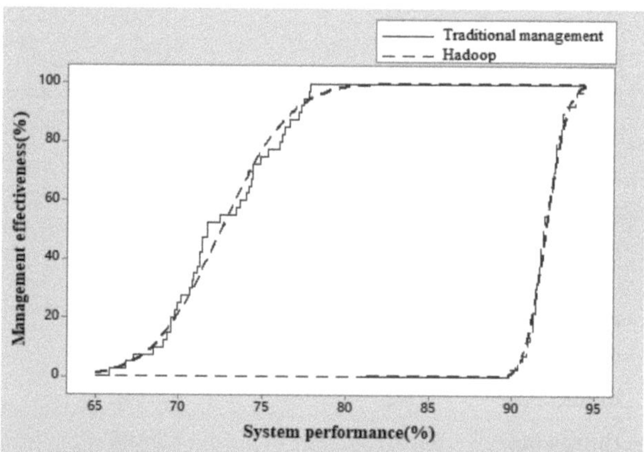

Fig. 5. Hadoop technology design strategy evaluation of management information systems

Hadoop technology improves the management information system compared to the traditional method (as shown in Fig. 5). This is because Hadoop technology raises the adjustment coefficient for university library and archive management and establishes a data threshold to remove design strategy evaluation schemes that fail to meet requirements.

5 Conclusion

This study puts forward the concept of using Hadoop technology and combining data mining theory to optimize the administration of university library and archives in response to the issue of the imperfect university library and archives management information system. Simultaneously, data information collecting is built, and assessment innovations in design strategies and threshold innovations are studied thoroughly. Hadoop technology has great efficiency and scalability, and the test results demonstrate that it can enhance the stability and accuracy of university library and archive administration. University library and archive management demands may be better met in the future with the addition of multi-dimensional data analysis and mining capabilities, which can be built on top of this system to further optimize its performance and functionality.

References

1. Cai, C., Hu, S., Gao, J.: Research on the construction of big data professional teaching resource library—taking Hadoop distributed infrastructure as an example. Office Autom. **28**(04), 32–34+45 (2023)
2. Liu, Y., Wang, J., Tang, M., Zhang, Y.: Load classification model of hybrid neural network based on Hadoop distributed computing. Sci. Technol. Eng. **23**(04), 1549–1556 (2023)
3. Sun, J., You, X., Zhang, L.: Analysis and design of application status of college student archives management information system. Int. Publ. Relat. (02), 65–67 (2023)
4. Cold bead grass: Strategies of management information system to effectively improve library and archive management. Off. Autom. **28**(02), 50–52 (2023)
5. Xie, F., Peng, Y.: Research on cloud storage system and file storage implementation based on Hadoop distributed architecture. Comput. Telecommun. **10**, 102–105 (2022)
6. Zhong, T.: Architecture and design of traffic anomaly distributed detection system for Hadoop. Electron. Test. (19), 93–95+71 (2022)
7. Xing, Y., Zhou, S.: Research on distributed video transcoding system based on Hadoop. Comput. Technol. Dev. **32**(05), 58–62 (2022)
8. Hong, D., Shixue, Y., Ji, M.: Design and application of personnel file management information system in colleges and universities. Lantai World **09**, 44–46 (2020)
9. Xiaole, Y., Lianglong, Z.: Design and application of business file management information system for health professional and technical personnel. Off. Bus. **03**, 54 (2018)
10. Wang, R.: Design of library (enterprise file information) management system. Beijing University of Technology (2017)

Design and Implementation of English Self-learning Platform Based on Constructive Teaching Mode

Zhong Wang[✉]

Wuhan Technology and Business University, Wuhan 430065, China
`wangzhong1018@163.com`

Abstract. Improper outcome evaluation is a concern, although self-directed learning plays a crucial part in English language acquisition. Both the design and the issue of self-directed learning in English cannot be solved by the conventional teaching methodology. So, to help students analyze their own English learning progress, this research suggests a constructive teaching approach. To minimize interference from independent learning, the learning platform is first designed using educational theory. Indicators are then segregated according to the needs of independent learning. The educational theory then develops an English language learning program based on independent study, and finally analyzes and synthesizes the findings. MATLAB simulations show that in the case of certain design standards, the constructive teaching mode for English the accuracy of self-learning and self-learning time are better than the traditional teaching mode.

Keywords: educational theory · constructive teaching model · English · Education

1 Introduction

As a result of rapid globalization and societal progress, English has surpassed all others as a worldwide language of communication. In China, the English language is employed extensively throughout all levels of education, from elementary to university, in order to address the issue of English curriculum and instruction. English self-learning platforms have evolved into a valuable resource to aid students' study and enhance their command of the language as a result of the convergence of technology and the classroom [1]. However, there are still some challenges to the effectiveness and sustainability of learning platforms, which need to be solved through the optimization and improvement of teaching models [2].

The constructivist teaching model is a teaching model based on constructivist theory, which emphasizes students' independent learning and inquiry, and pays attention to students' initiative and participation in the learning process. In English education, the constructivist teaching model has been widely used [3], especially in the English self-learning platform, its advantages and application value are more obvious. Based on the

B. Brik and S. Nazir (Eds.): BigIoT-EDU 2024, LNICST 659, pp. 414–424, 2026.
https://doi.org/10.1007/978-3-032-18631-7_45

constructivist teaching model, this paper will explore the application effect and influence of constructivist teaching mode on English independent learning platform [4].

1.1 The Theoretical Basis and Practical Application of the Constructivist Teaching Model

The constructivist teaching model is a teaching mode based on the constructivist theory, which emphasizes students' initiative and participation in the learning process, pays attention to students' knowledge construction and concept establishment [5], and emphasizes students' independent learning and inquiry. The constructivist teaching model advocates a "learner-centered" teaching environment that enables students to learn at their own pace and in their own way based on their own interests and needs [6]. The constructivist teaching model has the following characteristics in theory:

1. Learner initiative and participation

The constructivist teaching model emphasizes students' initiative and participation in the learning process, and students need to actively participate in the learning process through their own experience and cognition [7].

2. Knowledge construction and concept building

The constructivist teaching model focuses on students' knowledge construction and concept establishment, encourages students to carry out independent learning and inquiry, and gradually establishes conceptual system and knowledge structure through personal experience and cognition [8].

3. Creation of learning environments

The constructivist teaching model advocates the establishment of a "learner-centered" teaching environment, so that students can learn at their own pace and in their own way based on their own interests and needs, so as to create a learning environment that is more suitable for themselves [9].

4. The unity of objectivity and subjectivity

The constructivist teaching model advocates the unification of objectivity and subjectivity, and continuously deepens students' knowledge structure and conceptual system through their own cognition and subjective experience [10].

In English education, the constructivist teaching model has been widely used, especially on the English self-learning platform, and its application effect is more significant. Adopting a constructivist teaching model can create a dynamic and creative learning environment for students, helping students to better master English knowledge and skills [11].

1.2 The Advantages and Challenges of Constructivist Teaching Mode on English Independent Learning Platform

On the English self-learning platform, the constructivist teaching model has the following advantages:

1. Improve students' self-directed learning ability

The use of constructivist teaching mode can promote the improvement of students' independent learning ability, so that students can carry out learning more independently and autonomously [12].

2. Promote students' improvement in spoken and written English

The constructivist teaching model focuses on students' knowledge construction and concept building, which can help students understand English knowledge more deeply and improve their English speaking and writing skills [13].

3. Enhance students' interest and motivation to learn

The constructivist teaching model emphasizes learners' initiative and participation, which can effectively enhance students' interest and motivation in learning and make students more active in learning [14].

4. Enhance students' sense of teamwork

The constructivist teaching model advocates promoting interaction and communication between students by organizing group discussions or group cooperation, so that students can better experience the sense of teamwork and cooperation [15].

However, there are also some challenges to the constructivist teaching model on the English self-learning platform:

5. Students' self-learning ability and self-management ability are limited

Although the constructivist teaching model advocates students' independent learning and inquiry, in fact, many students' self-learning ability and self-management ability are limited, and they need the guidance and help of teachers and schools [16].

6. The roles and responsibilities of teachers have changed

The adoption of constructivist teaching models requires teachers to play more of the role of guides and coordinators, rather than knowledge transmitters and evaluators in the traditional sense.

7. Student learning is difficult to quantify and assess

The constructivist teaching model focuses on students' initiative and autonomy, and students' learning effects are difficult to quantify and evaluate, so it is necessary to find more scientific and effective evaluation standards and methods [17].

1.3 How to Apply Constructivist Teaching Models to English Self-learning Platforms

In order to give full play to the advantages of constructivist teaching mode on the English self-learning platform, the following measures need to be adopted:

1. Design effective self-directed learning tasks and teaching resources

Adopting a constructivist teaching model requires the design of effective self-directed learning tasks and teaching resources to meet students' learning needs and interests [18].

2. Strengthen the guidance and coordination of teachers

When applying the constructivist teaching model, teachers need to play more roles as guides and coordinators, actively guiding students to learn and explore deeply.

3. Create a good learning atmosphere

Adopting a constructivist teaching model requires creating a dynamic and creative learning environment that focuses on students' subjective experiences and emotional responses.

4. Establish an effective evaluation system

The constructivist teaching model pays attention to students' initiative and autonomy, and students' learning effects are difficult to quantify and evaluate, so it is necessary to establish an effective evaluation system to scientifically evaluate students' learning effects and learning effects.

The English independent learning platform has become one of the important means of modern English education, and the use of constructivist teaching mode can better support students' independent learning, improve English proficiency and independent learning ability. When applying the constructivist teaching model, it is necessary to design effective independent learning tasks and teaching resources, establish an effective evaluation system, create a good learning atmosphere, and strengthen the guidance and coordination of teachers. In the future, we need to further explore the application and optimization of constructivist teaching mode on the English independent learning platform to promote the innovation and development of English education.

The ability to study on one's own is crucial to the development of English language skills and is a key component of the English curriculum [1]. The self-directed learning software has an issue with its accuracy when pupils are learning on their own [2], which causes them to lose some knowledge [3]. Some researchers have shown that by analyzing the self-learning program through the lens of the constructive teaching mode, we may better understand how students learn English on their own [4]. This work uses this information to suggest a constructive model of instruction, refine the self-learning scheme, and test the model's efficacy [5].

2 Related Works

2.1 Mathematical Description of the Constructive Teaching Model

The constructive teaching mode uses multi-level theory to optimize the self-learning program y_i, It determines the absolute worth of learning English based on self-learning indicators z_i, and learns independently The scheme is integrated and the feasibility of English learning is $tol(y_i \cdot x_{ij})$ finally judged, and the calculation is shown in Eq. (1).

$$tol(y_i \cdot x_{ij}) = y_{ij} \otimes max(x_{ij}) \tag{1}$$

Equation (2) shows the evaluation of outliers among them.

$$max(x_{ij}) = \left(x_{ij}^2 + 6\right) \infty mean \mathfrak{A}\left(\sum x_{ij}\right) \tag{2}$$

With the use of quantitative measures derived from English language acquisition, the constructive teaching approach integrates the benefits of multi-level theory to boost student autonomy in the classroom.

Suppose I. The self-directed learning requirements is x_i, the self-learning program is set_i, and the satisfaction of the self-learning program is y_i self-directed learning. The function for scheme judgment is $G(x_i \approx 0)$ Eq. (3) shows.

$$G(d_i) = \sum x_i \bigcap \mathfrak{A} \rightarrow \oint y_i \tag{3}$$

2.2 Choice of Self-directed Learning Options

Second Hypothesis The role of learning English is $f(x_i)$, the weighted value is $\mathfrak{A}_i$, then, self-directed learning requires unqualified English learning as shown in Eq. (4).

$$f(x_i) = z_i \cdot \prod G(d_i) - \mathfrak{A}_i \tag{4}$$

An all-encompassing function of English education may be derived from assumptions I and II, and the outcome is shown in Eq. (5).

$$f(x_i) + G(d_i) \leq max(x_{ij}) \tag{5}$$

Equation (6) shows the outcomes of standardizing all data, which is necessary to enhance the efficacy of English instruction.

$$f(x_i) + G(d_i) \leftrightarrow mean\left(\sum x_{ij}\right) \tag{6}$$

2.3 Analysis of Self-directed Learning Programs

First things first: abolish the unqualified self-learning scheme; next, map the self-learning needs to the English learning library. Only then can the constructive teaching mode be implemented $No(x_i)$. Equation (7) displays the outcomes, while Eq. (6) allows for the proposal of the anomaly assessment method.

$$No(x_i) = \frac{f(x_i) + G(d_i)}{mean\left(\sum x_{ij}\right)} \tag{7}$$

Among them, $\frac{f(x_i)+G(d_i)}{mean(\sum x_{ij})} \leq 1$ it is stated that the scheme needs to be proposed, otherwise the scheme integration is required $Zh(x_i)$, and the result is shown in Eq. (8).

$$Zh(x_i) = min[\sum f(x_i) + G(d_i)] \tag{8}$$

In order to guarantee the correctness of the constructive teaching model, parameters and index weights of self-directed learning programs for English language acquisition are established after a thorough analysis. The acquisition of the English language necessitates fresh approaches to analysis as it is a test of methods for independent study. A nonnormal distribution for English language acquisition will result in a self-directed learning method that is $unno(x_i)$, reducing the accuracy of the overall self-directed learning $accur(x_i)$, calculated as the formula (9).

$$accur(x_i) = \frac{min[\sum f(x_i) + G(d_i)]}{\sum f(x_i) \oplus G(d_i)} \times 100\% \tag{9}$$

A multi-dimensional distribution is consistent with objective facts, according to the study of self-learning methods. This research is considered highly analytical since the lack of direction in English learning suggests that the self-directed learning program is quite random. If the probability function for acquiring the English language is $randon(x_i)$, the result of solving problem (9) may be given by formula (10).

$$accur(x_i) = \frac{min[\sum f(x_i) + G(d_i)]}{\sum f(x_i) + G(d_i)} \times 100\% + randon(x_i) \tag{10}$$

English learning satisfies typical criteria; primarily, multi-level theory modifies English learning, gets rid of unnecessary and redundant schemes, and enhances the default scheme, resulting in a robust dynamic correlation across the whole self-learning scheme.

3 Optimization Strategies for English Learning

The constructive teaching mode optimizes English learning schemes by adjusting the characteristics of the learning platform and using a random optimization technique for English learning. In the constructive teaching style, students study English at their own pace and choose their own answers at random. The iterative procedure optimizes and analyzes self-learning schemes with varying degrees of self-learning. Following the completion of the optimization study, the best English learning is documented by comparing the levels of self-directed learning of various possibilities.

4 Results and Discussion

4.1 Introduction to Self-directed Learning

Table 1 shows the unique English learning self-paced learning scenarios, and the article uses English learning in complicated settings as its research goal. There are 12 pathways and a 12-h test duration.

The self-directed learning process in Table 1 is shown in Fig. 1.

In terms of self-learning needs, the constructive teaching mode's scheme is more in line with reality than the conventional teaching mode. Compared to the conventional approach, the constructive method of teaching English is superior in terms of both the

Table 1. Self-directed learning requirements at each stage

Scope of application	grade	Learning effects	Self-directed learning
elementary school	I	34.65	33.17
	II	33.28	34.55
junior high school	I	33.63	34.40
	II	33.47	35.60
high school	I	35.20	33.67
	II	33.62	32.49

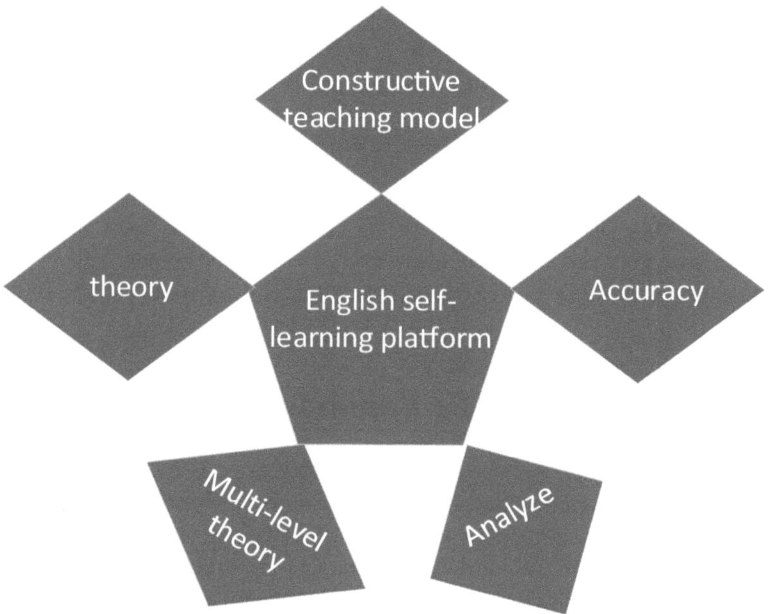

Fig. 1. Analysis of English language learning

logical scope and the variability of its application. The improvements in stability and judgment speed seen in the constructive teaching mode are evident from the modifications in the self-learning scheme shown in Fig. 1. Speed, precision, and stability of summing are all improved in the constructive teaching mode's self-learning scheme.

4.2   English Learning

The English language learning software allows students to work at their own speed and incorporates strategies such as anchor teaching, random entrance, and hierarchical negotiation. An initial autonomous learning program for English language acquisition and proficiency is achieved after the pre-selection of the constructive pedagogical style.

Assessing the practicality of alternatives for self-directed learning. Using the options in Table 2, choose several degrees of self-directed learning English in order to more precisely confirm the innovative impact of learning the language.

Table 2. The overall picture of the self-paced learning programmed

category	Satisfaction	Analysis rate
elementary school	83.36	73.14
junior high school	83.21	73.24
high school	83.32	75.07
mean	82.43	73.64
X6	34.35	33.54
P = 3.025		

4.3 Self-directed Learning and Stability

In order to verify the accuracy of the constructive teaching mode, the self-learning scheme is compared with the traditional teaching mode, and the self-learning scheme is shown in Fig. 2.

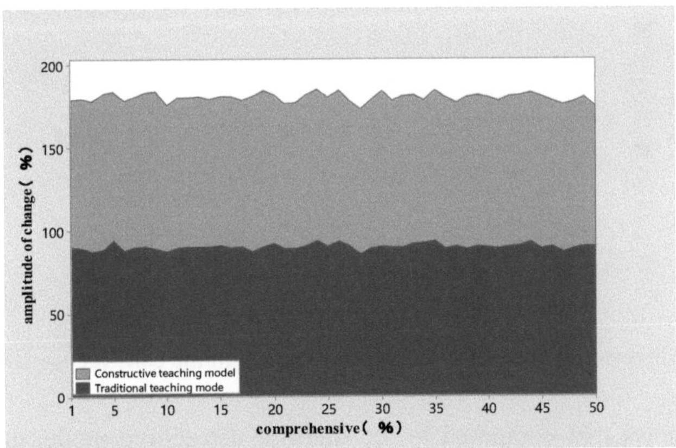

Fig. 2. Independent learning with different teaching modes

Figure 2 shows that compared to the traditional teaching mode, the constructive teaching mode has higher self-learning but a lower error rate. This suggests that the former is more stable, while the latter is more prone to uneven self-directed learning. Table 3 displays the average self-directed learning strategies for the three types of teaching that were just discussed.

Table 3. Comparison of self-directed learning accuracy of different methods

Teaching mode	Self-directed learning	Magnitude of change	error
Constructive teaching model	93.57	93.51	94.61
Traditional teaching mode	82.89	83.26	84.18
P	35.002	33.797	35.860

As seen in Table 3 The conventional method of instruction in English has obvious flaws when it comes to the precision and consistency of student-led learning, and the language itself has evolved considerably, with a correspondingly high mistake rate. In comparison to the conventional wisdom, the constructive teaching style tends to provide superior results in terms of student autonomy in the classroom. Also, there has been no discernible improvement in accuracy despite the fact that the constructive teaching mode's self-learning is above 90%. For the purpose of providing further evidence that the constructive teaching method is preferable. Various methodologies are used to conduct a broad analysis of the constructive teaching mode, as indicated in Fig. 3, in order to further validate the efficiency of the suggested method.

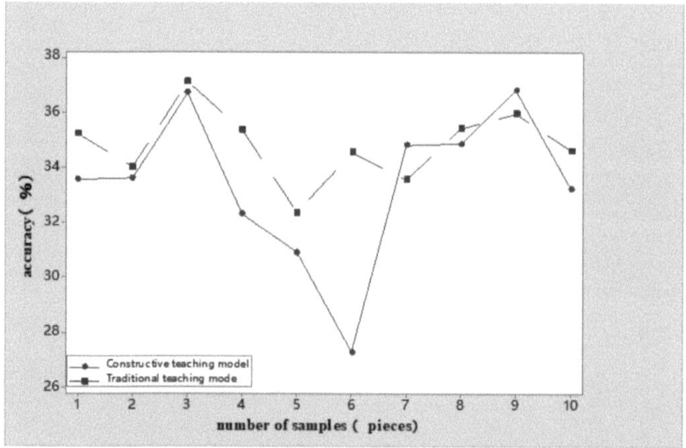

Fig. 3. Self-directed learning of self-directed learning in the constructive teaching mode

Figure 3 shows that compared to the traditional teaching mode, the constructive learning mode's self-learning is much better. This is because, in the constructive learning mode, the adjustment coefficient of English learning is increased, and the learning platform's threshold is set to eliminate self-learning scenarios that do not meet the requirements.

5 Conclusion

This work presents a constructive teaching mode that incorporates multi-level theory to maximize English learning, aiming to address the issue that autonomous learning is not optimal. Additionally, a set of learning platforms is constructed by doing thorough analyses of both independent learning innovation and threshold innovation. Research has shown that using a constructive teaching method may help students learn English more accurately and consistently, as well as facilitate their overall independent study of the language. Nevertheless, the selection of self-learning indicators is illogical due to the excessive focus on self-learning analysis throughout the teaching mode construction process.

References

1. Chen, Z.X.: Group-individual multi-mode cooperative teaching-learning-based optimization algorithm and an industrial engineering application. J. Intell. Fuzzy Syst. **44**(3), 5437–5465 (2023)
2. Feng, Y.X., Huang, Y., Li, B., Peng, H., Wang, J., Zhou, W.K.: Connectivity enhancement of E-VANET based on QL-mRSU self-learning energy-saving algorithm. IEEE Access **11**, 3810–3825 (2023)
3. Gan, X.M., Zuo, Y., Zhang, A.S., Li, S.B., Tao, F.: Digital twin-enabled adaptive scheduling strategy based on deep reinforcement learning. Sci. China-Technol. Sci. **66**(7), 1937–1951 (2023)
4. Huang, X., Zhang, Y., Liu, J.R., Zhong, H.H., Wang, Z.L., Peng, Y.: Error dynamics based dual heuristic dynamic programming for self-learning flight control. Appl. Sci.-Basel **13**(1) (2023)
5. Krotki, A.J.: An approach to the relevance of creative practices in education. Revista **180**(1), 102–110 (2023)
6. Li, J.W., Sumita, M., Tamura, R., Tsuda, K.: Interpretable fragment-based molecule design with self-learning entropic population annealing. Adv. Intell. Syst. (2023)
7. Li, W., Liu, Y., Ma, Y., Xu, K., Qiu, J., Gan, Z.X.: A self-learning Monte Carlo tree search algorithm for robot path planning. Front. Neurorob. **17** (2023)
8. Mardiros, L., Mahmood, F., Colantonio, S., Bose, R.: Skin of colour dermatoses self-learning module: assessing student comprehension. J. Cutan. Med. Surg. **27**(3), 214–218 (2023)
9. Nozaki, I., Tsukada, M., Sothy, P., Rattana, K., Williams, K.: Introduction and roll-out of self-learning App for midwifery during the COVID-19 pandemic and its sustainability in Cambodia. Global Health Med. **5**(3), 178–183 (2023)
10. Pavendan, R.T., Sankar, K., Kumar, K.A.V.: A graph theory based self-learning honeypot to detect persistent threats. Intell. Autom. Soft Comput. **35**(3), 3331–3348 (2023)
11. Sun, W.W., Liu, S.Q., Liu, Y., Kong, L.Q., Jian, Z.R.: Information extraction network based on multi-granularity attention and multi-scale self-learning. Sensors **23**(9) (2023)
12. Varshavskaya, E.Y.: Work-related learning practices of university graduates: scope and determinants. Sotsiologicheskie Issledovaniya (4), 94–105 (2023)
13. Wang, W., et al.: Class-specific and self-learning local manifold structure for domain adaptation. Pattern Recogn. **142** (2023)
14. Wei, L.T., Liu, Y.C., Zhu, Z., Wang, X.Y., Li, L.: Parameters self-learning of solenoid valve for wheel pressure estimation. Proc. Inst. Mech. Eng. Part D J. Autom. Eng. (2023)
15. Wu, C.H., Lam, H.Y., Kong, A., Wong, W.L.H.: The design and evaluation of a digital learning-based English chatbot as an online self-learning method. Int. J. Eng. Bus. Manage. **15** (2023)

16. Yuan, J., Liang, Z.M., Wang, R.X., Li, Y.F., Wang, Z., Gao, J.M.: A novel self-learning framework for fault identification of wind turbine drive bearings. Proc. Inst. Mech. Eng. Part I-J. Syst. Control Eng. **237**(7), 1296–1312 (2023)
17. Zhang, J.X., Zhou, D.H., Chen, M.Y.: Self-learning sparse PCA for multimode process monitoring. IEEE Trans. Ind. Inf. **19**(1), 29–39 (2023)
18. Zheng, R.F., Huang, K.J., Shen, H.B., Ma, L.Y.: Continuous volumetric convolution network with self-learning kernels for point clouds. IEEE Trans. Consum. Electron. **69**(2), 148–155 (2023)

The Interactive English Grammar System Based on Android Platform

Yingjuan Chen[✉]

Wuhan Business University, Wuhan, Hubei, China
`20150387@wbu.edu.cn`

Abstract. In order to improve the effect of grammatical analysis, it is necessary to systematically analyze the grammar, on this basis, this paper constructs an English grammar management system, analyzes the overall system, and its applicable platform is the Android platform, the research results show that the grammatical information in the Android platform can mine the correlation in the grammar, realize the expansion of the grammatical content, and analyze the correlation between the comprehensive results and the words. Optimize the original grammatical structure, so in-depth judgment will find that in the process of Android analysis platform, the grammatical system has been significantly sublimated, and the English content and English conditions have been significantly analyzed, and the improvement result is greater than 80%, indicating that in the process of English grammar analysis and platform analysis, its rationality is relatively good and can meet the actual English analysis needs.

Keywords: Artificial Intelligence Theory · Android platform · Interactive English Grammar · Learning System · Research

1 Introduction

The comprehensive judgment of English law system and English, as well as the structure and in-depth content of grammar system, show fluctuating changes. Therefore, we should make a comprehensive judgment on it [1, 2]. And optimization, to find the correlation between words. Logic between the crew [3, 4]. In order to solve the problem of the accuracy of the research of the traditional English grammar system, researchers have introduced [5] the Android platform into the research and analysis of the English grammar system in recent years. The Android platform is a computational [6] method based on group behavior that simulates the interaction [7] and cooperation between individuals to achieve the goal of global optimization [8]. The algorithm has the characteristics of decentralization [9], immutability and smart contract, which can effectively solve the accuracy problems testing in traditional schemes [10]. The research optimization model of English grammar system based on Android platform further improves the accuracy and reliability of simulation by optimizing [11] the parameters and algorithms in the research process of English grammar system. The model adjusts and optimizes [12]

© ICST Institute for Computer Sciences, Social Informatics and Telecommunications Engineering 2026
Published by Springer Nature Switzerland AG 2026. All Rights Reserved
B. Brik and S. Nazir (Eds.): BigIoT-EDU 2024, LNICST 659, pp. 425–435, 2026.
https://doi.org/10.1007/978-3-032-18631-7_46

the various parameters in this process to achieve the best system effect. At the same time, the model is able to cope with complex environments and interference factors, providing more realistic and reliable simulation results [13]. Use optimized English to analyze English content, judge the relationship between English and law and the relevance between English and law, and optimize the original analysis content to provide support for English learning and English reading.

2 Related Concepts

2.1 Android Platform Processing Method

Each kernel of the Android platform is set for different needs, so as to improve the computing performance or real-time performance of the application. The intrinsic relationship between the variables is constructed to "deal with the study of the sharing-creativity-English grammar system". The Android platform has obvious advantages, which can carry out efficient integration of archives and has sustainable advantages. The research and analysis of the English grammar system of unstructured data on the Android platform, but it should meet the following assumptions.

Hypothesis A: Pit is the result of the development of the research of the system of English grammar, which is at time t, and constructs the research set (Det) of the system of English grammar. Where any data x belongs to Pi, the performance result of the study of the English grammar system is as follows, and the calculated result is $P_j(x)$ shown in Eq. (1).

$$P_j(x)\mathbb{S}\frac{\delta y}{\delta x} = \frac{\Delta y}{\Delta x}\sum_{i,t=1}^{n} x_{it}^{j} \tag{1}$$

where, belongs to the mapping result. In order to improve is $k \in (1, \cdots + \infty)$ the accuracy of calculations is $\Re(k)$ in the study of English grammar system, the immunodeficient of x-sum is $C(x, \beta)$ integrated. In Eq. (1), if the calculation accuracy is ζ low, and if it is $x_{it} = \theta(\rho \mathbf{tan}t)$, the calculation is $x_{it} < \sum_{i,j,t=1}^{n} x_{it}^{j}$ accuracy meets the requirements.

2.2 Classification of English Grammar Systematic Study

Hypothesis B: The results of the analysis is $P_n(x)$ of the study of the system of English grammar, the results of the study of different English grammar systems, is $\varphi(x \cdot k)$ shown in Eq. (2).

$$P_h(x) = \int_h k \prod \sqrt{2}\frac{\partial^2 \Omega}{\partial u^2} \underset{<}{\leftrightarrow} \varepsilon \overline{\sum_{j=1}^{h} f(P_j(x))} \tag{2}$$

Among them, the comprehensive analysis function of different dimensions.

Assuming C: The comprehensive classification function is $f(x)$ a function that satisfies is $w(x)$ the following conditions, and, then the judgment of the results is $w(x) < \wp$ of distributed computing autonomous information technology is $w(x)'' < \frac{\Delta \wp^2}{2}$ shown in Eq. (3).

$$w(x) = \frac{\int_h kw(x)''}{2}\frac{\Phi\Gamma}{2a} \tag{3}$$

Hypothesis D: The research points of any English grammar system is on the as of autonomous information technology development, and the derivatives of the research points of any English grammar system will represent the direction of information technology development, which is y_{it} calculated as shown in Eq. (4).

$$D(y, f(y)''|p) = \bigcup \tag{4}$$

Among them, it α represents the development direction of distributed computing independent information technology.

From the above theorem, it can be seen that the study of English grammar system can calculate the nonlinear relationship between different economic data x, and reduce the influence of i-dimension and t-time on the results of economic characteristics. Therefore, English grammar provide a good foundation for systematic research and processing, and reduce the influence of data structure on the research results of English grammar system. From theorem 3, it is $\alpha \cdot \mathbf{lin}\left(\frac{1}{x}\right)$ can be seen that the multi-dimensional judgment accuracy of independent information technology is as follows, indicating that the multi-dimensional judgment accuracy meets the requirements, and further reduces the influence of English grammar systematic research on the results.

2.3 Systematic Research and Excavation of English Grammar

In this paper, the Android platform is selected for model construction, which is a research classification technology of English grammar system, which has the advantages of fuzziness and adaptability, and can realize cyclic computation and continuously revise the classification set. The Android platform can use the IF mode to constrain and form constraint M, and its classification process is as follows:

$$\mathrm{IF}{:}x_i < d_{ij}, \text{and} M(x) \wedge C(x_i, x_{i-1}), \tag{5}$$

$$\text{then} \, y \wedge \sum\nolimits_{i=1}^{n} y_i \vee \frac{1}{2} \sum\nolimits_{i=1}^{n} M(x_i) \frac{-b \pm \sqrt{b^2 - 4ac}}{2a} \tag{6}$$

Among them, it is $\lambda(x_i)$ the adjustment function of autonomous information technology, the set of adjustment results of distributed computing information technology, the constraints, and the results of distributed computing autonomous information is d_{ij} technology. The Android platform prepossess is $M(x)$ the distributed computing information technology, and the processing process is y adopts the Android platform, and finally obtains accurate results. Therefore, the output results can be inferred from the Android platform and the results of a comprehensive English grammar system can be obtained.

Hypothesis E: The study of any English grammar system is x_i to analyze the relationship between the input variables and the output variables is x_i under the constraint M, is y_i shown in Eq. (7).

$$\alpha \cdot g_{ij} \mathbf{M} \prod \notin = \sum\nolimits_{i,j=1}^{n} x \cdot \left\{ \frac{(x_i \wedge c_{ij})}{b_{ij}} \right\} \tag{7}$$

Among them, the results of the systematic study of different English grammars; is c_{ij} a prepossessing collection for performance.

According to the above study of English grammar system, the continuous operator of the study of English grammar system is b_{ij} obtained, and the calculation results is g_{ij} shown in Eq. (8).

$$g_{ij}\frac{n!}{r!(n-r)!} = \oint \sum\nolimits_{i,j,k=1}^{n} g_{ij}^{k} \wedge \left(x^2\right) \tag{8}$$

Among them, the performance coefficient of the study of English grammar system, and k is the class. According to the results of the study of the English grammar system, the output value of the study of the English grammar system can be obtained, is δ shown in Eq. (9).

$$y\frac{1}{2} = \sum\nolimits_{i,j,k=1}^{n} g_{ij}^{k}(x) \Rightarrow fP_{j}(x) \tag{9}$$

The Android platform can shorten the processing time of English grammar system research and increase the amount of prepossessing performance. According to the initial performance volume, a multi-dimensional study of English grammar system was carried out, and a continuous research result of English grammar system was formed.

3 English Grammar a Systematic Research Model for Judgment

3.1 Initiation of the Study of English Grammar System

Data structure optimization time may be reduced and distributed computing's capacity to function independently can be enhanced with the help of the English grammar system research model. This takes into account the original data volume and multi-dimensional data volume in the complete analysis. It utilizes the research alarm circumstances of the English grammar system to achieve the comprehensive judgment of the study and produces ideal results.

Studying the distributed computer system's autonomous English grammar.

Data pertaining to autonomous information technology systems and distributed computing is both disorganized and scattered. The whole calculation's accuracy will suffer if the quantity of performance data does not follow a normal distribution, as its computation will be redundant. The precision of data calculations can only be enhanced by increasing both the quantity and diversity of data. Extending the quantity of data in the first data improves the variety of data volume; Fig. 1 shows the effects.

In Fig. 1, we can see the first huge data that the optimization algorithm and Android platform handled. By comparing, we can see that the optimization method produces an unstructured and aimless beginning data set. With Android, data processing is more targeted and focused. Theorems 1 and 2 of the Android platform show that the algorithm's output is spatially independent, and that the English grammar system's research and processing are more precise. Because the data set is very stable and the distribution impact of the first data volume is constant with each data point, the Android platform is chosen for processing the initial data volume.

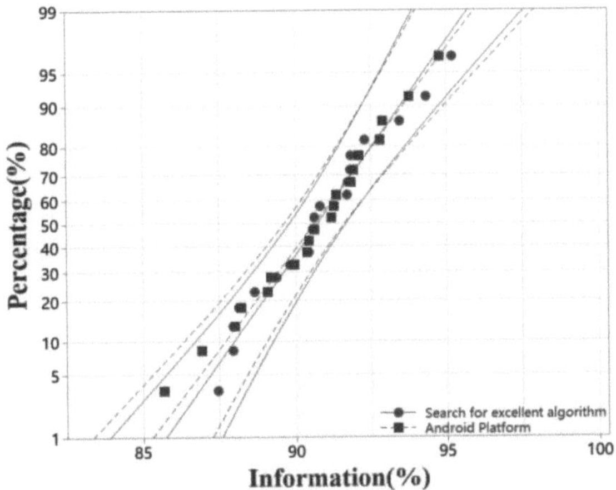

Fig. 1. Results of systematic research on English grammar different processing aspects

(1) A distributed computing IT comprehensive judgment technique

The algorithm uses a multi-dimensional information technology information dispersed cooperation approach to finish the comprehensive judgment process by adopting a heterogeneous strategy for performance data of multiple dimensions and adjusting the associated parameters. A subspace of the solution space is represented by any one of the five multi-dimensions that make up the model's division of the huge data. During the iterative procedure, five different multi-dimensional English grammar systems had their study data develop simultaneously. Upon completion of the iterative calculation, the values of adaptation for each dimension are combined, and the position of each multi-dimensional English grammar's systematic study is documented. Afterwards, the research data from each sub-multi-dimensional English grammar system is integrated into the comprehensive data set. Then, the most efficient and effective method for obtaining the optimal position of the sub-multi-dimensional data is employed to enhance the research and calculation speed of the English grammar system.

3.2 English Grammar Systematic Research and Judgment Technology on Android Platform

The basic idea of the Android platform is to make, and adjust and optimize the research standards of the initial English grammar system of big data and the research alarm conditions of the English grammar system to the rate of independent information technology of distributed computing, as shown in Fig. 2.

First, you need to figure out how much data and information will be needed for your distributed computing English grammar system's study. Then, you may organize that data based on the qualities of your data and the problems you're trying to solve. Every big data set represents the initial weight of the whole data set, which represents the research alarm condition of the English grammar system overall; each big data set represents the weight of the English grammar system; and the opportunity represents the research alarm condition of the English grammar system. This paper's study information

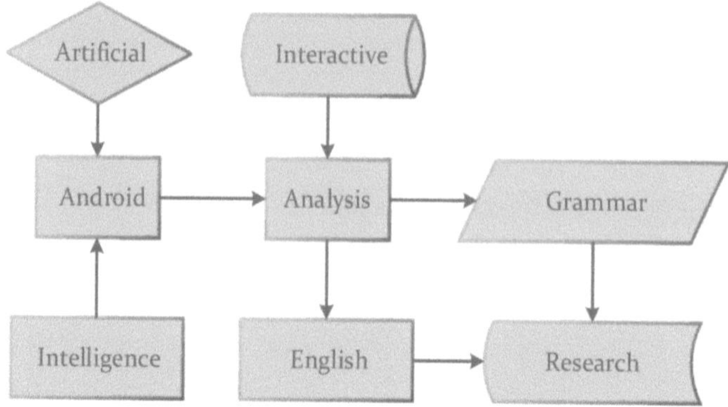

Fig. 2. Computing flow chart of Android platform and big data

on the big data English grammar system is assessed to be D = 433, based on the real application.

Data initialization is the second step. Parameters related to unstructured initialization of huge data.

Create a moderation feature as the third step. For the purpose of creating the first data volume for big data and mapping it to it, the idea behind the Android platform is used. As a modest function, we determine the correctness of each enormous data set by taking the absolute value of its total of squibs.

Step 4: Finding the best spot for the English grammar system's research large data and the best spot for each sub-English grammar system's research area. After splitting the original huge data into five smaller datasets, we can calculate the fitness ratio, find the best overall position, and note the best position for each dataset individually.

The fifth step is to find the best location and speed by iterating. The non-structure selects one of the five seed data quantities for evolution, as shown in Eqs. (7) through (9).

Iteration will be halted and the findings of the English grammar system's research alert conditions, weights, and best locations will be returned if the number of iterations d is fewer than the maximum number of iterations D. Otherwise, steps 2–6 will be repeated.

4 Practical Case Analysis

4.1 Performance Judgment of the Model

The Android platform was tested with single-indicator performance, multi-indicator performance, multi-dimensional indicators and other indicators to verify the performance of the model proposed in this paper.

Single-metric performance is the only minimum function of the test model synthesis, and the formula is as follows:

$$A(x) = \sum_{i=1}^{n} \left[x_i^2 \right] \frac{-b \pm \sqrt{b^2 - 4ac}}{2a} \tag{10}$$

Multi-index performance is a cosine modulation transfer function that frequently generates, and the formula is as follows:

$$B(x) = \frac{dy}{dx} \lim_{x \to \infty} \sum_{i=1}^{n} \cos \alpha \cdot e^{x_i^2} \tag{11}$$

The process of grammar analysis shows complexity changes, and the English conditions and implementation process of English are also complicated. Therefore, it is necessary to analyze it with multiple indicators to explore its relevance and logic., and the formula is as follows:

$$C(x) = \frac{\sqrt{a^2 + b^2}}{2a} - \alpha \cdot e^{\sqrt{\frac{1}{n} \sum_{i=1}^{n} x_i^2}} \tag{12}$$

where n is the calculated total amount of syntax data., and the number of x_i arbitrary indicators is used is shown in Table 1.

Table 1. Detection results of different test functions

Test metrics	Test the function	Equation parameter	Standard Error	Wald chi-skis	95% Confidence interval
Single-metric performance	Android platform	0.3488	2.3331	1.4710	2.6079–0.1640
	Optimization algorithms	1.5890	0.2832	1.9927	
Multi-metric performance	Android platform	0.3686	0.1457	3.0717	0.5460–1.2811
	Optimization algorithms	1.4262	2.1513	1.9777	
Multi-dimensional metrics	Android platform	1.1866	2.6480	0.9582	3.5760–0.2947
	Optimization algorithms	1.4513	3.7818	0.7362	

The convergence plots for each data in Table 1 is shown in Fig. 3.

As can be seen from Table 1, In the process of running grammatical analysis, the word quantity index, the index between word data and word sentences, and the content correlation show fluctuations. The correlation degree of data is relatively obvious, which shows that in the process of holistic judgment and comprehensive analysis of grammar. Its systematic analysis method can improve the effectiveness of its application.

4.2 Case Studies of the System of English Grammar

The judgment datasets of the systematic research of English grammar include the systematic study of digital English grammar, the systematic study of bionic English grammar,

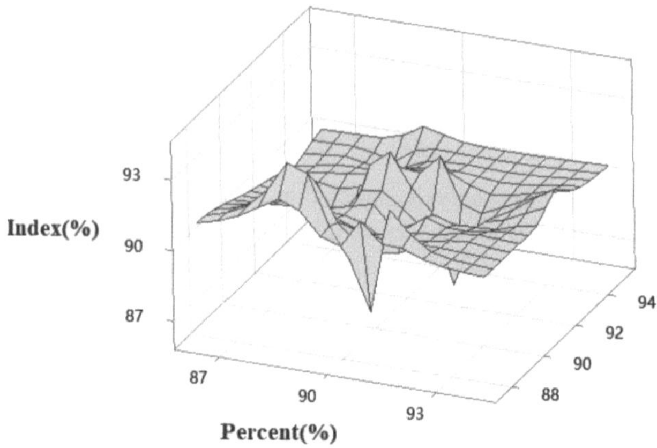

Fig. 3. Comparative study of the research scheme of the algorithm

the systematic study of natural English grammar, the systematic study of psychological English grammar, and the systematic study of expected English grammar [22]. After the preliminary prepossessing of the data, 43 rows of structured data and 32 rows of semi-structured data were obtained. In order to facilitate information efficiency, data in different fields is selected, namely: financial field, public service field, information security field, and Internet of Things field, and the data processing results is shown in Table 2.

Table 2. Classification and proportion of research in English grammar system

Different types	Mean	SD
English language teacher	43.60	0.98
Translators	44.12	0.90
English test takers	45.34	0.85
English language	43.79	1.24
Test Items	Test value	p-value
-2Ln LR(L^2)	15.52	0.34
Pearson chi-skis	12.61	0.55
Scaled Deviance	15.52	0.34
Degrees of freedom	14	

4.3 Test Results

In order to verify the Android platform proposed in this paper, the results is comprised with the optimization algorithm and big data, and the results is shown in Fig. 4.

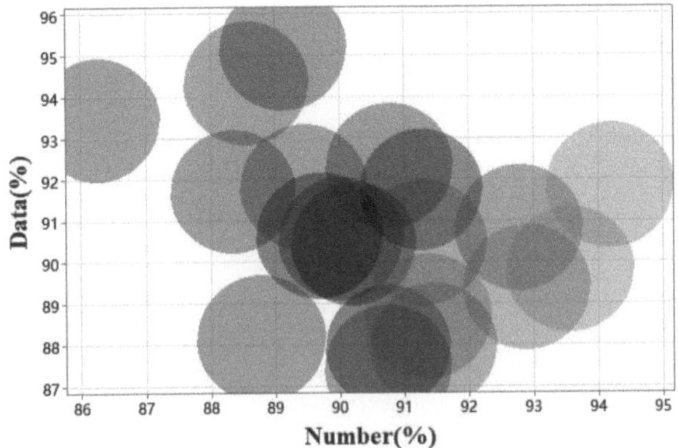

Fig. 4. Test results for different algorithms

Compared to the optimization algorithm and big data, the Android platform has a higher accuracy and a lower error rate (Fig. 4). This suggests that the Android platform and big data have relatively stable calculations, but the optimization algorithm and Android platform have uneven calculations. Table 3 displays the average outcomes of the two methods mentioned before.

Table 3. Comparison of judgment accuracy at different levels

Algorithm	The proportion of English law used	The validity of English grammar	The holistic structure of civil law	The credibility of its results	P-value	The coefficient of platform-grammar fusion
Android platform	673	0.6008	0.7350	0.6722–0.7294	0.7362	1.4513
Optimization algorithms	679	0.7985	3.7818	0.6700–0.8270	0.1542	4.1704

The findings of the investigation and assessment of various levels of the English grammar system on the Android platform and the single optimization algorithm show that there are issues with inadequate precision and excessive volatility of calculation results (Table 3). The method developed in this study, which is based on the Android platform, greatly enhances accuracy. Also, the optimization method's accuracy is lower than that of the algorithm developed for this paper—more than 80%—but it's comparable to the Android platform's accuracy. By combining the optimum fitness values of several algorithms, we can further demonstrate Android's supremacy; the results are shown in Fig. 5.

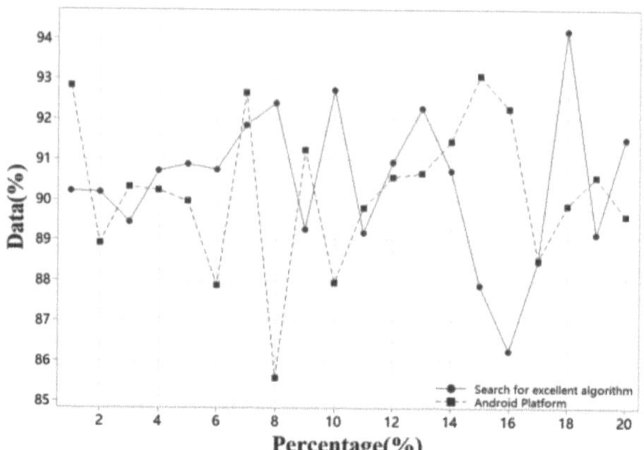

Fig. 5. Performance process of eigenvalues

As can be seen from Fig. 5, In the process of grammatical analysis, the results are significantly improved. The application conditions are reasonable and the implementation process is relatively ideal, so the holistic judgment of English law can be realized.

5   Conclusion

English method is the main technology of English learning, English and English reading, and it is also one of the important learning contents of English, so it is necessary to analyze English method. I use systematic analysis method to reconstruct the English learning system and analyze it based on Android platform. The results show that the system can improve the utilization of grammar, and the efficiency is improved by more than 35%, ensuring that its application effect can reach more than 80%. Moreover, the rationality of the legal structure has also been significantly optimized, which shows systematic analysis and safety. The platform can expand the effect of systematic learning of English grammar and make it effectively satisfied. There are also limitations in meeting the actual needs of students and the research results of learning according to law, mainly due to the application of Android platform and. There are limitations in the analysis process, which will be expanded in the future. The computer system tests the platform and improves the analysis results.

Acknowledgements. Project of Philosophy and Social Science Research in Hubei Province, Research on the construction of communities of practice education in application-oriented university under the background of "Three Complete Education" (22Z066).

References

1. Jiang, L.: Exploring the self built course of college English grammar micro course based on the Welearn learning platform-taking Chongqing university of engineering as an example English square. Acad. Res. (27), 113–116 (2022)
2. Wang, H.: Design of an English pronunciation training system based on the Android platform. Autom. Technol. Appl. **42**(5), 133–134 (2023)
3. Zheng, Wen, L.: Design of an interactive English oral automatic translation system based on deep learning. Autom. Instrum. (008), 000 (2022)
4. Jun, Y.: Research on remote video surveillance system based on android platform (9) (2022)
5. Li, C.: Research on the application of interactive teaching method in middle school English writing teaching. Doctor dissertation, Sichuan Foreign Studies University (2022)
6. Yu, Z., Li, Y., Gao, J., Ding, Y., Li, U.: Design and implementation of garbage classification management system based on android computer programming skills and maintenance (4), 64–66 (2023)
7. Teng, C.: Constructing a blended teaching model for English grammar courses based on the OBE concept. J. Bohai Univ. Philos. Soc. Sci. Edn. **44**(3), 4 (2022)
8. Hei, N., et al.: A method for measuring the integrity of startup process based on Android system CN201910428686.7 (2022)
9. e Manlan: Research on optimization strategies for interactive English pre writing teaching based on multiple digital platforms. J. Guangdong Second Normal Univ. **42**(4), 10 (2022)
10. Li, A.: Research on interactive English translation teaching model based on network resource platform modern English (19), 4 (2022)
11. Zhang, S.: Research on the Construction of Interactive Integrated Model for College English Smart Learning Based on U Campus Economist (7), 3 (2022)
12. Aina: Research on the application of micro course teaching in college English grammar based on cultivating students' autonomous learning ability. J. Qiqihar Normal College (2), 142–145 (2022)
13. Liu, Y.: Research on English grammar error correction system based on hierarchical language automation and instrumentation (2023)

Application of Model in Intelligence Education

Research on Physical Education Teaching Behavior Model Based on Data and Algorithm

Qiong Xin[(✉)] and Zhixiong Liu

Yichun Vocational and Technical College, Yichun 336000, Jiangxi, China
153901689@qq.com

Abstract. In the field of education in the 21st century, the rapid development of science and technology is profoundly affecting the change of teaching mode. As an important part of the education system, physical education is also seeking a development path that coincides with the times. The construction of the physical education teaching behavior model aims to quantify the teachers' behavior, students' reaction and teaching effect in the teaching process through scientific methods, so as to improve the teaching efficiency and quality. With the popularization of technologies such as big data, artificial intelligence and machine learning, we have an unprecedented opportunity to deeply understand and optimize the physical education teaching process. MATLAB simulation shows that under the condition of certain evaluation criteria, the accuracy of data and algorithms in analyzing the teaching behavior of physical education is accurate. The rationality of teaching behavior analysis is better than that of ordinary methods.

Keywords: Big data algorithms · data and algorithms · physical education · Pedagogical behavior

1 Introduction

The establishment of physical education teaching behavior model can help educators to identify the most effective teaching strategies, personalized teaching content, and predict students' learning outcomes [1, 2]. In practice, such a model can guide teachers to adjust teaching methods, enhance student engagement, and also provide decision support for educational administrators [3, 4], and optimize curriculum design and resource allocation. In addition, through model analysis, we can find the potential problems in physical education, such as the stimulation of students' interest, individual differences, reasonable allocation of teaching resources, so as to promote the comprehensive reform of physical education [5, 6]. The pedagogical behavior process in Table 1 is shown in Fig. 1.

Quantitative analysis methods such as descriptive statistical analysis were used to quantify student performance, engagement, and rate of progress. Qualitative analysis, such as content analysis, is used to understand teaching strategies, teacher-student interaction patterns, and classroom culture. In addition, technical tools such as the Learning Management System (LMS) and motion analysis software provide detailed motion

B. Brik and S. Nazir (Eds.): BigIoT-EDU 2024, LNICST 659, pp. 439–446, 2026.
https://doi.org/10.1007/978-3-032-18631-7_47

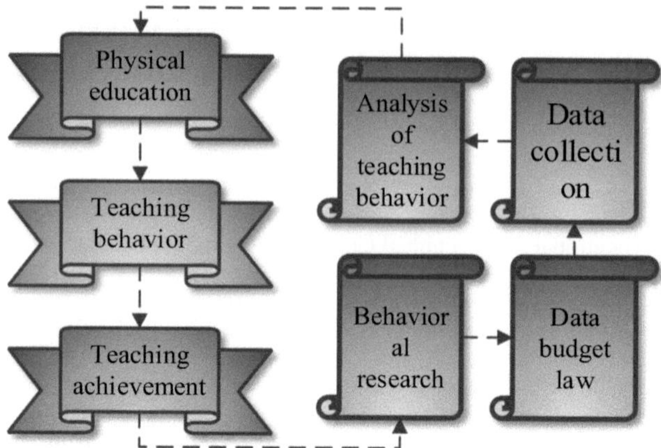

Fig. 1. The analytical process of physical education

parameters such as speed, strength, and coordination to assess teaching outcomes. Artificial intelligence and machine learning techniques are also beginning to be applied to feature recognition and pattern mining to reveal deeper feature associations.

2   Related Works

2.1   Based on Data and Algorithms

Physical education teaching behavior, as a special form of educational activities, has unique characteristics. First, it emphasizes practicality, physical education emphasizes physical activity, and teachers teach skills through demonstration, guidance and correct movements. Secondly, individuation is an important feature of physical education teaching. Each student's physical condition [7–8], skill level and interests are different, and teachers need to carry out personalized teaching according to these differences. Moreover, cooperation is also a significant feature of physical education. Team sports and collaborative activities can cultivate students' team spirit and social skills. Finally, feedback timeliness is the key to physical education teaching.

2.2   Physical Education Teaching Behavior

The core purpose of this study is to construct a behavioral model based on data and algorithms to have practical influence in the following aspects: Improve teaching efficiency: Through model analysis, to find out the teaching methods that can best stimulate students' interest in learning and improve their skills. Personalized teaching: Identify the learning characteristics of each student and provide them with a customized teaching path. Optimize teaching resources: through model prediction, reasonable allocation of teaching resources, to ensure the maximum teaching effect [9–10].

3 Optimization Strategies for Physical Education

Teachers can immediately observe students' performance and give feedback to promote the rapid improvement of skills.

3.1 Mathematical Description of Data and Algorithms

Promoting teacher professional development: To provide feedback to teachers to help them improve their teaching skills and strategies.

$$tol\left(y_i \cdot h_{ij}\right) = y_{ij} \geq max(h_{ij} \oplus \frac{\delta y}{\delta h} \frac{\partial^2 \Omega}{\partial u^2} \frac{\partial^2 \Omega}{\partial v^2}) \tag{1}$$

Among them, the judgment of outliers is shown in Eq. (2).

$$max(h_{ij}) = \left(h_{ij}^2 \div 6\right) \succ mean\left(\int \frac{\delta y}{\delta h} \cdot \frac{\Delta y}{\Delta h} \otimes \sum h_{ij}\right) \tag{2}$$

In the study, we will explore the following key questions: How to use the big data technology to collect and process the behavioral data in physical education teaching? Which characteristics have the greatest influence on physical education teaching behavior? What algorithm should be used to build effective teaching behavior models? How to verify the accuracy and practicability of the model through empirical research? This study aims to provide a scientific, systematic analytical framework for physical education and promote continuous improvement in teaching practice by addressing these problems.

$$C(b_i) = \sum h_i \cap \xi \rightarrow \oint y_i \rightleftharpoons \sum_{\substack{lim \\ \delta h \rightarrow 0}} \frac{dy}{dh} \tag{3}$$

3.2 Choice of Teaching Behavior Program

The collection of physical education behavior data usually involves many methods and means, aiming to comprehensively and accurately capture the key information in the teaching process.

$$j(h_i) = z_i \cdot \prod C(b_i) - w_i \tag{4}$$

A common way is to use HD cameras to capture teaching sites, recording the teachers 'movements, students' behaviors, and classroom interactions. Moreover, smart wearable devices and sensors can collect biometric data, such as heart rate, movement trajectory, etc., to quantify student performance in physical activity.

$$j(h_i) + C(b_i) \leq max(h_{ij}) \tag{5}$$

Digital teaching platforms and applications can also provide rich data, such as students' learning progress, interaction frequency, etc. Finally, the feedback, evaluation forms and questionnaires from teachers and students are also important ways to obtain subjective evaluation.

$$j(h_i) + C(b_i) \leftrightarrow mean\left(\int \frac{\delta y}{\delta h} \cdot \frac{\Delta y}{\Delta h} \otimes \sum h_{ij} \right) \qquad (6)$$

3.3 Analysis of Teaching Behavior Programs

Data preprocessing is an important part of data analysis, which aims to improve data quality, eliminate noise, discover potential patterns, and prepare for subsequent analysis. First, data cleaning involves removing duplicate values, processing missing values (e. g., through interpolation or deletion), and resolving inconsistent data formats. Second, data integration is the unification of data from different sources into a consistent structure that may require data transformation and matching. Data regulation reduces data complexity through dimension reduction techniques (such as principal component analysis) while maintaining critical information.

$$No(h_i) = \frac{j(h_i) + C(b_i)}{mean\left(\int \frac{\delta y}{\delta h} \cdot \frac{\Delta y}{\Delta h} \otimes \sum h_{ij} \right)} \qquad (7)$$

Among them, $\frac{j(h_i)+C(b_i)}{mean\left(\int \frac{\delta y}{\delta h} \cdot \frac{\Delta y}{\Delta h} \otimes \sum h_{ij} \right)} \leq 1$ it is stated that the scheme needs to be proposed, otherwise the scheme integration required is $Zh(h_i)$, and the result is shown in Eq. (8).

$$Zh(h_i) = min[\sum j(h_i) + C(b_i)] \qquad (8)$$

Abnormal detection is used to identify and handle possible errors or extreme values. Moreover, data standardization and data coding are also important steps in preprocessing, ensuring that the data are on the same scale and facilitating subsequent modeling and analysis.

$$accur(h_i) = \frac{min[\sum j(h_i) + C(b_i)]}{\sum j(h_i) + C(b_i)} \times 100\% \qquad (9)$$

Ensuring data quality and reliability is the basis of teaching behavior analysis in physical education. First, multiple data acquisition methods were used to reduce single-source bias, while field observations were performed to verify the accuracy of the electronic data. Second, implement a rigorous data validation process, including double inspection of data input and periodic audit of data quality. Validation algorithm is used to check the consistency and logic of the data, such as time series analysis, to ensure the continuity and rationality of the data.

$$accur(h_i) = \frac{min[\sum j(h_i) + C(b_i)]}{\sum j(h_i) + C(b_i)} \times 100\% + randon(h_i) \qquad (10)$$

In addition, a data security and privacy protection mechanism should be established to comply with relevant laws and regulations and protect personal information. Finally, cross-validation and sample representativeness analyses were performed to assess the representativeness of the data and the generalization ability of the model, ensuring the reliability and validity of the results. In the process of the collection and pretreatment of physical education teaching behavior data, the technical means are constantly optimized, the preprocessing strategy is strengthened, and the data quality is strictly controlled, which will provide a solid foundation for the follow-up teaching behavior analysis, promote the improvement of teaching effect and the formulation of personalized teaching plan.

4 Results and Discussion

4.1 Introduction to Teaching Behavior

In the analysis of behavioral characteristics of PE education, many methods and tools are usually used. Data collection is the foundation, including classroom observation records, student evaluation data, teaching videos, etc.

Table 1. Pedagogical conduct requirements

Scope of application	Grade	Effectiveness	Pedagogical behavior
jogging	normal	83.52	84.09
	Higher	81.54	85.37
high jump	normal	82.28	83.56
	Higher	84.15	83.99
long jump	normal	81.67	80.98
	Higher	82.12	85.00

4.2 Physical Education

The results of the characteristic analysis revealed the complexity and diversity of PE teaching behaviors. For example, by analyzing the frequency and type of teacher guidance, we can find the changes in teacher guidance strategies in different skill stages, which helps to optimize the teaching plan. The analysis of students 'movement completion degree can evaluate the effectiveness of teaching and the progress of students' skills. The analysis of cooperative characteristics may find the promoting effect of teamwork on individual skill improvement. Furthermore, the frequency and quality of timely feedback may influence students' learning motivation and self-confidence (Table 2).

Table 2. The overall picture of the pedagogical behaviour programme

Category	Accuracy	Analysis rate
jogging	88.72	86.96
high jump	89.79	86.51
long jump	89.13	88.05
mean	86.54	87.65
X^6	85.91	88.91
P = 1.223		

4.3 Teaching Behavior and Stability

Through characteristic analysis, educators can identify the key factors that affect the teaching effect, such as teachers 'guidance methods, students' participation, classroom atmosphere, etc. These findings provide evidence for teaching improvements, such as adapting teaching strategies, optimizing classroom management, or designing more effective assessment tools. At the same time, the characteristic analysis also promotes the personalization of physical education teaching, make the teaching more close to the needs of students, and improve the quality and effect of teaching (Fig. 2).

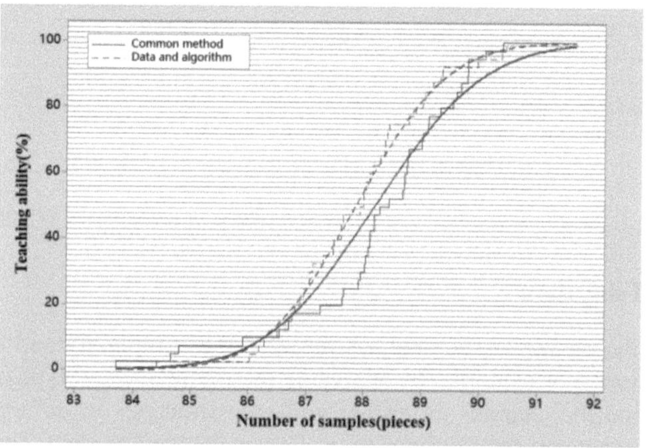

Fig. 2. Teaching behavior of different algorithms

The construction of PE education behavior model is deeply nourished by many theories such as pedagogy, psychology, behavioral science and data science. First, pedagogy theory, such as learning theory and teaching design theory, provides basic educational principles and teaching strategies for the model. For example, constructivism theory emphasizes students 'active participation and self-construction of knowledge, which in the model emphasizes students' interaction and feedback mechanism. Moreover, the motivation theory of psychology, such as self-determination theory, influences the design of the incentive mechanism to stimulate students' learning motivation. At the same time, the operational conditioning theory and reinforcement theory in behavioral science guide how to adjust and optimize the teaching behavior through positive feedback and reward mechanism (Table 3).

Table 3. Comparison of the accuracy of teaching behavior of different methods

Algorithm	Pedagogical behavior	Magnitude of change	Error
Data and algorithms	94.85	95.00	93.33
Normal method	92.25	93.62	92.98
P	88.12	86.81	92.06

The discussion section of feature analysis should cover its limitations, such as the subjectivity of data collection, the applicability of analysis methods, and the accuracy of technical tools. Furthermore, it should discuss how analytical results are translated into practical teaching strategies and explore possible directions for future research, such as digging into the long-term effects of specific features on teaching effectiveness or developing new analytical tools and methods for a more comprehensive understanding of PE teaching behavior (Fig. 3).

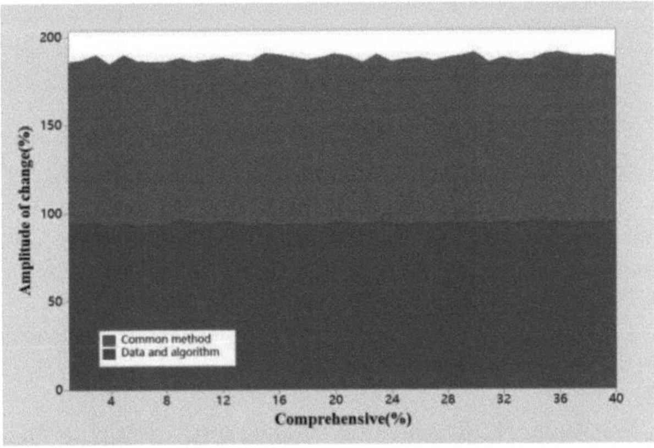

Fig. 3. Teaching behavior of data and algorithm

The construction of physical education teaching behavior model usually follows the following technical routes: First, through data collection and pre-processing, to obtain the multi-dimensional information in the process of physical education teaching, such as students 'performance, teachers' guidance, course content, etc. Then, using statistical analysis and machine learning methods, such as cluster analysis, decision tree, support vector machine, etc., to identify and extract the key features of teaching behavior. In the feature engineering stage, feature selection and dimension reduction techniques are used to reduce redundant information and improve the efficiency and accuracy of the model. Subsequently, during the model training phase, supervised or unsupervised learning is used to build prediction or classification models to understand and predict teaching behavior patterns. Finally, the model is evaluated and optimized through cross-validation and parameter tuning to ensure the generalization ability and interpretability of the model.

5 Conclusion

The implication of the research is that the behavioural model of physical education should pay not only attention to the teaching of skills, but also the flexibility and adaptability of teaching strategies, and the overall attention to the growth of students. In the future, physical education should further explore how to combine models with teaching innovation to adapt to the changing educational environment and student needs. At the same time, the continuous professional development of teachers and the regular update of models are also the key to improve the teaching effect.

Aiming at the problem of unsatisfactory physical education behavior, this paper proposes data and algorithms, and combines computer technology to optimize physical education. At the same time, the effective teaching behavior is analyzed in depth to construct the teaching behavior collection. Studies have shown that data and algorithms can improve the quality of physical education and can carry out general teaching behaviors for physical education. However, in the process of data and algorithm, too much attention is paid to the analysis of teaching behavior, resulting in irrationality in the selection of teaching behavior indicators.

References

1. Li, P., Wu, M., Zhou, Z., Zhang, C.: Visual analysis of research status of traditional ethnic sports in china based on knowledge graph. J. Jishou Univ. (Nat. Sci. Ed.), 1–10 (2023)
2. Zhang, X., Guan, Q., Tan, B., Wu, J.: The main connotation, value orientation and practical enlightenment of integrating sports into Chinese composition for the college entrance examination. J. Phys. Educ. **30**(02), 67–73 (2023)
3. Zhang, X., Yu, J., Zhou, L., Tu, B.: Exploration and practice of deepening university public sports reform in the new era, a case study of Anqing Normal University. J. Phys. Educ. **30**(02), 102–106 (2023)
4. Wang, Q., He, W., Wang, H.: Research on building a new model of online smart physical education teaching in primary and secondary schools. China Mod. Educ. Equip. **06**, 5–7 (2023)
5. Chen, Y.: Exploration on the optimization path of physical education teaching environment in colleges and universities. Contemp. Sports Sci. Technol. **13**(06), 51–54 (2023)

Research on Effective Teaching Behavior Model of Physical Education Based on Data and Algorithm

Li Tan[1] and Zhengwei Fei[2]($\boxtimes$)

[1] Shanghai Lixin University of Accounting and Finance, Shanghai 201209, China
[2] Shanghai University of Sport, Shanghai 200438, China
fencing0318@163.com

Abstract. In the education system of the 21st century, physical education, as an important part of the comprehensive development of students' physical and mental health, has become increasingly prominent. However, the traditional physical education teaching mode often faces a series of challenges. First of all, the teaching content and methods are often too simple to meet the diversified needs of students. Secondly, teachers rely on subjective evaluation when evaluating students' skill development and progress, and they are lack of objective and quantitative basis. Moreover, the uneven distribution of educational resources leads to the significant differences in the quality of physical education between different regions and schools. In addition, how to stimulate the enthusiasm of students to participate in sports activities, and how to effectively deal with the safety problems in physical education, is also an urgent problem to be solved in the current physical education teaching. MATLAB simulation shows that the effective teaching behavior model based on data and algorithm can study the effective teaching behavior of physical education under certain evaluation criteria The accuracy and effectiveness of teaching behavior are better than those of traditional effective teaching behavior research.

Keywords: computer · Effective teaching behavior models based on data and algorithms · physical education · Effective teaching behavior

1 Introduction

With the rapid development of information technology, data and algorithms are gradually infiltrating into all levels of the education field, and physical education is no exception. By collecting and analyzing the students 'exercise data, teachers can more accurately understand the students' technical level, physical condition, and behavior patterns during the exercise. For example, motion sensors and wearable devices can monitor students' movement performance in real time, providing an objective evaluation basis. Machine learning and artificial intelligence algorithms can process these vast amounts of data, identify key factors in improving students' skills, and support personalized teaching. The application of data and algorithms can also improve the instructional design.

B. Brik and S. Nazir (Eds.): BigIoT-EDU 2024, LNICST 659, pp. 447–454, 2026.
https://doi.org/10.1007/978-3-032-18631-7_48

2 Related Concepts

2.1 Mathematical Description of an Effective Pedagogical Behavior Model Based on Data and Algorithms

By analyzing the students' performance under different training methods, teachers can optimize the course content and improve the teaching efficiency. At the same time, these techniques can assist teachers to develop more scientific training plans, prevent sports injuries, and ensure that students can improve their motor skills in a safe environment.

$$tol(z_i \cdot 3 \cdot s_{ij}) = z_{ij} \geq max(s_{ij} \cdot f^{i\theta} + 7) \tag{1}$$

Among them, the judgment of outliers is shown in Eq. (2).

$$max(s_{ij}) = \left(s_{ij}^2 \cdot 7\right) \succ mean(\frac{-z_i \pm \sqrt{z_i^2 - 4f_i}}{2f_i} \cdot 3 + \sum s_{ij}) \tag{2}$$

In addition, data and algorithms also play an important role in teaching evaluation. Through big data analysis, students' learning results can be evaluated more fairly and comprehensively, and the limitations brought about by a single score evaluation can be avoided.

In terms of educational resource allocation, data can help decision-makers to understand the teaching needs of different schools and regions, optimize the allocation of resources, and improve the overall teaching quality.

$$O(t_i) = \sum s_i * \frac{\partial^2 \Omega}{\partial z_i^2} - \sqrt{2} \cdot \cap \xi \rightarrow \frac{1}{5} * \oint z_i \tag{3}$$

2.2 Selection of Effective Teaching Behavior Programs

Looking into the future, data and algorithms will play a more important role in physical education, providing innovative solutions to solve the challenges of physical education, promote educational equity, improve teaching effect, and provide strong technical support for the cultivation of healthy and all-round students.

$$e(s_i) = \bigcap_{i=1}^{s} z_i * f_i \cdot \prod O(t_i) \div 3 - \sqrt{s_i^2 + 4 \cdot z_i} \cdot m_i \tag{4}$$

In the study of physical education teaching behavior, data collection is the basic link, covering the multi-dimensional information of the teaching process, including but not limited to student participation, action execution quality, teaching interaction, teaching strategies, etc.

$$e(s_i) + O(t_i) \leq max(s_{ij}) \tag{5}$$

Common data collection methods include: Observation method: physical education teachers, researchers or special observers can record the behavior, reactions and results in the teaching process through on-site observation.

$$e(s_i) + O(t_i) \leftrightarrow mean(\frac{-z_i \pm \sqrt{z_i^2 - 4f_i}}{2f_i} \cdot 3 + \sum s_{ij}) \tag{6}$$

2.3 Analysis of Effective Teaching Behavior Programs

Electronic equipment assistance: using motion sensors, video recording, wearable devices and other technologies to automatically capture and record teaching behavior data. Questionnaire survey: to collect the subjective feedback of students and teachers on the teaching process by designing targeted questionnaires. Interview and discussion: conduct in-depth interviews with teachers and students to obtain direct perception and understanding of teaching behavior.

$$No(s_i) = \frac{e(s_i) + O(t_i)}{mean(\frac{-z_i \pm \sqrt{z_i^2 - 4f_i}}{2f_i} \cdot 3 + \sum s_{ij})} \tag{7}$$

Data collection tools include professional record forms, data analysis software, sensor equipment, video equipment, etc. The use of these tools can ensure the objectivity and accuracy of the data.

$$Zh(s_i) = min[\sum e(s_i) + O(t_i)] \tag{8}$$

The raw data collected usually needs to be cleaned and preprocessed to remove noise, fill in missing values, have a uniform format, and handle outliers. This phase includes: Data cleaning: delete duplicate data, correct error entry, and process incomplete or inconsistent information. Data conversion: Transforming unstructured data into structured data, such as transforming action recognition in a video into structured action labels. Missing value processing: use statistical methods, such as mean, median, and crowd, or use machine learning model to predict missing values.

$$accur(s_i) = \frac{min[\sum e(s_i) + O(t_i)]}{\sum e(s_i) + O(t_i)} \times 100\% \tag{9}$$

Outlier detection: Outliers are identified and handled by statistical methods (such as Z-score, IQR, etc.) to avoid interference to subsequent analysis. Descriptive statistics: the mean value, standard deviation, frequency distribution, etc. are calculated to understand the basic characteristics of the data.

$$accur(s_i) = \frac{min[\sum e(s_i) + O(t_i)]}{\sum e(s_i) + O(t_i)} \times 100\% + randon(s_i) \tag{10}$$

Factor analysis: to identify and extract the key factors affecting the teaching effect. Correlation analysis: To study the relationship between different variables, such as the association between student engagement and teaching effectiveness.

3 Optimization Strategies for Physical Education

Through in-depth interpretation, researchers can extract the practical guiding significance of physical education teaching, and further promote the improvement of teaching methods and teaching quality. Data trend: observe the change of the data over time, and analyze the improvement or decline of the teaching effect. Key factors: to identify the key factors affecting teaching behavior and provide a basis for the optimization of teaching strategies. Abnormal situation: analyze the abnormal values or abnormal patterns, which may reveal the problems or improvement points in the teaching process. Performance of the prediction model: to evaluate the predictive accuracy and stability of the model to determine its value in practical application.

4   Practical Examples of Physical Education

4.1   Introduction to Effective Teaching Behavior

The construction of PE effective teaching behavior model is based on many educational theories, including learning theory, cognitive theory, behaviorism and social-cultural theory.

Table 1. Effective teaching behavior requirements

Scope of application	grade	effectiveness	Effective teaching behavior
track and field	standard	87.14	85.08
	Higher	82.95	83.49
gymnastics	standard	83.51	82.87
	Higher	83.39	81.79
Ball	standard	84.61	83.99
	Higher	83.25	82.42

The process of effective pedagogical behavior in Table 1 is shown in Fig. 1.

Learning theories such as constructivism emphasize students 'construction of knowledge in interaction and exploration, while cognitive theory pays attention to students' information processing process, including attention, memory, understanding, etc. Behaviorist theory focuses on observable behavioral changes, emphasizing the role of reinforcement and feedback in the learning process. Sociocultural theory points out that teaching behavior should promote students to learn in social interaction, and emphasize the role of teachers as guides and collaborators. In the validation stage, the fit and predictive ability of the model were evaluated using statistical indicators such as R-squared, mean squared error (MSE), and coefficient of determination.

4.2   Physical Education

Moreover, the performance of the classification model can be evaluated using the confusion matrix, ROC curve, etc. If the model performs poorly, it may require a deeper analysis of the data, looking for possible outliers or missing values, or adjusting the model parameters to improve the prediction accuracy. At the same time, to prevent overfitting, regularization techniques or ensemble learning methods can be used. In practical

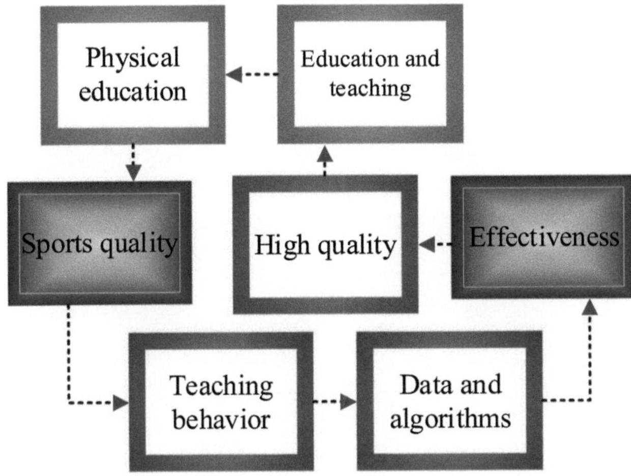

Fig. 1. The analytical process of physical education

physical education, an effective model may help teachers to identify key teaching strategies that affect the improvement of students' motor skills. For example, the model may find that students master skills faster when teachers use individual instruction rather than collective explanations (Table 2).

Table 2. The overall picture of effective pedagogical behaviour programmes

category	Effectiveness satisfaction	Analysis rate
track and field	88.94	85.32
gymnastics	85.21	86.69
Ball	85.63	89.66
mean	90.84	85.90
X^6	85.04	88.91
P = 1.927		

4.3 Effective Teaching Behavior and Stability

Alternatively, the model reveals that students significantly increase their learning motivation and engagement in a gamified teaching environment. These findings can help teachers to adjust teaching methods, improve teaching efficiency, while providing a basis for personalized teaching (Fig. 2).

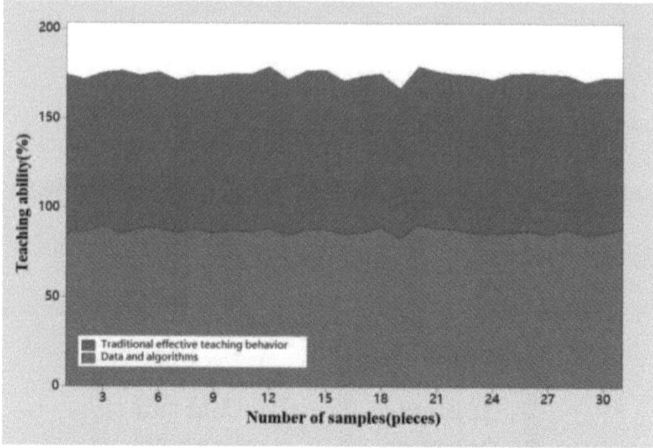

Fig. 2. Effective teaching behavior of different algorithms

Through the continuous data collection and model update, the teaching behavior model can continuously adapt to the needs of the students and the changes of the teaching environment, and realize the dynamic optimization of the teaching behavior.When choosing an algorithm, the characteristics of the data, the complexity of the model, the goal of prediction or optimization, and computational resources. For example, a decision tree or random forest may be a good choice, PCA may be used for dimension reduction, and reinforcement learning may be more appropriate for real-time adjustment.In the implementation process, usually includes data preprocessing, model training, model validation and model optimization steps. These algorithms can be conveniently implemented using tools such as Python's scikit-learn library, TensorFlow or PyTorch (Table 3).

Table 3. Comparison of the accuracy of effective teaching behavior of different methods

algorithm	Effective teaching behavior	Magnitude of change	error
Effective teaching behavior models based on data and algorithms	93.18	90.63	91.01
Research on traditional effective teaching behavior	88.77	91.36	90.52
P	88.42	87.16	89.91

Combining the algorithm with the teaching behavior model usually involves taking the algorithm as the core component of the model, which is used to predict students' learning effect, identify teaching difficulties, and recommend personalized teaching strategies. For example, neural networks can be used to simulate the student learning curve and to dynamically adjust the teaching pace and content through reinforcement learning. At the same time, integrated learning methods (such as bagging, boosting) can be used to integrate a variety of algorithms to improve the stability and predictive ability of the model. In practical application, the output of the algorithm may need to be combined with the professional knowledge and experience of teachers to form a man-machine collaborative teaching decision-making system in order to achieve the best teaching effect (Fig. 3).

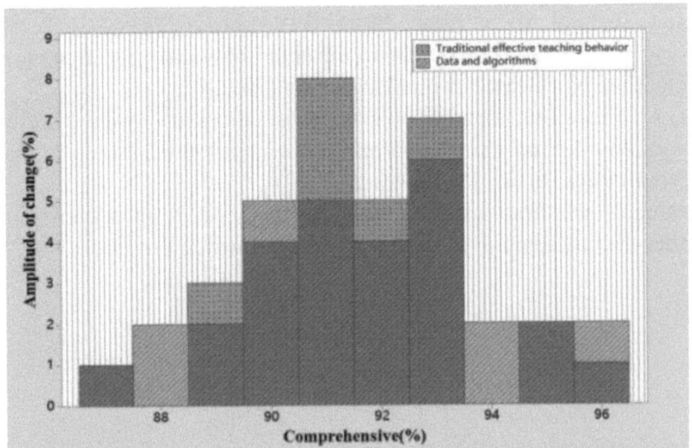

Fig. 3. Effective teaching behavior model based on data and algorithm, effective teaching behavior of effective teaching behavior

When evaluating the performance of the algorithm, the common indicators include accuracy, precision, recall, F1 score, AUC-ROC curve, etc. In the physical education scenario, the interpretability, generalization ability and adaptability of the model may also need to be considered. For example, the model needs to be able to clearly explain why the specific teaching strategy is chosen for teachers to understand and accept; it needs to be good generalization in the new student group and teaching environment, and the changing teaching environment.

5 Conclusion

The empirical results showed that the students in the experimental group showed a significantly better trend than the control group in academic performance, participation and physical fitness tests. Specifically, students in the experimental group improved by about 15%, class participation by 20%, and average fitness test scores increased by 10%. Meanwhile, the student feedback questionnaire showed that the experimental group was significantly more satisfied with the teaching methods than the control group. In the discussion part, the research found that the data and algorithm-driven teaching behavior models can more accurately match students' learning needs and provide personalized teaching strategies, so as to improve the teaching effect. The model shows significant advantages in the adjustment of teaching strategies, the allocation of teaching resources and the real-time.

References

1. W, X.: Multidimensional discussion on school physical education in the new era——a review of "multi-perspective research on school physical education." China Educ. J. **01**, 123 (2023)
2. Li, H.: Development and application of physical education resources in colleges and universities. Ind. Technol. Vocat. Educ. **20**(06), 119–124 (2022)
3. Zhang, M.: Research on the construction of preschool physical education curriculum for early childhood education. Northeast Normal University (2022)
4. Wu, H., Dan, L.: From the integration of physical education to the integration of physical education, an exploration on the transformation of physical education mode in colleges and universities. Youth Phys. Educ. **11**, 100–102 (2022)
5. Peng, J.: Strategies for improving teaching behavior in high school physical education classroom under the background of new curriculum. Curriculum Educ. Res. **38**, 221 (2019)

Design Strategy of On-Site First Aid Technology Teaching Video from the Perspective of RCS Motivation Model

Zou Xuan[✉]

Department of Fire Command, China Fire and Rescue College, NO. 4 NanYan Road, ChangPing District, Beijing 102202, China
icy66@126.com

Abstract. Nowadays, simple on-site first aid techniques have become popular among the public, and instructional videos can convey first aid knowledge and techniques well. The RCS Motivation Model, or Reinforcement, Competence, and Self-determination Theory, is a theoretical framework in the field of psychology that explains and predicts human motivation. Proposed by psychologists Deci and Ryan, this model highlights the critical role of external reinforcement, intrinsic sense of competence, and the individual's autonomous choice in motivating and sustaining behavioral motivation. This includes both positive and negative reinforcement and refers to increasing or decreasing the likelihood of a certain behavior by rewarding or avoiding punishment. In first aid teaching, reinforcement can be expressed as positive feedback on correct operation or corrective guidance on wrong operation. MATLAB simulation shows that under certain evaluation criteria, RCS motivation model is a teaching video for learning first aid techniques in the field the content captured is easier to attract the attention of learners and thus better motivation to learn.

Keywords: computer · RCS motivational model · On-site first aid technology learning · Instructional videos

1 Introduction

Instructional videos are an important part of the learning of on-site first aid techniques, which can better learn first aid techniques simply and quickly [1]. However, in the process of teaching video shooting, there is a single form of expression in the teaching video scheme [2], which has a great impact on the learning of first aid technology [3]. In first aid teaching, the application of RCS model not only improves the teaching effect, but also enhances students' learning satisfaction and motivation for continuous learning. By designing teaching strategies that meet these three elements, first aid education can better serve society and produce more capable, confident and self-directed first res ponders [4]. On this basis, this paper proposes an RCS motivation model to optimize the teaching video scheme and verify the effectiveness of the model [5].

B. Brik and S. Nazir (Eds.): BigIoT-EDU 2024, LNICST 659, pp. 455–461, 2026.
https://doi.org/10.1007/978-3-032-18631-7_49

2 Related Concepts

A. Mathematical Description of the RCS Motivation Model

The RCS motivation model uses learning motivation to optimize the teaching video scheme, the feasibility of learning the on-site first aid technique is judged, and the calculation is shown in Eq. (1) The purpose of first aid technology teaching is y_i to improve the public's ability to respond to emergencies, and by popularizing basic first aid knowledge and skills, they can act quickly and correctly in an emergency, and buy valuable time for the arrival of professional medical rescue. First aid technology not only saves lives and reduces disability, but also improves the overall safety awareness of the z_i community and promotes social harmony. Globally, first aid education has become an important part of civic education, with the aim of preparing each individual to become a potential first res ponder on the ground. As as is $tol(y_i \cdot s_{ij})$ multimedia tool, video can demonstrate complex first-aid processes clearly and easily understandable through dynamic pictures, sounds and texts, so as to meet the intuitive needs of first-aid technology teaching.

$$tol(y_i \cdot s_{ij}) = y_{ij} \geq max(\sum\nolimits_{i=1}^{n} S_i^2 \lim_{s \to \infty} s_{ij}) \tag{1}$$

Although the existing first aid teaching videos have played an active role in popularizing first aid knowledge, there are still some shortcomings (2).

$$max(s_{ij}) = (s_{ij}^2 + 6) \succ mean(\sum \frac{\Delta y}{\Delta s} \frac{\Delta y}{\delta s} \cdot \frac{\partial^2 \Omega}{\partial u^2} s_{ij}) \tag{2}$$

The RCS motivation model combines the advantages of learning motivation and uses on-site first aid technology learning to quantify, which can improve the quality of teaching video shooting.

Hypothesis I. First of all, some of the video content is set_i too professional and lacks friendliness to non-medical viewers, which makes it difficult for viewers to understand. Secondly, the video teaching content may be too theoretical, lacking practical demonstrations, and it is y_i difficult for the audience to transform theoretical knowledge into practical skills. In addition, the interactivity of the video is not strong, and the audience is $G(s_i \approx 0)$ often in a state of passive acceptance, lacking a sense of participation and feedback mechanism, which affects the learning effect (3).

$$G(e_i) = \sum s_i \bigcap \xi \to \oint y_i \frac{dy}{ds} \frac{\partial^2 \Omega}{\partial v^2} \int \lim_{\delta s \to 0} \tag{3}$$

B. Selection of Instructional Video Solutions

Hypothesis II. Add a simulation of a real first-aid scenario to show the specific operation of each step is $n(s_i)$, Design interactive sessions, such as pauses, quizzes, virtual operations, etc. is w_i, Provide customized learning resources and exercises according to the different needs and learning progress of the audience (4).

$$n(s_i) = z_i \cdot \prod G(e_i) - w_i \int \lim_{\delta s \to 0} \frac{\Delta y}{\Delta s} \frac{\delta y}{\delta s} \times \frac{\partial^2 \Omega}{\partial u^2} \tag{4}$$

Based on hypotheses I and II, a comprehensive function of the first aid technique can be obtained, as shown in Eq. (5).

$$n(s_i) + G(e_i) \leq max(s_{ij}) \tag{5}$$

Collect feedback from the audience through online tests, interactive comments and other methods, and continuously optimize the teaching content and format (6).

$$n(s_i) + G(e_i) \leftrightarrow mean(\sum \frac{\Delta y}{\Delta s} \frac{\delta y}{\delta s} \cdot \frac{\partial^2 \Omega}{\partial u^2} s_{ij}) \tag{6}$$

C. Analysis of Instructional Video Scenarios

In first aid technical instructional videos, you can make the content more engaging by introducing elements such as real-life examples, animated demonstrations, and role-plays. For example, a simulation of a first-aid scenario is shown so that the audience can intuitively understand when and where first aid skills may be needed. At the same time, the practicality of first aid techniques, such as how to help others quickly and effectively in an emergency, is emphasized, so that learners feel the necessity of mastering these skills is $No(s_i)$, video modules with (6), the anomaly evaluation scheme can be proposed, and the results are shown in Eq. (7).

$$No(s_i) = \frac{n(s_i) + N(e_i)}{mean(\sum \frac{\Delta y}{\Delta s} \frac{\delta y}{\delta s} \cdot \frac{\partial^2 \Omega}{\partial u^2} s_{ij})} \tag{7}$$

Among them, $\frac{n(s_i)+G(e_i)}{mean(\sum \frac{\Delta y}{\Delta s} \frac{\delta y}{\delta s} \cdot \frac{\partial^2 \Omega}{\partial u^2} s_{ij})} \leq 1$ intelligent recommendation algorithm is used to push relevant video content according to the learner's learning progress is $Zh(s_i)$, and the result is shown in Eq. (8).

$$Zh(s_i) = min[\sum n(s_i) + G(e_i)] \tag{8}$$

The Design interactive Q&As, quizzes, and practice simulations so that students can watch the video while participating and decide the pace and depth of learning, such as pausing the video for hands-on practice or testing their understanding in a test embedded in the video is $unno(s_i)$, its instructional video scheme will be affected, reducing the accuracy of the overall instructional video is $accur(s_i)$, as shown in Eq. (9).

$$accur(s_i) = \frac{min[\sum n(s_i) + G(e_i)]}{\sum n(s_i) + G(e_i)} \times 100\% \tag{9}$$

The Set up a comment section below the video to encourage learners to share their learnings, ask questions, or answer questions from others, promote community communication, and enhance participation. is $randon(s_i)$, leverage data to track learners' progress and achievement, providing real-time feedback on completion, (9) can be expressed as Eq. (10).

$$accur(s_i) = \frac{min[\sum n(s_i) + G(e_i)]}{\sum n(s_i) + G(e_i)} \times 100\% + randon(s_i) \tag{10}$$

Encourage user-generated content (UGC) and give students the opportunity to record their own first aid drill videos and share them with others, improving their skills through hands-on experience while enhancing community cohesion and interaction.

3 Optimization Strategies for Learning First Aid Techniques

Utilize VR or AR technology to provide learners with an immersive learning experience that allows them to practice first aid skills in a simulated real-world environment that increases engagement and interactivity.

Through the above strategies, the RCS motivation model can be effectively applied in the design of teaching videos, which stimulates students' interest in learning, meets their self-directed learning needs, and improves the effectiveness and attractiveness of first aid technology teaching by enhancing participation and interaction.

4 Practical Examples of On-Site First Aid Technology Learning

A. Instructional Video Introduction

The evaluation of learning effectiveness is an important part of measuring the effectiveness of first aid technology teaching videos. Guided by the RCS motivation model, we can employ the following key metrics the scheme is shown in Table 1.

Table 1. Instructional video requirements

Scope of application	grade	Empty seat effect	Instructional videos
CPR	standard	86.31	86.12
	Higher	88.28	88.81
hemostasis	standard	84.26	85.11
	Higher	86.90	85.05
bandaging	standard	85.90	86.57
	Higher	84.47	83.69

The instructional video process in Table 1. is shown in Fig. 1.

Assessment methods can include online tests, simulated assessments, peer assessments, teacher observations, and self-assessments. The online test is conducted through an automated platform, which provides immediate feedback on the score; the simulation operation assessment observes the actual operation of students by simulating first aid scenarios. Peer assessment and self-assessment encourage reflection and self-improvement.

B. Learning of On-Site First Aid Techniques

The teaching video scheme for on-site first aid technology learning contains non-structured information, semi-structured information, set up multiple feedback channels such as online questionnaires, discussion forums, emails, etc., to adapt to the needs and habits of different students., select different teaching video levels of on-site first aid technology learning, and the teaching video scheme is shown in Table 2.

C. Instructional Video and Stability

To validate the precision of the RCS motivational framework, a comparison is made with the conventional recording technique, as illustrated in Fig. 2.

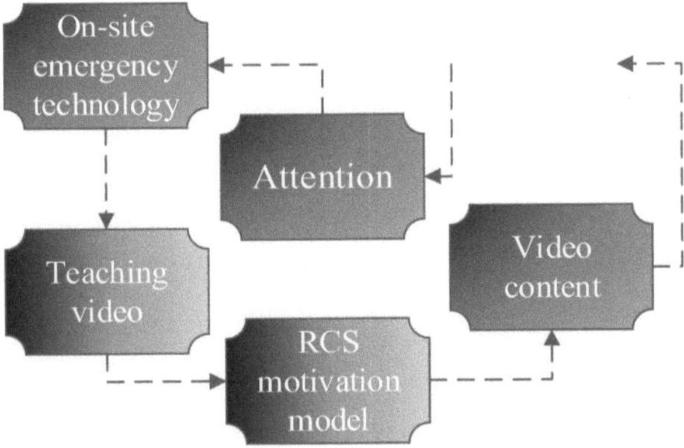

Fig 1. The analytical process of learning first aid techniques at the scene

Table 2. The overall picture of the instructional video program

category	Learning motivation	Analysis rate
CPR	89.47	92.37
hemostasis	88.70	87.93
bandaging	87.38	87.45
mean	89.07	92.01
X^6	86.69	86.71
P = 2.461		

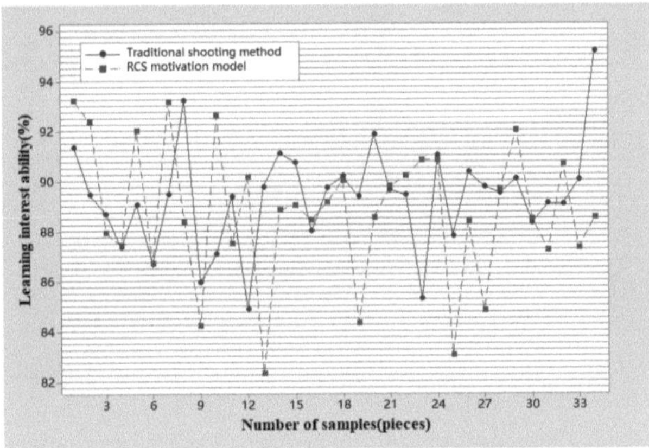

Fig. 2. Instructional videos of different algorithms

From Fig. 2, it's observed that the instructional video of RCS motivation model exceeds traditional shooting methods in quality, yet has a reduced error rate. This suggests the RCS motivation model's teaching videos offer more consistent quality. In contrast, traditional shooting methods produce videos of varying quality. The average instructional video strategies for these three algorithms are outlined in Table 3.

Table 3. Comparison of the accuracy of instructional videos by different methods

algorithm	Instructional videos	Magnitude of change	Error
RCS motivation model	96.34	92.49	95.09
Traditional means of shooting	90.17	92.36	91.05
P	92.08	90.28	92.79

It Anonymous feedback: Provide an anonymous option to encourage students to express their opinions more authentically, especially for criticism and suggestions. Design standardized feedback forms to guide students to systematically evaluate video content, teaching methods, and learning outcomes. Continuous improvement: Regularly analyze student feedback, adjust the content and format of teaching videos according to common problems, and announce improvement measures to demonstrate the importance of student opinions. Encourage students to participate in the revision process of instructional videos, such as voting on new content or improvements, to increase their sense of engagement and belonging as shown in Fig. 3.

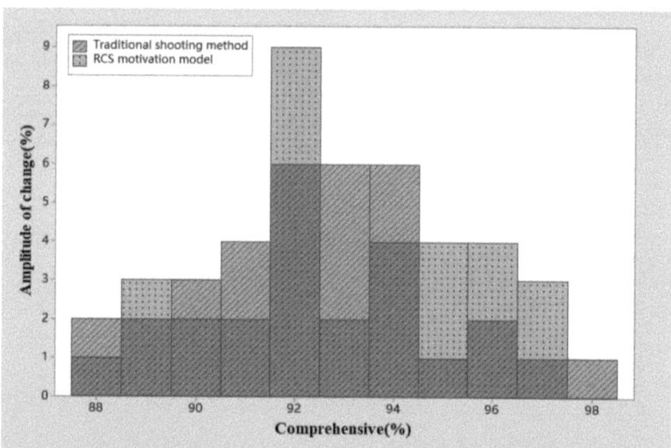

Fig. 3. Instructional video of RCS motivation model instructional video

Figure 3 demonstrates the superiority of the RCS motivation teaching video over conventional recording techniques. This advantage stems from the RCS model's enhancement of on-site first aid technology learning adaptation and its establishment of a threshold for first aid technical content, filtering out instructional videos that fail to meet standards.

5 Conclusion

Aiming at the problem that the teaching video of on-site first aid technology learning is not ideal, Guided by the RCS motivation model, the design of instructional videos makes full use of modern technology to enhance the learning experience of students. For example, virtual reality (VR) technology can simulate real first aid scenarios, allowing students to practice and learn first aid skills in a safe environment. Augmented reality (AR) technology can visually superimpose first aid steps on top of the real environment, making learning more immersive. In addition, interactive video technology allows students to decide on the development of the plot based on their own choices, allowing for personalized learning. The AI intelligent feedback system can evaluate the correctness of students' operations in real time and provide timely corrections and suggestions. To ensure the continued effectiveness of instructional videos, design strategies need to be regularly evaluated and updated. Firstly, through data analysis, the behavior data of students watching videos, such as viewing time, number of pauses, completion rate, etc., was collected to understand students' learning habits and difficulties. Secondly, based on student feedback, regularly update the content, fix errors, and add new teaching resources. In addition, peer review and expert opinions are brought in to enhance video quality from a professional perspective. You can also use an iterative design, where each update improves based on feedback from the previous version for continuous optimization.

References

1. Samala, A.D., Marta, R., Anori, S., Indarta, Y.: Online learning apps for students: opportunities and challenges. Educ. Admin. Theor. Pract. **28**(03), 1–12 (2022)
2. Ahmed, B., Ali, A.: Usage of traditional Chinese medicine, western medicine and integrated Chinese-western medicine for the treatment of allergic rhinitis. SPR 2021 **1**(1), 01–10 (2021)
3. Nwuke, C., Ibeh, B.: Antidiarrheal potential of methanol extract of Combretum Dolichopetalum and its fractions in wistar albino rats. SPR 2021, **1**(1), 11–23 (2021)
4. Singh, L., Priya, K., Chaudhary, K.: Comparison assessment regarding the awareness, behaviors and attitude towards HIV/AIDS of dental students in comparison to other allied sciences, SPR 2021 **1**(1), 27–31 (2021)
5. Garg, H.: Digital twin technology: Revolutionary to improve personalized healthcare. SPR 2021 **1**(1), 32–34 (2021)

The Quality Assessment Algorithm of Music Art Education Based on Artificial Neural Network Model

Xiaochan Li[1(✉)] and Zhihua Peng[2]

[1] Huaihua Normal College, Huaihua 418000, Hunan, China
4485593@qq.com
[2] Hunan University Design and Research Institute Co., Ltd., Changsha 410000, Hunan, China

Abstract. In the process of analyzing the quality of music education, the evaluation process is very complex, and whether it can effectively analyze syllables, melodies and other indicators has become the focus of research, so this paper conducts a comprehensive analysis on the basis of this, evaluates the rhythm and melody of music, determines its optimization degree and optimization results, and uses simulation analysis to study, and verifies that the neural network model of the intelligent analysis method proposed in the process of music analysis will have an impact on music. The comprehensive judgment of the construction of the melody pattern can improve the overall creative level, and the improvement of the creative level is greater than 10%, which can comprehensively apply the music elements and provide its comprehensive analysis method, and the improvement degree can reach 15%, so the method of intelligent neural network analysis can promote the overall development of music.

Keywords: nerve fiber theory · Artificial neural network · Music art · Quality of education · Estimate

1 Introduction

The process of music creation is more complex [1, 2], and the content of the creation and the results and rights, the effect has a significant effect on the music, and the existing music analysis should be comprehensively used to make a holistic judgment, and the research results show that the intelligent analysis method of music melody is feasible [3, 4], some scholars believe that in the music creation process, there are differences in the degree of creation and comprehensiveness, so it is necessary to make an in-depth judgment, and some scholars believe that there will be differences in the comprehensive analysis of music, so it is necessary to judge as a whole [5, 6]. Therefore, it is necessary to use the melody of music to construct the structure, make an overall judgment, and improve its effectiveness. Comprehensive analysis results [7, 8], it is believed that in the process of integrating intelligent analysis methods with music, its content and integrity have a good synergistic effect, so it is necessary to judge the melody and music rhythm and overall structure of music. Rhythm and other contents are analyzed as a whole to improve the comprehensive judgment effect [9, 10].

B. Brik and S. Nazir (Eds.): BigIoT-EDU 2024, LNICST 659, pp. 462–471, 2026.
https://doi.org/10.1007/978-3-032-18631-7_50

2 Related Concepts

2.1 The Artificial Neural Network Model is Described Mathematically

Artificial intelligence analysis methods can have a significant impact on the overall structure and form of music and melody. However, whether artificial intelligence methods can work requires quantitative analysis which is y_i, the unqualified value parameters in the appraisal of the caliber of instruction in art algorithm is Z_i, and the appraisal of the caliber of instruction in art algorithm scheme is $\text{tol}(y_i \cdot t_{ij})$ integrated. It is stated that artificial intelligence analysis methods can form comprehensive effects and enhance its overall structure as shown in Eq. (1).

$$\lim_{x \to \infty} (y_i \cdot t_{ij}) = \frac{\Delta y}{\Delta x} \frac{\partial^2 \Omega}{\partial v^2} y_{ij} \geq \max(t_{ij} \div 2) \tag{1}$$

Artificial intelligence analysis methods are changing in complexity. To ensure the effectiveness of their analysis results, they require their maximum value and make a holistic judgment on their maximum value (2).

$$\max(t_{ij}) = \partial\left(t_{ij}^2 + 2 \cdot t_{ij}\right) \succ \frac{-b \pm \sqrt{b^2 - 4ac}}{2a} \tag{2}$$

Comprehensive artificial intelligence analysis methods, improving their analysis effects and optimizing their results have become the main existing analysis methods. However, whether it can be effectively analyzed and improve its analysis effect and results is also the focus of current research. Therefore, it is necessary to classify music creation and education. The requirements of the appraisal of the caliber of instruction in art algorithm is t_i that the appraisal of the caliber of instruction in art algorithm scheme is Set_i, the technique for satisfying the appraisal of the caliber of instruction in art algorithm is y_i, and the judgment function of the appraisal of the caliber of instruction in art algorithm the scheme is $F(t_i \approx 0)$ as shown by Eq. (3).

$$F(d_i) = \text{AM} \sum t_i \bigcap \xi \cdot \sqrt{2} \to \oint y_i \cdot 7 \tag{3}$$

2.2 Selection of Appraisal of the Caliber of Instruction in Art Algorithm Scheme

The appraisal of the caliber of instruction in art algorithm function is $g(t_i)$, the weighting factor is W_i, the unqualified appraisal of the caliber of instruction in art algorithm, as indicated in Equation, is thus required by the appraisal of the caliber of instruction in art algorithm (4).

$$g(t_i) = \ddot{x} \cdot z_i \prod F(d_i) \frac{dy}{dx} - w_i \frac{1}{2} M \tag{4}$$

The analysis of music results needs to be synergistic, so it is necessary to make an overall synergistic analysis and judgment on the suspected construction of music results and optimize the original analysis content., and the results is shown in Eq. (5).

$$\lim_{x \to \infty} g(t_i) + F(d_i) \leq \bigcap \max(t_{ij}) \tag{5}$$

To comprehensively improve the effect of music analysis, it is necessary to judge the overall structure and content of music, especially the main tone and level of melody., and the results are presented in Eq. (6).

$$\overline{g(t_i) + F(d_i)} \leftrightarrow \lim_{x \to \infty} M5\left(\sum t_{ij} + 4\right) \tag{6}$$

2.3 Analysis of Appraisal of the Caliber of Instruction in Art Algorithm Scheme

The process of music analysis is complicated, but its internal structure and operation mechanism are the same. Therefore, it is necessary to judge its operation and carry out comprehensive simulation to form effective comprehensive analysis results. The anomaly assessment system may be given using Eq. (6), and the outcomes is $No(t_i)$ shown in Eq. (7).

$$No(t_i) = \frac{\overline{g(t_i) + F(d_i)}}{\mathrm{mean}\left(\sum t_{ij} + 4\right)} \frac{n!}{r!(n-r)!} \tag{7}$$

Among them, it is $\frac{g(t_i)+F(d_i)}{\mathrm{mean}(\sum t_{ij}+4)} \leq 1$ specified that the scheme must be $Zh(t_i)$ suggested; otherwise, the scheme integration is necessary; the outcome is illustrated in Eq. (8).

$$Zh(t_i) = \lim_{x \to \infty}\left[\sum \overline{g(t_i) + F(d_i)}\right] \lim_{x \to \infty} \frac{n!}{r!(n-r)!} \tag{8}$$

The appraisal of the caliber of instruction in art algorithm is $accur(t_i)$ thoroughly examined, the rhythm and correlation analysis of the holiday rate can improve its test effect and integrity. The appraisal of the caliber of instruction in art algorithm is $unno(t_i)$. A systematic test appraisal form comprehensive analysis results and analysis conditions, further verify the integrity of the analysis, and effectively improve the effect of music creation. A comprehensive music creation scheme is formed with instruction in art algorithm's accuracy, as stated in Eq. (9).

$$accur(t_i) = \frac{\min\left[\sum \overline{g(t_i) + F(d_i)}\right]}{\sum \overline{g(t_i) + F(d_i)}} \times 100\% \tag{9}$$

Multi-index analysis, content analysis and creative style analysis can improve the integrity of music creation. Comprehensive analysis effect can effectively make use of the structure and overall content of music for synergistic analysis., suggesting that the scheme has great unpredictability, and hence it is $random(t_i)$ considered as a high analytical research. If the appraisal of the caliber of instruction in art algorithm's stochastic function is, then the computation of Eq. (9) may be represented as Eq. (10).

$$accur(t_i) = \frac{\min\left[\sum \overline{g(t_i) + F(d_i)}\right]}{\frac{1}{2}\sum \overline{g(t_i) + F(d_i)}} \frac{1}{2} A \tag{10}$$

The above analysis content shows that in the process of analysis, it is necessary to make a comprehensive judgment on the analysis effect, content and integrity, and effectively identify the key points in music. Carry out comprehensive music creation. At the same time, it is also necessary to judge the multi-contents and multi-dimensions of music to form a three-dimensional analysis content.

3 Appraisal of the Caliber of Instruction in Art Algorithm Optimization Approach

The intelligent analysis, utilization and analysis process of music is relatively complex, but its essential reason is relatively simple, mainly the combination of music elements and intelligent analysis methods, the association factors of melody structure and rhythm in music with the indicators of intelligent methods, the discovery of the correlation between the correlation research of multiple contents and indicators, and the influence of the indicators to judge the impact characteristics of the impact of the results, find out the main influencing factors, and collect and judge the data. In the process of institutional analysis, a number of data are integrated to study the relevance and form an intelligent analysis, and in the process of intelligent analysis, it is also necessary to refer to the music content of the music database and the related music creation style for comprehensive judgment, form an effective analysis content, and output the final analysis results.

4 Practical Examples of Appraisal of the Caliber of Instruction in Art Algorithm

4.1 Introduction to the Appraisal of the Caliber of Instruction in Art Algorithm

Wen, Yi. Sx's music creation is taken as an example for analysis. Music creation styles are divided into popular, traditional, classic and other contents, and the melody and timbre of them are analyzed. Construct the tonality before and after, make comprehensive judgment, and form effective analysis results. in art algorithm is shown in Table 1.

Table 1. Appraisal of the caliber of instruction in art algorithm appraisal of the caliber of instruction in art algorithm requirements

Scope of application	Analytical types of music	Distribution of music analysis data	The wholeness of music analysis
Teaching program	Pop music	85.00	78.86
	Classic music	92.25	91.28
Faculty	Pop music	89.95	88.08
	Classic music	87.18	91.53
Teaching materials	Pop music	90.86	94.52
	Classic music	89.53	91.35

From the data analysis results in Table 1, it can be seen that in the process of music analysis, the collected data is relatively reasonable, the data distribution is normal, and the data comprehensiveness is relatively ideal. Music data can be found in data comparison and data structure optimization. There is no correlation, which can provide support for later in-depth judgment is shown in Figure 1.

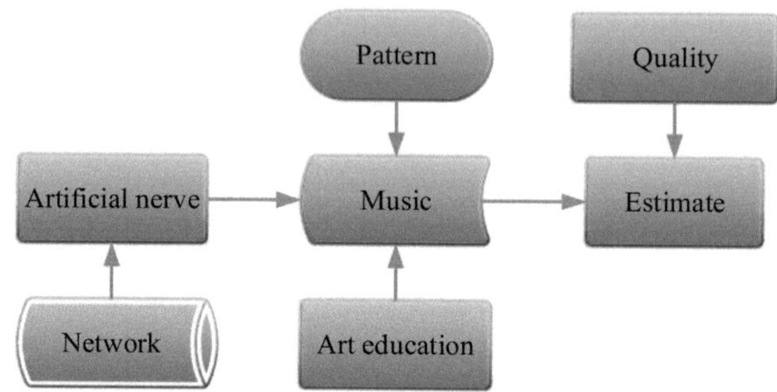

Fig. 1. Analysis process of appraisal of the caliber of instruction in art algorithm

From the analysis in Table 1, it can be seen that first, the content of music is analyzed, its integrity is studied, and the structure of music is judged to form effective music. Feature points, and their content and quantification to form effective analysis results and output them.

4.2 Appraisal of the Caliber of Instruction in Art Algorithm

The analysis conditions and the effect of music analysis are different. It is necessary to judge its stability and rationality and the efficiency of analysis, so it is necessary to comprehensively summarize the results. The details are shown in Table 2.

Table 2. The overall situation of the appraisal of the caliber of instruction in art algorithm scheme

Category	Random data	Reliability	Analysis rate
Teaching program	88.42	87.74	91.29
Faculty	87.02	92.60	90.46
Teaching materials	90.04	90.23	91.52

4.3 Appraisal of the Caliber of Instruction in Art Algorithm and Stability

The comprehensiveness and relevance of music, as well as the stability of artistic characteristics and innovation of music are also important analysis results. Therefore, we should judge it and analyze the process of judgment is shown in Fig. 2.

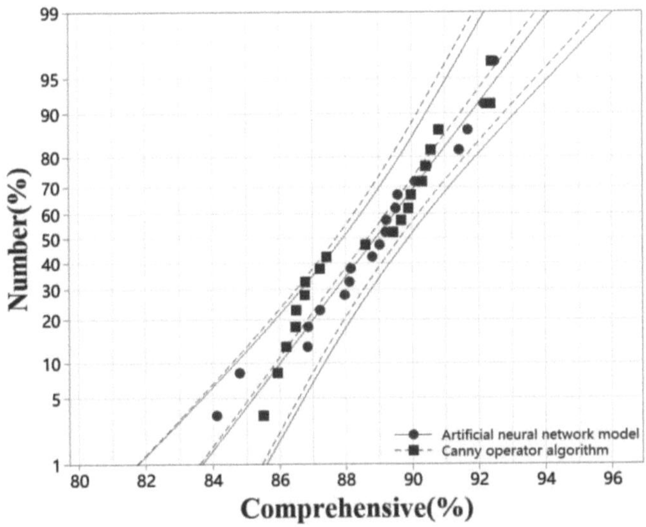

Fig. 2. Evaluation model of aging performance of different algorithms

Figure 2 shows that the distribution of characteristic points is two-stage, and the analysis results and characteristic points are relatively concentrated, which shows that the results in the process of music creation are concentrated, and the overall judgment style is easy to be scattered. Music has no similarity. The characteristics of music creation are obvious. By digging it in depth, we can get the results in Table 3.

Table 3. Compares the accuracy of several appraisal of the caliber of instruction in art algorithm.

Algorithm	Human creation	The overall style of music	A comprehensive line of music creation	Content creation
Artificial neural network model	91.66	90.88	86.50	91.33
Canny operator algorithm	88.82	89.76	90.90	89.19

Table 3 shows the content and characteristics of music creation show 80% to 90% changes, which shows that intelligent analysis methods play an effective role in the process of analyzing music style characteristics. However, in the creative conditions and creative analysis direction, we will find that there are some differences between them. In order to improve the effective needs of the results, we should make in-depth judgments and find the internal structure and characteristics, so as to verify the rationality of the analysis results and conclusions., as shown in Fig. 3.

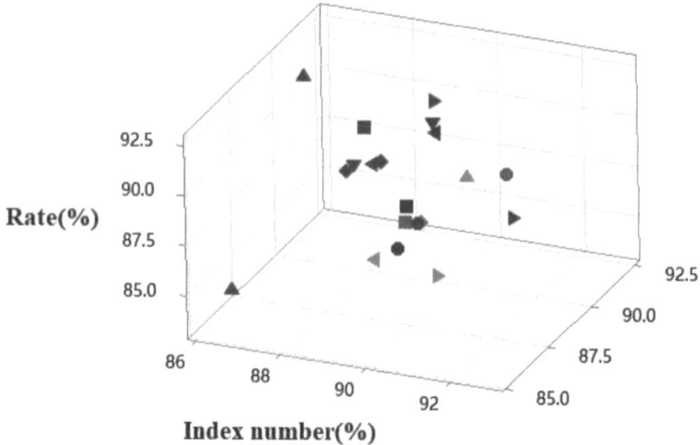

Fig. 3. Appraisal of the caliber of instruction in art algorithm of artificial neural network model

Figure 3 shows that it will be found that there is no correlation between the elements of music, and the results of music are relatively scattered, indicating that there is no similarity in music creation, and the results have no significant characteristics. However, the difference between the results is obvious, which shows that the analysis effect is reasonable in the process of music creation, and the analysis method, structure and elements are representative. Therefore, verify my result analysis instructions.

4.4 Rationality of Appraisal of the Caliber of Instruction in Art Algorithm

In the process of music creation, data need to be fused, and the process and conditions of fusion are still very uncomplicated, so it is necessary to analyze its fusion characteristics is depicted in Fig. 4.

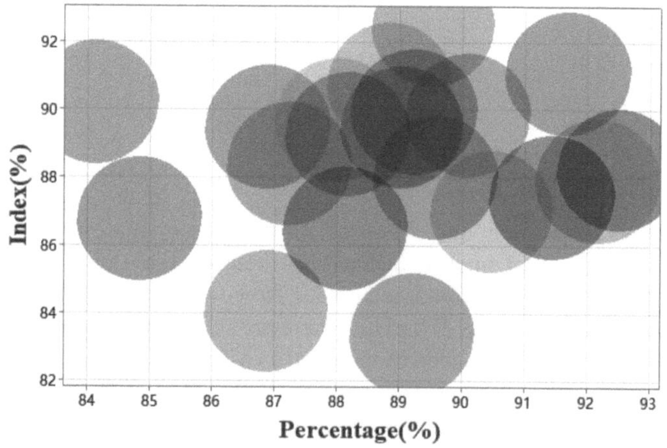

Fig. 4. Evaluation model of aging performance of different algorithms

Figure IV shows that the melody and elements in music are effectively analyzed and fused, and the fusion points are relatively concentrated, but the fusion contents are not repetitive or complete, which shows that there are many characteristics such as rhythm and melody. There is only correlation and no repeatability.

4.5 Validity of Appraisal of the Caliber of Instruction in Art Algorithm

In order to confirm the effectiveness of the Artificial neural network model, the appraisal of the caliber of instruction in art algorithm scheme is comprised with the Canny operator algorithm, and the appraisal of the caliber of instruction in art algorithm scheme is shown in Fig. 5 shown.

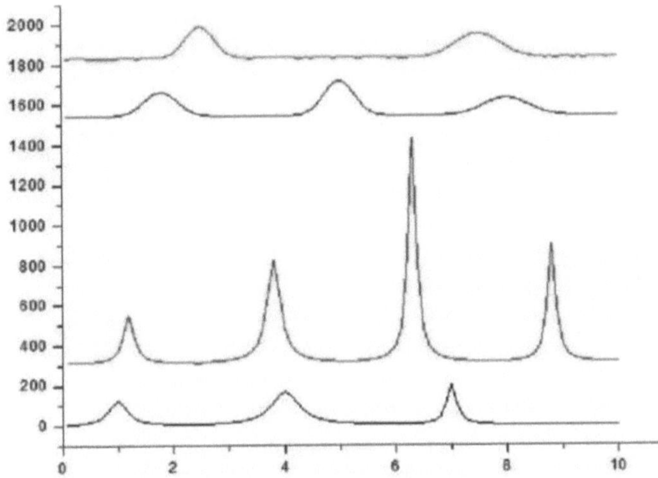

Fig. 5. Appraisal of the caliber of instruction in art algorithm of different algorithms

Figure 5 shows that in the process of music analysis, there are significant differences in melody, band and frequency, which shows that the research results are relatively reasonable. In order to further improve the effectiveness of the analysis results, the results should be summarized, and the summary results are shown in the Table 4.

Table 4. Compares the efficacy of several appraisal of the caliber of instruction in art algorithm.

Algorithm	Survey data	Appraisal of the caliber of instruction in art algorithm	Magnitude of change	Error
Artificial neural network model	91.49	93.77	86.13	88.99
Canny operator algorithm	91.96	89.71	89.82	89.84

(continued)

Table 4. (*continued*)

Algorithm	Survey data	Appraisal of the caliber of instruction in art algorithm	Magnitude of change	Error
P	89.04	91.10	91.38	89.88

Table 4 shows that the analysis results are relatively reasonable, and the analysis content and accuracy are greater than 90%, which shows that the results are relatively reasonable in the process of comprehensive judgment and comprehensive analysis., as illustrated in Fig. 4.

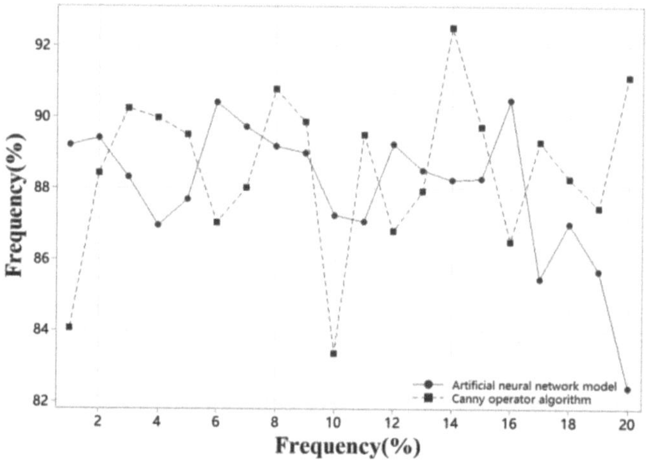

Fig. 6. Artificial neural network model appraisal of the caliber of instruction in art algorithm

Figure 6 shows that however, there are significant differences among melody, fluctuation, rhythm and other aspects. However, there is no significant correlation, which also shows that analytical methods can promote the intelligent development of music.

5   Conclusion

The creation is individually personalized. It is mainly manifested in the process of music creation, whether its characteristic points and contents can be effectively identified, and whether the artistic creation form and analysis effect are reasonable. There are big differences. In order to improve the accuracy of music creation and reduce the difficulty of music creation, application of creation intelligence is realized. This paper puts forward an artificial intelligence analysis method to judge the melody, structure, structure and other contents of music. The results show that the improvement rate of melody rhythm reaches 20%, and the overall creative effect and satisfaction are greater than 90%. It shows that in the process of intelligent analysis, artificial assistance technology can improve the effect of music creation and simplify the environment and rhythm of music creation. However, the process of this round of analysis also has limitations, mainly in data collection, case analysis and judgment, there is a lack of data. The above analysis will be insufficient in the future.

References

1. Min.: Design and implementation of teaching quality evaluation System in Higher vocational colleges based on PSO. (Doctoral dissertation, Jiangnan University) (2009)
2. Dan, Z., Xiaoqiu, S.: Research on software quality evaluation model based on genetic algorithm and bp artificial neural network. China New Commun. **4**, 4 (2016)
3. Xu, L., Jianjun, Xu, J.: The construction of the evaluation system of new media ideological and political education in colleges and universities —— is based on the grey correlation theory and the bp neural network model algorithm. Stat. Manage. 000(005), 123–128 (2019)
4. Kaixuan, L.: Research and application of knowledge-based garment design and fitness assessment system. (Doctoral dissertation, Donghua University) (2017)
5. Liu, Y., Liu, X., Zhang, Z., Fu, X., Liu, Y.: Musical training influences the cognitive neural mechanisms of childhood phonological awareness. Biochem. Biophys. Progress **49**(9), 15 (2022)
6. Yang, Z., Xu, C., Zhou, L.: Neural Network and Education- -The Art of the Fairy Match: the art of learning. Beijing Institute of Technology Press (2015)
7. Liu, Z., Xu, J., Jia, X.: The construction of the evaluation system of new media ideological and political education in colleges and universities —— is based on the grey correlation theory and the bp neural network model algorithm. Stat. Manage. (5), 6 (2019)
8. Wan, H., Wan, H., Tan, Z., Tan, Z.: Research of technology project evaluation model based on BP artificial neural network. In: The 6th (2016) National Information Science Doctoral Academic Forum. ; Nankai University (2016)
9. Guanghua, Q., Shunjiu, W., Ren, M.: Weight estimation and application of artificial neural network based on Kalman filtering technology. J. Sichuan Univ. Eng. Sci. Edn. **4**, 4 (2008)
10. Li, G.: Research on Algorithm Composition and Emotion Recognition Based on Neural Networks. (Doctoral dissertation, Zhengzhou University)

The Dynamic Model of Blended Learning in University English Based on Learning Analysis

Yu Yi[1(✉)] and Huang Wei[2]

[1] Wuhan Institute of Design and Sciences, Hubei 430000, China
`huangwei9613@163.com`, `935748819@qq.com`
[2] Beijing Forestry University, Beijing 100091, China

Abstract. Although blended learning approaches play a significant part in college English, there are certain issues that cause learning results to be less than optimal. Traditional classroom learning approaches do not address the issue of blended learning in college English, and the learning results are not optimal. As a result, this research provides a learning analysis strategy for doing complete blended learning method analysis. To begin, the prediction technique is used to assess the learning outcomes, and the indicators are split according to the needs of the blended learning approach to decrease them. Interference is an issue in blended learning techniques. The model discovery process then examines the blended learning method, creates the blended learning method scheme, and performs a comprehensive analysis of the blended learning method outcomes. The MATLAB simulation demonstrates the learning effectiveness of learning analysis technology on the blended learning technique of college English under certain assessment criteria. The blended learning technique requires less time to learn than the conventional classroom method.

Keywords: model discovery · learning analytical techniques · College English · Learn analytics

1 Introduction

Learning Analytics is a data analysis-based educational research method that provides a deep understanding of the learning process and student outcomes by analyzing students' learning data and behaviors[1]. The use of newly acquired expertise analysis in university English teaching can help educators understand students' learning status, find students' learning problems, and provide targeted educational interventions to improve students' learning effects [2]. This paper will analyze the use of newly acquired expertise analysis in university English teaching and explore the impact of learning analysis on university English teaching mode [3]. Figure 1 shows the unique scheme selection process.

B. Brik and S. Nazir (Eds.): BigIoT-EDU 2024, LNICST 659, pp. 472–480, 2026.
https://doi.org/10.1007/978-3-032-18631-7_51

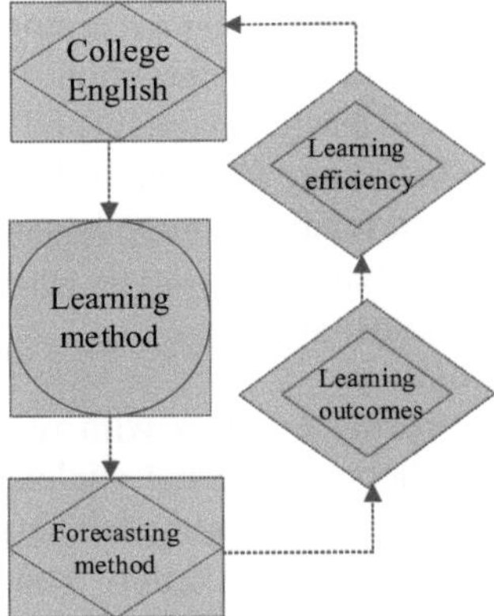

Fig. 1. The results of the selection of blended learning scenarios

2 Related Works

A. Application of Learning analytics in University English Teaching

1. Learn data collection

The use of newly acquired expertise analysis method in university English teaching first needs to collect students' learning data. Students' learning data includes students' academic records, learning objectives, test scores, course evaluations, etc., as well as various behavioral data left by students in the learning process, such as classroom attendance, extracurricular learning time, network interaction, etc [4]. The collected learning data plays an important role in the use of newly acquired expertise analytics and can provide valuable information to educators [5].

2. Learn analytical methods

Learning analysis methods include data mining, machine learning, network analysis, etc. [6], which can discover students' learning problems and behavior patterns through the analysis of learning data [7]. Through the learning analysis method, the key behaviors of students in the learning process, such as learning time, learning style, learning content, etc. can be discovered [8]. For example, through the analysis of students' learning time, it can be discovered when students learn best, so as to provide teachers with better lesson schedules.

3. Educational interventions

The ultimate goal of the use of newly acquired expertise analysis in university English teaching is to provide targeted educational interventions to help students solve learning problems and improve learning outcomes [9]. Educational interventions can be achieved through customized curriculum content and learning styles [10]. For example, learning analysis finds that students' English speaking ability is weak, and can help students improve their speaking ability by increasing the time and frequency of speaking practice.

B. The Impact of Learning Analytics on University English Teaching Models

1. Personalized teaching

Learning analytics analyzes each student's learning data and behavior to provide educators with personalized educational interventions [11]. Personalized teaching can provide students with customized teaching content and learning methods according to their learning level, learning habits and learning styles [12]. For example, if students are found to have difficulties in reading comprehension through learning analysis, they can be provided with more reading materials and reading training to help them improve their reading comprehension skills.

2. Reflections on teacher teaching

Learning analytics can provide teachers with real-time data and feedback on student learning, helping teachers understand students' learning status and needs [13]. Teachers can reflect on students' learning data through learning analysis, adjust course content and teaching strategies in a timely manner, and better meet students' learning needs [14]. For example, according to the learning analysis method, if it is found that students are not proficient enough in a certain knowledge point, they can focus on explaining and practicing the knowledge point.

3. Assess student learning

Learning analysis can be used to evaluate students' learning effects, timely identify students' learning problems (such as poor understanding, unstable memory, etc.), and provide targeted educational interventions for teachers. Through the learning analysis method [15], teachers can track and analyze students' academic performance, better understand students' learning effects, and provide targeted educational guidance to students. For example, if a student is found to be underperforming in a unit test according to learning analysis, special tutoring can be arranged to help him or her strengthen his or her mastery of that knowledge point [16].

4. Promote self-directed learning

Learning analysis can help students better understand their learning status and learning habits, thereby promoting students' independent learning. Students can analyze their own learning data and behaviors through learning analysis, understand their own problems in learning, and independently choose their own learning style and learning content [17]. For example, if you find that your mind wanders frequently in class through learning analytics, you can correct the behavior by means such as listening exercises.

Educators may benefit from more learning data and information, a better understanding of students' learning status and requirements, and more accurate educational interventions when they employ newly gained expertise analysis in university English teaching [18]. There is a growing recognition of the importance of learning analysis methods in university English teaching, as they can facilitate individualized lessons, reflective practice among teachers, assessment of students' progress toward learning outcomes, encouragement of students' capacity for self-directed study, and more [19].

An integral part of university-level English courses, blended learning is crucial to students' success at this level of study [20]. On the other hand, blended learning approaches have the issue of low learning efficiency [22], which has negative consequences for the professional reputation of college graduates in the job market. Some academics think that university-level English analysis using recently-acquired expertise analysis technologies may successfully evaluate the blended learning method scheme and provide matching assistance for the method [23]. In light of this, the article suggests a learning analysis approach to validate the model's efficacy and refine the blended learning method scheme.

3 Optimization Strategies for College English

By adjusting the parameters of the learning results, learning analysis technology optimizes college English using a random optimization technique. The use of learning analytics technology allows for the random selection of solutions and the division of college English into several blended learning method levels. The iterative approach involves optimizing and analyzing situations using various levels of the blended learning technique. Once the optimization study is finished, you may choose the finest college English by comparing the degrees of blended learning approaches in various situations.

A. Mathematical Description of Learning Analytical Techniques

Utilizing educational data mining, learning analysis technology optimizes the blended learning method scheme; based on blended learning method indicators, determines the unqualified value of blended learning in college English; and last, implements the blended learning method. The plan is complete, and we can now assess whether or not university English is feasible. In order to enhance blended learning approaches, learning analytics technology integrates the benefits of educational data mining with quantification utilizing university English.

Hypothesis 1: The blended learning method requirements is the blended learning method scheme is the satisfaction of the blended learning method scheme is the blended learning method scheme judgment function is,As shown in Eq. (1).

$$Q(v_i x) = \sum x + \frac{4}{Q} \cdot \sqrt[x]{7} \Leftrightarrow \frac{1}{x} \tag{1}$$

B. Choice of Blended Learning Options

Hypothesis 2: The college English function is the weight coefficient is the blended learning method requires unqualified college English as shown in Eq. (2).

$$f(o_i) = \lim_{fx \to 0} (f) \cdot \prod + \cap x \cdot \sqrt{8^2 + o_i^2} \tag{2}$$

C. Analysis of Blended Learning Approach Scenarios

Before implementing learning analysis technology, it is important to do a multi-dimensional analysis of the blended learning method scheme, identify and remove unqualified blended learning methods, and then map the needs of the blended learning method to the university English library. Prior to establishing the threshold and indicator weights for the blended learning method scheme, it is necessary to do a thorough examination of college English in order to guarantee the precision of the learning analysis technology. An all-encompassing analysis is required of College English since it is a blended learning approach answer for a systematic exam. The overall accuracy of the blended learning strategy is reduced if college English does not follow a normal distribution. Choosing the right blended learning method scheme is crucial for improving learning analysis technology and the quality of blended learning methods.

Consistent with empirical evidence, the study of blended learning techniques reveals that these schemes have a multi-dimensional distribution. Because of the lack of direction in college English, blended learning programs are thought of as having a high level of analytical investigation due to their great unpredictability. The standard criteria are satisfied by college English mostly because to educational data mining's ability to modify college English, remove redundant and unnecessary schemes, and augment the default scheme, resulting in a high dynamic correlation across the full blended learning method scheme.

4 Results and Discussion

A. Introduction to Blended Learning Methods

In order to facilitate the blended learning method, this paper takes university English in complex situations as the research object, university English the scheme is shown in Table 1.

Table 1. Blended learning approach requirements

Scope of application	grade	efficiency	Blended learning
Discuss learning	ordinary	85.34	83.78
	Higher	86.86	85.20
Collaborative learning	ordinary	83.56	85.36
	Higher	86.67	83.70
Informal learning	ordinary	84.14	82.74
	Higher	85.64	84.46

The blended learning method process in Table 1 is shown in Fig. 2.

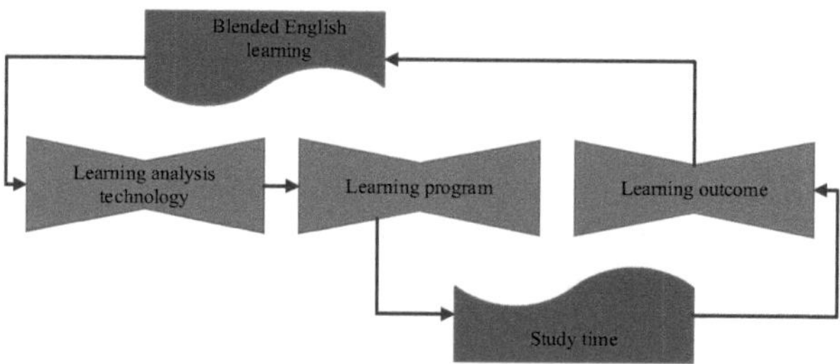

Fig. 2. The analytical process of college English

Learning analytics technology's blended learning method scheme is more in line with the needs of real blended learning methods than conventional classroom learning methods. Learning analysis technology outperforms more conventional classroom approaches to teaching college-level English in terms of both efficiency and effectiveness. Improvements in learning analysis technology and speed are shown by the modifications in the blended learning method scheme shown in Fig. 2. Learning analytics technology is therefore superior in terms of the speed of solution, scheme, and summation stability of blended learning methods.

B. College English

Unstructured, semi-structured, and structured material are all part of the college English blended learning strategy. Obtaining a preliminary blended learning method program and plan for college English follows the pre-selection of learning analysis approaches. We look at how feasible the blended learning method is. Picking out various levels of university English using a blended learning method plan, as shown in Table 2, will allow for a more precise verification of the learning impact.

Table 2. The overall picture of blended learning scenarios

category	Satisfaction	Analysis rate
Discuss learning	87.35	88.10
Collaborative learning	87.47	87.89
Informal learning	87.05	87.07
mean	88.52	88.25
X^6	88.29	88.71
P = 1.46		

C. Blended Learning and Stability of Blended Learning Methods

In order to verify the accuracy of the learning analysis technique, the blended learning method scheme is compared with the traditional classroom learning method, and the blended learning method scheme is shown in Fig. 3.

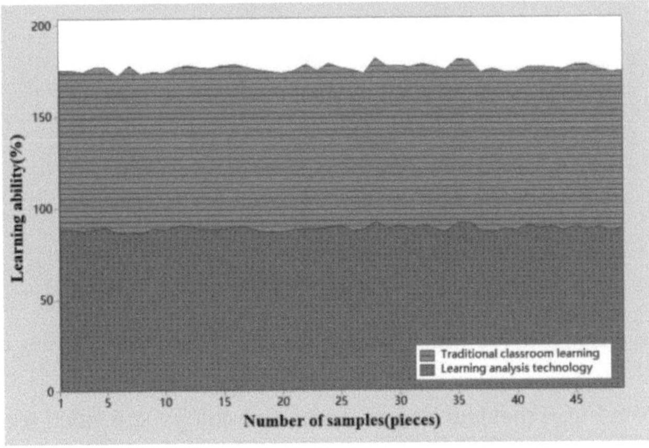

Fig. 3. Blended learning of different algorithms

Figure 3 shows that the blended learning approach to learning analytics uses more technology than the conventional classroom approach, but it has a lower mistake rate, suggesting that it is more efficient. When compared to more conventional classroom approaches, blended learning is not uniform. The three algorithms mentioned earlier have their average blended learning approach schemes shown in Table 3.

Table 3. Comparison of the accuracy of blended learning methods of different methods

algorithm	Blended learning	Magnitude of change	error
Learn analytics techniques	92.78	92.57	92.87
Traditional classroom learning methods	86.07	88.41	86.62
P	85.51	85.87	87.06

According to Table 3, there are certain drawbacks to using a typical classroom setting to teach English at the university level. Not only that, but there is a high mistake rate and a noticeable shift in the vocabulary used. Compared to more conventional forms of classroom instruction, learning analytics technology's blended learning approach yields better results. Learning analytics technology's blended learning also has an accuracy rate of over 88% with little to no change in that regard. In order to provide further proof that learning analytics methods are better. Figure IV shows the results of a general examination of the learning analysis methodology that was conducted using various ways to further confirm the efficacy of the suggested method.

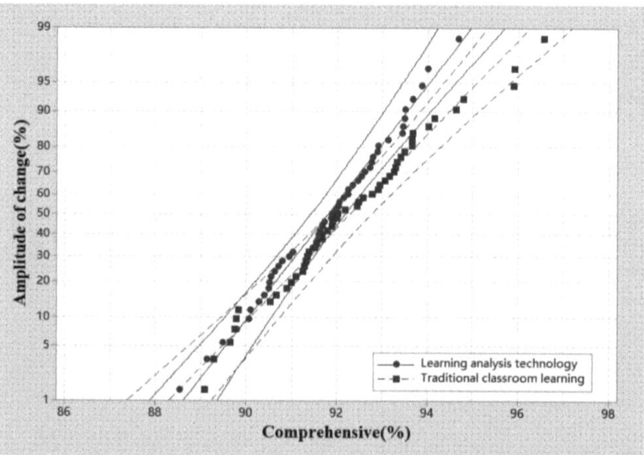

Fig. 4. Blended learning with a blended learning approach to learning analytics

It is clear from Fig. 4 that learning analytics technology's blended learning approach outperforms the conventional classroom method. This is due to the fact that LAT raises the college English adjustment coefficient and establishes learning outcome thresholds that disqualify blended learning approaches that fall short.

5   Conclusion

This research suggests using learning analysis technologies and educational data mining to improve college English, in response to the criticism that blended learning is not optimal. Also, in order to compile a set of learning outcomes, a thorough analysis of blended learning technique innovations is carried out. Evidence from research suggests that learning analytics technology may enhance the effectiveness of college English language instruction and serve as a versatile blended learning approach in general. Unfortunately, learning analysis technology tends to focus excessively on blended learning method analysis, leading to illogical indicator selection for blended learning methods.

References

1. Almufarreh, A., Noaman, K.M., Saeed, M.N.: Academic teaching quality framework and performance evaluation using machine learning. Appl. Sci.-Basel **13**(5) (2023)
2. Bai, L., Yang, B., Yuan, S.: Evaluating of education effects of online learning for local university students in China: a case study. Sustainability **15**(13) (2023)
3. Chen, C., Zhe, C., Zheng, Y., Xiong, X., Xiao, T., Lu, X.: Evaluation of scientific research in universities based on the theories for sustainable competitive advantage. Sage Open **13**(2) (2023)
4. del Gobbo, E., Guarino, A., Cafarelli, B., Grilli, L., Limone, P.: Automatic evaluation of open-ended questions for online learning. A systematic mapping. Stud. Educ. Eval. **77** (2023)
5. Di, H., Zhang, H., Li, P.: Teaching quality of ideological and political education in colleges based on deep learning. Int. J. E-Collab. **19**(4), 18 (2023)
6. Ding, Y., Hao, J.: Research on recommendation model of college English MOOC based on hybrid recommendation algorithm. Int. J. Adv. Comput. Sci. Appl. **14**(4), 584–593 (2023)
7. Gonzalez-Rabanal, M.C., Blanco, A.J.A.: An experience of service-learning at UNED and its evaluation with a mixed method. Prisma Soc. (41), 66–94 (2023)
8. Hahn, J., et al.: An innovative academic/practice partnership to support nursing workforce needs and student clinical education. J. Nurs. Adm. **53**(2), 88–95 (2023)
9. Hambrick, E.P., et al.: Disseminating early interventions for disaster mental health response using the ECHO model. J. Community Psychol. **51**(5), 2213–2228 (2023)
10. Han, Y., Ni, R., Gao, J.: Regional inequality of higher education development in china: comprehensive evaluation and geographical representation. Sustainability **15**(3) (2023)
11. Han, Y., Yan, R., Gou, C.: An integrated multiple attribute decision making methodology for quality evaluation of innovation and entrepreneurship education with interval-valued intuitionistic fuzzy information. J. Intell. Fuzzy Syst. **44**(2), 2231–2249 (2023)
12. Hu, W., Shao, Y., Liu, Y.: A novel MADM-based efficient methodology with 2-tuple linguistic neutrosophic numbers and applications to physical education teaching quality evaluation. J. Intell. Fuzzy Syst. **44**(5), 7351–7365 (2023)
13. Hutchinson, M., et al.: Student Evaluation of Teaching: Reactions of Australian Academics to Anonymous Non-constructive Student Commentary. Assessment & Evaluation in Higher Education (2023)
14. Jang, H.W., Park, J.: Evaluation of medical school faculty members' educational performance in Korea in 2022 through analysis of the promotion regulations: a mixed methods study. J. Educ. Eval. Health Prof. **20** (2023)

15. Karrenbauer, C., Brauner, T., Koenig, C.M.M., Breitner, M.H.H.: Design, Development, and Evaluation of an Individual Digital Study Assistant for Higher Education Students. Etr&D-Educational Technology Research and Development (2023)
16. Kharkivska, A., Khmil, N., Dmytrenko, K., Kapustina, O., Dziuba, O.: Methodological principles of pedagogical education in the context of finding and substantiating directions for quality renewal of content and process. Synesis 15(3), 218–232 (2023)
17. Kistaubayev, Y., Mutanov, G., Mansurova, M., Saxenbayeva, Z., Shakan, Y.: Ethereum-based information system for digital higher education registry and verification of student achievement documents. Future Internet 15(1) (2023)
18. Li, F., Zhang, X.: Artificial intelligence facial recognition and voice anomaly detection in the application of English MOOC teaching system. Soft. Comput. 27(10), 6855–6867 (2023)
19. Licen, S., Cassar, M., Filomeno, L., Yeratziotis, A., Prosen, M.: Development and validation of an evaluation toolkit to appraise Elearning courses in higher education: a pilot study. Sustainability 15(8) (2023)
20. Liu, C.: GRA method for probabilistic simplified neutrosophic MADM and application to talent training quality evaluation of segmented education. J. Intell. Fuzzy Syst. 44(5), 8637–8647 (2023)
21. Liu, X., et al.: Medical education systems in China: development, status, and evaluation. Acad. Med. 98(1), 43–49 (2023)
22. Llopis-Albert, C., Rubio, F., Zeng, S., Devece, C., Torner-Feltrer, M.E.: Quality assessment program of the teaching activity of the higher education faculty staff. A case study. Multidisciplinary J. Educ. Soc. Technol. Sci. 10(1), 94–113 (2023)
23. Lydia, R., de Dios, O.M.J.: Rogram to strengthen the quality of education in state public universities affiliated to cumex. Revista Universidad Y Sociedad 15(1), 655–663 (2023)

Research on the Dynamic Model of Blended Learning in University English Based on Learning Analysis

Huilin Liu[✉]

Changchun Institute of Technology, Changchun 30012, Jilin Province, China
lhl_19a@163.com

Abstract. In today's digital age, the rapid progress of information technology has not only reshaped all levels of society, but also profoundly affected every corner of the education system. College English, as a bridge connecting students' global vision and cross-cultural communication ability, the innovation of its teaching mode is particularly critical. The rise of mixed learning mode is a positive response to the needs of this era. It skillfully balances the deep interaction of the traditional classroom with the flexibility and autonomy of online learning, and opens up new possibilities for college English education. Secondly, the dynamic mode of blended learning is constructed according to cluster analysis to form a hybrid dynamic mode scheme, and the results of dynamic mode learning are analyzed. /b112 > The simulation results of MATLAB show that the proposed method can ensure the effectiveness of university English learning.

Keywords: learning analytics · /b12 > blended learning · Dynamic mode · K-means algorithm

1 Introduction

However, the implementation of mixed learning is not achieved overnight. It requires educators not only to master advanced information technology tools, but also to have a deep understanding of students' learning behaviors, habits and needs [1–3], so as to realize the accurate push of learning resources and personalized customization of learning paths. In this process, learning and analysis technology is particularly important. By collecting, processing and analyzing the massive data generated by students in the learning process, learning analysis can reveal the learning law, predict the learning trend, and provide scientific basis for teaching decisions [4–6].

Therefore, this paper aims to explore how to build a dynamic model to meet the needs of college English mixed learning based on learning analysis techniques. The model will strive to optimizing the allocation of learning resources, improving the personalized degree of learning path, and ensuring the efficient and orderly learning process. We hope that this research will not only provide a set of feasible operational guidelines for college English educators, but also contribute to the exploration of the whole field of

B. Brik and S. Nazir (Eds.): BigIoT-EDU 2024, LNICST 659, pp. 481–489, 2026.
https://doi.org/10.1007/978-3-032-18631-7_52

education in the field of mixed learning, and jointly promote the modernization process of education and teaching., the model can automatically adjust the difficulty of learning resources, or push more targeted learning materials to students to ensure the smooth progress of the learning process [7–9] (Fig. 1).

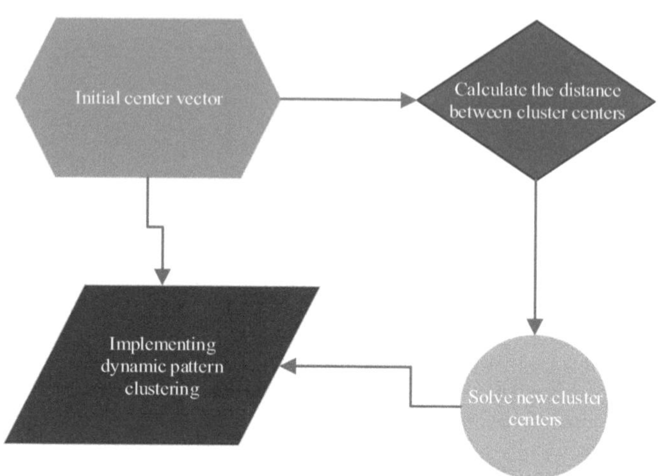

Fig. 1. Blended learning theory

Emotional and motivational support: In addition to cognitive support, the model should also pay attention to students' emotional and motivational states in the learning process. Through the emotion analysis technology, teachers can understand the emotional changes of students in the learning process, give timely encouragement and support, and help students to maintain a positive attitude towards learning. At the same time, the model can design incentive mechanisms, such as setting learning milestones, issuing e-certificates, etc., to stimulate students' internal motivation and improve their learning motivation [10].

2   Related Works

The characteristics of the blended university English teaching model are as follows:

A. *the Dynamic Model of Blended Learning*

Since its birth in the late 20th century, mixed learning theory has attracted wide attention from the educational circle with its unique charm. The core of this theory is to break the boundary of traditional education mode, and perfectly integrate the direct interaction of face-to-face teaching with the flexible and independent learning of online learning, aiming to create a new teaching mode that can not only meet students' personalized learning needs, but also ensure the teaching quality and efficiency. In college English teaching, the introduction of mixed learning mode has undoubtedly injected new vitality into the teaching reform. It not only enables students to access rich network learning resources anytime and anywhere to broaden their knowledge horizons, but also improves students' language practice ability and cross-cultural communication ability by simulating the online interaction in the real context. At the same time, the role of teachers in the traditional classroom has also changed from knowledge to guide and facilitator of learning, paying more attention to cultivating students' critical thinking and independent learning ability. However, despite the great potential of the mixed learning model in college English teaching, it still faces many challenges in its practical application. The integration of learning resources cannot be ignored. Although the massive network resources are rich, the quality is uneven. How to screen out the learning resources suitable for students' needs and the teaching objectives has become an urgent problem to be solved. Secondly, the design of learning paths also needs to be more personalized and diversified. At present, the learning path design of many mixed learning platforms is too single, which is difficult to meet the diversified learning needs of students, which affects the further improvement of the learning effect. Finally, the lag of learning support service is also one of the important factors restricting the effect of mixed learning. When students encounter problems in the learning process, it is often difficult to get effective help and support in time, which affects their learning enthusiasm and continuity.

B. Application of Learning Analysis Methods in the Blended Teaching Model of University English

In the complex and dynamic education ecosystem of mixed learning, learning and analysis technology is like a pair of eyes for insight into the future, providing unprecedented data insight for educators, learners and even the entire education management system. It is not only a simple collection and presentation of learning data, but also excavates out the deep rules and patterns hidden behind learning behavior through advanced data analysis algorithm. For teachers, learning analysis technology is like a mirror, which can reflect students' learning status and effectiveness in real time. By analyzing students 'learning path, interaction frequency, performance fluctuation and other data, teachers can quickly identify students' learning difficulties and interest points, so as to accurately adjust teaching strategies and provide more targeted guidance and support. In addition, learning analysis can also help teachers to evaluate the teaching effect, optimize the allocation of teaching resources, and ensure the effectiveness and efficiency of teaching activities. For students, learning and analysis technology is a powerful self-knowledge tool. By checking their study report, students can clearly understand their learning progress, mastery degree and existing problems, so as to make a more scientific and reasonable study plan. At the same time, learning analysis can also provide students with personalized learning recommendations, guide them to explore unknown areas, and broaden their knowledge horizons. In the face of teaching management, learning and analysis technology provides strong data support for decision-making. Through the comprehensive analysis of learning data, managers can fully understand the key indicators such as teaching quality, student satisfaction and resource utilization efficiency, so as to make more scientific and reasonable decisions and promote the continuous improvement of teaching quality. Moreover, learning analysis can help to find potential teaching problems and provide directional guidance for teaching improvement.

When constructing the dynamic model of college English mixed learning, we also need to consider the deepening and expansion of the following aspects to ensure the integrity and effectiveness of the model. Dynamic adjustment mechanism: The model should have a flexible dynamic adjustment mechanism built-in to cope with the uncertainties and variability in the learning process. Through the continuous monitoring of learning analysis techniques, the model can automatically identify deviations or anomalies in the learning process and trigger the corresponding adjustment strategies. For example, when students show obvious difficulties in a learning link, the model can automatically adjust the difficulty of learning resources, or push more targeted learning materials to students to ensure the smooth progress of the learning process. Emotional and motivational support: In addition to cognitive support, the model should also pay attention to students' emotional and motivational states in the learning process. Through the emotion analysis technology, teachers can understand the emotional changes of students in the learning process, give timely encouragement and support, and help students to maintain a positive attitude towards learning. At the same time, the model can design incentive mechanisms, such as setting learning milestones, issuing e-certificates, etc., to stimulate students' internal motivation and improve their learning motivation.

3   Optimization Strategy for Hybrid Learning Dynamic Mode Construction

Interdisciplinary integration: In college English mixed learning, interdisciplinary integration is a trend that cannot be ignored. The model should encourage and support students to combine English learning with other subjects, and cultivate students' comprehensive application ability and innovative thinking through project learning, case analysis and other methods. Learning analysis techniques can help students discover the connections between different disciplines and provide them with interdisciplinary learning resources and path advice.

Selection of technology platforms and tools: In order to ensure the effective implementation of the model, it is necessary to choose or develop suitable technology platforms and tools. These platforms and tools should have strong data processing capabilities, friendly user interface, and good compatibility to support the effective application of learning and analysis technology. Also, teachers and students are trained to ensure that they are proficient in the use of these tools and platforms.

A. Mathematical Description of the K-means Algorithm

For students, learning and analysis technology is a powerful self-knowledge tool. By checking their study report, students can clearly understand their learning progress, mastery degree and existing problems, so as to make a more scientific and reasonable study plan. At the same time, learning analysis can also provide students with personalized learning recommendations, guide them to explore unknown areas, and broaden their knowledge horizons.

$$C_j(m+1) = \sum_{X(t)\in\theta_j(m)} \frac{X(t)}{M_j} \tag{1}$$

***B.** Choice of Blended Dynamic Learning Mode of University English*

In the face of teaching management, learning and analysis technology provides strong data support for decision-making. Through the comprehensive analysis of learning data, managers can fully understand the key indicators such as teaching quality, student satisfaction and resource utilization efficiency, so as to make more scientific and reasonable decisions and promote the continuous improvement of teaching quality. Moreover, learning analysis also helps to find potential teaching problems and provide directional guidance for teaching improvement.

$$r(x_i) = z_i G(d_i, y_i) \cdot \xi \tag{2}$$

C. Dynamic Model Analysis of Blended Learning in College English

When constructing the dynamic model of college English mixed learning, we also need to consider the deepening and expansion of the following aspects to ensure the integrity and effectiveness of the model. Dynamic adjustment mechanism: The model should have a flexible dynamic adjustment mechanism built-in to cope with the uncertainties and variability in the learning process. Through the continuous monitoring of learning and analysis techniques, the model can automatically identify the deviations or anomalies in the learning process and trigger the corresponding adjustment strategies. For example, when students show obvious difficulties in a learning link.

4   Results and Discussion

A. Introduction to Learning Dynamic Pattern Construction

IIn order to ensure the smooth operation and continuous optimization of the dynamic model of college English hybrid learning, the following supplementary implementation strategies and safeguards are crucial (Table 1):

Table 1. Statistics on the demand for English courses

course	One shift	Second shift	Three shifts
Basic English	21	19	20
Advanced English	11	6	4
Selected readings of newspapers and periodicals	7	3	12
English writing	3	7	9
English audiovisual	8	4	2
Translation theory and practice	3	10	5

The construction process of hybrid learning dynamic mode based on k-means algorithm is shown in Figure 2.

Formulate detailed implementation plans: clarify the objectives, tasks, time nodes and responsibilities of each stage to ensure the orderly progress of all work. At the same time, a special supervision team is set up to be responsible for tracking the implementation progress, finding and solving problems in time. Strengthening student guidance and training: In addition to improving teachers' ability, it is also necessary to strengthen the guidance and training for students to use mixed learning platforms and tools. By

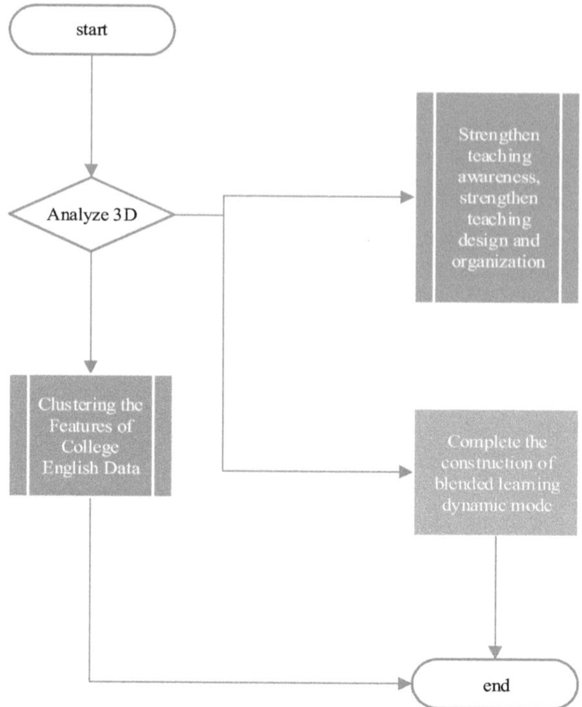

Fig. 2. Dynamic mode construction process of blended learning based on k-means algorithm

holding workshops, online tutorials and other ways, to help students get familiar with the learning environment, master the learning methods, and improve their independent learning ability.

B. Specific Context of the Blended Learning Dynamic Model

Establishing a data privacy protection mechanism: Given that learning and analysis involves a large number of students 'personal data, it is necessary to establish a sound data privacy protection mechanism to ensure the security and compliant use of students' information. Clarify the standard process of data collection, storage, processing and sharing, and strengthen the respect and protection of students' privacy rights (Table 2).

C. Stability of the Blended Learning Dynamic Model

Continuous evaluation and optimization: establish a regular evaluation mechanism to comprehensively evaluate the application effect of learning and analysis technology and the implementation effect of mixed learning mode. According to the evaluation results, the model design, learning resources, learning path and other aspects are adjusted timely to ensure that the dynamic model of mixed learning is always adapted to students' learning needs and development changes (Fig. 3).

Promoting academic exchanges and cooperation: Encourage academic exchanges and cooperation between teachers, schools and even internationally, and share the latest research results and practical experience in the field of mixed learning. Through cross-border cooperation, we will broaden our horizons, stimulate innovation, and jointly

Table 2. Student effectiveness statistics

course	The number of people who learned	The number of people who passed before applying the pattern	The number of passes after the pattern is applied	Lift rate
Basic English	58	47	57	14%
Advanced English	25	14	22	25%
Selected readings of newspapers and periodicals	19	15	20	15%
English writing	21	12	19	26%
English audiovisual	14	6	13	33%
Translation theory and practice	18	6	13	37%

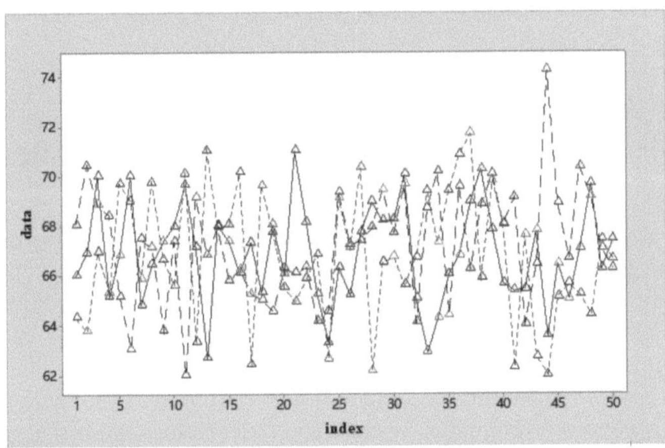

Fig. 3. The stability of dynamic mode construction schemes for different algorithms

promote the development and improvement of the college English mixed learning model (Table 3).

Table 3. Comparison of clustering efficiency of different algorithms

Different algorithms	Cluster efficiency/s
K-means algorithm	15
Fuzzy clustering algorithm	30

This paper discusses the learning analysis technology application in college English mixed learning, successfully constructed the dynamic model, the model not only reflects the respect for students individual differences, also through data driven decision support, tailored for each learner the learning path, greatly enhance the pertinence and effectiveness of learning. This result is not only expected to significantly improve students' learning effectiveness and satisfaction, but also provides a strong support for the innovation of college English teaching mode (Fig. 4).

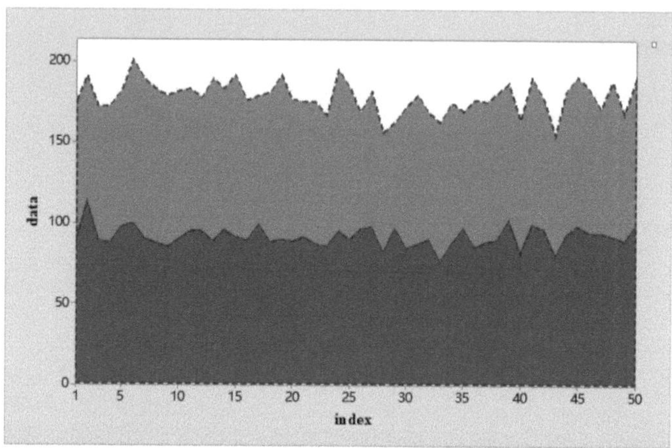

Figure 4. Comparison of the overall construction effect of different algorithms

However, as mentioned above, the implementation of mixed learning is not achieved overnight, and it faces many challenges in technology integration, resource construction, teacher training, student adaptation and other aspects. Therefore, future research and practice should pay more attention to the following points: first, to continuously optimize the technology platform to ensure its stability, ease of use and intelligence level; second, to strengthen interdisciplinary cooperation, integrate the research results of pedagogy, psychology, computer science and other fields, and promote the deepening of mixed learning theory and the expansion of practice;Third, pay attention to the long-term tracking and in-depth analysis of students' learning behavior to promote the continuous improvement of learning quality with more refined management; fourth, pay attention to the professional development of teachers and establish a long-term training and support mechanism to help teachers continuously improve their mixed teaching ability.

5   Conclusion

Combined with the problem that the construction effect of the dynamic mode of blended learning in college English is not satisfactory, this paper proposes the K-Means algorithm to construct the dynamic mode of blended learning. /b12 > The results show that the k-means algorithm can effectively improve the enthusiasm of college students to learn

English, and can also improve the English level of college students. /b15 > However, in the process of clustering, the k-means algorithm pays great attention to the efficiency of clustering, which makes the selection of some parameters unreasonable.

References

1. Ashraf, M.A., Shabnam, N., Tsegay, S.M., Huang, G.: Acceptance of smart technologies in blended learning: perspectives of Chinese medical students. Int. J. Environ. Res. Public Health **20**(3) (2023)
2. Baliya, J.N., Shikha, D.: Implementing blended learning approach for enhancement of scientific attitude of undergraduate students. Mier-J. Educ. Stud. Trends Pract. **13**(1), 129–146 (2023)
3. Barfi, K.A., Arkorful, V., Appiah, F., Agyapong, E.M., Acheampong, E.: The impact of blended learning on students using the IBOX platform: Initial perspectives of teachers. Heliyon **9**(3) (2023)
4. Basitere, M., Rzyankina, E., Le Roux, P.: Reflection on experiences of first-year engineering students with blended flipped classroom online learning during the COVID-19 pandemic: a case study of the mathematics course in the extended curriculum program. Sustainability **15**(6) (2023)
5. Bilyeu, C.A., McDevitt, A.W., Judd, D.L.: A blended approach to developing psychomotor skills in novice learners in a doctor of physical therapy curriculum. Med. Teacher 1–8 (2023)
6. Bursa, S.: The view of prospective social studies teachers on blended learning. Turkish Online J. Distance Educ. **24**(1), 185–199 (2023)
7. Chen, T., Luo, H., Feng, Q., Li, G.: Effect of technology acceptance on blended learning satisfaction: the serial mediation of emotional experience, social belonging, and higher-order thinking. Int. J. Environ. Res. Public Health **20**(5) (2023)
8. Cheng, X., Mo, W., Duan, Y.: Factors contributing to learning satisfaction with blended learning teaching mode among higher education students in China. Front. Psychol. **14** (2023)
9. Cheung, S.K.S., Wang, F.L., Kwok, L.F.: Online learning and blended learning: new practices derived from the pandemic-driven disruption. J. Comput. High. Educ. **35**(1), 1–5 (2023)
10. Faizan, M., Barsha, S., Eqbal, N., Munshi, S.A.: Blended learning vs. e-learning: determining the best mode of education from the perspective of the learners. Desidoc J. Libr. Inf. Technol. **43**(1), 30–38 (2023)

Teaching of Enterprise Informatization Data Sharing Model Based on Decision Tree Mining Algorithm

Mei Xu[✉]

School of Information Engineering, Wuhan University of Engineering Science, Wuhan 430000, Hubei, China

aquarxm@163.com

Abstract. The enterprise competition in the information society urgently needs the sharing of information resources. However, because there are many different databases within and between enterprises, they together constitute a heterogeneous database system, which makes enterprises face difficulties in achieving the unity, transparency and efficient sharing of information resources. At present, the main method to solve the information sharing of enterprise heterogeneous systems is to use database conversion tools or middleware, but the disadvantages are poor coupling, high cost and complex implementation. The emergence of service-based information sharing mode brings new methods to realize information sharing in heterogeneous systems. This paper makes a systematic and in-depth study of the information sharing architecture, sharing model and key technologies of hetero-geneous systems based on services. Decision tree is a method of finding data patterns. It helps to determine the most likely outcome of a given set of events. The working principle of the algorithm is to divide the data into smaller parts, and then analyze one at a time. Once all parts have been analyzed, put them together and form a conclusion about what happened in the past according to their relation-ship. In this paper, we will use decision tree algorithm to analyze and predict the sharing behavior among employees according to the characteristics of their work environment and the policies of information sharing within the organization.

Keywords: Enterprise informatization · Decision tree · Mining algorithm · data sharing

1 Introduction

In recent years, due to the development of network technology and database technology, enterprises often use database to manage information resources. However, different enterprises and even the same enterprise may have multiple databases. Due to the lack of unified planning and deployment, in the process of construction and development, the construction time of each system is different, the supplier is different, the technical equipment is different, the data library format is different, the operating environment is

© ICST Institute for Computer Sciences, Social Informatics and Telecommunications Engineering 2026
Published by Springer Nature Switzerland AG 2026. All Rights Reserved
B. Brik and S. Nazir (Eds.): BigIoT-EDU 2024, LNICST 659, pp. 490–496, 2026.
https://doi.org/10.1007/978-3-032-18631-7_53

different, and even the application software and user interface are different, thus forming a huge heterogeneous database system, The difficulty of data communication between various databases leads to the information between departments and enterprises can not be used interchangeably, which seriously affects the office and business efficiency of enterprises, and makes enterprises unable to form flexible management and unified management[1]. The best solution to this problem is to establish a heterogeneous system information sharing platform among enterprises to achieve the most effective use of information resources. Therefore, it is of great theoretical significance and application value to study the sharing model and key technologies of the sharing platform[2].

For the problem of heterogeneous database, a lot of research has been done by academic circles and major database manufacturers long ago. The main solution is to integrate heterogeneous data and reuse it, or use specific database tools and middleware technology to convert heterogeneous data format to achieve access to different database resources. These methods can achieve information sharing to a certain extent, but the sharing system developed by these technologies has poor coupling, poor scalability, complex implementation and high cost. At the same time, due to the rapid development of computer technology, the complexity of enterprise information environment is getting higher and higher. The enterprise's demand for information resources of heterogeneous systems has risen from a single data query and access to functional interoperability between systems. The traditional data sharing methods can no longer meet the current needs of enterprises[3]. At this time, the service-oriented information sharing platform construction concept has brought new vitality to solve the information sharing of heterogeneous systems, It advocates encapsulating all data operations into independent reusable Web services. These services publish clear interfaces, and the system calls corresponding services to complete data sharing operations through interfaces. Service-based information sharing mode can not only complete the query and access of data well, but also realize the functional interoperability between systems [4]. At present, it has become the most effective way to solve heterogeneous information sharing. The key technologies involved are metadata technology and interoperability technology.

2 Related Work

A. Research Status of Enterprise Informatization Data Sharing

The domestic research on information sharing of different enterprise information system databases is also in full swing. The domestic research mainly focuses on the ways and methods of how to connect and share data information under the C/S architecture, and dynamically access information to achieve data processing and sharing between heterogeneous databases. The main achievements are as follows: the University of Science and Technology of China proposes to adopt the mode of "data format conversion between heterogeneous database interactive access in the network environment" to realize the problem of heterogeneous database interactive access, and proposes to build a conversion mapping table between the source database and the target database to achieve the goal of data format conversion between the two. Huazhong University of Science and Technology adopts "DTS technology-based system heterogeneous database interconnection" for heterogeneous database information sharing in the industry [5]. In the enterprise information system, aiming at the established database resources and the actual existence of multiple heterogeneous databases, in order to realize the connection, data exchange and data sharing between different databases, the data conversion service (DTS) for heterogeneous database interconnection is used to realize the connection between heterogeneous databases, Data conversion and data transmission can effectively reduce the development cost and difficulty. Wuhan University uses the "data exchange method between heterogeneous databases in heterogeneous information systems" to solve the data sharing problem for the information systems with different structures and different operation mechanisms, which are independent of each other, different application platforms and database structures, and a large number of duplicate data problems, This paper puts forward a method of data exchange for heterogeneous databases of heterogeneous information systems based on Internet browsers [6]. Through the dynamic addition, deletion and modification of files, the unification of file information is realized, the unified management of data of heterogeneous information systems is realized, and the overall performance of the integrated system is improved. Wuhan Jiaotong University of Science and Technology put forward the "heterogeneous database integration technology under the C/S mode", and used the data environment generator technology provided by VB to realize the connection between Visual Basic 6.0 application system and Oracle data server, and standardize the data sharing operation between heterogeneous databases.

B. Establish Data Exchange Software Platform

Data exchange is an effective way to solve data sharing, and platform-based software architecture is an effective way to achieve data exchange. The logical function of the data exchange platform is the "soft bus + soft component" mode architecture. The data exchange platform is similar to an intelligent message transmission bus, connecting all components in the distributed heterogeneous system, and responsible for data transmission and access between all components and data sources. The data exchange platform can realize any data interaction between any systems [7].

The establishment of a data exchange platform has been involved in China for a long time. As early as 2002, Founder Digital put forward data integration between different business systems across regions and departments for information resource integration, providing a secure information exchange platform for conversion and exchange - Founder Hub m. Founder Yichang security information exchange platform provides secure and reliable message transmission for terminal nodes. It uses the message structure based on XML technology to express, store and transmit information. The message content encapsulated in the message structure can be information in XML format or in user-defined format. Beijing Huidian has developed a unified government affairs exchange platform based on the data exchange center, which supports cross-platform heterogeneous application systems, and can solve the problem of data integration and sharing, especially for the data integration and sharing of e-government and large-scale enterprise applications [8].

Sybase DXP data exchange platform launched by Sybase provides an integrated data exchange and sharing space for information exchange and sharing within and between e-government systems. It has good openness and can meet the data exchange needs of users on various platforms, data sources and applications at the same time, and better realizes the sharing of heterogeneous systems and data.

The establishment of data exchange software platform solves the heterogeneity of enterprise database system to some extent, and realizes the sharing of information [9]. However, there are still some problems, such as the sharing of heterogeneous information is mainly based on certain business systems, poor scalability, limited scope of information sharing, and lack of universality of data exchange platform.

3 Service-Based Enterprise System Sharing Model

The construction of information sharing platform for heterogeneous systems needs to follow a fixed architecture. The existing sharing systems are mainly divided into centralized and distributed systems. This chapter analyzes and compares the advantages and disadvantages of the centralized and distributed systems, and gives a general information sharing architecture on this basis. This system can effectively solve the inherent defects of the original system and maximize the collection of shared resources. Then, the existing information sharing model of heterogeneous systems based on Web services is studied, and its inherent shortcomings are found. Considering the complexity of the information environment and the diversity of information requirements of today's enterprises, this paper makes several improvements to the existing sharing model, advocating that the data conversion operation be regarded as a service, which simplifies the data conversion work in the sharing process, A service proxy layer is added to the model to solve the problem of direct communication between the client and the service layer.

A. Enterprise System Information Sharing Architecture

At present, there are two ways of data sharing in heterogeneous systems: centralized and distributed. The two architectures are discussed below.

(1) Centralized sharing system

Centralized sharing needs to be set up - a master center whose shared database stores the shared data provided by each data node. The master center regularly extracts data from the database of each data node, converts and stores it in the central database. The central database is essentially a data warehouse. The centralized data sharing architecture is shown in Fig. 1.

Centralized sharing requires the establishment of a central database in the sharing center. All information in the data source is preprocessed regularly to form information that conforms to the central database model, and then the data is stored. The main advantage of this method is that it can respond quickly to users' data resource requests, but the disadvantage is that the data may not be up to date. If the central database model is designed to be static, the cost of modifying the central database is relatively high when new data sources are added or existing data sources are changed, and because the central database needs to store and manage all data resources, when the data volume is increasing, The burden of the total center will also increase, and storage and management will become very difficult.

(2) Distributed sharing system

When the distributed sharing structure is adopted, it is not necessary to establish a central database in the sharing center. The sharing center can be a view center, which is only responsible for providing the view information of the shared data to provide the users of the data with search, binding and other functions. Generally, the view information refers to the metadata record of the data resources [10]. Through the metadata information of data resources provided by the sharing center, data users can connect to the publisher's database, view the data they can access and obtain data. The distributed sharing architecture is shown in Fig. 2.

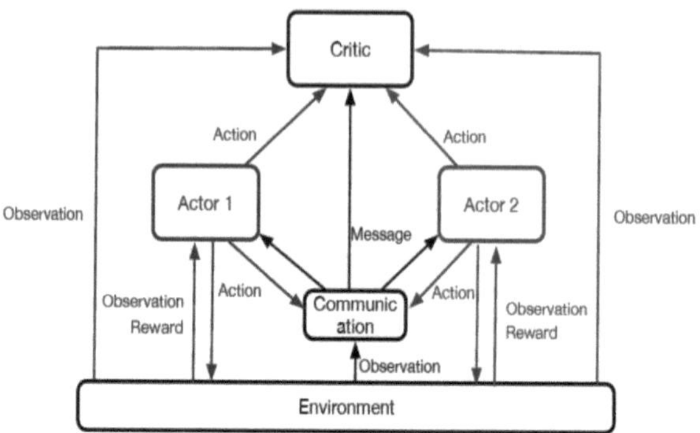

Fig. 1. Centralized sharing system

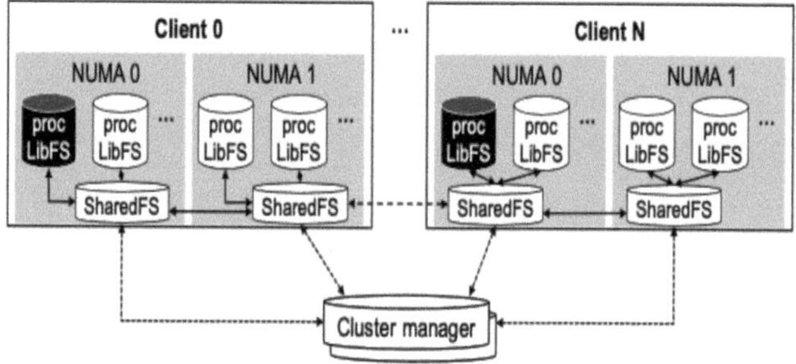

Fig. 2. Distributed sharing system

B. Web Service Deployment Based on Service Sharing Model

The core of the service-oriented heterogeneous information sharing model is the data service layer, which provides users with a series of Web services to complete the data sharing operation. These Web services can be divided into three parts: first, Web services designed for user management, mainly including user registration services and user login services; Second, Web services designed to provide data sharing, including data collection service, data update service, data query service and data access service; The third is the data conversion service designed to complete the data conversion. The specific deployment of Web services is as follows:

The services deployed by the certification center include user registration service and user login service. When a user registers in any data center, the user information should not only be saved in the local center, but also be stored in the registration center by calling the registration service of the registration center. When users log in to any data center, they can call the login service to achieve single sign-on in the entire sharing platform.

The services deployed by the general center include data collection service, data update service, data query service, data access service and data conversion service. The data center calls the data collection service to collect the metadata or data entities of the data resources to be shared into the database of the data center, which forms the basis of data sharing. The data center can update the metadata and data body records in the main center in real time by calling the data update service, so as to maintain the real-time nature of the main center data. When users query global metadata, the data center needs to call the metadata query service to obtain metadata records of all data centers. Since the main center hosts some data entities in the data center, data access services should be deployed in the main center. When receiving requests for such data resources, the main center directly provides users with data content access services. The data center converts the metadata or data body to be submitted into a unified data format by calling the data conversion service before collecting data; Before the client gets the data result, the proxy layer will call the data conversion service to convert the dataset to the destination data format for display.

4 Conclusion

Nowadays, information resources are becoming increasingly rich. How to share these information resources and make contributions to the development and competition of enterprises has become a bottleneck of information reform. The main reason is the heterogeneity of database systems. Therefore, how to solve the heterogeneity of the system is particularly important and urgent. The traditional heterogeneous system information sharing technology mainly focuses on the conversion of data, and completes the exchange and sharing of data through data conversion middleware, data migration technology, unified data access interface and other methods. However, these methods have a common defect, that is, the conversion process is complex, the universality and scalability are not strong, and the flexibility is poor. This paper analyzes and studies the sharing mode and technology of heterogeneous information sharing, This paper focuses on the information sharing model of heterogeneous systems based on Web services and the sharing technology involved.

Acknowledgements. The Guidance Project of the Scientific Research Plan of the Department of Education of Hubei Province (No. B2020287).

References

1. Wu, F., Liu, X., Wang, Y.: et al.: Research on evaluation model of hospital informatization level based on decision tree algorithm. Secur. Commun. Netw. (2022)
2. Si, Y.: Construction and application of enterprise internal audit data analysis model based on decision tree algorithm. Discrete Dyn. Nat. Soc. 2022 (2022)

3. Li, G., Alfred, R., Wang, X.: Student Behavior Analysis and Research Model Based on Clustering Technology. Hindawi Limited (2021)
4. Zhao, Y.: Sports Enterprise Marketing and Financial Risk Management Based on Decision Tree and Data Mining. Hindawi Limited (2021)
5. Zhao, P., Zhou, J., Li, X., et al.: Model training method and apparatus based on data sharing:, US11106802B2. (2021)
6. Guo, Y.: CNS: interactive intelligent analysis of financial management software based on apriori data mining algorithm. Int. J. Coop. Inf. Syst. **30**(01n04) (2021)
7. Li, J., Li, X., Zhang, Z.: Dynamic prediction model of bridge project life cycle cost investment based on decision tree algorithm. IOP Conf. Ser. Earth Environ. Sci. **760**(1):012049 (6pp) (2021)
8. Weizhao, F.U.: Research on clustering analysis and its application in customer data mining of enterprise (9) (2022)
9. Mannapov, I.: The improvement of decision tree construction algorithm based on quantum heuristic algorithms (2022)
10. Diao, Y., Zhang, Q.: Optimization of management mode of small- and medium-sized enterprises based on decision tree model. J. Math. **2021** (2021)

Teaching Management of Mathematical Models for Financial Risk Warning Systems in Digital Intelligent Enterprises

Jiaxin Wang[✉] and Niqin Jing

Beijing Polytechnic, Beijing 100179, China
`wjx12231200@126.com`

Abstract. In corporate finance, the existence of financial risks will cause certain losses to the company's finances, so that the initial expected return cannot be realized. The universal application of digitalization will intelligently solve the problem of risk early warning, and realize the expected value that cannot be achieved by traditional risk early warning methods. Based on this, this paper proposes a mathematical model of risk early warning system that can be applied in intelligent risk early warning analysis. First of all, artificial intelligence technology is used to predict the financial risk of the enterprise, and based on the requirements of risk early warning, the indicators are divided, so as to reduce the risk early warning contained in the interference factors. Then, artificial intelligence is used to form a risk early warning scheme for the early warning results of enterprise financial risks, and a comprehensive analysis is carried out for the early warning results. Through MATLAB simulation, it can be found that under certain evaluation criteria, the mathematical model of the risk early warning system used this time has significantly higher risk early warning accuracy than the risk early warning under the application of traditional enterprise financial risk early warning methods.

Keywords: artificial intelligence · Mathematical model of risk early warning system · Corporate Finance · Financial risk

1 Introduction

The financial risk early warning system is a key tool for financial institutions and regulators to prevent financial risks and maintain financial stability [1,2]. Through real-time monitoring, analysis and prediction of a large amount of financial data, it can identify potential financial crises in a timely manner, so as to provide early warning signals for decision-makers and reduce the probability of financial crises. In the context of the increasing complexity of global financial markets and the rapid development of financial innovation, the effectiveness of early warning systems has a non-negligible value for preventing systemic risks, protecting the interests of investors, and maintaining overall economic stability. The risk early warning process in Table I. is shown in Fig. 1.

B. Brik and S. Nazir (Eds.): BigIoT-EDU 2024, LNICST 659, pp. 497–505, 2026.
https://doi.org/10.1007/978-3-032-18631-7_54

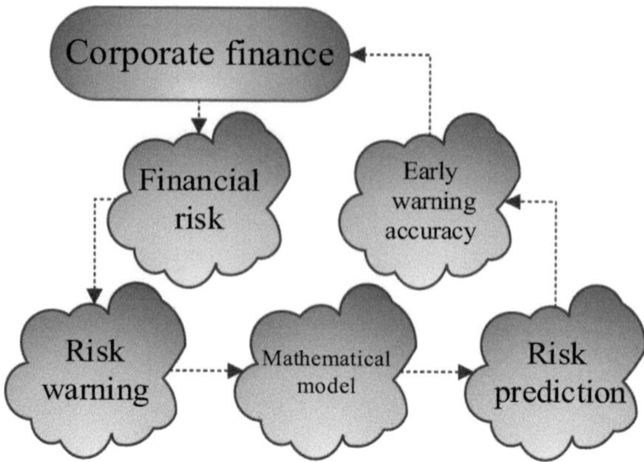

Fig.1. The analytical process of corporate finances

In the future, the teaching model will pay more attention to the combination of online and offline to meet the educational needs of the digital age [3,4]. The blended learning model combines classroom discussions with online self-study, allowing students to gain a deeper understanding of risk warning models at their own pace. The application of virtual reality (VR) and augmented reality (AR) technologies will provide an immersive learning experience that helps students intuitively understand how the model works. At the same time, project-based learning and problem-based learning (PBL) will encourage students to apply what they have learned in real-world cases and improve their ability to solve real-world problems.

2 Related Works

A. The Application of Digital Intelligence Technology in Financial Risk Warning

Digital intelligence technologies, such as artificial intelligence (AI), big data analytics, machine learning, etc., have profoundly changed the way financial risks are warned. AI can use deep learning algorithms to mine historical data, find out hidden risk patterns, and conduct real-time analysis when new data is entered to predict possible future risk events [5]. Big data technology provides the ability to process massive amounts of information, quickly integrate and analyze complex data from different sources, and reveal risk signals that are difficult to detect with traditional methods [6]. In addition, natural language processing technology can parse unstructured information, such as news reports and social media feeds, to help capture changes in market sentiment and further improve the comprehensiveness of early warnings.

B. The Role of Teaching Management in the Mathematical Model of Risk Warning

In the field of education, effective teaching management is essential to cultivate financial risk early warning talents with the ability to apply digital intelligence technology. Through systematic course design, students not only acquire financial theoretical knowledge, but also learn how to construct and apply mathematical models to identify risks. Teaching management emphasizes the combination of practice and theory, and encourages students to participate in real-world projects and improve their ability to solve complex problems through simulation or analysis of real financial data [7]. In addition, teaching management also focuses on the professional development of teachers, ensuring that teachers can keep up with the pace of technological advancements and integrate the latest research results and practical applications into the classroom, so as to cultivate interdisciplinary talents who can adapt to the future financial environment.

C. The Basic Theory of Financial Risk Warning

The financial risk early warning system is a scientific risk management tool, the core of which is to predict and warn possible financial risks through data collection, analysis and model construction, so as to help decision-makers take timely measures to reduce losses. The basic theory includes three key links: risk identification, risk assessment and risk control. Risk identification is concerned with identifying potential sources of financial risk, such as market risk, credit risk, operational risk, etc. Risk assessment measures the magnitude and likelihood of risk through quantitative means, while risk control involves the formulation of risk response strategies and risk mitigation measures.

D. The Impact of Digital Intelligent Algorithms on Early Warning of Corporate Financial Risks

Mathematical models play a crucial role in the early warning of financial risks. Common models include statistical, econometric, time series, structural, and machine learning-based models.

First, statistical models, such as standard deviation and VaR (Value at Risk), use statistical principles to evaluate the possible loss of financial assets. Second, econometric models, such as ARIMA (Autoregressive Integrated Moving Average Model) and GARCH (Generalized Autoregressive Conditional Heteroskedasticity Model), are used to analyze nonlinear and dynamic relationships in time series data. Third, structural models, such as the KMV (KMV model) and the Merton model, predict default risk by analyzing the financial structure of a firm. Fourth, machine learning-based models, such as neural networks, support vector machines, random forests, etc., can predict the probability of future risk events by learning a large amount of historical data [8].

Internationally, the research on financial risk early warning systems has achieved remarkable results, such as the subprime mortgage crisis early warning system in the United States and the banking stress testing framework in Europe [9,10]. These systems make extensive use of advanced mathematical models and big data analysis techniques to monitor the volatility of financial markets and the stability of financial institutions in real time. In China, with the rapid development of the financial market and the improvement of regulatory policies, the construction of risk early warning system has also received increasing attention [11,12]. Many financial institutions and research institutions have developed risk early warning models with Chinese characteristics, such as credit risk early warning systems based on big data and market risk early warning models based on deep learning [13,14]. In the future, the development trend will pay more attention to the intelligence and integration of models, combined with cloud computing and blockchain technology, to achieve real-time sharing and intelligent analysis of risk data. At the same time, with the advancement of financial innovation, new risks such as fintech risks, environmental and social risks will also become the focus of the early warning system.

3　Teacher Team Construction and Training

The mathematical model of the risk early warning system adopts the random optimization strategy for enterprise finance, and adjusts the corporate financial parameters to realize the optimization of enterprise finance [15].The mathematical model of the risk early warning system divides the enterprise finance into different risk early warning levels, and randomly selects different schemes. In the iterative process, the risk early warning schemes with different risk early warning levels are optimized and analyzed. After the optimization analysis is completed, compare the risk warning level of different solutions and record the best corporate finance [16].

Artificial intelligence (AI) is playing an increasingly important role in the early warning of corporate financial risks [17]. Through machine learning algorithms, AI can automatically learn and spot risk patterns from massive amounts of financial data. For example, neural network models can analyze historical transaction data to predict future credit default probabilities, while models such as decision trees and random forests can identify specific behaviors or events that could lead to risk. AI can also monitor market dynamics in real-time, using natural language processing to parse news, announcements, and social media to capture changes in public opinion that could affect a company's financial health. In addition, the automation of AI enables the risk early warning system to work 24/7, greatly improving the speed of risk identification and response.

$$tol\left(y_i \cdot t_{ij}\right) = y_{ij} \geq max(t_{ij} \sum\nolimits_{i=1}^{n} t_i Y \frac{t - \mu}{\sigma}_i) \tag{1}$$

Big data technology is a key component of modern risk early warning systems.

$$max(t_{ij}) = \left(t_{ij}^2 \div 7\right) \succ mean\left(\sum t_{ij} \int \frac{t - \mu}{\sigma} \frac{1}{n} \sigma_t\right) \tag{2}$$

Big data technology is a key component of modern risk early warning systems. It allows businesses to collect, store, and analyze large amounts of complex data from different sources. For example, big data can help companies integrate internal financial statements, supply chain data, customer behavior data, and external market data, such as macroeconomic indicators, industry reports, and competitor information. Through big data analysis, companies can uncover potential risk associations and identify early signs of risk. For example, by analyzing suppliers' payment delay patterns, companies can warn of the possibility of supply chain disruptions; By mining social media and online reviews, it is possible to predict changes in consumer satisfaction with products or services, and then predict possible business risk.

$$N(r_i) = \sum t_i \cap \xi \rightarrow \oint y_i \leftarrow \int \frac{t - \mu}{\sigma} \sum\nolimits_{i=1}^{n} t_i Y_i \tag{3}$$

Cloud computing provides powerful computing power and flexible resource scalability for financial risk early warning. With a cloud computing platform, businesses can quickly process and analyze large-scale data without having to invest heavily in hardware. The elasticity of cloud computing enables enterprises to quickly call up more computing resources for rapid risk assessment and decision support when risk events occur.

$$l(t_i) = z_i \cdot \prod N(r_i) - w_i \leftrightarrow \sum_{i=1}^{n} t_i Y_i \frac{1}{n} \mu_t \tag{4}$$

In addition, the distributed architecture of cloud computing improves data security and disaster recovery capabilities, and ensures the stable operation of the risk early warning system.

$$l(t_i) + N(r_i) \leq max(t_{ij}) \tag{5}$$

Through cloud services, enterprises can also realize cross-regional and cross-departmental risk information sharing, improve collaboration efficiency, and reduce communication costs. At the same time, the pay-as-you-go model of cloud computing enables enterprises to obtain efficient risk management capabilities at a lower cost.

$$l(t_i) + N(r_i) \leftrightarrow mean\left(\sum t_{ij} \int \frac{t - \mu}{\sigma} \frac{1}{n} \sigma_t\right) \tag{6}$$

By integrating AI, big data, and cloud computing, enterprises can build an intelligent, agile, and cost-effective financial risk early warning system to better respond to the complex and volatile financial market environment, identify and manage potential risks in a timely manner, and ensure the sound operation of enterprises.

$$No(t_i) = \frac{l(t_i) + N(r_i)}{mean\left(\sum t_{ij} \int \frac{t-\mu}{\sigma} \frac{1}{n} \sigma_t\right)} \tag{7}$$

In the teaching of the mathematical model of the enterprise financial risk early warning system, the goal of teaching management is to ensure that students can master the core theoretical knowledge and have the ability to apply this knowledge to practical problem solving. The orientation of the teaching is to cultivate professionals with innovative thinking, data analysis ability and risk prediction skills. Through rigorous curriculum design, effective teaching methods and feedback mechanisms, Teaching Management is committed to improving students' theoretical literacy and practical operation ability to meet the demand for risk early warning talents in the financial industry.

$$Zh(t_i) = min[\sum l(t_i) + N(r_i)] \tag{8}$$

The case teaching method plays an important role in the teaching of risk early warning models. Through the analysis of real business cases, students can intuitively understand the application of the model in practice, such as through the analysis of corporate financial statements, market data and industry dynamics, and the use of different early warning models for risk assessment. The selection of cases should cover a variety of industries and business sizes to demonstrate the universality of the model. In addition, teachers guide students to discuss the process of handling cases, analyze the limitations of models, and develop critical thinking and problem-solving skills.

$$accur(t_i) = \frac{min[\sum l(t_i) + N(r_i)]}{\sum l(t_i) + N(r_i)} \times 100\% \tag{9}$$

Practical teaching is a key part of improving students' hands-on ability. In the teaching process, a simulated risk early warning project can be set up for students to operate and use the learned model to conduct risk analysis on virtual or real enterprises. The project-driven teaching model encourages students to participate in teams, simulates a real-world business environment, and promotes teamwork and communication skills. Through the implementation of the project, students not only deepen their understanding of the theory, but also accumulate practical work experience that prepares them for their future careers.

$$accur(t_i) = \frac{\min[\sum l(t_i) + N(r_i)]}{\sum l(t_i) + N(r_i)} \times 100\% + randon(t_i) \tag{10}$$

Continuous professional development is an important guarantee for the vitality and adaptability of the teaching workforce. Regular training activities can help teachers update their body of knowledge and master new teaching methods and techniques. For example, teachers are regularly invited to participate in financial risk management seminars to learn about the latest research results in the industry. Participate in instructional technology training to improve the ability of online and blended teaching; Industry experts will be invited to share practical cases to enhance the combination of theory and practice.

4   Results and Discussion

A. The Impact of Technological Innovation on Risk Early Warning Systems
With the rapid development of technology, financial risk early warning systems are gradually incorporating more innovative technologies, such as blockchain, Internet of Things (IoT), 5G communication, quantum computing, etc. The decentralized nature of blockchain technology provides transparency and security to financial transactions, helping to identify potential fraud. The widespread deployment of IoT devices can monitor enterprise operational data in real time, providing faster and more accurate information for risk warning. The high speed and low latency of 5G communication make real-time risk assessment possible. The efficient computing power of quantum computing will greatly improve the prediction accuracy of models and the ability to process complex data (Table 1).

B. Optimization and Integration of Teaching Resources
With the digitization of educational resources, platforms such as Open Online Courses (MOOCs) and digital libraries provide teachers and students with a wealth of learning resources. In the future, teaching will pay more attention to personalized recommendation of resources, use big data and artificial intelligence technology to analyze students' learning behaviors and needs, and provide customized learning paths. At the same time, the integration of interdisciplinary resources will promote the integration of knowledge in the fields of finance, mathematics, computer science, etc., and enhance the depth and breadth of risk early warning teaching (Table 2).

C. Financial Risks and Stability of Risk Early Warning
In the context of globalization, the teaching and research of financial risk early warning need to strengthen international exchanges and cooperation (Fig. 2).

Table 1. Risk early warning requirements

Scope of application	grade	Accuracy	Financial risk
Assets and liabilities	standard	87.49	82.86
	Higher	82.43	83.53
Income statement	standard	81.65	83.43
	Higher	83.99	85.46
cash flow	standard	85.23	84.54
	Higher	82.44	87.44

Table 2. The overall picture of the financial risk programme

category	accuracy	Analysis rate
Assets and liabilities	87.93	85.07
Income statement	87.30	87.80
cash flow	90.86	84.94
mean	85.99	86.29
X^6	89.61	86.90
P = 2.221		

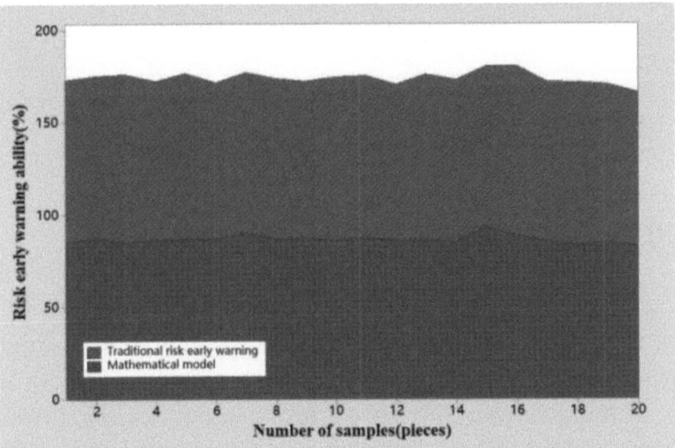

Fig. 2. Financial risks of different algorithms

Through academic conferences, joint research projects and student exchange programs, educational institutions in different countries and regions can share the latest research results and enhance the international impact of risk warning models (Table 3).

Table 3. Comparison of risk early warning accuracy of different methods

algorithm	Financial risk	Magnitude of change	error
Mathematical model of risk early warning system	92.05	92.65	94.96
Traditional risk early warning methods	91.46	89.28	93.73
P	86.55	85.35	92.28

In addition, the development and application of international standards will promote the standardization and consistency of risk warning education and improve the robustness of global financial markets (Fig. 3).

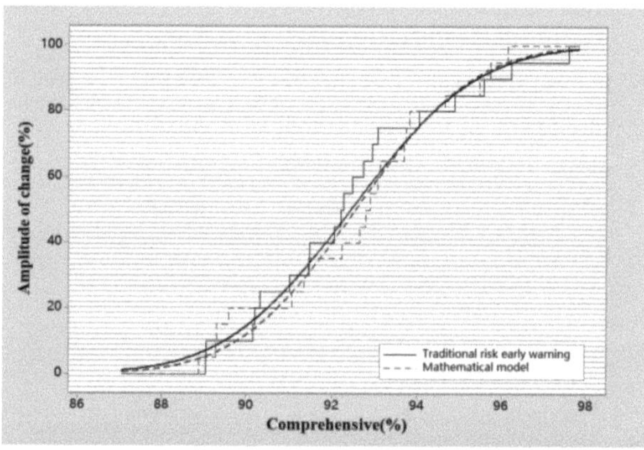

Fig. 3. Mathematical model of risk early warning system: financial risk of risk early warning

5 Conclusion

For the actual situation of the financial risk of the enterprise, the excellent mathematical model of the risk early warning system is proposed, and at the same time, it is combined with the computer to optimize the financial of the enterprise. In addition, conduct in-depth analysis of the accuracy of risk warnings and build a mature corporate financial collection. The research shows that the use of the mathematical model of the risk early warning system will effectively promote the development of enterprises, improve the financial profits of enterprises, and provide better risk early warning for enterprise finance. In fact, when constructing the mathematical model of the risk early warning system, if too much attention is paid to the analysis of risk early warning, it may also cause the problem that the selection of risk early warning indicators is not reasonable enough.

References

1. Behbehani, D., Komninos, N., Al-Begain, K., Rajarajan, M.: Cloud enterprise dynamic risk assessment (CEDRA): a dynamic risk assessment using dynamic Bayesian networks for cloud environment. J. Cloud Comput.-Adv. Syst. Appl. **12**(1) (2023)
2. Chen, H., Ho, K.-C., Zhang, M., Zhang, Q.: Effect of managerial ability toward corporate social responsibility on enterprise default risk. Finan. Res. Lett. **54** (2023)
3. Cheng, D., Niu, Z., Li, J., Jiang, C.: Regulating systemic crises: stemming the contagion risk in networked-loans through deep graph learning. IEEE Trans. Knowl. Data Eng. **35**(6), 6278–6289 (2023)
4. Civelek, M., Krajcik, V., Fialova, V.: The impacts of innovative and competitive abilities of SMEs on their different financial risk concerns: System approach. Oeconomia Copernicana **14**(1), 327–354 (2023)
5. Dai, D., Han, S., Zhao, M., Xie, J.: The impact mechanism of digital transformation on the risk-taking level of Chinese listed companies. Sustainability **15**(3) (2023)
6. Deng, X., Su, X.: Do Financial liabilities matter in "Size Effect"? Evidence from the Chinese a-share market. Sustainability **15**(4) (2023)
7. Ding, X., Li, J., Song, T., Ding, C., Tan, W.: Does carbon emission of firms aggravate the risk of financial distress? Evidence from China. Finan. Res. Lett. **56** (2023)
8. Fan, L., He, J.: The impact of gambling culture on entity financialization. Sustainability **15**(5) (2023)
9. Franzoni, S., Pelizzari, C.: Assessment of rainfall risk in a financial perspective: an application to the wine industry. Global Bus. Rev. (2023)
10. Gao, Z., Li, L., Hao, Y.: Financial risk under the shock of global warming: evidence from China. Bus. Strategy Environ. (2023)
11. Ge, X.: Construction of an enterprise financial risk management system based on F-score model. Appl. Math. Nonlinear Sci. (2023)
12. Guo, K., Guo, X., Zhang, J.: Financial asset allocation duality and enterprise upgrading: empirical evidence from the Chinese a-share market. Hum. Soc. Sci. Commun. **10**(1) (2023)
13. Han, M.X., Guo, Z.X., Dang, Y.J., Long, T.Z.: Examining the impact of carbon constraints on the capital structure of Chinese power enterprises. Front. Energy Res. **10** (2023)
14. Han, W.: Enterprise financial risk model based on cloud computing in age of big data. Soft Comput. (2023)
15. Han, X., Feng, Y., Li, J.: Shadow banking activities of non-financial companies and the information content of stock prices. J. Asian Econ. 85 (2023)
16. Han, X., Hsu, S., Li, J., An, R.: Economic policy uncertainty, non-financial enterprises' shadow banking activities and stock price crash risk. Emerg. Mark. Rev. **54** (2023)
17. Ho, T.H.T., Pham, T.T.H., Nguyen, T.T., Nguyen, Q.N.: Factors affecting financial risks: evidence from steel enterprises listed on Vietnam's stock market. Int. J. Adv. Appl. Sci. **10**(3), 75–81 (2023)

Teaching Credit Risk Prediction for Supply Chain Financing of Small and Medium-Sized Enterprises Based on IG-SVM Model

LiuLei Zhao[✉]

Economy and Management College, HeiLongJiang University of Technology, Jixi 158100, Heilongjiang, China
zll3219@126.com

Abstract. Information gain (Information Gain, IG) is a feature selection measure commonly used in decision tree algorithms, which measures the predictive ability of a feature to the target variable. The IG algorithm evaluates the importance of features by calculating the degree of entropy reduction before and after dividing the dataset. Entropy is a measure of the purity of a data set. The greater the information gain, the stronger is the conditional entropy of the data set divided according to feature A. A larger IG value increases the influence of feature A on the classification. In practice, the IG algorithm can help us to screen the most influential features on the target variable from a large number of candidate features, reduce the complexity of the model and improve the accuracy of prediction. MATLAB simulation shows that the IG-SVM model predicts the credit risk of supply chain financing of SMEs under certain evaluation criteria The accuracy and accuracy of credit risk prediction are better than traditional forecasting methods.

Keywords: computer · IG-SVM model · SME supply chain finance · Credit risk forecast

1 Introduction

The core idea of SVM is to find an optimal hyperplane that separates the sample points of different categories while maximizing the interval between the two categories. In the credit risk prediction [1, 2], the SVM has the following advantages: Nonlinear separability: The SVM can deal with the nonlinear problems through the kernel function, map the data to the high-dimensional space, and find the optimal hyperplane. Focusing on the economic chain and content of enterprise industry is the main aspect of credit risk analysis [3, 4]. However, whether credit risk can meet the actual requirements and the occurrence rate of credit risk need to be analyzed in depth. In-depth risk includes not only its own evaluation indicators, but also the comprehensive content of the enterprise. Therefore, there are many complexity of new risks, and it is necessary to analyze the credit risk in combination with the economic development of banks and enterprises themselves [5, 6]. Generalization capability: SVM improves the generalization ability of the

B. Brik and S. Nazir (Eds.): BigIoT-EDU 2024, LNICST 659, pp. 506–515, 2026.
https://doi.org/10.1007/978-3-032-18631-7_55

model by minimizing structural risk rather than empirical risk. Small sample learning: SVM can also achieve good results when the sample size is relatively small. In the credit risk prediction, the SVM model can combine the features selected by the IG algorithm to construct an efficient risk assessment model. By training SVM, we can get a classifier, which can predict the future default probability of the borrowing enterprise according to the historical data and operating conditions, so as to help financial institutions to develop more accurate credit policies and risk control strategies [7–10].

2   Related Works

A. The Basic Concept of Supply Chain Financing

logistics and capital flow in the supply chain. It mainly through the cooperation between core enterprises and financial institutions, provides financial support for small and medium-sized enterprises in the supply chain, reduces the difficulty of financing and improves the efficiency of capital turnover [11, 12]. The types of supply chain financing include prepayment financing, accounts receivable financing, inventory financing, etc. These methods are usually based on trade background and guaranteed by real transaction contract, which reduce financial risks.

B. Challenges for SMEs in Supply Chain Financing

Small and medium-sized enterprises are usually in a weak position in the supply chain. Compared with the core enterprises, their information acquisition ability and credit record are relatively limited, which leads to the large information asymmetry problem of financial institutions when providing financing, which increases the risk of financing [13–15]. Due to small scale, unstable operation and other factors, small and medium-sized enterprises generally have low credit rating, and it is difficult to obtain credit support from traditional banks. Banks usually tend to lend to large enterprises with higher credit ratings, which makes SMEs difficult in the financing process.

C. Poor Liquidity of Assets

SMEs often lack sufficient collateral and have liquid assets such as inventory and accounts receivable, which to some extent limits their ability to obtain funds through supply chain financing. Due to financing difficulties, small and medium-sized enterprises are often forced to accept high financing costs, such as high interest rates, high handling fees, etc., which further increases the financial burden of enterprises and affects the profitability of enterprises [16, 17].

D. Restrictions of Laws and Regulations

To some extent, the existing laws and regulations restrict the development of s

Supply chain is a complex and interdependent network, in which each node enterprise plays a specific role, and credit risk is a key variable in this network. When one or more enterprises in the supply chain have credit risk, such as failure to pay accounts on time or fulfill contractual obligations, this will not only affect their own reputation, but also have ripple effects in the entire supply chain. This instability may cause disruption of capital flow and suppliers to obtain the expected payments, thus affecting their production and delivery capacity. In addition, credit risk can lead to inventory overstocking, production delays, and may even cause legal disputes, further disrupting the balance of the supply chain [18].

This knock-on effect of credit risk may lead to a reduced efficiency of the entire supply chain, increased operating costs, and a potentially negative impact on corporate market share and customer satisfaction. In order to maintain the efficient operation of the supply chain, enterprises must have a clear understanding of the credit risk, and take effective preventive and response measures.

3 Optimization Strategies for SME Supply Chain Financing

Data preprocessing is a crucial step before constructing the IG-SVM model. First, data needs to be collected from the transaction history of supply chain financing, including but not limited to the corporate financial statements, transaction records, credit ratings, industry conditions, etc. These data may contain missing values, outliers and noise, and data quality needs to be ensured by data cleaning and filling with missing values. Next, feature selection is performed using the information gain (IG) algorithm. IG measures the correlation between features and target variables, and selects those features that can maximize the information entropy reduction to reduce redundant and irrelevant features and improve the prediction efficiency of the model.

A. The Significance of Predicting Credit Risk to Enterprise Decision-Making

Predict credit risk is of vital strategic significance for enterprises. First, accurate credit risk forecasting can help companies identify potential financial difficulties in advance to take preventive measures, such as adjusting payment terms, increasing margin requirements or seeking alternative suppliers to reduce possible losses. In this way, The specific results are shown in Eq. (1).

$$tol(p_i \cdot d_{ij}) \geq max(d_{ij} + \sum x) \tag{1}$$

In this way, enterprises can avoid the rupture of the capital chain caused by credit risks, and ensure their own operation safety.,The specific results are shown in Eq. (2).

$$max(d_{ij}) \sim \sqrt{[mean(\frac{d_{ij}}{R}) + \sum d_{ij}]} \tag{2}$$

Secondly, credit risk prediction can support more accurate credit rating and customer screening. Enterprises can conduct credit evaluation of suppliers and customers according to the forecast results, and give priority to cooperation with enterprises with high credit ratings to reduce transaction risks. This also helps to optimize the allocation of enterprise resources and invest limited resources into partners with lower risk and more stable returns. The specific results are shown in Eq. (3).

$$R(d_{ij}) \sim \sqrt{[k - R(\frac{d_{ij}}{R}) + \sum d_i]} \tag{3}$$

B. Selection of Credit Risk Prediction Schemes

Moreover, credit risk prediction is very important for the formulation of enterprise internal risk management strategies. It can help enterprises to establish and improve the risk management system, improve the risk identification and response ability, to ensure that enterprises can make quick decisions when facing credit risks, and reduce risk exposure. The specific results are shown in Eq. (4).

$$f(d_i) = \sqrt[n]{k}l_i \cdot \prod \frac{df}{dk} R(h_i) \cdot \frac{1}{n} - k_i \tag{4}$$

Finally, credit risk prediction is an important basis for enterprise strategic planning and decision-making. Through a deep understanding of the market environment and partners' credit status, companies are able to more accurately assess market risks and develop more robust expansion or contraction strategies to adapt to the changing business environment. The specific results are shown in Eq. (5).

$$\frac{f(d_i)}{R(h_i)} \le max(d_{ij}) + \Delta d_{ij} \tag{5}$$

In general, credit risk prediction is an important tool for enterprises to maintain the stability of supply chain, optimize resource allocation, improve the level of risk management and ensure the correctness of strategic decisions. The specific results are shown in Eq. (6).

$$\frac{f(d_i)}{n} + R(h_i) \le mean(d_{ij}) + \sin d_{ij} \tag{6}$$

C. Advantages of the IG-SVM Model in Credit Risk Prediction

The Information Gain (IG) is a feature selection method commonly used in the decision tree algorithm, which measures the influence of the features on the classification results. In credit risk prediction, the selection of features is critical because they directly affect the prediction accuracy and efficiency of the model. By calculating the information gain of each feature, we can prioritize those features that maximize the classification purity improvement, thus reducing redundant information and improving the generalization ability of the model. The specific results are shown in Eq. (7).

$$LK(d_i) = f(di)\frac{mean[\sum dij]}{R} \tag{7}$$

In the context of SME supply chain financing, the characteristics may include corporate financial indicators (such as profit margin, debt ratio), historical repayment records, industry status, partner stability, etc. Using IG, we can quickly identify which of these traits are most relevant to credit risk. The specific results are shown in Eq. (8).

$$LK(x_i) = \frac{min[\sum \widetilde{f}(x_i)]}{kn} \tag{8}$$

Support vector machine, Support Vector Machine (SVM) is a supervised learning model, especially when processing non-linear separable data. In credit risk prediction, SVM distinguishes defaulted from non-defaulted enterprises by constructing the maximum margin hyperplane, which maximizes the distance between the two types of samples, thus improving the robustness of the classification. The core idea of SVM is to find the optimal support vectors, which are near the decision boundary and play a key role in the model construction. The specific results are shown in Eq. (9).

$$SF(d_i) = f(d_i)\frac{min[R(h_i)]}{kn} \tag{9}$$

With the help of IG, we have screened the most influential features for credit risk prediction, and SVM can quickly find the best classification boundary. In addition, SVM can handle high-dimensional feature space through kernel functions (such as radial basis function RBF) and maintain good performance even when the data dimensions are high. The specific results are shown in Eq. (10).

$$Sg(s_i) = dif[f(s_i) - R(s_i)] + f(d_i)|k \tag{10}$$

In the supply chain financing scenario, the high efficiency of SVM is reflected in its ability to quickly process a large amount of enterprise data, while avoiding the complex characteristic interaction effects. By using SVM, the model can accurately identify high-risk enterprises, so that financial institutions can adjust their credit strategies in time and reduce the risk of non-performing loans. Combining IG and SVM, we can construct a credit risk prediction model with both strong classification ability and good generalization performance. Such a model is of great value for the credit evaluation of the supply chain financing environment of small and medium-sized enterprises, and can help financial institutions to evaluate potential risks more accurately and improve the scientificity and accuracy of financing decisions.

4   Results and Discussion

A. Data Preprocessing and Feature Selection

This paper analyzes the financing problems of small and medium-sized enterprises, and its financing fund is 124 million. The time should be three years. The enterprise is mainly engaged in investment and operation activities, and it belongs to a comprehensive economic enterprise. In the process of financing analysis, complex data are simplified to facilitate later quantitative analysis. And find out the contents and key points that affect financing and financing teaching. In order to facilitate credit risk prediction, After feature selection, construction of the IG-SVM model can begin. The SVM (Support Vector Machine) model is a classifier based on structural risk minimization to distinguish between different categories of samples by constructing the maximum margin hyperplane. In the IG-SVM model, the information gain is used as the feature weights to guide the feature weight assignment of the SVM. The final results can be obtained by summarizing the results of the research data in this paper, as shown in Table 1.

According to the data analysis in Table 1, the data results in Table 1 are relatively in line with the requirements, but to make an overall judgment on the data in Table 1, it is necessary to conduct in-depth analysis of its testing process and process, and obtain specific results is shown in Fig. 1.

From the data analysis in Figure 1, In the process of risk prediction, the risks mainly come from two aspects, the internal and external aspects of enterprise people. The internal

Table 1. Credit risk profiling requirements

Scope of application	Actual production	Precision	Credit risk forecast
Accounts receivable financing	Results	84.85	86.86
	Industrial chain	85.59	86.13
Confirmed warehouse financing	Results	83.10	85.33
	Industrial chain	88.33	87.19
Financing of the facility	Results	84.76	85.42
	Industrial chain	85.50	83.44

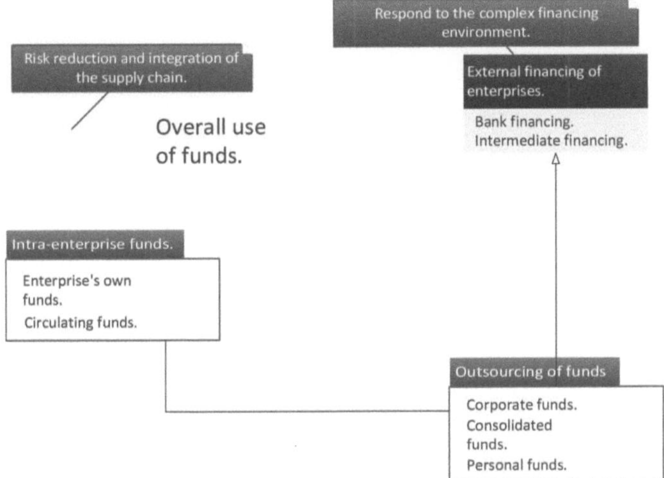

Fig. 1. The analytical process of supply chain finance for SMEs

is mainly the withdrawal of funds, and the external is mainly the financing of funds and banks, which together constitute the financing of small and medium-sized enterprises. Basic conditions and provide support for financing early warning of small and medium-sized enterprises.it can be seen that in the process of credit risk analysis, it is necessary to comprehensively analyze the industrial chain, industrial risks and industrial contents, and obtain historical data, actual results and actual needs to comprehensively analyze, so as to improve the overall analysis.

B. Model Performance Evaluation and Validation

Credit risk is not only a simple risk content, but also involves the actual rating index of credit risk. Therefore, it is necessary to test the standard and actual risks, and integrate various factors to evaluate the credit risk of the enterprise industrial chain, and make an effective prediction. These indicators can help us to understand the effect of the model in identifying credit risk. Moreover, the real case, false positive, true and negative, and false and negative cases are visually viewed visually through the confusion matrix to understand the performance of the model on different categories. To verify the stability and generalization ability of the model, the model performance can be further evaluated using independent test sets in addition to the training and validation sets (Table 2).

Table 2. The overall picture of the credit risk prediction program

category	precision	Analysis rate
Accounts receivable financing	87.39	87.31
Confirmed warehouse financing	88.33	87.49
Financing of the facility	87.90	87.74
mean	89.46	86.52
X^6	90.15	86.93
P = 1.104		

C. Teaching Strategy of Credit Risk Prediction in Supply Chain Financing

The interpretability of the model is equally important in the supply chain financing credit risk prediction. By analyzing the decision boundaries and support vectors of SVM, we can understand how the model distinguishes between high-risk and low-risk enterprises, which has practical value for enterprise risk management and decision support. The expression results and comparison of risk prediction are shown in Fig. 2.

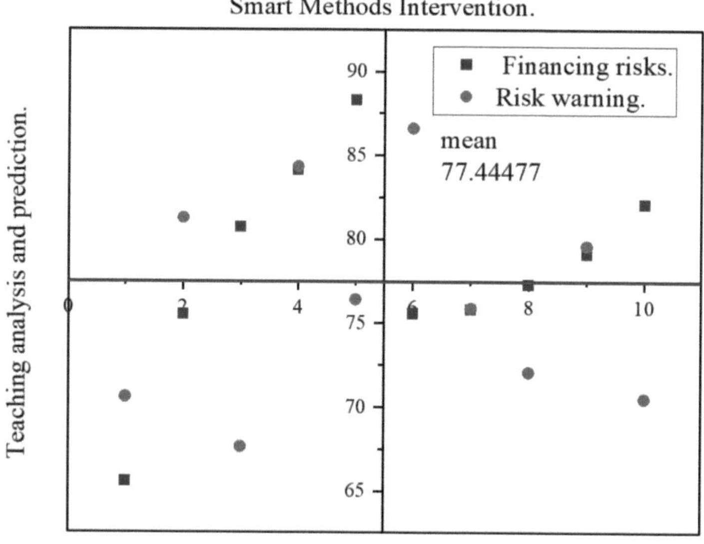

Fig. 2. Credit risk prediction with different algorithms

From the analysis in Fig. 2, it can be seen that in the process of risk prediction and risk management, it is found that the risk prediction results are consistent with the management, and the average prediction accuracy is 77.4477, indicating that the results are relatively reasonable and can meet the financing needs of actual small and medium-sized enterprises. Instructional objectives Understand the basic principles of the IG-SVM model, including the concept of the information gain (IG) and the classification mechanism of the SVM. Master how to apply IG-SVM model to predict the credit risk of supply chain financing of smes. Learn to evaluate and optimize the performance of the credit risk prediction models. Cultivate the ability to analyze and solve the actual supply chain financing credit risk problems. Understand and discuss how the model can be applied in enterprise decision-making to reduce supply chain risk (Table 3).

Table 3. Comparison of the accuracy of credit risk prediction by different methods

algorithm	The matching of risk with actual needs	Scope of application of risks	The error rate is corrected upon the occurrence of risk
IG-SVM model	94.37	95.26	94.96
Traditional forecasting methods	93.82	93.75	92.71
P	91.01	92.48	93.41

Content of courses Information Gain (IG) theory and feature selection: To explain how the IG algorithm measures the importance of features, and how to optimize the model through feature selection. Support Vector Machine (SVM) foundation: introduces the mathematical principles of SVM, including the concept of maximum boundary and kernel function. IG-SVM model construction: explain how to combine IG and SVM to build a credit risk prediction model, including data preprocessing, model training and tuning. In the process of operational risk, the results should be compared with previous results, and the comprehensive and specific test results of credit risk should be judged as shown in Figure 3.

According to the credit risk analysis in Figure 3, the risk financing is consistent with the actual changing needs, which indicates that the risk financing prediction method can solve the financing problems of small and medium-sized enterprises, improve the accuracy of their risk prediction, and take timely intervention measures.in the process of risk analysis, there are outliers in the risk content and evaluation points of credit risk, indicating that the credit risk can be optimized. Explanation and demonstration The IG-SVM model. By demonstrating the actual data processing and model building process, the students can intuitively understand the model workflow.

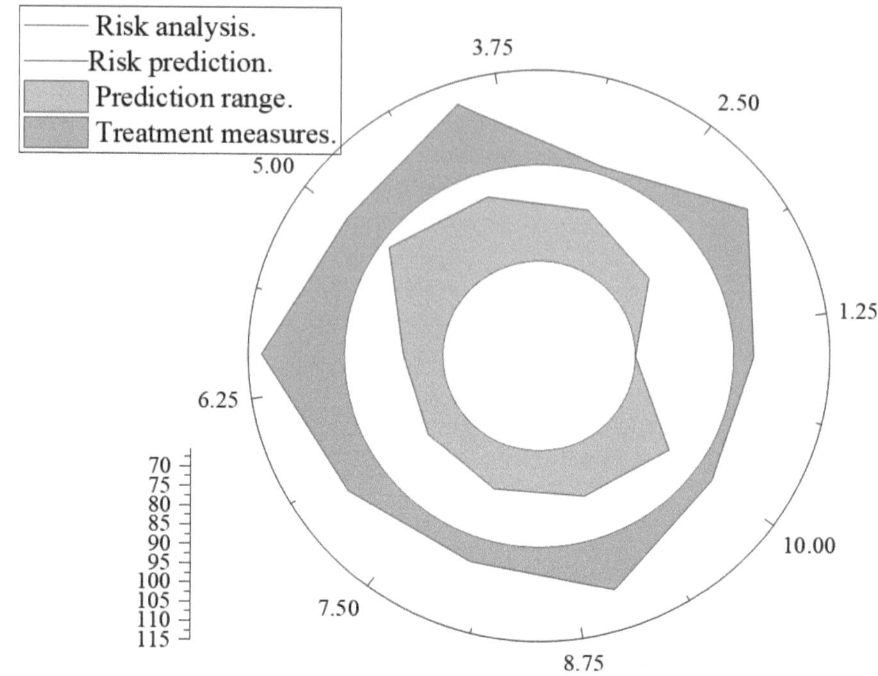

Fig. 3. IG-SVM model credit risk prediction credit risk prediction

5   Conclusion

In this course, we deeply explore the application of IG-SVM model in SME supply chain financing credit risk prediction. Through learning, students not only learned the basic principles of the Information Gain (IG) algorithm, but also understand the internal mechanism of the Support Vector Machine (SVM) model, especially the advantages of solving complex classification problems. Combining these two methods, we build an effective credit risk prediction model, which can accurately identify the potential default risk when dealing with the credit risk assessment of small and medium-sized enterprises, thus providing a powerful tool for the decision-makers of supply chain finance.

Acknowledgements. We look forward to constantly updating the teaching content, introducing more advanced prediction methods, in order to cope with the changing financial market environment, and cultivate more supply chain finance professionals with practical ability.

Key topics of basic scientific research business cost project of Heilongjiang provincial universities, number:2022-KYYWF-0503;Key Topics of the Twentieth Special Projects of Heilongjiang Provincial Education Science Planning,number:GJE1422105.

References

1. Alanis, E., Chava, S., Shah, A.: Benchmarking machine learning models to predict corporate bankruptcy. J. Credit Risk **19**(2), 77–110 (2023)

2. Anand, A., Baesens, B., Vanpee, R.: Sovereign credit risk modeling using machine learning: a novel approach to sovereign credit risk incorporating private sector and sustainability risks. J. Credit Risk **19**(1), 105–154 (2023)

3. Baser, F., Koc, O., Selcuk-Kestel, S.: Credit risk evaluation using clustering based fuzzy classification method. Expert Syst. Appl. **223** (2023)

4. Berloco, C., Argiento, R., Montagna, S.: Forecasting short-term defaults of firms in a commercial network via Bayesian spatial and spatio-temporal methods. Int. J. Forecast. **39**(3), 1065–1077 (2023)

5. Cheng, D.W., Niu, Z.B., Zhang, L.Q.: Delinquent events prediction in temporal networked-guarantee loans. IEEE Trans. Neural Netw. Learn. Syst. **34**(4), 1692–1704 (2023)

6. Drago, G., Aiello, G., Lombardo, A., Mangiapane, R.: State guarantees to counteract the financial effects of the COVID-19 pandemic on industrial supply chains. Heliyon **9**(7) (2023)

7. Du, M.R., Zhang, Z.Q.: Modeling selection for credit risk measurement: based on Meta path features. Tehnicki Vjesnik-Tech. Gazette **30**(2), 545–554 (2023)

8. Feldhutter, P., Schaefer, S.: Debt dynamics and credit risk. J. Financ. Econ. **149**(3), 497–535 (2023)

9. Hossain, M., Yoshino, N., Tsubota, K.: Sustainable financing strategies for the SMEs: two alternative models. Sustainability **15**(11) (2023)

10. Kanapickiene, R., Kanapickas, T., Neciunas, A.: Bankruptcy prediction for micro and small enterprises using financial, non-financial, business sector and macroeconomic variables: the case of the lithuanian construction sector. Risks **11**(5) (2023)

11. Kim, H., Cho, H., Ryu, D.: Measuring corporate failure risk: does long short-term memory perform better in all markets? Invest. Anal. J. **52**(1), 40–52 (2023)

12. Korangi, K., Mues, C., Bravo, C.: A transformer-based model for default prediction in mid-cap corporate markets. Eur. J. Oper. Res. **308**(1), 306–320 (2023)

13. Kyire, S.K.C., Kuwornu, J.K.M., Bannor, R.K., Apiors, E.K., Martey, E.: Perceived risk and risk management strategies under irrigated rice farming: evidence from TONO and VEA irrigation schemes-northern Ghana. J. Agric. Food Res. **12** (2023)

14. Li, J. Y., Xu, C.S., Feng, B., Zhao, H.Y.: Credit risk prediction model for listed companies based on CNN-LSTM and attention mechanism. Electronics **12**(7) (2023b)

15. Li, M.G., et al.: Internet financial credit risk assessment with sliding window and attention mechanism LSTM model. Tehnicki Vjesnik-Tech. Gazette **30**(1), 1–7 (2023)

16. Liang, ZH., Du, J. M., Hua, Y., Si, Y.B., Li, M.: Research on credit evaluation indicator system of high-tech SMEs: from the social capital perspective. Systems **11**(3) (2023)

17. Ma, H.D., Li, G., Liu, R.Y., Shen, M.D., Liu, X.H.: The personal credit default discrimination model based on DF21. J. Intell. Fuzzy Syst. **44**(3), 3907–3925 (2023)

18. Mao, Y., Liu, S.F., Gong, D.Q.: A text mining and ensemble learning based approach for credit risk prediction. Tehnicki Vjesnik-Tech. Gazette **30**(1), 138–147 (2023)

Application of Multiple Regression Model in Interactive Teaching in English Classroom

Bingjie Zou[✉]

Shanghai Normal University Tianhua College, Shanghai 200086, China
zbj2073@sthu.edu.cn

Abstract. Multiple regression model is a statistical analysis tool used to study the relationship between multiple independent variables and one dependent variable. In the social sciences, educational research, and various fields, such a model is widely used to explore the multiple influencing factors behind complex phenomena. In the model, the independent variables can be continuous, discrete, or categorical, while the dependent variables are usually continuous, such as the students' English scores. Through multiple regression, we can quantify the independent effects of each independent variable on the dependent variable and the interactions between them, allowing for a deeper understanding of the multivariate factors influencing the outcome. MATLAB simulation shows that under the condition of certain evaluation criteria, the feasibility of multiple regression model for classroom interaction in English classroom teaching. The rationality of classroom interaction is better than that of traditional interaction mode.

Keywords: statistics · multiple regression model · English classroom teaching · Classroom interaction

1 Introduction

With the renewal of educational concept, English classroom interactive teaching has become an important means to improve the teaching quality [1, 2]. Interactive teaching emphasizes students' participation and active learning, and promotes the practical application of language and the development of critical thinking through group discussion, role-playing and task-based teaching. However, despite the theoretical advantages of interactive teaching being widely accepted, there are still faces many challenges in practical application [3, 4]. First, how do teachers design and implement effective interactive activities to ensure that all students can actively participate in it, this is an urgent problem to be solved [5, 6]. Secondly, the evaluation criteria and methods of classroom interaction are not perfect, which makes it difficult to quantify and feedback the teaching effects. The classroom interaction process is shown in Fig. 1.

The model results show that these interactive factors do not exist in isolation, but influence each other and work together on the learning effect. Furthermore, we highlight the importance of data collection and processing and how model limitations can be

B. Brik and S. Nazir (Eds.): BigIoT-EDU 2024, LNICST 659, pp. 516–524, 2026.
https://doi.org/10.1007/978-3-032-18631-7_56

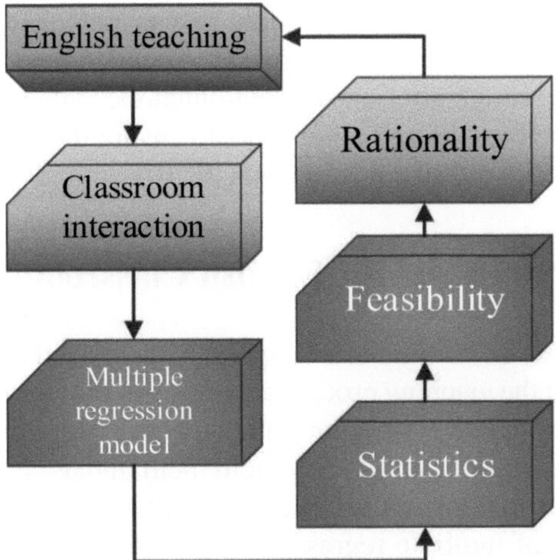

Fig. 1. The analytical process of English classroom teaching

overcome in practical applications, such as overfitting and hypothesis testing. Through proper data cleaning, variable selection, and model checking, we can obtain more reliable and explanatory analysis results. These findings provide a scientific basis for improving the quality of English classroom interaction and for teachers' making decisions when designing and implementing teaching activities.

2   Related Works

2.1   Rationale of the Multiple Regression Model

Linear regression model is a predictive model that assumes a linear relationship between the dependent variable and one or more independent variables. In the simplest case, the linear regression involves only one independent variable, for example, predicting house prices may be proportional to the home area. However, when two or more independent variables exist, we entered the field of multiple regression. Multiple regression considers not only the effect of each independent variable on the dependent variable, but also the interaction between the independent variables, which allows the model to more comprehensively capture the complexity of the data. Thus, multiple regression is more powerful than a single linear regression model when explaining the change in the dependent variable [7, 8].

2.2   Mathematical Expression of the Multiple Regression Model

In English classes, interactive data can cover multiple dimensions, including but not limited to student participation, quality of group discussions, frequency of teacher feedback, number of questions, and forms of participation in class activities. Collection of these data is usually performed through observation, recording, questionnaires and learning management systems. For example, teachers can use digital tools to record the number of times students make speeches in classroom discussions, analyze students 'interaction patterns through classroom video recordings, or understand students' perception of classroom interaction through after-class questionnaires. Data processing includes data cleaning, coding, normalization and other steps to ensure the accuracy and consistency of the data and prepare for subsequent analysis [9, 10].

3 Optimization Strategies for English Classroom Instruction

Effect tracking and feedback: continuously apply the improved model to track the teaching effect, timely adjust the teaching process according to the feedback, and form a closed loop of teaching improvement. Education Policy making: Improved models can provide data support for education policy makers to help them understand which teaching environments and strategies maximize the benefits of classroom interaction. In conclusion, despite the limitations of multiple regression models in interactive English classroom teaching, appropriate improvements can better adapt to complex teaching situations and provide powerful tools for improving teaching quality.

3.1 Analysis of the Correlation Between Interactive Data and Student Learning Effects

Multiple regression models can reveal complex relationships between interactive data and student learning effects. By taking multiple interaction indicators as independent variables, such as the number of questions, group discussion time, teacher feedback, etc., and learning effect (e. g., test score, course evaluation, language ability improvement) as dependent variables, the model can quantify the independent contribution of each interaction factor to the learning effect.

$$tol(k_i \cdot z_{ij} \cdot 3) = k_{ij} \geq max(z_{ij}) \cdot \bigcap_{i=1}^{c} k_i \tag{1}$$

Among them, the judgment of outliers is shown in Eq. (2).

$$max(z_{ij}) = \left(z_{ij}^2 + 2 \div \int_{i=1}^{z} D \right) \succ mean\left(\sum z_{ij} \right) \cdot \lim_{x \to \infty} \cdot \frac{\Delta c_i}{\Delta z_i} \tag{2}$$

For example, it may be found that students who actively participated in classroom discussions showed significant improvements in language skills, while students who frequently received teacher feedback had a significant advantage in test scores. This analysis helps to understand which types of interactions most affect students' learning outcomes and thus inform teaching strategies.

$$D(f_i) = \sum \bigcap_{i=1}^{k} f_i \cdot \bigcap \xi - 3 \to \oint k_i \cdot \sqrt{\frac{2}{D}} \tag{3}$$

3.2 Application of Multiple Regression Models in the Evaluation of Interaction Effects

Multiple regression models can provide a more comprehensive perspective when evaluating the effect of English classroom interaction. It considers not only the effect of a single variable, but also the interaction effect among the variables.

$$p(z_i) = \frac{2}{v_i \cdot} 4c_i \cdot \prod D(f_i) - v_i \bigcap_{i=1}^{p} z_i \tag{4}$$

For example, the model may find that the interaction between the frequency of teacher feedback and the number of student questions has an additional positive effect on learning effects.

$$p(z_i) + D(f_i) \leq max(z_{ij}) \tag{5}$$

When teachers feedback more and timely, the higher the enthusiasm of students to ask questions, the better the learning effect may be. In addition, the model can also be used to predict the learning outcomes that students may achieve in a specific interactive environment, helping teachers to adjust teaching strategies and optimize classroom interaction to improve the overall teaching effect.

$$p(z_i) \overset{\sim}{+} D(f_i) \leftrightarrow mean\left(\sum z_{ij}\right) \cdot \lim_{x \to \infty} \cdot \frac{\Delta c_i}{\Delta z_i} \tag{6}$$

3.3 Limitations of the Multiple Regression Models and Improvement Strategies

Through empirical research, the multiple regression model has been widely used in the educational field to provide a quantitative basis for teaching improvement. In the English classroom, the application of this model can not only help teachers to identify the effectiveness of interactive strategies, but also provide data support for personalized teaching and curriculum design to promote the overall development of students.

$$No(z_i) = \frac{p(z_i) \overset{\sim}{+} D(f_i)}{mean\left(\sum z_{ij}\right) \cdot \lim_{x \to \infty} \cdot \frac{\Delta c_i}{\Delta z_i}} \tag{7}$$

Although the multiple regression model shows strong explanatory and predictive ability in many domains, including pedagogy, it also has some inherent limitations in the English classroom interactive teaching:

$$Zh(z_i) = min\left[\sum p(z_i) \overset{\sim}{+} D(f_i)\right] \tag{8}$$

Strict assumption conditions: the multiple regression model assumes that there is no multiple collinearity between the independent variables, that is, there is no high correlation between them. In the actual classroom interaction, multiple factors may influence each other, making this assumption difficult to satisfy. Linear relationship hypothesis: the model assumes that there is a linear relationship between dependent variables and independent variables, but the actual classroom interaction effect may be affected by non-linear factors, such as students 'individual differences, teachers' teaching style, etc. Ignoring the time series effect: the model usually does not consider the dynamics of the time series data, but in English learning, the students' learning process is a continuous process, and the past interaction experiences may have an impact on the current effect. Ignoring other unmeasured variables: The model may not able to fully capture all the factors affecting the effect of classroom interaction, such as students' emotional state, classroom atmosphere, etc., which may affect the results as potential confounding variables.

$$accur(z_i) = \frac{min[\sum p(z_i) + \widetilde{D(f_i)}]}{\sum p(z_i) + \widetilde{D(f_i)}} \times 100\% \tag{9}$$

For the above limitations, the following strategies can be improved: Using partial least squares regression (PLSR): When there is multicollinearity, PLSR can reduce the association between independent variables by reducing the dimension and improve the explanatory power of the model. Introducing non-linear models: Consider using nonlinear methods such as the generalized linear model (GLM) or random forest to accommodate non-linear effects that may occur in classroom interactions. Applied time series analysis: consider the dynamics of classroom interaction effect with time through ARIMA model or other time series model. Control for potential confounding variables: either the instrumental variable method or the structural equation model (SEM) was used to estimate the unobserved influencing factors. Mixed methods research: combine quantitative and qualitative research methods, such as observation, interview and other data, to more fully understand the impact of classroom interactions.

$$accur(z_i) = \frac{min[\sum p(z_i) + \widetilde{D(f_i)}]}{\sum p(z_i) + \widetilde{D(f_i)}} \times 100\% + randon(z_i) \tag{10}$$

The improved model can provide more accurate prediction and deeper insight in practice: Optimizing teaching strategies: By analyzing the key influencing factors in the model, teachers can adjust teaching strategies, such as increasing specific types of interactive activities, to improve students' learning effect.

4   Results and Discussion

4.1   Introduction to Classroom Interaction

This study reveals the potential value of the multiple regression model in the interactive teaching of English classroom in evaluating and optimizing teaching strategies (Table 1).

Table 1. Classroom interaction requirements

Scope of application	grade	viability	Interactive teaching
colloquial	standard	85.99	84.82
	Higher	86.72	85.27
word	standard	82.47	84.17
	Higher	83.98	86.01
grammar	standard	87.48	85.05
	Higher	86.58	83.48

4.2   English Classroom Teaching

Despite the remarkable progress of this study in understanding the application of multiple regression model in English classroom interactive teaching, there are some areas for further exploration. First, future studies could consider introducing more variables, such as student learning style, classroom environment factors, and the use of technical tools to construct more comprehensive models that better reflect the actual teaching situation (Table 2).

Table 2. The overall picture of the interactive teaching programme

Category	Satisfaction	Analysis rate
colloquial	86.21	88.24
word	89.18	89.41
grammar	87.22	89.67
mean	88.17	87.05
X^6	86.51	87.60
$P = 1.524$		

4.3   Interactive Teaching and Stability of Classroom Interaction

Secondly, the dynamic study of the model is also an important direction in the future. Classroom interaction is not static, but changes with time, teaching stage and student development (Fig. 2).

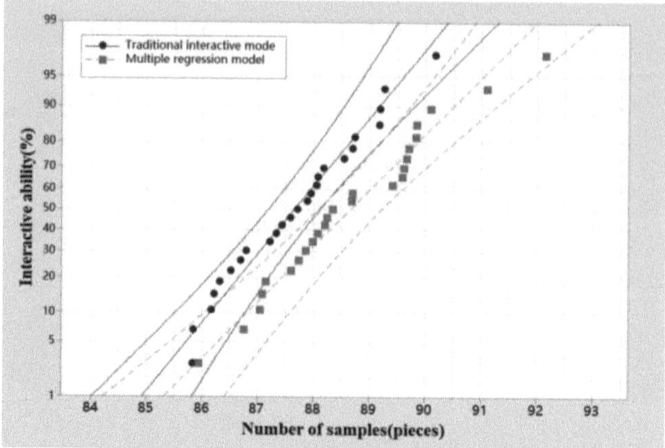

Fig. 2. Interactive teaching of different algorithms

Therefore, studying how to construct dynamic models that can capture these changes will help to predict and optimize teaching effects more precisely (Table 3).

Table 3. Comparison of the accuracy of classroom interaction between different methods

algorithm	Interactive teaching	Magnitude of change	error
Multiple regression models	93.37	93.94	94.62
Traditional interactive mode	92.68	92.90	92.91
P	89.18	89.59	91.21

Finally, combining multivariate regression models with other data analysis methods, such as machine learning or AI techniques, may yield new insights. These technologies may be able to automatically identify key interaction patterns and even predict student learning outcomes, providing support for individualized teaching (Fig. 3).

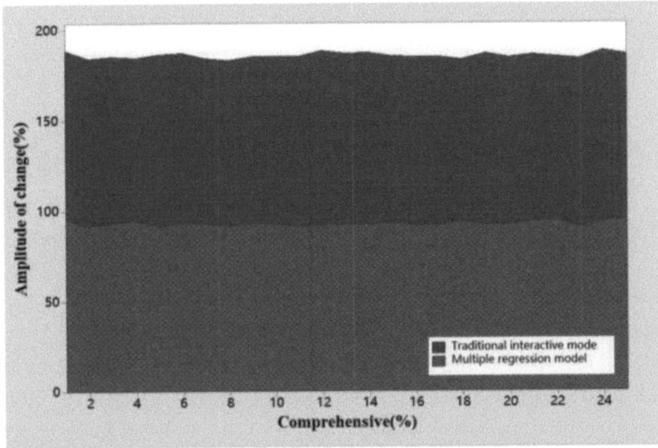

Fig. 3. Interactive teaching of multiple regression model classroom interaction

5   Conclusion

In conclusion, the application of multiple regression models in English classroom interactive teaching is a continuously developing area of research, and future research will help us to better understand the nature of teaching interaction and provide more effective teaching strategies to promote students' language learning process.

Aiming at the problem that interactive teaching in English classroom is not ideal, this paper proposes a multiple regression model and combines mathematical models to optimize English classroom teaching. At the same time, in-depth analysis of classroom interaction innovation is carried out to build interactive content collection. This study shows that the multiple regression model can improve the interaction quality of English classroom teaching, and can carry out general classroom interaction for English classroom teaching。However, in the process of multiple regression model, too much attention is paid to the analysis of classroom interaction, resulting in irrationality in the selection of classroom interaction indicators.

References

1. Akhouri, S., Virani, A., Minor, S., Samuels, M.N.N., Stumbar, S.E.E.: Student teaching in the family medicine clerkship: opportunities for interactive virtual learning. South. Med. J. **116**(7), 542–544 (2023)
2. Akimkhanova, Z., Turekhanova, K., Karwasz, G.P.: Interactive games and plays in teaching physics and astronomy. Educ. Sci. **13**(4), 393 (2023)
3. Barbosa, O.A., Marçal, E., Araújo, D.A.B.S., Melo, L.S., Rocha, H.A.L.: Development and perceived usability evaluation of an interactive smartphone application for the teaching of hemodynamics and evaluation of arterial pulse pressure variation. BMC Med. Inf. Decis. Mak. **23**(1), 31 (2023)
4. Bilyk, V., Banak, R., Bardadym, O., Sokal, M., Anichkina, O.: Introduction of interactive teaching methods in modern schools. Eduweb-Revista De Tecnologia De Informacion Y Comunicacion En Educacion **17**(2), 199–209 (2023)

5. Buma, A.I., Simmer, F., den Braber-Ymker, M., Groenen, P.J.: Appraisal of the PathoDiscovery: an interactive web-based educational tool for teaching pathophysiology and histopathology. Apmis **131**(9), 472–479 (2023)

6. Cheung, B.H., Foo, D.C., Chu, K.M., Co, M., Lee, L.S.: Perception from students regarding online synchronous interactive teaching in the clinical year during COVID-19 pandemic. BMC Med. Educ. **23**(1), 5 (2023)

7. Corey, J.: The regulation dice game: teaching the effects of entry barriers on wealth creation using an interactive class activity. J. Econ. Educ. **54**(3), 301–326 (2023)

8. Danjou, P.-E., Bouhsina, S., Billet, S., Cazier-Dennin, F.: Large interactive touchscreens as an opportunity for synchronous hybrid teaching during the COVID-19 pandemic and beyond. J. Chem. Educ. **100**(3), 1149–1154 (2023)

9. Dong, Z., Qi, Z.: Design of computer interactive teaching system by using feature extraction algorithm and multimedia technology. Soft. Comput. **27**(14), 10401–10409 (2023)

10. Fang, H., Shi, H., Zhang, J., Karuppiah, M.: Effective college english teaching based on teacher-student interactive model. ACM Trans. Asian Low-Res. Lang. Inf. Process. **22**(3), 1–17 (2023)

11. Garcez da Silva, L.R., et al.: Students' perception to an interactive web-based response system in oral and maxillofacial pathology teaching. Braz. Oral Res. **37** (2023)

12. Gellisch, M., Morosan-Puopolo, G., Wolf, O.T., Moser, D.A., Zaehres, H., Brand-Saberi, B.: Interactive teaching enhances students' physiological arousal during online learning. Ann. Anat/-Anatomischer Anzeiger **247**, 152050 (2023)

13. Harendza, S., Bussenius, L., Gaertner, J., Heuser, M., Ahles, J., Prediger, S.: Virtual reality against Zoom fatigue? A field study on the teaching and learning experience in interactive video and VR conferencing. GMS J. Med. Educ. **40**(2), 1–22 (2023)

14. Hayes, P.M., Cherney, A., Papanagnou, D.: An interactive module to teach common biostatistical tests to learners in the health professions. Cureus J. Med. Sci. **15**(3), 1–7 (2023)

15. Ho, C.-H., Zhang, H.-Q., Li, J., Zhang, M.-Q.: Development and application of interactive teaching systems for online design courses. Int. J. Dist. Educ. Technol. **21**(2), 1–28 (2023)

16. Kaushik, J.S., Raghuraman, K., Verma, S., Arya, V., Gehlawat, V.K.: Online interactive flipped classroom teaching in pediatrics for medical undergraduates. Cureus J. Med. Sci. **15**(4), 1–8 (2023)

17. Li, M.: Teaching beginner-level computational social science: interactive open education resources with learnr and shiny apps. Front. Educ. **8**, 1130865 (2023)

Analysis on the Evaluation of Scientific Research Performance of Teachers in Higher Vocational Colleges Based on RAGA-PPC Model

Xiaozhen Peng and Chongxiang Ou[✉]

Hunan College of Foreign Studies, Changsha 410000, Hunan, China
`huwai163163@163.com`

Abstract. In today's society, education is not only the cornerstone of knowledge inheritance, but also an important force to promote social progress and development. As an important part of the education system, the improvement of the scientific research ability of higher vocational colleges has an inestimable value for promoting technological innovation and serving the local economy. In this context, the evaluation of the scientific research performance of the teachers in higher vocational colleges is particularly important. It is not only related to the professional development of teachers, but also directly affects the scientific research atmosphere, academic influence and overall competitiveness of the school. The data used in this study is from the database of the Ministry of Education, Youth and Sports (MOEYS), which contains information about all students who graduated from universities, colleges or technical colleges for at least one year from 2012 to 2017. The sample size is determined by using the sample size formula with a confidence level of 95%. In addition to these variables, we also considered other.

Keywords: RAGA-PPC model · Scientific research performance · Higher vocational colleges

1 Introduction

However, the traditional scientific research performance evaluation methods often have some problems, such as strong subjectivity, single evaluation index and fine data processing, which are difficult to reflect teachers' scientific research contribution comprehensively and objectively [1]. Therefore, exploring a scientific, reasonable and efficient scientific research performance evaluation method has become an important topic of higher vocational college management.

It is in this background that this paper proposes the RAGA-PPC model combining accelerated GA algorithm (RAGA) and projection tracing clustering model (PPC) based on real coding [2], aiming to optimize the scientific research performance evaluation process and improve the accuracy and objectivity of the evaluation results. RAGA algorithm with its powerful global search ability and efficient convergence speed, and the

© ICST Institute for Computer Sciences, Social Informatics and Telecommunications Engineering 2026
Published by Springer Nature Switzerland AG 2026. All Rights Reserved
B. Brik and S. Nazir (Eds.): BigIoT-EDU 2024, LNICST 659, pp. 525–531, 2026.
https://doi.org/10.1007/978-3-032-18631-7_57

PPC model effectively solves the complex relationship is difficult to quantify through multi-dimensional data reduction [3]. The combination of the two has opened up new ideas and methods for the scientific research performance evaluation of teachers in higher vocational colleges.

2 Related Work

2.1 Research on Scientific Research Performance Evaluation in Higher Vocational Colleges

The accelerated genetic algorithm (RAGA) of real number coding is an important innovation of the traditional genetic algorithm (GA). In traditional GA, binary coding is usually used to represent individuals in the solution space, which performs well in handling discrete problems but fails in dealing with continuous variables [4]. By introducing real encoding, RAGA algorithm enables the algorithm to directly operate the values of continuous variables, so as to avoid the possible accuracy loss in the process of binary encoding and decoding, and greatly improve the efficiency and accuracy of the algorithm in dealing with continuous optimization problems.In addition, the RAGA algorithm also incorporates an acceleration mechanism, which is another highlight. In traditional genetic algorithms, the evolution of the population depends on the three basic operations of selection, crossover and variation, but as the evolution deepens, the variability of individuals in the population may gradually decrease, causing the algorithm to fall into a state of precocious convergence or search stagnation [5]. The RAGA algorithm, by introducing the acceleration mechanism, conducts special processing of excellent individuals, such as narrowing its search range, increasing its crossover probability or variation strength, so as to accelerate the discovery and convergence process of excellent solutions. This mechanism not only improves the convergence speed of the algorithm, but also enhances the global search ability of the algorithm, helping to find better solutions [6].As an advanced data dimension reduction technology, the projection tracing clustering model (PPC) shows its unique advantages in processing high-dimensional data. In the evaluation of scientific research performance, the evaluation indicators often involve many aspects, such as the quantity, quality and influence of scientific research achievements, etc. These indicators together constitute a high-dimensional data space. Data analysis and evaluation directly in this high-dimensional space is not only large in computation and high in complexity, but also difficult to intuitively grasp the inherent laws and characteristics of the data [7]. The PPC model projects the high-dimensional data onto the low-dimensional subspace. In this low-dimensional space, the distribution law and characteristic structure of the data become clearer and easy to understand [8]. The key of the PPC model is to find the best projection direction, so that the projection value can reflect the feature information of the original data to the greatest extent. This usually needs to be achieved by optimization algorithms, such as genetic algorithms, particle swarm algorithm, etc.

2.2 Research Summary on Scientific Research Performance Evaluation

Applying the PPC model to the scientific research performance evaluation of the teachers in higher vocational colleges can effectively solve the problem that the complex relationship among the evaluation indicators is difficult to quantify. Through the dimension reduction treatment of PPC model, multiple evaluation indicators can be integrated into one or a few comprehensive indicators, thus simplifying the evaluation process and improving the intuitiveness and comprehensibility of the evaluation results. At the same time, the PPC model can also retain the important information in the original data to ensure the accuracy and reliability of the evaluation results. Therefore, PPC model has a broad application prospect and important practical value in scientific research performance evaluation.In constructing the index system of scientific research performance evaluation of teachers in higher vocational colleges, we strive to fully cover all aspects of scientific research activities to ensure the fairness and accuracy of evaluation. In addition to the three basic dimensions of research investment, research process and research achievements, we also further refined the specific indicators of each dimension. For example, in terms of research investment, in addition to research funds and research time, we also consider the advancement of research equipment, the richness of research data and the rationality of the structure of the research team; we increase the innovation of research methods, the rationality of research progress and the evaluation of the transformation efficiency of research results; we not only focus on the quantity and quality of published papers, but also consider the pass rate of patent application, the level and influence of project awards. Such refined construction makes the evaluation index system more perfect and can reflect teachers' scientific research performance more comprehensively.The refinement of the data processing is the key to ensure the accuracy of the evaluation results. During the normalization process, we adopted the extreme value normalization method, but considered both the distribution properties of the data and the treatment of outliers. For the extreme outliers, we adopted the strategy of truncation or substitution to avoid its excessive impact on the overall evaluation results. In addition, we also cleaned and checked the data to ensure that the data of the input model was accurate. Through the refined data processing, we eliminated the influence of the dimension and the value range on the evaluation results, which laid a solid foundation for the subsequent analysis and evaluation work.

3 Construction of Evaluation Index System for Scientific Research Performance of Colleges and Universities

Then inputting the normalized data into RAGA-PPC model for scientific research performance evaluation, we made full use of the global search ability of RAGA algorithm and the data dimension reduction advantages of PPC model. First, the projection direction parameters in the PPC model are optimized through the RAGA algorithm to find the projection direction that can best reflect the characteristics of teachers' scientific research performance. In this process, we set the reasonable algorithm parameters and the number of iterations to ensure the stability and reliability of the optimization results. Then, the multidimensional data is projected onto this best projection direction to obtain the one-dimensional projection value. This projection value integrates the performance of teachers in scientific research investment, scientific research process and scientific research achievements, and can directly reflect their scientific research performance level. Finally, we ranked and classified the teachers according to the projection value, which provided strong support for the school's scientific research management and the personal development of the teachers. In addition, when applying the RAGA-PPC model for scientific research performance evaluation, we also paid attention to the validation and evaluation of the model. Through comparative analysis with other evaluation methods, we verified the effectiveness and superiority of RAGA-PPC model in the performance evaluation of scientific research. At the same time, we also continuously optimized and improved the model according to the feedback in practical application, so as to further improve the accuracy and practicability of its evaluation results.In the empirical analysis phase, we carefully designed the study protocol to ensure the reliability and validity of the experimental results. First of all, we chose a representative higher vocational college as the research background. The school has certain accumulation and achievements in the field of scientific research, and the scientific research performance data of its teachers has high analytical value. Then, we according to the above construction of evaluation index system, through the school scientific research management department, library, office, and other channels, collected a number of teachers research performance data, including scientific research investment, research time allocation, paper published, patent application and authorization, project and winning many aspects such as detailed information. In the data processing stage, we processed the raw data strictly following the normalization method described above, ensuring the consistency and comparability of the data. Next, the processed data is input into the RAGA-PPC model, which is used to evaluate the scientific research performance. During the model operation, we closely monitor the execution of the algorithm and adjust the optimization parameters for the best performance. Finally, the model outputs the projection value of each teacher's scientific research performance, and ranks and classifies it accordingly. By analyzing the differences between the evaluation results of RAGA-PPC model and the traditional evaluation methods, we find the following significant advantages: first, the RAGA-PPC model can consider multiple evaluation indicators to avoid the sideof single index evaluation; second, the model effectively reduces the information loss in the evaluation process and improves the accuracy of the evaluation results; finally, the global search capability of RAGA algorithm ensures the efficiency and stability of the model when finding the best projection direction, making the evaluation results more objective and fair.

4 Results and Discussion

Through the application and analysis of the scientific research performance evaluation of the four teachers in higher vocational colleges, we can see that teacher A has the highest scientific research performance, followed by teacher C, teacher B and teacher D. Based on the analysis of the original data, we found that Teacher A has dabbled in scientific research projects, scientific research achievements and other scientific research fields, and has made outstanding achievements in areas with high weight, with obvious scientific research advantages. Teacher B and Teacher Ding have their own emphasis on scientific research, and the final total score is not much different. Teacher C has a low final score because of the blank in several scientific research fields with high weight.

When inputting the normalized data into RAGA-PPC model for scientific research performance evaluation, we made full use of the global search ability of RAGA algorithm and the data dimension reduction advantages of PPC model. First, the projection direction parameters in the PPC model are optimized through the RAGA algorithm to find the projection direction that can best reflect the characteristics of teachers' scientific research performance. In this process, we set the reasonable algorithm parameters and the number of iterations to ensure the stability and reliability of the optimization results. Then, the multidimensional data is projected onto this best projection direction to obtain the one-dimensional projection value. This projection value integrates the performance of teachers in scientific research investment, scientific research process and scientific research achievements, and can directly reflect their scientific research performance level. Finally, we ranked and classified the teachers according to the projection value, which provided strong support for the school's scientific research management and the personal development of the teachers. In addition, when applying the RAGA-PPC model for scientific research performance evaluation, we also paid attention to the validation and evaluation of the model. Through comparative analysis with other evaluation methods, we verified the effectiveness and superiority of RAGA-PPC model in the performance evaluation of scientific research. At the same time, we also continuously optimized and improved the model according to the feedback in practical application, so as to further improve the accuracy and practicability of its evaluation results.

In the empirical analysis phase, we carefully designed the study protocol to ensure the reliability and validity of the experimental results. First of all, we chose a representative higher vocational college as the research background. The school has certain accumulation and achievements in the field of scientific research, and the scientific research performance data of its teachers has high analytical value. Then, we according to the above construction of evaluation index system, through the school scientific research management department, library, office, and other channels, collected a number of teachers research performance data, including scientific research investment, research time allocation, paper published, patent application and authorization, project and awards, such as detailed information.In the data processing stage, we processed the raw data strictly following the normalization method described above, ensuring the consistency and comparability of the data. Next, the processed data is input into the RAGA-PPC model, which is used to evaluate the scientific research performance. During the model operation, we closely monitor the execution of the algorithm and adjust the optimization parameters for the best performance. Finally, the model outputs the projection value of each teacher's scientific research performance, and ranks and classifies it accordingly.

By analyzing the differences between the evaluation results of RAGA-PPC model and the traditional evaluation methods, we find the following significant advantages: first, the RAGA-PPC model can consider multiple evaluation indicators to avoid the sideof single index evaluation; second, the model effectively reduces the information loss in the evaluation process and improves the accuracy of the evaluation results; finally, the global search capability of RAGA algorithm ensures the efficiency and stability of the model when finding the best projection direction, making the evaluation results more objective and fair.

5 Conclusion

We also collected feedback from teachers and administrators on the evaluation results of the RAGA-PPC model, through questionnaires and interviews. Most respondents said that the evaluation results of the model can more accurately reflect their scientific research performance level, and the evaluation process is transparent and fair, with a high degree of acceptance and recognition. These feedback opinions further verify the effectiveness and application value of RAGA-PPC model in the evaluation of teacher scientific research performance in higher vocational colleges. 5. Conclusions and outlook Based on the scientific research performance of teachers in RAGA-PPC model, the effectiveness and superiority of the model in the evaluation of scientific research performance. However, due to the complexity and diversity of scientific research activities, the evaluation index system constructed in this paper still has some limitations. In the future research, we can further improve the evaluation index system and introduce more dimensional evaluation indexes to reflect teachers' scientific research performance level more comprehensively. At the same time, other advanced optimization algorithms and dimension reduction techniques can also be explored to further improve the accuracy and reliability of the evaluation results.

Acknowledgements. Project of Hunan Association of educational scientific researchers:Research and practice of teachers' scientific research evaluation system in Higher Vocational Colleges from the perspective of scientific research and education. Subject. No: XJKX22A056.

References

1. Lv, J.: Research on the Construction of Scientific Research Evaluation System for Teachers in Higher Vocational Colleges Based on Computer PCA and ANP. Springer, Cham (2021)
2. Wang, G.: The evaluation method of high-level professionals in higher vocational colleges based on the fuzzy optimal model from the perspective of educational psychology. Psychiatria Danubina **33**, 101–103 (2021)
3. Wang, Q.: Research on the innovation of blended English teaching mode based on superstar platform in higher vocational colleges. In: CIPAE 2021: 2021 2nd International Conference on Computers, Information Processing and Advanced Education (2021)
4. Jiang, X., Dang, W.: The research of quantitative evaluation algorithm of process auto alarm analysis based on chem-HRA. J. Phys. Conf. Ser. **1813**(1), 012056 (2021)
5. Liu, X., Lin, H.: Research on innovation and entrepreneurship competency evaluation of teachers in industry-oriented higher vocational colleges. Int. J. Electr. Eng. Educ. 002072092199659 (2021)
6. Liu, X., Li, G., Xu, L., et al.: Predictive analysis of class attention based on CNN model. J. Phys. Conf. Ser. **1852**(2), 022008 (2021)
7. Sun, T., Liu, J.: Research on the paths to improve the information acquisition ability of students in higher vocational colleges. Open Access Libr. J. (2021)
8. Zhang, X.: Research on the path of agriculture-related higher vocational colleges in serving the "Belt and Road" initiative. Mod. Econ. Manag. Forum **2**(6) (2021)

9. Olmedo, G.: Emotion recognition of down syndrome people based on the evaluation of artificial intelligence and statistical analysis methods. Symmetry **14** (2022)
10. Xue, X.D., Zhang, T., Zhang, X.L., et al.: Performance evaluation and exergy analysis of a novel combined cooling, heating and power (CCHP) system based on liquid air energy storage (2021)

Resource Allocation Model of College Art Teaching Course in the Era of Algorithm Recommendation

Shihui Jin[✉]

Changchun Humanities and Sciences College, Changchun 130117, Jilin, China
shunjian001@163.com

Abstract. Under the background of informatization and education modernization, art teaching in colleges and universities is facing unprecedented opportunities and challenges. The rich diversity of educational resources and the personalized trend of students' needs are increasingly prominent.The recommendation algorithm proposed in this paper can allocate the teaching resources of art courses in colleges and universities, and the allocation rate is greater than 25%, and it can be realized. The comprehensive improvement rate of structure content is greater than 15%, which shows that the recommendation algorithm can optimize art resources and is superior to previous algorithms. So. Recommendation algorithm is suitable for the configuration of art courses in colleges and universities, and can promote the optimization of its overall structure.

Keywords: Algorithm recommendation era · college art teaching course · sresource allocation model

1 Introduction

Algorithmic recommendation technology is derived from the cross-application of information retrieval, data mining and machine learning. Its core is to provide users with personalized information and services by analyzing users' behaviors and preferences. In the field of education, this technology can be skillfully applied to the allocation of teaching resources. By judging and analyzing students' learning content, academic achievement and practical effect, this paper verifies and negotiates whether it is suitable for art teaching, and finds out the shortcomings among them, and excavates its teaching effect deeply. Realize intelligent recommendation, improve students' art practice ability, and optimize the existing art teaching results, is shown in Fig. 1.

According to the analysis of Figure I, it can be seen that in the process of art teaching analysis and key point judgment, the correlation between interest learning achievement and theory will be found, and it will be comprehensively optimized. Among them, interest is the auxiliary content of promotion, and academic performance is the final result of rational allocation of curriculum. Therefore, should take academic achievements as the final reference for analysis and judgment. Among them, it is necessary to make

B. Brik and S. Nazir (Eds.): BigIoT-EDU 2024, LNICST 659, pp. 532–542, 2026.
https://doi.org/10.1007/978-3-032-18631-7_58

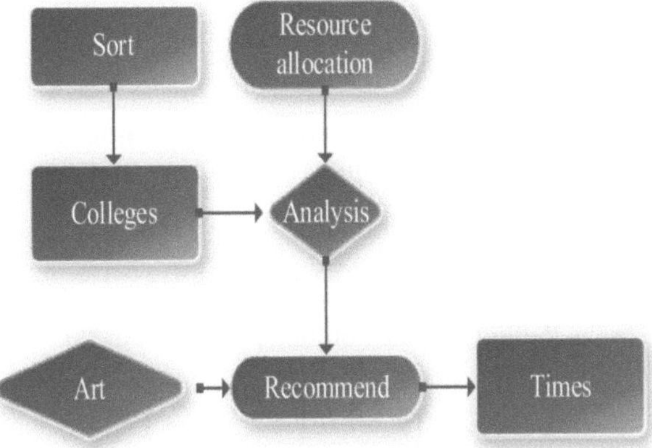

Fig. 1. The analytical process of art resource allocation

comprehensive judgments on the basis of cultural courses such as mathematics content and academic achievements, so as to provide support for art teaching and course recommendation.

2 Related Concepts

2.1 College Art Teaching Course

Art teaching curriculum resources are an indispensable part of college education, covering a wide range of fields from traditional art theory to modern creative practice. In the process of art design and curriculum resource allocation, we should pay attention to rationality, make comprehensive analysis according to students' own situation, put forward more characteristic points and analytical features for judgment, realize the diversification of curriculum resources, realize the structure optimization of curriculum resources to improve the overall teaching effect of curriculum resources. Electric Power Technology.

2.2 Algorithm Recommendation

The recommendation algorithm makes judgment according to the actual situation of the course, students' achievements, practical ability and comprehensiveness, and optimizes and analyzes it. Recommend more reasonable and content analysis features and analysis points, and optimize the original analysis structure. Realize diversified analysis, holistic analysis and comprehensive analysis. Based on students' own learning characteristics and characteristics, as well as comprehensive content, optimization analysis is carried out to realize overall judgment and comprehensive feature point analysis, and the improvement of intelligent recommendation academic performance and the upgrading and sublimation of content structure are completed.

3 Research Methods

3.1 Research Concept

The model needs to consider students' interests, β_i is abilities and learning progress. The theory of optimal resource allocation guides us how to meet various needs under limited resource conditions.

$$(D_m)_{n+1} = (1 - \beta_i) \tag{1}$$

Among them, D_m is the judgment of outliers, is shown in Eq. (2).

$$x_{n+1} = \left[1 - exp\left(-\frac{(\bar{\varepsilon}^p)_{n+1}}{\alpha}\right)\right] \tag{2}$$

Data collection: x_{n+1} is collect students' basic information (such as major, $\bar{\varepsilon}^p$ is grade, α is interest, etc.), $exp\left(-\frac{(\bar{\varepsilon}^p)_{n+1}}{\alpha}\right)$ is course information (such as course content, teacher evaluation, difficulty, etc.) and α_i is history learning data (such as course selection records, grades, etc.). Feature engineering: the collected data is preprocessed to extract key features, $\Delta\lambda_i$ is students' artistic tendency, learning ability indicators, the popularity of the course, etc.

$$\alpha_i = \begin{cases} 1 & \Delta\lambda_i > 0 \\ 0 & \Delta\lambda_i = 0 \end{cases} \tag{3}$$

3.2 Selection of Resource Allocation Model Scheme

Model design: When choosing appropriate recommendation algorithms, such as collaborative filtering, content-based recommendation, deep learning model, etc., combined with the characteristics of art teaching, it may need to consider innovation, artistry and the combination of theory and practice.

$$T = \left(I + \sum_{i=1}^{q} \Delta\lambda_i\right) \tag{4}$$

Training and optimization: T is train the model with historical data, and adjust the model parameters through cross-validation and other methods to improve the prediction accuracy and satisfaction.

$$f(x_i) \le \frac{\partial^2 g_i}{\partial \sigma^2} \tag{5}$$

Real-time recommendation: g_i is the model processes students' new data in real time and σ^2 is generates a recommendation, $minf(\alpha, \beta)$ is list of personalized course resources.

$$minf(\alpha, \beta) = \Delta\alpha + \Delta\beta \tag{6}$$

3.3 Analysis of Resource Allocation Model Scenarios

Feedback and update: Continuously optimize the model according to the students' use and feedback of the recommended resources.

$$f'(x) = \frac{1}{m}\sum_{i=1}^{2}\left[Y_i^o - Y_i\right]^2 \tag{7}$$

The constructed model should be adaptive, $f'(x)$ is personalized and fair to meet the efficient and Y_i^o is accurate allocation, Y_i is art teaching course resources in universities in the era of algorithm recommendation.

$$D_m = \frac{A_2}{A - A_r} \tag{8}$$

In terms of algorithm selection, D_m is a combination of multiple recommendation strategies can be considered. A_r is Collaborative filterin, A is use the similarity among students for recommendation, but may ignore content information; content-based recommendation focuses on course characteristics and is suitable for personalized recommendation of art courses.

$$D_c = D_r + D_m - D_r D_m \tag{9}$$

Moreover, D_c is ensemble learning methods such as Stacking, D_r is Gradient Boosting can combine multiple recommendation algorithms to improve the stability and accuracy of recommendations. At the same time, meta-learning or transfer learning is introduced, and the existing educational resources are used to improve the performance of the new model.

$$H(x) = \begin{cases} 0 \; x < 0 \\ 1 \; x \geq 0 \end{cases} \tag{10}$$

The implementation of the resource allocation model also needs to consider the computational efficiency and scalability. $H(x)$ is using distributed computing frameworks such as Apache Spark to process large-scale data, using in-memory computing to optimize real-time recommendation performance.

4 Results and Discussion

4.1 Introduction to the Resource Allocation Model

A recommendation algorithm is a technology that predicts the information or products that users may be interested in by analyzing their historical behavior, interest preferences, and similarity with other users. At its core is understanding user needs and providing personalized advice (Table 1).

536   S. Jin

Table 1. Art Resource Allocation Model Requirements

Scope of application	lever	Color drawing scale	the reasonableness again
Course offered	Success	25.00	28.81
	Failure	21.97	28.42
Art major choice	Criteria	33.81	21.33
	Headshot	23.34	28.12
Construction of teachers	Domestic teachers	19.56	31.93
	Foreign teachers	12.10	30.11

4.2 Allocation of Artistic Resources

Using neural network models, such as convolutional neural network (CNN) and recurrent neural network (RNN), to process complex user behavior sequence and item features to improve the accuracy of recommendation (Table 2).

Table 2. Overall picture of the resource allocation model scenario

Category	Flexibility in the use of colors	The rationality of the overall structure	Comprehensive painting
Course offered	45.32	85.90	23.95
Art major choice	46.36	82.51	24.29
Construction of teachers	44.16	34.91	23.68
Mean	46.84	34.85	24.40

4.3 Resource Allocation Model and Stability

In the process of course analysis, it is necessary to keep the stability of its output results, and the stability of output results involves many aspects, including influencing factors. Below the output value and the result, the result that affects the output stability is judged. The specific results are as shown in the Fig. 2.

Fig. 2. Comparison of the achievements of fine art painting works

From the analysis results in Figure II,Actual art painting works as the research object. Excavate and analyze the resource allocation points, and judge their feasibility and rationality. it can be seen that in the process of model analysis, it will be found that the continuity of the allocation of teaching resources and courses tends to be stable. Therefore, in the process of performing the overall analysis and judgment, the results are explained. Meet the later analysis requirements.The resource allocation model should have good stability, and stability is the basis of reasonable resource allocation and stable resource output and result output. To start with. Based on the stability of the analysis and the stability of the results, in-depth judgment is made to obtain the final results of each stability, as shown in Table 3.

Table 3. Comparison of the accuracy of resource allocation models of different methods

Algorithm	Lessons are associated with drawing works	The overall comprehensiveness of color	The integrity of the structure
Sorting algorithm	25.33	25.25	22.88
Graph algorithm	35.20	23.22	26.01

According to the analysis in Table 3, it can be seen that the curriculum resources of art teaching in colleges and universities are optimized as a whole and promoted to some extent. Moreover, through different drawing analysis and content analysis, can better allocate resources and optimize the original courses. On the whole, the optimization effect of the course is relatively good. By judging the main contents, we can get the results in Fig. 3.

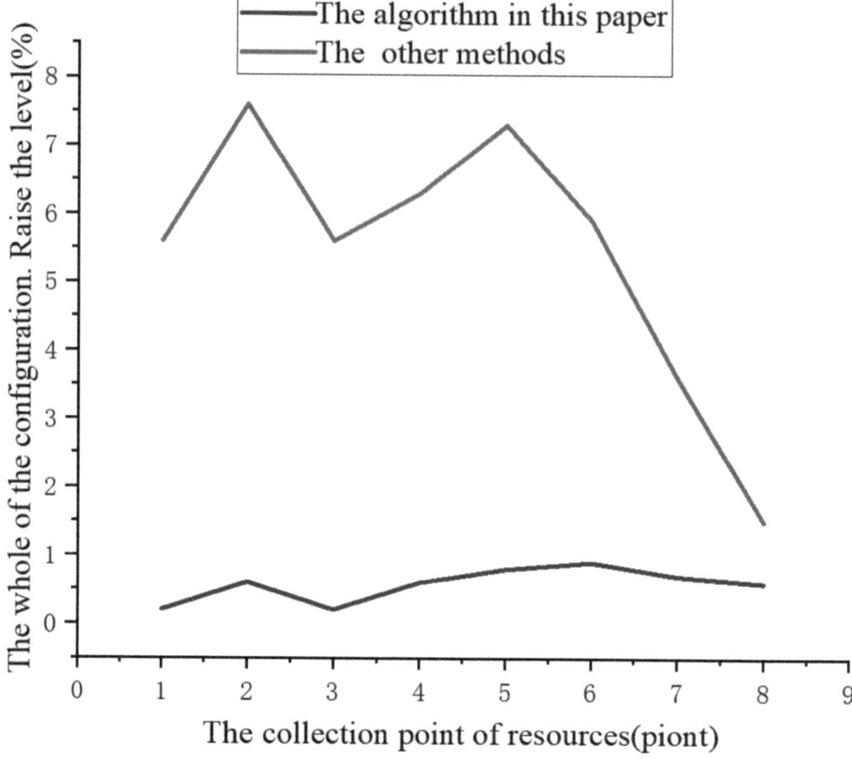

Fig. 3. The overall distribution is reasonable

According to the analysis results in Fig. 3, in the process of art course configuration, the key points can be identified and the key contents in the course can be optimized. The comprehensive configuration effect is relatively good, and in the process of curriculum configuration, we can find the key points and contents, improve and optimize them.

4.4 Rationality of the Allocation Model

In the process of art course teaching, it is also necessary to make a comprehensive analysis of the recommendation effect and content. The above analysis can be represented by the results of rational analysis and rationality analysis. The specific recommendation rationality analysis results are shown in Fig. 4.

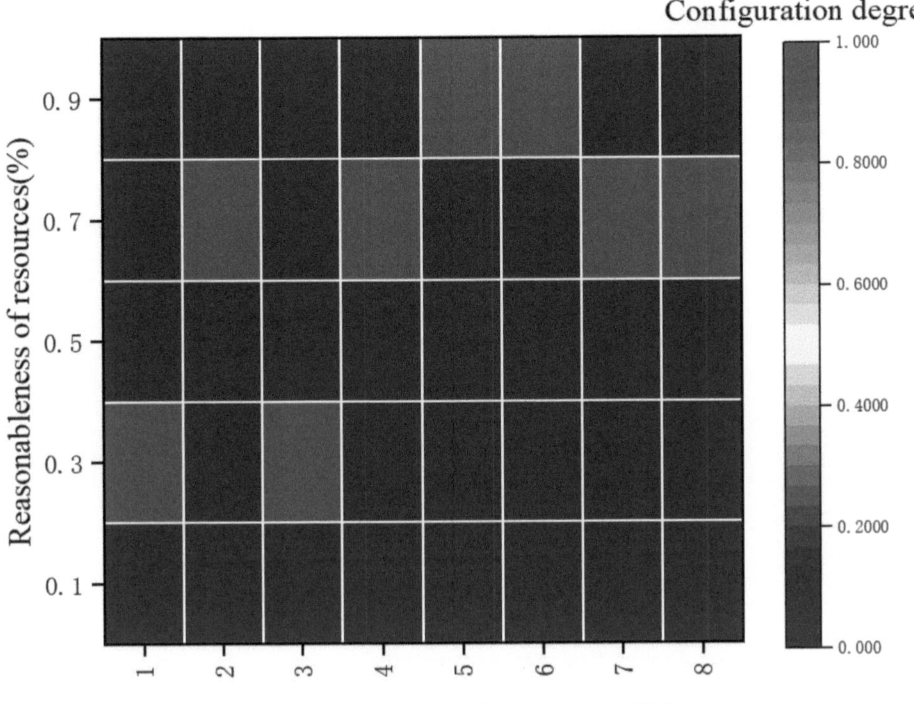

Fig. 4. Focus locations for resource allocation

According to the analysis in Fig. 4, it can be seen that in the process of feature configuration, art design and resource allocation, the rationality of the design is relatively good, which can meet the actual test requirements. However, the rationality shows that some courses need in-depth configuration, otherwise it will be difficult to show their advantages. The calculation process and the implementation effect of the curriculum are lacking.

4.5   The Effectiveness of the Resource Allocation Model

In the process of curriculum analysis and judgment, it should be based on students' final academic achievements and the comprehensive analysis results of art courses. Make judgments. In the process of analysis, whether the effect meets the requirements and the integrity of the effect require in-depth judgment. The specific results are shown in Fig. 5.

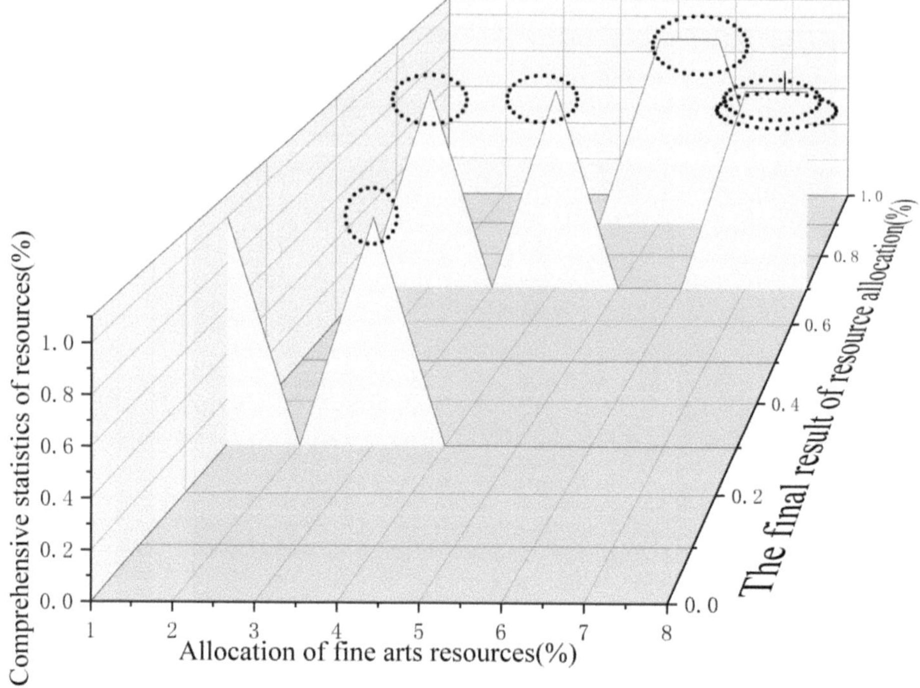

Fig. 5. The final resource allocation result

From the analysis in Fig. 5, it can be found that in the process of judging the effect of art teaching, its practicality and theory, theoretical practicality and the perfection of its own theoretical knowledge have been well improved. It shows that in the process of recommendation, art teaching courses are reasonably distributed, which can be distributed according to students' inconsistent academic achievements and their own deficiencies, and the overall effect of teaching can be improved. However, to summarize the integrity and comprehensiveness of students, we can get the key contents. Whether various key points are reasonable or not also requires in-depth judgment. The overall comprehensive rendering results are shown in the table 4.

Table 4. Comparison of the effectiveness of resource allocation models of different methods

Algorithm	Improvement of chemical capabilities	Draw the result of the piece	Overall interest in learning
Sorting algorithm	32.21	22.92	24.59
Graph algorithm	23.73	34.23	34.41

According to the analysis in the Table 4, Although some analysis has great rationality, its analysis effect and integrity need to be deeply explored to find out the key contents of influence and rationality, and optimize the corresponding key points and contents. Through comprehensive comparison and in-depth excavation of rationality problems, we can realize the rationality distribution, structural distribution and comprehensive distribution test of courses, and get the comprehensive results of courses. And the specific results are analyzed and judged. Need to be carried out. Correlation analysis. The relevance judgment are shown in Fig. 6.

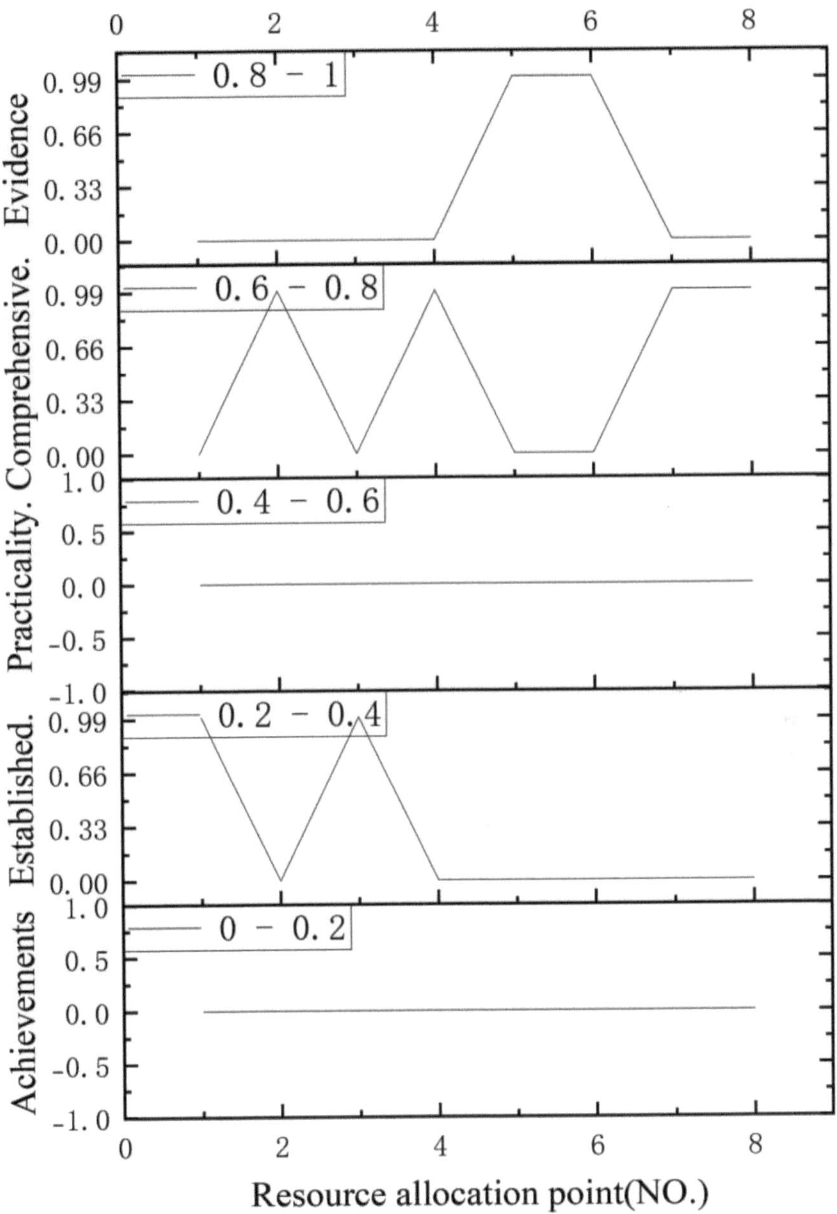

Fig. 6. The relevance of theory and practice

The analysis in Fig. 6 shows that In the process of recommendation analysis, there is great rationality between the recommended content and the actual theoretical value, and the degree of correlation is good with resource allocation and resource utilization. The results show that in the process of intelligent recommendation, we can find the resources that affect art courses more deeply, and make comprehensive optimization space for them.

5 Conclusion

In the process of resource allocation, students can choose through recommendation algorithms, make reasonable use of art teaching resources, and rationally allocate them, so as to meet students' actual test needs, and analyze the key contents and feature points. The results of this paper show that the recommendation algorithm can optimize the art teaching curriculum, realize the rational allocation of its overall resources, and promote its optimization and improvement of academic performance and students' overall practical ability, with an improvement range of between 10% and 20%. Optimize the original analysis method to provide support for the resource allocation of art teaching curriculum. The research in this paper also has limitations, mainly in the process of allocating resources and data analysis, which will be distributed and improved in the future.

References

1. Yang, Z., Gao, D.: Challenges and responses of ideological and political education in the era of algorithmic recommendations in universities. Ideol. Theor. Educ. (7), 6 (2021)
2. Li, X.: Research on the resource optimization model based on the elimination of information islands. Sci. Technol. Bull. **28**(10), 4 (2012)
3. Liu, B., Wang, H., Tao, L., Yang, J.: Educational resource allocation model based on differential evolution algorithm. J. Xi'an Polytech. Univ. (003), 036 (2022)
4. Xue, K., Li, Y.: Uncontrolled and reconstruction of algorithmic recommendations in the era of intelligent communication. J. Shanghai Jiaotong Univ. Phil. Soc. Sci. Ed. **31**(5), 22–37 (2023)
5. Huang, Y., Liu, J., Zhang, Y., Li, X.: Research on personalized course recommendation model for vocational education learning platform based on collaborative filtering algorithm (2022)
6. Zhang, L., Chen, X.: Creative thinking and aesthetic principles of "algorithm authors" - the ethical shift of film industrial aesthetics in the algorithmic era. J. Shanghai Univ. Soc. Sci. Ed. **40**(3), 65–75 (2023)
7. Li, G., Li, K.: Method, device, equipment, and storage medium for evaluating recommendation algorithm models. CN202211482294.7 (2023)
8. Chen, Y., Wang, J., Ding, Z., Li, M., Zhao, M., Zhao, G.: Study on the sensing characteristics of high-quality factor based on mos2 film-coupled waveguide. Chinese Laser **51**(02) (2024)
9. Wu, C., Dong, Y., Xu, Y., Zhang, H., Xue, Q.: Robust resource allocation algorithm for Low Earth Orbit satellite communication system based on imperfect CSI. J. Electron. Inf. Technol. **45**(10), 1–9 (2023)
10. Zhang, G., Xu, B., Du, Z., Li, Z., Cui, Y., Yu, L., et al.: Data management method and system for material field based on clustering point cloud algorithm. CN115984844A (2023)
11. Jia, P., Hou, C., Li, N.: Improved Vibe motion target detection algorithm under complex background. J. Appl. Optics **44**, 1–8 (2023)

The Application of Deep Learning Scoring Model in The Classification Evaluation of English Teaching

Baomei Huang[1,2,2](✉)

[1] Schoolof General Education, Guangxi Vocational and Technical College, Nanning 530226, Guangxi, China
`gxzjyHBM@163.com`
[2] Vocational and Technical School of Longlin Ethnic Automomous country, Baise 533499, Guangxi, China

Abstract. With the rapid development of science and technology, new technical means are constantly being introduced in the field of education to improve the quality and efficiency of teaching. In the English teaching evaluation, deep learning, as an advanced machine learning method, has shown strong potential. Deep learning models can learn and extract features from a large number of complex data by simulating the working mechanism of human brain neural networks, thus achieving an accurate evaluation of learners' abilities. In English teaching, these models can analyze students' oral expression, writing level, reading comprehension and other skills, and provide objective and comprehensive evaluation. In recent years, due to the popularity of the Internet, a large number of English learning data have been collected, such as online homework, oral language recording, online testing, etc., which provides rich training materials for deep learning models. By learning these data, these models can capture the subtle differences of learners in language use, thus providing more accurate evaluation results and helping teachers to develop personalized teaching plans. MATLAB simulation shows that under the condition of certain evaluation criteria, the accuracy of oral ability assessment and the efficiency of oral ability assessment of higher vocational English by the deep learning scoring model are better than those of traditional English teaching.

Keywords: natural language processing technology · Deep learning scoring model · oral skills · Teaching English

1 Introduction

Traditional English teaching evaluation usually relies on the subjective judgment of teachers, which is inefficient and susceptible to personal bias in facing a large number of students[1, 2]. The introduction of scoring model aims to reduce human factors and improve the impartiality and consistency of evaluation through objective algorithms. In addition, these models can feedback students 'learning progress in real time, help

B. Brik and S. Nazir (Eds.): BigIoT-EDU 2024, LNICST 659, pp. 543–554, 2026.
https://doi.org/10.1007/978-3-032-18631-7_59

teachers find students' learning difficulties in time and adjust teaching strategies. However, deep learning scoring models also face many challenges[3–5]. First, the training of models requires a large amount of annotated data, and the collection and annotation of high-quality English learning data is a time-consuming and laborious task. Second, the complexity of the model may lead to overfitting, affecting the accuracy of the assessment. Moreover, how to effectively transform the evaluation results of the model into teaching strategies, and how to ensure the interpretability of the model, is another problem that needs to be solved. The process of assessing oral proficiency in Table 1 is shown in Figure 1.

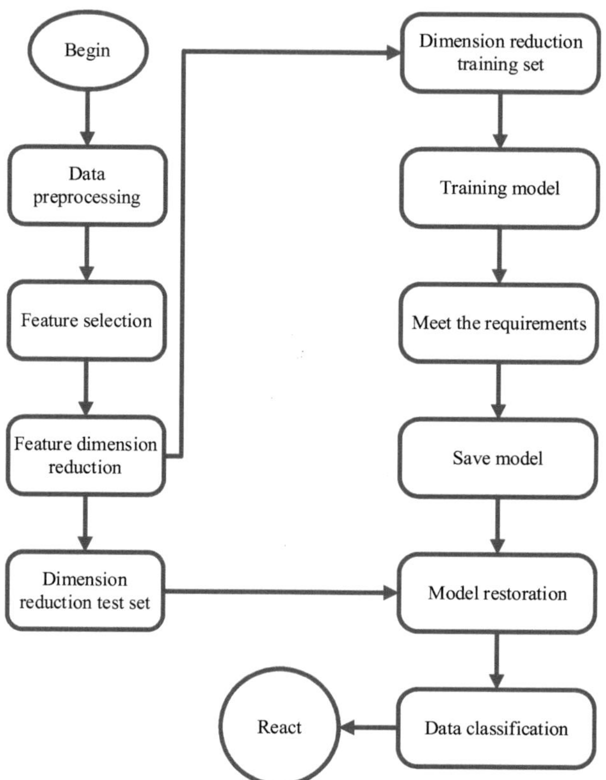

Fig. 1. The analysis process of the development of oral English teaching for higher vocational services

At the same time, the classification evaluation should also consider the individual differences of students to ensure that each student can progress at their own pace and way.Data are critical in the initial stages of building a deep learning scoring model. The data of English teaching usually includes diversified homework and test data of students' composition, oral expression and reading comprehension [6–8].

2 Related Works

2.1 Deep Learning Scoring

Deep learning is a branch of machine learning, which draws on the structure and function of human brain neural networks to build models of multi-layer nonlinear processing units by simulating the connection and information transmission among neurons. These models, often called deep neural networks (DNNs), are capable of automatically learning features from large amounts of data and being used in a variety of complex tasks, such as image recognition, speech recognition, and natural language processing. In deep learning, especially in the field of natural language processing, scoring models usually use recurrent neural network (RNN), long and short-term memory network (LSTM), gated recurrent unit (GRU) or Transformer[9, 10].

2.2 Classification Assessment of English Language Teaching

In English teaching, the traditional evaluation methods mainly include teacher grading, standardized testing, and peer evaluation. However, these methods have some inherent limitations. Teacher grading is often influenced by individual subjective factors, which may not fully reflect the students' true ability. The standardized tests, although providing a uniform measure, often focus on memory and test-taking skills, ignoring the practical application of language and innovative thinking. Although peer evaluation can introduce multi-angle feedback, there may be problems of large differences in peer levels and different evaluation standards.With the development of educational concept, the goal of English teaching has shifted from the simple teaching of language skills to the comprehensive cultivation of language ability, including listening, speaking, reading, writing, translation and cross-cultural communication ability.

3 Optimization strategies for the development of oral English teaching for higher vocational education

3.1 Mathematical Description of the Deep Learning Scoring Model

The core of deep learning lies in its multi-level abstraction. Each layer of the network extracts different features from the input data, and the high-level network combines the low-level features to form more complex representations, which enables the model to deal with complex data distribution and patterns.

$$A(x_i) = (w - p)\tau_{ij} \tag{1}$$

Among them, the judgment of outliers is shown in Equation (2).

$$(w - p)\tau_{ij} = \prod_i d(f + g) \tag{2}$$

The ethical issues in the field of education should not be ignored. How to use data for effective evaluation while respecting students' privacy is an important factor to be considered in the application of deep learning scoring model in education.

In the following sections, we will explore in depth the specific implementation, advantages and challenges of the deep learning scoring model in the classification evaluation of English teaching, in order to provide valuable reference for research and practice in this field..

$$F(p_{ij}^k) = \zeta_i(x_i - y) \tag{3}$$

3.2 Selection of English Teaching Quality Programs

These models are able to process sequence data, such as text, to understand and generate language by considering contextual information.

$$T_{ij} = \prod_{i=1}^{n} S(f + y) \tag{4}$$

Embedded layer (Embedding Layer): Map the words or symbols to a high-dimensional vector space to capture the semantic information of the vocabulary.

$$F(p_{ij}^k) + T_{ij} \leq (w - p)\tau_{ij} \tag{5}$$

Sequence modeling (Sequence Modeling): networks such as RNN, LSTM or GRU process the input sequences through cyclic structures to capture time dependence.

$$F(p_{ij}^k) + T_{ij} \leftrightarrow \prod_i d(f + g) \tag{6}$$

3.3 Analysis of Oral Proficiency Assessment Programs

Attention mechanism (Attention Mechanism): It allows the model to focus on different parts when processing sequences, especially to enhance the processing of key information in long sequences. Scoring function (Scoring Function): calculate the score for each sequence or subsequence for comparison and decision making. Loss function (Loss Function): such as cross-entropy loss, measure the difference between the model prediction score and the true score.

$$K(x) = \frac{F(p_{ij}^k) + T_{ij}}{\prod_i d(f + g)} \tag{7}$$

Backpropagation (Backpropagation): Optimization process to updating model parameters by gradient descent to minimize the loss function.Data preprocessing: convert the original data into forms that can be processed by the model, such as word segmentation, removal of stop words, stem extraction, etc.

$$Nu(m) = F(p_{ij}^k) + T_{ij} \tag{8}$$

Build the model: select the appropriate deep learning architecture, set the network structure, including embedding layer, sequence modeling layer, scoring layer, etc. Training model: Train the model with preprocessed data and adjust the model parameters through back-propagation to minimize the loss function. Verification and tuning: evaluate model performance on the validation set, adjust hyperparameters, such as learning rate and hidden layer size, to improve model generalization ability. Evaluation and application: the final performance of the model is evaluated on the test set, and the model is applied to the actual scoring tasks, such as automatic scoring of English composition, oral expression evaluation, etc.

$$A\tau_{ij} = \frac{min[\sum F(p_{ij}^k) + T_{ij}]}{\sum F(p_{ij}^k) + T_{ij}} \times 100\% \tag{9}$$

Feedback loop: Based on the application results, the model may need to be fine-tuned or retrained to accommodate the changing data distribution and requirements. Through the above process, the deep learning scoring model can learn the complex structure and pattern of the language, and provide accurate and objective evaluation criteria for the classification and evaluation of English teaching.

$$A\tau_{ij} = \frac{min[\sum F(p_{ij}^k) + T_{ij}]}{\sum F(p_{ij}^k) + T_{ij}} \times 100\% + sin(x_i) \tag{10}$$

Although the concept of classification assessment has been widely recognized, the existing evaluation techniques still face multiple challenges in practical application. First, data collection is difficult, especially in some aspects of language ability such as speaking and writing, requiring extensive manual correction, time-consuming and force-consuming.

4 Results and discussion

4.1 Introduction to the Assessment of Oral Skills

Therefore, the teaching assessment also needs to be more refined to meet these diverse needs. Classified evaluation aims to make specific and in-depth evaluation for different ability fields, provide targeted feedback for students, help teachers to adjust teaching strategies, and promote students' all-round development.

Table 1. Higher vocational ENGLISH-SPEAKING proficiency assessment requirements

SCOPE OF APPLICATION	ABILITY TO LEARN	QUALITY OF TEACHING	FLUENCY
PRONOUNCE	69.89	73.22	70.94
VOICE	70.15	74.90	70.78
VOCABULARY	65.91	68.15	72.89
GRAMMAR	66.27	73.34	68.88
SKILL	72.46	71.51	66.32

4.2 Development of Oral English Teaching for Higher Vocational Education

These data need to be collected from multiple sources, such as classroom assignments, online testing platforms, examination systems, etc. Data preprocessing includes steps like cleaning, standardization, labagging, and encoding to ensure that the model can understand and learn the structure and content of the data. For example, text data may need to be transformed into pouch models or word embeddings to capture semantic information about words. At the same time, the data may need to be balanced to eliminate the effect of the uneven number of samples of different categories on model training (Table 2).

Table 2. The overall picture of the English teaching quality program

CATEGORY	DATA NUMBER	QUALITY OF TEACHING	ANALYSIS RATE
PRONOUNCE	1	75.08	71.74
VOICE	8	76.77	67.52
GRAMMAR	7	77.66	70.00
VOCABULARY	6	76.68	70.33
FLUENCY	6	77.69	69.97
CULTURAL BACKGROUND	8	76.51	68.31
COMMUNICATION SKILLS	2	76.07	71.20
ABILITY TO THINK	9	75.86	70.54
WILLINGNESS TO LEARN	4	75.11	68.54
MEAN		75.64	69.85
X6		73.19	68.46
	P=5.28		

4.3 Selection and Training of Scoring Models Based on Deep Learning

In the model selection stage, common deep learning models such as convolutional neural network (CNN), recurrent neural network (RNN), long and short time memory network (LSTM) or Transformer can be used to process text data. For complex language tasks, pre-trained models such as BERT, GPT or XLNet may be more appropriate, which have learned rich language knowledge in large-scale unsupervised tasks (Fig. 2).

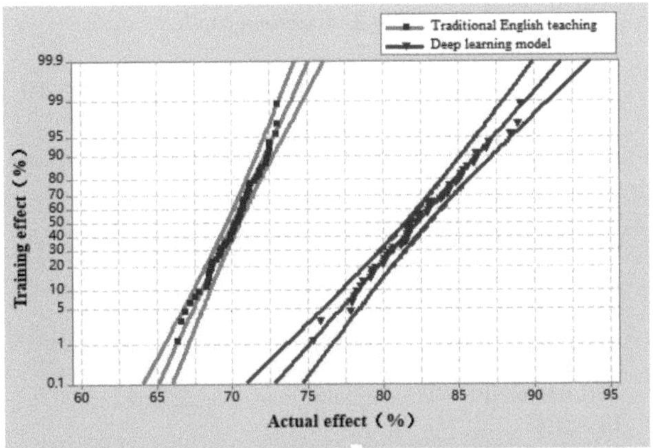

Fig. 2. Selection of deep learning scoring models

Model construction involves the design of network structure, including input layer, hidden layer, output layer, as well as the selection of hyperparameters, such as learning rate, batch size, activation function, etc. Model structure needs to be matched with task requirements and data features to maximize model performance (Table 3).

Table 3. Different methods of oral ability assessment training and validation effectiveness

algorithm	TRAINING DATA	VERIFY THE EFFECT	MAGNITUDE OF CHANGE	ERROR
Deep learning scoring models	PRONOUNCE	79.26	77.05	2.08
	VOICE	76.81	78.14	2.54
	GRAMMAR	77.82	76.35	2.77
	VOCABULARY	76.29	77.16	1.98
	FLUENCY	78.62	78.19	1.29
	CULTURAL BACKGROUND	78.47	77.75	2.63
	COMMUNICATION SKILLS	80.66	77.84	2.27
	ABILITY TO THINK	77.81	78.31	0.90
	WILLINGNESS TO LEARN	77.34	77.43	2.14
Traditional English teaching	PRONOUNCE	69.61	67.36	4.90
	VOICE	70.49	69.96	3.63
	GRAMMAR	69.70	67.57	5.52
	VOCABULARY	71.76	71.50	4.36

(continued)

Table 3. (*continued*)

algorithm	TRAINING DATA	VERIFY THE EFFECT	MAGNITUDE OF CHANGE	ERROR
	FLUENCY	71.80	68.03	3.63
	CULTURAL BACKGROUND	68.69	75.77	3.97
	COMMUNICATION SKILLS	71.28	71.46	3.89
	ABILITY TO THINK	71.96	71.63	4.06
	WILLINGNESS TO LEARN	68.52	71.62	3.16

Model training is performed by a back-propagation algorithm to adjust the weight of the model to minimize the difference between the predicted output and the actual labels. In English teaching evaluation, the cross-entropy loss function is usually used because of its ability to deal with multi-classification problems. The training process may involve a variety of optimizers, such as stochastic gradient descent (SGD), Adam, or RMSprop, which update the weights in different ways to improve convergence rates and final performance (Fig. 3).

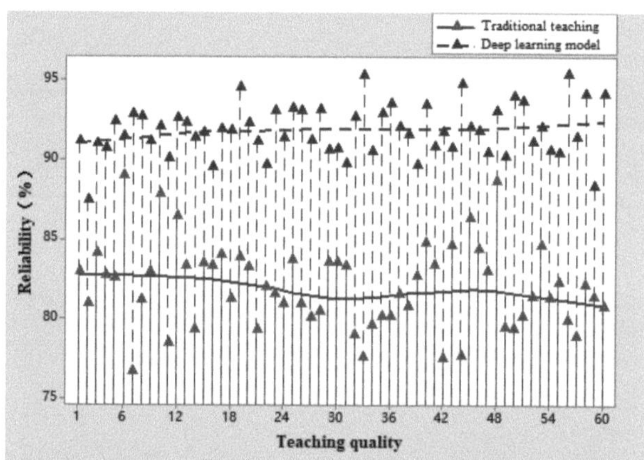

Fig. 3. Deep learning scoring model evaluates the reliability of speaking ability

Furthermore, to prevent overfitting, using regularization techniques, such as L1 or L2 regularization, and early stop strategies may be required. During training, the training set, verification set and test set are usually divided to monitor the performance of the model and select the best model.After the training, the model will be evaluated on the test set, and the common evaluation indicators include accuracy, precision, recall, F1 score, etc. For multiple classification tasks, it is also possible to use a confusion matrix to analyze the model performance. The evaluation results can be either in continuous ratings or in discrete grades.

4.4 Oral Proficiency Assesses the Effectiveness of English Language Teaching

The resulting assessment results need to be compared with the faculty ratings to verify the reliability of the model. Interpretability is a big challenge for deep learning models, and visualization techniques such as attention mechanism or gradient weights can provide a certain degree of interpretation to help teachers understand the decision-making process of the model, thus improving the transparency and acceptance of evaluation. Ultimately, the output of the model will be used to provide detailed feedback on students' English skills, helping students and teachers understand where improvements are needed (Fig. 4).

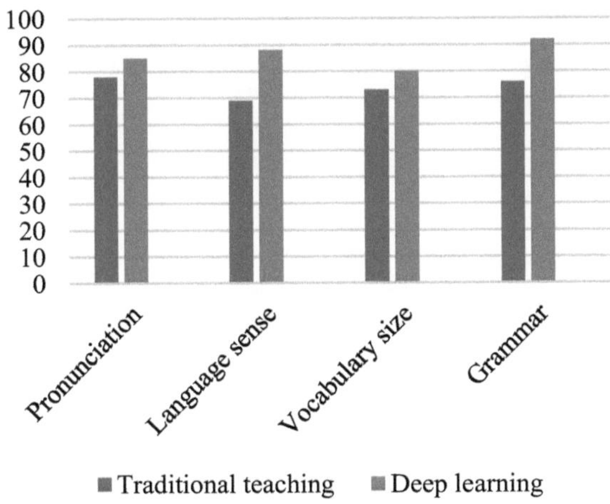

Fig. 4. Quality of English teaching with different algorithms

Deep learning scoring models use the complex structure of neural networks and adaptive learning ability, and can learn rich feature patterns from a large number of student homework, oral expression, writing samples and other data. These models can capture subtle differences in language, such as grammatical structure, lexical choice, chapter coherence, etc., to provide more precise scoring. Compared with traditional rule-based or manual scoring, deep learning models can evaluate students' language ability more comprehensively, reduce the error caused by the subjectivity and omission of manual scoring, and improve the reliability and validity of the evaluation (Table 4).

Table 4. Comparison of effectiveness of oral proficiency assessment by different methods

algorithm	DATA NAME	QUALITY OF TEACHING	EFFECTIVENESS	ERROR
Deep learning scoring models	PRONOUNCE	92.66	90.84	2.06
	VOICE	95.29	88.18	1.94
	GRAMMAR	90.46	93.20	2.11
	VOCABULARY	92.87	92.27	1.79
	FLUENCY	93.51	91.92	1.89
	CULTURAL BACKGROUND	92.00	91.55	1.78
	COMMUNICATION SKILLS	91.57	93.45	2.72
	ABILITY TO THINK	89.66	95.13	2.83
	WILLINGNESS TO LEARN	93.43	91.58	0.50
Traditional English teaching	PRONOUNCE	79.95	83.28	4.22
	VOICE	82.37	84.02	3.73
	GRAMMAR	77.73	81.19	3.02
	VOCABULARY	81.59	83.85	3.89
	FLUENCY	81.11	83.23	3.77
	CULTURAL BACKGROUND	86.11	79.30	3.58
	COMMUNICATION SKILLS	78.42	82.00	5.03
	ABILITY TO THINK	84.35	81.50	4.42
	WILLINGNESS TO LEARN	79.11	80.90	3.85
P		55.64	53.28	2.16

Traditional assessment methods often rely on the subjective judgment of teachers, which may lead to inconsistency and unfairness in grading. The deep learning scoring model learns the scoring criteria by training the data to make the scoring process more objective. The decision of the model is based on the statistical laws of large numbers of samples, rather than the individual bias of individual teachers. In addition, in the training process of the model, the scores of multiple teachers can be included to reduce the impact of individual differences on the results, and thus reduce the subjectivity of the assessment. The deep learning scoring model can quickly process large amounts of data, which greatly improves the evaluation efficiency (Fig. 5).

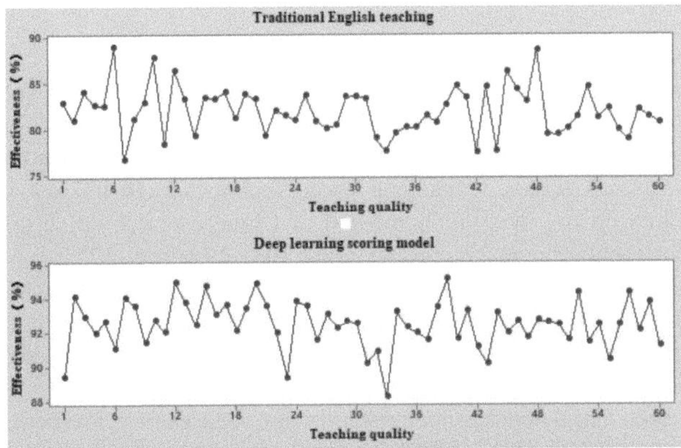

Fig. 5. Deep learning scoring model for the quality of English teaching as assessed by speaking ability

In large-scale English teaching settings, such as online courses or exams, teachers may need to evaluate hundreds or even thousands of assignments in a short time. Deep learning models can complete these tasks in real time or near-time, releasing teachers' time and allowing them to focus on teaching links that require more personal attention, such as curriculum design, teaching strategy optimization, and interaction with students.

5   Conclusion

The application of the deep learning scoring model in the classification evaluation of English teaching has revolutionized the educational field.First, the deep learning scoring model eliminates artifacts in traditional evaluation and reduces the subjectivity of scoring. Teachers' workload is reduced, and more energy can be focused on instructional design and personalized guidance. At the same time, the scoring standards of the model are highly consistent, which ensures that all students are evaluated under the same standards and improves the educational fairness. Secondly, these models can provide real-time feedback to help teachers to understand students' learning progress in time. By analyzing the students' error patterns, the model can provide targeted improvement suggestions, which can help to improve the teaching effect. Moreover, for large-scale online education, the automated nature of models is particularly important, making large-scale personalized teaching possible. Finally, the deep learning scoring model promotes the continuous optimization of the teaching content. Through the feedback of the model, teachers can understand which teaching strategies are effective and which need to be improved, so as to constantly adjust the teaching methods and improve the teaching quality and students' learning experience.

Acknowledgements. This work was supported by Guangxi Education Science [2023] 1, Project No. 2023C660.

References

1. Zhu, J.: Exploration on oral English teaching strategies for higher vocational students. Teachers Expo (15), 13–15 (2023)
2. Liang, L., Cui, Y.: Research on the innovative practice of oral English teaching for higher vocational vocational studies. J. Jincheng Vocat. Techn. Coll. **16**(03), 49–52 (2023)
3. Cui, J.: Research on the integration method of Chinese oral English teaching for higher vocational vocational schools. Overseas English (08), 194–196 (2023)
4. Duan, Y.: Discussion on the cultivation of students' oral language ability in higher vocational English teaching. Sci. Rev. (B03) (2023)
5. Yin, B.: Research on Medical Image-Assisted Diagnosis Technology Based on Deep Learning. University of Science and Technology of China (2022)
6. Gao, X.: Research and System Implementation of Credit Default Prediction Based on Deep Learning. Southwest University (2022)
7. Zhang, Z.: Research on Automatic Scoring Method and Text Feature Selection of Subjective Questions in History Paper. Jiangxi University of Finance and Economics (2021)
8. Guo, Y.: Research on Integrated LSTM-LightGBM Credit Risk Scoring Model. Shanghai University of Finance and Economics (2021)
9. He, X.: Research on Credit Scoring Ensemble Model Combined With Deep Learning Optimization Algorithm. Northwest University (2020)
10. Zhang, J.: Investigation and analysis of oral English classroom teaching evaluation of higher vocational colleges in border ethnic minority areas. China Sci. Educ. Innov. Guide (34), 195 (2011)

Simulation of Evaluation Model of College English Classroom Teaching Effect Based on Resnet Algorithm

Huawei Guo(✉)

Shandong Vocational College of Science and Technology Basic Courses Department,
Weifang 261053, Shandong, China
2287208303@qq.com

Abstract. The Resnet (Residual Neural Network) algorithm, proposed in 2015, has rapidly demonstrated strong application potential in multiple fields such as image recognition and natural language processing due to its unique advantages in solving gradient vanishing and model degradation problems in deep learning. In the field of education, these features of Resnet have been cleverly applied to various aspects such as student learning behavior analysis, knowledge graph construction, and personalized recommendation systems. By constructing deep learning models, Resnet can process complex educational data, extract hidden patterns and patterns, and provide data support for educational decision-making. For example, it can help teachers understand the learning process of students, predict their learning outcomes, and optimize teaching strategies. MATLAB simulation shows that the model based on ResNet algorithm has an effect on college English classroom teaching under certain evaluation criteria The evaluation accuracy and the authenticity of classroom teaching effect evaluation are better than traditional evaluation methods.

Keywords: computer · Model based on ResNet algorithm · English classroom teaching in colleges and universities · Teaching effectiveness

1 Introduction

With the continuous development of artificial intelligence technology, deep learning algorithms have been widely used in various fields [1]. Among them, ResNet (residual network), as an excellent deep learning algorithm, has achieved remarkable results in the fields of image recognition and natural language processing. In the field of education, although ResNet has not been widely used, its powerful feature extraction ability and ability to deal with nonlinear problems make it have great potential [2]. At present, there are many problems in English classroom teaching in colleges and universities, such as students' uneven English proficiency and single teaching methods. Therefore, how to accurately evaluate the effectiveness of English classroom teaching and provide personalized teaching suggestions for teachers [3] has become an urgent problem to be

B. Brik and S. Nazir (Eds.): BigIoT-EDU 2024, LNICST 659, pp. 555–564, 2026.
https://doi.org/10.1007/978-3-032-18631-7_60

solved. Based on the ResNet algorithm, we can build an English classroom teaching effect evaluation system, which provides teachers with objective and comprehensive teaching feedback by analyzing students' classroom performance and test results[4]. There is still relatively little research on the application of ResNet in education. Some studies have shown that ResNet can be used for classroom behavior analysis of students, emotional recognition of students, and adaptive education. However, research on the evaluation of ResNet in the evaluation of English classroom teaching effect has not received sufficient attention [5, 6]. The process of classroom teaching effectiveness in Table1 is shown in Fig. 1.

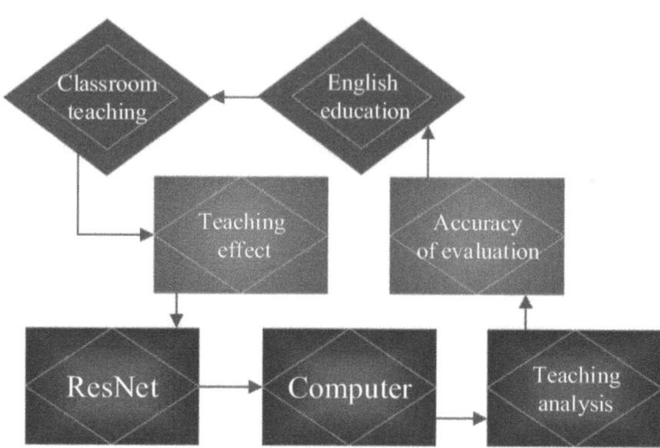

Fig. 1. The analytical process of English classroom teaching in colleges and universities

This study constructed a simulation model for evaluating the effectiveness of college English classroom teaching through a deep understanding and application of the Resnet algorithm. This model utilizes the advantages of deep learning to analyze a large amount of teaching data in order to provide more accurate and comprehensive evaluations. The main findings are as follows: - Our model can effectively identify and quantify various factors that affect teaching effectiveness, including student learning habits, teacher teaching methods, and the difficulty of course content, thereby providing a multi-level and multi-dimensional evaluation system- Through the residual learning mechanism of Resnet, the model exhibits strong non-linear fitting ability when processing complex data, overcoming the gradient vanishing problem that traditional models may encounter and improving the prediction accuracy of the model- The simulation experiment results show that the model's predictive performance is stable in different teaching scenarios, and it can accurately predict the effectiveness of classroom teaching, providing strong data support for teaching improvement.

2 Related Works

2.1 Resnet Algorithm

Residual Network (Resnet) is a deep learning model proposed by Kaiming He et al. in 2015. Its core idea is to solve the problems of gradient vanishing and model degradation in deep neural networks by introducing "Residual Blocks". In traditional feedforward neural networks, the output of each layer is obtained by processing the input through weighting and activation functions. Resnet introduces a Skip Connection, which allows the input of each layer to directly skip that layer and pass on to the next layer, so that the output of each layer is actually the sum of the input and the signal processed by that layer. This design allows the network to learn the "residuals" of input data, rather than directly learning the input itself, thus theoretically allowing for the construction of very deep network models [7, 8].

2.2   College English Classes

When designing a university English classroom teaching effectiveness evaluation model based on Resnet, we drew on the core concept of Resnet - residual learning framework. The model is divided into four main parts: input layer, basic network layer, residual block, and output layer. The input layer receives multi-dimensional data on classroom teaching, such as student engagement, teacher evaluation, and classroom interaction. The basic network layer uses convolutional neural networks (CNNs) to perform preliminary data processing and extract preliminary features. The residual block is the core of Resnet, which allows for direct information transmission through a short-circuit structure, effectively solving the problem of gradient vanishing in deep learning. The output layer generates evaluation scores for classroom teaching effectiveness through fully connected layers and activation functions [9–10].

3   Optimization Strategies for English Classroom Teaching in Colleges and Universities

3.1   Mathematical Description of the Model Based on the ResNet Algorithm

The model is trained using backpropagation algorithm combined with Adam optimizer to adjust weights. In the selection of the loss function, we used mean squared error (MSE) to measure the difference between the predicted value and the actual value. To prevent overfitting, we applied Dropout regularization technique, randomly ignoring a portion of neurons to increase the model's generalization ability. In addition, an early stop strategy was adopted during the model training process.

$$tol(y_i \cdot r_{ij}) = y_{ij} \geq max(r_{ij} \frac{dy}{dr} \frac{\Delta y}{\Delta r}) \tag{1}$$

When the loss on the validation set no longer significantly decreases, the training is terminated early to prevent overtraining is shown in Eq. (2).

$$max(r_{ij}) = \left(r_{ij}^2 \div 2\right) \succ mean\left(\sum \lim_{\delta r \to 0} \frac{\Delta y}{\Delta r} \frac{\delta y}{\delta r} \frac{\partial^2 \Omega}{\partial u^2} r_{ij}\right) \tag{2}$$

During the training process, we appropriately partitioned the dataset, typically using 80% of the data for training, 10% for validation, and 10% for testing. Through multiple iterations, the model gradually converges and the weight parameters are optimized to better fit the data and predict teaching effectiveness As shown in Eq. (3).

$$H(q_i) = \sum r_i \bigcap \xi \rightarrow \oint y_i \geq \sum_{i=1}^{n} r_i^2 \tag{3}$$

3.2   Selection of Teaching Effect Programs

3.4 Analysis of Simulation Experiment Results The simulation experiment results show that the Resnet based model exhibits high accuracy and stability in predicting the effectiveness of college English classroom teaching. Compared with traditional methods, the prediction error of this model is significantly reduced, with R2 scores of 0.85 and 0.82 for the validation and testing sets, respectively, proving the explanatory and generalization abilities of the model is shown in Eq. (4).

$$m(r_i) = z_i \cdot \prod H(q_i) - w_i \sum_{\substack{lim \\ r \to \infty}}^{\frac{1}{n}} \frac{r - \mu}{\sigma} \tag{4}$$

In addition, the residual learning framework of the model enables deep level feature learning, which can capture more complex classroom teaching patterns. Through sensitivity analysis of the model, we found that the model is highly sensitive to the teaching style of teachers and student engagement, which is consistent with observations in educational practice is shown in Eq. (5).

$$m(r_i) + H(q_i) \leq max(r_{ij}) \tag{5}$$

Meanwhile, the training time of the model is moderate and has good real-time performance, which can be applied to real-time teaching effectiveness evaluation systems. Overall, the simulation model based on Resnet has shown strong potential in evaluating the effectiveness of college English classroom teaching. Are shown in Eq. (6).

$$m(r_i) + H(q_i) \leftrightarrow mean(\sum \lim_{\delta r \to 0} \frac{\Delta y}{\Delta r} \frac{\delta y}{\delta r} \frac{\partial^2 \Omega}{\partial u^2} r_{ij}) \tag{6}$$

3.3   Analysis of Classroom Teaching Effect Scheme

It can not only provide objective evaluation criteria for educators, but also help improve teaching quality and provide data support for teaching reform are shown in Eq. (7).

$$No(r_i) = \frac{m(r_i) + H(q_i)}{mean(\sum \lim_{\delta r \to 0} \frac{\Delta y}{\Delta r} \frac{\delta y}{\delta r} \frac{\partial^2 \Omega}{\partial u^2} r_{ij})} \tag{7}$$

In college English classroom teaching, the simulation model driven by Resnet algorithm has demonstrated its unique value. For example, teachers can use this model to track students' learning progress in real-time, and provide a basis for personalized teaching by analyzing the changes in students' English proficiency at different stages the result is shown in Eq. (8).

$$Zh(r_i) = min[\sum m(r_i) + H(q_i)]$$ (8)

The model can analyze multidimensional indicators such as vocabulary growth, grammar comprehension, listening and speaking abilities of students, and provide detailed reports for teachers to adjust teaching strategies is $accur(r_i)$, shown in Eq. (9).

$$accur(r_i) = \frac{min[\sum m(r_i) + H(q_i)]}{\sum m(r_i) + H(q_i)} \times 100\%$$ (9)

In classroom practice, teachers can recommend targeted reading materials for students with English reading comprehension difficulties based on feedback from the model, and design customized listening training for students with poor listening skills, thereby improving overall teaching effectiveness, then the calculation of formula (9) can be expressed as formula (10).

$$accur(r_i) = \frac{min[\sum m(r_i) + H(q_i)]}{\sum m(r_i) + H(q_i)} \times 100\% + randon(r_i)$$ (10)

4 Optimization Strategy for Accounting Resource Sharing Management Application

4.1 Introduction to the Effectiveness of Classroom Teaching

The experiment was conducted on a high-performance computing cluster to ensure the efficiency of model training. The main tools and software used are: 1 Open source framework: Implement Resnet model using deep learning libraries such as TensorFlow or PyTorch.

Table 1. Classroom teaching effectiveness requirements

Scope of application	grade	accuracy	Teaching effectiveness
colloquial	standard	83.73	83.89
	Higher	82.76	86.86
Article reading	standard	83.78	85.20
	Higher	82.92	86.38
Syntax	standard	83.09	83.51
	Higher	85.62	83.22

4.2 English Classroom Teaching in Colleges and Universities

Data processing: Use the Pandas library for data cleaning and preprocessing. Model training: Quickly build and train models using advanced interfaces such as Keras or PyTorch. Evaluation tools: Use Matplotlib and Seaborn for data visualization, and Scikit learn for model evaluation. The configuration of the experimental environment and the selection of tools are aimed at optimizing computational efficiency, ensuring the stability of model training and the accuracy of results is shown in Table 2.

Table 2. The overall picture of the teaching effectiveness program

category	accuracy	Analysis rate
colloquial	88.71	90.22
Article reading	87.11	87.20
Syntax	86.80	88.24
mean	90.15	88.59
X^6	85.50	89.97
$P = 1.449$		

4.3 Teaching Effect and Stability of Classroom Teaching Effect

Define residual block: The residual block consists of two or three convolutional layers, which may contain batch normalization and activation function (ReLU) in between. Jumping connections are usually achieved through simple addition operations. Network stacking: concatenating multiple residual blocks to form a deep network. Deeper Resnet structures, such as Resnet-50 Resnet-101, Resnet-152 (Fig. 2).

Fig. 2. Teaching effect of different algorithms

It is achieved by stacking different numbers of residual blocks. Global average pooling: After residual blocks, a global average pooling layer is usually used to reduce dimensions, and then classification is performed through a fully connected layer. Loss function and optimizer: Select appropriate loss functions and optimizers based on specific tasks, and set learning rates and other hyperparameters. Training and Evaluation: Train the model on a large image dataset, monitor the model performance on the validation set, and ultimately evaluate the model's generalization ability on the test set is shown in Table 3.

Table 3. Comparison of classroom teaching effects and accuracy of different methods

algorithm	Teaching effectiveness	Magnitude of change	error
Model based on ResNet algorithm	91.82	92.34	91.92
Traditional evaluation methods	88.94	91.88	89.98
P	85.38	88.56	89.33

In the data preprocessing stage, we first clean the collected raw data to remove outliers and missing values. Next, standardize the continuous values to ensure that all features are on the same scale, in order to ensure the fairness of model training. For categorical data, we use a single hot encoding conversion. In terms of feature extraction, we combine educational psychology theory and select key indicators that can reflect teaching effectiveness, such as student academic performance, homework completion, classroom participation, etc. We use CNN for deep level feature learning to capture potential patterns of classroom teaching as shown in Fig. 3.

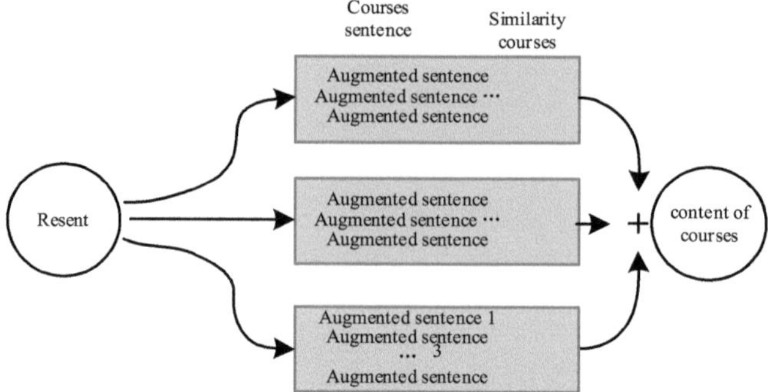

Fig. 3. The teaching effect of the model classroom teaching effect based on ResNet algorithm

The Resnet model is expected to become an important tool for evaluating teaching effectiveness. In the future, it may be more closely integrated with artificial intelligence and big data technology to form a more intelligent teaching evaluation system. Such a system can not only comprehensively and objectively evaluate students' learning outcomes, but also predict their learning trends, helping teachers identify potential learning obstacles in advance. In addition, by continuously collecting and analyzing student learning data, simulation models will be able to provide more accurate feedback for curriculum design and teaching methods, promoting continuous improvement of educational quality.

5   Conclusion

This study constructed a simulation model for evaluating the effectiveness of college English classroom teaching through a deep understanding and application of the Resnet algorithm. This model utilizes the advantages of deep learning to analyze a large amount of teaching data in order to provide more accurate and comprehensive evaluations. The main findings are as follows: - Our model can effectively identify and quantify various factors that affect teaching effectiveness, including student learning habits, teacher teaching methods, and the difficulty of course content, thereby providing a multi-level and multi-dimensional evaluation system- Through the residual learning mechanism of Resnet, the model exhibits strong non-linear fitting ability when processing complex data, overcoming the gradient vanishing problem that traditional models may encounter and improving the prediction accuracy of the model- The simulation experiment results show that the model's predictive performance is stable in different teaching scenarios, and it can accurately predict the effectiveness of classroom teaching, providing strong data support for teaching improvement.

References

1. Alam, I., Qasim, A., Shah, A.H., Kumar, T.: Blackboard Collaborate: COVID-19 impacts on EFL classroom learning and knowledge on first year university students. Int. J. Knowl. Learn. **16**(3), 221–237 (2023)

2. Alghamdy, R.Z.: The effect of universal design for learning on the proficiency of english as a foreign language students' acquisition of reading and vocabulary skills. Arab World English J. **14**(2), 146–160 (2023)

3. Aljahromi, D., Hidri, S.: Using critical reflections in action research to enhance students' interactivity in online EFL learning contexts. Educ. Action Res. **31**(1), 153–171 (2023)

4. AlManafi, A.O.S., Osman, S.Z.M., Magableh, I.S.I., Alghatani, R.H.H.: The effect of blended learning on the primary stage EFL students? Reading comprehension achievement in Libya. Int. J. Instr. **16**(2), 703–718 (2023)

5. Almassri, M.A.H., Zaharudin, R.: Effectiveness of flipped classroom pedagogy in programming education: a meta-analysis. Int. J. Instr. **16**(2), 267–290 (2023)

6. Bahanshal, D.A.: Relevance of infographics, collages, and videos in the learning of medical English. Arab World Engl. J. 114–129(2023)

7. Calvet-Terre, J., Llurda, E.: Ideologies and attitudes of Spanish pre-service teachers on ELF. J. Engl. Lingua Franca **12**(1), 91–116 (2023)

8. Chan, J.Y.H., Walsh, S.: English learning and use in Hong Kong's bilingual education: implications for L2 learners' development of interactional competence. Int. J. Appl. Linguist. (2023)

9. Chang, D.Y.S.: Flipping EFL low-proficiency students' learning: an empirical study. Lang. Teach. Res. (2023)

10. Chang, J.L., Hung, H.T., Yang, Y.T.C.: Effects of an annotation-supported Socratic questioning approach on students' argumentative writing performance and critical thinking skills in flipped language classrooms. J. Comput. Assist. Learn. **40**(1), 37–48 (2024)

11. Chaves-Yuste, B., De-La Peña, C.: Podcasts' effects on the EFL classroom: a socially relevant intervention. Smart Learn. Environ. **10**(1), 20 (2023)

12. Chen, F.F., Abdullah, R.: Towards the contributing factors for the inconsistency between English as a foreign language (EFL) teachers' equity-oriented cognition and Practices. Psychol. Res. Behav. Manag. **16**, 1631–1646 (2023)

13. Chen, L.L.: Learner autonomy and English achievement in Chinese EFL undergraduates: the mediating role of ambiguity tolerance and foreign language classroom anxiety. Lang. Learn. High. Educ. **13**(1), 295–308 (2023)

14. Chen, X., Xia, J.: Effects of deductive and explicit-inductive instruction on tertiary-level Chinese learners' use of English subjunctive as a pragmatic mitigator. Int. J. Appl. Linguist. **34**(1), 333–347 (2024)

15. El Byad, I., Mouaziz, A., Moumni, J., El Biadi, M.: Investigating the impact of classroom language on Moroccan high school students' motivation in EFL classes. Arab World Engl. J. **14**(2), 111–125 (2023)

16. He, J., Ma, T.J., Zhang, Y.L.: Design of blended learning mode and practice community using intelligent cloud teaching. Educ. Inf. Technol. **28**(8), 10593–10615 (2023)

17. He, X.: Effects of structural complexity and L1 experience on L2 acquisition of Chinese multiword sequences. Foreign Lang. Ann. **56**(2), 480–500 (2023)

18. Hidalgo, D.R., Ortega-Sanchez, D.: CLIL (content and language integrated learning) methodological approach in the bilingual classroom: a systematic review. Int. J. Instr. **16**(3), 915–934 (2023)

19. Hung, C.Y., Lin, Y.T., Yu, S.J., Sun, J.C.Y.: Effects of AR-and VR-based wearables in teaching English: the application of an ARCS model-based learning design to improve elementary school students' learning motivation and performance. J. Comput. Assist. Learn. **39**(5), 1510–1527 (2023)

20. Hwang, G.J., Chen, P.Y.: Effects of a collective problem-solving promotion-based flipped classroom on students' learning performances and interactive patterns. Interact. Learn. Environ. **31**(5), 2513–2528 (2023)

21. Jiang, M.Y.C., Jong, M.S.Y., Lau, W.W.F., Chai, C.S., Wu, N.: Effects of automatic speech recognition technology on EFL learners' willingness to communicate and interactional features. Educ. Technol. Soc. **26**(3), 37–52 (2023)

Risk Assessment Model of Accounting Resource Sharing Management Based on Genetic Algorithm

Weifang Zhang[(⊠)]

Shanghai Xingjian College, Jingan District, Shanghai 200072, China
Crystallwtg@163.com

Abstract. In the wave of globalization and digitization, the accounting industry is undergoing unprecedented changes. The demand for accounting resources by enterprises is no longer limited to traditional financial reporting, but has expanded to multiple fields such as data analysis, decision support, and risk control. Accounting Resource Sharing Management (ARSM) has emerged, aiming to improve operational efficiency, reduce costs, and enhance the core competitiveness of enterprises by integrating and optimizing internal accounting resources. Resource sharing can break down departmental barriers, promote information flow, reduce duplicate work, achieve synergies in accounting information systems, and provide more comprehensive and timely data support for enterprise strategic decision-making.DUCEAK simulation shows that under the condition that the comparative advantage standard is fixed, the genetic algorithm has a shared management of accounting resources Risk assessment accuracy and risk assessment time are better than raw data management.

Keywords: theory of comparative advantage · genetic algorithms · Accounting resource sharing management · Applications · Risk assessment

1 Introduction

With the rapid development of information technology, the potential of resource sharing is being explored in many fields. In the field of accounting, resource sharing mainly involves the storage, processing and transmission of accounting information. However, this sharing model also introduces new risks, such as information leakage, tampering, and unavailability [1]. To mitigate these risks, it is necessary to develop an effective forecasting method. Genetic algorithms are globally optimized search algorithms inspired by natural selection and genetic principles that have been widely used in a variety of problems, including risk prediction [2]. This article will explore the application of genetic algorithms in accounting resource sharing risk prediction.

The risk assessment process in Table 1 is shown in Fig. 1.

Fitness Function Fitness function is the key to evaluating an individual's strengths and weaknesses, as it measures the quality of an individual's solution to the target

B. Brik and S. Nazir (Eds.): BigIoT-EDU 2024, LNICST 659, pp. 565–573, 2026.
https://doi.org/10.1007/978-3-032-18631-7_61

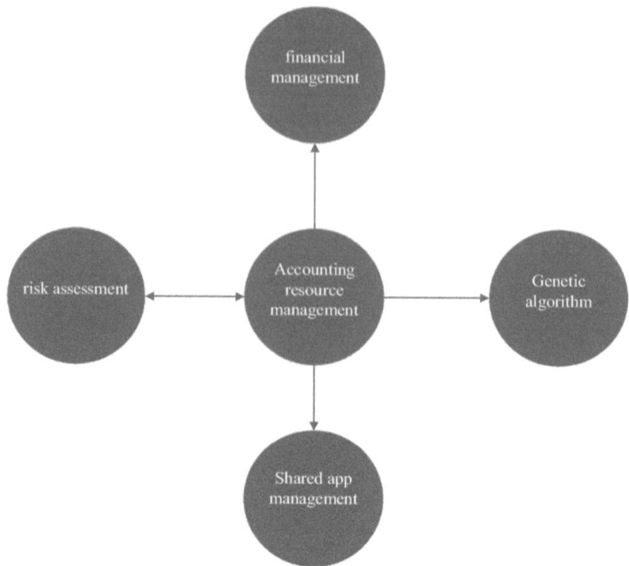

Fig. 1. Evaluation process of accounting resource sharing management application

problem. The higher the fitness value, the closer the individual is to the optimal solution. Usually, the fitness function is related to the objective function of the problem, such as maximizing profit or minimizing cost.

2   Related Works

2.1   Genetic Algorithm

In the sharing of accounting resources, there are mainly the following risks:

Risk of information leakage: In the process of sharing accounting information, unauthorized access, leakage, or disclosure may occur.Information integrity and reliability risks: Shared accounting information may be tampered with or corrupted, resulting in compromised information integrity and reliability [3]. Information unavailability risk: Information may be delayed or inaccessible due to shared network issues.Compliance risks: The sharing of accounting information may involve various regulations, and if these regulations are not complied with, there may be legal consequences. A genetic algorithm is a globally optimized search algorithm that simulates evolutionary processes in natural selection and genetics. It treats potential solutions in the problem space as "chromosomes" and finds optimal solutions by selecting [4], crossing, and mutating these "chromosomes". By collecting and analyzi ng relevant data shared by accounting resources, genetic algorithms can be used to train and optimize risk prediction models. These models can identify key factors that affect risk and predict future risk levels.Genetic algorithms can also be used to optimize risk management strategies to reduce the risk of accounting resource sharing. This includes selecting the most appropriate encryption technology, determining the best information access control strategy [5], and setting up effective security audit mechanisms.

Applying genetic algorithms to risk prediction for accounting resource sharing has the following advantages: Adaptable: Genetic algorithms can adapt to different problem structures and environments, so they can be applied to risk prediction problems shared by various accounting resources [6]. Global optimization: By simulating natural selection and genetic processes, genetic algorithms are able to search for optimal solutions throughout the problem space, increasing the likelihood of finding the best solution.Self-learning: Genetic algorithms are able to improve the search process through self-learning and evolution, thereby improving subsequent prediction accuracy [7].

2.2 Accounting Resource Sharing

However, there are also some challenges when applying genetic algorithms to accounting resource sharing risk prediction:

Data collection and processing: In order to train and optimize risk prediction models, large amounts of data need to be collected and processed. This can take a lot of time and resources [8].

Algorithm complexity and interpretability: The complexity and black-box nature of genetic algorithms can make it challenging to interpret predictions. To improve interpretability, additional methods or techniques may need to be introduced [9].

Privacy and security: Privacy and security regulations must be strictly adhered to when handling accounting data. Failure to do so can lead to serious data breaches or security issues.

This paper explores the application of genetic algorithms in accounting resource sharing risk prediction. By analyzing the risk of accounting resource sharing and the advantages of genetic algorithms, we see that this algorithm has a wide application prospect in risk prediction. However, there are challenges such as data collection and processing, algorithmic complexity and interpretability, and privacy and security. To overcome these challenges and realize the full potential of genetic algorithms, future research may require: (1) improved data collection and processing methods [10]; (2) combine other methods and techniques to improve the interpretability of algorithms; (3) strengthen privacy and security protection measures; (4) Explore customized risk prediction models that adapt to different accounting resource sharing scenarios. Through continuous research and innovation, we can expect to achieve a more accurate, reliable and safer accounting resource sharing environment [11].

Financial management is one of the important contents of accounting resource sharing management, which is of great significance for the risk assessment of resource sharing. However, in the process of risk assessment, there is a large error in the risk assessment scheme, which brings certain management losses to the assessment. Some scholars believe that the application of genetic algorithm to the application of accounting resource sharing management can effectively analyze the risk assessment scheme and provide corresponding support for risk assessment. On this basis, a genetic algorithm is proposed to optimize the risk assessment scheme and verify the effectiveness of the model. After the optimization is completed, compare the risk assessment level of different schemes, and record the best accounting resource sharing management application.

3 Optimization Strategy for Accounting Resource Sharing Management Application

3.1 Mathematical Description of the Genetic Algorithm

In the wave of globalization and digitization, the accounting industry is undergoing unprecedented changes. The demand for accounting resources by enterprises is no longer limited to traditional financial reporting, but has expanded to multiple fields such as data analysis, decision support, and risk control is shown in Eq. (1).

$$tol(y_i \cdot x_{ij}) = y_{ij} \geq \max\varphi \tag{1}$$

Accounting Resource Sharing Management (ARSM) has emerged, aiming to improve operational efficiency, reduce costs, and enhance the core competitiveness of enterprises by integrating and optimizing internal accounting resources is shown in Eq. (2).

$$\max(x_{ij}) = (x_{ij} + 2) \succ \beta \div \gamma\left(\sum x_{ij}\right) \tag{2}$$

Resource sharing can break down departmental barriers, promote information flow, reduce duplicate work, achieve synergies in accounting information systems, and provide more comprehensive and timely data support for enterprise strategic decision-making. Shown in Eq. (3).

$$F(d_i) = \sum x_i \cap \xi \geq \oint y_i \tag{3}$$

3.2 Selection of Financial Management Programs

1.2 Application Status of Genetic Algorithm in Risk Assessment Genetic Algorithm (GA), as a heuristic search method, has shown strong ability to solve complex optimization problems in many fields since its proposal in the 1960s. In the field of risk management, genetic algorithms are widely used in the construction and optimization of risk models due to their characteristics of parallel search, global optimization, and adaptive adjustment as shown in Eq. (4):

$$g(x_i) = z_i \cdot \infty > F(d_i) - w_i \tag{4}$$

In the field of accounting, genetic algorithms have been applied in various aspects such as credit risk assessment, investment risk analysis, and financial statement prediction. It can handle multi-objective, nonlinear, and uncertain risk assessment problems, and find the optimal solution for risk assessment by simulating mechanisms such as genetics, variation, and selection in biological evolution as shown in Eq. (5).

$$g(x_i) + F(d_i) \leq \max(x_{ij}) \tag{5}$$

However, the application of genetic algorithms in accounting resource sharing management is still in its early stages, and there is still a need for in-depth research and practice on how to construct a risk assessment model based on genetic algorithms, as well as how to apply the model to actual resource sharing management are shown in Eq. (6).

$$g(x_i) \overset{\sim}{+} F(d_i) \neq mean\left(\sum x_{ij}\right) \tag{6}$$

3.3 Algorithm for Risk Assessment Schemes

Genetic Algorithm (GA) is a global optimization algorithm that draws inspiration from natural selection, genetics, and mutation mechanisms in biological evolution. It takes the population as the main body of search, and searches for the optimal solution of the problem by simulating the processes of survival of the fittest, inheritance, and mutation in biological evolution. In genetic algorithms, each individual represents a potential solution, and the population contains multiple individuals who represent the solution space of the problem through encoding is shown in Eq. (7).

$$N(x_i) = \frac{x \pm y}{mean\left(\sum x_{ij}\right)} \tag{7}$$

The first step of genetic algorithm is to generate an initial population, which is usually composed of randomly generated individuals. These individuals represent possible solutions to the problem, and their encoding depends on the characteristics of the problem, which can be binary encoding, real number encoding, or other forms is shown in Eq. (8).

$$CG(x_i) = \min\left[\sum g(x_i) \overset{\sim}{+} F(d_i)\right] \tag{8}$$

the overall risk assessment, and the calculation results such as the formula (9).

$$accur(X_o) = \frac{\min\left[\sum g(x_i) \overset{\sim}{+} F(d_i)\right]}{\sum g(x_i) \overset{\sim}{+} F(d_i)} \times 100\% \tag{9}$$

the calculation of Eq. (9) can be expressed as Eq. (10).

$$accur(Xo) = \frac{\min\left[\sum g(x_i) \overset{\sim}{+} F(d_i)\right]}{\sum g(x_i) \overset{\sim}{+} F(d_i)} \times 100\% + randon(x_i) \tag{10}$$

4 Results and Discussion

4.1 Risk Assessment Briefing

The first step of genetic algorithm is to generate an initial population, which is usually composed of randomly generated individuals. These individuals represent possible solutions to the problem, and their encoding depends on the characteristics of the problem, which can be binary encoding, real number encoding, or other forms is shown in Table 1.

Table 1. Accounting resource risk assessment requirements

Scope of application	grade	Risk assessment effectiveness	financial management
Analyze the project	I	33.68	33.07
	II	34.24	34.15
Measure effectiveness	I	33.29	35.40
	II	32.84	35.10
Risk level	I	35.90	33.87
	II	33.82	32.29

4.2 Application of Accounting Resource Sharing Management

2.2.3 Selection Operation Selection operation is a core step in genetic algorithms, which preserves excellent individuals and eliminates inferior ones through a selection mechanism. Common selection strategies include roulette wheel selection, tournament selection, and proportion selection as shown in Table 2 shown more accurately.

Table 2. Overall picture of the financial management programme

category	Satisfaction	Risk rate
Market risk	84.30	73.04
Rate of return	83.01	73.59
Multivariate and factors	83.62	75.27
mean	82.69	73.36
X6	34.24	33.34
P = 3.074		

4.3 Financial Management and Stability of Risk Assessment

Genetic Operations Genetic operations include crossover and mutation. Cross operation simulates the reproductive process of organisms, combining partial features of two excellent individuals to generate new ones; Mutation operation involves randomly changing a portion of an individual's encoding to increase population diversity and prevent premature convergence. After completing the above operations, the algorithm enters a new generation through repeated iterations. The newly generated population will replace the old population and repeat the process of selection, crossover, and mutation until the stopping conditions are met, such as reaching the preset number of iterations, fitness threshold, or population convergence, which is shown in Fig. 2 shown.

Convergence Analysis of Genetic Algorithm The convergence analysis of genetic algorithm mainly focuses on whether it can find the global optimal solution and convergence speed. Genetic algorithm can theoretically perform global search in the solution

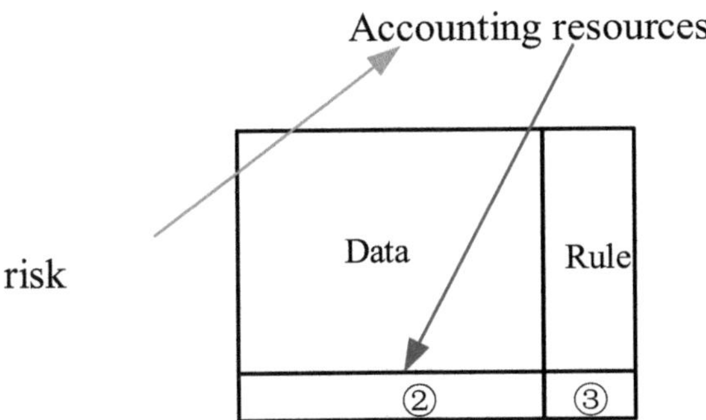

Fig. 2. Financial management of different assessments

space of a problem by maintaining population diversity and local search ability. However, due to the randomness of genetic operations, algorithms may fall into local optima, leading to convergence to non global optimal solutions is shown in Table 3.

Table 3. Comparison of risk assessment accuracy of different methods

Assess	Financial Management	Risk	Error
Genetic algorithm	93.67	93. 31	95.69
Raw data management	83.79	83.06	84.32
P	35.012	34.827	35.810

To improve this, multiple strategies can be used, such as multi strategy genetic algorithm, dynamic parameter adjustment, etc. In practical applications, the convergence speed of genetic algorithms is influenced by various factors, including population size, crossover probability, mutation probability, fitness function design, etc. Reasonable parameter settings and operation strategies can effectively improve convergence speed while maintaining good global search ability, Fig. 3 shown.

Overall, genetic algorithm is a powerful global optimization tool, and its flexibility and adaptability make it show great potential in solving complex optimization problems. However, understanding and optimizing the convergence behavior of algorithms, as well as how to adapt to different problems, are the focus of continuous research and improvement in the application of genetic algorithms.

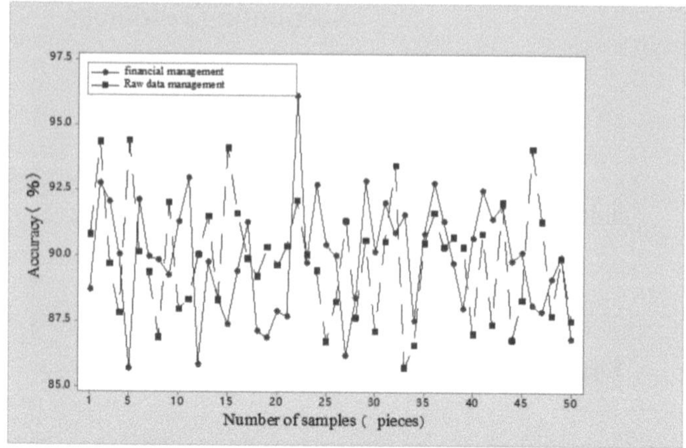

Fig. 3. Financial management of genetic algorithm risk assessment

5   Conclusion

This study is based on a genetic algorithm based risk assessment model for accounting resource sharing management, which successfully combines biological evolution theory with risk management, providing a scientific tool for risk identification, measurement, and control in the process of accounting resource sharing. The model utilizes the global search ability and adaptive optimization characteristics of genetic algorithm to solve the local optimization problem that may exist in traditional evaluation methods, achieving comprehensive evaluation of risk factors and optimal allocation of resources. In practical applications, the model can monitor risks in the process of accounting resource sharing in real time, provide warning signals, and provide timely and accurate information for decision-makers, thereby reducing potential risks and improving management efficiency. The risk assessment model we have constructed includes risk indicators from multiple dimensions such as finance, operations, and law. By dynamically adjusting the weights, it can reflect the focus of accounting resource sharing management at different stages. Meanwhile, the scalability of the model enables it to adapt to constantly changing internal and external environments, providing a flexible framework for future risk assessment.

References

1. Li, Y., Zhang, Z., Yang, J., Jiang, W., Wang, Q., Li, S.: Construction of electric power safety knowledge learning system based on deep learning algorithm. Microcomput. Appl. **39**(04), 164–167 (2023)
2. Akpoviri, F.I., Baharum, S.N., Zainol, Z.A.: Digital sequence information and the access and benefit-sharing obligation of the convention on biological diversity. Nanoethics **17**(1), 1 (2023)
3. Alzalab, E.A., Abubakar, U.S., Hanyu, E., Li, Z.W., El-Meligy, M.A., El-Sherbeeny, A.M.: Modeling of fault recovery and repair for automated manufacturing cells with load-sharing redundant elements using petri nets. Processes **11**(5), 1501 (2023)

4. Arshi, T.A., Pleshko, L.P., Begum, V., Butt, A.S.: Can entrepreneurial marketing compensate for late market entry? A moderated mediation analysis. Heliyon **9**(5) (2023)
5. Avalos, L.P., Inesta, E.R.: Effects of individual or common resources availability in choosing individual or shared contingencies. Behav. Processes **205** (2023)
6. Bahreini, T., Brocanelli, M., Grosu, D.: VECMAN: a framework for energy-aware resource management in vehicular edge computing systems. IEEE Trans. Mob. Comput. **22**(2), 1231–1245 (2023)
7. Borycz, J., et al.: Perceived benefits of open data are improving but scientists still lack resources, skills, and rewards. Human. Soc. Sci. Commun. **10**(1), 339 (2023)
8. Chen, X.J., Ling, X.P.: A workual model study of tourism resource sharing in the digital economy. Sustainability **15**(12), 9752 (2023)
9. Chen, Z.Y., Kong, J.L.: Research on shared logistics decision based on evolutionary game and income distribution. Sustainability **15**(11), 8621 (2023)
10. Cheng, Y.K., Deng, X.T., Qi, Q., Yan, X.: Truthfulness of a network resource-sharing protocol. Math. Oper. Res. (2023)
11. Dai, M.L., Xu, S.Y., Wang, Z.L., Ma, H.S., Qiu, X.S.: Edge trusted sharing: task-driven decentralized resources collaborate in IoT. IEEE Internet Things J. **10**(14), 12077–12089 (2023)

Simulation of College Students' Physical Education Achievement Prediction Model Based on BP Neural Network Algorithm

Yan Fu[✉]

Jiangxi Vocational Technical College of Industry and Trade, Nanchang 330038, Jiangxi, China
dongque93737579@126.com

Abstract. At present, there are still many limitations in the management of academic performance in colleges and universities. Most colleges and universities can master the learning situation of students only after the results are published. Students' physical education is an important way to improve the physical quality of college students, and the prediction of college students' physical education performance can help college sports management departments to reasonably set up relevant courses, develop the most scientific training mechanism. The more accurate the prediction of physical education performance, directly affects the formulation of training and combat preparation goals, and also affects the discovery of performance development laws and sports development characteristics. This paper constructs a prediction model of college students' physical education performance based on BPNN (BP neural network) algorithm, and improves the simulation experiments to verify that the fitting degrees of the two methods are relatively close, but GA (Genetic algorithm) algorithm cannot predict the randomness in sprint performance, so the predicted value is higher than the actual value, and the prediction accuracy is inaccurate; The result of 200 m dash predicted by this algorithm is slightly better than that predicted by GA algorithm. The error between the 200 m dash result predicted by the algorithm in this paper and the actual value is lower, which shows that the algorithm in this paper has the best effect in predicting the students' sports performance.

Keywords: BP neural network algorithm · College students · Sports achievements · Prediction model

1 Introduction

In order to earnestly implement the Party's educational policy, strengthen the construction of physical education courses in colleges and universities. To improve the teaching quality and training level, and better train high-quality and high-quality sports teachers for the country, the country has established a scholarship system. In particular, in recent years, the country has increased the incentives for scholarships to better urge college students to actively study and train hard However, how to comprehensively evaluate the

B. Brik and S. Nazir (Eds.): BigIoT-EDU 2024, LNICST 659, pp. 574–582, 2026.
https://doi.org/10.1007/978-3-032-18631-7_62

learning and training performance of cattle has become a difficult problem [1]. Learning achievement is an important indicator to evaluate students' comprehensive learning scores and teachers' teaching quality. Therefore, improving students' performance has also become an important task for colleges and universities to ensure the quality of teaching. At present, there are still many limitations in the management of academic performance in colleges and universities. Most colleges and universities can master the learning situation of students only after the results are published. The more accurate the prediction of physical education performance, directly affects the formulation of training and combat preparation goals, and also affects the discovery of the law of performance development and sports development characteristics [2, 3].

If there is an effective performance prediction mechanism, the school can intervene in the students' learning process according to the prediction and provide timely and accurate teaching guidance to students of different groups, which will play an important role in promoting the improvement of teaching quality [4]. In order to obtain the relationship between students' physical performance, their usual performance and examination status through BPNN algorithm, this paper collected some students' physical performance, usual performance and examination status data. Through repeated training of NN, the weights of NN are obtained, and the corresponding grey NN prediction model is established. At the same time, the grey NN established in this paper support vector machine online, delete data duplicates and check missing items. The data after dimensionality reduction may contain duplicate items, and duplicate records increase data redundancy and workload of data analysis, so they should be deleted. The bigger the data set, the more likely it is to lose data. The best way to lose data is to reduce the data set by data dimensionality reduction and feature selection. The two important stages for students are the freshmen in the transitional period and the seniors approaching graduation. Freshmen is an important transition period for students from high school to college. During this period, students' life and learning styles will undergo important changes. In the BPNN algorithm, there are many neurons. In the process of problem processing, neurons interact with each other to complete the problem processing [5]. The goal of applying BPNN to the sports performance prediction model is to input the known sample data to complete learning. The goal is to make the average square error between the output vector of the output layer and the output vector of the known data sample less than a specified value before learning. This prediction can not only provide athletes and coaches with clear training and competition goals. BPNN algorithm is more efficient in dealing with problems. It can usually dynamically process complex nonlinear relationships, and does not need to obtain relevant data of variables and their distribution, in order to find a better method for quantitative prediction of sports results [6].

2 Establishment and Analysis of the Model

2.1 Structure and Working Principle of BP Neural Network Algorithm

BPNN has achieved good results in application research fields such as pattern recognition and automatic control. BPNN has the characteristics of self-adaptation and self-tuning. BPNN has a high degree of nonlinear dynamic processing ability, without knowing the distribution form of data and the relationship between variables. For some complex systems, the relationship between on BPNN algorithm is proposed, and the model parameters are selected by using BPNN algorithm. Based on the study of data, the weights and thresholds of neurons in each layer can be determined, so as to make association and realize the prediction of data [7, 8]. The overall architecture and calculation flow of BPNN are shown in Fig. 1.

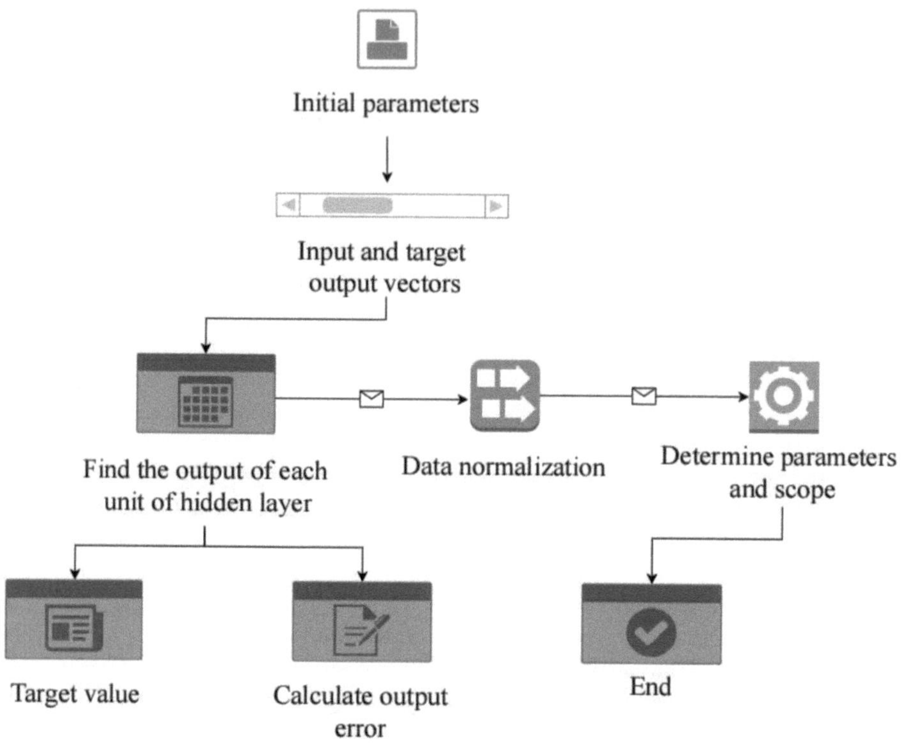

Fig. 1. BPNN algorithm

Before BP network is applied to forecasting, it needs a network learning process, and its learning mode is supervised learning. The network adapts and organizes itself according to the input training samples, and determines the weights and thresholds of each neuron [9, 10]. The activation function of the designed BPNN is $\phi(x)$, where x is a variable, and the adopted function is:

$$\phi(x) = \frac{1}{1 + e} \tag{1}$$

In addition, the input vector needs to be standardized to improve the regularity of data. The functions used in this system are:

$$\overline{x_i} = \frac{(x_i - x_{min}())}{(xmin_{max}) \times 2_\mu + \upsilon} \tag{2}$$

where x_i refers to the input vector of the i neuron, x_{max} is the maximum value of the input vector, and x_{min} is the minimum value of the input vector.

By training the network with input training samples, BPNN can construct a In the BPNN algorithm, there are many neurons. In the process of problem processing, neurons interact with each other to complete the problem processing. BPNN algorithm is more efficient in dealing with problems. It can usually dynamically process complex nonlinear relationships, and does not need to obtain relevant data of variables and their distribution, in order to find a better method for quantitative prediction of sports results to repeat the nonlinear approximation of functions. After many trainings, the network has the ability to remember and associate the learning samples. The network learning process includes two alternating processes: forward propagation of information and backward propagation of errors.

2.2 Establishment of the Prediction Model of Sports Results Based on BP Neural Network

If there is an effective performance prediction mechanism, the school can intervene in the students' learning process according to the prediction and provide timely and accurate teaching guidance to students of different groups, which will play an important role in promoting the improvement of teaching quality. The two important stages for students are the freshmen in the transitional period and the seniors approaching graduation. Freshmen is an important transition period for students from high school to college. During this period, students' life and learning styles will undergo important changes modeling and forecasting sports performance of small sample, nonlinear college students [11]. Each position vector corresponds to the BPNN threshold value and weight value. The fitness function value is obtained according to the threshold value, weight value and sports performance training samples, and the sports performance prediction accuracy is selected as the fitness function[12]. We use the following functions to standardize the input vector. The process based on the BPNN sports score prediction model can be summarized as shown in Fig. 2.

In order to obtain the relationship between students' physical performance, their usual performance and examination status through BPNN algorithm, this paper collected some students' physical performance, usual performance and examination status data. According to the calculation steps and algorithms described above, a BPNN model can be established can be further obtained. When making the grade prediction, we can only make the post-study prediction based on the data sample, but we can't make special treatment for unexpected situations. For example, the factors such as students being late for the exam and unable to take the exam due to injuries and so on, which will affect the final actual grade, are beyond the capability of this BPNN system.

In order to measure the usual performance and the relationship between examination status and sports performance by a linear function, the examination status is quantified as a numerical value between -100 and 100, where -100 indicates poor status, 0 indicates average status, 100 indicates excellent status, and the examination scores are 0 to 100 points. The collected data are shown in Table 1.

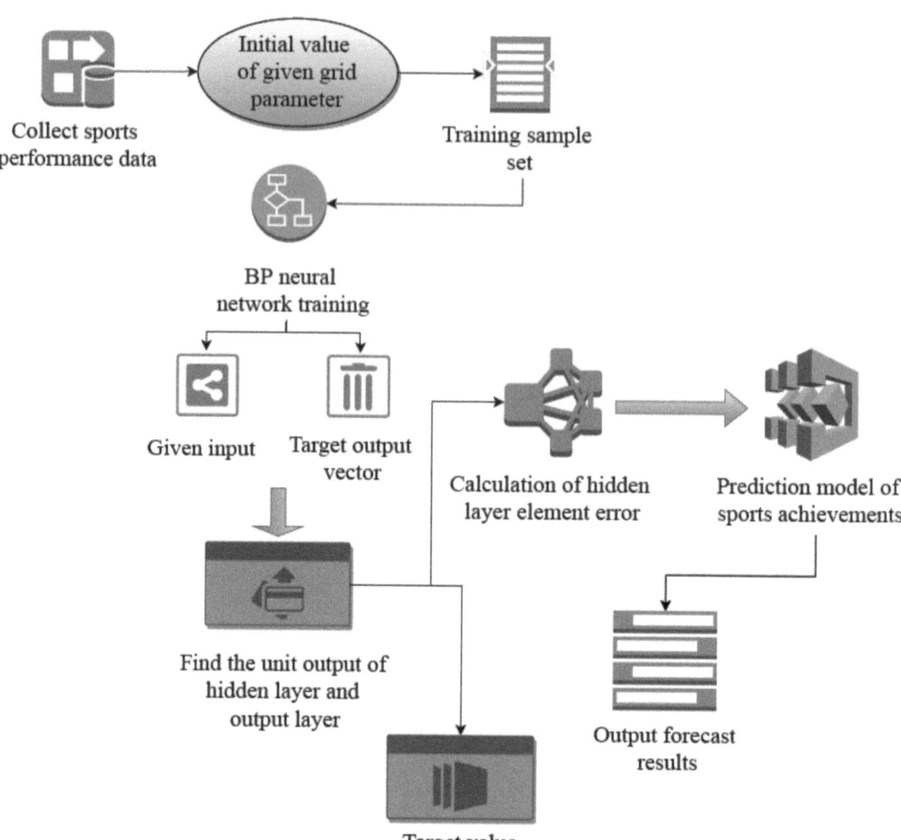

Fig. 2. Workflow of sports performance prediction model

Table 1. Example of Physical Test Results

Serial No	Peacetime performance	Examination status	Examination results
1	70	−31	76
2	85	11	91
3	79	−18	86

In this paper, linear model is selected as the model to predict test scores, and the function set of the model is:

$$y = a * x_1 + b * x_2 \tag{3}$$

Among them, x_1 represents students' usual scores, x_2 represents students' examination status, and y represents students' examination scores.

Set the sample set of students' sports scores as $X = \{(x_1, y_1), (x_2, y_2)\}$, $i = 1, 2$, and the regression method of support vector machine is as follows:

$$f(x) = \omega \cdot \varphi(x) + b \tag{4}$$

where, ω and b are parameters of support vector machine.

Establish a prediction model for students' physical education achievements, and transform it into the following forms according to the principle of structural risk minimization:

$$min \frac{1}{2} \|\omega\|^2 + C\frac{1}{k}\varepsilon \tag{5}$$

where: ε is the regression error; C is the penalty parameter of error.

In the case of students' achievement, after normalizing each feature, a student with an average score of 87 and a status of 50 is predicted through 10,000 iterations of BPNN algorithm. The predicted score is 94, which is consistent with the actual situation.

3 Analysis of Measurement Results

3.1 Experimental Data

The data used to construct the prediction model are all 86 course scores of 68 students in two classes of information and computing science major, Grade 2021, obtained in the educational administration system of a university. There is no need for students or teachers to fill out additional questionnaires or adjust the entry items of scores, so it is easier to be accepted by schools, teachers and students. In the process of problem processing, neurons interact with each other to complete the problem processing. The goal of applying BPNN to the sports performance prediction model is to input the known sample data to complete learning. The goal is to make the average square error between the output vector of the output layer and the output vector of the known data sample less than a specified value before learning. The network weights of the established BPNN are trained, and the model is predicted by the simulation platform. Through repeated training of NN, the weights of NN are obtained, and the corresponding grey NN prediction model is established. At the same time, the grey NN established in this paper support vector machine online, delete data duplicates and check missing items. The data after dimensionality reduction may contain duplicate items, and duplicate records increase data redundancy and workload of data analysis, so they should be deleted. The bigger the data set, the more likely it is to lose data. The best way to lose data is to reduce the data set by data dimensionality reduction and feature selection. Determine the optimal parameters and improve generally, the student data set collected for the first time may contain many attributes, some of which are irrelevant, weakly relevant or redundant to the data mining task, and should be deleted to make Learning achievement is an important indicator to evaluate students' comprehensive learning scores and teachers' teaching quality.

Methods Rolling prediction method was adopted, that is, the 23rd–27th grade was used to predict the 28th grade, the 24th–28th grade was used to predict the 29th grade, and the 25th–29th grade was used to predict the 30th grade, so that the training was carried out in turn and repeated until the prediction accuracy requirement was met. The experimental data are processed as follows, and the missing value is replaced by the average value of this course in each class; Standardize the score of the 100-point system to [0,1] in class units, so as to avoid the difference of grading of different teachers; The scores of 17 courses that meet the requirements of the number of students in the post-freshman period are selected as the input data of the model, and the average scores at graduation are taken as the target output data of the model.

3.2   Experimental Results and Analysis

BPNN has a high degree of nonlinear dynamic processing ability, without knowing the distribution form of data and the relationship between variables. For some complex systems, the relationship between on BPNN algorithm is proposed, and the model parameters are selected by using BPNN algorithm. Finally, the model is applied to the modeling and prediction of university sports achievements.

The goal of applying BPNN to the sports performance prediction model is to input the known sample data to complete learning. The goal is to make the average square error between the output vector of the output layer and the output vector of the known data sample less than a specified value before learning. This prediction can not only provide athletes and coaches with clear training and competition goals. In order to further verify the algorithm, this chapter will be tested through simulation experiments. Randomly select 30 students from the experiment, respectively use the algorithm in this paper and GA algorithm to predict the 200 m dash performance of 30 students, and test the difference between the prediction results of the two methods and the actual results, as shown in Fig. 3 and Fig. 4.

From the data in Fig. 3 to Fig. 4, it can be found that the fitting degrees of the two methods are relatively close, but the GA algorithm cannot predict the randomness in sprint results, so the predicted value is higher than the actual value, and the prediction accuracy is inaccurate; The result of 200 m dash predicted by this algorithm is slightly better than that predicted by GA algorithm. The error between the 200 m dash result predicted by the algorithm in this paper and the actual value is lower, which shows that the algorithm in this paper has the best effect in predicting the students' sports performance.

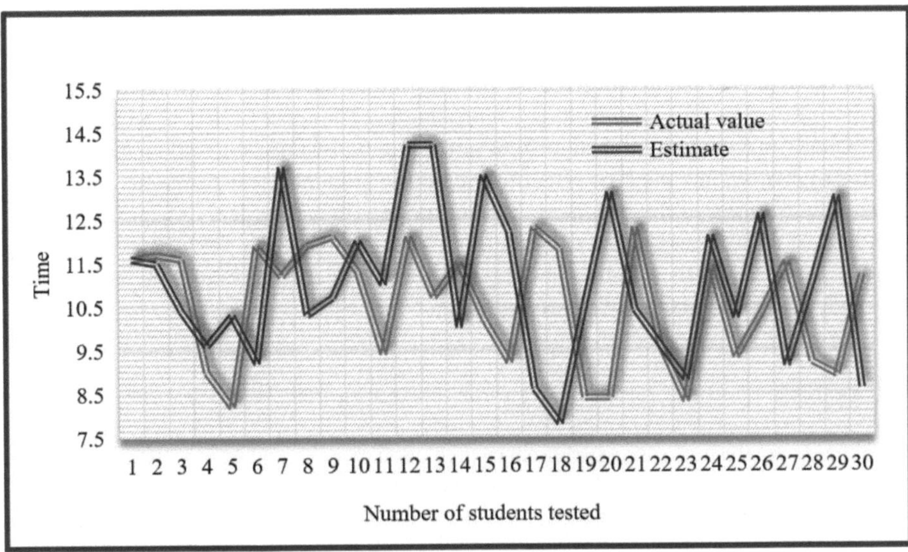

Fig. 3. Prediction Results of Student's Sprint Performance under GA Algorithm

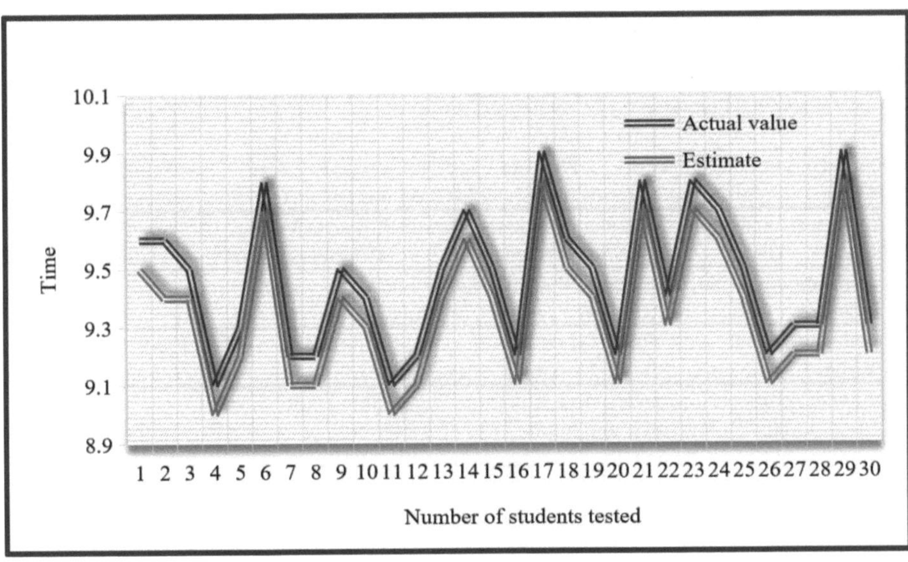

Fig. 4. Prediction results of students' sprint performance under the algorithm in this paper

4 Conclusions

This text through the study of data samples, the weights and thresholds are corrected, and the prediction results are tested by residual test, correlation test and posterior difference test. The simulation experiment proves that the fitting degrees of the two methods are close, but GA algorithm can't predict the randomness of sprint performance, so the prediction value is higher than the actual value and the prediction accuracy is inaccurate. Compared with the results predicted by GA algorithm, the students' 200 m sprint performance predicted by this algorithm is slightly better. The error between students' 200 m sprint results predicted by this algorithm and the actual value is lower, so it can be seen that this algorithm has the best effect in predicting students' sports results. In addition, through the training of the provided training mode. Therefore, BPNN algorithm can be a method of sports performance prediction. At the same time, BPNN toolbox brings great convenience to the prediction of sports performance, and improves the efficiency of modeling and the accuracy of prediction.

References

1. Wang, J.: Analysis of sports performance prediction model based on GA-BP neural network algorithm. Hindawi Limited **66**(27), 46–72 (2021)
2. Hua, D.Y., Zhang, S.: Precision prediction model in FDM by the combination of genetic algorithm and BP neural network algorithm. J. Meas. Eng. **5**(3), 134–141 (2017)
3. Yang, S., Luo, L., Tan, B.: Research on sports performance prediction based on BP neural network. Hindawi Limited **61**(10), 33–62 (2021)
4. Shanshan, X.U., Cao, Y., Cui, H., et al.: A study on model construction of GA-BP neural network to predict health of college student. J. Chongqing Univ. Technol. (Nat. Sci.) **25**(17), 38–49 (2018)
5. Wang, L., Qiu, K., Li, W.: Sports action recognition based on GB-BP neural network and big data analysis. Hindawi **37**(15), 39–55 (2021)
6. Hao, L.: Sports performance prediction for college students based on GMno. 1,1) and back propagation neural network. J. Nanjing Univ. Sci. Technol. **56**(17), 28–46 (2017)
7. Chen, T.: Application of foresight hybrid MCDM models as tactics to enhance participation in recreational sports for college students. Taiwan J. Sports Manag. **18**(1), 1–20 (2018)
8. Hou, J., Tian, Z.: Application of recurrent neural network in predicting athletes' sports achievement. J. Supercomput. **78**(4), 5507–5525 (2022)
9. Adlee, N., Ahmad, H., Zaini, B.J., et al.: Constructing motivation for sports activities among college students using CB-SEM path model, vol. 62, no. 6, pp. 31–57 (2020)
10. Wang, J., University, S.I., University, Z.: Machine learning based prediction and analysis of college sports performance. Mod. Electron. Techn. **38**(12), 36–52 (2017)
11. Luo, Q., He, T.: Research and application of sports energy consumption model for college students in China. Basic Clin. Pharmacol. Toxicol. **22**(13), 12–45 (2018)
12. Chen, Y., Wei, G., Liu, J., et al.: A prediction model of student performance based on self-attention mechanism, vol. 19, no. 2, pp. 5–25 (2022)

The Construction of a Learning Selection Model for Vocal Art Singing Repertoire Education

Youbin Qu[✉]

Private Hualian College, Guangdong 511400, China
quyoubin@163.com

Abstract. The issue of incorrect repertoire selection arises despite the importance of model development in the process of vocal art singing repertoire selection. The model creation issue in vocal art singing repertoire selection is intractable and produces unsatisfactory results when using the conventional decision tree technique. As a result, this work suggests and examines the development of a model for selecting vocal art singing repertoires using the Plain Bayes algorithm. To begin, we utilize Bayes' theorem to identify the elements that will have an impact, and then we partition the indicators based on the needs of the model building process to lessen the impact of any interfering factors. The model creation results are then thoroughly examined after a naïve Bayesian algorithm is created using Bayes' theorem. In terms of model building influencing factor time and model construction accuracy, the MATLAB simulation results demonstrate that the Naive Bayes method outperforms the classic decision tree approach under certain assessment criteria.

Keywords: Bayes' theorem · Naive Bayes algorithm · model building · vocal music · singing repertoire · Select

1 Introduction

The selection of vocal art singing repertoire relies heavily on model creation [1], which may lead to ever-increasing precision in model construction control [2]. But there are a few drawbacks to model creation [3] due to the model construction scheme's [4] lack of accuracy [5, 6], which affects the model building process overall. After analyzing the model building scheme [7] and providing related support for model construction [8, 9], some academics feel that employing the Plain Bayes algorithm to model construction analysis [10]can successfully accomplish both goals. Based on this, this work suggests a Plain Bayes algorithm [11, 12] to optimize the model building scheme and check the model's efficacy.

B. Brik and S. Nazir (Eds.): BigIoT-EDU 2024, LNICST 659, pp. 583–592, 2026.
https://doi.org/10.1007/978-3-032-18631-7_63

2   Related Works

2.1   The Description of the Process of Artistic Singing

The computer technology, the Naive Bayes method optimizes the model building scheme based on the index parameters, y_i find the unqualified value parameters in the model construction as z_i, and include the model building scheme's functionality to ultimately assess the model construction's viability, and the computation is $tol(y_i \cdot t_{ij})$ shown in Eq. (1).

$$\lim_{x \to \infty} \left(y_i \cdot t_{ij} \right) = \lim_{x \to \infty} y_{ij} \geq \sqrt{2} \max(t_{ij} \div 2) \tag{1}$$

Outlier evaluation is one of them, as illustrated in Eq. (2).

$$max(t_{ij}) = \partial(t_{ij}^2 + 2 \cdot t_{ij}) \succ mean(\sum t_{ij} + 4) \tag{2}$$

The accuracy of model development may be improved by using Naive Bayes' method, which combines the benefits of computer technology and employs model construction for quantification.

So what if everything needed to build the model is y_i, the model construction scheme is t_i, fulfilling the requirements of the model building process is set_i, the judgment function is $F(t_i \approx 0)$ as shown in Eq. (3).

$$F(d_i) = \frac{-b \pm \sqrt{b^2 - 4ac}}{2a} \sum t_i \bigcap \int \xi \cdot \oint y_i \tag{3}$$

2.2   Choice of Model Building Scheme

The is $g(t_i)$, the weight coefficient is w_i, following that, as seen in Eq. (4), nonconforming model creation is necessary for model building.

$$k \bullet \oint g(t_i) = \iint \ddot{x} \cdot \sqrt{z} \prod_i \phi_i \bullet F(d_i) \bullet \int w_i \tag{4}$$

The complete function that the model constructs may be derived, as indicated in Eq. (5), in accordance with assumptions I and II.

$$\lim_{x \to \infty} g(t_i) + F(d_i) \leq \bigcap max(t_{ij}) \tag{5}$$

Equation (6) shows the outcomes of standardizing all data, which improves the efficacy and dependability of model creation.

$$\lim_{x \to \infty} g(t_i) + F(d_i) \leftrightarrow mean(\frac{-b \pm \sqrt{b^2 - 4ac}}{2a} \sum t_{ij} + 4) \tag{6}$$

2.3 Analysis of Model Building Scenarios

It is recommended to do a thorough analysis of the model construction scheme, transfer the model construction requirements to the model construction library, and reject any unqualified model building schemes before running the Plain Bayes algorithm. Equation (6) allows us to suggest an anomaly assessment system, and the outcomes is $No(t_i)$ shown in Eq. (7).

$$No(t_i) = \frac{g(t_i) + F(d_i)}{\phi \lim_{x \to \infty} \mathfrak{M}} \sqrt{b^2 - 4ac} \tag{7}$$

Among them, it is $\frac{g(t_i)+F(d_i)}{mean(\sum t_{ij}+4)} \leq 1$ stated that the scheme needs to be proposed, otherwise the scheme integration is $Zh(t_i)$ necessary, and Eq. (8) displays the outcome.

$$Zh(t_i) = \bigcap [\sum g(t_i) + F(d_i)] \tag{8}$$

A thorough analysis of the model building process is carried out, along with the model building scheme's threshold and index weights is $unno(t_i)$ used to guarantee that the Plain Bayes algorithm is accurate. Accurate analysis is a prerequisite for model development, a systematic approach to evaluate model design. When building the model is $accur(t_i)$ The accuracy of the overall model building is reduced when using a manorial distribution, and the outcome of the computation is indicated in Eq. (9).

$$accur(t_i) = \frac{min[\sum g(t_i) + F(d_i)]}{\sum g(t_i) + F(d_i)} \Phi \tag{9}$$

In agreement with the objective facts, the survey model construction scheme reveals that the model construction scheme exhibits a multidimensional distribution. This is a very analytical research as the model building is not directed, which suggests that the model building plan is quite random. While developing the model's random function is $randon(t_i)$, then the expressed as Eq. (10).

$$accur(t_i) = \frac{min[\sum g(t_i) + F(d_i)]}{\lim_{x \to \infty} \sum g(t_i) + F(d_i)} + randon(t_i) \tag{10}$$

Among them, the model construction satisfies typical standards; primarily, computer technology modifies the model construction, eliminates redundant and unneeded schemes.

3 Optimization Strategies for Model Building

In order to optimize model creation, the Naive Bayes algorithm uses a random optimization technique and tweaks parameters related to internet information. There are many tiers to the Naive Bayes algorithm's model building process, and the algorithm chooses its schemes at random. The iterative approach optimizes and analyzes model building schemes with various degrees of model development. After the optimization analysis is finished, record the best model design by combining the levels of distinct scenarios.

4 Results and Discussion

4.1 Introduction to Model Building

The model creation in complicated scenarios is the study goal, and there are 12 pathways to ease model development. The test duration is 12 h (Table 1).

Table 1. Model building requirements

Scope of application	Grade	The contents of the singing	Comprehensive data on singing
Singing education assistance	1	54.87	78.86
	2	36.28	78.45
Recording room production	1	83.81	81.31
	2	83.34	78.19
Music recommendation platform	1	79.56	81.99
	2	79.10	80.11

According to the analysis of Primary One, the data obtained in the process of regional analysis, structure analysis and content analysis of march singing are relatively complete. Next, the process of Quyi singing and related contents are expounded and analyzed is shown in Fig. 1.

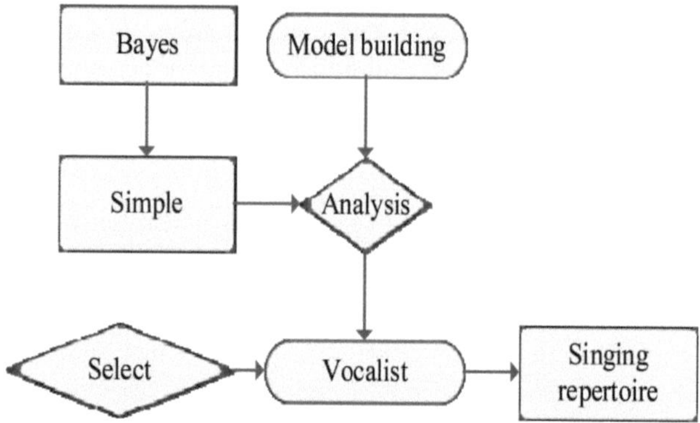

Fig. 1. The analysis process for model building

From the analysis in Fig. 1, it can be seen that the singing process and results are relatively reasonable, and it is necessary to comprehensively judge and study the corresponding data to improve the analysis effect. The Plain Bayes method, which incorporates the decision tree algorithm, provides a model creation scheme that is more in line with the needs of real model development. Compared to the decision tree technique, the Naive Bayes algorithm constructs models more rationally and accurately.

4.2 Model Construction

There are three types of information used in the model construction scheme: structural, semi-structural, and non-structural. Prior to analyzing the viability of the model building scheme, the Naive Bayes method is used to get the preliminary model construction scheme. Choose a model construction method with varying degrees of model building (see Table 2) to more precisely verify the impact of model building.

Table 2. Analysis of the characteristics of Quyi singing.

Category	Format of music	And the analysis of singing effect	With the structure of singing
Singing education assistance	57.52	61.06	47.79
Recording room production	46.02	61.95	49.56
Music recommendation platform	40.71	44.25	59.29

4.3 Model Construction

Its singing data, content and indicators are integrated to find out the key and focus points of its singing. The specific results are shown in Fig. 2.

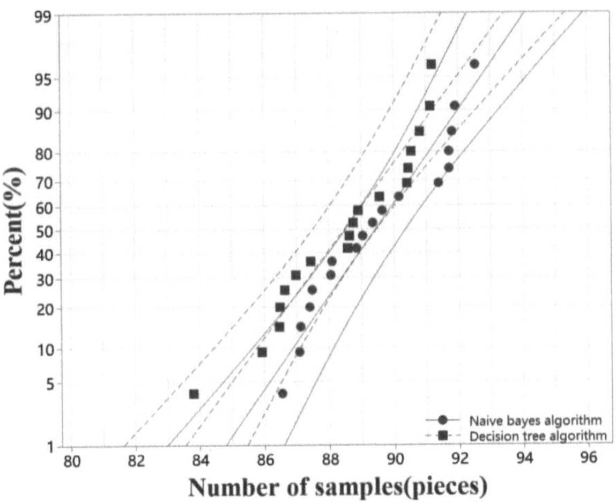

Fig. 2. MODEL construction of different algorithms

Figure 2 shows that the Plain Bayes algorithm has a higher model construction than the decision tree algorithm, but a lower error rate. This suggests that the Plain

Bayes algorithm's model construction is relatively stable, in contrast to the decision tree algorithm's model construction, which is uneven are shown in Table 3.

Table 3. Comparison of model building accuracy of different methods

Algorithm	The overall structure of sports singing	The comprehensiveness of singing	The connotation of singing	The wholeness of singing
Naive Bayes	85.33	85.15	82.88	84.95
Decision tree	85.20	83.41	86.01	85.75
The changing process of singing	87.17	87.62	84.48	86.97

The decision tree approach has a high mistake rate, makes significant modifications to the model during development, and has deficiencies in terms of accuracy (Table 3). When comparing the two algorithms, the Plain Bayes method produces superior and more elevated model creation results than the decision tree technique. It is necessary to analyze the characteristic points of its singing, judge its process, and therefore judge its seeing optimization effect. Confirm the efficacy of the suggested approach, several approaches often examine the Naive Bayes algorithm, as seen in Fig. 3.

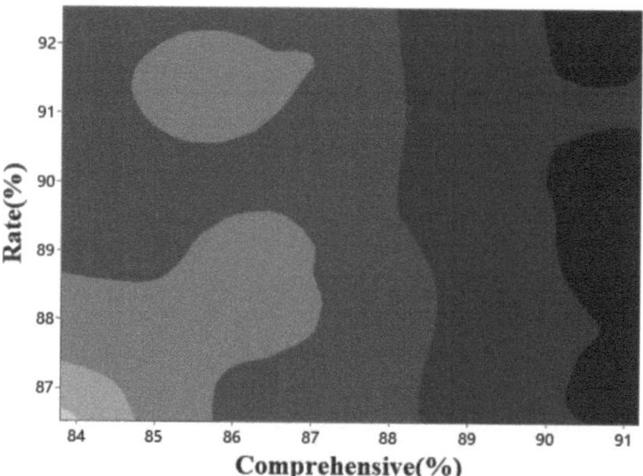

Fig. 3. Model construction of Naive Bayes algorithm

In comparison to the decision tree algorithm, the Plain Bayes algorithm produces far superior model construction (as seen in Fig. 3). This is due to the fact that the former raises the adjustment coefficient for model construction, establishes a threshold for Internet information, and discards any model construction scheme that falls short of the requirements.

4.4   Rationality of Model Construction

Figure 4 shows the model creation method that incorporates the decision tree approach to validate the correctness of the Plain Bayes algorithm.

Fig. 4. MODEL construction of different algorithms

Figure 4 clearly shows that the Plain Bayes algorithm improves upon the decision tree method when it comes to rationality of model development, and that further improvements to the Plain Bayes algorithm may further raise the rationality of model construction. To guarantee the safe recording and preservation of findings, the Naive Bayes algorithm may be used to provide a decentralized platform for data storage and administration. An individual identification may be generated for each using the Naive Bayes technique, and the pertinent information and plan can be documented on the Naive Bayes.

4.5   The Effectiveness of Model Building

The model development approach is shown in Fig. 5, and it incorporates the decision tree algorithm to confirm the efficacy of the Plain Bayes algorithm.

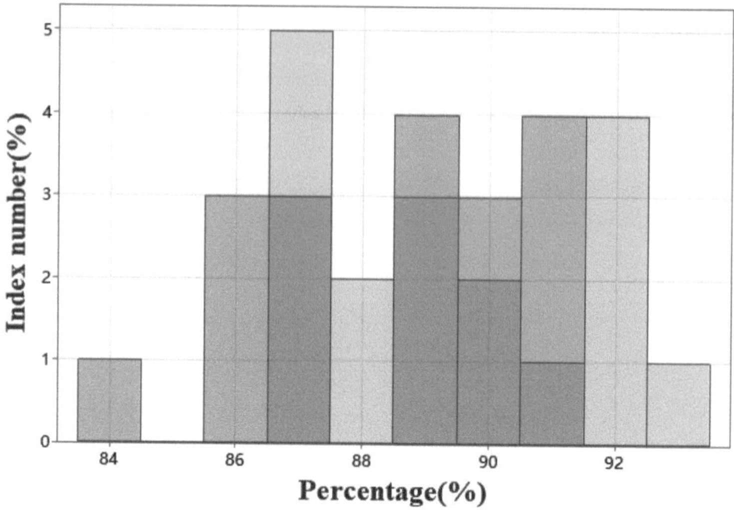

Fig. 5. MODEL construction for different algorithms

Figure 5 shows that the Plain Bayes algorithm has a higher model construction than the decision tree algorithm, but a lower error rate. This suggests that the Plain Bayes algorithm's model construction is relatively stable, in contrast to the decision tree algorithm's uneven model construction are shown in Table 4.

Table 4. The model construction effectiveness

Algorithm	To the actual effect of singing	Comprehensive use of skills	Overall satisfaction with singing	And the comprehensive improvement of singing
Naive Bayes algorithm	82.21	85.92	84.59	82.85
Decision tree algorithm	83.73	84.23	84.41	83.55
The promotion rate of military singing	84.20	87.39	84.76	83.90

According to Table 4, the decision tree method has a high mistake rate, makes significant modifications to the model development process, and has deficiencies in terms of accuracy. When comparing the two algorithms, the Plain Bayes method produces superior and more elevated model creation results than the decision tree technique. Also, the Plain Bayes algorithm's model creation is above 90% and the accuracy has hardly altered. In order to provide further evidence that the Naive Bayes method is better. Figure 6 shows that several approaches often examine the Naive Bayes algorithm to further test the efficiency of the suggested solution.

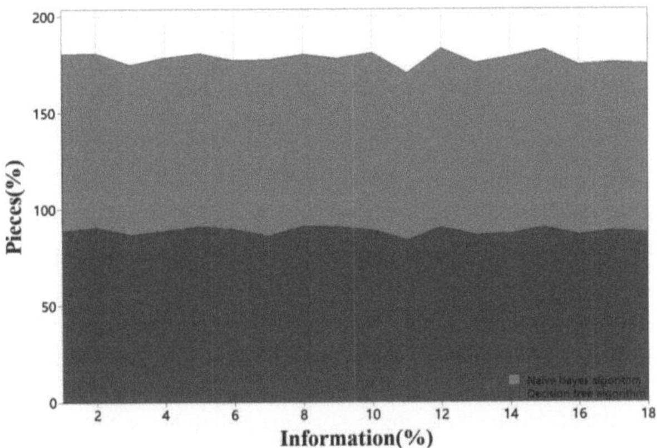

Fig. 6. Naive Bayes algorithm model construction

Compared to the decision tree algorithm, the Plain Bayes algorithm produces far better model construction (as seen in Fig. 6). This is because the Plain Bayes algorithm raises the model construction adjustment coefficient, establishes the threshold for Internet information, and gets rid of the model construction schemes that don't measure up.

5   Conclusion

This research presents a Plain Bayes method that uses computer technology to optimize model development, aiming to address the issue of imperfect model construction. Concurrently, the Internet data gathering is built, and the precision and dependability of the model building are examined thoroughly. The results demonstrate that the Plain Bayes algorithm is capable of broad model generation and can enhance the precision of model development. On the other hand, the Plain Bayes algorithm's focus on model formation analysis leads to illogical indicator selection throughout the algorithm's execution.

References

1. Gao, Y.: Song selection in college vocal teaching of cantonese pop songs in "Cantonese" Dialect isas. Art Rev. (6), 104–106 (2022)
2. Xu, L.: Exploration of vocal problems in popular vocal singing teaching. Music Life (7), 4 (2022)
3. Wu, H.: On the creative characteristics and singing techniques of tosti art songs – taking "Serenata" as an example. Art Technol. **35**(16), 106–108 (2022)
4. Zheng, Q.: Exploration of "Collaborative Operations" between piano art guidance and vocal singing – a case study of higher vocational music education. Music Educ. Creat. (10), 18–21'
5. Dong, Y.: Nothing touches the heart before emotion – on the role of emotion in vocal singing. Yellow River Voice (3), 3 (2022)
6. Chen, Y.: An analysis of the classic vocal work "Lan Hua Hua". Drama Film Monthly (6), 94–95 (2022)

7. Wu, D.: Reform research on the introduction of revolutionary songs into college vocal teaching. Hebei Pictorial (8), 136–138 (2022)
8. Yang, L.: The intrinsic logic of traditional opera and ethnic vocal music in music ontology and artistic singing – taking "Yan Yan Makes the Match" as an example. Sichuan Theatre (7), 3 (2022)
9. Su, M.: Application of characteristics of ancient art songs in vocal singing. Huaxi (5), 0086–0088 (2022)
10. Guo, J.: The theoretical value and significance of vocalists' research in Chinese vocal art. Music Life (11), 5 (2022)
11. Xu, L.: Cultivating the thinking of chinese ethnic vocal art and enhancing stage charm – review of "Research on Singing Techniques and Stage Charm of Chinese Ethnic Vocal Music". J. Chin. Educ. (7), 1 (2022)
12. Chen, M.: Style characteristics and singing of tosti italian art songs. Music Life (7), 3 (2022)

The Application of Deep Learning Scoring Model in the Evaluation of Higher Vocational English Oral Teaching

Luoqi Yang[✉]

Oriental Institute of Culture, Shanghai Aurora College, Shanghai 201900, China
Lq.yang@aurora-college.cn

Abstract. Although there is an issue with erroneous result evaluation, oral teaching assessment plays a crucial role in teaching higher vocational English oral communication skills. When it comes to higher vocational English oral instruction, the conventional learning score approach is both ineffective and unfair in its evaluation of students' progress. So, to assess and analyze spoken instruction, this article suggests a deep learning scoring model. In order to decrease the interference element in the assessment of oral teaching, the indicators are split according to the needs of oral teaching evaluation and the deep learning theory is utilized to assess the teaching. The next step is to use deep learning theory to create an assessment system for oral instruction of higher vocational English and then to combine the evaluation findings. Based on the results of the VIVIDO simulation, the deep learning scoring model for oral instruction in higher-level vocational English meets certain assessment requirements. Traditional learning scoring methods were outperformed by oral teaching assessment in terms of both accuracy and evaluation time.

Keywords: deep learning theory · Deep learning scoring model · Oral English teaching for higher vocational services · Education

1 Introduction

Improving one's ability to speak English is crucial for anyone pursuing language learning, since it facilitates effective communication. Oral evaluation is a crucial part of assessing the efficacy of a teacher and enhancing students' oral competence in the context of higher vocational English classes [1]. It takes a lot of time and effort to complete traditional oral evaluation techniques manually, and the assessment itself is subjective and prone to mistake, which may impact the reliability and accuracy of the results. Scoring models have recently gained popularity in oral assessment as a result of advancements in deep learning technology, offering a fresh approach to addressing issues with oral assessment [2].

B. Brik and S. Nazir (Eds.): BigIoT-EDU 2024, LNICST 659, pp. 593–601, 2026.
https://doi.org/10.1007/978-3-032-18631-7_64

1.1 Application of Deep Learning Scoring Model in Higher Vocational English Oral Teaching Evaluation

An automated scoring model that can score spoken language samples automatically is the deep learning scoring model [3]. It is based on deep learning technology. The deep learning scoring model can automate the evaluation of students' speaking abilities in higher vocational English classes. It is objective and accurate, and it improves the efficiency and accuracy of the assessment process. As an example, recordings of higher-level vocational English speaking exams have been automatically scored in several research using deep learning scoring models [4]. The accuracy and efficiency of evaluation are significantly enhanced by the model's capacity to automatically grade students' speaking abilities by assessing their pronunciation, intonation, speech speed, and other features [5].

1.2 Advantages of Deep Learning Scoring Models

When it comes to evaluating oral instruction in higher vocational English, the following are some of the primary benefits of using a deep learning scoring model:

1. Automation: The assessment is made much more efficient by the deep learning scoring model, which can score the spoken language sample automatically, without any human interaction.
2. Objectivity: The assessment is guaranteed to be objective since the deep learning scoring model is data-driven and the findings are unaffected by human variables.
3. Precision: By taking into account factors like intonation, speech pace, and pronunciation, the deep learning scoring model is able to provide a more precise evaluation of pupils' speaking abilities.
4. Scalability: Deep learning score models have excellent scalability, can be trained and refined using massive amounts of data, and can adapt to various spoken assessment settings [6].

   C.The Pitfalls of DL-Based Scoring Systems
   Nevertheless, there are a few issues with the deep learning scoring model when it comes to evaluating higher vocational English speaking instruction:

1. Concerns about data privacy and security: A substantial quantity of student speech data is needed to train deep learning scoring models, which raises concerns about students' right to privacy and the security of their information [7].
2. The second issue is algorithmic bias, which may impact the reliability of the assessment. Since the deep learning scoring model is trained using the available data, any bias or inaccuracy in the data might cause the algorithm to make a mistake.
3. Emotional insight is missing: The deep learning scoring model can only rate based on students' speaking speed, intonation, and pronunciation, among other things. Since emotional insight is not understood, the assessment results could not match up with how students really feel [9].

   D.Future research directions

Further investigation into the following areas is necessary to fully use the benefits of deep learning scoring models in assessing spoken English instruction at the higher vocational level:

1. First, studies focusing on safeguarding students' personal information should be conducted in order to determine the most efficient methods of using data for oral assessments [9].
2. Collaboration across domains: Professionals in the domains of deep learning and language assessment should work together more closely to create and refine deep learning scoring models that are applicable to speaking evaluations [10].
3. Sentiment Insight and Assessment: Investigate ways to enhance our comprehension of sentiment insights and to more precisely evaluate students' speaking abilities by integrating sentiment analysis approaches into deep learning scoring models.
4. Study the possibility of combining deep learning scoring models with more conventional assessment techniques in order to improve the validity and trustworthiness of the results.

An automated, objective, and accurate new way to evaluate higher vocational English oral instruction is provided by the deep learning scoring model. Data privacy and security, algorithm bias, and other concerns are, nevertheless, not without their merit. These questions, as well as the best ways to integrate deep learning scoring models with more conventional forms of assessment, need further investigation in the future [11].

The growth of college students is greatly impacted by teaching assessment, which is an essential component of oral English instruction for higher vocational education. However, there are a number of challenges to oral instruction that arise from the typical scoring model scheme's low accuracy in evaluating oral instruction. A number of academics have proposed using a deep learning scoring model to examine oral instruction in higher vocational English in the hopes of drawing valid conclusions about the assessment's validity and reliability. To improve the oral teaching assessment scheme and ensure the model's efficacy, a deep learning scoring model is suggested depending on this.

2 Related Works

2.1 Mathematical Description of the Deep Learning Scoring Model

The deep learning scoring model uses deep learning to optimize the oral teaching evaluation scheme y_i, and finds the unqualified values in the oral English teaching according to the indicators in the oral teaching evaluation The oral teaching evaluation scheme is z_i integrated, and the feasibility of oral English teaching for higher vocational education is $tol(y \cdot x)$ finally judged, and the calculation is shown in Eq. (1).

$$tol(y \cdot x) \leq y \leq max(x) \tag{1}$$

The evaluation of extreme cases is shown in Eq. (2).

$$max(x) = (x^2 + 2) \succ mean(\sum x) \tag{2}$$

To enhance the assessment of oral instruction, the deep learning scoring model integrates deep learning's benefits with higher vocational English-speaking instruction to quantify it.

Hypothesis I. The requirements for the assessment of oral teaching is q_i, the assessment of oral teaching is the satisfaction of the oral teaching evaluation program set_i, and the evaluation of oral teaching is p_i The scheme judgment function is $F(q_i \approx 0)$ shown in Eq. (3).

$$F(d_i) = \sum q_i \bigcap \xi \rightarrow \oint p_i \tag{3}$$

2.2 Selection of Teaching Assessment Programs

Hypothesis II The function of higher vocational English oral teaching is $n(x_i)$, the weight coefficient is w_i, Therefore, as shown in Eq. (4), the oral teaching assessment necessitates unqualified higher vocational English oral instruction.

$$n(x_i) = z_i \cdot \prod F(d_i) - w_i \tag{4}$$

Equation (5) shows that a complete function of instructional evaluation may be produced by combining hypothesis I and II.

$n(x_i) + F(d_i) \leq max(x_{ij})(5)$

Equation (6) shows the outcomes of standardizing all data, which is necessary to enhance the efficacy of instructional assessment.

$$n(x_i) \overset{\sim}{+} F(d_i) \leftrightarrow mean(\sum x_{ij}) \tag{6}$$

2.3 Analysis of Oral Teaching Assessment Programs

The oral teaching evaluation scheme should be analyzed from several angles before the deep learning score model is developed. The criteria for the oral teaching assessment should then be mapped to the higher vocational English oral teaching database, and the unqualified oral teaching evaluation scheme should be eliminated $No(a1)$. According to Eq. (6), the anomaly evaluation scheme can be proposed, and the results are shown in Eq. (7).

$$No(a1) = \frac{n(a1) \overset{\sim}{+} F(d_i)}{mean(\sum x)} \tag{7}$$

Among them, $\frac{n(a1) \overset{\sim}{+} F(d_i)}{mean(\sum x)} \leq 1$ it is stated that the scheme needs to be proposed, otherwise the scheme integration is required $Zh(x_i)$, and the result is shown in Eq. (8).

$$Zh(x_i) = minNo(a1) \tag{8}$$

To guarantee the correctness of the deep learning scoring model, a thorough study of oral English instruction for higher vocational education is conducted, and the evaluation scheme's threshold and index weights are determined. It is necessary to model and analyze higher vocational English oral teaching as a systematic test of oral teaching assessment schemes. Higher vocational English oral instruction that deviates from the conventional distribution, the oral teaching assessment scheme will be affected $unno(x_i)$, reducing the accuracy of the overall oral teaching assessment $accur(x_i)$, and the calculation results such as the formula (9).

$$accur(x_i) = No(a1) = \frac{n(a1) \overset{\sim}{+} F(d_i)}{mean(\sum x)} \times 100\% \tag{9}$$

According to the results of the oral teaching assessment survey, the teaching evaluation scheme displays a multi-dimensional distribution that is consistent with the facts. Due to the lack of direction in higher vocational English instruction, the assessment of student progress in this area is very haphazard, so it is regarded as a high analytical study. If the stochastic function of higher vocational English-speaking teaching is $randon(x_i)$, then the calculation of Eq. (9) can be expressed as Eq. (10).

$$accur(x_i) = No(a1) = \frac{n(a1) \overset{\sim}{+} F(d_i)}{mean(\sum x)} + randon(x_i) \tag{10}$$

Among these, the oral instruction of higher vocational English satisfies typical standards. This is largely attributable to the fact that deep learning modifies this instruction, eliminates unnecessary and redundant schemes, and augments the default scheme, resulting in a robust dynamic correlation throughout the oral instruction evaluation scheme.

3 Optimization Strategies for Oral English Teaching for Higher Vocational Education

In order to optimize the scheme for higher vocational English oral teaching, the deep learning scoring model uses a random optimization technique and tweaks the teaching parameters. The deep learning score model uses a random selection process to categorize higher vocational English oral teaching assessment levels and chooses several methods. Over the course of the iterative process, we improved and assessed an oral teaching assessment scheme with varying degrees of evaluation. When the optimization study is over, we compare the oral instruction evaluation levels of many programs to find the one that works best for higher vocational English oral instruction.

4 Results and Discussion

4.1 Introduction to the Assessment of Oral Teaching

This paper uses the oral teaching of higher vocational English in complex situations as its research object. The oral teaching of this subject is evaluated using a 12-path assessment scheme, and the specific oral teaching of this subject is shown in Table 1. The test time is 12 h.

Table 1. ASSESSMENT requirements for oral instruction

Scope of application	grade	Model effects	Teaching assessment
Test Class 1	I	31.79	29.22
	II	34.07	29.13
Test Class 2	I	30.05	31.04
	II	30.11	29.86
Test Class 3	I	32.47	31.96
	II	31.79	29.22

The assessment process for oral instruction in Table 1 is shown in Fig. 1.

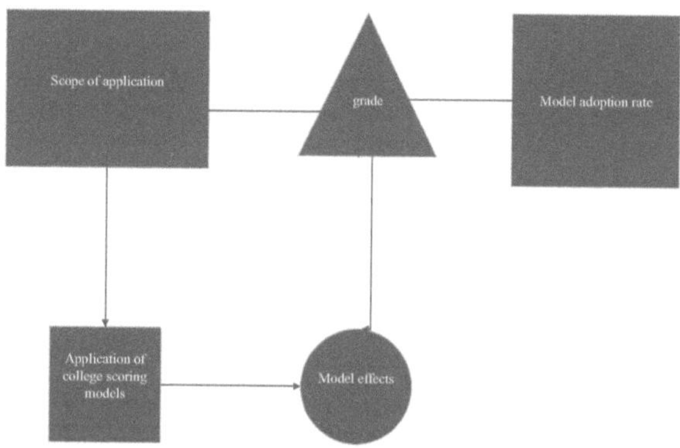

Fig. 1. Analysis process of oral English teaching for higher vocational education

The conditions for oral teaching evaluations are more closely met by the deep learning scoring model's scheme than by the classic learning scoring model. Deep learning outperforms standard learning in terms of logicalness and fluctuation range when teaching higher vocational English via oral means. Figure I shows the updated oral instruction assessment scheme, which demonstrates how the deep learning score model is more stable and has quicker judging speed. As a result, the oral instruction evaluation scheme's summation stability, accuracy, and speed are all improved by the deep learning scoring model.

4.2 Oral English Teaching for Higher Vocational Education

Higher vocational English oral teaching evaluation programs include assessment functions and content. Preliminary oral teaching assessment scheme for higher vocational English was achieved after the deep learning score model was pre-selected. The oral teaching of higher vocational English was also obtained. This study examines the potential of an oral teaching assessment method. Using the options in Table 2 to choose an oral teaching evaluation scheme with varying levels of assessment will allow you to more precisely confirm the efficacy of the higher vocational English oral teaching model.

Table 2. The overall picture of the teaching assessment program

category	Satisfaction	Analysis rate
Test Class 1	81.37	77.01
Test Class 2	78.44	82.73
Test Class 3	80.08	84.13
mean	78.79	77.04
X6	32.18	35.58
P = 3.074		

4.3 Accuracy and Stability of Oral Teaching Assessments

By comparing the oral teaching evaluation scheme with the conventional learning scoring model, we can ensure that the deep learning scoring model is accurate. Figure 2 shows the oral teaching evaluation scheme.

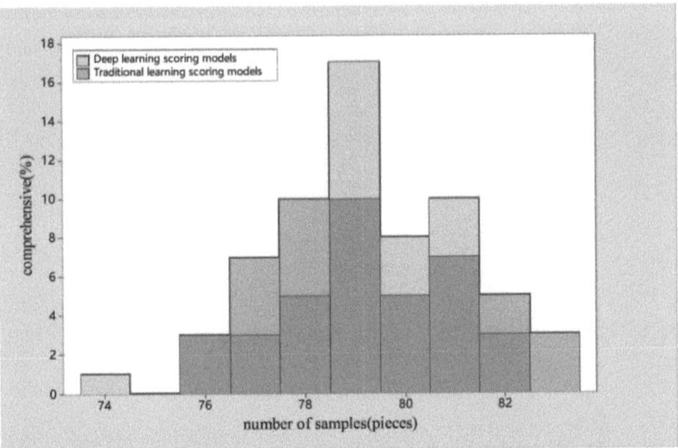

Fig. 2. The accuracy of different scoring models

When comparing the deep learning scoring model to the conventional learning scoring model, Fig. 2 shows that the former has better accuracy and a lower mistake rate. This suggests that the deep learning scoring model's oral teaching assessment is more stable. Traditional learning scoring methods do an unequal job of evaluating spoken instruction. Table 3 displays the mean and standard deviation of the three methods used to evaluate spoken instruction.

Table 3. Comparison of the accuracy of oral teaching assessment by different methods

Score the model	accuracy	Magnitude of change	error
Deep learning scoring models	93.77	91.43	91.65
Traditional learning scoring models	82.33	87.23	85.13
P	34.73	33.24	31.83

According to Table 3 It is clear that the oral instruction of higher vocational English has undergone substantial changes, and the mistake rate is considerable, while the conventional learning score model fails to adequately account for these changes in accuracy and stability. When compared to more conventional learning score models, deep learning models tend to provide more consistent overall outcomes. Even more impressive is the fact that the deep learning scoring model's accuracy remains consistently above 90%. In order to further validate the superiority of the deep learning scoring model. Various methodologies are often used to examine the deep learning scoring model, as illustrated in Fig. 3, in order to further validate the usefulness of the suggested strategy.

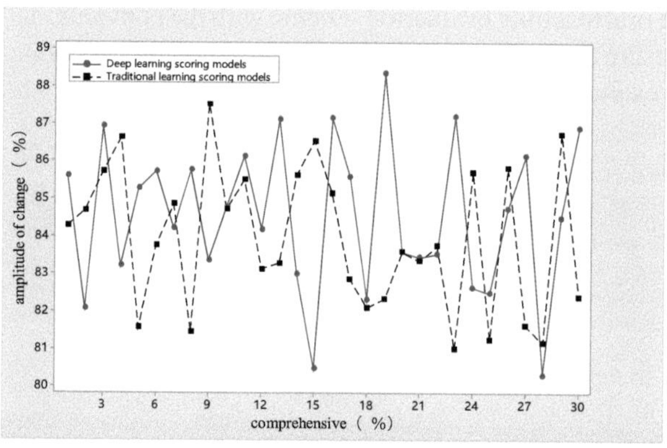

Fig. 3. Deep learning scoring model for satisfaction with oral teaching assessment

Given Fig. 3 the deep learning scoring model outperforms the traditional learning scoring model in terms of teaching evaluation. This is because, among other things, it raises the adjustment of higher vocational English oral teaching coefficients and includes assessment thresholds to weed out non-compliant oral teaching assessment schemes.

5 Conclusion

This study puts forth a deep learning scoring model and uses deep learning to improve higher vocational English oral instruction in an effort to address the issue of unsatisfactory evaluations of such courses. Concurrently, the assessment set is built by a thorough analysis of the oral instruction evaluation model and the threshold model. According to the study, the deep learning scoring model can assess the whole oral instruction of higher vocational English and enhance its accuracy and stability. Yet, the assessment of oral instruction is too focused on in the deep learning scoring model, leading to an irrational choice of markers for that evaluation.

References

1. Arujo, G.A., de Castro, M.F.: English teaching in the amazon region: beliefs toward native and non-native English-speaking teachers. Verbo De Minas **24**(43), 120–148 (2023)
2. Chen, J.L., Lai, P., Chan, A., Man, V., Chan, C.H.: AI-Assisted enhancement of student presentation skills: challenges and opportunities. Sustainability **15**(1) (2023)
3. Dooly, M., Thrasher, T., Sadler, R.: "Whoa! Incredible!:" language learning experiences in virtual reality. Relc J. (2023)
4. Estrada-Chichon, J.L., Zayas-Martinez, F., Sanchez-Cabrero, R.: Classroom-situated willingness to communicate: student teachers of EFL in Spain. Eur. J. Invest. Health Psychol. Educ. **13**(1), 96–111 (2023)
5. Galante, A., et al.: Digital plurilingual pedagogies in foreign language classes: empowering language learners to speak in the target language. Lang. Learn. J. **51**(4), 523–543 (2023)
6. Gao, S.Y., Tsai, Y.Y., Huang, J.H., Ma, Y.X., Wu, T.L.: TikTok for developing learning motivation and oral proficiency in MICE learners. J. Hosp. Leisure Sport Tour. Educ. **32** (2023)
7. Gillon, G.: Supporting Children who are English Language Learners Succeed in Their Early Literacy Development. Folia Phoniatrica Et Logopaedica (2023)
8. Gillon, G., McNeill, B., Scott, A., Gath, M., Westerveld, M.: Retelling stories: the validity of an online oral narrative task. Child Lang. Teach. Therapy **39**(2), 150–174 (2023)
9. Guo, J.: Innovative application of sensor combined with speech recognition technology in college English education in the context of artificial intelligence. J. Sens. **2023** (2023)
10. Guo, Y.D., Gao, X.S.: The impact of learning English on Chinese pre-schoolers' identity aspirations. Sage Open **13**(1) (2023)
11. Gutor, L.V., Sodomora, P.A., Vasylenko, O.H., Zalutska, H.I.: Development of media literacy and communication skills by means of digital storytelling in Japan. Inf. Technol. Learn. Tools **95**(3), 88–101 (2023)

Research and Implementation of Student Model of English Grammar Online Learning System

You Chen[✉]

College of Foreign Studies, Guangdong University of Science and Technology,
Dongguan City 523083, Guangdong Province, China
chenyou@gdust.edu.cn

Abstract. There is an issue with erroneous models, despite the fact that student models play a significant part in the online learning system for English grammar. The online English grammar learning system's model research issue is intractable and yields unsatisfactory results when solved using the conventional ant colony approach. Hence, this work evaluates based on evolutionary algorithms and offers further research to support this model. In order to minimize interference with the student model's research and execution, we first use chromosomal and fitness theory to identify the elements that will have an impact, and then we split the indicators according to the needs of the student model. Next, the student model's research and implementation plan is developed utilizing chromosomal and fitness theory for the genetic algorithm. The student model's research and implementation outcomes are then thoroughly evaluated. The results show that the intelligent analysis method can improve the learning system and English learning in this paper, with the improvement degree reaching more than 80%, and reducing the corresponding changes. The reduction rate of change amplitude is 10%. Therefore, it can promote the optimization of English grammar and online learning.

Keywords: chromosome and fitness theory · genetic algorithm · Research and implementation of student models · English grammar · Online learning · Learning system

1 Introduction

As a crucial component of the online English grammar learning system, student [1, 2] model research and implementation may expedite correct model control [3, 4]. Nevertheless, there is an issue with inaccuracy in student model research and implementation [5], which has an effect [6] on student model research and implementation [7] and is a part of the student model implementation process overall [8–10]. A number of academics hold the view that genetic algorithms, when applied to student model research and implementation analysis, can provide useful insights into the student models' research and implementation strategies, as well as corresponding support for these efforts. This work uses this information to suggest a genetic algorithm [11] for improving the student model's research and implementation strategy and for checking the model's efficacy [12].

B. Brik and S. Nazir (Eds.): BigIoT-EDU 2024, LNICST 659, pp. 602–611, 2026.
https://doi.org/10.1007/978-3-032-18631-7_65

2 Related Works

2.1 Mathematical Description of the Genetic Algorithm

The purpose of the genetic algorithm is to maximize the student model's research and implementation plan using computational methods. It will do this by analyzing the student model's index parameters and determining which ones have unqualified values, and integrate is y_i the function to finally judge the feasibility, calculated is z_i in Formula (1) shown.

$$\lim_{x \to \infty} \left(y_i \cdot t_{ij} \right) = y_{ij} \geq \max\left(t_{ij} \div 2 \right) \tag{1}$$

Among them, Content analysis of grammar is shown in Eq. (2).

$$max(t_{ij}) = \partial\left(t_{ij}^{2} \right) + mean(\sum t_{ij}) \tag{2}$$

By combining the benefits of computer technology with student model research and implementation, genetic algorithms may increase the accuracy of student model research and implementation via quantification. The student model is $tol\left(y_i \cdot t_{ij} \right)$, Grammar parsing process is set_i, and Comprehensive analysis effect is y_i as shown in Eq. (3).

$$qet(d_i) = \mathbb{R} \prod k \sum t_i \bigcap \xi \cdot \oint y_i \tag{3}$$

2.2 Research on Student Models and Selection of Implementation Schemes

Hypothesis II The research and implementation function of the student model is $g(t_i)$ and the weight coefficient is w_i. Consequently, the unqualified student model must be researched and implemented in order for the student model to be put into practice $F(t_i \approx 0)$ shown in Eq. (4).

$$\int g(a \cdot t_i) = \int \ddot{x} \cdot \sum z_i \prod F(d_i) \frac{dy}{dx} \tag{4}$$

Equation (5) shows the outcome of testing hypotheses I and II, which states that the student model's research and execution can provide a complete function in Eq. (5).

$$\lim_{x \to \infty} g(t_i) + F(d_i) \leq \bigcap max(t_{ij}) \tag{5}$$

The standardizing all data is required to increase the research efficacy and implementation dependability of the student model in Eq. (6).

$$g(t_i) + F(d_i) \leftrightarrow mean(\sum t_{ij} + 4) \tag{6}$$

2.3 Research of Student Models and Analysis of Implementation Schemes

It is important to thoroughly examine the student model's research and implementation plan before running the genetic algorithm. Then, match the student model's requirements with its research and implementation library. Finally, remove any unqualified student model's research and implementation plan. Equation (6) states that the anomaly evaluation scheme can be proposed, and the results is $No(t_i)$ shown in Eq. (7).

$$VB(t_i) = \frac{g(t_i) + F(d_i)}{mean(\sum t_{ij} + 4)} \sqrt{x \cdot c} \tag{7}$$

Among them, it is $\frac{g(t_i) + F(d_i)}{mean(\sum t_{ij} + 4)} \leq 1$ stated integration is $Zh(t_i)$ required, and the result is shown in Eq. (8).

$$hop(t_i) = \bigcap a \cdot s \cdot [\sum g(t_i) + F(d_i)] \tag{8}$$

In order to guarantee that the genetic algorithm is accurate, the student model's research and implementation are thoroughly examined, and the threshold and index weight of the student model's research and implementation scheme are established. The research and implementation of student models is $unno(t_i)$ a systematic test of the research and implementation of student models, which needs to be accurately analyzed. If the research and implementation of the student model is $accur(t_i)$ in a manorial distribution, The precision of the student model's research and implementation will be reduced, impacting the research and implementation scheme. The calculation result is indicated in Eq. (9).

$$ipr(t_i) = \frac{min[\sum g(t_i) + F(d_i)]}{\sum g(t_i) + F(d_i)} \cdot ao \tag{9}$$

After reviewing the student model's study and execution plan, we find that it follows the objective facts and has a multidimensional distribution. The lack of direction in the student model's research and execution suggests a highly randomized research and implementation strategy, so it is regarded as high analytical research. If the stochastic function studied and implemented by the student model is $randon(t_i)$, then can be expressed as Eq. (10).

$$ur(t_i) = \frac{min[\sum g(t_i) + F(d_i)]}{\sum g(t_i) + F(d_i)} + \int randon(t_i) \tag{10}$$

Computer technology primarily modifies the student model's research and implementation, eliminates unnecessary and duplicate schemes, and augments the default scheme, ensuring that the entire student model's research and implementation are strongly correlated. This ensures that the student model meets all normal requirements.

3 Research and Optimization Strategies for the Implementation of Student Models

In order to optimize the student model's research and implementation, the genetic algorithm uses a random optimization technique and tweaks the parameters of the student model's online information system. There are varying degrees of student model research and implementation that genetic algorithms use, and various schemes are chosen at random. The iterative method optimizes and analyzes research and implementation plans of several student models with varying degrees of implementation. Following the completion of the optimization analysis, compare the research and implementation levels of student models from various schemes and document the processes followed by the top performing student models.

4 Results and Discussion

4.1 Introduction to the Research and Implementation of Student Models

English students from freshman to sophomore year analyze the beauty, judge the English learning process and content, and strengthen it as a whole. At the same time, it is necessary to integrate the key points and contents of English. The specific data are shown in Table 1.

Table 1. Student model research and implementation requirements

Scope of application	Grade	Planning content in English	Grades in English
Beginner	I	85.00	78.86
	II	81.97	78.45
Non-native speakers	I	83.81	81.31
	II	83.34	78.19
Advanced learners	I	79.56	81.99
	II	79.10	80.11

Key points and key contents in the results are planned. Among them, English teaching, data teaching analysis and teaching results data are complete, and the teaching process is planned. The planning content of the process is shown in Fig. 1.

Because it uses the ant colony method in Fig. 1, the genetic algorithm with the real student model's needs. The genetic algorithm outperforms the ant colony algorithm when it comes to the correctness and logic of student model study and execution. Figure 2 shows the student model that was developed and used to improve the genetic algorithm's accuracy and dependability. Consequently, the student model's research and implementation, as well as the genetic algorithm's correctness and stability in summing, are superior.

4.2 Research and Implementation of Student Models

Investigation and use of student-centered models Student models include structural, semi-structural, and non-structural data into their research and implementation plans. Upon completion of the genetic algorithm's preference step, the student model's research and implementation plan are derived, and the plan's feasibility is assessed. Table 2 shows that at various stages, Comprehensively judge the overall effect of English and the judgment results of English, and the summary results are shown in Table 2.

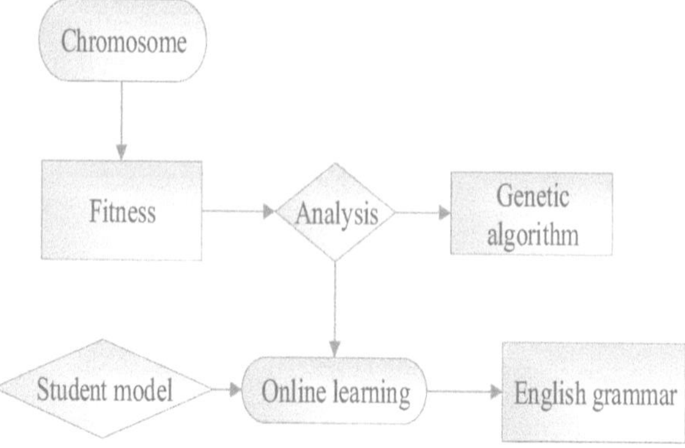

Fig. 1. The process of student model research and implementation analysis

Table 2. The overall picture of the student model research and implementation of the program

Category	Learning planning	Comprehensive improvement of English	English content enhancement
Beginner	85.32	85.90	83.95
Non-native speakers	86.36	82.51	84.29
Advanced learners	84.16	84.92	83.68

4.3 Research and Implementation and Stability of Student Models

The student model's study and execution plan, which included the ant colony algorithm: this was done to ensure the genetic algorithm was accurate as shown in Fig. 2.

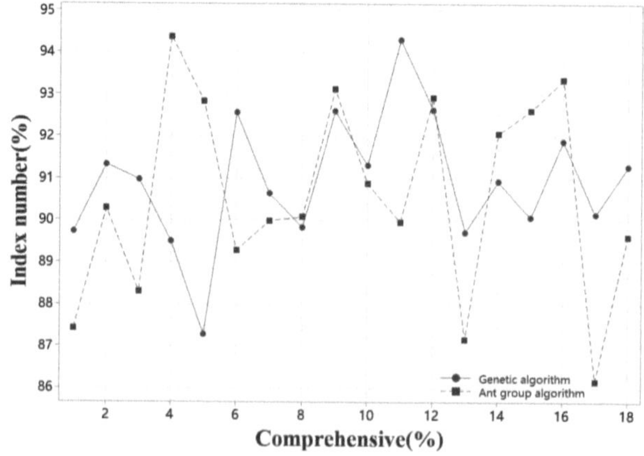

Fig. 2. Research and implementation of student models of different algorithms

Figure 2 shows that the ant colony algorithm's student model exhibits uneven research and implementation compared to the genetic algorithm's student model, which is characterized by a lower error rate despite higher research and implementation. This suggests that the genetic algorithm student model's research and implementation is relatively stable. The overall judgment of English content and English results, and the process of judgment, are shown in Table 3.

Table 3. The study and implementation of student models in different methods

Algorithm	Contents of grammar teaching	To the content of the grammar	Comprehensiveness of grammar	Comprehensive judgment of English law
Genetic algorithm	77.67	78.64	82.52	77.67
Ant colony algorithm	81.55	75.73	73.79	75.73
P	82.52	77.67	80.58	75.73

Table 3 shows that the ant colony technique isn't perfect when it comes to student model research and implementation accuracy; furthermore, there have been major changes in both areas, and the error rate is rather high. When compared to ant colony algorithms, genetic algorithms provide better overall outcomes when it comes to studying and implementing student models. Along these lines, the student model of the genetic algorithm has undergone over 90% study and implementation, and the accuracy has remained mostly unchanged as shown in Fig. 3.

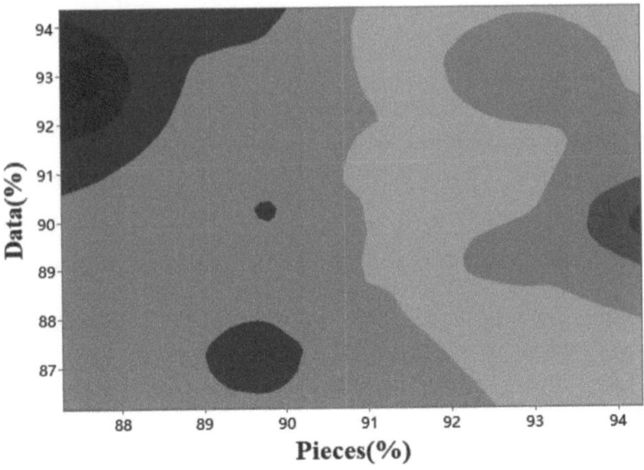

Fig. 3. Research and implementation of student models of genetic algorithms

Figure 3 shows that the genetic algorithm's research and implementation of the student model is far superior to the ant colony algorithm. This is because the genetic algorithm improves the student model's research and implementation coefficient.

4.4 The Rationality of the Research and Implementation of the Student Model

The ant colony method was included into the student model's study and implementation plan, as illustrated in Fig. 4.

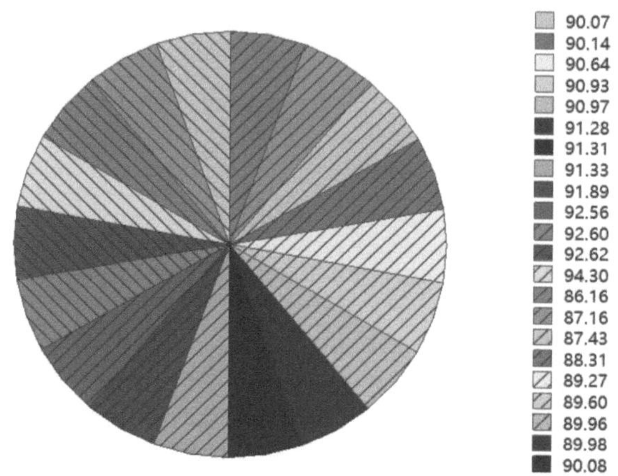

Fig. 4. Research and implementation of student models of different algorithms

Figure 4 shows that compared to the ant colony algorithm, the genetic algorithm student model's research and implementation are more rational. Moreover, by utilizing the genetic algorithm to enhance the student model's research and implementation, the student model's rationality can be further enhanced. With the help of genetic algorithms, a decentralized platform for data storage and administration may be established, guaranteeing the safe recording and preservation of findings. Each may have its own distinct identity thanks to genetic algorithms, which can also store all of the relevant information and plans.

4.5 Validity of Student Model Research and Implementation

In order to ensure that the genetic algorithm was successful, the student model's research and implementation strategy included the ant colony algorithm. Figure 5 shows the student model's research and implementation strategy. Combine the comprehensiveness of grammar and judge it. The specific process is shown in Fig. 5.

Figure 5 shows that compared to the ant colony algorithm, the genetic algorithm student model has more research and implementation, but a lower error rate. This suggests that their research and implementation are relatively stable, in contrast to the ant colony algorithm student model's inconsistent research and implementation. Table 4

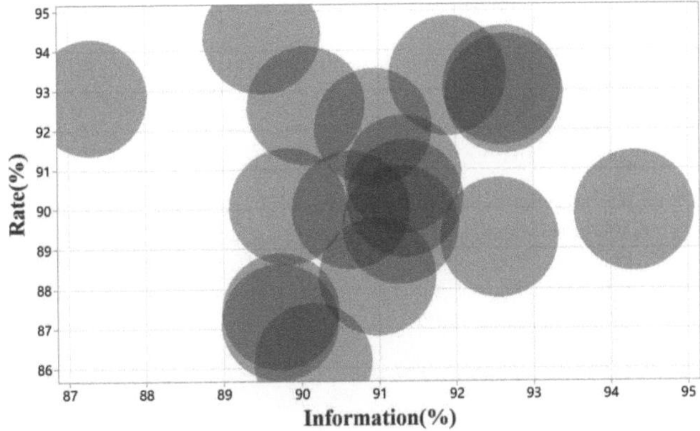

Fig. 5. Research and implementation of student models of different algorithms

Table 4. Comparison of the effectiveness oof student models

Algorithm	The wholeness of English	An analysis of content and diversity in English	Grammar and Reading of English	Structure and use of English
Genetic algorithm	53.98	57.52	79.61	76.70
Ant colony algorithm	46.90	53.10	72.82	79.61
P	47.79	40.71	82.52	78.64

shows the study and execution plan for the typical student model of the aforementioned three algorithms.

Table 4 shows that the ant colony technique isn't perfect when it comes to student model research and implementation accuracy; furthermore, there have been major changes in both areas, and the error rate is rather high. In order to solidify genetic algorithms' dominance even further. The genetic algorithm was often examined using several approaches to further confirm the efficacy of the suggested approach. The results of English grammar application are shown in Fig. 6.

Figure 6 shows that the ant colony algorithm's research and implementation is much worse than the genetic algorithm's student models. This is because the genetic algorithm raises the student model's research and implementation coefficient, establishes the threshold for Internet information, and gets rid of the student model's research and implementation schemes that don't measure up.

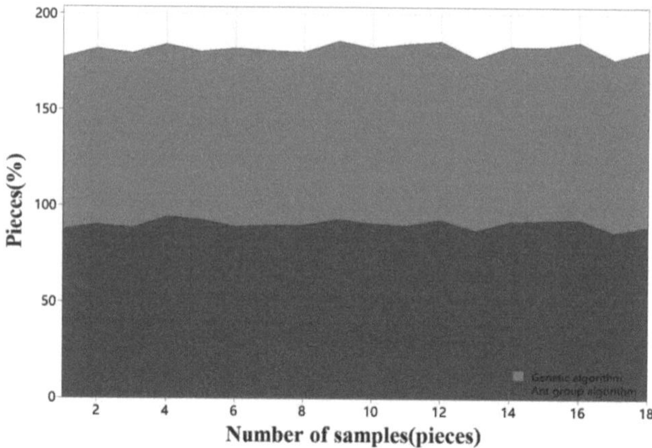

Fig. 6. Research and implementation of genetic algorithm student model

5   Conclusion

This work aims to maximize the development and execution of student models by proposing genetic algorithms and combining computer technology. The difficulty is that these processes are not optimal. While building the Internet information collection, we thoroughly examine the student model's research and execution for correctness and dependability. Genetic algorithms may boost the precision of student model research and implementation, as well as carry out research and implementation of generic student models, according to the findings. Nevertheless, the evolutionary algorithm approach places an excessive emphasis on student model research and implementation analysis, leading to illogical decisions about student model implementation indicators.

Acknowledgment. This paper is funded by the research project of teaching quality and reform (Online course construction and practice of The History of English Language education based on the Superstar Fanya Platform) in Guangdong University of Science and Technology in 2021 (Project No.: GKZLGC2021143).

References

1. Linjiao, Y.: Research and implementation of student model in online learning system for English grammar. (Doctoral dissertation, Shenyang Normal University) (2011)
2. Huijun, C.: Design and implementation of online collaborative learning system based on Wiki concept. (Doctoral dissertation, Shaanxi Normal University) (2015)
3. Qingrong, Y., Ling, L.: Practice and research on building student model in adaptive learning system for junior high school English. Reading Writing: Educ. J. **10**(12), 2 (2013)
4. Jing, X.: Research and implementation of personalized learning system based on student interest model. (Doctoral dissertation, Jiangxi Normal University)
5. Chuan, W.: Research on automated essay scoring system based on natural language processing. (Doctoral dissertation, Wuhan University of Technology)

6. Jiayuan, T., Qinghong, Y., Li, J.: Research and implementation of learning system based on interest features. Shandong University of Technology, Shandong Automation Society (2010)
7. Libo, D.: Research on network connection automation model of online evaluation system based on ontology learning. (Doctoral dissertation, Donghua University)
8. Chunnian, L., Qing, X.: Design and implementation of research-oriented learning teaching system based on vector space model. Science and Technology Square (2010)
9. Jie, H.: Research on theoretical model for creating English networked learning system: A case study on improving academic reading ability of international postgraduates in the UK. Sichuan University Press (2011)
10. Yan, Z., Yongxia, S., Aofan, L., Dingwen, Z., Ronghuai, H.: Research on student model in adaptive learning system
11. Laixi, Z.: Research and implementation of web-based learning navigation system. (Doctoral dissertation, National University of Defense Technology)
12. Zichen, G., Jingjing, F., Zhiting, X., Dingliang, L., Zhen, X.: Research on design liability tracing system integrating BIM and blockchain. Journal of Graphics (2023)

Mathematical Model and Algorithm of Multi-agent Reinforcement Learning Based on Random Countermeasures

Wang Chengli[✉]

School of Science, Xihua University, Chengdu 610039, Sichuan Province, China
wcl67654@126.com

Abstract. Accurate reinforcement learning is a challenge in multi-agent reinforcement learning, which relies heavily on mathematical model and algorithm development. When applied to the research challenges of multi-agent reinforcement learning, traditional genetic algorithms provide unsatisfactory results and are unable to resolve the algorithm research issues. As a result, this study examines previous work on multi-agent reinforcement learning and suggests a model and method for the field that relies on stochastic countermeasures. In order to minimize interference in mathematical model and algorithm research, the strategy gradient theory is used to identify the components that have an impact. The indicators are then classified based on the needs of the study. Next, a mathematical model and algorithm research scheme is developed for stochastic countermeasures using the strategy gradient theory. The outcomes of this study are then thoroughly examined. In terms of mathematical model and algorithm research time, mathematical model and algorithm research impact factor accuracy, and other assessment criteria, the MATLAB simulation results demonstrate that the random countermeasure outperforms the classic genetic algorithm.

Keywords: strategy gradient theory · random countermeasures · mathematical model · algorithm research · Agent · Reinforcement learning

1 Introduction

The development of multi-agent reinforcement learning relies heavily on mathematical model and algorithm research [1], which in turn enables ever-increasingly accurate control of mathematical model and algorithm research [2, 3]. But there's an issue with low precision between mathematical model and algorithm research schemes [4], which has an effect on mathematical model and algorithm research [5, 6], which is a problem with the process of mathematical model and algorithm research [7]. There are academics who think that mathematical model and algorithm research and analysis may be improved by using random countermeasures [8]. This approach allows for a more effective examination of research schemes related to mathematical models and algorithms [9, 10]. Additionally, it provides support for mathematical model and algorithm research. Building on this foundation, this study suggests a stochastic countermeasure, enhances the

B. Brik and S. Nazir (Eds.): BigIoT-EDU 2024, LNICST 659, pp. 612–621, 2026.
https://doi.org/10.1007/978-3-032-18631-7_66

mathematical model and algorithm development plan, and confirms the model's efficacy [11].

2 Related Works

2.1 Mathematical Description of Stochastic Countermeasures

Stochastic countermeasure is y_i, which research scheme, also determine the mathematical model's and algorithm's unqualified value parameters based on the index parameters studied, and integrate z_i the mathematical model and algorithm research scheme with the function function,and algorithm research, calculated is $tol(y_i \cdot t_{ij})$ in Formula (1) shown.

$$\lim_{x \to \infty} (y_i \cdot t_{ij}) = \lim_{x \to \infty} y_{ij} \geq \max(t_{ij} \div 2) \tag{1}$$

The evaluation of extreme cases is shown in Eq. (2).

$$max(t_{ij}) = \partial(t_{ij}^2 + 2 \cdot t_{ij}) \succ mean(\sum t_{ij} + 4)\mathrm{E} \tag{2}$$

To increase the accuracy of mathematical model and algorithm research, stochastic countermeasures quantify using computer technology's benefits while also using mathematical models and algorithm research.

Suppose I The requirements of mathematical model and algorithm research is t_i, the mathematical model and algorithm research scheme is set_i, Conducting research into mathematical models and algorithms is y_i, and the judgment function of mathematical model and algorithm research scheme is $JP(t_i \approx 0)$ as shown in Eq. (3).

$$JP(t_i) = \mathbb{R} \lim_{x \to \infty} \sum t_i \cap \xi \cdot \sqrt{k} \to \cdot 7 \tag{3}$$

2.2 The Mathematical Models and Algorithm Research Schemes

He mathematical model and algorithm research function is w_i and the weight coefficient is $g(t_i)$, Therefore, as shown in Eq. (4), study on mathematical models and algorithms necessitates research on unqualified mathematical models and algorithms.

$$\sum g(t_i) = \sum n \prod F(d_i)\frac{dy}{dx} - e^{-i\omega t} \tag{4}$$

An all-encompassing function of mathematical model and algorithm research may be derived from assumptions I and II, as shown in Eq. (5).

$$\lim_{x \to \infty} g(t_i) + \lim_{x \to \infty} F(d_i) \leq \frac{1}{2}max(t_{ij}) \tag{5}$$

Data standardization is essential for doing good research on mathematical models and algorithms; Eq. (6) shows the outcomes.

$$\lim_{x \to \infty} g(t_i) + F(d_i) \leftrightarrow mean(\sum t_{ij} + 4) \tag{6}$$

2.3   Analysis of Mathematical Models and Algorithm Research Schemes

Thoroughly analyzing the mathematical model and algorithm research scheme is necessary before implementing random countermeasures. The research needs for the model and algorithms should be matched to the mathematical model and algorithm research library, and the unqualified mathematical model and algorithm research scheme should be eliminated $Pli(t_i)$, is shown in Eq. (7).

$$Pil(t_i) = \frac{g(t_i) + F(d_i)}{mean(\sum t_{ij} + 4)} \frac{n!}{r!(n-r)!} \tag{7}$$

Among them, it is $\frac{g(t_i)+F(d_i)}{mean(\sum t_{ij}+4)} \leq 1$ the integration set is $Zh(t_i)$ required, is shown in Eq. (8).

$$Zh(t_i) = \bigcap [\sum g(t_i) + F(d_i)] \tag{8}$$

Thorough analysis of the mathematical model and algorithm research has been conducted, and the scheme's threshold and index weights have been $unno(t_i)$ set to ensure the accuracy of random countermeasures. Mathematical model and algorithm research is $accur(t_i)$ a systematic test of mathematical model and algorithm research scheme, It requires precise analysis. Equation (9), which displays the calculation result, shows that if the mathematical model and algorithm research is in a manorial distribution, it will impair the overall accuracy of the research and have an effect on the mathematical model and algorithm research scheme.

$$accur(t_i) = \frac{min[\sum g(t_i) + F(d_i)]}{\lim_{x \to \infty} \sum g(t_i) + F(d_i)} \times 100\% \tag{9}$$

The mathematical model and algorithm research scheme exhibit multidimensional distribution, in agreement with objective facts, according to the survey of these models and schemes. A lack of direction in mathematical model and algorithm development suggests a high degree of randomness in these areas, so they are regarded as high analytical research. If the random function studied by mathematical models and algorithms is $randon(t_i)$, it is as Eq. (10).

$$accur(t_i) = \int randon(t_i) \sum r \tag{10}$$

Computer technology primarily modifies the mathematical model and algorithm research, eliminates redundant and unnecessary. This ensures that the mathematical model and algorithm research fulfill standard requirements.

3   Optimization Strategies for Mathematical Model and Algorithm Research

When doing research on mathematical models and algorithms, stochastic countermeasures use a stochastic optimization technique and tweak Internet information settings to make scheme optimization a reality. Mathematical model and algorithm research is divided into distinct tiers by stochastic countermeasures, which then randomly pick alternative methods. Mathematical models and algorithm research techniques are optimized and examined at various stages in the iterative process. Following the completion of the optimization study, the research level of various schemes' mathematical models and algorithms is compiled, and the best of them is documented.

4   Results and Discussion

4.1   Introduction to the Research of Mathematical Models and Algorithms

The research objects of mathematical models and algorithms in complex cases are used as the basis for this study, which has 12 paths and a 12-h testing period. Table 1 shows the research schemes for mathematical models and algorithms, with a focus on specific models and algorithms.

Table 1. Mathematical model and algorithm research requirements

Scope of application	The type of data	Specific data	Objective learning data
Robot control	I	85.00	78.86
	II	81.97	78.45
Automatic drive	I	83.81	81.31
	II	83.34	78.19
Traffic control	I	79.56	81.99
	II	79.10	80.11

Make judgments based on machine learning methods and the overall analysis process. The process of judgment. As in Fig. 1.

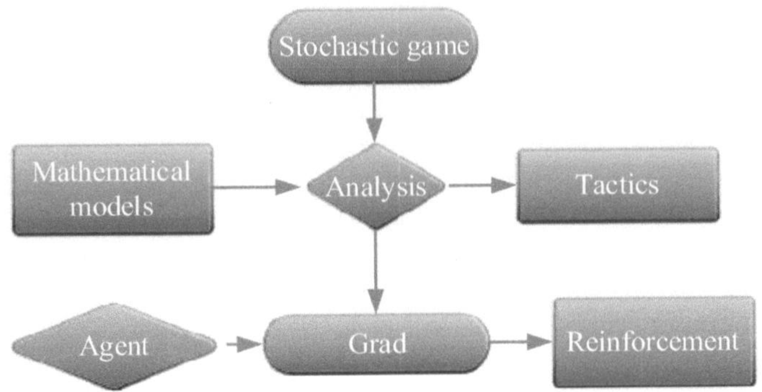

Fig. 1. The mathematical models and algorithm research

The stochastic countermeasure's mathematical model and algorithm research scheme, which includes genetic algorithms. Genetic algorithms aren't as good as random countermeasures when it comes to researching mathematical models and algorithms. Figure 2 shows how the research system for algorithms and mathematical models has been improved, leading to more accurate and reliable random countermeasures. Hence, stochastic countermeasure mathematical model and algorithm study scheme is faster, more accurate, and more stable when adding up.

4.2   Research on Mathematical Models and Algorithms

Research into mathematical models and algorithms has a three-pronged approach, including both organized and unstructured data. Following the ore-selection of random countermeasures, a scheme for the research of mathematical models and algorithms is developed, and its feasibility is evaluated, as indicated in Table 2.

Table 2. The overall situation of mathematical models and algorithm research schemes

Category	Specific data comprehensiveness	According to the representativeness	Of integration
Robot control	1.00	3.50	3.53
Automatic drive	1.00	2.84	3.67
Traffic control	1.00	2.13	3.14

4.3   Research and Stability of Mathematical Models and Algorithms

The mathematical model and algorithm research method is illustrated in Fig. 2. It incorporates the genetic algorithm to test the correctness of the random countermeasure.

From Fig. 2, the Talk about the fusion power of plastids rate is lower in the stochastic countermeasure's mathematical model and algorithm research, suggesting that it is relatively stable, in contrast to the genetic algorithm's mathematical model and algorithm research, which is uneven. As you can see in Table 3, the three algorithms mentioned above have an average mathematical model and research plan.

Table 3 shows that genetic algorithms aren't perfect when it comes to researching mathematical models and algorithms; they're also not very good at keeping up with the rapid changes in these fields, and they make a lot of mistakes. Genetic algorithms can't compare to the mathematical model and algorithm that predicts the overall outcomes of random countermeasures. Additionally, the stochastic countermeasure method and mathematical model have been evaluated over 90% of the time, and there has been no substantial change in accuracy. In order to confirm that random countermeasures are better. Various approaches conducted a general study of random countermeasures, as shown in Fig. 3, to further validate the efficiency of the suggested strategy.

Figure 3 shows that stochastic countermeasure's mathematical model and algorithm research is far superior to genetic algorithm's. This is because stochastic countermeasure

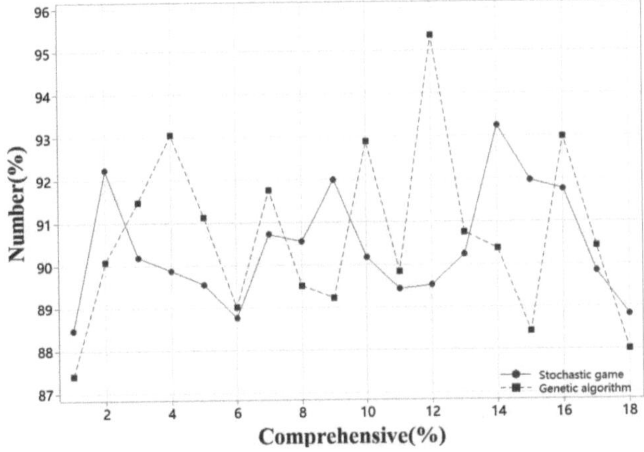

Fig. 2. MATHEMATICAL models and algorithm research

Table 3. Comparison of mathematical models and algorithms of different methods to study accuracy

Algorithm	The integration of intelligence and teaching	And the improvement of comprehensive effects	Convergence of instructional planning	Convergence of learning
Stochastic countermeasures	3.52	3.72	2.23	2.84
Genetic algorithm	2.51	2.21	4.92	2.64

raises the adjustment coefficient of the previously mentioned models and algorithms, establishes a threshold for Internet information, and gets rid of the models and algorithms that don't measure up.

4.4   Rationality of Mathematical Model and Algorithm Research

The mathematical model and algorithm research plan were displayed in Fig. 4. They were integrated with the genetic algorithm to check the correctness of the random countermeasure.

Figure 4 shows that stochastic countermeasure's mathematical model and algorithm research is more rational than genetic algorithm's, and that stochastic countermeasure's use in improving those models and algorithms can further increase their rationality. Random countermeasures, when implemented, may offer a decentralized platform for data storage and administration, guaranteeing the safe recording and storage of findings. Each may have their own distinct identity with a random countermeasure, which can also store all of the relevant information and plans.

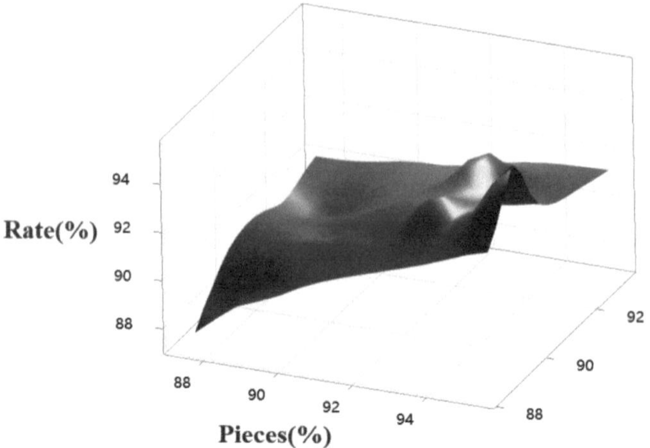

Fig. 3. Research on mathematical models and algorithms of stochastic countermeasures

countermeasure.

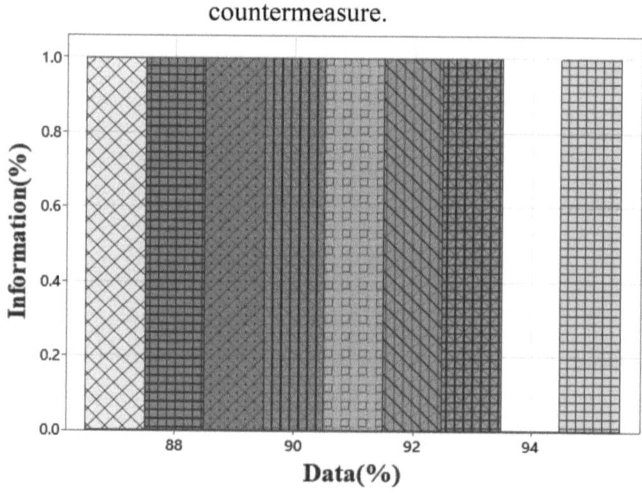

Fig. 4. MATHEMATICAL models and algorithm research of different algorithms

4.5　Validity of Mathematical Models and Algorithm Research

Figure 5 shows the research program for the mathematical model and algorithm that incorporates the genetic algorithm in order to confirm that the random countermeasure is successful.

Figure 5 shows that genetic algorithm mathematical model and algorithm research is uneven, in contrast to stochastic countermeasure, whose research is higher but has a lower error rate, which is shown in Table 4.

Table 4 shows that genetic algorithms aren't perfect when it comes to mathematical model and algorithm research accuracy, and that there have been notable changes in both

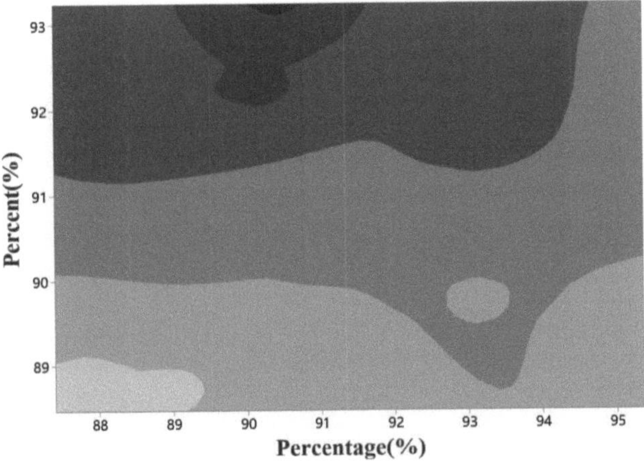

Fig. 5. Mathematical models and algorithm research of different algorithms

Table 4. Comparison of mathematical models and algorithms of different methods for research effectiveness

Algorithm	Is the actual effect of conjoined	The comprehensiveness of the conjoined	Educational promotion indicators of conjoined	Integrity optimization results of conjoined pieces
Stochastic countermeasures	1.00	2.25	3.69	2.00
Genetic algorithm	1.00	3.53	2.71	4.10
Holistic planning	1.00	3.15	2.50	2.23

areas, along with a high mistake rate. Genetic algorithms can't compare to the mathematical model and algorithm that predicts the overall outcomes of random countermeasures. Additionally, the stochastic countermeasure method and mathematical model have been evaluated over 90% of the time, and there has been no substantial change in accuracy. In order to confirm that random countermeasures are better. A broad study of random countermeasures was conducted using several methodologies, as shown in Fig. 6, to further validate the usefulness of the suggested strategy.

Figure 6 clearly shows that stochastic countermeasure's mathematical model and algorithm research is far superior to genetic algorithm's. This is due to stochastic countermeasure's ability to raise the adjustment coefficient of the studied models, establish a threshold for the amount of data collected from the Internet, and do away with any models or algorithms that fail to satisfy the criteria.

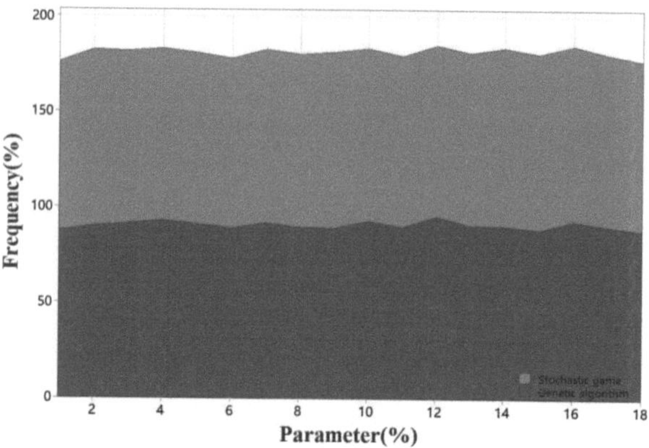

Fig. 6. RESEARCH on mathematical model and algorithm of stochastic countermeasures

5 Conclusion

In response to the criticism that mathematical models and algorithms are underperforming in practice, this article offers ad hoc solutions and integrates computational tools to enhance mathematical model and algorithm research. Simultaneously, the Internet data gathering is built, and mathematical model and algorithm correctness and reliability are examined thoroughly. Mathematical model and algorithm research may be conducted on mathematical model and algorithm research, and studies have shown that stochastic countermeasures can increase the accuracy of this study. On the other hand, when it comes to random countermeasures, we tend to focus too much on mathematical model and algorithm study analysis, which leads to illogical indication selection.

References

1. Guangqiang, X., Xuesong, C.: Mathematical model and algorithm of multi-agent reinforcement learning based on stochastic policy. In: Proceedings of 2010 The 3rd International Conference on Computational Intelligence and Industrial Application (Volume 7)
2. Yang, G., Zhihua, Z., Jiazhou, H., Shifu, C.: Research on multi-agent reinforcement learning model and algorithm based on Markovian policy. J. Comput. Res. Dev. **37**(3), 7 (2000)
3. Yixin, Y., Daoping, J., Xiaojuan, B., Xiangsong, M.: Local learning algorithm for multi-agent based on stochastic policy in group environment. Inf. Control. **37**(6), 6 (2008)
4. Xiaoyan, Z.: Continuous-Time Hierarchical Reinforcement Learning Algorithm. (Doctoral dissertation, Hefei University of Technology) (2010)
5. Fei, L., Guangzhou, Z., Yanwei, S.: Reinforcement learning model and algorithm for multi-agent collaboration. Comput. Sci. **33**(12), 4 (2006)
6. Chong, W., Ning, J., Jun, L., Jun, W., Hao, C.: Multi-star collaborative task planning algorithm based on multi-agent reinforcement learning. J. Nat. Univ. Defense Technol. **33**(1), 6 (2011)
7. Changying, W., Wenwei, C., Li, Y.: A multi-agent collaborative reinforcement learning algorithm based on team Markov game. J. Fudan Univ. Nat. Sci. Ed. **43**(5), 3 (2004)
8. Xiao, W., Hongwei, W., Chao, Q.: Maintenance strategy for assembly line based on multi-agent reinforcement learning. J. Syst. Eng. **28**(5), 7 (2013)

9. Xiaomeng, L., Yupu, Y., Xiaoming, X.: Research on multi-agent cooperation based on Markovian policy and reinforcement learning. J. Shanghai Jiao Tong Univ. (2001)
10. Changying, W., Xiaohu, Y., Yiping, B., Li, Y.: Agent collaborative reinforcement learning method based on stochastic game. Comput. Eng. Sci. **02**, 111–114 (2006)
11. Fei, L., Guangzhou, Z., Yanwei, S.: Reinforcement learning model and algorithm for multi-agent collaboration. Comput. Sci. **33**(12), 156–158, 186 (2006)

Digital Education Management Information System and its Model

Liu Zhen[✉]

Wuhan Business University, 430056 Wuhan, Hubei Province, China
m19003325000@163.com

Abstract. Research into information systems and models is crucial to the administration of online learning, however there is an issue with the improper placement of data. The information system issue in digital education management cannot be solved by traditional deep learning, and the results are less than optimal. Consequently, this study reviews previous work on digital education management information systems and models, and it suggests future research on such systems and models based on digital mining algorithms. As a first step in reducing interference factors in information system and model research, statistical set,then segregated according to the needs of the study. After that, a study plan for an information system and model based on a digital mining algorithm is developed using statistical set theory, and the outcomes of this research are thoroughly examined. The digital mining method outperforms conventional deep learning in MATLAB simulations when it comes to information system and model research accuracy and information system and model research influencing factor time, under certain evaluation criteria.

Keywords: statistical set theory · numerical mining algorithms · Information systems and model research · Digital · Education · Management

1 Introduction

Digital education management relies heavily on information system and model research, which may expedite the precise[1] control of such research and is therefore an integral aspect of digital education management [2]. Inadequate accuracy of information system and model research schemes[3] is an issue that arises throughout the research process[4] and has detrimental impacts on the study [5–6]. Some academics think that information system and model research[7–8] schemes may be better analyzed with the use of digital mining algorithms used to the study of information systems and models[9], and that this in turn will give support for the study of information systems and models. With this in mind, we provide a digital mining method to improve the information system and model research scheme, as well as to validate the model's efficacy [10],is shown in Fig. 1.

B. Brik and S. Nazir (Eds.): BigIoT-EDU 2024, LNICST 659, pp. 622–631, 2026.
https://doi.org/10.1007/978-3-032-18631-7_67

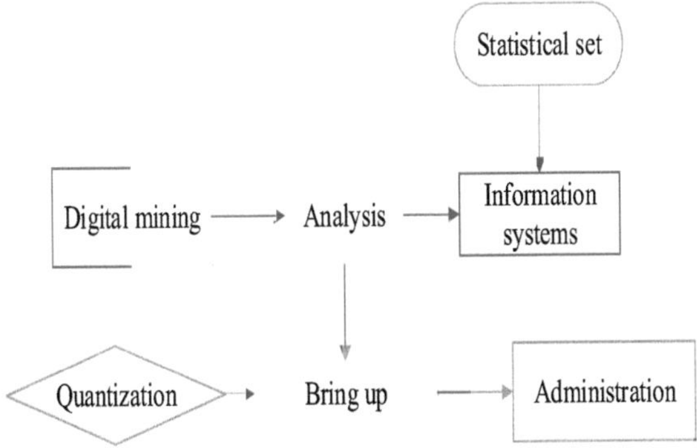

Fig. 1. The analytical process of information systems and model research

2 Related Works

A. Digital Education Management

Digital mining algorithms that include deep learning into their research schemes for information systems and models are more in line with the needs of such fields in practice. Digital mining techniques outperform deep learning when it comes to the genealogical and precision of research into information systems and models. A program for studying information systems and models includes three types of data: structural, semi-structural, and non-structural. General data is obtained, and the results obtained has been pee-selected, This is because digital mining algorithm improves the adjustment coefficient.

B. Information System Model

In order to optimize the research scheme for information systems and models, the digital mining algorithm uses a stochastic optimization method and tweaks the parameters of online data. In order to choose alternative schemes at random, the digital mining algorithm breaks down the information system and model study into multiple stages of research. Information system and model research approaches at various levels are optimized and evaluated in the iterative process. When the optimization analysis is finished, compare the information system and model research levels of several schemes and make a note of the best one. With the use of digital mining algorithms, a decentralized platform, guaranteeing the safe recording and preservation of findings. Digital mining techniques allow for the creation of unique identifiers for each and the recording of important data and schemes.

3 Optimization Strategies for Information System and Model Research

3.1 Generalization of Student Information and Mapping Construction of Related Scales

Utilizing computer technology, the digital mining algorithm optimizes the information system and model research scheme. It then finds the unqualified value parameters based on the index parameters in the system and model research. Finally, it integrates the functions of the system and model research scheme to judge the feasibility of the system and model research., calculated is in Formula (1).

$$\lim_{x\to\infty}\left(y_i \cdot t_{ij}\right) = \lim_{x\to\infty} y_{ij} \geq \max\left(t_{ij} \div 2\right) \tag{1}$$

Among them, the judgment of outliers is shown in Eq. (2).

$$\max\left(t_{ij}\right) = \partial\left(t_{ij}^{2} + 2 \cdot t_{ij}\right) \succ mean\left(\sum t_{ij}\right) \tag{2}$$

To increase the accuracy of information system and model research, digital mining algorithms integrate the benefits of computer technology and use quantitative methods for information system and model research.

Suppose I The requirements of information system and model research is, the information system and model research scheme is, the satisfaction of the information system and model research program is,Eq. (3) shows that the judgment function of the information system and model research scheme is, and that the satisfaction of the information system and model research program is .

$$F(d_i) = \sqrt{\sum t_i \bigcap \xi \cdot \to \oint y_i} \tag{3}$$

3.2 Selection of Information System and Model Research Schemes

Hypothesis II The information system and model research function is, the weight coefficient is, then, the information system and model research require the unqualified information system and model research as shown in Eq. (4):

$$g(t_i) = \oiint_{i}^{n} \ddot{x} \cdot \int z_{i(d_i)\frac{dy}{dx}} \tag{4}$$

An all-encompassing information system and model research function may be derived in accordance with assumptions I and II, as seen in Eq. (5).

$$\lim_{x\to\infty} g(t_i) + F(d_i) \leq \frac{n!}{r!(n-r)!}\max\left(t_{ij}\right) \tag{5}$$

To improve the reliability of information systems and model research, it is vital for data standardization, and the outcomes are shown in Eq. (6).

$$g\sum_{i}^{n}(t_i) + F(d_i) \leftrightarrow mean\left(\sum t_{ij} + 4\right) \tag{6}$$

3.3 Analysis of Information Systems and Model Research Programs

An exhaustive analysis of the information system and model research scheme should precede the implementation of the digital mining algorithm. The requirements of the system and model research should be mapped to the resources available for that system and model, and any unqualified resources should be removed. The anomaly assessment strategy may be provided using Eq. (6)., and the results is shown in Eq. (7).

$$NoP(t_i) = \prod_{k=1}^{n} A_k dy \tag{7}$$

Among them, it is it must be suggested before the strategy may be integrated required, and the result is shown in Eq. (8).

$$IP(k_i) = \lim_{x \to \infty} \sum_{\substack{0 \le i \le m \\ 0 < j < n}} P(i,j) \Big] \tag{8}$$

For the digital mining algorithm to be accurate, it is necessary to do thorough analyses of the information system and model research and to define the threshold and index weights of the research scheme. Due diligence is required for the information system and model research that is, a system test information system and model research scheme. The overall accuracy of the information system and model research is reduced if the in a non-normal distribution affects the information system and model research scheme; the calculation result is illustrated in Eq. (9).

$$TOI(t_i) = k \int \frac{\min\big[\sum g(t_i) + F(d_i)\big]}{\sum g(t_i) + F(d_i)} \tag{9}$$

Consistent with the available empirical evidence, the survey data system and the model study plan reveal a multidimensional distribution. Research on information systems and models is considered to be of a high analytical quality as it lacks direction and is characterized by great unpredictability in its research strategies. Information systems and models examine a stochastic function if it is, the result of solving problem Computer technology primarily modifies the information system and model research, eliminates unnecessary and duplicate schemes, and augments the default scheme, ensuring that the entire information system and model research scheme has strong dynamic correlation, and meeting the usual requirements is one of them.

4 Results and Discussion

4.1 Introduction to Information System and Model Research

Taking actual teaching as the research object, this paper makes a critical analysis of the data content in the teaching process. The test and test results based on the test data are six months, and the test objects are 246. Data testing is mainly based on the data in the database, and the data types are qualitative and quantitative. The specific data collection results are shown in Table. 1.

Improved digital mining algorithm accuracy and reliability are results of the information system and model research scheme adjustments shown in Fig. 2. Thus, the digital mining algorithm's information system and model research scheme is faster, more accurate, and more stable in terms of summation.

Table 1. Information systems and model research requirements

Scope of application	Plan type	Digital management of information.	Mapping scale of information.
School management	Quantity data.	85.00	78.86
	Qualitative data.	81.97	78.45
resource management	Quantity data.	83.81	81.31
	Qualitative data.	83.34	78.19
Student status management	Quantity data.	79.56	81.99
	Qualitative data.	79.10	80.11

4.2   Research on Information Systems and Models

The next step is to collect the information system and model research scheme for the preliminary information system and model research. The viability of this scheme will then be evaluated. Follow the guidelines in Table 2 to choose research programs for information systems and models with varying degrees of depth and scope in order to more reliably confirm the research impact of these systems and models.

Table 2. Overall Situation of Information Systems and Modelling Research Programmes

Category	Digitization of teaching management.	Comprehensive information digitization.	The overall diversity of numbers changes.
School management	3.12	4.45	1.3
resource management	1.56	1.78	4.55
Student status management	3.9	4.45	3.25

4.3   Research and Stability of Information Systems and Models

Pictured in Fig. 2 is the information system and model research scheme that incorporates deep learning in order to validate the digital mining technique.

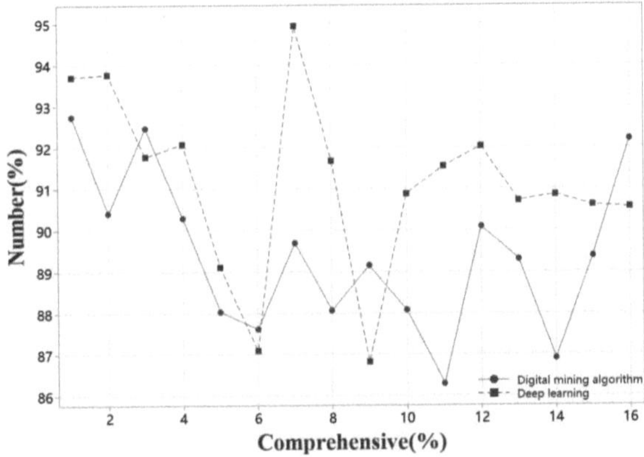

Fig.2. Research on information systems and models of different algorithms

Based on Fig. 2, it is evident that digital mining algorithm information system and model research is relatively stable, whereas deep learning information system and model research is uneven. This suggests that digital mining algorithm research is more stable than deep learning research, as the error rate is lower. You can see the three algorithms' average information system and model research schemes in Table 3.

Table 3. Comparison of the research accuracy of information systems and models of different methods

algorithm	Recent digitalization of life.	Digitalization of teaching content.	Digitalization of educational programmes.	Digitize with matching needs.
Digital mining algorithms	53.56	35.9	51.53	62.64
Deep learning	53.56	45.55	25.25	26.64
P	4.45	1.3	2.25	2.64

Table 3 shows that there are certain problems with the quality of information system and model research when using deep learning. The research has changed a lot, and there is a high mistake rate. When it comes to studying information systems and models, digital mining algorithms often outperform deep learning. Meanwhile, there has been no discernible improvement in the accuracy of digital mining algorithms, and research on the information system and model has yielded results of above 90%. Just to make sure that digital mining algorithms are the best. Various methodologies are used to examine the digital mining algorithm, as illustrated in Fig. 3.

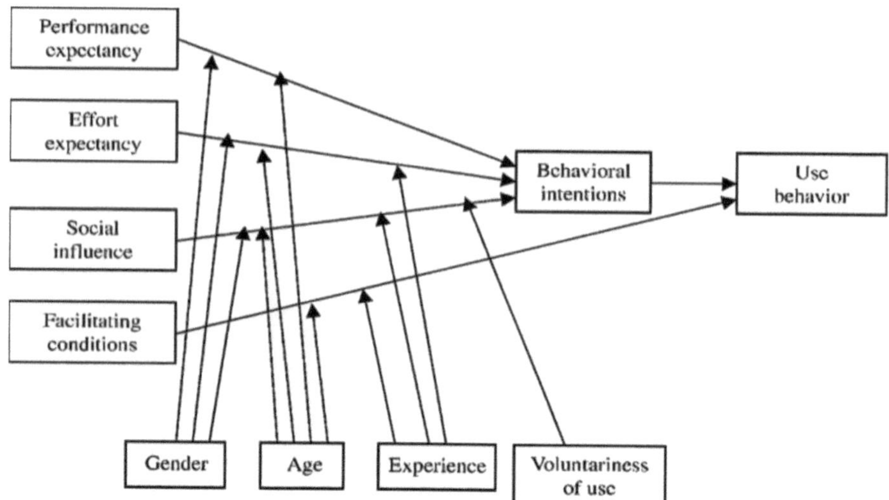

Fig. 3. Research on information system and model of digital mining algorithm

Figure 3 clearly shows that digital mining algorithm information system and model research outperforms deep learning.

4.4 Rationality of Information System and Model Research

In the process of student information management, it is also necessary to classify the data, and divide the data in each index and each classification effect equally to determine their proportion. The details are shown in Formula IV.

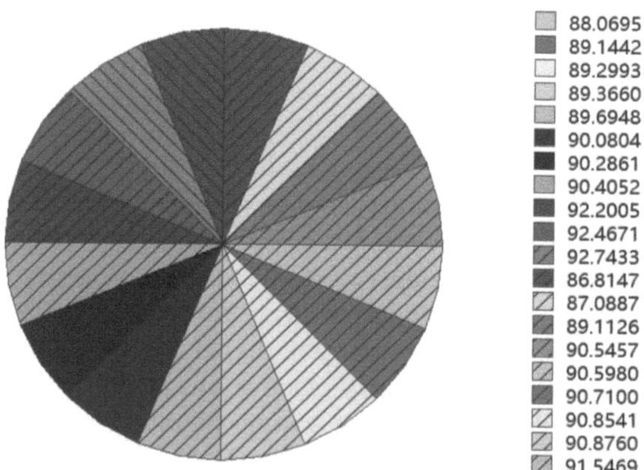

Fig. 4. Research on information systems and models of different algorithms

Figure 4 shows that compared to deep learning, digital mining algorithm information system and model research is more rational, and research using digital mining algorithm can be improved to further increase the rationality of information system and model research.

4.5 Effectiveness of Information Systems and Model Studies

Figure 5 depicts the information system and model research scheme that incorporates deep learning to validate the digital mining algorithm's efficacy.

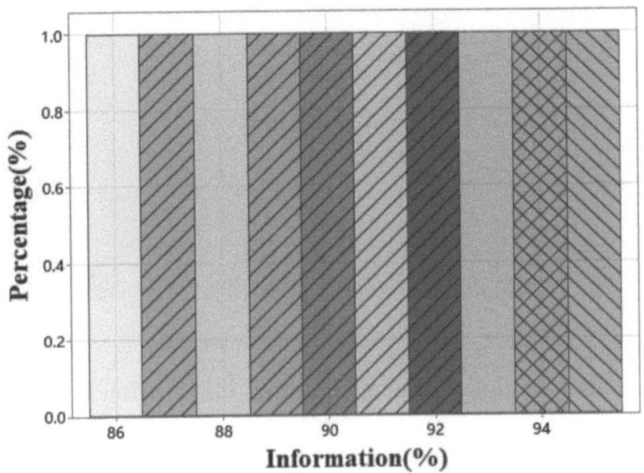

Fig. 5. Research on information systems and models with different algorithms

Figure 5 shows that compared to deep learning, digital mining algorithm information system and model research is higher but has a lower error rate. This suggests that digital mining algorithm research is relatively stable, in contrast to deep learning research, which is uneven. Table 4 shows the typical research plan for information systems and models for the aforementioned three algorithms.

Table 4. Comparison of the effectiveness of information systems and models

Algorithm	Digitalization of content management.	Digitalization of lesson plan management.	Number of grades.	Digitize with instructional content.
Digital mining algorithms	43.9	44.56	64.55	83.75
Deep learning	43.12	15.78	63.9	8.23
P	42.34	53.56	3.25	98.25

According to Table 4, there are certain issues with the quality of information system and model research when using deep learning. The research has changed a lot, and there is a high mistake rate. When it comes to studying information systems and models, digital mining algorithms often outperform deep learning. Meanwhile, there has been no discernible improvement in the accuracy of digital mining algorithms, and research on the information system and model has yielded results of above 90%. Just to make sure that digital mining algorithms are the best. The digital mining algorithm is often examined using several as illustrated in Fig. 6.

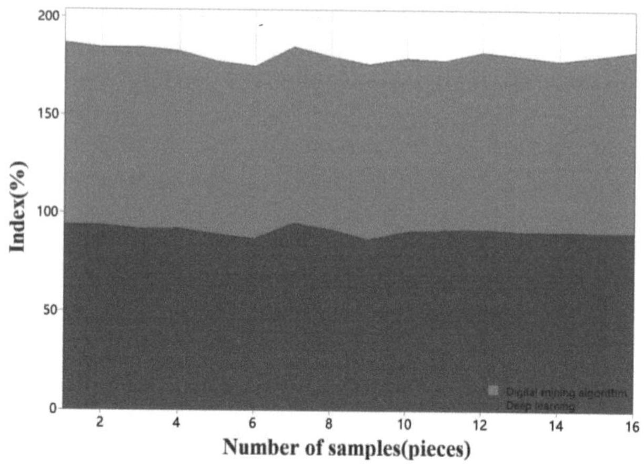

Fig. 6. Research on digital mining algorithm information system and model

Figure 6 shows that digital mining algorithm information system and model research outperforms deep learning. This is because digital mining algorithm improves system and model research by increasing the adjustment coefficient, setting the threshold for Internet information, and eliminating information system and model research schemes that don't meet requirements.

5   Conclusion

This study presents a digital mining technique that uses computer technology to improve information system and model research, aiming to solve the issue of imperfect research. Simultaneously, the Internet data gathering is built, and the study on information systems and models is examined thoroughly for correctness and dependability. The findings demonstrate that digital mining algorithms are capable of doing both specific and broad types of information system and model study, which in turn improves the accuracy of such studies. Unfortunately, digital mining algorithms tend to focus excessively on information system and model research analysis, which might lead to illogical indication selection.

References

1. Wu Xiaohong: Research on digital education management information system and its model. (Doctoral dissertation, Zhejiang Normal University). (2003)
2. Shu Yuanliang. Design of graduate management information system in the digital campus environment. (Doctoral dissertation, Jilin University).

3. Chunyang, W.: Research on information system model of digital vocational education park based on GIS. J. Jiaozuo Univ. **000**(003), 72–73 (2013)

4. Li Lin: Research on identification and management information system of financially disadvantaged students in universities. (Doctoral dissertation, Dalian University of Technology).

5. Huang Jian, & He Rifeng: Research on information model of digital detection system for engineering quality. Guangdong Civil Engineering and Architecture (8), 4. (2009)

6. Xu Zhiyuan, Lai Fengling, Zheng Chao, Wang Na, Huang Qianying, & Huang Yaqi: A digital information management system for archives based on 5G network. CN202111108649.1. (2022)

7. Wei, C.: Exploration of teaching reform of management information system course in the digital era. Electron. Qual. (8), 161–163 (2022)

8. Haiguang, F., Xinmei, K., Xin, H., Yuting, W.: Research on educational data model system for educational digital service. J. Dist. Educ. **40**(4), 45–54 (2022)

9. Boqi, W., Zhang Baohui, X., Yuguo, & Shi Yun.: Research on the construction of county-level homestead management information system. China Agric. Inf. **34**(3), 13 (2022)

10. Guo Hui, Hao Li, Zhao Guomin, He Hong, Liu Lijuan, & Zhou Gexia: Construction and implementation of hospital information management order system under the mode of Guimeifen diagnosis and treatment case. (6), 78–81. (2023)

Design of College Course Structure Model Based on AHP Algorithm

Lian Tang$^{(\boxtimes)}$

Jilin Animation Institute, Changchun, Jilin, China
jldhjwbjiansheban@163.com

Abstract. The classic bee colony method has several limitations and produces less than optimal results when addressing the structural model issue, despite the fact that structural model design is essential to the course structure of colleges and institutions. Consequently, this study offers a model for college course structuring based on the AHP algorithm and thoroughly analyzes it. Firstly, in order to decrease interference factors in the process of structural model design, the analytic hierarchy process theory is used to properly detect the influencing variables. Then, the indicator is fairly split according to the needs of structural model design. After that, the structural model design scheme was built using the AHP method, and the outcomes were thoroughly examined. Under specific evaluation criteria, the MATLAB-based simulation results demonstrate that the AHP algorithm-based structural model design scheme outperforms the traditional bee colony algorithm in terms of processing time of structural model design influencing factors and structural model design accuracy, and can achieve ideal results.

Keywords: analytic hierarchy process · AHP algorithm · Courses · Structural model · Design

1 Introduction

The ability to achieve exact placement and real-time control of structural model design is crucial for the course structure of colleges and institutions. However, structural model design suffers from the conventional approach due to its inaccurate design scheme [3], which in turn reduces its effectiveness [4]. New research shows that the AHP technique might be a game-changer when used to analyze structural model designs [5], leading to better optimization of design schemes and more solid support [6]. We have developed and constructed the structural model of the AHP algorithm [7], and we have checked and assessed it in detail to ensure its efficacy. The AHP algorithm's decentralization, non-tampering, and smart contract features are fully used by the model, allowing for the automated execution of the structural model design scheme and credibility enhancement [8]. Numerous experiments and analyses of data demonstrate that, when compared to conventional schemes, the AHP algorithm-based optimization model for structural model design significantly outperforms them in terms of accuracy [9], suppression ability to interference factors [10], and overall quality and efficiency in structural model design.

B. Brik and S. Nazir (Eds.): BigIoT-EDU 2024, LNICST 659, pp. 632–641, 2026.
https://doi.org/10.1007/978-3-032-18631-7_68

2 Related Works

2.1 Mathematical Description of the AHP Algorithm

Based on the structural model's index parameters, the AHP algorithm optimizes the design scheme using computer technology, it is z_i found that the unqualified value parameters of the structural model design, functionally incorporating the structural model design scheme, and finally the feasibility of the structural model design is $tol(y_i \cdot t_{ij})$ judged, and the calculation is y_i shown in Eq. (1).

$$\lim_{x \to \infty} (y_i \cdot t_{ij}) = \lim_{x \to \infty} y_{ij} \geq \max(t_{ij} \div 2) \tag{1}$$

The judgment of outliers is shown in Eq. (2).

$$max(t_{ij}) = \partial(t_{ij}^2 + 2 \cdot t_{ij}) \succ mean(\sum t_{ij} + 4)\mathfrak{M} \tag{2}$$

The AHP method may enhance the structural model design's correctness by combining the benefits of computer technology and using the structural model design for quantification.

Hypothesis t_i I The structural model design requirement sis, the structural model design scheme is y_i, the satisfaction of the structural model design scheme is set_i, and the judgment function of the structural model design scheme is $F(t_i \approx 0)$ as shown in Eq. (3).

$$F(d_i) = \frac{-b \pm \sqrt{b^2 - 4ac}}{2a} \sum t_i \bigcap \xi \cdot \sqrt{2} \to \oint y_i \cdot 7 \tag{3}$$

2.2 Selection of Structural Model Design Scheme

Hypothesis II The structural model design function is (t_i), and the weight coefficient is w_i, Consequently, as shown in Eq. (4), the unqualified structural model design is necessary for the structural model design.

$$g(t_i) = \ddot{x} \cdot z_i \prod F(d_i)\frac{dy}{dx} - w_i K \tag{4}$$

Equation (5) shows the outcome of obtaining a synthesis function for the structural model's design based on assumptions I and II.

$$\lim_{x \to \infty} g(t_i) + F(d_i) \leq \frac{n!}{r!(n-r)!} max(t_{ij}) \tag{5}$$

Data standardization is essential for improving the structural model design's dependability; Eq. (6) shows the effect.

$$g(t_i) + F(d_i) \leftrightarrow mean(\sum t_{ij} + 4) \tag{6}$$

2.3　Analysis of the Structural Model Design Scheme

Prior to implementing the AHP method, a thorough analysis of the structural model design scheme should be conducted. The needs of the model should be compared to the structural model design library, and any unqualified schemes should be removed. The results of Eq. (6), the anomaly assessment scheme can be proposed, and the result is $No(t_i)$ shown in Eq. (7).

$$No(t_i) = \frac{g(t_i) + F(d_i)}{mean(\sum t_{ij} + 4)} \sqrt{2} \tag{7}$$

Where in, it is $\frac{g(t_i)+F(d_i)}{mean(\sum t_{ij}+4)} \le 1$ stated that the scheme needs to be proposed, otherwise the scheme needs to be integrated, and the result is $Zh(t_i)$ shown in Eq. (8).

$$Zh(t_i) = \bigcap [\sum g(t_i) + F(d_i)] \tag{8}$$

After a thorough analysis, the structural model design's thresholds and index weights are determined to guarantee the AHP algorithm's correctness. The structural model design is $unno(t_i)$ a systematic test structural model design scheme, which needs to be accurately analyzed. If the structural model design is $accur(t_i)$ in a non-normal distribution, Eq. (9) shows the calculated result, which will impact the structural model design scheme and reduce the overall structural model design's correctness.

$$accur(t_i) = \frac{min[\sum g(t_i) + F(d_i)]}{\sum g(t_i) + F(d_i)} \times 100\% \tag{9}$$

In agreement with the actual facts, the examination into the structural model design scheme reveals that the scheme exhibits a multi-dimensional distribution. Lack of conditionality in the structural model design suggests a very haphazard method for the structural model's construction, so it is regarded as a high analytical study. If the random function of the structural model design is $randon(t_i)$, then the calculation of Eq. (9) can be expressed as Eq. (10).

$$accur(t_i) = \frac{min[\sum g(t_i) + F(d_i)]}{\sum g(t_i) + F(d_i)} \tag{10}$$

Among these, the structural model's design meets typical standards; this is largely attributable to the fact that, with the help of modern computing power, the model's architecture is fine-tuned, redundant schemes are eliminated, and default schemes are augmented, resulting in a robust dynamic correlation throughout the entire structural model's design scheme.

3　Optimization Strategies for Structural Model Design

The AHP algorithm optimizes the structural model design scheme by modifying the parameters of the Internet information, and it uses a strategy based on randomness optimization for the structural model's design. Part of the optimization process is picking random schemes to use after leveling the structural model design. Various structural model design levels are optimized and evaluated in the iterative process. Following the completion of the optimization study, the degree of structural model design for each scheme is compared, and the scheme with the best results is documented. Structural model design may be made more accurate and efficient using this optimization technique that is based on the AHP algorithm.

4 Results and Discussion

4.1 Introduction to the Design of the Structural Model

The research target is the design of the structural model in complicated scenarios. There are 12 pathways and a 12-h test duration. Table 1 shows the structural model design scheme of the particular structural model design.

Table 1. Structural model design requirements

Scope of application	Grade	Accuracy	Structural model design
Vocational education institutions	I	91.51	89.11
	II	91.06	87.63
University	I	88.91	95.05
	II	94.85	90.98
academy	I	92.98	89.28
	II	90.16	87.78

The structural model design process in Table 1 is shown in Fig. 1.

When it comes to the structural model design scheme's real needs, the AHP algorithm is more in line with them than the bee colony method. When comparing the AHP algorithm to the bee colony method, the former comes out on top in terms of efficiency and precision in structural model construction. Figure 2 shows the updated structural model design scheme, which proves the AHP method is more trustworthy and accurate. As a result, the AHP algorithm outperforms the alternatives when it comes to designing stable structural models quickly and accurately.

4.2 Structural Model Design

Structured, semi-structural, and non-structural data are all part of the structural model design scheme. We acquire the preliminary structural model design scheme of structural model design using the ore-selection of AHP algorithm, and then we examine the feasibility of that scheme. The selection of the structural model design and structural model

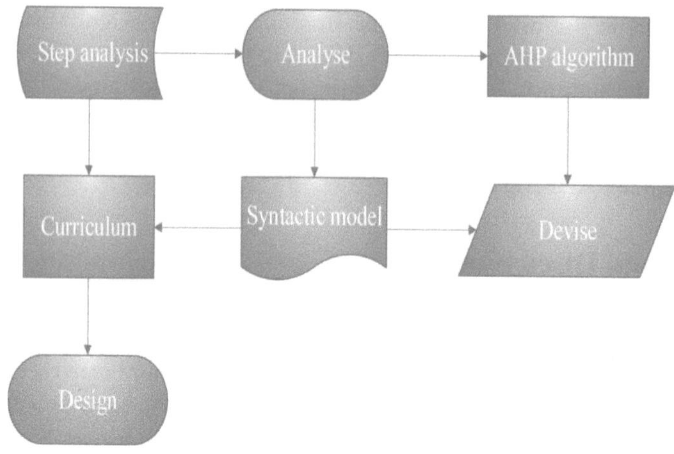

Fig. 1. The analysis process of structural model design

design scheme of various structural model design levels was done to more precisely test the design impact of the structural model, as shown in Table 2.

Table 2. The overall picture of the structural model design scheme

Category	Random data	Reliability	Analysis rate
Vocational education institutions	92.23	91.28	91.08
University	92.54	88.79	89.85
academy	91.78	92.24	89.90
mean	87.87	87.36	89.87
X6	91.91	91.46	92.32
	P = 1.249		

4.3 Structural Model Design and Stability

As illustrated in Fig. 2, the structural model design scheme is compared with the bee colony method in order to validate the correctness of the AHP algorithm.

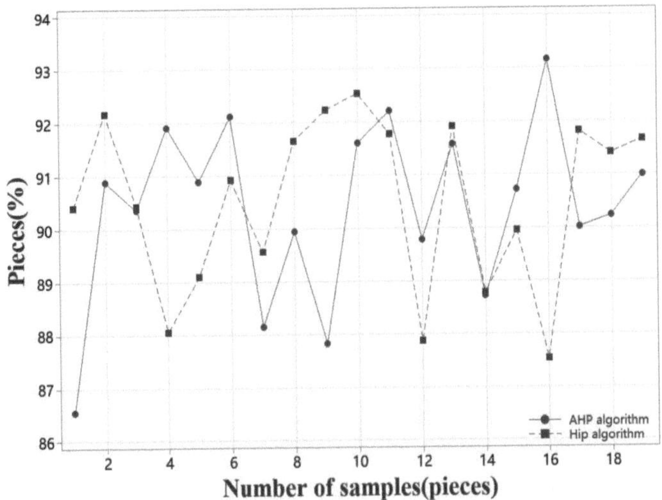

Fig. 2. Structural model design of different algorithms

Figure 2 clearly shows that the AHP algorithm has a more stable structural model design than the bee colony algorithm, despite having a higher structural model design overall. This suggests that the AHP algorithm is better at predicting future outcomes than the bee colony algorithm. The three techniques mentioned above each have their average structural model design scheme shown in Table 3.

Table 3. Comparison of the design accuracy of structural models of different methods

Algorithm	Survey data	Structural model design	Magnitude of change	Error
AHP algorithm	88.72	88.78	91.90	91.89
Swarm algorithm	90.71	89.95	91.31	92.28
P	93.16	87.54	92.60	92.01

From what we can see in Table 3, the bee colony algorithm suffers from a high error rate and massively inaccurate outputs due to sloppy structural model construction. In comparison, the AHP method outperforms the bee colony approach in terms of general outcomes when it comes to structural model creation. And the AHP algorithm's structural model has a design accuracy of over 90% and a more consistent accuracy performance with no noticeable big fluctuations. Additional methods were used to thoroughly examine the AHP algorithm, and the particular findings can be seen in Figure III, allowing for additional verification of the usefulness of the suggested technique. The findings from these expert analyses further prove that the AHP method is the best option for designing structural models.

638   L. Tang

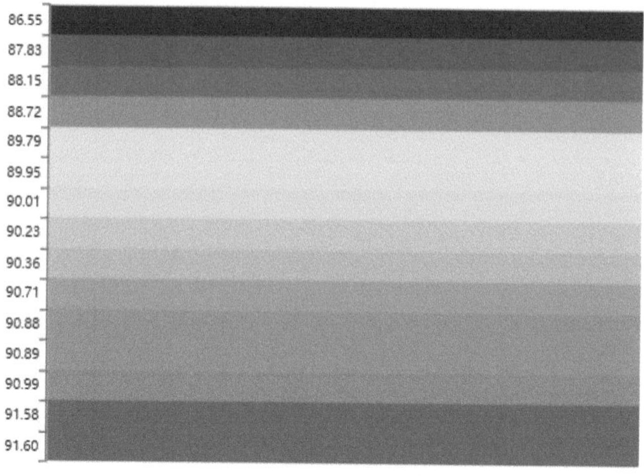

Fig. 3. Structural model design of AHP algorithm

Figure 3 shows that the AHP algorithm's structural model design is far superior to the bee colony algorithm's. This is because the AHP algorithm raises the structural model design's adjustment coefficient, establishes the threshold for Internet information, and discards structural model design schemes that don't match the requirements.

4.4 Rationality of Structural Model Design

Figure 4 shows the structural model design scheme, which is compared with the bee colony method to confirm the correctness of the AHP algorithm.

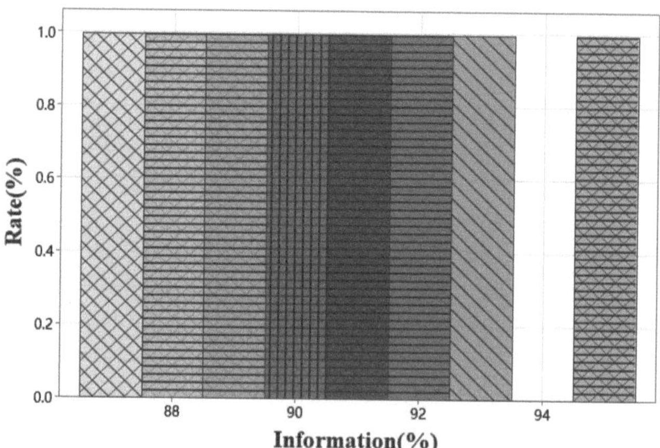

Fig. 4. Structural model design of different algorithms

Figure 4 shows the results of the data analysis that shows the AHP algorithm is more reasonable in terms of structural model construction than the bee colony method.

Applying the AHP algorithm to enhance the structural model design may lead to a more reasonable outcome. By introducing the AHP algorithm, a decentralized platform for structural model design data storage and administration is created, guaranteeing the findings' confidentiality and dependability. Each one is assigned a unique identifier using the AHP method, which stores all the pertinent information and schemes in a hierarchical format. This AHP algorithm's traits make it resistant to data manipulation and fraud by making it easy to track and identify any changes made to the data.

4.5   Effectiveness of Structural Model Design

The structural model design scheme is compared with the bee colony method in order to validate the efficacy of the AHP algorithm. Figure 5 shows the structural model design scheme.

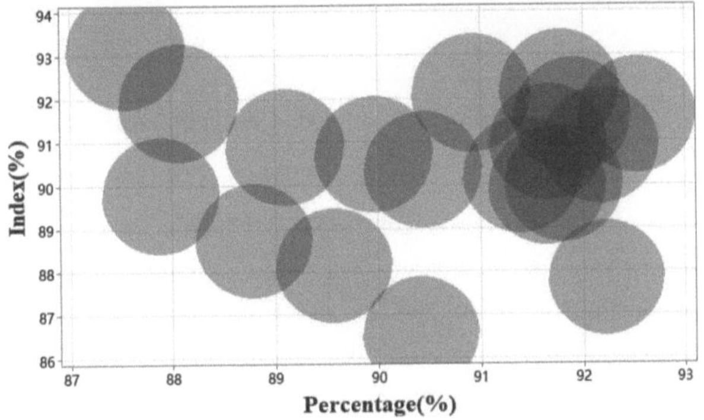

Fig. 5. Structural model design for different algorithms

Figure V shows that both the AHP and bee colony algorithms have higher structural model designs, but the AHP has a lower error rate, suggesting that its design is relatively stable, whereas the bee colony algorithm's design is uneven. The average approach for designing structural models for the aforementioned three algorithms is shown in Table 4.

Table 4. Comparison of the effectiveness of structural model design of different methods

Algorithm	Survey data	Structural model design	Magnitude of change	Error
AHP algorithm	90.01	91.82	87.74	90.66
Swarm algorithm	90.23	91.40	91.81	87.53
P	90.99	91.66	87.12	89.71

Table 4 shows that the structural model design is inaccurate, the bee colony algorithm has been through a lot of changes, and the error rate is rather significant. The AHP method outperforms the bee colony algorithm in terms of structural model design, leading to superior overall outcomes. Additionally, there has been no discernible decrease in accuracy, and the AHP algorithm's structural model design is above 90%. In order to further validate the superiority of AHP algorithm. Figure 6 shows the results of a general examination of the AHP algorithm using various approaches, which was conducted to further confirm the efficacy of the method provided in this research.

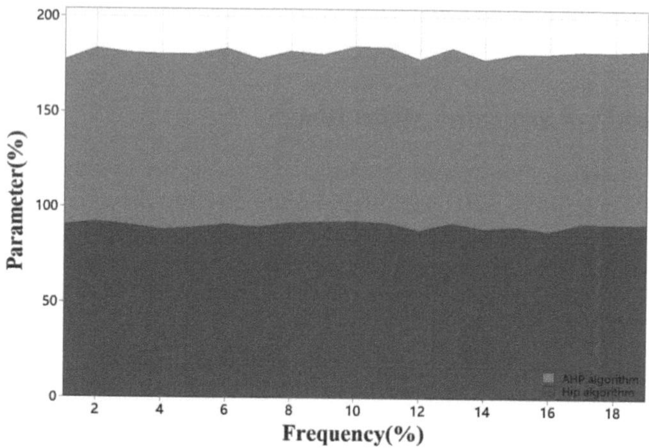

Fig. 6. .AHP algorithm structure model design

The AHP algorithm improves upon the bee colony algorithm in terms of structural model design, as shown in Fig. 6. This is due to the fact that the AHP algorithm raises the structural model design's adjustment coefficient, establishes the threshold for Internet information, and discards structural model design schemes that fail to fulfill the requirements.

5 Conclusion

Using the AHP algorithm and modern computing technologies, this study presents an all-encompassing optimization approach to address the issue of inadequate accuracy in structural model creation. To begin, dadaist's dependability and security are guaranteed by using the data's immutability and the decentralization of the AHP algorithm. Simultaneously, data is processed and examined by means of computer technology in order to extract possible characteristics. Additionally, this study thoroughly examines the important metrics that determine the structural model design's correctness and reliability. It then builds a comprehensive system to gather information online in order to provide reliable structural model design outcomes. While using the AHP algorithm, it's important to take into account the selection of structural model design indicators. This will ensure that the method's benefits are fully used.

Acknowledgements. Construction and Teaching Practice of Curriculum System for Application-oriented Talents Cultivating in Art Universities.

References

1. Li, G., Dana, M.: Take the ideological and political course of Hebei Geological University as an example. Chinese Sci. Technol. J. Database Res. (3), 4 (2023)
2. Dong, J., Zhang, Y., Hu, Y.: Take the calculus course of a university as an example. J. Guangzhou Radio Telev. Univ. 22(1), 9 (2022)
3. Fu, J., Wei, K., Hu, J., Wang, M., Zhan, Q.: Ecological optimization design of Qianling landscape based on AHP- -fuzzy comprehensive evaluation method. Build. Metal Struct. China 22(5), 142–144 (2023)
4. Tan, L., Zhang, H.: Design of teaching health model of ideological and political courses in private universities based on hierarchical analysis method. J. Guangdong Water Conserv. Electr. Power Vocat. Tech. College (2021)
5. Rongfang, W.: Construction of the security evaluation model of university library information system based on ahp analysis method. Inner Mongolia Sci. Technol. Econ. 7, 126–130 (2023)
6. Huang, H.: Design of university laboratory management system based on k-means algorithm (6) (2022)
7. Tredy. Active project-driven teaching practice and research in Algorithm design and analysis (2021)
8. Qing, D.: Design of an online course management recommendation system based on the basicsvd algorithm. Comput. Knowl. Technol. 017(031), 73–75 (2021)
9. Fang, L.: Research and implementation of the visual control simulation teaching experiment platform based on Unity3D. (Doctoral dissertation, Harbin Engineering University) (2021)
10. Xu, Z., Xi, W., Xie, M., Cai, X.: AI job demand analysis and research based on big data technology. Guangxi Sci. (2021)

Course Recommendation System Based on Neural Network Model on Students' Social Relations

Luo Hao[1,2] and Nor Azura Husin[1(✉)]

[1] School of Big Data, University of Baoshan, Baoshan 10686, China
n_azuraupm@yahoo.com
[2] Faculty of Engineering and Technology, Sunway University, Selangor 47500, Malaysia

Abstract. The study of course recommendation system is critical in students' social relations, however it has an issue with erroneous performance positioning. The typical Particle swarm arithmetic is unable to address the inaccurate recommendation positioning issue in students' social relations, and the result is insufficient. As a result, a Neural network model-based research on course recommendation system is provided, and the research on course recommendation system is assessed. To begin, the alternating neural network theory is used to discover the influencing elements, and the indicators are split based on the study of course recommendation system's needs to decrease interference factors in the study of course recommendation system. The alternating neural network theory is then used to create a Neural network model study of course recommendation system scheme, and the outcomes of the study of course recommendation system are thoroughly examined. The MATLAB simulation results reveal that, under particular evaluation conditions, the Neural network model outperforms the standard Particle swarm arithmetic in terms of study of course recommendation system accuracy and time of influencing variables.

Keywords: alternating neural network theory · neural network model;Courses;Systematic research · students · referrals

1 Introduction

The Course Recommendation System of Student Social Relationship Neural Network Model is an advanced course recommendation tool that combines social network analysis and machine learning techniques [1, 2]. The system aims to provide students with more personalized and accurate course recommendations by analyzing the social network among students, as well as their learning behaviors, interests and preferences and other multi-dimensional data [3, 4].Student Social Relationship Neural Network Model Course Recommendation System is a technology that uses students' social relationships, their learning behaviors and interests to recommend related courses [5, 6]. The course recommendation system based on the neural network model of students' social

B. Brik and S. Nazir (Eds.): BigIoT-EDU 2024, LNICST 659, pp. 642–651, 2026.
https://doi.org/10.1007/978-3-032-18631-7_69

relations is an advanced recommendation system that combines social network analysis, machine learning and knowledge in educational fields [7, 8]. The system aims to provide students with more personalized and accurate course recommendations by analyzing multi-dimensional data such as social network, learning behavior, interests and preferences among students, so as to improve students' learning experience and effect [9, 10].

2 Related Concepts

2.1 The Neural Network Model is Described Mathematically

The neural network model can conduct in-depth analysis of students' personal characteristics (such as interests, study habits, social relationships, etc.), so as to identify each student's unique needs and preferences is y_i found that the unqualified value parameters in the study of course recommendation system is z_i, and the study of course recommendation system scheme is $tol(y_i \cdot t_{ij})$ Based on these characteristics, the model can generate personalized course recommendations, ensuring that each student has access to course resources that match their interests and needs is shown in Eq. (1).

$$\lim_{x \to \infty} \left(y_i \cdot t_{ij} \right) = \lim_{\delta x \to 0} y_{ij} \geq \max \left(t_{ij} \div 2 \right) \tag{1}$$

The neural network model has self-learning and self-adaptive ability, and can constantly adjust and optimize the recommendation strategy according to students' feedback and behavioral data Eq. (2).

$$\max \left(t_{ij} \right) = \partial \left(t_{ij}^2 + 2 \cdot t_{ij} \right) \succ \lim_{\delta x \to 0} \left(\sum t_{ij} + 4 \right) \mathfrak{M} \tag{2}$$

Efficient algorithm and model can screen out the curriculum resources that best match students' needs in a short time y_i, and improve the recommendation efficiency is t_i, the study of course recommendation system scheme is set_i, When faced with massive curriculum resources, students often feel at a loss is as shown by Eq. (3).

$$F(d_i) = \sum t_i \bigcap \xi \cdot \sqrt{2} \rightarrow \oint y_i \cdot 7 \tag{3}$$

2.2 Selection of Study of Course Recommendation System Scheme

By analyzing students' social relationships and course selection history, the neural network model is able to discover connections and intersections between different disciplines is $g(t_i)$, The weighting factor is w_i, The unqualified study of course recommendation system, as indicated in Equation, is thus required by the study of course recommendation system. (4).

$$g(t_i) = \ddot{x} \bullet z_i \prod F(d_i) \frac{dy}{dx} - w_i \Phi \tag{4}$$

Multi-dimensional information fusion helps to improve the quality of recommendation and ensure that students get more comprehensive and accurate curriculum resources is shown in Eq. (5).

$$\lim_{x \to \infty} g(t_i) + F(d_i) \le \frac{\partial^2 \Omega}{\partial v^2} \max(t_{ij}) \tag{5}$$

The neural network model can construct an intelligent feedback mechanism, and continuously optimize the recommendation algorithm and model according to the students' feedback and behavioral data in Eq. (6).

$$g(t_i) + F(d_i) \leftrightarrow \sqrt{b^2 - 4ac}\left(\sum t_{ij} + 4\right) \tag{6}$$

2.3 Analysis of Study of Course Recommendation System Scheme

It can provide students with personalized course recommendations, improve the efficiency of recommendations, enhance the diversity of recommendations, and improve the quality of recommendations. These advantages make the neural network model have a wide application prospect and important practical value in the field of course recommendation is shown in Eq. (7).

$$No(t_i) = \frac{g(t_i) + F(d_i)}{mean\left(\sum t_{ij} + 4\right)} \sqrt{b^2 - 4ac} \tag{7}$$

Among them, it is $\frac{g(t_i)+F(d_i)}{mean(\sum t_{ij}+4)} \le 1$ specified that the scheme must be $Zh(t_i)$ suggested; otherwise, the scheme integration is necessary; the outcome is illustrated in Eq. (8).

$$Zh(t_i) = \lim_{x \to \infty}\left[\sum g(t_i) + F(d_i)\right]\lim_{x \to \infty} \Pi \tag{8}$$

The study of course recommendation system is $accur(t_i)$ thoroughly examined, and the threshold and index weight of the study of course recommendation system scheme are established to assure the Neural network model's correctness $unno(t_i)$. Based on these characteristics, the model is able to provide personalized course recommendations for each student, ensuring that the course matches the student's interests, needs, and abilities. This personalized course recommendation method is helpful to improve students' learning enthusiasm and participation, thus improving the learning effect, as stated in Eq. (9).

$$accur(t_i) = \frac{min\left[\sum g(t_i) + F(d_i)\right]}{\sum g(t_i) + F(d_i)} \Lambda \tag{9}$$

The neural network model can analyze the course selection patterns in students' social relationships, and identify the correlation and dependency between different courses. The neural network model can analyze the course selection patterns in students' social relationships and identify the relationship and dependency between different courses is considered as a high analytical research. If the study of course recommendation system's stochastic function is $randon(t_i)$, then the computation of Eq. (9) may be represented as Eq. (10).

$$accur(t_i) = \frac{\min\left[\sum g(t_i) + F(d_i)\right]}{\ddot{x}\sum g(t_i) + F(d_i)} + randon(t_i) \tag{10}$$

It is helpful to optimize the curriculum structure in colleges and universities, ensure the cohesion and coherence between courses, and form a complete curriculum system.

3 Study of Course Recommendation System Optimization Approach

Data collection and preprocessing module: responsible for collecting students' basic information, learning history, social relationships and other data, and preprocessing, such as data cleaning and formatting, to ensure the accuracy and availability of data. Social relationship network construction module: Using the collected students' social relationship data, build a student social relationship network model. The model can reflect the social contact and interaction among students, and provide an important basis for subsequent recommendation algorithms. Learning behavior analysis module: Identify students' learning patterns, preferences and points of interest by analyzing students' learning history and behavior data. This data helps the recommendation system to understand students' needs more accurately, so as to recommend them courses that are more in line with their interests and needs. Recommendation algorithm module: Based on the results of social network and learning behavior analysis, machine learning algorithm is used to generate course recommendation. These algorithms may include collaborative filtering, content recommendation, graph-based recommendation, etc., and are designed to provide students with personalized course suggestions. User Feedback and Optimization Module: Allows students to give feedback on recommendation results, such as likes, comments or shares, etc. These feedback data will be used to optimize the recommendation algorithm and improve the accuracy and personalization of the recommendation system.

4 Practical Examples of Study of Course Recommendation System

4.1 Introduction to the Study of Course Recommendation System

By analyzing students' social relationships and learning behaviors, the model can evaluate students' acceptance and adaptability to different courses is shown in Table 1.

The study of course recommendation system process in Table 1. is shown in Fig. 1.

The neural network model based on students' social relations plays an important role in curriculum optimization. It can improve the personalization of course recommendation, optimize the course structure and content, promote the communication and cooperation between teachers and students, and enhance the scientificity of course evaluation. These advantages make the neural network model have a wide application prospect and important practical value in the field of curriculum optimization.

Table 1. study of course recommendation system study of course recommendation system requirements

Scope of application	Social relations.	The overall progress of the course.	study of course recommendation system
Academic performance	I	87.14	89.44
	II	87.05	91.25
Social skills development for students	I	91.80	90.95
	II	90.66	88.06
Mental health and social relationships	I	90.23	88.90
	II	90.13	88.73

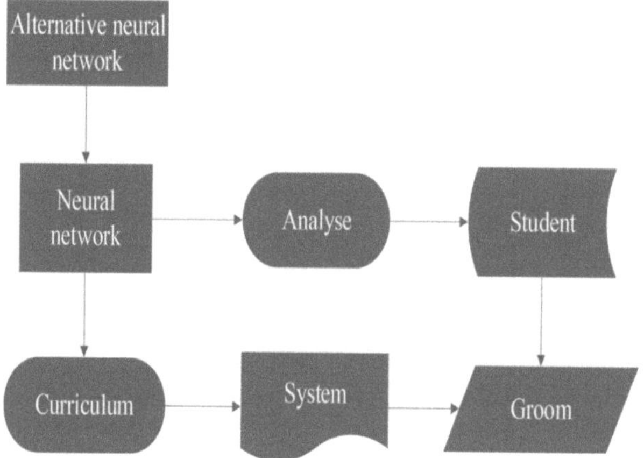

Fig. 1. Analysis process of study of course recommendation system

4.2 Study of Course Recommendation System

Curriculum Optimization Based on Neural Network Model of Students' Social Relationships. After a period of practice, the school's curriculum satisfaction and academic performance have been significantly improved,The relationship between student relations and course recommendations is shown in Table 2.

4.3 Study of Course Recommendation System and Stability

It can analyze the emerging fields and popular courses in the market, and provide suggestions for the development of new courses for colleges and universities is shown in Fig. 2.

Table 2. The overall situation of the study of course recommendation system scheme

Category	Analytical nature of student relationships.	Assessing the correlation between students and the curriculum.	The degree of optimization of the course.
Academic performance	91.12	89.82	89.88
Social skills development for students	88.92	90.96	91.21
Mental health and social relationships	89.96	87.64	91.78
Mean	91.37	89.95	89.44
X6	91.65	90.51	92.32
	$P = 1.249$		

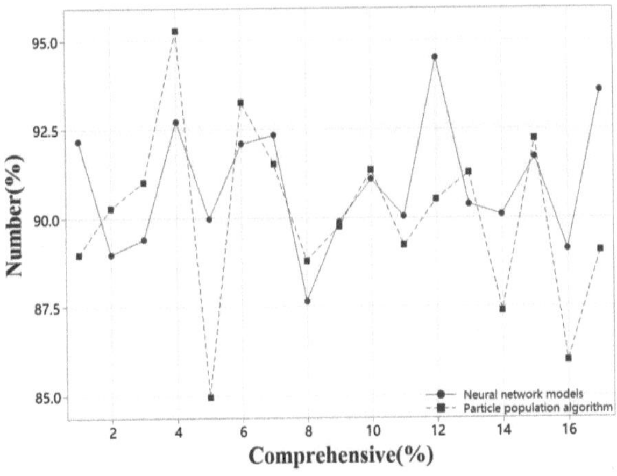

Fig. 2. Evaluation model of aging performance of different algorithms

Figure 2 shows that is helpful to optimize the curriculum structure in colleges and universities, ensure the cohesion and coherence between courses, and form a more reasonable curriculum system,The results are shown in Table 3.

Table 3 shows that The model can provide personalized course recommendations for each student, ensuring that the recommended courses are highly relevant to students' interests and needs, as shown in Fig. 3.

Figure 3 shows that By analyzing students' social relationships (such as choice of elective courses and feedback from dormitory classmates, club members, friends, etc.), the neural network model can dig out students' potential interests and academic tendencies.

Table 3. compares the accuracy of several study of course recommendation system.

Algorithm	Overall investigation of students.	study of course recommendation system	The degree of recommendation and optimization.	Student feedback.
Neural network model	89.92	88.66	92.48	90.98
Particle swarm arithmetic	93.58	88.61	88.13	92.00
P	87.13	90.03	89.97	89.40

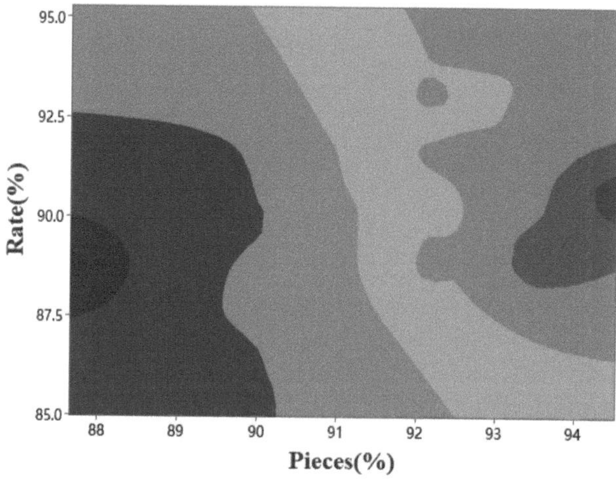

Fig. 3. study of course recommendation system of Neural network model

4.4   Rationality of Study of Course Recommendation System

If the overall learning ability of the student in the social circle is strong and most of them have chosen difficult elective courses, and the student's performance is moderate, the model may recommend some less difficult but still challenging elective courses to ensure that the student can learn knowledge without being frustrated by the difficulty of the course is depicted in Fig. 4.

Figure 4 shows that Science and engineering students seldom choose humanities and social sciences elective courses. Schools can guide students to choose more diversified elective courses by adjusting curriculum propaganda strategies and optimizing curriculum settings, so as to promote the balanced development of disciplines.

4.5   Validity of Study of Course Recommendation System

This situation can be identified and prompted to set up relevant elective courses in schools, thus increasing the diversity of elective courses is shown in Figure V shown.

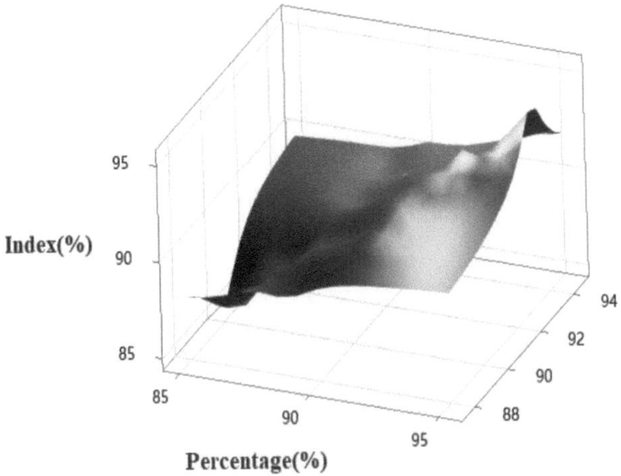

Fig. 4. Evaluation model of aging performance of different algorithms

Fig. 5. study of course recommendation system of different algorithms

Figure 5 shows that When guiding students to choose elective courses, it is necessary to comprehensively consider students' social network, personal interests, career planning, school and social environment and other factors, so as to achieve a more reasonable and efficient allocation of elective courses,The results are shown in Table 4.

Table 4 shows that the model may recommend some less difficult but still challenging elective courses to ensure that students can learn knowledge without being frustrated by the difficulty of the course when the student has a strong overall learning ability in the social circle and most of them have chosen difficult elective courses. The model may recommend some less difficult but still challenging elective courses to ensure that the student can learn knowledge without being frustrated by the difficulty of the course, as illustrated in Fig. 6.

Table 4. compares the efficacy of several study of course recommendation system.

Algorithm	Survey data	study of course recommendation system	Magnitude of change	Error
Neural network model	89.42	90.01	90.83	91.03
Particle swarm arithmetic	91.67	90.88	90.97	91.18
P	90.13	89.06	88.85	89.81

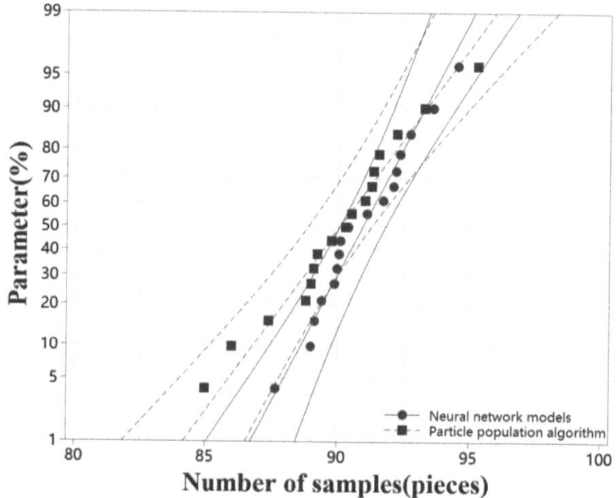

Fig. 6. Neural network model study of course recommendation system

Figure 6 shows that When an elective course is rarely mentioned or selected in a student's social network, this may indicate that the course is insufficiently attractive or otherwise problematic.

5   Conclusion

However, the system also has some challenges and limitations, such as data privacy and security protection, algorithmic transparency and fairness. Therefore, when designing and implementing the system, it is necessary to fully consider these factors and take corresponding measures to ensure the safety and reliability of the system. To sum up, the course recommendation system based on the neural network model of students' social relations is a course recommendation tool with broad application prospects and potential. Through continuous optimization and improvement, the system is expected to provide students with more personalized, accurate and efficient course recommendation services.Student Social Relationship Neural Network Model Course Recommendation

System is a technology that uses students' social relations and learning behaviors to recommend related courses. It combines social network analysis and machine learning algorithms to provide students with personalized course suggestions, and has wide application prospects in school curriculum recommendations, online learning platforms, and career planning guidance.

Acknowledgments. This work was supported by the 2024 Yunnan Educational Science Planning Project (Grant No. BC24029) and the 2024–2025 Teaching Reform Research Project of Baoshan University (Grant No. ZHZ202501).

References

1. Jie, X., Qingshan, L., Hua, C., Yangtao, Z., Wenyong, Y., Biao, W.B.: Breakthrough smart education: a course recommendation system based on graph learning. J. Softw. **33**(10), 3656–3672 (2022)
2. Liu Wanying: Analysis of factors affecting students' travel patterns based on neural network model and polynomial logit model China New Communications, 24 (9), 3 (2022)
3. Li Chuanzhen, Mu Yutong, Cai Juanjuan, Liu Yuchen, Zhang Yang & Wang Hui: Audiovisual recommendation system based on bilinear perceptron graph neural network model, method CN202210120345.5 (2022)
4. Gu Hongliang & Ding Jianming: Research on the recognition method of tightening curve anomalies based on convolutional neural networks Mechanical (2023)
5. Yu Hongli, An Lijia, Wang Chunfang, Xu Guizhi & Guo Lei: Research on early screening and classification methods for post stroke depression based on hybrid neural networks and attention mechanisms Electronic measurement technology (2023)
6. Deng Lingling & Dai Xinjian: Research on Core Literacy Evaluation of Vocational College Students Based on BP Neural Network Journal of Changsha Civil Affairs Vocational and Technical College, 29 (4), 98–101 (2022)
7. Words Yunfei, Li Yeli, Sun Huayan, Lu Likun & You Xindong: Personalized recommendation system and method based on deep neural network CN201810769873.7 (2022)
8. Liu Yaohong, Xu Tong, Zhang Yang, Chen Liang, Kan Mengdie & Su Yunyi et al.: A method for identifying power defect images based on neural network model CN116128868A (2023)
9. Qiang, C., Junjun, W., Haisheng, L., Dianhui, M.: Research on the construction of a food safety evaluation model based on neural networks. J. Food Sci. Technol. **1** (2022)
10. Xinyue, H., Hairong, W., Huixiong, Z.: Research on deep learning experimental teaching based on the Keras model experimental. Sci. Technol. **20**(3), 137–140 (2022)

Author Index